W9-BNW-889

Youth Drug Abuse

Youth Drug Abuse

Problems, Issues, and Treatment

Edited by
George M. Beschner
National Institute on Drug Abuse

Alfred S. Friedman
Philadelphia Psychiatric Center

Lexington Books
D.C. Heath and Company
Lexington, Massachusetts
Toronto

Library of Congress Cataloging in Publication Data

Main entry under title:
Youth drug abuse.

1. Drugs and youth–United States–Addresses, essays, lectures. 2. Drug abuse–United States–Addresses, essays, lectures. 3. Drug abuse–United States–Prevention–Addresses, essays, lectures. I. Beschner, George M. II. Friedman, Alfred S. [DNLM: 1. Drug abuse–In adolescence. 2. Drug dependence–In adolescence. WM270.3 Y83]
HV5824.Y68Y68 362.7'8'2930973 78-21197
ISBN 0-669-02804-5

Second printing, May 1980

Published simultaneously in Canada.

Printed in the United States of America.

International Standard Book Number: 0-669-02804-5

Library of Congress Catalog Card Number: 78-21197

Contents

List of Figures

List of Tables

Foreword

Attempts to define the problems of drug abuse in our society have proved to be frustrating. Different analysts have considered different factors essential to any such definition, for example, the different classes and types of drugs, their pharmacological properties, the intended purposes for which they are used, the consequences of use, and the psychological makeup of the user. Not only is drug abuse multifaceted, it is also a dynamic phenomenon and, as such, it is subject to fads, shifting patterns, and changing values. Diverse viewpoints regarding the use of different substances and levels of abuse have often been in conflict.

One particular aspect of the drug-abuse issue, abuse among youth, has generated a continuing debate. Concern about youthful drug abuse has focused principally on substances used: marihuana, various inhalants, fad drugs such as PCP and quaaludes, and heroin. Those who must plan and administer programs of drug-abuse prevention and treatment are becoming increasingly concerned about the spread and patterns of use in this population.

In that context, this volume is particularly timely and important. The chapters assembled encompass a number of the major unresolved issues that workers in this field must address on a daily basis. Moreover, a single data base collected from a large number of youth-oriented drug-abuse treatment programs has been used by the various authors to explore the issues. The range of topics addressed guarantees the utility of this volume to anyone with youth issues. In the preface and introductory chapter, the editors offer a summary and a guide to the remaining chapters in the book. The chapters themselves are written with a premium of technical language, permitting an ease of understanding even by persons who are only casually familiar with the drug-abuse field. Some chapters will be of interest to all in the field; others will be of interest to particular specialties. A ready audience should exist among planners and policy makers at the local, state, and national levels. Persons working in prevention programs, educators, and training, treatment, and rehabilitation personnel will find much important information. Throughout, subject matter regarding issues of research methodology and the presentation of data and findings is made available for the first time.

Much of the data used in the various chapters is from the same relatively recent sources and thus provides a unifying theme for the book. Many of these chapters document and make similar points concerning both the rapid changes in the complex nature of youthful drug abuse, and about trends which have been observed over time. Such trends as, for example, decreasing age of first use and increasing numbers who have ever used are of great importance to all who work with youthful drug abusers.

The book does not pretend to give easy answers to the difficult questions of youthful drug abuse. It does, however, provide a definition and a prescription of drug abuse in youthful populations and it will permit the careful reader to be in a better position to understand and address that complex problem area. *Youth Drug Abuse: Problems, Issues, and Treatment* may be read as a basic reference by those working in this difficult and potentially rewarding area.

Carl Akins, Ph.D.
Executive Director, National Association
of State Alcohol and Drug Abuse Directors, Inc.

Preface

Plan of the Book

The issues to be addressed in this book are the methodology of research on drug abuse; the epidemiological, social, psychological, pharmacological, and legal aspects of the youth drug-abuse problem; and the implication for planning drug-abuse treatment and prevention programs and for the determination of policy. Of course, not equal weight or space is devoted to each of these issues, and there is more focus on epidemiology and drug-abuse patterns of youth than on any other issue.

This book is a comprehensive and definitive data-based report on the current status of the drug-abuse problem among youth, covering most of the major issues in the field. The principle data sources for this book are (1) the three national drug-abuse data bases (CODAP,[1] DAWN,[2] DARP,[3]), from which youth subsamples were extracted and new analyses conducted, and (2) the new National Youth Polydrug Study (NYPS) national data base. In addition, the authors were asked to contribute to their particular topics from their own empirical resources (their own research studies and other local statewide studies) and their own perspectives. The new National Youth Polydrug Study (NYPS) sampled clients in youth drug treatment programs around the country. The allocation of various parts of the results of this study to each of a number of the chapters, appropriate to the topics of the chapters, provides continuity and a unifying theme for this book.

Each author has met in his or her own way the challenge of integrating his or her own knowledge and research findings with the findings from the national data bases. Thus, although the book presents a variety of points of view, it achieves wholeness and integrity by virtue of the fact that each author (1) relates to his or her assigned part of the same central data bases and the findings of the same national surveys and studies, and (2) brings to it his or her own background, and approaches it from his or her own vantage point.

This particular way of organizing the data presentation has both some advantages and some disadvantages. There is a strength in the multiple and heterogeneous data sources, including the four national-level data bases and a number of data reports from local and state research studies conducted by the various authors. The plan enables each author to report the findings of his or her local research against the background of the findings from the national studies. The plan encompasses the various methods and approaches of a group of experts, experienced investigators, and authors to the analysis of the NYPS and other data bases and, in addition, encompasses their various perspectives to the interpretation of the findings from these analyses.

If this book had been planned so that only the NYPS study and data were presented, the result would be a clearer, more straightforward, and somewhat more integrated presentation for the reader. The interspersing of parts of the NYPS data with the findings of other research makes for a more comprehensive consideration of the various issues, but at the same time may be considered a disadvantage in that it is a more complex and unwieldly way of addressing the issues.

The book opens with an introduction, by the co-editors of the book, which sets the tone and develops the background for consideration of the new data and information to be presented in subsequent chapters. This first chapter includes a brief history of youth drug use and abuse in the United States, a look at the federal government's policy and response to the problem, a brief review of the current theories of causes and contributing factors to youth drug abuse, and a short presentation of some of the most important current problems and some of the key research, treatment, and policy and planning issues related to youth drug abuse which will be examined in more depth and detail in subsequent chapters of the book.

In chapter 2, Judith Green begins Part I of the book by presenting an overview of the findings of recent published research reports on prevalence rates, drug-use patterns, and characteristics of youth drug users in national school surveys, stratified sample household surveys, and other large-scale state surveys. This information on the drug-use problem in the community at large provides the setting in which the drug-use patterns and problems of youth in treatment will later be presented.

In chapter 3, Leon Hunt, Edward Farley, and Rachel Hunt study a particular issue regarding the epidemiology of drug abuse. They assess survey data collected on an annual basis from California and Florida school districts, and focus on the changes from year to year in first use, or in incidence, for each drug and for each youth cohort.

In chapter 4, O'Donnell and Clayton utilized data from two research studies of their own and from the NYPS in a special type of analysis to show (1) how the incidence of first use of marihuana is related to the incidence of first use of heroin, (2) the degree to which marihuana use is antecedent to other "deviant" and other illegal behavior, and (3) characteristics of young heroin users.

Part II of the book is composed of two chapters on methodology. There is a systematic review of methodological issues in drug-abuse research by Lavenhar in chapter 5 which includes issues of drug survey research, evaluations of drug treatment programs, and evaluation of drug education prevention programs.

Santo's chapter 6 presents the methodological issues and procedures that were involved in the National Youth Polydrug Study, including an assessment of the reliability of the data collection procedure, a description of the study sample, and a comparison of this sample with the largest sample available of youth in drug treatment, derived from the CODAP data base. Thus the reading of this chapter is essential for an adequate understanding of the findings of the NYPS study presented in a number of later chapters.

Part III deals with specific issues and aspects of youth drug abuse. In chapter 7, Farley et al. present some of the main findings of the NYPS study, including the drug-use prevalence of youth applying for treatment, an analysis of the large variety of combinations of drug use, and racial differences in drug-use patterns. A special feature of this chapter is the presentation of the dramatic and disturbing data on the extensive number of different harmful "hard" drugs, in addition to marihuana and alcohol, which the average adolescent client applying for drug greatment today has already used and abused. The need for increased national concern for and attention to this serious polydrug and youth multiple drug-abuse problem, which in the past has been overshadowed by the public concern with the heroin problem, is discussed.

Beschner and Treasure's chapter 8 provides a comprehensive review of research findings and issues on female adolescent drug use, including data on sex differences. The authors discuss attitudes toward the young female drug abuser, the nature and extent of drug use in the female adolescent population, and the need for the development of more appropriate treatment services for this hitherto neglected population.

Luekefeld and Clayton's chapter 9 on the relationship of youth drug use to delinquent and illegal behavior presents findings from the NYPS on the degree of association of eight selected substances with various types and categories of illegal behavior.

In chapter 10, Cohen and Santo discuss the interaction of drug-use behavior with the educational experiences of youth. It is one of the most extensive reports of systematic data in the literature on the educational deficits of drug-abuse youth in treatment and the inadequacies of school systems in coping with the problems of these students.

In chapter 11, on the pharmacologic aspects of drug abuse among youth, Schnoll highlights issues of street drug pharmacology and the problem of drug interaction for the multiple drug abuser. He considers the potential for physiological addiction and abuse of the major types of drugs, examines cross-tolerance and cross-dependency, and dispels some of the myths about different drugs.

In chapter 12, DuPont, in his recent role as director of the National Institute of Drug Abuse, presents in very coherent fashion (1) the federal administration policy on marihuana use, (2) projections for increased spread of marihuana use among youth in the future, (3) health issues related to marihuana use, (4) the rationale for decriminalization of marihuana use in the near future would be unwise public policy, particularly in view of the problems related to legal use of alcohol in this country.

Part IV of the book consists of three chapters about specific types of drugs that are common to youth populations, have special implications for youths who use them, and constitute various degrees of hazard for youth.

The serious problem posed by use of inhalants and solvents by young children as well as adolescents is presented by Sidney Cohen in chapter 13. This chapter includes a detailed description of the variety of products and substances abused, their pharmacology, the history of their use, the techniques of usage, the extent of the problem, the signs of intoxication, physical and mental effects of use, causative factors, and implications to the user and to society.

The various aspects of the special problem posed by PCP (phencyclidine) use is comprehensively presented in chapter 14 by Burns and Lerner, including the history of PCP use and its spread across the country, its methods of manufacture, economic factors, laboratory and medical findings, and explanations of the rapid increase in popularity and use of the substance among youth. The chapter includes a report on the long-term harmful medical effects on a sample of chronic PCP users studied in a western city and a report from the NYPS data on the characteristics of young PCP users in treatment.

Heroin use and addiction has traditionally been more of an adult phenomenon, and relatively little has been reported in the literature on heroin use by youth under nineteen years of age. In chapter 15, McCoy reviews the evidence for the increased involvement of youth in heroin use during the past decade. He also discusses the reasons for the relatively long "deferral" period from the time of starting heroin use to the time of getting into treatment, and presents evidence on youth who have used heroin only "experimentally" or sporadically rather than on a regular daily basis and have not become addicted.

Five chapters follow in Part V of the book on special youth populations. Four of these chapters are on specific minority ethnic youth groups, and the fifth is on a rural youth population. In chapter 16, Kirk reviews the limited information available on drug use among rural youth, compares their drug-use patterns with those of urban youths, and reports on a study he conducted of youths in rural Vermont high schools in which he compared groups of users of various types of drugs on their personality traits, attitudes, and perceptions of their parents.

In chapter 17, Oetting and Goldstein report on drug use in Native American adolescent populations. Drug problems are reviewed in the context of such factors as the cultural heritage, the acculturation process, the multiple life problems, and the impoverished socioeconomic conditions of the six tribes studied in several Southwestern states. The drug-use prevalence rates are compared with those reported in a nationally representative sample to show the differences in drug involvement. Native American drug-using youths are also compared with peers who do not use drugs, on their personal and social characteristics, values, and attitudes toward the major social institutions in their lives (tribe, family, religion, school, law, etc.).

The core of Brunswick's chapter 18 is an indepth report on youth drug abuse in the black community in New York City's Harlem. It is not surprising that this study found the highest prevalence of heroin use and addiction of any recent representative household community survey or high school survey reported. (Nevertheless, an earlier report by Graeven of a heroin "epidemic" that occurred in a West Coast high school among middle-class white students is cited as evidence that race or color is not the determining factor, but rather that other historical, situational, and social factors are implicated.)

In chapter 19, Szapocznik et al. report on drug use and abuse and subjective psychological distress factors among Hispanic, primarily Cuban, youths in Miami. They draw on ideas regarding the adolescent life phase, identity formation, intergenerational conflict in immigrant families, and acculturation and deculturation to discuss how these factors impact differentially on male and female adolescents and relate to their respective drug-use patterns. Szapocznik et al. also present the differences in drug-use patterns between their adolescent Miami sample and their young-adult (19 to 30 years) Miami sample.

Carlisi's chapter 20 is unusual in that it focuses on white "ethnic" groups as minorities, rather than the more typical focus on nonwhite minority groups. Each youth ethnic group has its own history and culture and its own unique problems. Four white inner-city ethnic communities (Italian-American, Irish-American, German-American, and Polish-American) were studied in four cities (Baltimore, Detroit, Cincinnatti, and Providence). The differences between these four groups regarding drug prevalence rates, frequencies of use, onset patterns, and drug preferences are reported and discussed. Comparisons are made with samples of white ethnic drug-using groups drawn from the NYPS data on youth in treatment; and the drug prevalence rates and onset profiles for Carlisi's various ethnic youth groups turned out to be proportionate to those of the same ethnic groups in the treatment sample. The implications of the findings for future prevention and intervention efforts in the various ethnic communities are discussed.

Part VI of this book has as its mission the description of the treatment resources, facilities, and services that are available for drug-abusing youths; an assessment of what has been learned about what types of treatment are successful with youth; a report on the evaluation of the outcome and effects of various treatment environment and modalities; a description of the relative success of these various types of treatment, at discharge and at long-term followup; and the demographic, drug-use, and psychosocial factors that predict to successful treatment outcome.

Thus far there is very little valid and reliable information available to parents, judges, and other referral sources regarding what types of treatment settings and modalities are effective. In chapter 21, Smith, Levy, and Striar describe the different treatment services and programs generally thought to be successful with drug-abusing youth. In addition, these authors review some of the key treatment issues and problems experienced by agencies that attempt to treat youthful drug abusers. While many treatment approaches have been developed, no one particular model of treatment has been sufficiently established as effective for the majority of drug-abusing youth who come to treatment.

The research methods required to accomplish the treatment evaluation task are complex and difficult, and require the following conditions: (1) that the client population be adequately homogeneous and adequately described and defined, and that the clients be randomly assigned to different treatment conditions by an automatic blind assignment procedure; (2) that the treatment methods be administered to clients in a relatively uniform, standardized manner and adequately described and defined for the treatment staff; (3) that the outcome criteria (indexes of improvement and progress) be adequately defined; and (4) that the treating personnel be relatively homogeneous in training, experience, and relevant key personality characteristics, or that each treatment staff person treat equal numbers of randomly assigned clients by all the treatment methods being compared.

In chapter 22, Sells and Simpson present a study of the outcome effectiveness of treatment for the youth subsample of the national Drug Abuse Reporting Program (DARP) file, including during-treatment data for black and white youths in the DARP, and a follow-up study of the status of two youth client cohorts 4 to 6 years after admission to treatment. The treatment outcomes are compared for four types of treatment environments (modalities): outpatient methadone maintenance, therapeutic community, outpatient drug-free, and detoxification.

In chapter 23, Rush reports on another large-scale treatment outcome study. The sample studied includes youths in treatment in all the drug treatment programs in the Commonwealth of Pennsylvania. These programs participate in a centrally coordinated uniform data-collection system and report the status of each client on a standardized form at admission and at discharge. The treatment outcomes are reported for four groups: adolescents in outpatient drug-free (counseling and psychotherapy) programs, adolescents in residential (therapeutic community, etc.) programs, and a group of young-adult clients (18 to 20 years of age) in each of the same two types of treatment environments. The comparison of the treatment outcomes by age group provides information on whether or not the treatment programs, which were originally developed primarily for young-adult drug-abuse clients, are equally effective for adolescents. The treatment interventions studied were found to make more impact overall on young adults than on adolescents. Some of the findings on treatment outcome reported in this chapter are similar to those reported in chapter 22. These two research evaluation studies therefore tend to reinforce each other and thereby provide a degree of confidence for generalizing from their findings.

This latter chapter also presents a profile of the characteristics of young drug-abuse clients at admission which predicts to successful outcome of treatment. In general, those clients who engaged in more productive activities and less socially unacceptable and deviant behavior before treatment were more likely to show improvement at the end of treatment.

Although this book attempts a broad, comprehensive coverage of youth drug-abuse issues, it obviously cannot address all the important relevant issues. It is primarily a data-based book, reviewing recent and new research findings. It does not treat in any depth or detail the sociological and sociohistorical theories of youth drug abuse, or the sociopolitical and economic aspects and implications of drug abuse. It does not attempt to cover, and so contains little information on, the problems related to the supply, selling, and manufacture of illegal drugs or the enforcement of laws regarding drug traffic.

Acknowledgments

A number of persons have contributed significantly and directly to the work involved in developing this book. Major portions of the book, most specifically the National Youth Polydrug Study, grew out of studies conducted under the joint auspices of the Services Research Branch, Division of Resource Development of the National Institute on Drug Abuse (Grant #81 DA0 1657), and the Philadelphia Psychiatric Center. Most of the work of developing the book was conducted and coordinated at the Polydrug Research Center of the Philadelphia Psychiatric Center. The members of this team who contributed their effort and expertise to the book were research supervisor Yoav Santo; senior research associate Edward C. Farley; research associates David Speck and Arlene Utada; research assistant Andy Finkel; secretaries Tybie Levit, Marian Little, and Harriet Schwartz. We wish to express our thanks and our gratitude to all of them for their cooperation and assistance.

Yoav Santo and Edward C. Farley functioned as assistants to the editors of the book. The daily continuing effort and the dedication of these two team members in implementing all the various aspects of the data coordination, in communicating with the contributing authors, and in editing of the chapters, was pivotal to the development of the book.

Notes

1. Client Oriented Data Acquisition Process (CODAP), Division of Scientific and Program Information, NIDA.

2. Drug Abuse Warning Network (DAWN), Information Management Systems, America, Ltd., Ambler, Pa.

3. Drug Abuse Reporting Program (DARP), Institute of Behavioral Research, Texas Christian University.

Youth Drug Abuse

1 Introduction

George M. Beschner and
Alfred S. Friedman

The Drug Problem: Background in the Sixties and Seventies

There was a period of upheaval and social crisis in the United States in the late 1960s. Its manifestations were the civil rights struggle and the Black Power revolution, riots and burning in the large inner cities, increased crime in the streets, assassinations of national leaders, protests of the Vietnam war, and a revolution in lifestyles among youths. These young people, localized primarily on college campuses, challenged traditional values, social norms, and attitudes. An integral part of their revolt was the widespread use and abuse of licit and illicit drugs. Large urban "hippie" communities, such as Haight-Ashbury in San Francisco and Greenwich Village in New York City, became the scene for a new drug subculture involving regular use of such mood-altering drugs as marihuana, psychedelics, hallucinogens, and LSD. In addition, during the late sixties, heroin use began to spread from the traditional older groups in low-income ghetto communities to youth populations in urban, suburban and rural communities.

In the youth culture, patterns of drug use are constantly changing. One of the most complex and disturbing drug trends is the increasing involvement of youths in multiple drug-use patterns. Surveys now show that young people are using a wide variety of substances, including marihuana, alcohol, barbiturates, amphetamines, inhalants, hallucinogens, PCP, etc., in combination or in sequence with one another. As the drug-abuse problem has spread and grown during the 1970s, ever younger cohorts of users have joined the ranks of drug users. Multiple drug use has become common practice; youngsters are beginning to experiment with drugs at earlier ages, and some dangerous and harmful substances have become popular "fad" drugs. High schools, middle schools or junior high schools, and even grade schools have become places for the sale, exchange, and group or solo use of drugs and alcohol. Young people receive their illicit drug education very early today.

One of the most startling findings from recent survey data is the degree to which youngsters are now involved in drug use. According to the National Survey on Drug Abuse conducted in 1976-1977, more than one-fourth (28.2 percent) of the youths aged 12 to 17 report marihuana experience and about one-sixth (16.1 percent) report use in the past month. For adults (ages 18 and over), the lifetime prevalence rate of 24.5 percent is lower than that of youth, and current use (8.2 percent) is half that reported by youngsters. Probably more noteworthy is the reported increase over the previous year, in both prevalence and current use of marihuana among youths—increases of 5.7 and 3.7 percent, respectively.

One in ten youths report using drugs stronger than marihuana, including such drugs as inhalants (9 percent), hallucinogens (4.6 percent), cocaine (4 percent), stimulants (5.2 percent), tranquilizers (3.8 percent), and sedatives (3.1 percent). Only a small percentage of youngsters (1.1 percent) ages 12 to 17 admit having used heroin, but this is not so different from the adult population (1.4 percent). However, 6.1 percent of the youths report using other opiates, including methadone.

Drugs of Use

There is relatively little reliable information about the extent of drug use in youth populations during the 1950s and 1960s. Good epidemiological studies are lacking for the period, and problems of gathering accurate information on illicit drug use were (and continue to be) formidable. Much of what was learned came from small school surveys, reports from the criminal justice system, treatment data, and studies of special populations. Although accurate statistics are not available on the extent of use of such drugs as marihuana, amphetamines, and barbiturates during the 1960s, considerable information was produced on the types and patterns of drug use. For example, nonmedical use of amphetamines became popular after World War II. They were used by soldiers, vehicle drivers, students, and athletes to counteract fatigue and increase performance. Available commercially in a variety of forms and mixtures, amphetamines became well known as a street drug in the late sixties. Slang terms used for these drugs are "speed," "crystal," "bennies," "uppers," and "pep pills." Recent surveys indicate that these drugs are still widely used by youth populations.

Barbiturates, which gained wide medical usage as sedatives and hypnotics, have also become popular street drugs. Referred to as "barbs," "goof balls," and "downers," barbiturates are available in a variety of forms and are frequently marketed in mixtures with other drugs. Nonmedical use has been widespread across age groups. Youngsters frequently use barbiturates in combination with amphetamines and other drugs. High doses produce sedation, drowsiness, and sleep, but the effects of small quantities can be unpredictable.

The nonmedical use of psychotherapeutic (psychotropic) drugs (barbiturates, sedatives, amphetamines, and antidepressants, considered together) currently ranks second to marihuana among youth. One in eight young people report having some nonmedical experience with these drugs. Among youth 12 to 17 years of age, 7.5 percent have used a prescription drug nonmedically, while 5.5 percent have used an over-the-counter drug nonmedically.[1]

In addition, LSD (lysergic acid diethylamide) gained notoriety in the 1960s. Called "acid" and popularized as a consciousness-expanding drug, LSD was used primarily by youth populations. It appears that adverse reactions to this drug, including prolonged psychoses, discouraged more widespread use. Ninety-two percent of the high school seniors interviewed in a recent national survey indicated that they disapproved of using LSD even once or twice, and 64 percent felt that there was a "great risk" in trying this drug.[2] One in twenty-two youths (4.6 percent) have tried hallucinogens according to the George Washington Survey (1977).

The use of inhalant and solvent substances has for a long time constituted a special risk for the very young (as described in detail in chapter 13 of this book). In 1977, one in eleven young people 12 to 17 years of age (9 percent) were found to have used these substances. It is known that there are, in addition, a considerable number of children under 12 years of age who have engaged in the harmful use of inhalants and solvents.

Periodically, we hear of new drugs being marketed to youth populations. Phencyclidine hydrochloride, more commonly known as "PCP" or "angel dust," is an example of a drug that has recently become popular. In a national survey of youths in drug abuse treatment during 1977, it was learned that more than 31 percent of the youthful clients had current or past use of PCP, with males and females having similar exposure rates.[3] PCP was the second most frequently implicated drug in hospital emergency room admissions involving youth during 1977, having skyrocketed from thirteenth place in 1975. The Drug Abuse Warning Network (DAWN), a national reporting system jointly sponsored by the National Institute on Drug Abuse and the Drug Enforcement Agency, listed nearly 4,000 emergencies involving PCP in 1977, including some deaths. It is currently being predicted by some that PCP may be just one of a new series of "fad" drugs among the many which can be made in the cottage industry of small amateur laboratories, and which find their way into the street and into the hands of experimenting youths.

Currently there is more information available on the consequences of marihuana use than on the consequences of most other drugs, since there has been so much research devoted to this substance. Some of the preliminary findings regarding the consequences of marihuana use are cause for concern. Regarding physical health hazards, the *Sixth Annual Report to the U.S. Congress on Marihuana and Health* states, "While experimental use at typical U.S. levels is usually without significant hazard, more frequent, and especially chronic use, may have quite different implications." There is already some evidence that marihuana use is associated with lung problems; there are still unanswered questions about possible adverse effects on reproductive function, the body's immune response, and basic cell metabolism.

There are also some socio-psychological findings reported in the research literature that could be taken as cause for alarm. For example, several studies have found that the more or the earlier a youngster in high school is involved in marihuana use, the more likely he or she is to be failing at school and to be rated as functioning poorly on measures of personal competence and social responsibility—at least as defined in terms of the expectations of parents who hold traditional middle-class values.[4] However, at least one longitudinal study, conducted by the University of California at Berkeley, found that marihuana use did not predict poorer academic attainment and "did not have any negative consequences that are independent of other prior characteristics of users compared to nonusers."[5] It is not clear yet whether drug use causes such failures, whether the failures lead to drug use, or whether both are caused by other factors. In fact, some attributes and values have been associated with marihuana use in normal youth samples studied by Jessor et al. In these samples marihuana use has been associated with "greater value on independence, greater tolerance of transgression, greater orientation to peers than parents."[6]

Some investigators have reported a direct relationship between marihuana and other drug use. Nevertheless, the *Marijuana and Health* report concluded that, "Although marihuana use does not 'cause' other drug use in the way once simplistically believed, it is often associated with other drug use."[7] There is evidence that individuals who use one drug are more likely to use other drugs than those who do not use drugs at all. For example, marihuana use is found not to substitute for, but to be used concurrently with alcohol in both high school survey samples and in samples of youths in treatment. The consumption of alcohol and tobacco has actually increased among youths who use marihuana. Other researchers have reported a stepwise progression from beer, liquor, and cigarettes to marihuana, barbiturates, amphetamines, phencyclidine and other "fad" drugs, and ultimately heroin.

Different research approaches to the question of whether marihuana use predisposes one to heroin use will be found in chapter 4. O'Donnell and Clayton, utilizing one type of analysis, present evidence that more young subjects who started with marihuana later used heroin than did subjects who had never used marihuana. Other chapters present evidence to show that the majority of subjects who start using marihuana never progress to use of other drugs. Brunswick, in chapter 18, concludes that her study of the New York City sample "demonstrates the negligible impact of marihuana use in increasing the probability of hard drug use." Not all the research is yet completed in this area, nor are all aspects of the problems involved adequately understood.

Has the rapidly accelerating trend in use of drugs and alcohol among youths peaked yet? What impact does drug use have on society? What is the social cost? It is very difficult to determine the severity of and social cost associated with this drug problem, and the studies that have been conducted so far are limited in scope. The *Sixth Annual Report to the U.S. Congress on Marihuana and Health* states, "The rise in drug use among adolescents has generated concern about possible consequences of use in this group, especially when such use becomes an escape from the demands of preparing for later life." The report goes on to state, "A better understanding of the motivations for heavy use may permit the development of means for early intervention to avert possible lifelong patterns of drug dependency."[8]

The Federal Response

In 1971, the government launched a major effort to address what were considered to be the major drug-abuse problems in America. Public Law 92-255 provided that a permanent National Institute on Drug Abuse (NIDA) be established in the Department of Health, Education and Welfare to manage the federal drug-abuse treatment, rehabilitation, and research activities. The overall federal drug-abuse strategy involved a two-pronged effort to reduce the supply of illicit drugs through law enforcement programs and international control agreements and to reduce the demand for drugs through prevention and treatment efforts. The strategy focused on the problem of heroin abuse, which had emerged in the mid-1960s as a major social problem. It was estimated that there were more than 500,000 heroin users in the United States by the early seventies and that the cost of this problem to the nation could be as high as $117 billion a year.

This general policy–giving priority to the heroin problem–has continued to the present time. It has been based on the rationale that not all drug use is equally destructive, and therefore, the limited resources which are available should be devoted to the problems which pose the greatest risk to society at large. This policy has been reflected in state and local treatment efforts across the nation. In 1976 it was estimated that, of the 130,000 patients receiving treatment for opiate abuse, approximately 60 percent were in methadone treatment. Methadone maintenance proved to be of considerable value in stabilizing hard-core heroin addicts while they participated in rehabilitation programs.

On February 10, 1978, the Carter administration announced that heroin-related deaths in the United States had declined by 40 percent from the previous year. Within a 2-year period (1976-1977), some important trends seemed to occur. Most significant was the apparent stabilization of heroin prevalence rates and a sharp increase in the use of other drugs such as marihuana, cocaine, and phencyclidine. Although a huge investment is required to maintain the treatment system that has been established, the problems of drug abuse in our society are now quite different from what they were in 1971 when the federal drug strategy was launched. Problems of drug use and abuse have continued to increase in complexity.

The government has learned that drug-prevention activities must be undertaken with great care. More has probably been learned about what *not* to do in developing prevention strategies than about how to develop appropriate prevention strategies. There is a growing concern about the advisability of educating school children about drugs. In the past, many prevention campaigns were based on moralistic appeals and scare tactics that attempted to persuade youngsters not to experiment with drugs.

Studies have reported that many youngsters were first attracted to drugs after learning about them on the television and reading about them in the newspapers. Some youngsters are simply lured by the excitement that accompanies the risk of drug taking. As a result of the problems with past prevention strategies, a moratorium was imposed on all federally supported prevention programs, in 1973. With the publication of the "Federal Guidelines for the Production of Prevention Material" in January 1974, the moratorium was lifted. Given the reality that there is always going to be some risk in attempting to educate youngsters about drugs, the current federal prevention strategy makes the following basic assumptions: The prevention message must be nonglamorizing, realistic, and factual. Youngsters who have some experience with drugs will write off information that is erroneous, misrepresented, exaggerated, or deceptive.

The total amount of money used for funding for drug-abuse treatment in 1977 from both public and private sources was $511 million. Drug-free treatment accounted for the largest portion of the total capacity of 260,000 treatment slots–about two-thirds of all slots. Of the total number of clients in treatment, only 12.7 percent (or about 33,000) were under 18 years of age.

Recent Drug Issues

During the concentrated effort to address what was considered to be a national crisis (heroin abuse) in the 1970s, three other drug issues surfaced and received considerable attention by the media:

The movement to decriminalize marihuana

Changing patterns of psychotherapeutic drug use

The increase in multiple-substance-abuse patterns

The National Commission on Marihuana and Drug Abuse recommended decriminalization of marihuana in 1972. Since then there has been growing public sentiment in support of the position to decriminalize the possession of small quantities (1 ounce or less) of marihuana and casual accommodation (not for profit) transfers between users. This change in attitude was due primarily to several factors:

Greater understanding of the social costs associated with imprisonment

More knowledge of marihuana and its effects and greater understanding of the issues by the public

Publicity of some of the injustices (long-term imprisonment) associated with the criminal justice response

More individuals with direct experience with the drug

Regular users who smoke the drug at least once a week are now estimated at more than 15 million. It is estimated that 5,500 tons of marihuana are consumed annually in the United States. Until new legislation is passed, the federal government's policy is to prevent and discourage marihuana use in a way that is least harmful to the users and the public. The primary methods currently employed include:

Prohibiting use in public places

Developing detection methods for identifying individuals driving under the influence of marihuana

Decreasing trafficking in the drug

Despite recent developments, adult attitudes on the use of marihuana appear not to have changed since 1974. Surveys indicate that adults still feel that first offenders for either marihuana possession or use should be required to have treatment and second offenders should go to jail. However, there was some change noted in the attitudes of the high school class of 1976: they favored marihuana use more than the class of 1975. In 1976, fewer young people believed that marihuana users risk harming themselves and fewer disapproved of the use of marihuana. These attitudes and beliefs about marihuana use have shifted in conjunction with more prevalent use of this drug among young people.

National surveys conducted in the early seventies brought a new drug problem to the attention of the American public: the growing use of prescription and over-the-counter drugs and the problems associated with these types of drugs. One survey, conducted on the national patterns of psychotherapeutic drug use in 1970 and 1971, reported that 13 percent of the men and 29 percent of the women interviewed had used prescription drugs, particularly minor tranquilizers and daytime sedatives, most of which were legally obtained.[9] It was also learned that the over-the-counter drugs were being used to satisfy essentially the same needs as their counterparts among the more potent prescription drugs.

Sedative-hypnotics have become the most prescribed drugs in the world, accounting for 27 million prescriptions and over 1 billion doses in 1976. Valium is the particular drug within this class of drugs that has the most widespread use, as both a legally prescribed drug and an illegal street drug. Barbiturates were implicated in almost 5,000 drug-related deaths and accounted for 25,000 hospital emergency room visits in 1976. Over the past five years the Drug Abuse Warning Network (DAWN) and other government-sponsored information systems have shown a consistently higher frequency of drug-related overdoses, suicides, and accidental deaths associated with barbiturates and other popular sedative-hypnotic drugs. The primary medical use of amphetamines is for weight reduction, but it has long been apparent that there is a major abuse problem when they are used as stimulants, mood alterers, etc.—sometimes even when they are obtained by legal prescription.

Nonmedical use of drugs has continued to spread downward by age, crossing social and class lines, and adolescent females now seem to be using drugs at the same rates as adolescent males. This phenomenon—the expansion in drug use—can be seen most dramatically in the recent reports of phencyclidine (PCP) use. Between 1976 and 1977, the use of phencyclidine, principally among youngsters 12 to 18, doubled from 3 to 6 percent, spreading rapidly across the country from the West Coast to the Midwest, Northeast, and South, and down to the Southwest. This startling increase in use during a 1-year period appears to have resulted from the ease of manufacturing the drug, making it inexpensive to produce and widely available. In a recent study of PCP users in treatment centers, it was learned that the average PCP user who applied for treatment had taken at least five other drugs.

Factors Influencing Drug-Abuse Behavior

In addition to youngsters in school, there are large numbers of school dropouts, youngsters "running around loose," or runaways from home, unemployed, aimless, without adequate guidance and supervision, and without adequate interest, goals, or meaning in their lives. Unfortunately, the central interest and activity of these young people too often becomes drug use. By becoming involved in a drug culture, youngsters are more likely to develop experience in illegal activities and thus come into contact with the criminal justice system.

Random statements by such adolescents 13 to 17 years of age, when asked why they use drugs, are informative: "What else is there to do?" "It makes you feel you're in another world." "It doesn't hurt you and it feels good, so why not?" "People are funnier and get along better stoned." "I like it; I'm funny and can really talk." "Nothing bothers me when I'm stoned." "When I'm stoned, I can't think about the things that bring me down; I'm someplace else, where there's no bring-downs, like my family." "It's easier to make friends getting stoned."

Adolescents' reasons for using specific drugs are directly related to the particular effects of a substance. For example, they may use alcohol, marihuana, or heroin to produce pleasure. Barbiturates, amphetamines, or sedative-hypnotics may be used to help cope with moods or feelings the individual wishes to alter or escape from, such as depression, tension, or anxiety. Psychedelic drugs are usually taken in attempts to expand awareness.

Recent surveys have shown that youngsters are more likely to use drugs during the weekdays and alcohol during the weekends. Drugs are easier to conceal than alcohol, which is an important factor to youngsters who intend to use intoxicants while at school. It is sometimes difficult for school teachers to determine whether students are under the influence of drugs. Youngsters can be "intoxicated" on marihuana and yet still be able to act reasonably well in a school situation.

The drug patterns of young people are often broken down into the following categories: (1) occasional use, (2) experimental use, (3) regular use, and (4) compulsive use. Most adolescent drug users fall into the experimental or casual use category. Drug experimenters may terminate their involvement voluntarily, but they may progress to greater involvement if relevant or meaningful alternatives are not found for the benefits perceived as deriving from drug use. Among regular users, "getting high" is a primary coping mechanism and begins to dominate the individual as he or she uses drugs with greater frequency. One's energies may be almost completely consumed by the drug life. During this stage, there is a noticeable decrease in overall functioning and a high risk of bad trips, overdoses, and other adverse reactions.

Factors often considered to influence youthful drug abuses (in addition to the general effect of the emerging new cultural values and lifestyles of the "now" generation and current fads) include the quality of the parental relationship, the individual's attitudes toward society and the Establishment, peers who are involved in drug use, and the stormy nature of adolescence itself. Midway between childhood and adulthood, adolescence is a time to experiment—to try out new lifestyles and to rebel against authority and childhood limitations. To many young people, involvement in the drug culture may be a passing phase. Criminalization of a young person during this time may confirm his or her involvement and drive him or her deeper into this culture and into drug use.

Most young people use drugs because they perceive taking them as a new, interesting, or exciting experience to share with their friends and peers and as a way of belonging to, identifying with, and being accepted by a particular group. For many, however, whether they are aware of it at the time or not, involvement in drug use is a response to or an escape from some complex personal or family problem or conditions in their lives which appear to be insoluble. Those for whom drug use serves these latter purposes tend to be the youngsters who use drugs in a more extreme, unbalanced, and self-destructive way. Such youngsters may also be more likely to engage in behavior that is confusing, erratic, violent, or disturbing to their families and others, and as a result of these drug effects and behavior, they tend to become psychologically and socially dysfunctional and thus more likely to require treatment. In family therapy sessions, the wide gulf (more than the usual "generation gap") that exists between youngsters and their parents is more easily understood. This gulf may have widened since involvement of the young people in drugs, but it is likely that it preceded the drug use. In learning of their child's involvement with drugs such as marihuana, many parents become alarmed that their youngster will inevitably progress into hard drug use such as heroin addiction. In most instances, parents lack an understanding of the problem and how it evolved. These parents tend to overreact to the situation, which leads to an unhappy progression of the underlying factors (conflict, poor communication, etc.) that initially contributed to the drug use.

Multiple Causation

Youngsters take drugs for many different reasons and under many different circumstances and conditions. Obviously, adolescent substance abuse is a broadly based and multiply determined phenomenon, inbedded in its own cultural milieu and social structure, so that the study of some of the more important factors does not lend itself easily to precise quantitative analysis. The drug-use patterns of youth require interpretation and reassessment at frequent intervals, since these patterns are fluid and constantly changing. The changes are determined not only by the availability of various substances at a given time, but also by the patterns and habits of use that become institutionalized by various groups of users and by the appearance of new fads.

No one factor—whether it be pursuit of pleasure, relief from boredom or psychic distress, peer influence, or family problems such as a broken home—can adequately explain why a youngster becomes involved with drugs. How much of present adolescent substance abuse is related to ready availability? Had these substances existed earlier, and had they been as easy to get, perhaps rates and patterns of abuse in earlier years might have been different. For example, drugs are not as readily available and thus are used less in rural areas compared with some urban and suburban areas. How much drug use is related to the value systems of some subcultures? In some ghetto areas, exposure to drugs and pressure to experiment can hardly be escaped. For example, Dembo has reported that the specific features which youth select out, orient toward, and affiliate themselves with from the sociocultural and community environment in which they live are among the most critical elements in determining whether such youth become involved and stay involved in drug use.[10] Their interest in and attitude toward the tough street-wise role models in their neighborhoods are key determinants of drug use.

How much drug use was due to the youth revolt of the sixties, lending a sanction to continued drug use? How much is due to the often-blamed "pill popping" and alcohol-abuse examples of parents? Drugs and alcohol are an integral part of the youth scene in the seventies, and they are interwoven into the social and cultural fabric of the time, along with rock music, new dances, television, the movies, etc. Drug use during the adolescent years is a social phenomenon most often starting as a group experience with peers, considered by many youth as a way of growing up, getting with it, and leaving childhood and parental control behind. Taking drugs, and particularly the use of marihuana, may be considered at the present time to be institutionalized as part of the adolescent phase of life.

Research studies show that peer and family behavior and standards are, for most youngsters, the sources of greatest influence. Several investigators found relationships between students and their parents' use of drugs and between students and their closest friends' use of drugs.

It is not easy to sort out cause from effect or the coincidental and concomitant factors associated with drug use. For example, do such symptoms of psychopathology as depression and thought disorder lead the individual to use illicit drugs for self-medication purposes? Are these symptoms the effects of drug abuse, or are they not relevant to the drug abuse at all? What is the causal connection between drug use and delinquent or criminal behavior? It has been shown by a number of studies that there is a strong statistical association between using illicit drugs and engaging in other forms of illegal behavior, particularly in theft, burglary, and robbery. Some studies, however, such as that by Johnson, et al. have shown that, at least for nonaddictive drugs, other forms of delinquency tend to precede drug use: "This may simply reflect the fact that proneness toward deviancy is expressed through different behaviors at different ages."[11] Or, as Chein has asked in his classic work *The Road to H,* "Does the given personality pattern actually precede the addiction or does it emerge only afterward? Is it not conceivable, for instance, that everyone has these characteristics to some degree and that the life of the addict strengthens them while weakening and submerging compensatory contradictory characteristics? The obvious answer is to study addicts before they become addicted."[12]

Treatment for Youthful Drug Abusers

There are several reasons for the low percentage of youngsters in treatment. As indicated earlier, the treatment system was established by the federal government to reach and treat hard-core heroin addicts. Only a small fraction of the youthful drug users fall into this category. Physical and/or psychological dependency on drugs generally develops over time and becomes more problematic to the user at a later age. Intervention or treatment may, however, be indicated before physical addiction or psychological dependency develops. Even those who are more seriously involved in drug use are not apt to see the need for treatment at this age.

It is recognized that in many ways the drug-abuse treatment system has not been responsive to the special needs of youths. Current treatment modalities do not have the kind of services required to meet these special needs, and there has not been enough attention paid to the task of creating treatment and rehabilitation environments that will attract youngsters. Many drug clinics tend to be bureaucratic in structure and are viewed by youngsters as extensions of parental authority. Many youngsters find it degrading to seek help from a drug-abuse treatment program. Parents are also sensitive to the stigma associated with drug-abuse treatment and are often reluctant to refer their children to such programs for help.

One of the ideas that has been advanced for making a treatment program more acceptable to young drug abusers is the employment of former drug users. Such people are usually respected and trusted by young drug abusers, and they can be used to make contact with and to initiate treatment with youth who are at high risk of becoming dysfunctionally involved with drugs. Some professionals also can earn the trust of young drug abusers if they are capable and willing to meet them on their own level and in their own territory.

In recognition of the complexities involved, there is a need to develop a realistic treatment approach. First, it must be made clear that the problem associated with youthful drug abuse cannot be addressed by the drug field alone. Drug agencies need to develop better working relationships with other health delivery systems and social service organizations. It must be understood that in attempting to address the problems of drug-abusing youth, one must take a holistic approach. There is also a need to identify, develop, and test early intervention and treatment models which offer alternatives that are of interest to youngsters.

The findings of treatment evaluation and outcome studies have reinforced the conviction of workers in the field that their treatment efforts are beneficial. These studies have credited treatment programs with achieving marked reductions in drug use and illegal behavior and with increasing employment. However, since these studies have not used "no-treatment" control groups as a basis for comparison with the groups receiving treatment, it is not known to what extent the improvement can be attributed to the influence of the specific treatment programs. With a stringent research design and procedure, one can begin to find partial answers to the following general question: What kinds of treatment, provided in what kinds of settings, are relatively more or less effective, compared with other kinds of treatment, for what kinds of clients, based on what kinds of outcome criteria?

Conclusion

In the sixties, drug use among young people was symbolic of the counterculture movement. It was a period when many young persons were involved in political activism and rebellion against Establishment values. There were a number of causes to protest against, including the Vietnam war, the Watergate scandal, the pollution of natural resources, and discrimination against minority groups. Through such protest activities, participants established their own set of values and gained a sense of identity. Nonconformity and the quest for self-expression were manifestations of the counterculture. Drug use was often a part of this trend toward self-exploration and continued to grow in popularity. During the seventies, we have witnessed the growth and spread of drug use among adolescents and children. These youngsters, who have not yet worked through adolescence, come into contact with drugs at an age when they are groping for acceptance, understanding, and identity. The many factors contributing to their interest and involvement in using drugs are detailed in the chapters that follow.

It is clear that the children of today face a new set of challenges. Drugs are promoted more aggressively and used more freely than at any other time in our history. At the same time, youngsters have less family involvement, less participation in school activities, increased peer pressure, and more freedom for exploration and experimentation. It is time to consider the eighties and what actions might be taken to reverse this trend in drug use. One of the dilemmas regarding youth drug use is the difficulty in defining the problems associated with such use. Perhaps, to achieve any understanding, the issues must be viewed from different perspectives.

Most youngsters who use drugs do not view their drug use as a problem. In fact, many feel that drugs enhance their performance or make them feel better at times when they experience tension, ambivalence, and other pressures associated with growing up in a complex society. We know very little about the reasons youngsters start using drugs, how they experience different drugs, and the consequences of such use over time. These patterns of use are of particular concern to most parents, teachers, and other concerned adults. Drug use by youths often appears to be out of their control. Living with the fear that drugs are readily available and potentially harmful to youth, yet being in a position to do little about the situation, parents and other adults who work with youth often experience feelings of frustration.

It is time to consider courses of action that can be taken. First, there is a need to continue to increase our understanding of youth drug use, its causes, and manifestations. It is hoped that this book will prove to be a step in this direction. Ethnographic studies may also prove useful in advancing our knowledge. Second, we must explore methods of reaching youngsters during the critical years when drugs become an alternative. At the very least, we must be in a position to give them the accurate information they need, in order to make responsible decisions about their own drug use. Beyond this, we must remember how to set and enforce realistic limits on youthful behavior. Third, as adults, we must accept the fact that we set the example for youth. The current drug trend is surely a reflection of our own behavior and confusion about the use of different chemical substances, including alcohol, caffeine and tobacco. We must remove the confusion that exists regarding our own use of drugs. We must be prepared to meet the challenge of the eighties if we intend to reverse this drug trend of the seventies.

References

1. H.I. Abelson and P.M. Fishburne, *A Nationwide Study–Youth, Young Adults, and Older People,* Vol. 1, Main Findings. NIDA National Survey on Drug Abuse, U.S. Department of Health, Education and Welfare, 1977.

2. L. Johnston, J. Bachman, and P. O'Malley, *Drug Use Among American High School Students,* Vol. 1, Main Findings. NIDA National Survey on Drug Abuse, U.S. Department of Health, Education and Welfare, 1977.

3. A.S. Friedman, Y. Santo, E. Farley, and D. Speck, *Phencyclidine Use Among Youths in Drug Abuse Treatment.* Washington, D.C.: National Institute on Drug Abuse, 1978.

4. G.M. Smith, and C.P. Fogg, Psychological predictors of early use, late use, and nonuse of marihuana among teenage students, in D.B. Kandel (ed.), *Longitudinal Research on Drug Use: Empirical Findings and Methodological Issues.* New York: Wiley, 1978.

5. G.D. Mellinger, R.H. Somers, S. Bazell, and D.I. Manheimer, Drug use, academic performance, and career indecision: Longitudinal data in search of a model, in Kandel (ed.), *Longitudinal Research on Drug Use.*

6. R. Jessor, and S.L. Jessor, Theory Testing in Longitudinal Research on Marihuana Use, in Kandel (ed.), *Longitudinal Research on Drug Use.*

7. *Sixth Annual Report to the U.S. Congress on Marihuana and Health.* U.S. Department of Health, Education and Welfare, Rockville, Maryland, 1976.

8. Ibid.

9. L.H. Parry, M.B. Balter, G.D. Mellinger, I.H. Cisin, and D. Manheimer, National patterns of psychotherapeutic drug use, *Arch. Gen. Psychiat.* 28 (June 1973):769-783.

10. R. Dembo, Neighborhood Relationships and Drug Involvement Among Junior High School Youths, paper presented at the National Drug Abuse Conference, Seattle, 1978.

11. L.D. Johnston, P.M. O'Malley, and L.K. Eveland, Drugs and delinquency: A search for causal connections, in Kandel (ed.), *Longitudinal Research on Drug Use.*

12. I. Chein, *The Road to H.* New York: Basic Books, 1964, pp. 253-254.

Part I
Epidemiology

2 Overview of Adolescent Drug Use

Judith Green

Introduction

In recent years, increasing numbers of adolescents have become involved in experimentation with psychoactive agents and in the regular and often multiple use of these substances. Moreover, average age at first use has declined. Since extensive involvement with drugs during the critical years of adolescence is not only a symptom of distress but may adversely affect psychosocial or even physical development (Litt and Schonberg 1975), the effects of early use without intervention may contribute to long-range as well as immediate problems for the individual and the community.

The last decade has witnessed numerous surveys of drug use among adolescents and young adults. Samples for study have been selected using local, regional, or national bases. In attempts to characterize and differentiate users and nonusers of drugs, a variety of sociodemographic factors have been investigated for potential epidemiological significance. Although the intent of this chapter is to focus in detail on the prevalence and patterns of nonmedical drug use among youths, an introduction to later chapters is provided in a brief sketch of some features which have been found in large or repeated studies to distinguish between those individuals who are nonusers or experimenters and those who are more seriously involved in the use of psychoactive agents.

In the current review of the extent of and the sociodemographic correlates of substance use among youth in the United States, major emphasis has been placed on the findings of (1) studies which are national in scope, and (2) more regionally limited studies which through design or analysis have made unique contributions to the understanding of drug use. An extensive review of studies which are limited geographically, in sample size or in sampling techniques, is beyond the scope of this chapter, although corroborating or contrasting findings of some of these studies have been included when appropriate.

Scope of Adolescent Drug Use

Overview

Experimentation with drugs by adolescents in the United States has been shown to be extensive. Studies of youth, however, permit only limited conclusions. A simple decline in age of onset of drug use, for example, would result in elevated drug-use rates in youthful samples but would not reveal whether changes in eventual lifetime prevalence of use in the current population had occurred. It is only through studies of rates of drug use among individuals comprising a wide spectrum of age groups, however, that it is possible to determine whether the overall prevalence of drug use in our society has altered in any long-range manner or whether earlier inception of drug use has occurred without change in the ultimate proportions of individuals to be affected.

Clear evidence of increase in the prevalence of use of most psychotropic agents has been provided by the work of Abelson and Fishburne (1976) in an investigation of a national household probability sample. Whereas only a fifth of adults 26 years of age or older have reported ever using an illicit drug, nearly one-third of youths aged 12 to 17 and well over half the young adults aged 18 to 25 have reported illicit drug experience. Thus lifetime prevalence of illicit drug use in youths and young adults far exceeded usage rates in the older adult population. These data indicate that increased proportions of individuals in the current younger generation, as compared with prior generations, are becoming involved with drug use, at least on an experimental basis. Data pertaining to the frequency of current use of most psychotropic agents suggest that drug use at all levels of intensity has increased in youths and young adults, although experimentation remains the most common pattern. Since more intense drug-use practices develop over time, it is not surprising that much higher percentages of older adolescents and young adults are involved in frequent drug use as compared with youths in early teen years.

Substances which must be excluded at present from generalizations concerning increased lifetime prevalence of use include cigarettes, which are currently used by greater proportions of adults than youths, and alcohol, for which lifetime prevalence has apparently not yet been determined in the various age cohorts. In the case of alcohol, it is unlikely that dramatic increases in lifetime prevalence of use could occur since the vast majority of adults have had experience with alcohol.

While surveys indicate that marked rises in drug use have occurred in the last decade, a plateau in prevalence and new incidence of substance use appears to have commenced (Blackford 1977; Johnston et al. 1976; Abelson and Fishburne 1976). It is important to note that although increases in prevalence rates have diminished, the percentages of young people involved and continuing to become involved in substance use are substantial. For example, in the nationwide household survey conducted by Abelson and Fishburne (1976), it was found that more than 30 percent of the youths and almost 60 percent of the young adults had ever used an illicit drug at some time. Among nationally representative high school seniors in public and private schools in 1977, 62 percent claimed to have illicit drug experiences (Johnston et al. 1978). Approximately 9 percent of the youths and 18 percent of the young adults sampled in households reported illicit drug experience with marihuana only, while 22 and 29 percent of individuals in these cohorts had experience with other illicit drugs as well (Abelson and Fishburne 1976). According to Johnston et al. (1978), more than one-third of high school seniors report having used one or more illicit substances other than marihuana.

Similarly, in a representative survey of more than 8,000 high school students in New York, Kandel et al. (1976) reported that 90 percent of the youths had ever used one or more psychoactive drugs (including both licit and illicit drugs). While 55 percent of the students used licit drugs only, primarily alcohol and cigarettes, 35 percent had tried an illicit drug at some time. The data from surveys concerning the use of any drugs, licit drugs, and illicit substances by adolescents are presented in table 2-1.

Use of Licit Drugs

It is clear from the majority of studies that alcohol is the substance most frequently tried and most regularly and heavily used among young people of all classes and ethnic groups sampled. The data in table 2-2 compare adolescent use of alcohol with that of cigarettes and marihuana.

In New York State, more than 82 percent of high school students surveyed were reported to have ever used alcoholic beverages, and 27 percent were considered current regular drinkers of beer or wine (six or more times in the last

Table 2-1
Prevalence of Use of Any Drugs, Licit Drugs Only, and Illicit Drugs by Adolescents

Study[a]	*Year of Survey*	*Subject Age or Grade Level*	*Sample Size*	*Ever Used Any Drug (%)*	*Ever Used Legal Drugs Only (%)*	*Ever Used Illicit Drug (%)*	*Only Illicit Drug Marihuana (%)*	*Ever Used Other Illicit Drug (%)*
(1)	1975-1976	12-17 yrs.	985	–	–	30[c]	9.3	22
		18-25	–	–	–	57[c]	18.1	39
(2)	1977	HS students	22,000	90[b]	–	–	–	–
(3)	1976	HS seniors	17,000	92	–	60[c]	–	33[c]
(4)	1974-1975	Jr. and Sr. HS students	8,500	83	–	35	19	13
(5,6)	1971	HS students	8,000	90	55	35	11	19

[a](1) Abelson and Fishburne 1976; (2) Blackford 1977; (3) Johnston et al. 1976; (4) N.Y. State Offices of Drug Abuse Services 1975; (5) Single et al. 1975; (6) Kandel et al. 1976.

[b]During preceding year.

[c]Approximate calculation.

Table 2-2
Comparison of Prevalences of Lifetime, Current, and Frequent Use of Alcohol, Cigarettes, and Marihuana among Adolescents at Various Age or Grade Levels

Drug	*Study*[a]	*Year of Study*	*Subject Age or Grade*	*Ever Used (%)*	*Used in Past Month (%)*	*Regular Current Use*[b] *(%)*	*Daily or Nearly Daily Use (%)*
Alcohol	(1)	1975-1976	12-17	54	32	5	i
	(7)	1971	HS students	65[c]	39[c]	9[c]	–
				82[d]	–	27[d]	–
	(4)	1974-1975	13-18	82	–	6[e]	–
	(6)	1974	13-18	80	–	23	2
	(2)	1977	HS students	88[f]	–	25	–
	(3)	1976	HS seniors	92	69	41[g]	6
	(1)	1975-1976	18-25	–	69	>17	7
	(5)	1974-1975	19-30[h]	97	85	–	–
Cigarettes	(1)	1975-1976	12-17	–	23	–	23
	(7)	1971	HS students	72	–	–	23
	(2)	1977	HS students	57[f]	–	25	–
	(3)	1976	HS seniors	75	–	–	–
	(1)	1975-1976	18-25	–	49	–	49
	(5)	1974-1975	19-30[h]	88	–	–	–
Marihuana	(1)	1975-1976	12-17	22	12	>7	–
	(7)	1971	HS students	30	19	8	–
	(4)	1974-1975	13-18	32	–	6[e]	–
	(2)	1977	HS students	58[f]	–	23	–
	(8)	1973-1974	HS students	48	22	19	6
	(3)	1976	HS seniors	53	32	16[g]	–
	(8)	1973-1974	College students	64	35	31	8
	(1)	1975-1976	18-25	53	25	>15	–
	(5)	1974-1975	19-30[h]	55	26	–	–

[a](a) Abelson and Fishburne 1976; (2) Blackford 1977; (3) Johnston et al. 1976; (4) N.Y. State Offices of Drug Abuse Services 1975; (5) O'Donnell et al. 1976; (6) Rachal et al. 1975; (7) Single et al. 1975; (8) Yankelovich et al. 1975.

[b]Frequency of once a month or greater.

[c]Hard liquor.

[d]Beer or wine.

[e]31 or more times in last 6 months.

[f]During preceding year.

[g]Three to nineteen times in past month.

[h]Men only.

[i]Less than 0.5 percent.

30 days) (Kandel et al. 1976). Among 1,987 nationally representative high school and college students, 58 percent of high school and 79 percent of college students were classified as current drinkers although the criteria used were not clear (Yankelovich, Skelly and White, Inc. 1975). Of more than 7,000 urban and suburban high school students 85 percent had tried alcohol, and 56 percent

reported themselves continuing to drink (Yancy et al. 1972). In 1976, more than 92 percent of high school seniors reported having used alcohol. Nearly 70 percent had used alcohol within the last 30 days, and 41 percent reported using alcohol regularly (three to nineteen times in the last month) (Johnston et al. 1976). It is important to note that in this study, daily or near daily users of alcohol constituted 6 percent of the high school seniors, a percentage that is compatible with estimates of excessive drinking in the general population.

Data collected in longitudinal studies suggest that first use of alcohol is occurring at earlier ages. For example, in San Mateo County in 1977, nearly 23 percent of males in grade 7 had used alcohol within the last 6 months as compared with approximately 11 percent in 1969 (Blackford 1977). Since alcohol is tried at some time during life by nearly everyone, these data reflect a decline in age of first use rather than an increase in prevalence of alcohol use per se. In Blackford's study, a 20 to 30 percent increase in the recent use of alcohol was observed in high school students between 1968 and 1977. Similarly, the reported prevalence of current alcohol usage (use within the last month) in adolescents aged 12 to 17 increased between 1972 and 1975-1976 (Abelson and Fishburne 1976), with the percentage of 14- and 15-year-olds who reported themselves as current drinkers rising from 21 percent in 1972 to 31 percent in 1975-1976. Among 16- and 17-year-olds, the increase in current drinking was from 35 to 47 percent. In at least one study, the prevalence of current alcohol use was found to reach a peak (exceeding 90 percent) in men by age 19 (O'Donnell et al. 1976). Since few studies have addressed the relationship between age and intensity of drinking, it is difficult to determine whether there have been any changes in the age at which serious involvement with alcohol first occurs.

In a number of studies, cigarettes have been found to rank second to alcohol in prevalence of lifetime and current use among youth. Of a nationally representative sample of youth aged 12 to 17, 23 percent reported themselves as current smokers (approximately half the sample had tried cigarettes), while 41 percent of all adults 18 years of age or older claimed to smoke (Abelson and Fishburne 1976). Consistent with these data, 29 percent of high school seniors reported themselves as daily smokers, with 19 percent smoking at least half a pack of cigarettes per day (Johnston et al. 1978). As with many other drugs, the prevalence of cigarette use has reportedly increased among adolescents. In 1976, 23 percent of youths claimed to be smokers versus only 15 percent in 1971 (Abelson and Fishburne 1976). Whether increased proportions of individuals in the adolescent population as compared with the current adult population will become smokers cannot be determined with certainty, since at present considerably greater percentages of adults are smokers. However, it appears from this and other longitudinal studies (Johnston et al. 1976) that more individuals are becoming smokers at younger ages. Interestingly, an overall decline in cigarette use among students in grades 7 to 12 in San Mateo County has been observed since 1974 (Blackford 1977), which was accounted for primarily by decreased smoking among boys. Rates of smoking appear to have actually increased among high school girls in San Mateo County. However, in the high school senior sample in 1977, little difference was found between prevalences of men and women who smoked ten or more cigarettes per day (20 versus 19 percent respectively); within this group of regular smokers, men appeared to be somewhat heavier smokers than women (Johnston et al. 1978).

The high proportions of smokers are of particular interest since early cigarette use has been implicated as an antecedent factor in the excessive use of alcohol and the use of illicit drugs in adulthood (Tennant and Detels *in press*). In addition, many studies have indicated that the use of cigarettes is correlated with the use of other drugs, both licit (Seltzer et al. 1974) and illicit (Block 1975; Josephson et al. 1972; Gould et al. 1977; Roth 1972; Wolfson et al. 1972; Single et al. 1975). In a large study of patients at the Kaiser-Permanente Medical Group (Seltzer et al. 1974), it was found from medical records that teenagers who smoked tended to be several times more likely than nonsmokers to have been prescribed such psychoactive drugs as barbiturates, codeine, morphine, and amphetamines. Similarly, youths who were smokers were approximately three times as likely to have used nonmedically prescribed psychotherapeutic drugs, marihuana, and other illicit substances (Abelson and Fishburne 1976). Single et al. (1975) reported that almost all New York State high school students who had ever tried an illicit drug had previously smoked cigarettes (89 percent) or used alcohol (at least 94 percent).

Since cigarette use generally precedes experimentation with marihuana and "hard" illicit drugs, it may prove fruitful to address the preventive implications of these known smoking correlates. Screening for smokers may provide an efficacious procedure for the identification of adolescents at high risk for drug misuse, particularly at the younger age levels. Combined with poor academic performance, there is evidence that smoking implies an attempt to achieve status in an alternative outside of school and more deviant subculture (Tamerin 1973).

Illicit Drug Use

The results of several studies suggest that between 30 and 60 percent of adolescents have experimented at some time with one or more illicit drugs, most frequently with marihuana (Abelson and Fishburne 1976; Single et al. 1975; Johnston et al. 1976). It is clear that while the percentage of young people claiming extensive use of illicit drugs is considerably smaller, the numbers of individuals involved are appreciable, particularly among the older teenagers and young adults. Table 2-2 shows the prevalence of lifetime, current, and frequent use of marihuana as compared with licit drugs at various age, school, or grade levels.

Marihuana. Data from several large annual studies indicate that marihuana use has increased substantially among young people in the last decade, and although the rate of increase may have diminished in the last few years, new incidence continues to rise in young adults. Among youth aged 12 to 17, those who had tried marihuana increased from 14 to 23 percent in 1974, a level which appeared to remain stable for the succeeding 2 or 3 years. Among those aged 18 to 25, the prevalence rose from 39 percent in 1971 to 53 percent in 1974 and 1975-1976 (Abelson and Fishburne 1976). An even greater rise was observed since 1969 in a study of male high school seniors (Johnston et al. 1976). A threefold increase in those who had tried marihuana was reported in this study, the rate burgeoning from 20 percent in 1969 to 59 percent in 1976. In 1978 the same authors reported that among male and female high school seniors the proportion of those who had used marihuana rose from 47 percent in 1975 to 56 percent in 1977, suggesting another acceleratory trend in the use of this agent.

Assessments of intensity of marihuana use in adolescents indicate that parallel increases in nonexperimental use of this substance has occurred concomitantly. In San Mateo County, the rate of regular marihuana use by high school students (on fifty or more occasions in the preceding year) rose from 16 percent in 1970 to an apparently stable rate of 24 percent in 1974 (Blackford 1977). Some data, however, have suggested that current regular use of marihuana may be continuing to increase. Johnston et al. (1978) reported that in 1977, 9 percent of high school seniors were smoking marihuana daily or nearly daily, whereas 6 percent claimed such use in 1975 and 8 percent did so in 1976. Thus, although the experimental use of marihuana seemed to have reached a plateau in the middle 1970s, data gathered later in the decade suggest an acceleratory trend, and it is likely that more extensive involvement with this substance has continued to increase also.

It is interesting, too, that among high school seniors the regular, daily or near daily use of marihuana has become more prevalent (9 percent of the sample in 1977) than comparably frequent use of alcohol (6 percent). In this regard, Kandel et al. (1976) noted that although in New York State more high school students had tried hard liquor (65 percent) than marihuana (29 percent), among those who had tried either, higher percentages of marihuana than alcohol experimenters became regular users of the respective substances (29 versus 14 percent).

New incidence of marihuana use has been found to be similar in the 1974 and 1975-1976 surveys of Abelson and Fishburne (1976): 8 to 9 percent in the 12- to 17-year-old cohort and 2 to 3 percent for all adults. The age groups which revealed the highest incidences of new marihuana use in 1975-1976 were 16- to 17-year-olds (13 percent) and 18- to 21-year-olds (11 percent). These data represent a small shift toward first usage of marihuana at older ages, but the strength of the trend has not been determined.

The use of hashish, a more purified form of cannabis, while less common than marihuana, is nonetheless of much greater magnitude than the use of "harder" illicit drugs. Hashish use has been reported by nearly 10 percent of youths and 29 percent of young adults (Abelson and Fishburne 1976). In contrast to marihuana use, regular use of hashish (five or more times in the past month) is low: 7 percent of adolescents and 15 percent of young adults reported current regular use of marihuana, whereas less than 1 percent of youths and only 1 percent of young adults reported similar levels of hashish use.

Other Illicit Drugs. Table 2-3 presents a summary and comparison of the findings of major drug surveys conducted in recent years. It has been found that psychedelic drugs, stimulants, barbiturates, and sedatives are the most widely used of the "hard" illicit drugs. Examination of survey data suggests that although experimentation with such drugs is widespread, the regular use of any of these substances is limited. Moreover, both experimental and more extensive use of these agents appears to have declined in the last few years. For example, whereas more than 13 percent of high school students in San Mateo County used LSD in the past year, 3 percent had used it (on ten or more occasions) during that year, and 1 percent had used it regularly (on fifty or more occasions) (Blackford 1977). Thus only about one in ten students with current-year hallucinogen experience admitted to regular use. Moreover, rates of both any past year use and regular past year use of hallucinogens showed modest decreases in recent years as compared with the early 1970s.

In the 1975-1976 national household probability sample (Abelson and Fishburne 1976), 8 percent of youths aged 12 to 17 claimed to have ever used hallucinogens, but only 2 percent had used such drugs in the past year, and less than 1 percent reported current usage (within the past month). Current use rates were reported to be stable from 1972, when data were first obtained, to 1975-1976, although the prevalence of any use increased slightly from 6 to 8 percent. These data suggest that even while experimentation with hallucinogens may have increased during the early to middle 1970s, continued usage rates did not. In fact, fewer than 0.5 percent of individuals in any age group reported current regular use of hallucinogens (five or more times in the past month). In addition to these findings, Johnston et al. (1978) reported a decline in the lifetime prevalence of hallucinogen use among high school seniors from 16 percent in 1975 to 14 percent in 1977.

The San Mateo student data for barbiturate and amphetamine use are strikingly similar to those for hallucinogens (Blackford 1977). While 11 percent of high school students had used some kind of barbiturate during the past year (assessed in 1977), only 1 percent claimed to have used such drugs fifty or more times during the same period. Again, both the "any use" and "frequent use" figures represented declines from the early 1970s. In 1971, 18 percent of high school students reported some kind of barbiturate use during the preceding year, and 3 percent claimed regular use.

Amphetamine use fell among high school students from more than 23 percent in the "any" category in 1971-1972 to 15 percent in 1977, and from approximately 4 percent in the early 1970s to 2 percent in the "frequent" (fifty or more times) category.

Other longitudinal studies have indicated increased trial of hallucinogens,

Table 2-3
Comparison of Prevalences of Lifetime, Current, and Regular Use of Illicit Drugs Other Than Marihuana among Adolescents at Various Age or Grade Levels

Drug	*Study*[a]	*Year of Study*	*Subject Age or Grade*	*Ever Used (%)*	*Used in Past Month (%)*	*Regular Current Use (%)*	*Daily or Nearly Daily Use (%)*
Amphetamines	(1)	1975-1976	12-17	4	–	–	–
	(6,7)	1971	HS students	14	–	–	–
	(4)	1974-1975	13-18	9	–	h	–
	(2)	1977	HS students	15[c]	–	2[c]	–
	(3)	1976	HS seniors	23	8	4[d]	0.6
	(1)	1975-1976	18-25	17	–	–	–
	(5)	1974-1975	19-30[e]	27	5	–	–
Barbiturates (Sedatives)	(1)	1975-1976	12-17	3	–	–	–
	(6,7)	1971	HS students	12	–	–	–
	(4)	1974-1975	13-18	9	–	h	–
	(2)	1977	HS students	11[c]	–	1[c]	–
	(3)	1976	HS seniors	17	4	1[d]	h
	(1)	1975-1976	18-25	12	–	–	–
	(5)	1974-1975	19-30[e]	20	3	–	–
Opiates	(1)	1975-1976	12-17	0.5[f]	*	*	–
	(6,7)	1971	HS students	3[c,f]	–	–	–
				8	–	–	–
	(4)	1974-1975	13-18	4	–	*	–
	(2)	1977	HS students	3[f]	–	–	0.8[f]
	(3)	1976	HS seniors	2[f]	f,h	*	–
				10	2	0.7[d]	*
	(1)	1975-1976	18-25	4[f]	*	*	–
	(5)	1974-1975	19-30[e]	6[f]	1[f]	–	–
LSD	(1)	1975-1976	12-17	5[g]	1[g]	*	–
	(6,7)	1971	HS students	9	–	–	–
	(4)	1974-1975	13-18	6	–	*	–
	(2)	1977	HS students	13[c]	–	1	–
	(3)	1976	HS seniors	11	2	*	*
	(1)	1975-1976	18-25	17[g]	1[g]	*	–
	(5)	1974-1975	19-30[e]	22[g]	2[g]	–	–
Cocaine	(1)	1975-1976	12-17	3	1	*	–
	(6,7)	1971	HS students	4	–	–	–
	(3)	1976	HS seniors	10	2	0.6[d]	–
	(1)	1975-1976	18-25	13	2	*	–
	(5)	1974-1975	19-30[e]	14	2	–	–

[a](1) Abelson and Fishburne 1976; (2) Blackford 1977; (3) Johnston et al. 1976; (4) N.Y. State Office of Drug Abuse Services 1975; (5) O'Donnell et al. 1976; (6) Single et al. 1975; (7) Kandel et al. 1976.

[b]Frequency of once a month or greater.

[c]During the preceding year.

[d]Three to nineteen times in the past month.

[e]Men only.

[f]Heroin.

[g]Psychedelics.

*Less than 0.5 percent.

stimulants, and depressants in the past decade. Among nationally representative male high school seniors sampled throughout the last 9 years, approximately three-fold increases in any use of these drugs has occurred. Rates of usage among the "pills" are again seen to be highest for amphetamines, perhaps reflecting the dieter's interest in these agents.

The drugs least used are those with the greatest legal sanctions, namely the opiates and cocaine. Although cocaine is a central nervous system stimulant similar in its effects to the amphetamines, it is far less available for casual use.

In one study (Abelson and Fishburne 1976), estimates of any cocaine use ranged from 4 percent for the 12- to 17-year-olds to 13 percent for young adults. Relative constancy in cocaine usage since 1974 was reported for both age groups with respect to lifetime prevalence and current involvement. Fewer than 1 percent of 12- to 17-year-olds claimed to have used cocaine in the past month; the highest current usage rate, 2 percent, was found in the 18- to 25-year cohort.

Data obtained from high school seniors was comparable for 1975-1976. Lifetime prevalence of cocaine use remained at 9 to 10 percent in 1975 and 1976 (Johnston et al. 1976) in contrast to 2.5 times greater but also stable amphetamine-use rates. It may be of some importance to note that the proportion of seniors reporting any use of cocaine increased to 11 percent in 1977, indicating a gradual increase in the experimental use of this potent stimulant. In addition, although current use of cocaine remained stable at 1 to 2 percent during 1975-1976, a significant increase in this rate to 3 percent (p = .001) occurred between 1976 and 1977 (Johnston et al. 1978). Thus it is clear that although the rates of cocaine use at all levels of intensity are low and that these rates have not been subject to the major changes which have characterized the use of most other drugs during the last decade, attention to these recent increases in use is merited.

The rates of experimentation with heroin are also low. Fewer than 3 percent of New York State high school students sampled in 1971 had ever used heroin (Single et al. 1976), a rate which has remained remarkably constant (Blackford 1977). When youths were sampled over a wider age range (12 to 17 years), the prevalence of any use of heroin was only 0.5 percent, suggesting that age of first use of heroin tends to occur during later adolescence. This inference is reinforced by the finding that nearly eight times as many young adults as adolescents had ever used heroin (Abelson and Fishburne 1976).

Further evidence of stability in the usage rates of heroin across the nation was provided in a number of surveys. For example, current use of heroin by adolescents was reported to have remained below 0.5 percent from 1972 to 1975-1976 (Abelson and Fishburne 1976), and similar data were reported for high school seniors from 1975 to 1977 (Johnston et al. 1978).

In summary, it is important to point out the observations of Kandel et al. (1976) that with the exception of those young people using marihuana and hashish, regular users of other psychoactive substances (six or more times in the past month) were rare, constituting only about 1 percent of the student population. Whereas there was a tendency for persistent use of cigarettes, alcohol, marihuana, and heroin among significant percentages of those who had ever tried such substances, the use of amphetamines, depressants, tranquilizers, and psychedelics very seldom became regular. Thus, current regular use of beer and wine (27 percent), cigarettes (23 percent), hard liquor (9 percent), and marihuana and hashish (8 percent) were substantial, but only 1 percent of high school students used any illicit drug other than marihuana on a regular basis.

A follow-up survey administered to the same New York State students 5 months later (Kandel et al. 1976) indicated that experimentation rates increased sharply during high school years, with the percentage of new users in each of the drug categories greatly exceeding the percentages who stopped using drugs. But it is significant that much of the regular use reported in the initial survey was no longer reported in the follow-up survey 5 months later; the regular users in the second survey largely represented new users. Thus, with the important exceptions of alcohol, cigarettes, and marihuana, for which cumulative increases in use occur with age, the regular use of drugs tends to be intermittent and scarce.

Relationships between Drugs

Much evidence has accumulated indicating that a large proportion of youths who become involved in illicit drug use also become multiple drug users. In New York State nearly all high school students who ever tried an illicit drug had prior experience with alcohol, and 89 percent had smoked cigarettes (Single et al. 1975). Thus there appeared to be a high correlation between the use of illicit drugs and prior usage of licit drugs. In addition, there was also a strong relationship between illicit drug use and a pattern of multiple use of illicit drugs. Of those who tried any illicit drug, 70 percent tried more than one other.

A finding of particular significance in the New York State study was the relationship between the degree of involvement with marihuana and the use of other drugs, both licit and illicit. Among heavy users of marihuana (sixty or more times), 84 percent used pills, 78 percent used LSD, and 62 percent used cocaine, heroin, or other narcotics. In addition, daily users of marihuana consumed more alcohol, suggesting that legalization of marihuana would not be likely to lead either to diminished alcohol consumption or to a diminution of the effects of excessive drinking. Similar findings with regard to the relationship between marihuana use and drinking have been reported by others (Block 1975; Wolfson et al. 1972).

There are indications that the prevalence of multiple drug use has also increased among adolescents (Gould et al. 1977; Vaillant 1970). Probably because multiple drug use is an index of the seriousness of drug-seeking behavior, it is associated with a poorer prognosis for abstinence by age 30 to 35 than is the use of a single drug (Robins and Murphy 1967).

Stages in Drug Involvement

From the number and kinds of drugs reported and the order in which they are first used, scalogram analyses of data gathered from high school students has indicated that there are progressive, though by no means inevitable, stages of involvement in drug use (Kandel 1975; Gould et al. 1977; Hamburg et al. 1975). Among those adolescents who used any drugs, Kandel (1975) found that beer and/or wine were usually tried first (stage 1), in many cases followed by cigarettes or hard liquor (stage 2). Marihuana was generally the next drug used (stage 3). Those young people who eventually tried other illegal drugs (stage 4) usually did so after experimentation with or regular use of marihuana. Two other investigative groups have reported further progression within Kandel's stage 4 (Gould et al. 1977; Hamburg et al. 1975). Among individuals who used illicit substances other than marihuana and hashish, the drugs tried next were stimulants, depressants, and psychedelics. Lastly, and involving therefore the smallest percentage of youth, cocaine and narcotics were used.

Demographic Factors

Data concerning demographic factors have frequently been assessed in surveys of drug use. Unfortunately, few attempts have been made to study demographic correlates of drug use with appropriate controls for social and psychological variables as well as other peer pressure, conventionality, or relationships with parents. It is quite possible, for example, that the increases in drug use observed to occur with increasing age actually reflect progressive intensification of difficulties in relationships with parents during adolescence. Thus age itself may have little direct effect on drug use except insofar as it correlates with other variables.

Despite the methodological problems encountered in the literature, data concerning demographic factors in drug use are reviewed here to provide an overview of current knowledge in this area. Demographic correlates may serve as useful descriptors even when the relationships to other such variables and to underlying factors are uncertain.

Age

It is abundantly clear that the use of licit and illicit drugs increases with age during adolescence. While relatively few 12- to 13-year-olds experiment with any drugs, large proportions of high school seniors have experimented with or entered into regular use of psychoactive agents. Kandel et al. (1976) reported that age-related increases in drug use appeared to reach a peak in the early twenties. These findings were recently corroborated by Abelson and Fishburne (1976) in a large national sample.

To some extent the correlation between age and rate of drug use reflects the increasing time and opportunity for contact with drugs in older groups. Why the inception of drug use occurs at certain ages and not others and why these ages have changed in recent years remain intriguing questions. In any event, as the numbers of adolescents using drugs grow, peer pressure also mounts, leading at least in part to the exponential rather than linear relationship between age and drug use.

The data in table 2-4 are arranged to illustrate the relationship between age and the use of the most common drugs: alcohol, cigarettes, and marihuana. Although the data are most plentiful for lifetime prevalences, it is clear that the amount of recent and regular drug use increases with age as well. With the exception of inhalants, which are largely restricted in use to younger age groups, these generalizations are also valid for the use of illicit drugs other than marihuana.

Licit Drugs. In the national household survey (Abelson and Fishburne 1976), approximately 55 percent of youths aged 12 to 17 claimed to have ever tried alcohol; the comparable figure for young adults aged 18 to 25 was 84 percent. Current drinking (any use in the last month) was reported by more than twice as many young adults (69 percent) as youths (32 percent). Drinking on a regular basis (five or more times in the past month) was reported for 5 to 6 percent of youths, but for many times more young adults (31 percent). Regular drinkers among adults aged 26 or more years constituted 27 percent of that cohort. Daily or near daily drinking was reported in fewer than 1 percent of youth, in more than 7 percent of young adults, and in 12.5 percent of older adults. Although daily or near daily alcohol use appeared to increase with age beyond the early twenties, the data suggest that the *quantity* of alcohol consumed on an average day reached a peak in young adulthood. Thus 9 percent of youths, 28 percent of young adults, and 17 percent of older adults reported taking three or more drinks on an average alcohol-use day. These data correlate with findings in a study of American men aged 21 to 59 in which problem drinking was most common in the group aged 21 to 24 years (Cahalan and Room 1972).

Rates of cigarette use were shown to increase substantially with age, reaching a peak in young adulthood (49 percent) (Abelson and Fishburne 1976). Apparently the majority of those who become smokers have tried cigarettes by grade 8 or 9 (Kandel et al. 1976; Blackford 1977).

Marihuana. Several survey groups have reported that the experimental use of marihuana increases sharply with age. In their most recent study, Abelson and Fishburne (1976) found that 6 percent of 12- to 13-year-olds, 21 percent of 14- to 15-year-olds, 40 percent of 16- to 17-year-olds, and 53 percent of 18- to

Table 2-4
Relationship of Lifetime, Recent, and Regular Drug Use to Age

Drug	*Study*[a]	*Subject Age or Grade Level*	*Ever Used (%)*	*Used in Past Month (%)*	*Regular Current Use*[b] *(%)*
Alcohol	(1)	12-13	–	19	–
	(2)	Grade 7	72	–	8
	(5)	⩽13	62	–	–
	(1)	14-15	–	31	–
	(2)	Grade 9	84	–	20
	(4)	Grade 9	51[c]	–	–
			73[d]	–	–
	(5)	15	75	–	–
	(1)	16-17	–	47	–
	(2)	Grade 11	90	–	34
	(4)	Grade 11	72[c]	–	–
			79[d]	–	–
	(5)	17	83	–	–
	(1)	18-21	–	66	–
	(2)	Grade 12	91	–	40
	(4)	Grade 12	74[c]	–	–
			81[d]	–	–
	(3)	Grade 12	91[e]	–	–
			93[f]	–	–
Cigarettes	(1)	12-13	–	11	–
	(2)	Grade 7	–	–	6[e]
			41	–	5[f]
	(1)	14-15	–	20	–
	(2)	Grade 9	62[e]	–	24[e]
			51[f]	–	16[f]
	(4)	Grade 9	48	–	–
	(1)	16-17	–	39	–
	(2)	Grade 11	62[e]	–	34[e]
			54[f]	–	22[f]
	(4)	Grade 11	55	–	–
	(2)	Grade 12	59[e]	–	34[e]
		Grade 12	52[f]	–	22[f]
	(4)	Grade 12	54	–	–
	(3)	Grade 12	75[e]	–	–
			76[f]	–	–
	(1)	18-25	–	49	–
Marihuana	(1)	12-13	6	3	–
	(2)	Grade 7	15[e]	–	2[e]
			23[f]	–	4[f]
	(1)	14-15	21	13	–
	(2)	Grade 9	43[e]	–	16[e]
			48[f]	–	12[f]
	(4)	Grade 9	16	–	–
	(1)	16-17	40	21	–
	(2)	Grade 11	63[e]	–	25[e]
			65[f]	–	31[f]
	(4)	Grade 11	33	–	–
	(1)	18-21	52	25	–
	(2)	Grade 12	61[e]	–	24[e]

Table 2-4 continued

Drug	*Study*[a]	*Subject Age or Grade Level*	*Ever Used (%)*	*Used in Past Month (%)*	*Regular Current Use*[b] *(%)*
			64[f]	–	34[f]
	(4)	Grade 12	41	–	–
	(3)	Grade 12	53	32	24[g]

[a](1) Abelson and Fishburne 1976; (2) Blackford 1977; (3) Johnston et al. 1976; (4) Kandel et al. 1976; (5) Rachal et al. 1975.

[b]Frequency of once a month or greater.

[c]Hard liquor.

[d]Beer or wine.

[e]Female.

[f]Male.

[g]Three or more times in the last month.

25-year-olds had acknowledged ever trying marihuana. Current use rates (during the past month) were approximately half that of lifetime prevalence for each of these age groups. Thus for both any and current use, about an eight-fold rise in rate occurred between age 12 and young adulthood.

Other Illicit Drugs. The evidence derived from major surveys conducted in recent years indicates that congruent with licit drugs and marihuana, the lifetime prevalence and rates of regular use of amphetamines, barbiturates, hallucinogens, and opiates all increase several times between the twelfth and eighteenth years. Although the extent of experimentation with each of these substances varies (table 2-3), the proportion of users who reported regular involvement with each drug was constant across age levels. At all ages, large proportions of those who had tried alcohol, cigarettes, marihuana, or opiates used these drugs regularly, while much smaller proportions of those who ever tried hallucinogens, amphetamines, or barbiturates apparently became regular users.

With increasing age and drug experience, the likelihood of multiple substance use has been reported to increase. Gould et al. (1977) observed that as new drugs are tried, generally in a sequential pattern over time, previously used drugs are often not abandoned. Thus multiple substance users tend to be older individuals who have expanded the scope of their drug use to include illicit as well as licit drugs.

Sex

Although the data are not entirely consistent, recent studies indicate that previously reported sex-related differences in drug use among youth during high school and years immediately following have narrowed or disappeared (Wechsler and McFadden 1976). Traditionally, males were more likely to use drugs. Currently the severalfold higher rates of alcoholism and heroin addiction in males attest to the greater probability that males become involved in intensive, protracted substance use. However, in less severe forms of drug involvement, sex-associated disparities appear at present to be relatively insignificant when compared with other correlates of drug use. In 1971, few differences were found in the percentages of male and female high school students in New York State who had tried legal or illegal drugs (Kandel et al. 1976), although there was a tendency for males to use more alcohol (especially hard liquor) and females to use more pills (barbiturates and amphetamines). The probability of ever trying marihuana was similar for students of both sexes. Lavenhar et al. (1972) reported that males tended to use marihuana to a greater extent.

The findings in more recent studies suggest that limited sex differences in drug use do exist. Some evidence has indicated that males begin drinking at earlier ages than females, although by high school these differences have disappeared (Blackford 1977). Among youngsters in seventh grade, 72 percent of males and 64 percent of females reported using alcohol in the past year, while the comparable figures among ninth graders were 84 and 82 percent. Males, however, maintained consistently higher prevalences of *regular* alcohol use (on at least fifty occasions during the past year) (Blackford 1977). In twelfth grade, 40 percent of males and 32 percent of females claimed regular drinking practices. Rachal et al. (1975) also found that males (aged 13 to 18) were considerably more likely than females to be regular users of alcohol. It is important to note that although smaller percentages of females acknowledged serious involvement with alcohol, these rates of female involvement were far from insignificant.

In addition, the likelihood of being a *current* user of alcohol (within the last month) was greater for males than for females in the 12- to 17-year age range (Abelson and Fishburne 1976). Among young adults (18 to 25 years old), the difference was striking, with 79 percent of males and 58 percent of females reporting themselves to be drinkers. This disparity in current drinking was apparent in older adults as well, although it is not possible to predict whether current youth will conform to similar drinking practices in later life.

Perhaps the most striking sex difference in drug use concerns cigarettes. At least two recent studies based on large samples of youth suggest that smoking rates have declined in males while increasing modestly in females. The end result of these opposing trends has been a slight decline in overall smoking, with higher proportions of adolescent females now reporting themselves to be smokers. Since at present the strength of these trends is uncertain, interpretations require caution. However, it is tempting to speculate that males have been influenced to a relatively greater extent by campaigns to educate the public about the hazards of smoking, while females have been impressed by the advertising approaches which link female liberation, or the new feminism, with smoking. In any case, smoking in women presents dual hazards. Not only is the health of the individual woman jeopardized, but the normal development of a fetus may be impeded by smoking during pregnancy (Cope et al. 1973; Mausner 1973; Bergman and Wiesner 1976; Meyer and Tonascia 1977).

Race

Numerous studies have investigated race as a possible correlate of drug use, although the degree to which racial and other sociodemographic factors have been successfully differentiated is not always clear. Unfortunately, when analyzing racial data, few surveys have controlled for other factors, such as socioeconomic status or peer influence.

In recent years, accompanying the general increase in adolescent drug use, race-related (black versus white) differences in prevalence appear to have diminished or, in some cases, to have reversed. In one study, the prevalence of lifetime marihuana use was the same for black and white youths born in 1953-1954, but was greater for blacks than whites among the older groups of males (O'Donnell et al. 1976). In addition, reversing earlier trends, white youths born in 1953-1954 reported higher rates of use than blacks of sedatives, stimulants, psychedelics, and heroin. With regard to current use of drugs, there also appeared to be a convergence in prevalence rates between races which was most notable for the drugs traditionally used by larger proportions of blacks, that is, marihuana, opiates, and cocaine. For example, current use of marihuana in the youngest cohort of males was 51 percent for blacks and 49 percent for whites as contrasted with 39 percent and 21 percent, respectively, for black and white males born about 20 years earlier. In the youngest age cohort, 10 percent more whites than blacks used sedatives, whereas there was no race-related difference in use for the oldest males sampled.

In the national household survey (Abelson and Fishburne 1976), no overall differences in lifetime prevalence or current use of marihuana were found between white and nonwhite youth or adult populations. However, white young adults (18 to 25 years old) were more likely to have tried marihuana (55 percent) than nonwhites (48 percent), whereas more nonwhite older adults (17 percent) than white adults (12 percent) had used this substance. No appreciable overall differences were found between blacks and whites in the use of nonmedically prescribed psychotherapeutic drugs (sedatives, stimulants, and tranquilizers), although there was a tendency for whites in all age categories to use more sedatives and stimulants than nonwhites. These data corroborate the finds of O'Donnell et al. (1976) that in recent years traditional race-related differences in drug use have become obscured among youth.

One notable race-related difference, however, concerns alcohol use. More whites than nonwhites reported themselves to be current drinkers, particularly in the group of young adults sampled (Abelson and Fishburne 1976). While 34 percent of white and 23 percent of nonwhite youth (aged 12 to 17) considered themselves current drinkers, 72 percent of white young adults (aged 18 to 25) and only 54 percent of comparable nonwhites so reported. Rachal et al. (1975) also found drinking rates to be higher among white youths. White adolescents, in addition to a higher probability of ever having used alcohol, were considerably more likely than blacks to acknowledge regular (once a week or more) drinking practices (42 versus 27 percent).

The disparity between drinking rates in whites and nonwhites was shown to be related to a much steeper rise in the use of alcohol by white youth in recent years (Abelson and Fishburne 1976). Between 1972 and 1975-1976, current drinkers increased by nearly 50 percent in white youths but by less than 25 percent in nonwhite youths. The highest rates of drinking have been found in young white males.

Among high school students in New York State, whites were more likely than blacks to have tried alcoholic beverages, marihuana, pills, psychedelics, and inhalants and less likely to have tried cocaine or heroin (Kandel et al. 1976). These data suggest that black youths begin experimenting with drugs at older ages than white youths, an observation corroborated in a more recent study (Carlisi 1978). In addition, although among white adolescents drug use seemed to follow a stepwise progression from legal drugs through marihuana to "hard" illegal drugs, black students showed more variability in the *order* in which drugs were first tried (Single et al. 1976). The implications of these findings are not clear.

Other racial and ethnic differences in drug use have been noted, some of which appear to be more striking than those currently observed between blacks and whites. Kandel et al. (1976) reported that Hispanic high school students in New York State were less likely than either whites or blacks to have tried alcohol, cigarettes, or marihuana, yet they were intermediate in likelihood of having tried pills, psychedelics, and heroin and more likely to have tried cocaine. Although American Indian students constituted only a small subsample in the New York State study, the results that relate to them bear noting. Members of this minority group were most likely, often by large percentage differentials, to have tried all psychoactive drugs except heroin. Orientals, who also constitute a small subsample, showed dramatically lower rates of drug use compared with all other ethnic groups, a finding consistent with those of other studies (Seltzer et al. 1974). Undoubtedly subcultural differences in values concerning both drug taking itself and also the relative status of the various drugs play a major role in determining racial and ethnic differences in drug use patterns.

Place of Residence and Socioeconomic Status

Except for alcohol and tobacco, the prevalence of both lifetime and current drug use has been observed to vary directly with the size of the city of residence

(O'Donnell et al. 1976). Low social position and large city of residence were the leading correlates of problem drinking among males (Cahalan and Room 1972). Lower-middle- and middle-class high school students in a small industrial city were more likely to drink liquor and to have been intoxicated than middle- and upper-middle-class students from a comparable town (Wechsler and Thum 1973). At present, however, the use of hard liquor may be associated differently with socioeconomic status than are most other psychoactive drugs. Nonalcohol drug use among nationally sampled adolescents was greater in urban than rural areas; it was also greater among groups with higher socioeconomic status (Josephson et al. 1972). Similarly, in the New York City area, more high school youths had ever tried illicit drugs (with the exception of heroin) than had inner-city racially mixed students of lower socioeconomic status (Haberman et al. 1972).

It is of interest that when other factors were controlled, urban-rural drug use differences were nullified, suggesting that lower rates of drug use in rural areas may be a function of such factors as religiosity, conservative attitudes, and low peer usage rates (Kandel 1975) rather than degree of urbanization as such. In a carefully controlled study of Vietnam veterans, inner-city residence failed to correlate either with opiate addiction while in service or with opiate use after return to the United States. However, inner-city residence was associated with increased willingness to experiment with narcotics while in Vietnam (Helzer et al. 1975-1976). Thus, with appropriate controls, a correlation between drug use and place of residence may actually reflect a composite of other sociodemographic factors.

The Social Milieu

The Peer Group

Although it is uncertain whether peer influence encourages drug use in youths who would otherwise abstain or whether sharing of similar interests in a particular life orientation which includes drug use draw certain groups of individuals together, it is clear that adolescents who are involved with drugs or alcohol have significantly more friends who also use these substances than do nonusers (Jessor 1975; Lawrence and Velleman 1974; Roth 1972; Tec 1972; Wechsler and Thum 1973). Moreover, peer group behavior, particularly, perceived and self-reported marihuana use by a best friend, was the factor which correlated most strongly with the probability and frequency of marihuana use among high school students, outranking personal, family, or sociodemographic variables (Kandel 1975). However, among students who progressed beyond marihuana to the use of other illicit drugs, parental and personal attributes were found to increase while peer influence decreased in importance as correlates. Thus depression, school performance, educational aspirations, closeness to parents, and parental self-reported drug use (of stimulants, depressants, and tranquilizers) were factors which assumed increased importance with respect to the probability of adolescents using illicit drugs other than marihuana.

Parental Factors

Two main areas of parental influence have been studied with regard to adolescent drug use: the quality of the parent-adolescent relationship, and parental drug use or deviant behavior in the parental generation. Several studies have indicated that significantly higher percentages of nonusers than users of drugs report close or good relationships with parents; this is particularly true when nonusers have been compared with adolescents with extensive drug or alcohol experience (Block 1975; Lavenhar et al. 1972; Roth 1972; Russell 1972; Wechsler and Thum 1973). Disruption of ties with parents may be expected to occur more frequently in broken homes, and disruption is inevitable when a parent is lost. Drug use has been found associated both with broken homes (Lavenhar et al. 1972; Lawrence and Velleman 1974; Tennant et al. 1975; Wechsler and Thum 1973) and with loss of a parent (Vaillant 1970). Early father absence in particular has received attention as a correlate of serious drug involvement (Robins and Murphy 1967).

There is evidence suggesting a generational continuity of behavior patterns. Evidence exists that the use of drugs (Kandel 1974), particularly cigarettes, barbiturates, tranquilizers (Lavenhar et al. 1972), and hard liquor (Kandel 1975), and involvement in deviant behavior other than drug use on the part of parents (Goodwin et al. 1975) are factors correlated with drug use in the young. Maternal drug use patterns seemed of particular importance in one study (Lawrence and Velleman 1974), and a history of alcoholism or arrests in fathers was a predictor of alcoholism in Vietnam returnees (Goodwin et al. 1975). Carlisi (1978) found that perception of drinking problems in mothers and sisters correlated highly with drug use in all categories.

According to one view, parental absence, emotional or physical, results not only in lack of an emotionally supportive environment, but in the inadequate setting of consistent behavioral controls. In such a poorly structured environment, healthy identification with a parent figure is difficult to achieve and feelings of inadequacy are engendered. In this context, drug use may be seen as a coping mechanism in the search for peer approval, acceptance, and identification (Woody 1972). Although the role of unconscious parental wishes in the deviant behavior of children has not been systematically assessed, some psychoanalysts support the view that such motivation, although not always readily apparent, has significant impact (Levy 1972); that is, children may fulfill unconscious parental desires to engage in prohibited antisocial acts.

Personal Attributes

Conformity versus Nonconformity

A preponderance of evidence from surveys tapping a variety of attitudinal and behavioral indicators of conformity or deviance suggests that young drug users, especially those who are extensively involved in drug use, are less conformist, more tolerant of deviance, and more likely to have a predrug history of delinquent behavior. Employing behavioral (O'Donnell et al. 1976) and psychological (Berman and Benierakis 1972) assessments of conventionality, drug users were found to be less conventional than nonusers.

Religiosity and Political Orientation

Numerous studies have indicated that religious denomination is relatively unrelated to drug use or nonuse. However, religiosity, as assessed by reports of regularity of church attendance and the subjective value of religion to the individual, has been found highly correlated with nonuse of drugs, while lack of religious activity or affiliation has correlated with use (Jessor 1975; Kandel 1975; Lavenhar et al. 1972; Pearlman et al. 1972; Tennant et al. 1975). Consistent with the finding that drug users were less traditional in their attitudes toward religion is the further observation that they also tended to be more liberal in political orientation than nonusers (Kandel 1975).

School Orientation and Performance

Drug users and nonusers have been repeatedly differentiated by grade point averages (Jessor 1975; Lavenhar et al. 1972; Lawrence and Velleman 1974; Russell 1972; Wechsler and Thum 1973), but since even occasional marihuana users were found to have an increased prevalence of low grades, it is likely that the poor school performance so frequently noted among drug users is related to factors other than the effects of the drugs (Lavenhar et al. 1972). The correlation between poor school performance and drug use was increased in those adolescents who progressed beyond marihuana to regular use of other illicit drugs (Kandel 1975). In general, drug users have been found to be less interested in formal education, to be less involved in organized activities such as athletics, and to have fewer well-defined goals than nonusers (Lavenhar et al. 1972; Tec 1972). In one study, marihuana users were found to score significantly lower than nonusers on a "purpose in life" test (Shear and Fechtmann

1971). Experimentation with drugs has been found to be greater among high school dropouts than graduates (Robins and Murphy 1967), and in two studies strong predictive correlations were found between a history of high school dropout and delinquency and opiate addiction (Helzer et al. 1975-1976; Robins and Murphy 1967).

Delinquency

There is much evidence that extensive drug use is often a symptom and not a cause of delinquent behavior. Roff (1972) reported that in a population of servicemen who had been delinquent in the early 1960s, drug offenses tended to occur as part of a pattern of antisocial behavior rather than as isolated events. In a study of opiate addicts (Vaillant 1970), more than half admitted to delinquent behavior prior to drug involvement, and many addicts, regardless of social class, were unable to maintain stable employment patterns prior to addiction or during periods of abstinence. Trouble in school (truancy and expulsion) was one of four predictors of alcoholism among Vietnam returnees (Goodwin et al. 1975), and suspension from school correlated with marihuana use (Roth 1972). Among teenagers, heavy drinkers were several times more likely than light drinkers to have been involved in a wide range of antisocial behaviors (Wechsler and Thum 1973), as were drug users in comparison to nonusers in high schools and college (Yankelovich, Skelly and White, Inc. 1975). In a normal population of young black males, significantly more high school dropouts than graduates were drug users or heroin addicts (Robins and Murphy 1967). Juvenile delinquency, based on court records, proved to be a predictor of heavy drug use or addiction, and although delinquent and nondelinquent dropouts had equally elevated probabilities of drug experimentation, delinquent dropouts were at significantly greater risk of becoming heroin addicts (Robins and Murphy 1967). Father absence when coupled with delinquency provided a major determinant of heroin addiction in drug experimenters.

Personality Characteristics and Mood

Adolescents who use drugs heavily have been described both clinically and in survey investigations as manifesting more psychopathology than nonusers. Symptoms include depression, feelings of inadequacy, frustration, and helplessness; immaturity; self-alienation (Dodson et al. 1971; Levy 1972); poor object relations; and major deficiencies in ego structure and functioning (Amini et al. 1976). It is generally acknowledged that heavy drug users tend to have poor impulse control (Krug and Henry 1976; Rosencrans and Brignet 1972). Undoubtedly, a relative lack of social inhibitions, when coupled with psychic turmoil, leads some individuals to engage in a wider range of deviant behaviors, including drug use, than are manifested in their more-stable, less-impulsive counterparts. Green and Jaffe (1977) have discussed the possibility that an inadequate capacity to experience reward, whether psychologically or biologically determined, can result in a chronic depressed state which may underlie compulsive drug-seeking behavior.

Discussion

It is clear that the average age at which drug use begins has become lower resulting in increasing proportions of adolescent drug users in the United States. Although most adolescent drug use is experimental, occasional, or only intermittently regular, the proportion of young people involved in persistent and multiple drug use is sufficient to justify concern. A variety of indicators suggest that serious medical and psychological sequelae of drug use have increased in recent years (Citron et al. 1970; Klinge and Vaziri 1975; Lemere 1966; Kolansky and Moore 1971 and 1972).

Since early signs of deviance, including substance use, can often be traced to preteen years, and since early drug use is correlated with serious drug involvement in later life, an increased focus on prevention and intervention efforts directed toward grade school children seems indicated. For those adolescents without major deficiencies in ego functioning, the mere forestalling of drug use through alternative involvements might be sufficient to provide some with the time necessary to develop more socially adaptive coping mechanisms. For adolescents with gross deficiencies in ego assets who ultimately seek drugs to fill a void or for other psychopathological reasons, alternative preventive strategies are yet to be developed.

Involvement with drugs during adolescence appears to follow a steplike, though by no means inevitable, progression (Kandel 1975; Hamburg et al. 1975; Gould et al. 1977). Legal drugs, which are used most widely and regularly, are tried at the youngest ages and by an overwhelming majority of adolescents. Marihuana, the most commonly used illicit drug, is tried by a large percent of those who have used alcohol or smoked cigarettes, and its use precedes involvement with any other illicit drug. Regular users of marihuana tend to be multiple drug users, and although they constitute only a small percentage of adolescents, they may represent a group of individuals at particularly high risk for deviant behavior.

It appears that in recent years a convergence of drug use rates has occurred in black and white youth (O'Donnell et al. 1976). White adolescents seem to begin using drugs at earlier ages than blacks, and there is evidence that the prevalence rates are slightly higher among whites for use of many drugs. Sex differences in drug use prevalence have also diminished, further suggesting the need for reevaluation of treatment programs traditionally oriented toward older, nonwhite males.

Specific sociodemographic factors seem to be only modestly associated with drug use. Other than age, which is essentially the time function over which increasing numbers of young people try and use drugs, other demographic factors seem of little importance per se except insofar as they reflect attitudes and values. Thus religious denomination is far less important than religiosity, and size of city of residence, when adequately controlled, may reduce to attitudinal factors, religiosity, and level of peer support. Whether values are stable or in transition seems to be important also (Brod 1975; Vaillant 1966), as reflected in high drug use rates in postimmigrant generations and the new suburban populations. Further expressions of values include place of residence (urban, suburban, rural), attitudes toward authority, political views, and religiosity. In general, the prevalence of drug use is greater in change-oriented urban and suburban youth who declare themselves religiously inactive than in more conservative rural adolescents satisfied with the status quo.

Age factors in relation to drug use are of special interest. An association between age of onset of drug use and the eventual extent of involvement in drugs has been shown in several studies. It is likely that early involvement in drug use is another aspect of the patterns of deviant behavior repeatedly observed in serious drug seekers. Among males, early first use of alcohol, cigarettes, or coffee (at or prior to age 12), correlated with excessive use of alcohol and the use of illicit drugs during adulthood (Tennant and Detels *in press*). Very early first use of alcohol (prior to age 9) correlated with hashish use (Tennant et al. 1975). In a comparison of heroin addicts and controls, Vaillant (1970) found that addicts tended to be multiple drug users who generally began experimenting with drugs at younger ages than their peers. Age of first use of drugs also appeared to be an important predictor of the extent of involvement with drugs in young black males (Robins and Murphy 1967), just as early age of first drunkenness was a predictor of alcoholism in Vietnam returnees (Goodwin et al. 1975). Since extensive involvement with drugs often follows early use, the implications for prevention and early intervention efforts are clear, particularly if they are to help in building the social coping skills required to emerge successfully from the conflicts of adolescence.

Although peer group drug use practices appear to be of major significance in experimentation with drugs, other personal factors seem to be of increased importance when drug use is extensive (Kandel 1974). For example, studies have shown that parents greatly influence the drug use behavior of their children through the quality of parent-adolescent relationships (Muller 1976), the behavioral models parents provide, parental expectations, and the degree to which deviance is tolerated in the household.

References

Abelson, H.I. and Fishburne, P.M. 1976. *Nonmedical Use of Psychoactive Substances. 1975-1976. Nationwide Study Among Youth and Adults.* Princeton: Response Analysis Corp.

Amini, F., Salasnek, S., and Burke, E.L. 1976. Adolescent drug abuse: Etiological and treatment considerations. *Adolescence* 11:281-299.

Bergman, A.B., and Wiesner, L.A. 1976. Relationship of passive cigarette-smoking to sudden infant death syndrome. *Pediatrics* 58:665-668.

Berman, G., and Benierakis, C. 1972. Characteristics of student marijuana users. *Canad. Psychiat. Assn. J.* 17:37-40.

Blackford, L. 1977. *Summary Report–Surveys of Student Drug Use, San Mateo County, California.* San Mateo County Dept. of Public Health and Welfare.

Block, J.R. 1975. Behavioral and demographic correlates of drug use among students in grades 7-12. In *Predicting Adolescent Drug Abuse: A Review of Issues, Methods and Correlates.* Research Issues 11, NIDA.

Brod, T.M. 1975. Alcoholism as a mental health problem of Native Americans. A review of the literature. *Arch. Gen. Psychiat.* 32:1385-1391.

Cahalan, D., and Room, R. 1972. Problem drinking among American men aged 21-59. *AJPH* 62:1473-1482.

Carlisi, J.A. 1978. Unpublished data.

Citron, B., Halpern, M., McCarron, M., Lundberg, G., McCormick, R., Pincus, I., Tatter, D. and Haverback, B. 1970. Necrotizing angiitis associated with drug abuse. *N. Eng. J. Med.* 283:1003-1011.

Cope, I., Lancaster, P., and Stevens, L. 1973. Smoking in pregnancy. *Med. J. Australia* 1:673-677.

Dodson, W.E., Alexander, D.F., Wright, P.F. and Wunderlich, R.A. 1971. Pattern of multiple drug abuse among adolescents referred by a juvenile court. *Pediatrics* 47:1033-1036.

Goodwin, D.W., Davis, D.H., and Robins, L.N. 1975. Drinking amid abundant illicit drugs. *Arch. Gen. Psychiat.* 32:230-233.

Gould, L.C., Berberian, R.M., Kasl, S.V., Thompson, W.D. and Kleber, H.D. 1977. Sequential patterns of multiple drug use among high school students. *Arch. Gen. Psychiat.* 34:216-222.

Green, J., and Jaffe, J.H. 1977. Alcohol and opiate dependence. A review, *J. Stud. Alcohol* 8:1274-1293.

Haberman, P.W., Josephson, E., Zanes, A. and Elinson, J. 1972. High school drug behavior: a methalogic report on pilot studies. In S. Einstein (ed.), *Proceedings of the First International Conference on Student Drug Surveys.* Farmingdale, N.Y.: Baywood Publ. Co.

Hamburg, B.A., Kraemer, H.C., and Jahnke, W. 1975. A hierarchy of drug use in adolescence: behavioral and attitudinal correlates of substantial drug use. *Am. J. Psychiatry* 132:1155-1163.

Helzer, J.E., Robins, L.N., and Davis, D.H. 1975-1976. Antecedents of narcotic use and addiction: A study of 898 Vietnam veterans. *Drug Alc. Dependence* 1:183-190.

Jessor, R. 1975. Predicting time of onset of marihuana use: a developmental study of high school youth. In *Predicting Adolescent Drug Abuse: A Review of Issues, Methods and Correlates.* Research Issues 11, NIDA.

Johnston, L.D., Bachman, J., and O'Malley, P. 1976. Statement to the press, Washington, D.C.

Johnston, L.D., Bachman, J.G., and O'Malley, P.M. 1978. *Highlights from Drug Use Among American High School Students 1975-1977.* National Institute on Drug Abuse, DHEW Publication No. (ADM) 78-621.

Josephson, E., Habernan, P., Zanes, A., and Elinson, J. Adolescent marijuana use: Report on a national survey. In S. Einstein (ed). *Proceedings of the First International Conference on Student Drug Surveys.* Farmingdale, N.Y.: Baywood Publishing Co.

Kandel, D. 1974. Inter- and intragenerational influences on adolescent marijuana use. *J. Social Issues* 30:107-135.

Kandel, D. 1975. Some comments on the relationship of selected criteria variables to adolescent illicit drug use. In *Predicting Adolescent Drug Abuse: A Review of Issues, Methods and Correlates.* Research Issues 11, NIDA.

Kandel, D. 1975. Stages in adolescent involvement in drug use. *Science* 190:912-914.

Kandel, D., Single, E., and Kessler, R.C. 1976. The epidemiology of drug use among New York State high school students: distribution, trends, and change in rates of use. *AJPH* 66:43-53.

Klinge, V., and Vaziri, H. 1975. EEG abnormalities in adolescent drug abusers. *Adolescence* 10:1-10.

Kolansky, H., and Moore, W.T. 1971. Effects of marihuana on adolescents and young adults. *JAMA* 216:486-492.

Kolansky, H., and Moore, W.T. 1972. Toxic effects of chronic marihuana use. *JAMA* 222:35-41.

Krug, S.E., and Henry, T.J. 1974. Personality, motivation and adolescent drug use patterns. *J. Consult. Psychology* 21:440-445.

Lavenhar, M.A., Wolfson, E.A., Sheffet, A., Einstein, S. and Louria, D.B. 1972. Survey of drug abuse in six New Jersey high schools: II: Characteristics of drug users and nonusers. In S. Einstein (ed.), *Proceedings of the First International Conference on Student Drug Surveys.* Farmingdale, N.Y.: Baywood Publ. Co.

Lawrence, T.S., and Velleman, J.D. 1974. Correlates of student drug use in a suburban high school. *Psychiatry* 37:129-136.

Lemere, F. 1966. The danger of amphetamine dependency. *Am. J. Psychiatry* 123:569-572.

Levy, N.J. 1972. The use of drugs among teenagers. *Canad. Psychiat. Assn. J.* 17:31-36.

Litt, I.F., and Schonberg, S.K. 1975. Medical complications of drug abuse in adolescents. *Med. Clinics N. Amer.* 59:1445-1452.

Meyer, M.B., and Tonascia, J.A. 1977. Maternal smoking, pregnancy complications and perinatal mortality. *Am. J. Obs. Gyn.* 128:494-502.

Masner, J.S. 1973. Smoking and pregnancy. *Ann. Internal Med.* 79:272.

New York State Office of Drug Abuse Services. Winter 1974-1975. *A Survey of Substance Use among Junior and Senior High School Students in New York State.* Report No. 1. Prevalence of Drug and Alcohol Use. New York.

O'Donnell, J.A., Voss, H.L., Clayton, R.R., Slatin, G.T., and Room, R. 1976. *Young Men and Drugs–A Nationwide Survey.* NIDA Research Monograph 5, NIDA, Rockville, Md.

Pearlman, S., Philip, A.F., Robbins, L.C., Robbins, E., Robinson, E.E. and Schmitter, B. 1972. Religious affiliations and patterns of drug usage in an urban university population. In S. Einstein (ed.), *Proceedings of First International Conference on Student Drug Surveys.* Farmingdale, N.Y.: Baywood Publ. Co.

Rachal, J.V., Williams, J.R., Brehm, M.L., Cavanaugh, B., Moore, R.P., and Eckerman, W.C. 1975. *A National Study of Adolescent Drinking Behavior, Attitudes and Correlates.* Research Triangle Institute, Center for the Study of Social Behavior, Report to NIAAA.

Robins, L.N., and Murphy, G.E. 1967. Drug use in a normal population of young negro men. *AJPH* 57:1580-1596.

Roff, M. 1972. *The Service-Related Experience of Juvenile Delinquents. IX. A Preliminary Study of the Later Significance of Adolescent Drug Use.* Report No. 72-11. National Technical Information Service, U.S. Dept. Commerce, Springfield, Va.

Rosencrans, C.J., and Brignet, H.P. 1972. Comparative personality profiles of young drug abusers and non-users. *Ala. J. Med. Sci.* 9:397-402.

Roth, R. 1972. Student drug use in southeastern Michigan and profiles of the abusers. In S. Einstein (ed.), *Proceedings of the First International Conference on Student Drug Surveys.* Farmingdale, N.Y.: Baywood Publ. Co.

Russell, J.S. 1972. Composite pattern of drug use. In S. Einstein (ed.). *Proceedings of the First International Conference on Student Drug Surveys.* Farmingdale, N.Y.: Baywood Publ. Co.

Seltzer, C., Friedman, G.D., and Siegelaub, A.B. 1974. Smoking and drug consumption in white, black and Oriental men and women. *AJPH* 64:466-473.

Shean, G., and Fechtmann, F. 1971. Purposes in life scores of student marijuana users. *J. Clin. Psychol.* 27:112-113.

Single, E., Kandel, D., and Faust, R. 1975. Patterns of multiple drug use in high school. *J. Health Soc. Behav.* 15:344-357.

Tamerin, J.S., 1973. Recent increase in adolescent cigarette smoking *Arch. Gen. Psychiat.* 28:116-119.

Tec, N. 1972. Socio-cultural context of marijuana. In S. Einstein (ed.), *Proceedings of the First International Conference on Student Drug Surveys* Farmingdale, N.Y.: Baywood Publ. Co.

Tennant, F.S., and Detels, R. *In press.* Relationship of alcohol, cigarette and drug abuse in adulthood with alcohol, cigarette and coffee consumption in childhood. *J. Prev. Med.*

Tennant, F.S., Detels, R., and Clark, V. 1975. Some childhood antecedents of drug and alcohol abuse. *Am. J. Epidemiology* 102:377-385.

Vaillant, G. 1966. Parent-child cultural disparity and drug addiction. *J. Nerv. Ment. Dis.* 142:534-539.

Vaillant, G. 1970. The natural history of narcotic drug addiction. *Seminars in Psychiatry* 2:486-498.

Wechsler, H., and McFadden, M. 1976. Sex differences in adolescent alcohol and drug use; A disappearing phenomenon. *J. Stud. Alcohol* 37:1291-1301.

Wechsler, H., and Thum, D. 1973. Teen-age drinking, drug use and social correlates. *Quart. J. Stud. Alcohol* 34:1220-1227.

Wolfson, E.A., Lavenhar, M.A., Blum, R., Quinones, M.A., Einstein, S., and Louria, D.B. 1972. Survey of drug abuse in six New Jersey high schools: I: Methodology and general findings. In S. Einstein (ed.), *Proceedings of the First International Conference on Student Drug Surveys* Farmingdale, N.Y.: Baywood Publ. Co.

Woody, R. H. 1972. Therapeutic techniques for the adolescent marijuana user. *J. School Health* 42:220-224.

Yancy, W.S., Nader, P.R., and Burnham, K.L. 1972. Drug use and attitudes of high school students. *Pediatrics* 50:739-745.

Yankelovich, Skelly and White, Inc. 1975. *Students and Drugs.* Drug Abuse Council, Inc., Washington, D. C.

3 Spread of Drug Use in Populations of Youths

Leon G. Hunt,
Edward C. Farley, and
Rachel G. Hunt

Introduction

The spread of drug use has been widely studied in populations of abusers, typically heroin addicts whose drug use ultimately led them to treatment (de Alarcon 1969; Hughes, Crawford, and Jaffe 1971; Hunt 1973; Hunt 1974). Much less is known about patterns of spread of other drugs in normal populations, those much larger groups that contain many drug users who do not seem to experience difficulties. Are the processes of spread alike in these two groups, or are they different and specific to each? Is there something unique about spreading drug *abuse* (use leading to problems) as compared with the general spread of all use, one-time casual, and experimental as well as heavy and frequent?

This chapter tries to answer these questions by examining the growth of new drug use in two large high school populations where such use is just beginning. Growth or spread of drug use is measured by the rate of new cases, that is, by first use (Hunt 1977). Even though there might be many active users of a drug, use is not spreading or growing unless new cases occur. We therefore consider incidence of first use or changes in the rate of active users to see where a drug is spreading.

Our results are not strictly longitudinal behavior characterizations of fixed high school populations. In each new survey year, the student population is being augmented and reduced as new students enter and old students leave their high school years. Thus we will analyze the changing nature of high school drug use by examining sequential cohorts of classes.

Of further interest are questions concerning the spread of drug use among classes in the same school. Each class is not an isolated population. We know that drug abuse spreads in peer and friendship groups, but such groups are not

This chapter is based on the secondary analysis of survey data. We are grateful to Lillian St. Clair Blackford, Biostatistician, formerly of the Department of Public Health and Welfare, San Mateo County, California, and Coke Barr, Research and Program Evaluation Section School Board, Duval County, Florida, for sharing their material with us and their suggestions and interpretations. In addition, the Drug Abuse Epidemiology Center, (DAEC), Institute for Behavior Research, Texas Christian University, which is the repository for the original data from these surveys, helped us by making a large number of special computer runs. We are grateful for DAEC's assistance in data processing.

limited to a single high school class (Hunt and Chambers 1976). Any adolescent may have friends who are both younger and older than himself. Therefore spread of drug use in one class may be influenced by what has occurred (or is occurring) in contiguous classes of both older and younger students. Does the effect of such influence die out as the difference in ages increase? If so, does new drug use cluster in groups of classes during the same historical period, or is there a uniform "handing down" of new use from older to younger classes, which continues regularly and uninterrupted year after year?

These questions could be answered definitely if year of first use of each drug for each student was known for a series of classes in the same schools. But comprehensive incidence-of-first-use data are not usually available. Sometimes we must rely on a surrogate measure of new use, change in prevalence rates as recorded by surveys. However, the difficulties involved in using prevalence changes in place of incidence of first use are many, as we shall see.

Analysis

The size of a drug-using population is constantly changing. In any year, new use spreads locally, active users from elsewhere immigrate and former users who had been inactive resume use, all adding to the previous year's population of users. During the same year, of course, some of the preceding year's active users emigrate, others stop use, and some die, all subtracting from the active population. The difference in last year's population of active users and this year's is the sum of these effects: new use, in-and-out-migration, resumption and cessation of use, and mortality (figure 3-1).

Under certain conditions, new use is the dominant term in this sum. If in-and out-migration are balance, if cessation and resumption of use are equal (or negligible), and if mortality is low, then changes in prevalence are largely the result of *new* use. In this situation, the difference between this year's prevalence of active use and last year's is a rough measure of new use.

When we lack a direct measure of incidence of first use, I_n, we shall use the prevalence change. Thus in any year n, ΔP_n substitutes for the incidence of first use. That is, we assume $\Delta P_n = P_n - P_{n-1} \approx I_n$.

For the populations studied here, in which mortality is low and drug use is just beginning, the only crucial defect in this approximation might come from radical differences in in-and out-migration (of drug users, not total migration). We are unable to assess the importance of net migration effects.

Data Sources

In San Mateo County, California, and Duval County, Florida, drug use in school populations (grades 7 through 12 and 6 through 12, respectively) has been

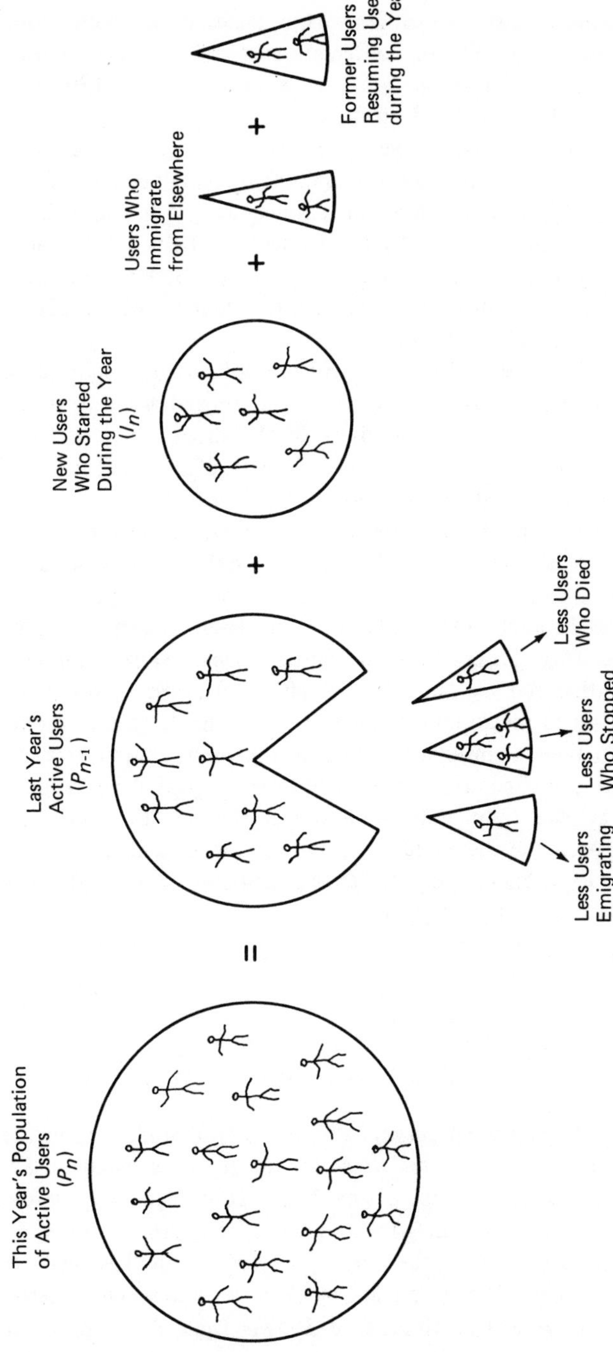

Figure 3-1. Year-to-Year Changes in the Population of Active Users.

described in a series of surveys. While these data are not strictly longitudinal, as noted before, because of changes within classes during their school careers, they are at least the results of consistent answers to similar questions asked of institutionally similar populations over a series of years, 1967 through 1977 in San Mateo County and 1973 through 1976 in Duval County.

San Mateo County's surveys are actual censuses of their 7th through 12th graders, involving from 18,000 to 35,000 students annually. Duval County, on the other hand, utilized a random sampling survey design. Thus, only 5,000 to 10,000 of its 6th through 12 grade students participated annually. Our analysis of spreading drug use has concentrated on increases among the male students only. The actual numbers of male students enrolled in each grade for each survey year are given in table 3-1 and 3-2.

Our chief interest in these survey results is the reported percentages of students in each class in each year who started using a given drug *or* the percentages who were active users of the drugs. The first is a measure of incidence of new use, while the second leads to ΔP_n, our substitute measure for incidence of new use described above.

San Mateo and Duval Counties are demographically similar in many ways. Both are in highly developed regions containing both urban and suburban populations, and both have grown rapidly in recent years from their 1970 populations of about half a million. San Mateo County lies just south of San Francisco, while Duval County contains Jacksonville, Florida, so both are directly influenced by large central cities. National surveys have found that youths living in metropolitan areas are more likely to use or experiment with drugs than their counterparts living in non metropolitan areas (Abelson et al 1977). The causal connections between urban social changes and the growth of drug use are not fully understood and are beyond the scope of our analysis. However, both the metropolitan counties examined in this chapter have been subjected to urbanization influences, and thus we might expect to find somewhat similar drug use growth rates.

Findings

San Mateo County

The series of ten annual surveys (1968-1977) of student drug and alcohol use showed a rapid rise in rates of active use for all substances. For the school system as a whole, the use of marihuana continued to grow throughout the period. The average use rates for amphetamines, barbiturates, and LSD (including other hallucinogens) peaked in the early 1970's and has declined since. These prevalence trends for the San Mateo County's entire school system have been ably reported elsewhere (Blackford 1977). Table 3-3 displays the prevalence

Table 3-1
Number of Male Youth Respondents in the San Mateo School Surveys for 1968 through 1977 by Grade

	Survey Year									
Youth in Grade	*1968*	*1969*	*1970*	*1971*	*1972*	*1973*	*1974*	*1975*	*1976*	*1977*
7	–	530	2,267	2,619	2,765	2,015	2,498	2,644	2,609	2,379
8	–	553	2,215	2,636	2,698	2,247	2,651	2,481	2,630	2,357
9	2,349	3,115	3,160	3,077	2,628	2,557	2,332	2,346	1,541	1,591
10	2,332	2,827	3,183	2,804	2,453	2,451	2,124	2,060	1,426	1,438
11	2,064	2,578	3,019	3,037	2,370	2,288	2,126	1,920	1,410	1,387
12	1,799	2,034	2,352	2,491	2,043	1,686	1,679	1,527	1,077	1,178
Total	8,544	11,637	16,195	16,664	14,957	13,444	13,410	12,978	10,691	10,330

Source: L. Blackford, *Summary Report–Surveys of Student Drug Use, San Mateo County, California*, San Mateo County, California, Department of Public Health and Welfare, 1977.

Table 3-2
Number of Male Youth Respondents in the Duval County School Surveys for 1974 Through 1976 by Grade

	Survey Year		
Youth in Grade	*1974*	*1975*	*1976*
6	452	410	420
7	418	403	423
8	448	423	417
9	407	464	424
10	425	309	451
11	371	369	406
12	327	291	285
Totals	2,848	2,669	2,826

Source: C. Barr, *Drug and Alcohol Opinionnaire and Usage Survey, 1973, 1975, 1976,* Duval County School Board, Jacksonville, Florida.

rates of 4 drugs for 10 consecutive years of San Mateo County male senior classes. The prevalence rates found among these male seniors are unusually high when compared to other youth surveys. For instance, table 3-4 compared the San Mateo senior class of 1969 with Lloyd Johnston's national random sample. For these selected substances, both groups report marihuana use highest, followed by amphetamines, hallucinogens, and last, barbiturates. However, for the San Mateo male seniors, the rates of use are more than double the national rate. The prevalence trends displayed for 10 consecutive classes of San Mateo male seniors in table 3-3 are quite similar to the trends reported by Blackford for the entire San Mateo school system. As with the entire school system, prevalence for male seniors peaked in 1971 and 1972 for amphetamines, LSD, and barbiturates. The rate of marihuana use rises continuously except for a temporary setback in 1976. Overall, the prevalence profiles from year to year appear quite similar.

Table 3-3
Rate of Use for San Mateo Male High School Seniors 1968-1977
(Percent of Sample Reporting Any Use during Preceding Year)

	Survey Year									
Drug (Ranked)	*1968*	*1969*	*1970*	*1971*	*1972*	*1973*	*1974*	*1975*	*1976*	*1977*
Marihuana	44.6	50.1	50.9	58.6	60.7	61.0	61.9	63.6	61.1	64.5
Amphetamines	20.5	25.6	18.6	26.7	25.8	21.1	22.2	21.2	18.4	20.6
LSD[a]	16.6	23.0	17.4	20.9	21.2	20.0	20.1	19.6	17.8	18.3
Barbiturates	NA	NA	14.4	18.5	15.4	14.0	14.7	13.1	12.2	12.8

Source: L. Blackford, *Summary Report—Surveys of Student Drug Use, San Mateo County, California,* San Mateo County, California, Department of Public Health and Welfare, 1977.
[a]Other hallucinogens including PCP were defined within this category.

Table 3-4
Drug-Use Comparisons of Male High School Seniors from the Class of 1969
(In Percentages)

Drugs (Ranked)	*National Random Sample*[a] *(n = 1,798) Any High School Use*	*San Mateo County*[b] *(n = 2,034) Any Use Preceding Year*
Marihuana	20.7	50.1
Amphetamines	10.0	25.6
Hallucinogens	6.9	23.0
Barbiturates	6.3	NA[c]

[a]L. Johnston, *Drugs and American Youth,* Institute for Social Research, Univ. of Michigan, Ann Arbor, Michigan, 1973.

[b]L. Blackford, *Summary Report Surveys of Student Drug Use, San Mateo County, California,* San Mateo County, California, Department of Public Health and Welfare, 1977.

[c]14.4 for class of 1970.

We are interested in studying the growth of *new* use of each drug in each class. To examine new use, each class is followed as it enters the seventh grade and progresses through the twelfth (except for those that were already past the seventh grade when the surveys started in 1968). Figure 3-2 shows rates of marihuana use for two of these class cohorts of males. Cohort A started the seventh grade in 1969, while cohort B began the seventh grade in 1970. For both, each succeeding year brings higher prevalence rates, but the building up of active use is not uniform. The greatest increase for cohort A ($\Delta P = 21.7$ percent) occurred in 1971 when this class was in the ninth grade. For cohort B, the maximum increase ($\Delta P = 19.3$ percent) was also in 1971, the year these students were in the eighth grade. In general, the changes in prevalence for both cohorts rise and fall in the same *year,* but not in the same *grades.*

This matching growth, year by year but not grade by grade, suggests that these two classes are behaving as a single population. Is such clustering a consistent phenomenon? To examine this question, we look at changes in use for marihuana, amphetamines, barbiturates, and LSD for all nine cohorts over their entire recorded school careers.

Figures 3-3 through 3-6 show that drug use has grown episodically among these seventh through twelfth grade males in San Mateo County during the last ten years. For most drugs, periods of rapidly spreading use occurred at about the same year, cutting across several different classes of different ages. Instead of each class following its own separate pattern of progressive growth in new use, several continuous classes show use developing simultaneously.

The curves contain striking regularities. New use (as measured by ΔP_n) of marihuana, amphetamines, and barbiturates peaked in 1971 for a succession of

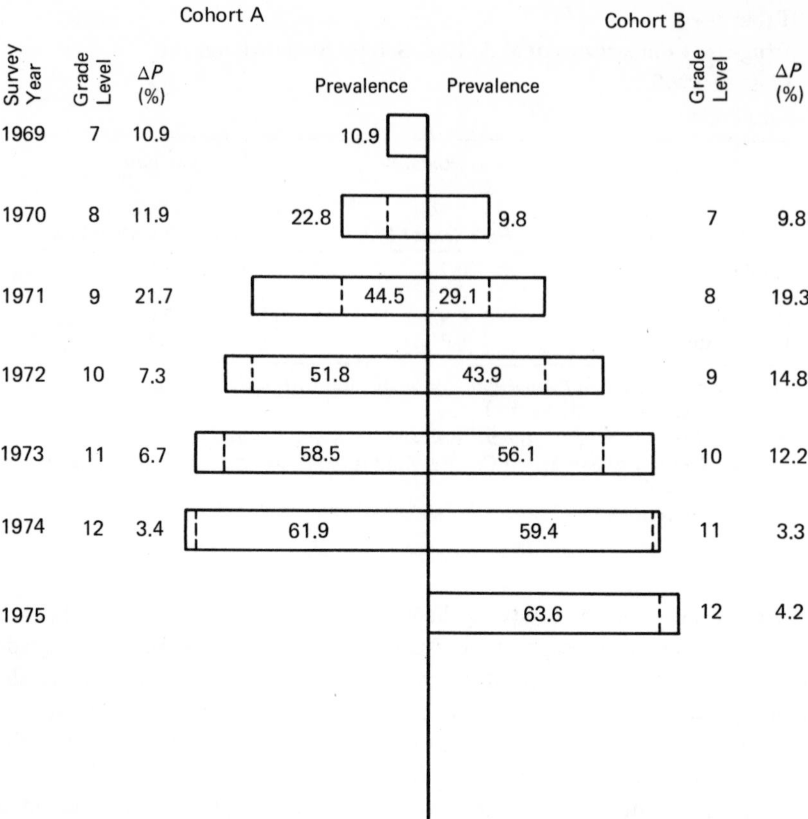

Source: L. Blackford, *Summary Report–Surveys of Student Drug Use, San Mateo County, California,* San Mateo County, California, Department of Public Health and Welfare, 1977.

Figure 3-2. Marihuana Prevalence among Two Cohorts of Male Students in San Mateo.

classes, at least those who were seventh graders from 1967 through 1970, and perhaps for later cohorts. For these later cohorts seventh grade in 1971 and afterward, the curves are much less regular (note especially amphetamine and barbiturates use, figures 3-4 and 3-5).

New use of LSD (hallucinogens) has behaved roughly the same way, but it shows more of a tendency for progressive growth of use in each class. There is, however, distinct clustering of maximum growth in pairs of classes (figure 3-6).

Taken together, figures 3-3 through 3-6 suggest that drug use has *not* grown independently in each class, but just the opposite, that rapid spread in a higher grade is transmitted to lower grades (younger classes) during the same year. For

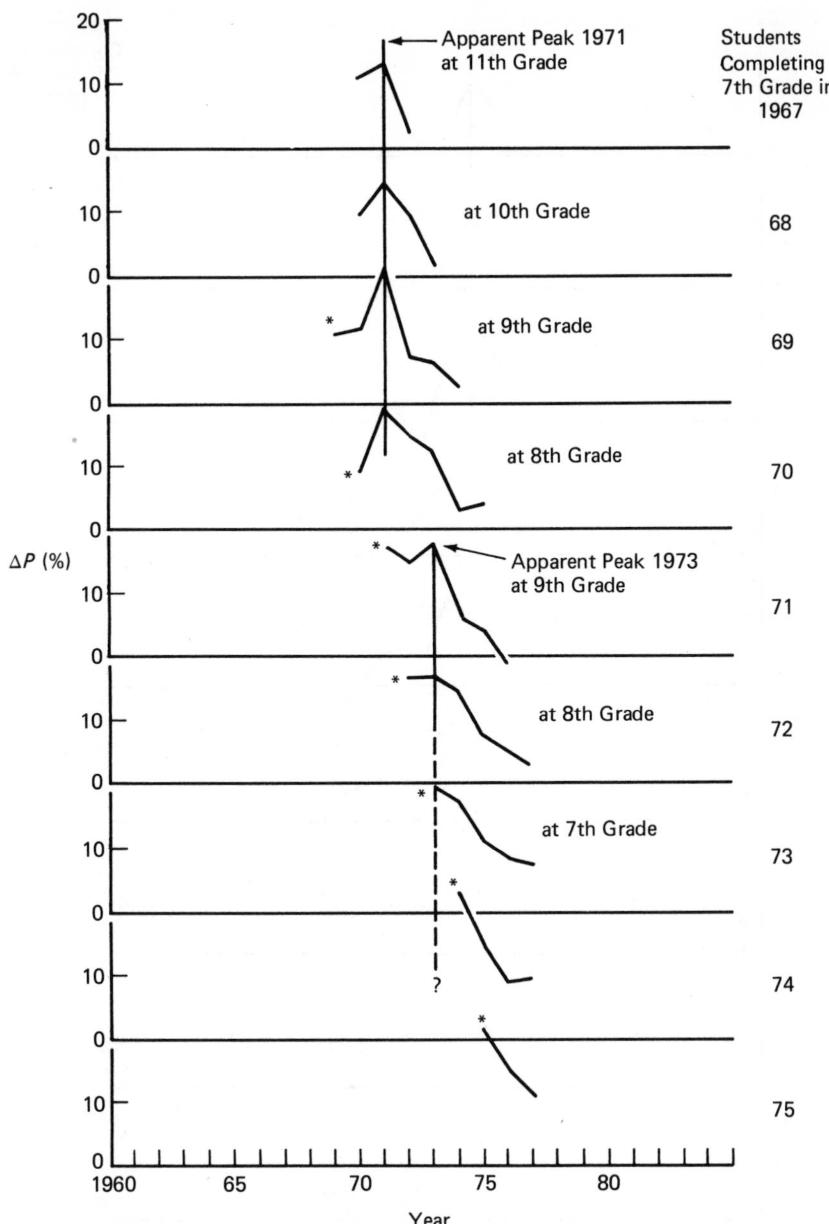

*P_n instead of ΔP_n if $P_{n-1} < \Delta P_n$, then so is ΔP_{n-1}, *a fortiori.*

Source: San Mateo School Surveys, 1968-1977.

Figure 3-3. San Mateo: Change in Percentage of Active Marihuana Users (ΔP_n), Males.

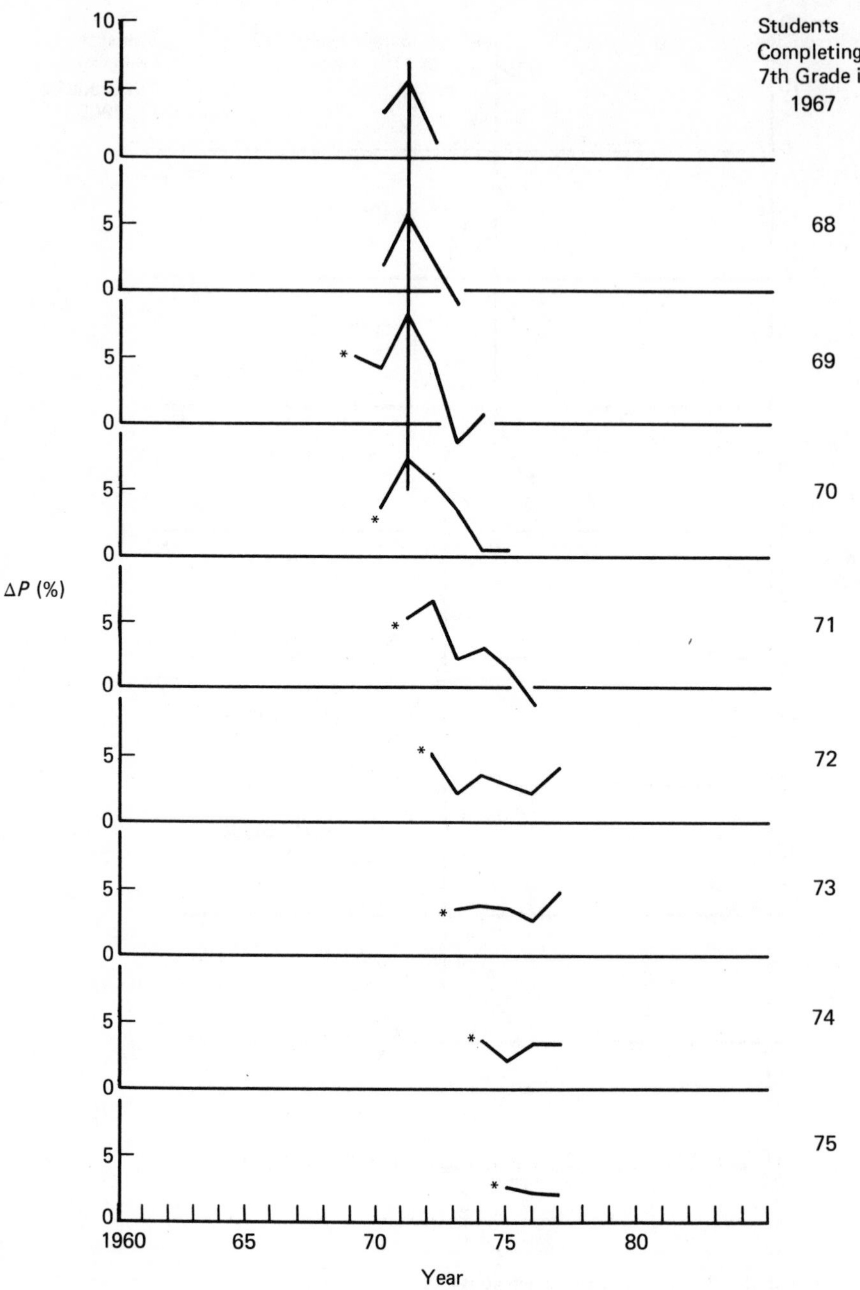

Source: San Mateo School Surveys, 1968-1977.

Figure 3-4. Change in Percentage of Active Amphetamine Users (ΔP_n), Males.

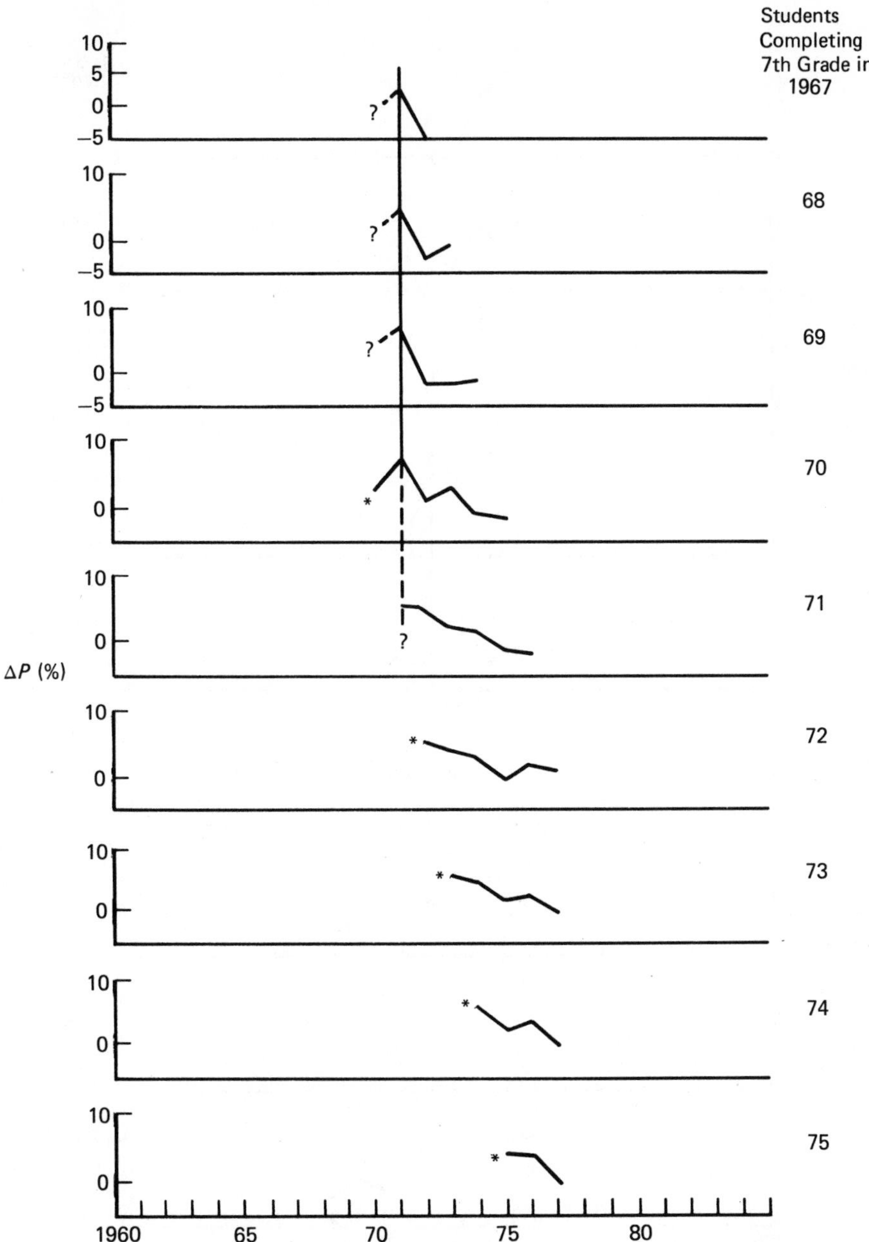

Source: San Mateo School Surveys, 1968-1977.

Figure 3-5. San Mateo: Change in Percentage of Active Barbiturate Users (ΔP_n), Males.

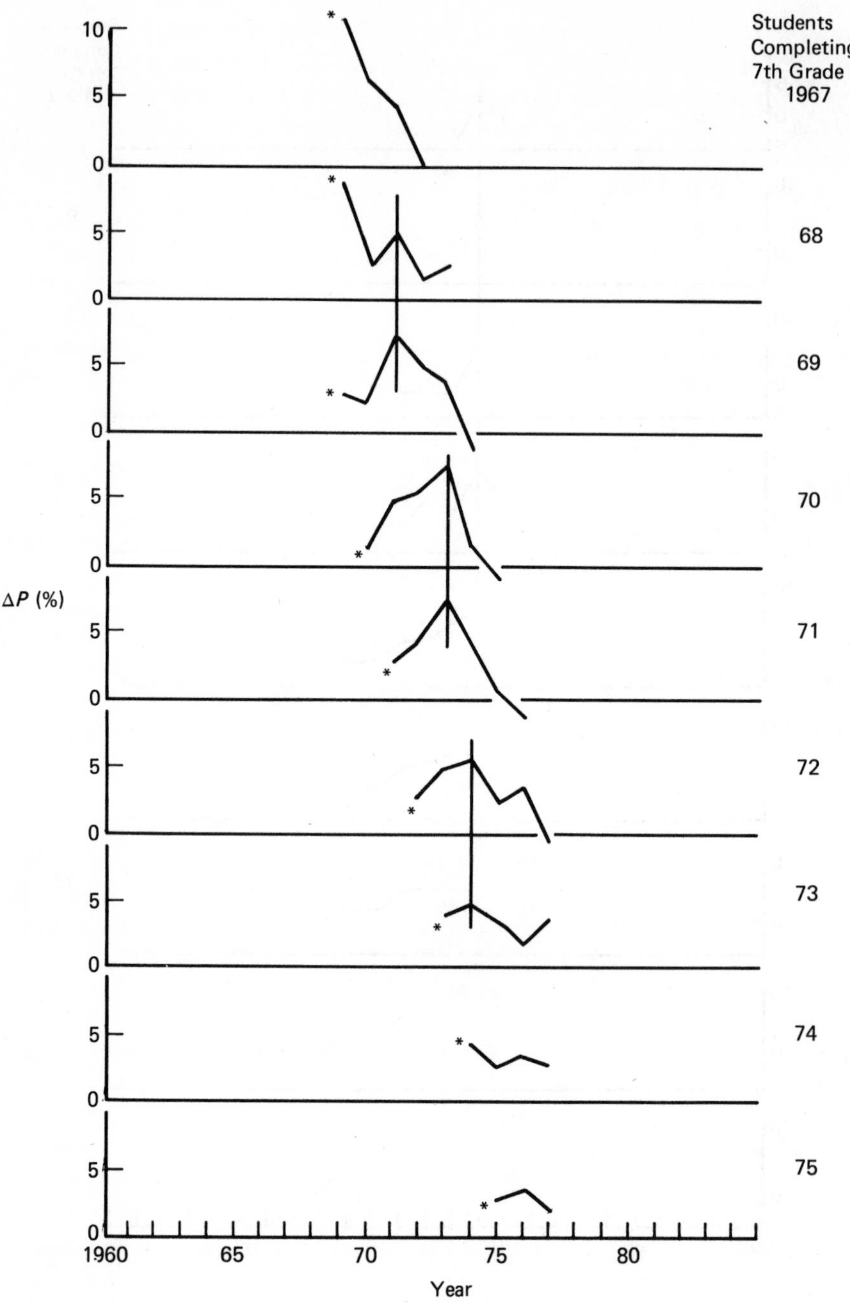

Source: San Mateo School Surveys, 1968-1977.

Figure 3-6. San Mateo: Change in Percentage of Active LSD Users (ΔP_n), Males.

instance, for marihuana (figure 3-3), the 1967 cohort (top curve) apparently experienced peak new use in its junior year in 1971. The same year the next three younger classes, who were then in the tenth, ninth, and eighth grades, also had maximum values of ΔP_n. Moreover, amphetamines and barbiturates show the same pattern. We conclude that the year 1971 was one in which use of these drugs suddenly became very popular in San Mateo County.

These data should not be overinterpreted, however: P_n is not precisely incidence of first use. It is complicated, as noted before, by migration and other population changes. For instance, the drop in the surveyed population in 1976 (see table 3-1) was the result of a high school refusing to continue its participation in the San Mateo survey. In this case, the effect of the population change on prevalence rates is reported as non significant. (Blackford 1978)

Duval County

The sixth through twelfth graders enrolled in Duval County schools reported considerably less drug use compared to their counterparts in San Mateo. However, both school systems reported identical relative prevalence rankings, with marihuana being used the most frequently, followed by amphetamines, hallucinogens and barbiturates. The magnitude of the Duval County prevalence rates are more comparable to Johnston's national rates than to San Mateo County. For instance, senior male marihuana users from Duval County constituted 33.0 percent in 1973 and 43.2 percent in 1976 of their classes (Barr 1973, 1976).

The youth in Duval County could be viewed as having more typical American drug prevalence levels than their San Mateo counterparts, although both school populations have similar prevalence profiles. How has drug use developed in this "average" American suburban community compared to San Mateo's rather drug-intense area? Quite differently, as we shall see.

Figures 3-7 and 3-8 show true incidence of first use for marihuana and for combined barbiturates and sedatives for successive class cohorts derived from Barr's 1973, 1975, and 1976 Duval County school surveys. Unlike the San Mateo data, these curves are estimates of actual incidence of first use. Survey respondents stated whether they had first used a drug "this year," "last year," or "before last year," and these responses can be used to calculate a direct measure of incidence of first use. However, such estimates are subject to sampling error, because the Duval County surveys employed samples rather than a total census of the school populations. Part of the yearly changes in the curves of figures 3-7 and 3-8 are therefore purely statistical fluctuations, and our conclusions are less certain than for San Mateo County data.

Fortunately, we do not seek absolute values of incidence, but only relative comparisons. We are looking for the coincidence of peaks in the curves.

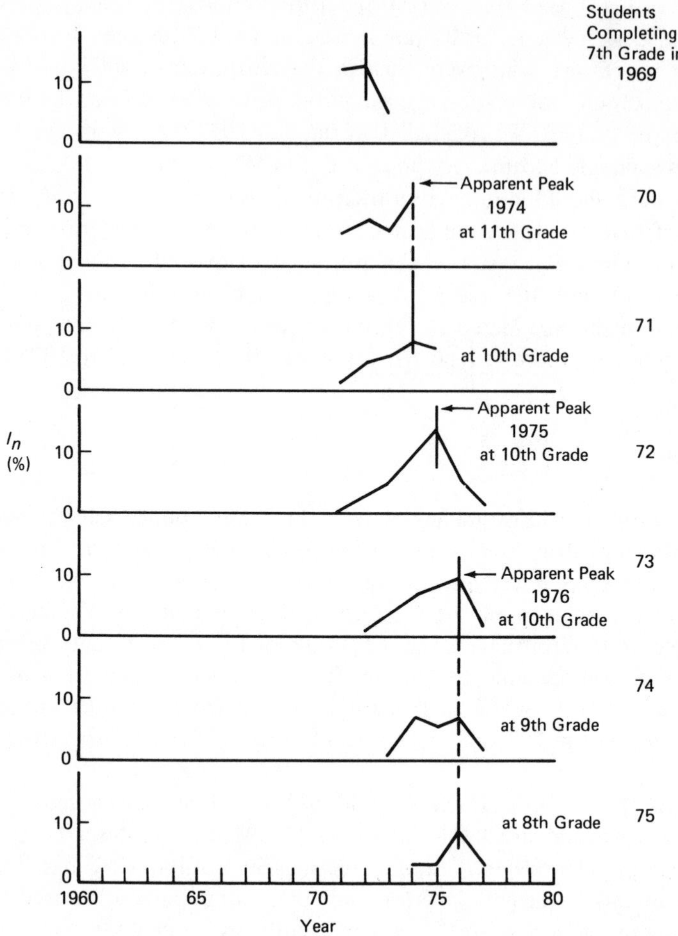

Source: Duval Co. School Surveys, 1968-1977.

Figure 3-7. Duval County, Florida: Percentage of New Marihuana Use (I_n) by Grade and Survey Year, Males.

Comparisons of the history of each cohort in figures 3-7 and 3-8 suggest that new use has developed differently here than in San Mateo County. Clustering of peak years of first use does occur, but it is clear only for later cohorts. The only apparent period of rapid growth was 1975/1976.

If these data are relatively correct—that is, if the shapes, but not necessarily the exact magnitudes, of the curves are true—they suggest interesting conclusions. Recall that Duval County's drug prevalence levels were not as high as those

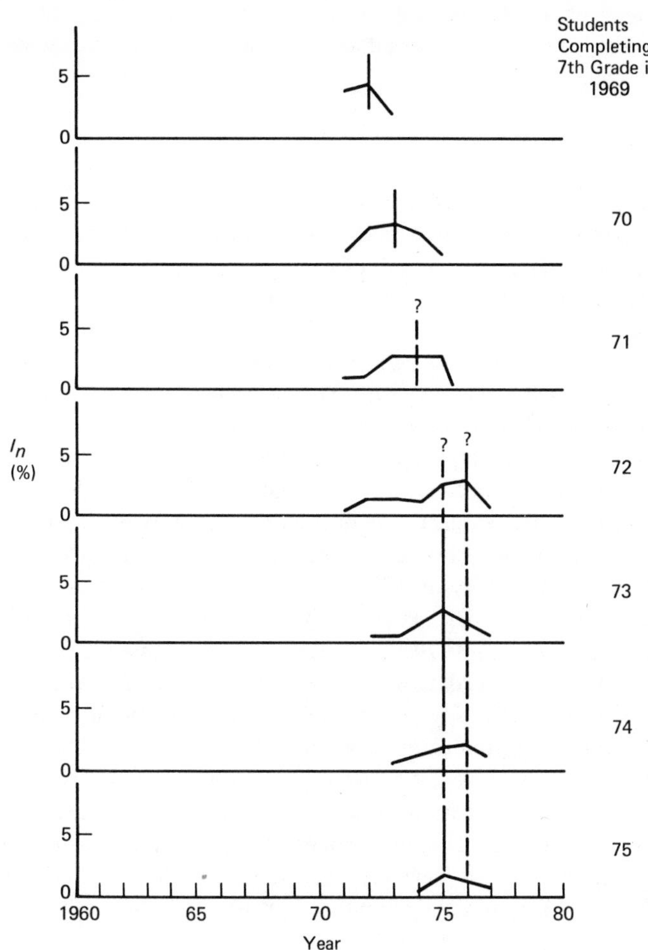

Source: Duval Co. School Surveys, 1968-1977.

Figure 3-8. Duval County, Florida: Percentage of New "Downer" Use (I_n) by Grade and Survey Year, Males.

observed among their contempories in San Mateo; yet, quite similar to levels found among America's youth in general. A comparison of figures 3-3 with 3-7, and of 3-5 and 3-8 would indicate that in Duval County the surge in new users occurred much later among its high school males when compared to their counterparts in San Mateo. The west coast students appeared to have experienced rapid growth in new use some three years earlier than the Florida students. In both counties, however, a common pattern is observed that involves different age cohorts. Often, regardless of what drug is being examined, two or more adjacent high school grades experience quite similar incidence curves.

Conclusions

These data describe growth of new drug use in high school populations in widely separated locales. Though not exactly comparable, the two measures of new use reveal a common tendency: growth of new use has been sudden and sporadic for entire school populations rather than regular and consistently repeated in succeeding classes.

Whether one chooses to call this tendency an *epidemic* is a matter of preference. It is clear that use spreads more quickly during some years than during others. Such behavior suggests that networks of friends and peers are able to transmit new use rapidly, in spite of considerable age differences.

The geographical contrasts in these data are striking. Nearly all growth curves for San Mateo County are declining (except two or three classes for amphetamines use), and have been since the early 1970s. During this same period (at least until 1975 or 1976), most of the Duval County curves were rising. We conclude that San Mateo's "epidemic," for all these substances, was a phenomenon of the early 1970s; a similar era of rapid growth might, of course, have occurred in the preceding decade, which we cannot see with these data. A similar period of accelerating growth did not occur in Duval County until the mid-1970s for the same populations of students.

More generally, we conclude that use of marihuana and other drugs spreads in these high school populations in about the same way that heroin has spread among known treated addicts, in episodes of sudden rapid growth followed by periods during which little new use occurs. Such patterns are characteristic of most forms of fad behavior and are not unique to psychotropic drug use.

References

Abelson, H.I., Fishburne, P.M. and Cisin, I., *National Survey on Drug Abuse 1977.* NIDA 78-618, 1977.

Barr, C. *Drug and Alcohol Opinionnaire and Usage Survey, 1973, 1975, 1976.* Duval County School Board, Jacksonville, Florida.

Blackford, L. Personal communication to E. Farley. March 1, 1978.

Blackford, L. *Summary Report, Surveys of Student Drug Use, San Mateo County California.* San Mateo County, California, Department of Public Health and Welfare, 1977.

de Alarcon, R. The spread of heroin in a community. *Bulletin on Narcotics.* July-September 1969, pp. 17-22.

Hughes, P. Crawford, G., and Jaffe, J. Heroin epidemics in Chicago. *Proceedings of the World Congress of Psychiatry*. Mexico City, 1971.

Hunt, L. *Heroin Epidemics: A Quantitative Study of Empirical Data.* Drug Abuse Council, Washington, D.C., 1973.

Hunt, L. *Recent Spread of Heroin in the United States.* Drug Abuse Council, Washington, D.C., 1974.

Hunt, L., and Chambers, C. *Heroin Epidemics*. New York: Spectrum, 1976.

Hunt, L. *Assessment of Local Drug Abuse.* Lexington, Mass: Lexington Books, D.C. Heath, 1977.

Johnston, L. *Drugs and American Youth.* Institute for Social Research, University of Michigan, Ann Arbor, Michigan, 1973.

4 Determinants of Early Marihuana Use

John A. O'Donnell and *Richard R. Clayton*

Introduction

Among the illicit drugs, marihuana is usually the first one used and the one used by most people. It also usually precedes the nonmedical use of licit drugs like the narcotics, sedatives, and stimulants and exceeds them in number of users. As the most relevant example, marihuana was used by 90 percent of both males and females in the National Youth Polydrug Study (NYPS), while no other drug (except alcohol) was used by more than 50 percent of either sex. In a nationwide study of nonmedical drug use among young men which will be described later, marihuana was used by 55 percent, with the next highest figure, 31 percent, for opiates.

In the National Youth Polydrug Study, the mean age at first use of marihuana was 12.8 years for males and 13.1 years for females. In both cases, these means are lower than for all other drugs, except alcohol. The time difference between first use of marihuana and first use of later drugs was not great in this sample, but this is largely due to the population from which the samples were drawn. When a sample is selected from a population under 19 years of age, all drugs that have been used must have been used at an early age. In other treatment samples with no limit on age and in samples from the general population, the time difference between first use of marihuana and first use of other drugs may be appreciable.

The fact that marihuana has been so widely used is the obvious reason for a chapter on marihuana use. The additional fact that it is usually the first illicit drug, plus other considerations to be discussed later, explain why the focus here will be on the age at which this use begins. (*Age at first use* is to be taken literally—the person's age at the time he or she first tried marihuana. *Age at first continuing use* might be preferable, but is not always available.) In addition to the interest in and importance of marihuana use in its own right, there is another reason to study it: such study may help to solve some of the problems that have proved recalcitrant in the study of other, more serious forms of drug use.

Studies of the etiology and natural history of heroin use, for example, have been limited by the fact that for practical purposes, the only heroin users available for study have been those who are arrested and incarcerated or who are treated, usually with only a minor aspect of voluntary action in their applications for treatment. If there have been users of heroin who keep their use sporadic enough to avoid addiction, or addicts with enough income to avoid illegal activities and minimize contact with the drug subculture, or users who quit their use without treatment, such users are unlikely to appear in prisons or treatment agencies. Those who were studied were therefore biased samples of users. Inferences based on such samples would almost inevitably fail to apply to users not represented in the studies.

One of the firmest conclusions based on the study of available samples of addicts was that relapse after treatment was inevitable, or almost inevitable, and usually rapid. Witness the fact that Lindesmith (1968) built a "tendency to relapse" into his definition of addiction. Early follow-up studies, usually covering only brief follow-up periods, seemed to confirm this. But Robins and Murphy (1967) reported that the small number of blacks they identified as having been addicts in St. Louis had ceased using narcotics. In the late 1960s a number of studies (Ball and Pabon 1965; Vaillant 1966; O'Donnell 1969) were conducted in which the follow-up period was long, up to 15 to 20 years after the index period of treatment. These studies clearly indicated that even among hard-core addicts, some eventually became abstinent and many were abstinent for periods of years even if use resumed. Addiction was clearly a cyclic pattern of periods of use, incarceration, and abstinence while not incarcerated. In addition, the patterns of use varied; some included little voluntary abstinence, while others included periods of years of abstinence.

Such studies should have established that relapse was not inevitable, but the lesson was not learned. If it had been, Robins' (1974) finding that only a minority of men who were addicted in Vietnam relapsed after their return to the United States would not have generated such a reaction of surprise. But it was clear that the major difference between her Vietnam follow-up study and previous follow-up studies was that the early studies used samples of incarcerated or treated addicts, the end product of a series of selection processes, while hers was essentially a sample from the *general* population of young men.

What had happened was reminiscent of what had happened earlier in another area, alcoholism. Early concepts of alcoholism were based on studies of skid-row populations and hospitalized alcoholics, and they had to be modified when studies of drinking practices among the general population were done (Cahalan et al. 1969; Cahalan 1970; Cahalan and Room 1974; Straus 1972). Studies of heroin use and other forms of drug use were clearly needed in samples drawn from the general population.

Some such studies have been done in recent years—the Marihuana Commission nationwide survey of 1971 (Abelson et al. 1972) and its repetitions in 1974 (Abelson and Atkinson 1975) and 1975-1976 (Abelson and Fishburne 1976), a nationwide survey of drug use among young men (O'Donnell et al. 1976) from which data will be used for this chapter, and two continuing panel studies by Johnston and his associates (Johnston 1973; Johnston and Bachman 1975). In addition, there have been several surveys of states or smaller units. If the responses given in these surveys can be taken at face value, the following conclusions seem justified.

1. Large and growing numbers of people in the general population have used heroin, other narcotics, and other drugs at some time in their lives. Johnston reports that 19 percent of male high school seniors in 1969 had used marihuana, while 54 percent of the 1975 class had used it by their senior year. The corresponding figures for heroin were 1.2 and 2.7 percent (Press release, Washington, D.C., October 1, 1975). The series of national studies that began with the Marihuana Commission survey showed a steady upward trend in lifetime prevalence of marihuana use among adults: 1971, 15 percent; 1972, 16 percent; 1974, 19 percent; 1975-1976, 21 percent. These figures are for all adults over age 17; among young adults, those 18 to 25 years old, the 1975-1976 survey showed 53 percent had used marihuana at some time in their lives, and 25 percent had used it in the past month. In the same survey, 1.2 percent of all adults, but 3.9 percent of young adults, had used heroin (Abelson and Fishburne 1976). In the survey which the present writers, with others, conducted, 55 percent of men 20 to 30 years old had used marihuana, and 6 percent had used heroin (O'Donnell et al. 1976).

2. Much of this use, however, was experimental–defining *experimental* as use less than ten times. While 55 percent of young men had used marihuana, almost one-third of them used it less than ten times, and half of the heroin users used it that infrequently (O'Donnell et al. 1976). Exactly equivalent definitions cannot be used for other studies, but Johnston reports that 48 percent of his 1975 high school seniors, males and females combined, had used marihuana: 18 percent of the users had used it only once or twice, and an additional 31 percent less than twenty times. For heroin, less than one half of the 2.3 percent who were users had used it more than twice (Press release, Washington, D.C., October 1, 1975).

3. Even when the use was more than experimental, much of it did not amount to addiction, since it was sporadic and did not progress to daily use. Even when addiction may reasonably be inferred, it did not usually lead to treatment. In the survey of young men, for example, of the 148 who had ever used heroin, 47 reported using daily at some time, so that physical dependence was probably present, but only 16 of them reported treatment for their heroin use. Asked if they had "ever been physically or psychologically dependent on any drug, or addicted to any," 43 said they had been on heroin, but only 15 of these had been in treatment (O'Donnell et al. 1976). In this survey, only 20 had been treated for heroin use out of the 148 who had used heroin–though of course it remains possible that more have entered or will enter treatment after the date of the interview.

4. In all the surveys, the figures for current use of any drug (except tobacco and alcohol) are much lower than for lifetime use. This appears to be true even for those who at some time used the drug heavily or were addicted to it,

although at this time the only firm data supporting the statement come from the survey of young men. From the preceding paragraph, it would appear that some 43 or more (about 30 percent) of the 148 heroin users had been addicted, but only 15 percent reported any use of heroin in the 4 months before the interview. It would thus appear that some drug users, and perhaps many, are able to give up their drug use, and do so without formal treatment.

These considerations make it seem almost certain that those heroin and other narcotic addicts who appear in our prisons and treatment agencies are the product of a long winnowing process and constitute a minority, rather than most, of those who began to use narcotics at any given time. If one is interested in the question "Why do people begin to use heroin?" it is evident that data must be sought from all who have begun to use it (and their peers who did not begin), not just from treated and incarcerated populations. To understand why some people learn to fly, one does not restrict questions to airline pilots.

For many questions about drug use, then, we need a sample of the general population. Surveys can provide such samples, but in addition to all their other difficulties, they are not efficient for locating samples of heroin users. Such use is still rare (even in a nationwide probability sample of males 20 to 30 years old, only 6 percent had ever used heroin), so enormous samples would be needed to produce a sizable number of users.

The surveys cited earlier located only small numbers of users of narcotics and fewer addicts, but they identified many users of other drugs, especially of marihuana. If it could be established, therefore, that some inferences based on the study of marihuana users, or of a clearly defined subset of marihuana users, also apply to heroin users, we would be able to learn about a hard-to-locate group by studying one that is relatively easy to locate and study.

One set of conditions under which such extrapolation of findings on marihuana users to heroin users would be legitimate would be where:

1. A variable is shown to be a cause of marihuana use.
2. Marihuana use is shown (or assumed) to be a cause of heroin use.
3. The variable is inferred to be a cause of heroin use.

We believe the second statement to be true, given a specific definition of causality. The case for it will be made in another publication, but the essential points are briefly noted in the following section. It is not crucial that the reader agree with our belief, because the central focus of this chapter will be on the first statement. The method used will be one form of causal model, path analysis.

The rhetoric of path analysis freely uses words like *cause, direct effect,* and *indirect effect,* although it is based only on correlational data, plus assumptions about temporal or causal priority. We will follow this convention, and will not trouble to couple every cause-effect expression with a disclaimer. Many readers may be uncomfortable with the inference of causality from correlations. For them, we suggest that they not be too troubled by the philosophical implications, but mentally translate *cause* into *predictor.* The third statement in the preceding list is not as logically compelling if *cause* is replaced by *predictor* each time it appears, because predictive power attenuates rapidly along a chain, but it would at least remain true that any variable shown to be a predictor of marihuana use would be worth testing as a possible predictor of heroin use. This, however, is secondary and for the future. The immediate focus will be on the causes, or predictors, of marihuana use.

The Samples

The analysis will be based on two sets of data. The first was obtained by interviews, lasting from 30 minutes to several hours, with a nationwide probability sample of young men in the United States who were 20 to 30 years old, inclusive, in 1974, when most of the interviews were done. The sample was restricted to males because it was desired to locate a sizable number of users of such drugs as heroin, and it was assumed that the rates for males were still appreciably greater than those for females. Similarly, the upper age limit served to restrict the sample to the age group where use would be highest. The lower age limit was imposed by the fact that the sample was drawn from records of Selective Service Boards, where men registered on reaching age 18. In theory, 19-year-olds could have been included, but these would have been men born in 1955 who registered in 1973, when there was some confusion about the need to register, and records were incomplete. They were therefore not included.

Sample size was originally 3,024, of whom 36 were found to be deceased and 7 incompetent and incapable of being interviewed, so there were 2,981 potential interviewees. Of these, 2,510 (84 percent) were interviewed, with 6 percent refusing to be interviewed and 10 percent who could not be located. Sampling procedure is described in more detail in O'Donnell et al. (1976), but it may be said that this sample can be taken as representative of all young men of their age range in the United States, except for Alaska and Hawaii.

The primary interests in interviews with men of the national sample were epidemiological, and interview items focused on obtaining details about drug use and its correlates. Items on early life experiences which might be seen as predictors or causes of the later drug use had to be cut to a bare minimum to keep the interview short enough to be tolerated by respondents. Since heroin use is a relatively rare form of behavior, it was expected that the number of respondents with a history of such use would be small, and indeed only 6 percent had used heroin.

A second sample was drawn from those areas in the Borough of Manhattan, New York City, which had been identified as areas of high drug use by reports to the City Registry in the late 1960s. It was expected that the proportion of heroin users in this sample would be much higher than in the national sample, as indeed it was (25.5 percent reported having used heroin at least once). Many of the items in the national interview schedule were deleted to make room for a set of new items on childhood experiences which might be analyzed as possible causes or predictors of drug use.

The original size of the New York sample was slightly over 600, but only 294 interviews were completed. Part of the reason was that it was much more difficult to locate men in New York, where whole areas had been razed. Part was the fact that the research team felt it was more important to achieve a high completion rate of interviews for the national sample, so this was given priority, and time and funds for field work were depleted before all the New York interviews could be done.

The New York sample was originally a probability sample, just as much as the national, but the population to which inferences would be statistically justified was an artificial one; the sample represented the high-drug-use areas of Manhattan, but these were not contiguous, and there is no natural geographical area to which generalizations would be applicable. In addition, the completion rate of under 50 percent means that the interviewed men may differ from the target sample in unknown and unknowable ways.

The one great advantage of the New York sample is that it is a sample of the general population, not of the treatment or arrested population on which most drug studies are based. Nonusers of drugs, those who tried drugs but did not continue, and those who continued but quit use on their own had as good a chance to be selected into the sample (perhaps, however, a different probability of being interviewed) as those users who are found in prisons or in treatment. Further, the sample was drawn from areas where up to half the young men were *known* as heroin users. Thus the question can sensibly be asked about the New York, but not the national, sample—Why do some young men *not* become drug users?

In the technical sense, then, it would not be justifiable to extrapolate any findings on the New York sample to any known population or area. In a practical sense, however, such findings will be at least plausible hypotheses about high-drug-use areas in New York and other cities, at least until such time as similar data are available on such areas and are found to differ. Depending on their nature, the findings might also suggest plausible hypotheses about drug use anywhere in the United States. To the extent that drug use is found to depend on a drug subculture, on the availability of drugs, and on the presence of many who are already using drugs, the explanation would be restricted to high-drug-use areas. But to the extent it might be found to depend on family background or non-drug-specific peer influences, the explanations could have wider applicability.

Age at First Use of Marihuana as a Strategic Variable

Table 4-1 shows that there is a strong association between marihuana use and heroin use in both samples. The same association has been found in many other studies (see Goode 1974, p. 315). The time order of the two variables is clear. In the national sample, there were 147 men who had used both drugs, and from 90 to 93 percent had used marihuana first (3 percent had used both drugs for the first time in the same month, and time order was uncertain). In the New York City sample, 74 men had used both drugs, and from 75 to 86 percent had used marihuana first.

The association between marihuana use and heroin use could, however, be a spurious one; both could be effects of some earlier variable and have no connection except that common cause. If this were so, a statistical control on the common cause would make the marihuana-heroin relationship disappear. To test for spuriousness on the data from the national sample, there were thirty-two variables which were clearly, or possibly, antecedent to marihuana use and heroin use in time. Controls on these, one at a time, failed to reduce the marihuana-heroin association.

In the New York City sample, there were forty-one variables prior in time to

Table 4-1
Relationship between Marihuana and Heroin Use, Based on Lifetime Extent of Use
(Numbers of Respondents)

Number of Times Heroin Used	Number of Times Marihuana Used: *0*	*1-9*	*10-99*	*100-999*	*1,000+*	*Total*
A. National Sample (gamma = .876)						
0	1,127	419	343	296	177	2,362
1-9	1	4	6	22	39	72
10-99	0	0	2	14	25	41
100-999	0	0	4	4	9	17
1,000+	0	0	1	2	15	18
Total	1,128	423	356	338	265	2,510
B. New York Sample (gamma = .634)						
0	73	35	43	38	30	219
1-9	0	2	1	5	8	16
10-99	0	1	3	7	4	15
100-999	1	3	4	3	9	20
1,000+	0	1	3	3	17	24
Total	74	42	54	56	68	294

marihuana use, and therefore also to heroin use, which could be used for control. The need to examine racial-ethnic groups separately meant that numbers became small in subtables and limited the testing of combinations of control variables, but controls on these variables one at a time also produced no significant reductions in the marihuana-heroin association.

While combinations of the control variables in tabular analysis are severely limited, these limits are removed if one is willing to accept the construction of twelve composite variables, described in a later section on predictors, from the forty-one, and the treatment of these as interval-level variables, although in fact they are ordinal. It then becomes possible to use partial correlation to control the twelve composite variables simultaneously and see if this affects the marihuana-heroin relationship.

The product-moment correlation between age at first use of marihuana and extent of heroin use (computed from the ordered categories shown in table 4-1) was –.398. With simultaneous controls on the twelve composite variables, the partial correlation was –.269; this is a reduction, but still significantly different from zero at the .001 level. If extent of opiate use replaces extent of heroin use, the zero-order correlation with age at first use of marihuana is –.484, and the partial correlation is –.365; again smaller, but again significantly different from zero at the .001 level.

A similar approach with the variables of the national sample led to similar results. Even simultaneous controls on all the available prior variables which might be producing spurious relationships failed to destroy the relationship in both samples.

The arguments of the preceding paragraph can be used to assert that by the usual three criteria employed by sociologists to infer causality from cross-sectional data—statistical association, temporal order, and no evidence of spuriousness—marihuana use should be regarded as a cause of heroin use. This is not, however, central to this chapter. Here the argument is simpler. Marihuana use and later heroin use are so closely connected that any explanation or predictors of marihuana use will be plausible hypotheses about the explanation or the predictors of heroin use. This is not to say, however, that the fact of marihuana use is, by itself, sufficient to predict heroin use; since only a small minority of marihuana users go on to heroin use.

For reasons that will become evident, we choose to take as dependent variable not marihuana use, but age at first use of marihuana. Table 4-2 displays this variable separately for the two samples, and by race within the samples. Several points about the table should be noted. There are differences between the races on many variables, which make it necessary to examine the races separately, but this produces *N*'s of 125, 98, and 71 in the New York City sample. When these are further divided on another variable, percentage estimates will become somewhat unstable.

No reason is known why the whites and blacks in New York City should not

Table 4-2
Age at First Use of Marihuana, by Race, in Two Samples
(Percentages)

	White		Black		Other	
Age at First Marihuana Use n	*National (2,103)*	*NYC (98)*	*National (303)*	*NYC (125)*	*National (104)*	*NYC (71)*
14 or earlier	–	5	–	22	–	11
15 or 16	10	17	20	24	16	20
17 or 18	13	17	14	22	12	11
19 or 20	14	34	16	14	9	21
21 or older	17	–	15	–	14	–
Never used	46	28	35	18	49	37
Total	100	99	100	100	100	100

be compared with the corresponding groups in the national sample, but the comparison for "others" is questionable. The "others" in the New York sample are largely men of Puerto Rican descent. In the national sample, those of Spanish descent are primarily Mexican rather than Puerto Rican, and about half the "others" are not of Spanish descent. The data on "others" will be presented in some tables to follow, but inferences will be based mainly on the white-white and black-black comparisons.

The two samples differ appreciably on the age at which marihuana use began. In the New York sample, enough began at age 14 or earlier to identify this as a separate category. In the national sample, only 2 percent used marihuana at that age, too few for separate analysis, so these are grouped with the 15 to 16 category in table 4-2 and following tables. For the national sample, therefore, 15 to 16 should be read as "16 or earlier," but for the large majority in this row, use did begin at 15 or 16.

Similarly, over 15 percent of the national sample began marihuana use after age 20, while a very small proportion of the New York sample began that late. These are included with the 19 to 20 group, which therefore should be read, for the New York sample, as "19 or older." Again, no confusion should be caused by this, and analysis will be facilitated.

It is evident in table 4-2 that a much higher proportion of men in the New York sample than in the national sample had used marihuana, and that the New Yorkers started use earlier. Much of the difference is accounted for, in tables not shown, by the older men in the sample, those who were 25 to 30 years old at the time of interview. In the national sample, the percentage of users in these cohorts was lower than in the younger cohorts, and the age at onset higher. In other words, during the 1960s there was a clear increase in use among younger men; less than 40 percent of the oldest cohorts, but over 60 percent of the youngest, had used marihuana. Further, the younger men began their use earlier;

median age at first use dropped from 25 in the oldest cohorts to 17 in the youngest (see O'Donnell et al. 1976, pp. 48-61). It is consistent with the data to speak of an epidemic of marihuana use for the nation. Depending on the size of the increase one chooses to use as the criterion for the start of the epidemic, it began with a year or two before or after 1965.

These changes are not seen in the New York sample. The percentage of users is high for all age subgroups, and early onset was as common among the oldest cohorts as among the youngest. If an epidemic of marihuana use in New York City did occur, it began before 1960, too early for its start to be estimated from these data. In view of the fact that the New York sample was selected from areas known to be high in drug use, it is reasonable not to think in terms of an epidemic at all, but rather of a high endemic rate of use.

That age at first use of marihuana is associated with use of other drugs is shown in table 4-3. In this table, age at first use is related to an index which measures the extent of use of other drugs, excluding marihuana itself, as well as tobacco and alcohol, which normally preceded use of marihuana. The drugs in the index are psychedelics, stimulants, sedatives, heroin, other opiates, and cocaine. For each sample, one item recorded the man's estimate of the total number of times he had used the drug, or class of drugs, in the five categories used in table 4-1 (that is, no use, use less than 10 times, 10 to 99 times, 100 to 999 times, and 1,000 or more times). The index was constructed by a method suggested by Lu (1974). Weights were assigned to each category by the proportion of cases in the national sample that were found in these categories and scores computed for each man in both samples by these weights, so that scores represent the extent of individual use in relation to the extent that the same drugs were used by the national sample as a whole (see O'Donnell et al. 1976, chap. 10, for a full discussion of this index). In table 4-3, the possible range of scores on this index is divided into four equal parts, and those in each age of onset of marihuana use are distributed in these parts.

Perhaps the first point to note in table 4-3, though an expected one, is that the use of psychedelics, stimulants, sedatives, heroin, other opiates, and cocaine was appreciably higher in the New York sample than in the national sample. Among whites, 44 percent of the New Yorkers fall in the two higher categories compared with 30 percent for the national sample. The corresponding figures for blacks are 49 and 36; for others, 32 and 24.

The important point from these data is best seen in the subtable for whites of the national sample, where the *N* is largest and random fluctuations least to be feared. The pattern is clear: the older the man was when he began using marihuana, the less likely he was to use other drugs, and those who never used marihuana at all were least likely to use other drugs or to use them extensively. Conversely, the earlier a man began to use marihuana, the greater was the likelihood that he would use other drugs and that his use would be extensive.

There are minor reversals in the figures for blacks and others in the national

Table 4-3
Extent of Use of Drugs Other Than Tobacco, Alcohol, and Marihuana for Two Samples, Using an Index Based on the National Sample, by Race and Age at First Use of Marihuana

	National Sample					NYC Sample				
		Drug-Use Index					Drug-Use Index			
Age at First Marihuana Use	*n*	*1 (Low)*	*2*	*3*	*4 (High)*	*n*	*1 (Low)*	*2*	*3*	*4 (High)*
A. Whites:										
14 or earlier	–	–	–	–	–	(5)	0	20	20	60
15-16	(210)	11	11	17	60	(17)	6	6	18	71
17-18	(274)	28	15	26	31	(17)	29	12	29	29
19-20	(289)	35	21	26	18	(33)	42	18	21	18
21 or older	(360)	43	26	22	9	–	–	–	–	–
Never used	(970)	79	12	8	*	(26)	85	12	4	0
Percent in column		53	16	16	14		43	13	17	27
B. Blacks:										
14 or earlier	–	–	–	–	–	(28)	0	4	25	71
15-16	(61)	23	5	21	51	(30)	37	20	17	26
17-18	(42)	36	14	10	40	(28)	43	4	21	32
19-20	(48)	33	17	25	25	(17)	41	29	18	12
21 or older	(45)	62	9	13	16	–	–	–	–	–
Never used	(107)	87	6	6	0	(22)	86	9	4	0
Percent in column		55	9	14	22		39	12	18	31
C. Other:										
14 or earlier	–	–	–	–	–	(8)	12	0	25	62
15-16	(17)	24	0	24	53	(14)	36	21	14	29
17-18	(13)	62	23	8	8	(8)	25	12	25	38
19-20	(9)	33	0	56	11	(15)	53	20	7	20
21 or older	(14)	43	43	7	7	–	–	–	–	–
Never used	(51)	88	8	4	0	(26)	92	4	4	0
Percent in column		64	12	12	12		56	11	11	21

*Less than 0.5 percent.

sample, and for all three groups in the New York sample, but these are explainable as the instability of percentages based on smaller numbers. It is evident that the pattern is identical in these subtables, and that age at first use of marihuana is negatively and strongly associated with use of other drugs for all racial groups in both samples.

The Lu index is a fairly abstract measure, is a recent addition to the literature, has not been widely used, and therefore may not convey enough to the reader. Table 4-4 therefore presents, in terms of percentages, how heroin use and opiate use in general are associated with age at first use of marihuana. With only minor exceptions—surprisingly few in view of the small number of cases on which some percentages are based—each column in each section of the table shows a marked decrease from top to bottom. The probability of heroin use, or of opiate use, is clearly much greater as the age at first use of marihuana is lower.

Several points should be made about table 4-4. If one looks only at a use-no use dichotomy for marihuana and heroin use, one finds relationships like 147 heroin users among 1,382 marihuana users and only 1 heroin user among 1,128 who never used marihuana (10.6 percent against less than 0.1 percent) in the national sample. The same 2 X 2 table for the New York sample gives 33.6 percent against 1.4 percent. These are extremely strong relationships, but they would not suffice for prediction, since in both cases only a minority of marihuana users go on to heroin use.

Table 4-4
Percentage of Heroin Users and Opiate (Including Heroin) Users in Two Samples, by Age at First Use of Marihuana and Ethnic Group

	White			*Black*			*Other*		
Age at First Marihuana Use	*n*	*Heroin Use (%)*	*Opiate Use (%)*	*n*	*Heroin Use (%)*	*Opiate Use (%)*	*n*	*Heroin Use (%)*	*Opiate Use (%)*
A. National Sample									
14 or earlier	–	–	–	–	–	–	–	–	–
15-16	210	25	69	61	26	69	17	29	59
17-18	274	8	45	42	26	50	13	8	23
19-20	289	7	41	48	19	46	9	0	33
21 or older	360	1	30	45	11	31	14	0	29
Never used	970	0	17	107	1	11	51	0	8
B. New York Sample									
14 or earlier	5	60	60	28	75	82	8	75	89
15-16	17	29	88	30	40	53	14	36	50
17-18	17	12	47	28	46	54	8	12	50
19-20	33	3	30	17	12	47	15	20	33
21 or older	–	–	–	–	–	–	–	–	–
Never used	26	0	4	22	4	14	26	0	4

In a larger table, such as table 4-1, some prediction might appear to be possible, at least for those men in New York who have used marihuana 1,000 times or more; more than half of them were also heroin users. But knowledge of this amount of marihuana use would be available only several years after use started, and probably in many cases this level would not be reached until after heroin use had begun, so it would not be a useful predictor of heroin use.

But age at first use of marihuana is a variable for which data are easy to get, which is, as tables 4-3 and 4-4 show, highly predictive of later drug use, including heroin or opiate use, but not restricted to them, and which normally could be available for predictive purposes before heroin use, or use of other drugs, has started. We suggest that if, among the hundreds who have in recent years conducted surveys of marihuana use among samples of youth, some have data on age at first use and are planning follow-up studies, it would be valuable to check on the predictive power of this variable.

A variable that is in some ways as important as drug use is the illicit sale of drugs. The selling of drugs is theoretically important as an indicator of involvement in a drug subculture and practically important in a number of ways. Principal among them is that drug sales may be more likely to result in arrest and imprisonment than just the use of drugs. More data on drug sales were available for the New York sample than for the national sample, but the variable used in table 4-5 is restricted to what was common to both samples. It is seen as an ordinal scale with three categories: no drug sales, selling of marihuana only, and selling of other drugs, usually but not necessarily including marihuana.

Table 4-5 shows first that more men in the New York sample sold drugs. For whites and blacks, over 30 percent of New Yorkers, as opposed to less than 20 percent in the national sample, had sold drugs. The difference is in the same direction, but smaller and probably negligible.

While selling of drugs was more common in New York, this sample was so highly selective that no useful generalization from it seems possible. But it is worth calling attention to how widespread the selling of drugs was among young men in the United States, as indicated by the national sample. No less than 30 percent of the marihuana users had sold drugs. Perhaps an even more striking way of putting it is that 17 percent of all young men, regardless of whether or not they had ever used drugs themselves, admitted to having sold drugs. The population of young men represented by the sample was approximately 19 million, so this would mean that over 3 million admitted an offense which could have led to a prison term.

More relevant for the concern of this chapter, however, is the fact that the selling of drugs is related to the age at which marihuana was first used, just as heroin use, opiate usage, and drug use in general were related. The earlier marihuana was used, the more likely were drug sales, and these were almost though not completely absent among men who never used marihuana. The linearity of the association is again clearest for whites in the national sample where numbers are large, but the pattern is essentially identical for whites in New York and for other groups in both samples.

Table 4-5

Self-Reported Sales of Drugs for Two Samples, by Race and Age at First Use of Marihuana

(Percentages)

	National Sample				NYC Sample			
Age at First Marihuana Use	*n*	*No Drug Sales*	*Marihuana Only*	*Other Drugs*	*n*	*No Drug Sales*	*Marihuana Only*	*Other Drugs*
A. Whites:								
14 or earlier	–	–	–	–	(5)	40	20	40
15-16	(210)	36	25	39	(17)	29	29	41
17-18	(274)	67	17	16	(17)	59	29	12
19-20	(289)	76	11	13	(33)	73	24	3
21 or older	(360)	84	10	6	–	–	–	–
Never used	(970)	99.5	*	*	(26)	100	0	0
Percent in column		83	8	9		69	19	12
B. Blacks:								
14 or earlier	–	–	–	–	(28)	39	14	46
15-16	(61)	57	23	20	(30)	50	13	37
17-18	(42)	62	10	29	(28)	61	7	32
19-20	(48)	83	8	8	(17)	71	18	12
21 or older	(45)	87	4	9	–	–	–	–
Never used	(107)	97	1	2	(22)	96	0	4
Percent in column		80	8	11		61	10	29
C. Other:								
14 or earlier	–	–	–	–	(8)	50	0	50
15-16	(17)	47	12	41	(14)	64	14	20
17-18	(13)	92	0	8	(8)	62	0	38
19-20	(9)	89	11	0	(15)	93	0	7
21 or older	(14)	86	7	7	–	–	–	–
Never used	(51)	100	0	0	(26)	100	0	0
Percent in column		88	4	9		82	3	16

*Less than 0.5 percent.

The available data on criminal behavior are less comprehensive than would be desirable. Men were asked only about specific offenses which were expected to be associated with drug use, and if they had ever committed any of these, they were asked in what year it first happened and when it last happened. But other crimes were not asked about at all, and even for those which were asked about, no estimates of the total number of offenses were obtained. The data therefore cannot be used to construct a measure of the extent of criminal behavior, nor is it even safe to see the data as indicating the variety of crimes a man engaged in. For what it may be worth, however, a crime variable was constructed with three categories: denied all the specified offenses, admitted one or more minor offenses (public intoxication, driving while intoxicated, shoplifting, illegal gambling, or auto theft), and admitted one or more of the more serious offenses (breaking and entering, armed robbery, stealing face to face, or bad checked).

A table omitted here to save space suggests that the crime measure may be useful because its association with age at first use of marihuana is similar to that seen for drug use and drug sales—the earlier the first use, the more likely the user was to report involvement in criminal behavior, and in the more serious crimes.

Three behaviors, then—drug use other than tobacco, alcohol, and marihuana; drug sales; and crime—are associated with age at first use of marihuana, and only data on time order are needed to say they are predicted by age at first use. For drug use, the data are available and show that the use of other drugs (except tobacco and alcohol) normally follows use of marihuana. This is not universally true, but it is true in the large majority of cases (see O'Donnell et al. 1976, p. 103). For drug sales, information on time order is not available. It is clear that drug sales can precede marihuana use; witness a few cases in table 4-5, where men who never used marihuana had sold drugs. But such cases are few. Further, it seems plausible that sales would follow use in most cases, and those studies which have collected data on this point confirm this (see, for example, Johnson 1973, p. 73). The data on the time order of crime and drug use are very complex (see O'Donnell et al. 1976, pp. 81-97; Voss 1976), and it appears that the question must be asked separately for each crime. Some crimes, like shoplifting, auto theft, and public intoxication, occur very early in some cases and may antedate marihuana use. Others, like those treated as "more serious" offenses, tend to occur later; they almost certainly follow marihuana use for those whose use is early, but may precede it for some.

On balance, then, age at first use of marihuana is a variable which seems to predict later drug use and sales and is associated with crime, although it may not predict crime. These are serious behaviors, and indeed it is the fact of the illicit market and the association of drug use with crime that largely account for regarding the drug problem as a serious one. To understand what determines age at first use of marihuana, therefore, may be to understand much about the drug problem in general.

The preceding arguments for the strategic importance of the variable age at first use of marihuana should not be surprising; they merely assert in specific terms a general principle, that early onset of deviant behavior is likely to be associated with more involvement in, or longer continuation of, the same or related kinds of deviant behavior. Thus early onset is regarded as an unfavorable prognostic sign in neurosis (Dollard and Miller 1950, p. 236). Kinsey et al. (1948) reported that males whose sexual activity began early were later more involved in premarital intercourse and homosexual activity. More recently, in the national sample of young men cited above, Clayton and Voss (1977) found that the younger the men were at first sexual intercourse, the more likely they were to report a history of cohabitation and currently to be cohabitating (defined as nonmarital heterosexual unions). Glaser (1964) states as a general finding: "The younger a prisoner was when first arrested, convicted, or confined for any crime, the more likely he is to continue in crime." With specific reference to drugs, O'Donnell (1969, p. 87) has reported that the earlier the onset of addiction, the greater is subsequent involvement in the drug subculture. Finally, in a paper which came to our attention only when this chapter had been drafted, Jessor (1976) reported that sexual intercourse, problem drinking, and activist protests were more common among high school students with early than with later onset of marihuana use, and more common among both than among nonusers.

There are, then, theoretical reasons to expect that early onset of marihuana use should be predictive of later drug use and deviance. As shown in the preceding pages, there are empirical data indicating that age at first use of marihuana *is* predictive of subsequent involvement in various forms of "deviant" or non-conformist behavior.

Predictors of Age at First Use of Marihuana

The remainder of this chapter will focus on data from the New York City sample. It has already been mentioned that in the interview schedule for this sample it was possible, at the cost of deleting some items used for the national sample, to include new items on early experiences which might be seen as predictors or causes of later drug use. Most of these items were phrased to apply to "when you were 13 to 15 years old." This choice for the time reference represented a compromise among estimates. It was desirable to make the reference as recent as possible to minimize errors due to memory, but to date it before drug use was likely to have begun so that the time order of variables would be clear.

As it turned out, the time reference was a little too recent for the New York sample. Fourteen percent of the men in that sample (22 percent of the blacks) began to use marihuana *before* age 15. In retrospect, it might have been better to phrase questions as of "when you were 12 or 13 years old." However, the major purpose seems to have been served. Time order is clear for the bulk of the sample, and even for those whose marihuana use began early, the items probably refer to the time prior to use if 13 to 15 indicates, as it was intended to indicate, the entrance into the teen years. A few items were asked twice, as of ages 13 and 16, and here only the responses for age 13 are used. A few other items referred to when an event first occurred, and those used here include only the events that occurred at age 14 or earlier.

The content of the items was suggested by a variety of theories which have been advanced to explain deviance: Merton's anomie theory (Merton 1957), Sutherland's differential association theory (Sutherland and Cressey 1970), Reckless's containment theory (Reckless et al. 1956), Hirschi's (1969) social control theory, and the labeling perspective, as exemplified by Becker (1963) and others. There was no intention of testing these theories, or trying to measure their relative explanatory power; the attempt was simply to identify variables which the theories suggested as important and for which measures with some degree of face validity could fairly easily be devised. Indeed, a number of the items which were included could as easily have been suggested by several theories other than the one from which they were first identified.

As one example, the importance of early family experiences is explicit or implicit in almost all theories which attempt to explain the beginning of deviant behavior, as well as in much empirical work that is less theoretically oriented, like the Gluecks' (Glueck and Glueck 1974) studies of delinquency. Family influences are specifically mentioned in Hirschi's concept of attachment and in Reckless's emphasis on socialization, and clearly implied in Merton's thinking about the internalization of goals and norms governing means and in Sutherland's emphasis on learning in primary groups.

Five variables relating to family background were constructed. The items used and the scoring procedures are described in appendix 4A, so a brief description will suffice here. A two-letter symbol is attached to each variable to facilitate later discussion and tabular presentations. The family variables are:

1. *Family control* (FC): A combination of several items on whether or not parents knew where the respondent was when he was not at home, whether they set and enforced a time to be home, and how many of his friends his mother knew.
2. *Closeness to mother* (CM): A single item, with categories ranging from very close to not close at all.
3. *Closeness to father* (CF): A single item, parallel to CM.
4. *Communication with parents* (CP): Each respondent was asked, for each of six different subjects, if he often, seldom, or never discussed it with his parents.
5. *Father as a model* (FM): A single item, asking if the boy had wanted to be like his father, with five responses ranging from "in every way" to "not at all."

The importance of peer influences is perhaps most stressed by Sutherland (Sutherland and Cressey 1970) and Cohen (1955) at the level of theory, and has been established in many studies of delinquents (for example, Short and Strodtbeck 1965). Two variables were designed to tap this area:

6. *Peer delinquency* (PD): Four items on the frequency of stealing, gang fights and arrests among the respondent's friends, and on whether neighborhood adults perceived them as delinquents.
7. *Peer drug use* (PU): Use of alcohol, marihuana, and other drugs by respondent's friends, dated as of age 13.

School difficulties have been described, perhaps most thoroughly by Cohen (1955), as an important cause of later delinquency, at least for lower-class boys. One school variable was used:

8. *School adjustment* (SA): Three items on grades, liking school, and getting in trouble with teachers or school officials.

The labeling perspective stresses later stages in a deviant career and pays little attention to the first deviant act or its causes. The major labeling variables included in the study, like arrest record and self-perception as an addict, can hardly explain early marihuana use. Still, the perspective is inherently vague about what is labeled and how a label attached to one kind of behavior may affect other kinds of behavior, so a measure of labeling prior to drug use was sought. The one used is:

9. *Labeling* (LA): Three items asking how strongly friends, teachers, and parents would have predicted that the boy, at 13 to 15, was headed for trouble with the law.

Hirschi (1969) specifies involvement in conventional activities as one factor that would be negatively associated with delinquency. Logically, one would expect that early signs of deviance make later deviance more probable, and there is much evidence that one of the better predictors of future delinquency is current delinquency (for example, Elliott and Voss 1974). Two variables on the early behavior of the respondent were therefore included:

10. *Conventional activities* (CA): Extent to which leisure time was spent in watching television, in boy scouts, and in school or YMCA sports.
11. *Early deviant behavior* (ED): Extent to which leisure time was spent hanging around on the street, playing pool, pitching pennies, shooting craps, playing con games or stealing, plus three items if they occurred at age 14 or earlier: running away from home, being suspended or expelled from school, and sexual intercourse.

A twelfth and final independent variable relates to the perceived availability of drugs. Many have pointed out that if a drug is not available, no one will use it. Aside from this extreme, clearly not applicable to the areas from which the New York sample was drawn, we are convinced that "availability" is not something to be predicated of a drug alone, but must be conceptualized as a relationship between the drug and the potential user. Drugs are available to youth primarily through peer networks, and it can happen that one youth can easily obtain drugs through the peer groups of which he is a member, while another youth on the same block or even in the same apartment house who is a member of different groups can not obtain them at all.

But the research team saw no way to identify and inquire about all groups of which the respondent had been a member. The best that could be done, it was felt, was to measure the respondent's perception of drug availability when he was a boy. The variable constructed was:

12. *Perception of drug availability* (DA): Four items were used, of which two asked how many people in the boy's neighborhood were using marihuana or heroin. One asked if he knew anyone in the neighborhood who was selling drugs. The last asked if he knew of any place where heroin could be bought, and if so, how close this place was to his home.

The variables are all ordinal measures, constructed mainly by adding scores of component items, with minor judgmental use of weights (see appendix 4A). Tabular analysis, using nonparametric statistics, would have been the more conservative method of analysis. But it was clear, from the tables earlier in this chapter, that the three racial/ethnic groups must be analyzed separately. Their sizes ranged from 71 to 125, and these small numbers would not have permitted multivariate analysis by tabular controls. The decision therefore was to treat the variables as if they were interval-level measures, so that parametric statistics could be used. One such use was the employment of partial correlation to test the marihuana-heroin and marihuana-opiate associations for spuriousness, as described earlier.

Data were missing on a few items used in the independent variables, but not for many respondents, and among them on no more than four variables in one case and three in another. Rather than eliminating these cases, missing data on an item were replaced by the mean score of the racial/ethnic group on the item. The dependent variable age at first use of marihuana was scored as the actual age reported. For users, the highest score possible was 30, since no men were older. A score of 35 was arbitrarily assigned to nonusers so that correlations and regressions could be done.

All the five family variables were expected to be positively correlated with age at first use of marihuana. The same was predicted for school adjustment and involvement in conventional activities. The remaining five were predicted to have negative correlations. In short, bonds to the family, school, and conventional activities were expected to prevent or delay marihuana use, while delinquency and drug use among peers, labeling, early deviant behavior by the boy, and his perception of drug availability were expected to lead to early use of marihuana.

Findings

From this point on, the focus will be on blacks and whites. Data on others will be omitted (but may be obtained from the authors) both to save space and because generalizations are not clearly justified.

In table 4-6 the mean scores on the twelve predictor variables and on age at first use of marihuana are shown by race. First it may be noted that the mean score on AF is much lower for blacks than for whites. But it will be recalled that this scale was constructed by assigning a score of 35 to nonusers, so the difference reflects not only the difference in mean age at first use among users (16.2 for blacks, 18.7 for whites) but also the fact that there were more nonusers among whites. Table 4-2 accurately reflects both differences.

Of more interest is the fact that on all the variables which were predicted to have negative associations with age at first use, the mean score for blacks is significantly higher than that for whites. This includes early deviant behavior, peer delinquency, peer drug use, and labeling and perception of drug availability—variables suggested by one theory or another as predictors of drug use.

Table 4-6
Means on Twelve Predictor Variables and Age at First Use of Marihuana by Race

		Blacks		*Whites*	
Variables		*Mean*	*S.D.*	*Mean*	*S.D.*
Family control	(FC)	10.504	2.465	10.501	2.116
Communication with parents	(CP)	12.495	2.476	13.102	2.550
Closeness to mother	(CM)	4.476	.788	4.082	.904***
Closeness to father	(CF)	3.444	1.472	3.653	1.176
Father as role model	(FM)	1.936	1.413	2.592	1.291***
School adjustment	(SA)	9.962	1.894	9.663	1.855
Involvement in conventional activities	(CA)	4.752	1.795	4.469	1.682
Early deviant behavior	(ED)	13.064	3.726	11.143	3.149***
Peer delinquency	(PD)	8.699	4.116	6.969	4.045**
Peer drug use	(PU)	2.656	2.244	2.071	1.801*
Labeling	(LA)	6.224	3.144	4.865	2.357***
Perception of drug availability	(DA)	11.469	5.099	7.429	4.502***
Age at first use of marihuana	(AF)	19.496	7.699	23.020	7.773***

*Means different at .05 level by *t* test.

**Different at .01 level.

***Different at .001 level.

Among the five family variables, only two show significant differences; blacks score higher on closeness to mother and lower on father as a role model. It should perhaps be noted about the latter measure that 25 blacks, as opposed to 7 whites, could not score high because they had no father or father substitute about whom the question could be asked, but this does not necessarily make the finding artifactual. If the perception of a father figure as a role model is a variable of importance, it may or may not matter if the absence of that perception is due to the absence of the father or to the rejection of a present father.

The remaining family variables (except possibly communication with parents), school adjustment and involvement in conventional activities, show nonsignificant differences between whites and blacks.

Space limitations preclude tabular presentation of the next steps in analysis, but what was done *and* the findings can be described briefly. First, correlation matrices of the twelve independent variables and age at first use were constructed for blacks and whites. These showed the following:

1. The correlations of the predictor variables with age at first use were all in the predicted direction for whites and all except one for blacks. The CP-AF correlation for blacks was –.03.
2. For both blacks and whites, the correlations of AF with ED, PD, PU, LA, and DA were statistically significant. The AF correlations with SA and CA were barely below significance at the .05 level for whites (each was .18). For blacks the AF-SA correlation also approached significance, but the AF-CA *r* was almost zero.
3. Among the five family variables, only one correlated significantly with AF for blacks (FM-AF = .24) but two others (FC and CF) approached significance. For whites, CM and CF correlated significantly with AF, and the other family variables did not fall far short.
4. No pair of independent variables showed both a high correlation and similar patterns of correlations with other variables, to suggest that they were merely alternative measures of the same underlying reality.
5. No variable showed such low correlations with all others that it could be dropped from the analysis. The weakest showed at least three significant correlations in one group and more in the other.

The next procedure, again separately for blacks and whites, used the twelve predictor variables in a stepwise multiple regression, with age at first use as the dependent variable. No order for entrance into the regression equation among the predictor variables was specified. The results of this were:

1. Among blacks, the twelve variables accounted for 42 percent of the variance in AF, but DA accounted for 27 percent, LA for another 6 percent, and none of the remaining ten contributed a statistically significant amount.

2. For whites, 32 percent of variance was explained, with DA accounting for 16 percent, CF another 6 percent, and PD just under 2 percent. None of the other variables contributed statistically significant amounts, and LA and SA did not even enter the equation.
3. The orders in which the variables entered the equations for blacks and whites were substantially different. Perception of drug availability was first for both groups, but after that there was little correspondence. Labeling, for example, ranked second for blacks, but for whites was not even one of the ten that entered the equation. A Spearman's ρ on the rank order of entrance into the equation showed that the difference in ranks was statistically significant.

The result of the stepwise regressions, in short, was that perception of drug availability emerged as by far the most important predictor of age at first use in both groups, while variables of clear theoretical importance contributed little or nothing to prediction. Such a result, however, would be consistent with a causal model in which perception of drug availability intervened between the other variables and age at first use. If it (DA) were closer to the dependent variable in the underlying true model, it would wash out and conceal the effects of other variables in the model, which is assumed by a multiple regression equation.

As the next step toward a causal model, the stepwise multiple regressions were repeated, dropping age at first use and treating perception of drug availability as the dependent variable. The results were similar to those in the first regressions.

1. For blacks, 39 percent of the variance was explained, but only two variables, ED and PD, contributed statistically significant amounts.
2. For whites, 60 percent of variance was explained, with three variables contributing statistically significant proportions.
3. The orders in which variables entered the equations were again completely different for the two groups. Only one variable, peer drug use, appeared among the significant variables in both regressions, second in rank in both cases. Early deviance ranked first for blacks and tenth for whites, while peer delinquency ranked first for whites and seventh for blacks.

In one sense, these findings were not unexpected. The multiple regression model assumes that all the independent variables are each directly related to the dependent variable. The true underlying model with this set of variables is far more likely to be one in which some variables, for example, the family variables, are causally prior to others, which in turn cause perception of drug availability and age at first use of marihuana. If this were so, it would be expected that the variables more closely contiguous to the dependent variable would show up strongly and would conceal the indirect causative power of prior variables. So the appearance of perception of drug availability as the only strong determinant of age at first use was no surprise.

What was not expected was the marked difference between the regressions for blacks and whites. The findings clearly suggested that no single model would serve equally well to explain age at first use in the two groups. What was needed next was an attempt to identify plausible causal models for the two.

No way was seen to do this with the full list of twelve independent variables; there were simply too many possible models and no basis to choose among them. The next step, therefore, was to reduce the number of variables. The five family variables were combined into one, family influence (FI), simply by adding the scores from the five family variables. Peer delinquency and peer drug use were combined into peer influence (PI), again by adding scores. Early deviant behavior and involvement in conventional activities were combined into early behavior (EB) by reversing the scoring on the second of the pair and adding scores. School adjustment, labeling, and perception of drug availability remained unchanged, so there were now six independent variables: family influence, peer influence, early behavior, school adjustment, labeling, and perception of drug availability.

The correlation matrix of these six variables and age at first use is shown in table 4-7; coefficients for blacks are shown above the diagonal, for whites below it. The *n* for blacks is 125, and an *r* of .176 or higher is significantly different from zero at the .05 level; for whites, with an *n* of 98, an *r* of .199 is required.

Among whites, all but one (SA-AF) of the correlations are significant; for blacks, the SA-DA, FI-AF, and SA-AF correlations fall short of significance, though not by much in the latter two. Of the twenty-one correlations for blacks,

Table 4-7
Correlation Matrix, Six Independent Variables and Age at First Use of Marihuana, by Race

		FI	*EB*	*SA*	*PI*	*LA*	*DA*	*AF*
Family influence	(FI)	–	–.234	.369	–.398	–.385	–.265	.172
Early behavior	(EB)	–.292	–	–.318	.427	.472	.469	–.346
School adjustment	(SA)	.375	–.399	–	–.255	–.379	–.106	.153
Peer influence	(PI)	–.355	.634	–.268	–	.543	.476	–.471
Labeling	(LA)	–.410	.538	–.548	.645	–	.416	–.437
Perception of drug availability	(DA)	–.265	.509	–.276	.745	.505	–	–.515
Age at first use of marihuana	(AF)	.292	–.282	.179	–.284	–.252	–.401	–
Mean (blacks)		32.85	13.06	9.96	11.35	6.22	11.47	19.50
S.D. (blacks)		5.20	3.73	1.89	5.35	3.14	5.10	7.70
Mean (whites)		33.93	11.14*	9.66	9.04*	4.86*	7.43*	23.02*
S.D. (whites)		4.95	3.15	1.86	5.26	2.36	4.50	7.77

Note: blacks above diagonal, whites below.
*Mean difference significant at .001 level; FI and SA differences not significant, even at .10 level.

only three are not significant; and for whites, only one. On the other hand, for blacks, only two are as high as .5. For whites, one is over .7, two more over .6, and four more over .5. Multicollinearity should thus not be a problem.

In a stepwise regression using the new variables, perception of drug availability emerged first for both whites and blacks, as before. There were still differences, but not as marked as before, in the order of appearance of other variables.

There is a loss of explained variance: twelve variables explained 42 percent of variance in age at first use for blacks, while the six explain only 36 percent. For whites the corresponding figures are 32 and 21. This, however, indicates only that the combination of the original variables into new ones was not the most efficient combination possible. Using the original five family variables as an example, multiple regression forms the best possible linear combination of them, *best* meaning the combination that produces the highest R^2. Simply adding the five scores would almost never be the best linear combination.

An R^2 approaching the original R^2 could be achieved with the six variables if the new ones were constructed by adding weighted (by beta) values of the original variables. But a high R^2 would be an illusory goal (Duncan 1975, p. 65); the goal here was to interpret the pattern of relationships among the variables, and the method was to seek a causal model.

Development and Testing of Causal Models

In trying to design a causal model containing the six independent variables, the problem was that while all were known to precede marihuana use, there were no data on their relative time order–all were dated as of "when you were 13 to 15 years old." While the assumptions used seem plausible to us, it should be kept in mind that from this point on, the analysis is based on theory-guided assumptions about causal order.

It seemed safe to place perception of drug availability immediately prior to the dependent variable, age at first use of marihuana, for two reasons. First, the logical connection is strong. In the extreme case, drug use would be impossible if the potential user did not perceive the drug as available; in the more usual case, it seems plausible that the probability of experimenting with a drug would increase with perception of the drug's availability. Second, the findings of the multiple regressions indicated that the direct effect of drug availability on age at first use was strong and that several other variables probably acted indirectly through drug availability.

The labeling variable was placed next in order (working backwards from the dependent variable) on the grounds that labeling was much more likely to be an effect of the other variables, like early behavior, school adjustment, and the peer associations implied by peer influence, than a cause of them. At the other end of the causal model it seemed reasonable to place family influence first. While this variable was, like the others, operationally measured as of "13 to 15 years old," the various items in the measure are not likely to have differed greatly in those years from earlier years. It is therefore assumed that the measure applies to years earlier than those specified in the interview items.

These considerations fixed the first, fifth, sixth, and seventh positions in a seven-variable causal model. No equally cogent arguments seemed available for relative placement of the remaining three variables. But these three provided only six combinations, if the others were taken as fixed, so the six possible models were run and examined separately for whites and blacks.

Three of the six showed a zero direct effect of family influence on early behavior, although they did allow for indirect effects. A fourth showed higher but statistically insignificant values for both of the ethnic groups for the same relationship. These findings were rejected as theoretically untenable. Given the content of the items used in the operational definitions of early behavior and family influence, it is difficult to see how the latter could fail to have some direct effect on the former.

This left two models, each with family influence first and early behavior second, differing in the placement of school adjustment and peer influence in third and fourth places. Either, it may be noted, presents early behavior as a cause of peer influence rather than the reverse. This fits the specific content of the measures, since several items in the former can be seen as indicating exposure to conventional or street influences. There was really not much basis for a choice between the two models. The major difference was that the causal direction between peer influence and school adjustment was reversed in the two models, and each of them measured the direct effect as zero. We found it more plausible that school adjustment would have no effect on peer influence than the reverse, and on this basis, we placed school adjustment third and peer influence fourth in the model.

With the relative positions fixed for EB, SA, and PI in the model, path coefficients for the full seven-variable model were produced separately for blacks and whites. For parsimony of explanation, it was desirable to drop as many of the twenty-one paths as could reasonably be omitted.

For blacks, four paths were close to zero, with coefficients under .05 positive or negative; these were PI-SA, DA-FI, AF-SA, and AF-EB. One more, AF-FI, was under .10. It was clearly safe to omit these five paths. In addition, LA-FI (–.130), DA-LA (.147), and DA-SA (.148) had coefficients that were not statistically significant. With these omitted as well, and with coefficients recalculated to fit the revised model, the result is shown in figure 4-1A.

For whites, PI-SA, DA-LA, DA-FI, DA-EB, AF-LA, and AF-SA were under .05. Three more were under .10; LA-FI, LA-EB, and DA-SA. The AF-EB path had a value of –.127, not significantly different from zero, so this too seemed safe to omit. The only questionable omission for whites was AF-PI, with a

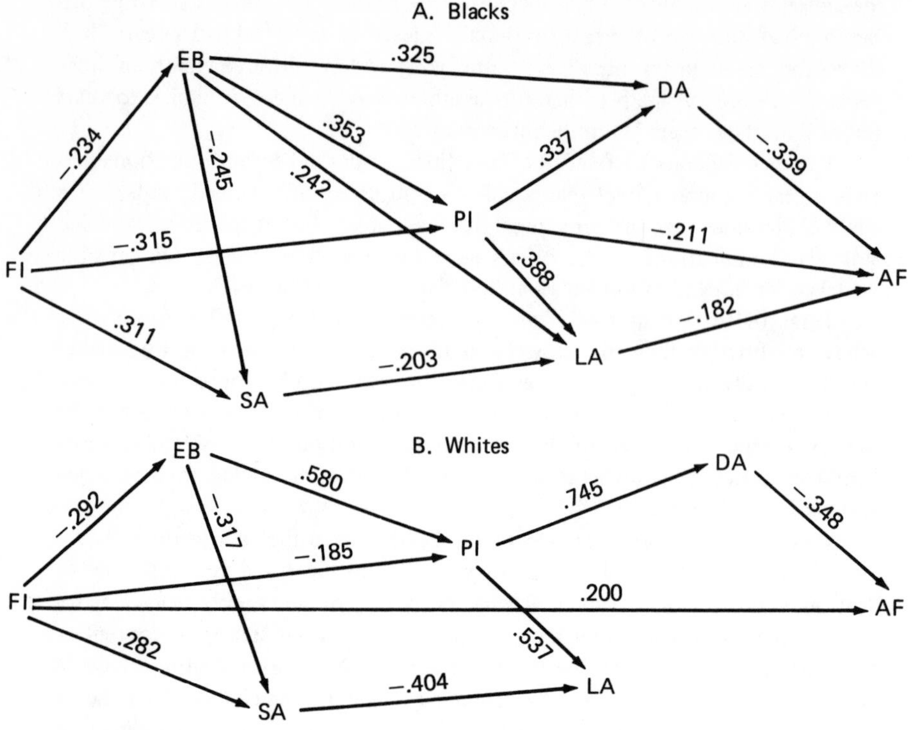

FI = family influence
EB = early behavior
SA = school adjustment
PI = peer influence
LA = labeling
DA = perception of drug availability
AF = age at first use of marihuana

Figure 4-1. Tentative Path Models, with Path Coefficients.

coefficient of –.193, but this too was nonsignificant and was dropped in the interest of parsimony. The result (with path coefficients recalculated to fit the revised model) is shown in figure 4-1B.

The two models in figure 4-1 are clearly different. The model for whites contains one path (FI-AF) not included for blacks and omits several of the paths in the model for blacks. The number of paths and the values of the path coefficients differ in the two models. The path analysis thus confirmed what had been suspected from the earlier regressions, that no single model would fit blacks and whites equally well.

While these models would not serve as final models, for reasons to be discussed later, we sought some assurance that they were on the right track. It was evident that the models could be tested by the Blalock (1964) method of predicting that certain partial correlations will be zero. For model A there are eight prediction equations, each asserting that a given partial *r* value (for example, FI-AF, with controls on the remaining five variables) will be zero.

For blacks in model A, three of the eight partial *r* values are below .05 and two more are below .10; all these show significance levels of .14 or higher. Two more partials are .137 and .147, with significance levels of .066 and .054, respectively. Only one of the eight, a partial of .159, with a significance level of .041, must be regarded as significantly different from zero, using the .05 level of significance. Model A is thus a good fit for blacks and would not be a bad fit for whites either. Only one of the eight partials (.207) is significantly different from zero for whites.

It was model B, however, which was suggested as more appropriate for whites. This model provides eleven prediction equations. For whites, six partials are below .05, three more are .10 or below, and the remaining two are –.117 and .116, not significant even at the .10 level. All eleven can thus be regarded as zero and as confirming the predictions. These findings can be contrasted with those for blacks on the same model: six of the 11 partials for blacks are significantly different from zero at the .05 level.

These findings provided strong support for the suggestion that model A fitted the data for blacks and model B for whites, but the models could be simplified further. Given that the purpose of the models was to explain age at first use, visual inspection of model B showed that neither SA nor LA contributed to this explanation. Neither had any direct or indirect influence on AF. Both could be dropped from model B.

No equally obvious changes were visible for model A. But when direct and indirect effects were computed for blacks, SA was found to have neither direct nor indirect influence on AF; all the correlations were found to be spurious. So SA could be dropped from model A too. This was not, however, true for LA, which had an appreciable direct effect on AF.

These changes produce models C and D in figure 4-2. The coefficients have been recomputed but show only minor changes from figure 4-1. These models too can be tested by the Blalock method. Four prediction equations are found for each model, but additional predictions that lower-order partials will be zero can be made from visual inspection of the models. These too are included in table 4-8.

It may be seen in table 4-8 that the four prediction equations for model C are confirmed for blacks; none of the observed partials approaches a value significantly different from zero at the .05 or even the .10 level. Three of the observed values for whites would be an equally good fit, but the fourth, involving the FI-AF relation, is very bad.

The reverse is found for model D. The fit is excellent for whites at the .05

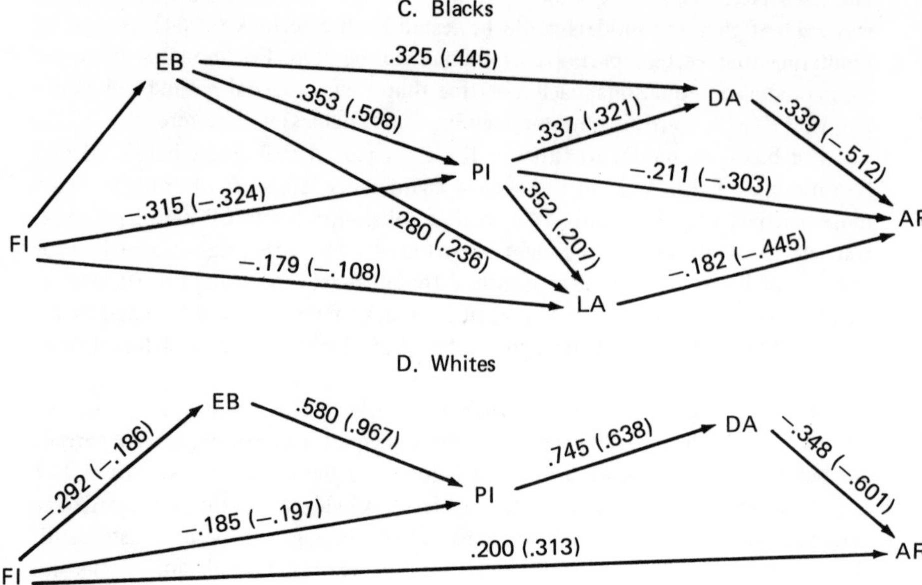

FI = family influence
EB = early behavior
PI = peer influence
LA = labeling
DA = perception of drug availability
FA = age at first use of marihuana

Figure 4-2. Revised Path Models (Unstandardized Coefficients, in Parentheses, Follow Standardized Coefficients).

or .10 levels, but very poor for blacks on EB-DA and PI-AF and on one of the secondary equations for EB-AF. The Blalock tests therefore provide support for retaining model C as a strong candidate for blacks and model D for whites.

Another test of the models gives a more ambiguous answer. This is the attempt to reproduce from the path coefficients those correlation coefficients which were not used in computing the path coefficients. For four such correlations in the model for whites, three reproductions fail to match by differences of .307, .046, and .060. There are three discrepancies among four correlations for blacks of .053, .055, and .080. There is no consensus in the literature as to how many, and how large, discrepancies are acceptable. Those found here are well within the criterion of Loether and McTavish (1976), that "differences of .05 or .10 are likely to be considered small unless a meaningful alternative model is able to make closer predictions." They are too large for the rule-of-thumb criteria used by others; Mueller et al. (1977), for example, suggest that the maximum discrepancy should be ".02 or, in some instances, .05."

Table 4-8
Prediction Equations for Models C and D and Observed Values of Partial Correlations for Blacks and Whites

Partials Predicted		Expected Value	Blacks		Whites	
			Partial	Significance	Partial	Significance
Model C:						
FI-AF	.EB,PI,LA,DA	0	−.100	.137	.206	.023*
	.EB,PI,LA	0	−.079	.194	.193	.030*
	.PI,LA,DA	0	−.100	.136	.209	.021*
FI-DA	.EB,PI,LA	0	−.049	.295	.013	.450
	.EB,PI	0	−.073	.212	.005	.482
EB-AF	.FI,PI,LA,DA	0	−.016	.430	−.102	.165
	.PI,LA,DA	0	−.017	.428	−.108	.150
LA-DA	.FI,EB,PI	0	.108	.118	.035	.367
	.EB,PI	0	.120	.092	.033	.374
Model D:						
FI-DA	.EB,PI	0	−.073	.212	.005	.482
	.PI	0	.094	.149	−.002	.453
EB-AF	.FI,PI,DA	0	−.068	.230	−.105	.155
	.FI,PI	0	.184	.021*	−.122	.119
	.FI,DA	0	−.134	.070	−.062	.274
EB-DA	.FI,PI	0	.330	.001**	.072	.244
	.PI	0	.334	.001**	.071	.243
PI-AF	.FI,EB,DA	0	−.281	.001**	.117	.130
	.FI,DA	0	−.302	.001**	.080	.219

*Significant at .05 level.
**Significant at .001 level.

Since there is no objective criterion for testing such discrepancies, Land (1973) suggests instead a formal chi-square test. This is based on logarithms of ratios between the residual sum of squares in each equation in which coefficients have been set at zero and the corresponding sum in that equation with all prior coefficients included. By this test, models C and D are highly acceptable: chi-square for model C is 3.422; for model D, 2.225.

The models have thus been subjected to three tests. On one, the reproduction of correlation coefficients, the result may be borderline, but there is no accepted criterion on this test. The other two, Blalock's predicted partial correlations and Land's chi-square, are statistical tests, and the models pass both tests.

In table 4-9, the standardized and unstandardized path coefficients are used to examine the direct and indirect effects of each variable on age at first use of marihuana. The noncausal (spurious) components in the relationships of each with the dependent variable are also included. In panels A and B these components are included in the total column for readers who might want to

Table 4-9
Effects of Independent Variables on Age at First Use of Marihuana, Based on Standardized and Unstandardized Path Coefficients in Models C and D

Variable		*Effects*			
		Direct	*Indirect*	*Not Causal*	*Total*
A. Blacks, Standardized Coefficients:					
1. Family influence		.000	.225	.000	.225
2. Early behavior		.000	−.314	−.021	−.335
3. Peer influence		−.211	−.178	−.082	−.471
4. Labeling		−.182	.000	−.229	−.411
5. Drug availability		−.339	.000	−.162	−.501
B. Whites, Standardized Coefficients:					
1. Family influence		.200	.092	.000	.292
2. Early behavior		.000	−.150	−.072	−.222
3. Peer influence		.000	−.259	−.071	−.330
4. Drug availability		−.348	.000	−.053	−.401
C. Unstandardized Coefficients:					
1. Family influence	B	.000	.333	.000	.333
	W	.313	.145	.000	.458
2. Early behavior	B	.000	−.617	−.075	−.617
	W	.000	−.371	−.179	−.371
3. Peer influence	B	−.303	−.256	−.118	−.559
	W	.000	−.383	−.105	−.383
4. Labeling	B	−.445	.000	−.561	−.445
	W	(Not included in model for whites.)			
5. Drug availability	B	−.512	.000	−.244	−.512
	W	−.601	.000	−.091	−.601

compare some reconstituted correlation coefficients with those in table 4-7. The spurious components are excluded from the totals in panel C, so totals there represent only effects.

The standardized coefficients in panels A and B may be used to make comparisons *within* the racial groups, for example, on the relative importance of variables. They could not legitimately be used, however, to compare the two groups. For this purpose the unstandardized coefficients must be used.

Looking at total effects as measured by the standardized coefficients (direct plus indirect effects only), peer influence ranks first for blacks, at −.389. Drug availability ranks second, at −.339, and early behavior third but almost equal, at −.314. Family influence and labeling rank fourth and fifth, not differing much, at .225 and −.182.

The rank order of total effects is quite different for whites. Drug availability is first, at −.348. Family influence is second rather than fourth, at .292; and peer influence is third rather than first, at −.259.

For comparing blacks and whites, the unstandardized coefficients of panel C in table 4-9 should be used, but in comparing the total effects it should be kept in mind that the numerical comparisons can be misleading because the model for blacks explains more variance than does the model for whites.

Family influence has an appreciable direct effect for whites and an additional indirect effect. For blacks, there is no direct effect, but the indirect effect is not much smaller than the total effect for whites. Early behavior has only indirect effects for both groups, and these seem to be much more important for blacks. Peer influence also appears to have more effect on age at first use for blacks than for whites. The fact that much of this is a direct effect for blacks while all is indirect for whites should not be misinterpreted. This is one of the variables for which the reconstituted correlation does not fit the observed correlation well. Model D could easily include a direct connection between PI and AF, which would make some of the effect for whites direct rather than indirect.

When allowance is made for the spurious components in the correlation between perception of drug availability and age at first use, the total effect does not seem to differ much in the two groups. The greatest difference between the models is that labeling has no effect on age at first use for whites; all the correlations for that relationship are found to be spurious. For blacks, on the other hand, while it is true that more than half the LA-AF correlation is spurious, there is a sizable direct effect from LA to AF.

Discussion

Whether they are later confirmed or modified by data from future studies, the models up to this point have been based firmly on the data cited here. The models are, aside from the considerations on which causal order was postulated, little more than a parsimonious description of the data. In this section, some of the possible meanings and implications of the models will be considered. These, it must be emphasized, are speculative. They were not hypotheses advanced prior to analysis of the data and thus supported by the data, but are instead post hoc attempts at interpretation.

Why should labeling have an appreciable effect for blacks, but none for whites? One explanation might be that labeling affects blacks more than whites, and it would not be impossible to find some arguments for the proposition. The fact of being black in the United States today is itself a kind of label, so perhaps the marginal effects of additional labeling would be more perceptible. Or perhaps, for unknown reasons, the items used to measure labeling in this study constitute a better measure for blacks than for whites. We cannot rule out such explanations, but we also cannot develop much enthusiasm for them.

It may be recalled that the measure of labeling was three items on the extent to which parents, teachers, and friends would have predicted, when the boy was 13 to 15 years old, that he was "headed for trouble with the law." On the face of it, such predictions would seem to relate to delinquency in general rather than to the specific behavior of drug use. The question may be not so much why labeling fails to show this specific effect for whites, as why it does show it for blacks.

Framed in these terms, the explanation could be that marihuana use (and age at first use) are more closely correlated with delinquency among blacks than among whites. Perhaps the labeling variable predicts delinquent behavior for both groups but marihuana use only for blacks because only for them is the marihuana-delinquency correlation high. The correlation between labeling and early behavior, which includes several delinquent or predelinquent activities, cannot be used as a test for this hypothesis because early behavior has been argued to precede rather than follow labeling. A full test of the hypothesis must await further analysis of delinquent behavior after age 15, but the data on crime cited earlier lend some support to it. Blacks were twice as likely as whites to report serious involvement in crime, and this involvement was more closely related to AF for blacks than for whites.

This explanation would be consistent with the observed fact that early behavior shows a stronger effect on AF for blacks; many studies show that one of the better predictors of delinquency at time 2 is a measure of delinquency at time 1. It can also be seen as consistent with the lack of direct effect of family influence on AF for blacks. The general hypothesis would be that for blacks the conditional probability of marihuana use, given delinquency, is fairly high, so any predictor of delinquency will predict marihuana use, but the early predictors are likely to act indirectly through later variables in the causal model. For whites, on the other hand, the conditional probability of marihuana use, given delinquency, is lower, and predictors may differ for drug use and other forms of delinquency.

It should be emphasized again that the preceding is speculation and rests on the assumption that the marihuana-delinquency correlation differs for blacks and whites. It should be noted that there may be a purely technical explanation for some of the differences between blacks and whites. It was seen in table 4-6 that the mean scores for whites were significantly lower than for blacks on such variables as early deviance and labeling. When these are used as independent variables, there is less variation on them for whites, and this would tend to reduce the correlation between them and any dependent variables.

Why is perception of drug availability so central and important in explaining age at first use of marihuana? It was noted earlier that the correlation between these variables is higher for blacks, but a higher proportion of the correlation is spurious and the total effect—all direct—appears to be about equal for blacks and whites or higher for blacks. DA was the first variable to enter a stepwise multiple regression for both groups and was the only variable explaining a large proportion of variance for both groups. But the specific content of the items in the DA measure should be kept in mind. One item asked how many persons in the boy's neighborhood were smoking marihuana, but the others were not specific to marihuana. The second item asked how many parents were using heroin. The third asked if the boy knew anyone "in the neighborhood who was selling drugs–heroin, marihuana, or any other illegal drug." And the final question was on knowledge of, and proximity of, places where heroin could be bought.

The DA variable, it may be repeated, does not measure the degree to which drugs were objectively available, but rather the boy's perception of that degree. Further, the degree of availability refers more to heroin and other drugs than specifically to marihuana. Why should a boy's perception of the availability of other drugs affect the age at which he began to use marihuana?

The answer may be simple. It seems reasonable to assume that in New York in the 1960s and early 1970s, marihuana would be present wherever heroin and other illegal drugs were present. It would therefore be reasonable to assume that the variable does measure perception of the availability of marihuana, even if several items refer to other drugs.

How would a boy acquire such a perception? There are probably two major sources of such knowledge–the boy's own observations (plus enough sophistication to interpret what he sees) and information obtained from his friends. In this connection, it is worthy of note that the model for blacks shows DA as directly affected by two variables, early behavior and peer influence, while only the latter appears in the model for whites. Review of the items in the early behavior variable will verify that a high score on this variable implies both delinquent or predelinquent behavior and some degree of "street wisdom" and therefore suggests learning from one's own observations.

These considerations, together with the fact that the mean score on DA was much higher for blacks than for whites, suggest the following picture. In the black neighborhoods, marihuana use was more prevalent and was more visible, perhaps literally, but mainly in the sense that it existed in more social networks. A black could therefore observe it and interpret it for himself, and was more likely to do so the more streetwise he was. The same knowledge would come to him through peer groups and would come more surely the more his peers themselves were engaged in delinquency or drug use.

The fact that, for whites, early behavior is only an indirect cause of DA does not mean, of course, that it was impossible for a white boy to observe drug use and traffic for himself. But it does suggest that in addition to the fact that the white was less exposed to delinquency, in white neighborhoods the prevalence of marihuana use may have been lower and restricted to fewer social networks, so his chance to perceive it was less than the black's. Further, he may have been less able to identify correctly fleeting and ambiguous signs of use, and the number of cases in which both perception and recognition occurred may have been small enough not to show a significant direct effect on DA. His perception would be heavily dependent on his peers, on the extent to which they were engaged in delinquency and drug use. This is reflected not only in the absence of a path from EB to DA in model D, but in the path coefficient from PI to DA, the highest coefficient by far in either model, .745.

If this argument is correct, the white boy was unlikely to perceive the availability of drugs on his own, but learned of it through his friends. But how could this be, if his friends were in the same situation he was in? One obvious answer would be that for the boy who learned, his friends were not in the same situation, they knew more about drugs than he did because they were using drugs.

It may be recalled that peer influence includes the original measures of peer delinquency, referring to age 13 to 15, and peer drug use, referring *to age 13*. Obviously, since very few white boys began marihuana use before age 15 (see table 4-2), drug use among their peers was likely to have increased by then. One possibility, therefore, was that DA for whites might really be a measure of peer drug use later, in the age period 13 to 15.

This hypothesis can be checked in several ways. First and most direct, the data include not only peer drug use at age 13, but also at age 16. Using only the item "When you were 16, were more than a few of your friends using marihuana? (Yes or No)," the hypothesis is that the mean score on DA will be significantly higher for those who answer "Yes."

Second, all studies with which we are familiar show that at the time a person begins using marihuana, some or most of his friends are using it (for examples, see O'Donnell et al. 1976; Johnson 1973). This leads to the hypothesis that among those whose friends were using marihuana when they were 16, the mean score on AF will be lower than among those whose friends were not then using it.

Another hypothesis is that if a measure of peer drug use at age 16 is constructed following exactly the scoring procedures that had been used for the original measure at age 13, this will be more closely correlated with DA and AF than the original measure was.

These hypotheses were all suggested by ways in which the data on whites differed from those on blacks. But if they are correct, if DA is really a later measure of peer drug use, the measure should apply to blacks as well as to whites.

The hypotheses were supported by the data. For blacks and whites, the mean score on DA was much higher for those who at age 16 had friends smoking marihuana than for those who did not, and the differences were highly significant. Similarly, their mean score on AF was much lower, and there too the differences were highly significant.

Finally, the new measure of peer drug use at age 16 (PU 16) was computed and its correlations with DA and AF compared with the original measure, PU 13.

Placing PU 16 first and PU 13 second, their correlations with DA were .527 and .389 for blacks and .653 and .594 for whites. Their correlations with AF were –.544 and –.342 for blacks and –.443 and –.308 for whites. In each case, the correlation of the use variable at age 16 with DA and AF was higher than the corresponding correlation of the use variable at age 13.

But the correlations, while high, do not approach 1.0. The subhypotheses were supported, but the major hypothesis which led to them, that DA might be no more than a later measure of peer drug use, must be rejected. The two concepts are closely related, but not identical.

Looking at the two models in more general terms, they make some theoretical contribution to understanding marihuana use and therefore, indirectly, other forms of drug use. Probably the major findings are that the road to drug use is not the same for blacks and whites and that there exist some indications of where to seek explanations for the difference.

The models are unsatisfactory in one sense and must be regarded as the beginning rather than the culmination of a process of analysis. One value of an ideal path model is that it allows one to predict along the lines of "other things being equal, an increment of x more years of education would produce, on the average, y more dollars of lifetime income." The dependent variable in the models here, age at first use of marihuana, is as concrete and specific as dollars of income, but the independent variables are constructs and too abstract to be of much value for prediction. Age at first use possesses a natural unit, years, but there is no clear meaning for a unit of family influence or peer influence.

One of the next steps in analysis, therefore, will be to try to break these composite variables down into their specific components and measure the effects of the latter. Now that the general models are reasonably well established, the composite variables can be replaced by the original variables from which they were contructed, singly or in combination. In later reports, instead of speaking of family influence, it may be possible to specify the relative importance of closeness to mother, closeness to father, communication with parents, control by parents, and acceptance of father as a role model. Similarly, it may be possible to identify which of the many items included in early behavior are the ones which contribute more to its predictive efficiency and causal efficacy. It might be instructive to replace peer influence with its two components, peer delinquency and peer drug use. And, of course, the model can be extended by adding variables on behavior that occurred after the onset of marihuana use, such as heroin use and criminal behavior.

There is, in short, much more to be done before this analysis can be regarded as complete. The analysis to date, however, implies some suggestions for future studies on drug use.

One, which we hope is well established by the introductory pages of this chapter, is that in any drug study, age at first use of marihuana (or age at first use of any illicit drug) is likely to be a very important variable. What has here been called perception of drug availability is also an important variable, but on this, further conceptual work to clarify the meaning of the variable and probably further empirical work on how to measure it are needed.

One specific suggestion which relates to peer influence and probably to perception of drug availability can be made. Many studies ask if, or how many, friends were using marihuana (and/or other drugs) when the respondent began using the drug. It is a common finding that most had using friends when they began use. Analysis tends to end there, partly because the respondents began using at different ages, but mainly because no comparable question was asked of those who never used the drug. Much more revealing analyses would become possible, and could include nonusers as well as users, if questions were asked about friends' use of drugs over a range of years, for example, when the respondent was 12, 14, or 16. Practical considerations may keep the range of ages small, and the range should differ in different studies, depending on the expected findings about age at first use in different populations, but a judicious selection would have two values. First, it would permit a more accurate measure of the influence of drug use by peers than previous studies have provided. Second, it would permit resolution of a perennial problem, the extent to which drug use by friends influences one's use of drugs and the extent to which one's use of drugs restricts one's choice of friends to drug users.

Theoretical Implications

The first section of this chapter suggested that findings on marihuana users might be transferrable to some extent to heroin users, but later sections have focused on age at first use of marihuana and its predictors. It may now be asked, is there any evidence for or against the hypothesis that the findings, or some of them, will also apply to heroin use? A proper answer to that question will require a paper as long as this chapter, but a few facts may be noted which suggest that the findings may well be transferrable or, in more specific terms, that the models constructed here will remain intact when heroin use is added as a dependent variable.

One indication is a byproduct of the tests for spuriousness of the marihuana-heroin relationship in the national sample. In a procedure not included in the earlier discussion, extent of heroin use was taken as a dependent variable and fourteen variables prior to heroin and marihuana use were taken as independent variables in a multiple regression equation. Five of these variables showed significant beta values; one of them, early deviance, was identical to the measure used for the New York data and another, peer problems at age 13, was similar to but not identical with the peer influence variable used for the New York data. Extent of marihuana use was next entered into the regression as an additional independent variable. The marihuana variable then had by far the largest beta value. Two of the five betas that had been significant became insignificant, and for the other three, including the two previously mentioned, their F values were halved.

Such a pattern of findings would fit a model in which these variables were presented as distal causes of heroin use, with some or all of their causal influence indirect, through the proximal effect on marihuana use.

At least partial support for the suggestion is also found in several papers of a recent National Institute on Drug Abuse Publication, *Predicting Adolescent Drug Abuse.* Smith and Fogg (1976) studied seventh and eighth graders–mostly white and middle class–annually for 5 years. Their sample fell into three groups at the end of the fifth year: 222 who had used no drugs, 216 who had used marihuana only, and 104 who had used "hard" drugs (opiates, hallucinogens, stimulants, or depressants). One part of their analysis concerned the relationship between drug use, as measured by these groups at the end of year 5, and twenty-three variables that had been measured in year 1.

In a one-way analysis of variance, all but one of the twenty-three variables showed F values significant or beyond the .05 level. The finding that is more relevant here, however, is that on twenty-two of the twenty-three, the mean score for marihuana users was intermediate between the means for nonusers and hard drug users. Smith and Fogg do not interpret their findings in causal terms, but the findings might fit a viewpoint which saw the variables as measuring causes of drug use, with a greater degree of the variable leading to more serious forms of drug use.

Even more relevant is a paper by Jessor (1976), also based on a longitudinal study. His analysis was based on 432 boys and girls who were in grades 7, 8, and 9 in 1969 and who completed questionnaires then and annually for the next 3 years, with the last three containing a question on marihuana use. From these data, four groups emerged; 258 nonusers, 45 who began marihuana use in 1971-1972, 48 who began in 1970-1971, and 69 who began before 1970. These groups therefore constitute a measure of time of onset of marihuana use but not necessarily of age at onset, since three grades and therefore presumably three age cohorts are in the sample and not distinguished in the four groups. Jessor's measure is analogous to but not identical with the measure used in this chapter.

Using nineteen variables measured in 1970, when only one of the groups had had experience with marihuana, Jessor found that all but one were significantly related with time of onset. With minor exceptions, the pattern on each variable was that nonusers were at one extreme, old users at the other, and the more recent initiates between them in the order of onset of use.

Jessor's explanatory variables were constructed within a sociopsychological theoretical framework which he and his colleagues have been developing for a decade or more to explain "problem behavior" or "deviance." Much problem behavior in adolescence, he points out, is relative to age-graded norms; it consists in acts forbidden to youths, though they will be permitted or even expected in older people. He shows that marihuana onset is related to other such "transition-marking" behaviors—early sexual intercourse, problem drinking, and participation in activist protests. He concludes that the course of adolescent development is significantly related to whether and to when marihuana onset occurs.

Jessor's sample was almost entirely white, middle class, and drawn from a small city in the Rocky Mountain region. The data on which the models of this chapter were based came from a sample only one-third white, largely lower class, and in the most crowded areas of New York City. Despite these major differences, Jessor's theory should apply to them. Insofar as there is some similarity between his sociopsychological independent variables and those used in the New York study and in the fact that both show early onset of marihuana use to be associated with early sexual intercourse and unconventional behavior, it seems probable that it does apply.

Jessor had no data on heroin use, and it is not at all clear that he would extend his theory to cover it and expect his independent variables to predict it. To the extent that what they predict is precocity, excessively early behavior that would later be acceptable, one would not expect them to predict heroin use, because it is not socially acceptable at any age. But the variables include personality characteristics like alienation, self-esteem, and inner controls, and it is not difficult to see these as possible predictors of heroin use. We suggest, therefore, that Jessor's sociopsychological model may be applicable to heroin use as well as to marihuana use.

Also relevant is Kandel's (1975) study of 1,100 high school students in New York State. She documents "a cumulative and hierarchical pattern of drug use which ranges from beer and wine on the one end to heroin on the other," and she concludes:

> The identification of stages in drug behavior has important implications for studying the factors that predict, differentiate, or result from drug use. First, it draws attention to the fact that in each of the stages different types of variables and different processes may be involved.... Second, whereas most studies compare youths within a sample on the basis of their use or nonuse of a particular substance, our results suggest a different strategy. Since each stage represents a cumulative pattern of drug use and generally contains fewer adolescents than the preceding stage in the sequence, comparisons should be made among users and nonusers of the restricted group of respondents who have already used the drug(s) at the preceding stage(s). Unless this is done, the attributes identified as apparent characteristics of a particular group of drug users may actually reflect characteristics important for involvement in drugs at the preceding stage (Kandel 1975, p. 357).

If this advice were correct, the approach used in this chapter would be wrong and suggestions for its extension still more wrong. But we believe Kandel's advice applies only within the limits of the analytic method to which she restricted herself. It led her to results like the following:

> It is evident that while many factors were related to marihuana use, many of the relationships disappeared when all other factors were controlled for. Substantively, the sociodemographic characteristics examined had little effect on marihuana use, especially when the confounding effect of other variables was controlled (Kandel 1975, p. 349).

She used multiple classification analysis, essentially multiple regression with dummy variables, and her variables fell into three classes: sociodemographic, personal attributes, and interpersonal influences of peers and family. In causal model terms, the sociodemographic variables can be seen as affecting the other two classes of variables, which in turn affect marihuana use (and later illicit drug use). When all variables are entered simultaneously into a single regression equation, the coefficients for the demographic variables might be small, but this could mean not that they have "little effect," but only that they have little *direct* effect on marihuana use.

Even those who reject the approach used in this chapter, whether because they question the causal model approach or refuse to use parametric statistics on ordinal variables, or because of other reasons, should question Kandel's advice. It will be noted that her practice, and advice, is to seek explanations for use of illicit drugs *only among those who have used marihuana.* In one sense, she thus defines marihuana use as a cause of illicit drug use—it becomes a necessary condition. But its efficacy as a cause cannot be compared with that of other variables, because marihuana use is no longer a variable (though extent of use may be). We may be wrong in seeing marihuana use as a cause of heroin use, but the hypothesis should be tested against data, not disposed of by a definition.

In brief summary, there are at least three recent studies of marihuana use and its predictors, two of which also provide data on other illicit drug use, which seem to be consistent with the position taken in this chapter. Insofar as findings can be compared, this and other studies seem to point in the same direction. Further, nothing in these other studies, after analysis, seems to contradict the suggestion made here that the predictors of marihuana use are likely to be predictors of heroin and other illicit drug use.

Summary

It is argued that the understanding of marihuana use is important not only because of interest in marihuana, but also because this understanding is likely to apply to other and more serious forms of drug use. This likelihood arises from the strong association between marihuana use and later use of other drugs, which may well be a causal connection, but at least can be used for predictive purposes.

Age at first use of marihuana is demonstrated to be a variable of strategic importance in that it is easily measured, is potentially available prior to the occurrence of the behaviors one would like to predict, and is strongly associated with the fact and extent of later use of other drugs, including opiates or heroin. It is also strongly associated with drug sales and criminal behavior. The chapter next takes age at first use of marihuana as a dependent variable and seeks to explain it in terms of a large number of items related to early behavior, family influences, peer influences, perceptions of drug availability, and labeling by others as a potential delinquent.

These items were all retrospective responses with a time reference to the general period "when you were 13 to 15 years old" or specific references to age 13 or 16; they thus refer to a period preceding first use of marihuana for at least the large majority of the sample studied. The items were combined first into twelve and later into six predictor variables, all constructed as ordinal variables but treated as interval variables to permit use of correlation and multiple regression. A path model leading to age at first use of marihuana was sought, but analysis showed that no single model would fit blacks and whites. Two separate models were therefore developed.

The findings of the study thus include, not surprisingly, that the roads to drug use in New York in the late 1960s and early 1970s were different for blacks and whites. A major explanatory variable for both groups was perception of drug availability; this was of more central importance for whites, in the sense that it acted as a filter through which most of the other variables acted on age at first use, while for blacks these variables had additional direct or indirect paths. Blacks scored much higher than whites on perception of drug availability, and the data indicate that this was probably because both delinquency and drug use were higher and more closely associated for the blacks in the sample. Family influence seemed to be more effective among whites in preventing or delaying marihuana use, while peer influence and early deviant behavior by the respondent seemed to have stronger effects on blacks in leading to marihuana use or earlier use of marihuana. These differences, however, have to be discounted to some extent because the model for blacks accounts for more variance in the dependent variable than does the model for whites.

Several recent studies on predicting adolescent marihuana use are reviewed and shown to be consistent with the findings and the suggestions of the chapter.

Bibliography

Abelson, H.I., and Atkinson, R. 1975. *Public Experience with Psychoactive Substances: A Nationwide Study Among Adults and Youth.* Princeton, N.J.: Response Analysis Corp.

Abelson, H., Cohen, R., and Schrayer, D. 1972. Public attitudes toward marihuana: A nationwide study of beliefs, information and experience. *Marihuana, A Signal of Misunderstanding*, Vol. II, Part 5, Appendix. Washington: Government Printing Office.

Abelson, H.I., and Fishburne, P.M. 1976. *Non-Medical Use of Psychoactive Substances.* Princeton, N.J.: Response Analysis Corp.

Ball, J.C., and Pabon, D.O. 1965. Locating and interviewing narcotic addicts in Puerto Rico. *Sociology and Social Research* 49:401-411.

Becker, H.S. 1963. *Outsiders.* New York: Free Press.

Blalock, H.M. 1964. *Causal Inferences in Nonexperimental Research.* Chapel Hill, North Carolina: Univ. of North Carolina.

Cahalan, D. 1970. *Problem Drinkers: A National Survey.* San Francisco, Calif.: Jossey-Bass.

Cahalan, D., Cisin, I., and Crossley, H.M. 1969. *American Drinking Practices*, Monograph No. 6. New Brunswick, N.J.: Rutgers Center of Alcohol Studies.

Cahalan, D., and Room, R. 1974. *Problem Drinking Among American Men.* New Brunswick, N.J.: Rutgers Center of Alcohol Studies.

Clayton, R.R., and Voss, H.L. 1977. Shacking up: Co-habitation in the 1970s. *Journal of Marriage and the Family* 39:273-283.

Cohen, A.K. 1955. *Delinquent Boys.* New York: Free Press.

Dollard, J., and Miller, N.E. 1950. *Personality and Psychotherapy.* New York: McGraw-Hill.

Duncan, O.D. 1975. *Introduction to Structural Equation Models.* New York: Academic.

Elliott, D.S., and Voss, H.L. 1974. *Delinquency and Dropouts.* Lexington, Mass.: Lexington Books, D.C. Heath.

Glaser, D. 1964. *The Effectiveness of a Prison and Parole System.* Indianapolis: Bobbs-Merrill.

Glueck, S., and Glueck, E. 1974. *Of Delinquency and Crime.* Springfield, Ill.: Charles C. Thomas.

Goode, E. 1974. Marihuana use and the progression to dangerous drugs. In L.L. Miller (ed.), *Marihuana: Effects on Human Behavior.* New York: Academic.

Hirschi, T. 1969. *Causes of Delinquency.* Berkeley, Calif.: Univ. of California Press.

Jessor, R. 1976. Predicting time of onset of marihuana use: A developmental study of high school youth. *Journal of Consulting and Clinical Psychology* 44:125-134. Also in D.J. Lettieri (ed.), 1975. *Predicting Adolescent Drug Abuse.* Rockville, Md.: National Institute on Drug Abuse, pp. 285-298.

Johnson, B.D. 1973. *Marihuana Users and Drug Subcultures.* New York: Wiley.

Johnston, L.D. 1973. *Drugs and American Youth.* Ann Arbor, Mich.: Institute for Social Research, University of Michigan.

Johnston, L.D., and Bachman, J.G. 1975. *Monitoring the Future: A Continuing Study of the Life-Styles and Values of Youth.* Descriptive brochure, Ann Arbor, Mich.: Institute for Social Research, University of Michigan.

Kandel, D. 1975. Comments on the relationship of selected criteria variables to adolescent illicit drug use. In D.J. Lettieri (ed.), *Predicting Adolescent Drug Abuse.* Rockville, Md.: National Institute on Drug Abuse, pp. 345-361.

Kinsey, A.C., Pomeroy, W.B., and Martin, C.E. 1948. *Sexual Behavior in the Human Male.* Philadelphia: Saunders.

Land, K.C. 1973. Identification, parameter estimation, and hypothesis testing in recursive sociological models. In A.S. Goldberger and O.D. Duncan, *Structural Equation Models in the Social Sciences.* New York: Seminar.

Lindesmith, A.R. 1968. *Addiction and Opiates.* Chicago: Aldine.

Loether, H.J., and McTavish, D.J. 1976. *Descriptive and Inferential Statistics.* Boston: Allyn and Bacon.

Lu, K.H. 1974. The indexing and analysis of drug indulgence. *International J. of the Addictions* 9:785-804.

Merton, R.K. 1957. *Social Theory and Social Structure.* New York: Free Press.

Mueller, J.H., Schuessler, K.F., and Costner, H.L. 1977. *Statistical Reasoning in Sociology.* Boston: Houghton Mifflin.

O'Donnell, J.A. 1969. *Narcotic Addicts in Kentucky.* Washington: Government Printing Office.

O'Donnell, J.A., Voss, H.L., Clayton, R.R., Slatin, G.T., and Room, R.G.W. 1976. *Young Men and Drugs: A Nationwide Survey.* Rockville, Md.: National Institute on Drug Abuse.

Reckless, W.C., Dinitz, S., and Murray, E. 1956. Self concept as an insulator against delinquency. *Am. Soc. Rev.* 21:744-746.

Robins, L.N. 1974. *The Vietnam Drug User Returns*, Special Action Office Monograph A2. Washington: Government Printing Office.

Robins, L.N., and Murphy, G.E. 1967. Drug use in a normal population of young Negro men. *AJPH* 57:1580-1596.

Short, J.E., and Strodtbeck, F.L. 1965. *Group Process and Gang Delinquency.* Chicago: Univ. of Chicago Press.

Smith, G.M., and Fogg, C.P. 1975. Teenage drug use: A search for causes and consequences. In D.J. Lettieri (ed.), *Predicting Adolescent Drug Abuse.* Rockville, Md.: National Institute on Drug Abuse, pp. 279-282.

Straus, R. 1972. Alcoholism and Social Policy. Paper presented at conference on New Directions in Graduate Training: Policy Implications of Sociological Research, American Sociological Association, Carmel, California, December 6-9, 1972.

Sutherland, E.H., and Cressey, D.R. 1970. *Criminology,* 8th ed. Philadelphia: Lippincott.

Vaillant, G.E. 1966. A twelve-year follow-up of New York narcotic addicts: I. The relation of treatment to outcome. *Am. J. Psych.* 122:727-737.

Voss, H.L. 1976. Young men, drugs and crime. In Research Triangle Institute, *Drug Use and Crime.* Washington: National Technical Information Service, pp. 351-368.

Appendix 4A Construction of Variables

1. *Perception of drug availability* (DA):
   a. Still thinking of the time you were 13 to 15 years old, as far as you knew at that time how many persons in your neighborhood were smoking pot?
   b. How about heroin? When you were 13 to 15, how many persons in your neighborhood were using heroin?

   Both questions used the same response categories and were scored as follows:

Half or more	= 5
Quite a few, but less than half	= 4
A few	= 3
Only one or two	= 2
None	= 1

   c. When you were 13 to 15, did you know of anyone in your neighborhood who was selling drugs—heroin, marihuana, or any other illegal drug?

Yes	= 5
No	= 1

   d. Did you know about any places where heroin could be bought, whether in your neighborhood or outside of it? (Yes/No; coded together with question e)
   e. (If Yes to question d) How close to your home was the nearest place where you knew heroin could be bought?

Yes—on the same block	= 5
Yes—within a couple of blocks	= 4
Yes—more than a couple of blocks away	= 3
No	= 1

   The variable score was the sum of the scores on the separate items. Range was therefore from 4 to 20, with high scores indicating more perception of drug availability. The prediction was a negative association between perception of drug availability and age at first use of marihuana.

2. *Peer delinquency* (PD):
   a. Did many of the adults in your neighborhood think of your friends as delinquent?

      Yes = 5
      No = 1

   b. Did any of your friends or the people you ran around with when you were 13 to 15 have trouble with the police, like being arrested and taken to the station? (Yes/No; coded together with question c)
   c. (If Yes to question b) Among all your friends together, did that happen:

      Yes–very often = 5
      Yes–fairly often = 4
      Yes–only a few times = 3
      Yes–only once = 2
      No = 1

   d. When you were 13 to 15, did any of your friends or the boys you ran around with ever go out stealing or boosting? (Yes/No; coded with question e)
   e. (If Yes to question d) Did that happen: Scoring as in question c.
   f. How about gang fights? Did you and your friends ever get into a fight with another gang? (Yes/No; coded with question g)
   g. Did that happen: Scoring as in question c.

   The variable score was the sum of the four item scores, with a range of 4 to 20. High scores indicate more delinquency among respondent's peers, and a negative association with age at first use of marihuana was predicted.

3. *Peer drug use* (PU):
   When you were 13 . . . were at least *some* of your friends:
   a. Drinking beer, wine, or liquor at times (Yes/No)
   b. Smoking marihuana (Yes/No)
   c. Using other drugs (Yes/No)

   A score of 1 was assigned to everyone. For use of alcohol, 1 point was added; for use of marihuana, 2; and for use of other drugs, 4. The variable score thus ranged from 1 to 8, with high scores indicating more drug use by peers. A negative association with age at first use of marihuana was predicted.

4. *Family control* (FC):
   a. Now a few questions about your relations with your family when you were 13 to 15 years old. When you were not at home, did your (parents/mother/father) know where you were:

Usually = 4
Sometimes = 3
Rarely = 2
Never = 1

b. Did your (parents/mother/father) set a definite time for you to be home at night when you were 13 to 15? (Yes/No; coded together with question c)
c. (If Yes to question b) Did you usually get home by the time they set?

Yes–Yes = 5
Yes–No = 3
No = 1

d. About how many of your friends did your mother know? Was it:

All = 4
Most = 3
Some = 2
None = 1

The variable score was the sum of the preceding three scores, so the range was 3 to 13. High scores indicate more control over respondent by his family. A positive correlation with age at first use of marihuana was predicted.

5. *Closeness to mother* (CM):
   a. When you were 13 to 15 years old, how close did you feel to your mother?

Very close = 5
Fairly close = 4
Not close but not distant = 3
Not close at all = 2
No mother or substitute = 1 (2 cases)

Only one item was available, so the range of the variable was 1 to 5, with high scores indicating more closeness. A positive correlation with age at first use of marihuana was predicted.

6. *Closeness to father* (CF):

The item was the same as for closeness to mother, so again the variable range was 1 to 5, with high scores indicating more closeness. There were forty-one cases with no father or father substitute. The prediction was a positive correlation with age at first use of marihuana.

7. *Communication with parents* (CP):
When you were 13 to 15 years old, about how often did you discuss each of the following with your (parents/mother/father)? How about:

a. Things related to school?
b. Your friends?
c. Future plans?
d. How you spent your leisure time?
e. Girls?
f. News and national events?

The predesignated responses were "Often," "Seldom," or "Never" for each of the six subjects, with these responses scored, respectively, 3, 2, and 1.

The variable score was the sum of the six item scores, so the range was 6 to 18, with high scores indicating more communication. The prediction was a positive correlation with age at first use of marihuana.

8. *Father as a model* (FM):
   a. When you were 13 to 15 years old, did you want to be the kind of person your father was?

In every way	= 5
In most ways	= 4
In some ways	= 3
In just a few ways	= 2
Not at all	= 1
No father or substitute	= 0

Only one item was used. The computing procedure used excluded zero scores from correlations and regressions, so the effective range of the variable was 1 to 5, with high scores indicating more seeing the father as a model. The prediction was a positive correlation with age at first use of marihuana.

(There were forty-one men who were not asked the question because they had no father or father substitute. We could not find a satisfactory rationale to assign a mean score, or any score, to these men so that they could be included in the computation or correlations, so it seemed safest to assign the zero, which would drop them from such computation.)

9. *Labeling* (LA):
   a. When you were 13 to 15, suppose we had asked your teachers if they thought you were headed for trouble with the law. Would they have said:

Definitely yes	= 5
Probably	= 4
Not sure	= 3

Probably not = 2
Definitely not = 1

b. Same question, for "your friends." (Responses and scoring as in question a)
c. Same question, for "your (parents/father/mother)." (Responses and scoring as in question a)

The variable score was the sum of the three item scores, so the range was 3 to 15, with high scores indicating more labeling as a potential delinquent. Prediction was a negative correlation with age at first use of marihuana.

10. *School adjustment* (SA):

a. How were your grades in school at the time, that is, at age 13 to 15? Were they:

Excellent = 4
Good = 3
Fair = 2
Poor = 1

b. Some 13- to 15-year-old boys like school, some do not. How did you like school at that age? Did you:

Like school a lot = 5
Like school fairly well = 4
Not care one way or another = 3
Dislike school = 2
Really hate school = 1

c. How often did you get in trouble with teachers or school officials at age 13?

Not at all = 4
A few times = 3
Quite often = 2
All the time = 1

The variable score was the sum of the three item scores, so the range was from 3 to 13, with high scores indicating better school adjustment. The prediction was a positive correlation with age at first use of marihuana.

11. *Involvement in conventional activities* (CA):

Think now about how you spent your leisure time when you were 13 to 15 years old. For each of the activities on card 3, tell me if you spent a total of a couple of hours or more a week doing that activity. Did you spend at least a total of a couple hours a week:

a. Watching TV? (Yes/No)
b. In boy scouts? (Yes/No)
c. In school or YMCA sports? (Yes/No)

In scoring, everyone was assigned a score of 1. "Yes" responses to the preceding, respectively, added 1, 2, and 2.

After the complete list of activities, which included the deviant activities in the next variable, respondent was asked "At which of these would you say you spent the most time?" and all "Yes" activities were read. If a, b, or c above was given as the response, an additional 2 points were added.

The range of the variable was therefore 1 to 8, with high scores indicating more conventional activities. The prediction was a positive correlation with age at first use of marihuana.

12. *Early deviant behavior* (ED):
Additional activities listed under the item described above were:

a. Hanging around on the street? Add 1
b. Playing pool? Add 1
c. Pitching pennies? Add 1
d. Shooting craps? Add 2
e. Playing con games or stealing Add 3

As in the previous variable, if one of these was named as the activity on which most time was spent, more points were added, 1 if it was one of the first three, 2 if one of the last two. Three additional items were available from a self-administered questionnaire completed during the interview in which the men were asked if they had ever engaged in certain behaviors and the age at which these had first occurred. For each of the following items, points were added if the respondent said he had done it at age 14 or earlier:

f. Ran away from home Add 2
g. Was suspended or expelled from school Add 2
h. Had sexual intercourse Add 2

With an initial score of 1 assigned to everyone, the range of the variable was 1 to 17, with high scores indicating more deviant behavior when the respondent was 13 to 15 years old. The prediction was a negative correlation with age at first use of marihuana.

Part II
Methodology

5 Methodology in Youth Drug-Abuse Research

Marvin A. Lavenhar

In response to the problem of widespread illicit drug use in the late 1960s, many communities perceived the need to do something, and to do it quickly. Numerous intervention and prevention programs were instituted in the absence of careful planning and tested hypotheses. A great amount of resources in time, energy, and money has been expended in preventive efforts. As the costs of these programs have spiraled upward, with few apparent successes, the trend has been toward critical assessment of the efficacy of these efforts. Most of the evaluative designs have not been based on objective scientific principles. As a matter of fact, there is currently little empirical evidence available to demonstrate that community programs have indeed been effective in reducing the problem of drug dependency.

A comprehensive community-based program to combat drug abuse addresses all three levels of prevention, where prevention is used in the epidemiological sense. The different phases of drug-abuse prevention can be defined as follows (Smith et al. 1973):

Primary prevention: Prevention of drug abuse in a previously uninvolved population.

Secondary prevention: Prevention of the progression of drug abuse in an involved population which does not as yet have residual disability from its drug usage.

Tertiary prevention: Rehabilitation of the drug-abusing population which has significant residual disability as a consequence of its drug involvement.

The traditional approach to primary and secondary prevention has been through legislation and law enforcement designed to prevent or reduce drug misuse and through policies aimed at limiting the available supply of drugs. During the drug-abuse epidemic of the 1960s, it became apparent that legal sanctions and efforts to limit the supply of drugs were not sufficient to stem the tide of illicit drug use, particularly among the young. Preventive drug education was proposed as a logical alternative or complement to the legal approach. A

Adapted with permission from "Methodology in Community Research" from *The Communities' Response to Drug Use*, Dr. S. Einstein, editor. New York: Pergamon Press, 1979

wide variety of drug education programs has been employed during the past decade, but their impact has rarely been rigorously tested.

Historically, up until the late 1950s, drug addiction was considered to be primarily a problem of "deviants" who could be handled by legal means, and incarceration was regarded as the only appropriate "treatment." In recent years, the trend has been toward treating drug abuse as more of a medical than criminal problem. Various treatment approaches to tertiary drug-abuse prevention have been instituted but few have been scientifically evaluated.

Community planners and policymakers must have knowledge of local drug-use patterns in order to evaluate the impact of community drug-abuse programs and to allocate resources in an efficient manner. However, at the present time we have no reliable means of estimating the number of people who use or misuse various drugs and their drug-using behavior patterns.

Many questions about drugs cannot be answered in the laboratory or in clinical research. Community research is needed. Unfortunately, it is seldom possible, in the community setting, to attain the level of control provided by scientific experimentation in the laboratory.

The following discussion considers the limitations of some of the research methodologies that have been used in drug-use intervention programs. The focus is on the community rather than on drugs or drug users. Major emphasis is given to three aspects of community research in the field of drug use: estimating the magnitude of the problem, treatment evaluation, and drug education evaluation.

Estimating the Magnitude of the Problem: Incidence and Prevalence

The task of estimating the extent of illicit drug use, abuse, and addiction in any community has always been, and continues to be, extremely difficult. Because of serious reporting gaps, much of the data needed for estimates are not available, and much of the available data are suspect. Other confounding factors include the large number of drugs that are being abused, the variable composition of illicitly produced drugs, the widespread deceptions in the illegal drug market, and the wide range of frequency of use and dosages employed. The latter points to another major obstacle to estimating the scope of illicit drug use—there is no general agreement on what constitutes drug abuse or addiction. Indeed, these terms defy precise definition. Smart (1971) studied the distribution of drug-use scores among Canadian high school student drug users and concluded that the distribution was a smooth one with no discontinuities, implying that there is no clear-cut differentiation of drug users into discrete categories (for example, users, abusers, addicts) on the basis of drug consumption alone.

The two measures most frequently used to characterize the extent of illicit drug use in a community are incidence and prevalence. Incidence pertains to the number of new drug addicts (abusers) that come into being during a specified period of time (for example, 1 year). Point prevalence attempts to estimate the number of drug addicts (abusers) on hand at a given point in time. Period prevalence describes the number of cases that were observed during a specified period of time (for example, 1 year). All three statistics are usually expressed as a rate per 1,000 individuals.

Inasmuch as incidence rates are tied in with onset of illicit drug use, they are important in epidemiological investigations of cause and effect and in studies evaluating the impact of preventive drug education programs. On the other hand, prevalence data are most useful for effective planning and utilization of treatment and rehabilitation facilities.

Since incidence and prevalence statistics may be derived from several different sources of information which may have different reporting needs, there is a wide variability in reporting.

Sources of Incidence and Prevalence Data

Police Records. Historically, police records have been the major source of incidence and prevalence estimates even though drug-related arrest data obtained from police records represent only the visible or known drug abuser and provide no indication of those who may not be known to law enforcement agencies. Moreover, arrests are unevenly distributed among different socioeconomic classes and groups. They are concentrated in people in the lower socioeconomic classes and therefore are likely to grossly underestimate middle- and upper-class illicit drug use. Furthermore, police records cannot provide the data needed to estimate the extent of misuse of licit drugs.

Case Registers. A case register is a system for collecting registration and follow-up information on a population with a particular disease or problem based on cases reported by agencies or individuals (Fishman, et al. 1971). Most drug registers have focused on cases of narcotics addiction.

The U.S. Bureau of Narcotics and Dangerous Drugs (BNDD) maintains a national register of drug addicts which depends on voluntary reports. Since its prime contributors are law enforcement agencies, it is subject to the same limitations as police records as a useful source of incidence and prevalence data.

Growing concern over the problem of narcotics addiction in the 1960s lead to the establishment of several localized, community-based narcotics case registers to provide incidence and prevalence information. Two of the most ambitious narcotics register projects were the ones developed by the New York City Department of Health (Kavaler et al. 1968; Fishman et al. 1971) and by the Narcotics Treatment Administration in Washington, D.C. (Dupont and Piemme

1973). The kinds of case information reported to these registers include name, address, sex, age, ethnicity, birthdate, amounts and types of drugs used, occupation, marital status, and arrests and convictions.

The development of any register population for the purpose of providing meaningful indicators of incidence and prevalence requires a comprehensive reporting base (hospitals, addiction services, police and correctional institutions, private physicians, and other health and social services agencies). A register must also carefully define the criteria for reporting. For example, the New York City Narcotics Register defines an addict as any individual who is reported by a medical source or is accepted for treatment by a hospital, clinic, or established social service agency.

The three major requirements of an effective register are completeness, representativeness, and accuracy. Inasmuch as registers generally must depend on unpaid reporters and on largely unenforceable reporting requirements, they are not likely to count all cases. For example, the New York City Register receives few reports from industrial physicians, schools, and agencies working with young people (Andima et al. 1973). Moreover, a case register population is not likely to be representative of the entire addict population, but only of the known or visible addicts. The extent to which it is representative of the latter group depends largely on the relative absence of errors introduced by inaccurate reporting and inadequate reporting processing and register maintenance.

It is conceded, by even the staunchest supporters of the case-register approach, that an addict register will never be able to provide a precise addict count. The major problem lies in estimating the number of addicts who do not come into contact with official agencies and who manage to escape detection by reporting sources. Several attempts have been made to develop a workable method for estimating the total addict population in localities where there is some reporting of addicts to a central register. These efforts, designed to overcome incomplete reporting, are based on extrapolation from a register population on the basis of testing against an independent outside data system, that is, one in which cases are reported on the basis of some criterion other than narcotics use. However, since extrapolation based on tenuous assumptions are extremely risky, these estimates should be used with caution and corroborated with as many external populations as possible (death certificates, treatment records, arrests).

Treatment Program Records. Estimates of the incidence and prevalence of drug addiction obtained from treatment program records are not only incomplete to an unknown degree but are also likely to be biased for a number of reasons (Hunt 1974). First, many treatment programs depend largely on voluntary admissions and attract only the highly motivated segment of the addict population. Second, there is no standard definition of addiction–programs admit users of all description. And third, other factors such as the physical location of the program, the nature of treatment, admission policies, and program capacities all influence the number and types of addicts entering a program. Even though treatment incidence may not be representative of the entire addict population, it can provide an indication of trends in treatment demand, which is of utmost interest to the health planner.

Polls and Surveys. Patterns of drug abuse in individuals not known or identifiable by any agency requires study by the use of polls or surveys. Polls that include questions on the use of drugs (for example, Gallup Poll) are seldom adequate for estimating the scope of the problem because they generally provide gross measures of drug use. Surveys tend to be more comprehensive and frequently elicit information about knowledge of and attitudes toward drugs in addition to drug-using behavior.

The survey is the most used (and perhaps most abused) means of estimating the incidence and prevalence of drug abuse in a given population. Glenn and Richards (1974) provided a comprehensive compendium, bringing together statistics from recent published and unpublished surveys of nonmedical drug use reported in 1971 or later.

If properly designed and implemented, surveys can provide useful information to help assess the magnitude of the drug problem in a given population and to generate baseline data essential for the evaluation of educational programs in drug-abuse prevention. However, data obtained from surveys have frequently been rather superficial and especially vulnerable to bias introduced by one or more of the following:

1. Inadequate sampling techniques (lack of randomization)
2. Insufficient sample size
3. Inclusion of loaded or leading questions
4. Lack of standardization of data-gathering instruments and collection procedures
5. Large nonresponse
6. Invalid responses

If these sources of bias are not controlled or accounted for, it becomes very difficult to interpret and draw inferences from survey data, and the utility of survey results is of questionable value. Moreover, since drug-use patterns tend to change rapidly, survey results become obsolete in a short period of time.

Reliable, valid estimates for generalization to wider groups and populations are possible only if the following requirements are met (Glenn and Richards 1974; Lavenhar 1973):

1. A random sample is selected from the target population (if 100 percent sampling is not considered necessary or is not feasible).

2. The sample size should be a compromise between the desired precision of estimates and the resources available, but should be sufficiently large to provide meaningful estimates of the extent of use of even the rarely used drugs.
3. It should be possible to estimate the potential bias due to nonresponse from statistically acceptable data.
4. The questionnaire should be carefully designed and pretested on a population similar to the target population prior to use in the actual survey.
5. Reliability and validity checks should be instituted to screen out misleading data.
6. The administration of the survey should follow a carefully worked out standardized protocol.
7. If survey results are based on responses elicited from a random sample of the target population, then estimates of drug use should be accompanied by an indication of the range of variability (for example, confidence intervals).

Utility of Drug Surveys. The proliferation of mainly one-time surveys of diverse populations in scattered locations using a wide variety of sampling techniques, data-gathering instruments, and survey methods has become a cause for concern among a growing group of researchers who have begun to raise questions as to the usefulness of drug survey data for program planning and development. The diversity of methods employed (for example, categories of drug use) makes comparison among surveys difficult.

The basic questions are the extent to which sample survey data are generalizable to and representative of the population under study and the extent to which the data are applicable to other similar populations. In an attempt to answer these questions, attention has recently been focused on the issues of reliability and validity of survey data. *Reliability* is defined as the degree to which a survey would yield similar estimates if repeated several times. *Validity* refers to the extent to which estimates drawn from a sample reflect the true characteristics of the total population.

Survey data are subject to two sources of error: *random error*, which is readily measurable, and *nonrandom error* or *bias*, which is frequently difficult to measure. Some of the main sources of bias and the measures that may be taken to minimize them have previously been outlined. In view of the legal and social implications of nonmedical drug use, a major concern in questionnaire surveys is the validity of the respondents' reports of their drug use. Clearly, even the most sophisticated survey designs may yield invalid data if the respondents are less than truthful in their replies. The issue of response validity in drug surveys has attracted much attention in the recent literature.

The accuracy of self-reported drug use is influenced by many factors, including the specific drug category involved, the respondent's memory, the ability of the respondent to correctly identify drugs taken on prescription or purchased in the illegal drug market, fear of reprisals, and changing peer group pressures which make drugs more socially acceptable than others.

Several investigators (Johnston 1974; Porter et al. 1973; Smart et al. 1973; Smart and Jackson 1969; Haberman et al. 1972; Petzel et al. 1973) have used one or more validity checks in their drug-use surveys of diverse populations, and all agreed that dishonest responses were likely to have little effect on results. On the basis of a critical review of four studies that examined the question on validity and one study that focused on test-retest reliability in surveys of drug-using behavior among adolescents, Whitehead and Smart (1972) concluded that "there is reason to have confidence in the validity and reliability of self-reports of drug use."

Assessment of Drug-Use Trends. Most of the earlier surveys of drug use were small-scale, one-time studies conducted in widely scattered local schools and communities. They were useful in providing a direct estimate of the prevalence of drug-using behavior in a given population at a particular point in time. However, the one-time survey could not yield direct estimates of incidence and provided limited information on drug-use trends over time. In recent years, the scope of drug-use surveys has broadened and the trend has been toward more repeated cross-sectional surveys which can assess overall changes in the target population and toward longitudinal surveys to assess changes in the individual.

Although the longitudinal approach to trend analysis is theoretically desirable, it creates a major logistical problem in surveys of sensitive issues. Longitudinal studies require that subjects be identified in some manner so that they may be periodically resurveyed, making it difficult to guarantee the privacy and confidentiality of the data. To address this problem, several attempts have been made recently to develop techniques for ensuring data security and respondent anonymity (Haberman et al. 1972; Kandel 1973; Astin and Boruch 1970). The search for new approaches to this problem will undoubtedly continue until the overall question of the rights of the researcher, with regard to the protection of the privacy of his subjects, is resolved.

The Epidemic Approach. Because there are certain similarities between the spread of heroin use and the spread of infectious diseases, there has been some development of epidemic models which purport to describe the spread of heroin use. These models use sophisticated analytical techniques to examine the incidence of heroin use over a long period of time by geographical area. A detailed description of this approach is provided by Hunt (1973, 1974).

Evaluation of Treatment Programs

In the late 1960s, the increasing incidence of drug dependence and the substantial recidivism among drug offenders demonstrated the ineffectiveness of the predominantly punitive approach to drug abuse and triggered the proliferation of newly established drug treatment facilities in an attempt to find a therapeutic solution to the problem. Although the medical professions have been studying and treating drug dependence for more than a century, there is still a great deal of uncertainty and confusion about the causes and nature of drug dependence and about the rationale behind treatment. Confusion about the nature of drug dependence has resulted in confusion about its treatment. Although a wide range of treatment approaches has been employed, no method of treatment has been proven generally effective.

While the earlier treatment programs tended to be limited in scope and generally focused on a single treatment modality, many current programs offer a wide range of treatment methods and techniques to a large number of clients. The five most common types of treatment modalities are:

1. Detoxification (mainly hospital inpatient)
2. Outpatient drug-free therapy
3. Therapeutic community
4. Methadone maintenance
5. Multimodality programs

Until recently, there has been little demand for scientific assessment of treatment programs. Evaluation in the past relied almost entirely on naturalistic observation of therapy as practiced. Systematic data collection and feedback have been, in general, nonexistent or extremely primitive. It has been assumed that reasoned judgment and experience were all that was needed to develop and administer treatment programs, and judgments as to program effectiveness have been based generally on minimally documented evidence.

The recent proliferation of treatment programs has placed a strain on the public and private resources needed for their support. Therefore, it has become imperative to determine which programs are effective enough to warrant retention and further support. While much has been learned from naturalistic observation, there is a clear need for more scientific methods of evaluation which allow for manipulation and control over the wide range of variables interacting in the present-day treatment setting.

Although some progress has been made in recent years in the development of objective evaluative models, most attempts at program evaluation have taken the form of one-shot intramural efforts at a definitive evaluation. This approach generally has had little practical impact on the administration, planning, or delivery of treatment services (Putnam et al. 1973). In general there has been a lack of sound and detailed extramural evaluations of treatment efficacy.

The most pressing problems encountered in evaluative studies have generally been lack of funds for indepth evaluation, a lack of expertise, and a lack of objectivity. There have also been, and still are, many specific obstacles to effective evaluation which are extremely difficult to overcome. Some of these include:

1. Limited generalizability of evaluative findings
2. Lack of agreement on aims, objectives, and criteria for effectiveness of treatment
3. The unavailability of appropriate outcome measures
4. Difficulties in obtaining objective and reliably measured data
5. Practical difficulties in applying experimental designs
6. Practical difficulties in patient follow-up

Future Directions in Treatment Evaluation

Evaluation research in the treatment of drug abuse has, in the past, been primarily concerned with the impact of the total program. The trend has been toward focusing on subcomponents of the treatment program to determine which specific intervention procedures produce the most desirable changes in which patients under which conditions. This requires greater explicitness in defining treatment goals and techniques as well as a clearer understanding of the specific mechanisms of change. The latter can be achieved only through the application of scientific methodology which permits isolation and manipulation of variables in order to evaluate their effect.

Since it has been clearly established that not all patients respond equally well to a given treatment, the focus of evaluation research has transgressed beyond assessment of treatment efficacy to a search for those patient characteristics which discriminate between successful and unsuccessful treatment rehabilitation. This approach assumes that if it is possible to identify demographic, social, and/or psychological indexes which, on the average, differ significantly in groups of successfully and unsuccessfully treated patients, then it may be possible to measure prospective patients on one or more discriminating variables and predict their likelihood of success in a given treatment program or modality. This approach and some of its limitations are discussed in the recent literature (Hunt and Odoroff 1969; Chambers et al. 1970; Snowden et al. 1973; D'Orban 1974).

Guidelines for Treatment Program Evaluation

Following are some recommended guidelines to be used to obtain optimal results in treatment evaluation efforts:

1. Evaluation should be a continuous process providing timely feedback to program administrators and staff.

2. Any evaluation effort must start with an explicit statement of the treatment objectives and the criteria for effectiveness.
3. There is no single criterion measure that is sufficient to assess treatment effectiveness.
4. Program evaluation should be systematic, objective, and based on empirical data.
5. Systematic data collection should be conceived as an integral part of the day-to-day treatment routine at the inception of the treatment program and should not impose an unreasonable burden on the program staff.
6. Assessment of treatment efficacy should be based on at least a quasi-experimental research design when true experimental methodology is not feasible.
7. Evaluation of treatment efficacy should be based on the measurement of criteria before, during, and after exposure to treatment programs.
8. Evaluation should focus on the impact of specific components of the treatment program as well as the impact of the total program.
9. Extramural evaluation is generally preferable to intramural evaluation.

Evaluation of Drug Education Programs

Until the last decade, community drug-abuse prevention programs were identified exclusively with the law. Once it became apparent that the use of illicit drugs could not be effectively controlled by the exclusive use of harsh legal penalties, police surveillance, and efforts to curtail the influx of drugs, then communities turned to drug education as the best means of prevention. It was generally assumed that communication of information about illegal substances would dissuade people from trying drugs or cause them to stop if they were already using them.

Drug education is a relatively new field which gained momentum in the late 1960s when illicit drug use among adolescents and young adults reached epidemic proportions. In fact, most of the formal drug education programs have been directed at adolescents through the school systems. Little headway has been made in educating adults and nonschool populations—the vast potential of the mass media as an educational tool has not been fully exploited.

Most school drug education programs have focused on primary prevention in young populations. Swisher (1974) defined *drug education* as "a series of activities and experiences with young people which occur before decisions have been made about drug involvement and which, if fully explored, will result in fewer negative consequences for the individual." The fact that most drug education programs are narrow in scope, focusing on student groups rather than on the population as a whole, has detracted from their usefulness. Other problems which have prevented the field of drug education from realizing its full potential include: (1) lack of clearly defined goals; (2) competition from mass media and other sources; (3) lack of well-trained, effective teachers; and (4) lack of clear understanding of the individual's motivation to use drugs (Smart and Fejer 1974).

Despite the fact that a great quantity of resources in time, activity, and money has been expended on drug education efforts, several recent published reviews of research on these programs (U.S. National Commission on Marihuana and Drug Abuse 1973; Braucht et al. 1973; Goodstadt 1974; Smart and Fejer 1974) reached the same conclusion—there is little scientific evidence available to assess the effectiveness of drug education. Few evaluative research studies have been undertaken, and most of these have been scientifically unsound. Compared with the large number of implemented drug education programs, it was recently reported that not more than a few dozen have employed the principles of scientific experimentation, no more than eight programs have utilized a no-treatment control group, and fewer than eight programs have studied their impact on drug use (Smart and Fejer 1974).

Not only has there been virtually no empirical evidence confirming the hypothesis that drug education can prevent or reduce drug use, but it has been suggested that under certain circumstances drug education may even encourage drug usage by allaying fears and by arousing curiosity (Bourne 1973) and also may, in effect, prove to be a costly distraction from the more important moral and political issues underlying the drug problem (Halleck 1971). In view of the uncertainty as to the impact of drug education, the U.S. National Commission on Marihuana and Drug Abuse (1973, p. 357) recommended a moratorium on all new school drug education programs until operating programs have been tested for effectiveness. The value of drug education is currently being seriously scrutinized in light of its generally questionable past performance. The answers to the critical questions regarding program effectiveness will not be forthcoming until the major problems in evaluative research are resolved. It has been argued that scientific evaluation is too costly in terms of effort, time, and funding. However, drug education itself is very costly, and unless it is objectively evaluated, there is no way of assuring its effectiveness.

Research Shortcomings of Drug Education Evaluation Studies

Most of the research limitations attributed to treatment program evaluation are equally applicable to the vast majority of studies evaluating drug education programs. The methodological requirements for effective evaluation are frequently difficult to attain in real-life situations. Most of the reported evaluative studies in drug education suffer from one or more of the following methodological shortcomings:

1. Educational goals and outcome criteria were not clearly defined.
2. Difficulties were encountered in measuring behavioral changes.
3. Subjects were not randomly assigned to experimental and control groups.
4. No provision was made for the use of control groups consisting of individuals who were not exposed to any educational programs (or to the usual program).
5. No attempt was made to assess the validity and reliability of criterion measurements.
6. Possible selection bias was introduced by the use of volunteer subjects.
7. Possible response bias was introduced by the subjects' awareness of the program objectives.
8. Possible response bias was introduced by the differential loss to follow-up of subjects in the experimental and control groups.
9. The sample size was inadequate.
10. The program content was too brief.
11. Follow-ups were held too soon to measure lasting change in knowledge and behavior.
12. Preprogram baseline data were unavailable for comparison (posttest only design).
13. Difficulties were encountered in matching subjects in long-range longitudinal studies.
14. The study design precluded the control of exposure of the study population to variables extraneous to the educational program (for example, information obtained from the mass media, peer group pressure).
15. There was questionable generalizability of the evaluative results beyond the study population.
16. Too much emphasis was placed on assessing the impact of the total educational effort and not enough on the specific approaches to drug education.

The evaluator has not only been faced with significant methodological problems, but has frequently been confronted with strong opposition to scientific evaluation of school-based drug education programs by parents and school administrators. Parents may not react favorably to a program which assigns their children to a control group which receives no drug education. They may also object to requiring their children to answer questions on drug use on the grounds that this constitutes invasion of privacy. School administrators may feel threatened by attempts to test the effectiveness of educational programs. Many evaluation efforts have been unsuccessful because the evaluators did not take the time to educate, motivate, and involve the community.

Future Directions in Evaluations of Drug Education Programs

Despite the fact that drug education programs have proliferated during the past 5 years, it is still not possible to make an objective judgment as to whether or not they have been generally effective in preventing or reducing the use of illicit drugs or in controlling the indiscriminate use of various medically approved drugs and medicines. In order to make sound decisions as to the future directions of drug education, it is not only essential to be able to assess the overall impact of programs, but it is also critical to ascertain the relative levels of effectiveness of different approaches to drug education with different target populations in attaining different educational goals.

Clearly, more scientific research is needed to measure the effects of drug education programs. However, it is also important to gain greater understanding of the underlying factors which determine the effectiveness or ineffectiveness of these efforts. In particular, some of the specific questions which merit further consideration are:

1. What, realistically, should be the goals of drug education?
2. How do knowledge, attitudes, and behavior interact in the decision-making process?
3. What are the relative influences of variables associated with the educator, the message, the delivery approach, and the audience in the communication process?
4. How does the duration of exposure to an educational program relate to the longevity of its impact?
5. To what extent do largely uncontrolled environmental factors, such as parental and peer use of licit and illicit drugs, counteract the impact of drug educational efforts?
6. What are the potential risks of obtaining adverse effects as a consequence of drug education?

To provide the information that will be needed for future community intervention, two basic forms of study will be needed: (1) large-scale, controlled longitudinal studies of intended outcomes to investigate the long-term (3 to 5 years) impact of programs; and (2) smaller-scale experimental studies to measure the impact of different approaches to drug education, with emphasis on determining which components of successful programs contribute the most to producing the intended outcomes. It may be the case that the most effective approaches to education have already been discovered. If so, the task remains to isolate these from the large set of available approaches.

Guidelines for Drug Education Program Evaluation

1. All newly established drug education programs should have a built-in evaluation mechanism.
2. Goals should be well defined and realistic.
3. A variety of criteria for effectiveness should be considered, with emphasis placed on changing attitudes and behavior in addition to increasing knowledge.
4. An attempt should be made to assess the reliability and validity of data-gathering instruments.
5. A strong attempt should be made to approximate experimental conditions.
6. Studies should be of sufficiently long duration to permit the assessment of long-range effects of education.
7. In addition to measuring overall program impact, studies should focus on the specific effects of variables associated with the educator, the message, the method of delivery, and the audience.

Summary and Conclusions

There has been a plethora of newly established community drug-abuse intervention programs during the past decade. Until recently, the effectiveness of most programs was not critically evaluated. While the costs of community drug programs have increased dramatically, there is little scientific evidence to demonstrate their efficacy. The trend has been toward more critical assessment of these programs to determine whether or not they merit continuing public and/or private support.

Some progress has been made in applying scientific principles to research and evaluation problems in the field of drug abuse, but much has yet to be done. Unfortunately, it is extremely difficult in the community setting to attain the level of control required for true scientific experimentation.

An attempt is made in this chapter to identify some of the difficulties encountered in applying scientific methodology, to suggest ways in which these difficulties may at least partially be overcome, and to recommend techniques and procedures that might be used in community research.

Major emphasis is given to three aspects of community drug research: estimating the magnitude of the problem, treatment evaluation, and drug education evaluation. The weaknesses and strengths of various sources of incidence and prevalence data are elucidated, guidelines are established, and future directions are suggested for the evaluation of community treatment and drug education programs.

Although the imposition of rigorous scientific control in community research may not often be possible, it is usually feasible to approximate the true experimental environment by means of quasi-experimental research designs which can yield useful information. If researchers take the appropriate steps to maximize the reliability and validity of their data and to exercise some degree of statistical control, then workable estimates of the incidence and prevalence of drug abuse and addiction and meaningful assessments of the efficacy of community intervention programs are attainable.

References

Andima, H., Krug, D., Bergner, L., Patrick, S., and Whitman, S. 1973. A prevalence estimation model of narcotics addiction in New York City. *Am. J. Epidemiol.* 98:56-62.

Astin, A.W., and Boruch, R.F. 1970. A "Link" system for assuring confidentiality of research data in longitudinal studies. *Am. Educational Research J.* 7:615-624.

Bourne, P.G. 1973. Is drug abuse a fading fad? *J. Am. Coll. Health Assoc.* 21:198-200.

Braucht, G.N., Follingstad, D., Brakarsh, D., and Berry, K.L. 1973. Drug education. A review of goals, approaches and effectiveness, and a paradigm for evaluation. *Q.J. Stud. Alcohol* 34:1279-1292.

Chambers, C.D., Babst, D.V., and Warner, A. 1970. Characteristics predicting long-term retention in a methadone maintenance program. *Proc. Third Nat'l Conf. on Methadone Treatment* 1:140-143.

D'Orban, P.T. 1974. A follow-up study of female narcotic addicts: Variables related to outcome. *Br. J. Psychiatry* 125:28-33.

Dupont, R.L., and Piemme, T.E. 1973. The estimation of the number of narcotic addicts in an urban area. *Med. Ann. D.C.* 42:323-326.

Fishman, J.J., Conwell, D.P., and Amsel, Z. 1971. New York City narcotics register: A brief history. *Int. J. Addict* 6:561-569.

Glenn, W.A., and Richards, L.G. 1974. *Recent Surveys of Nonmedical Drug Use: A Compendium of Abstracts.* National Institute on Drug Abuse, Rockville, Md.

Goodstadt, M. (ed.). 1974. *Research on Methods and Programs of Drug Education.* Toronto: Addiction Research Foundation of Ontario.

Haberman, P.W., Josephson, E., Zanes, A., and Elinson, J. 1972. High school drug behavior: A methodological report on pilot studies. In S. Einstein and S. Allen (eds.), *Proc. First International Conf. on Student Drug Survey.* Farmingdale, N.Y.: Baywood Publishing Co.

Halleck, S. 1971. The great drug education hoax. *Addictions* 18:1-13.

Hunt, L.G. 1973. *Heroin Epidemics: A Quantitative Study of Current Empirical Data.* Washington, D.C.: The Drug Abuse Council, Inc.

Hunt, L.G. 1974. Recent spread of heroin use in the United States. *Am. J. Public Health* 64:16-23 (Supplement).

Hunt, G.H., and Odoroff, M.E. 1969. Follow-up study of narcotic drug addicts after hospitalization. In: H.C. Schulberg, A. Sheldon, and R. Baker (eds.), New York: Behavioral Publications, pp. 393-415.

Johnston, L.D. 1974. Drug use during and after high school: Results of a national longitudinal study. *Am. J. Public Health* 64:29-37 (Supplement).

Kavaler, F., Denson, P.M., and Krug, D.C. 1968. The narcotics register project: Early development. *Brit. J. Addict.* 63:75-81.

Kandel, D. 1973. Adolescent marihuana use: Role of parents and peers. *Science* 181:1067-1070.

Lavenhar, M.A. 1973. The drug abuse numbers game. *Am. J. Public Health* 63:807-809.

Petzel, T.P., Johnson, J.E., and McKillip, J. 1973. Response bias in drug surveys. *J. Consult Clin. Psychol.* 40:437-439.

Porter, M.R., Vieira, T.A., Kaplan, G.J., Heesch, J.R., and Colyar, A.B. 1973. Drug use in Anchorage, Alaska. *JAMA* 223:657-664.

Putnam, D.G., McCaslin, F.C., Stewart, A., Senn, R.M., Bent, R.J., and Kiesler, D.J. 1973. A model for program evaluation and development. *Proc. 5th Nat'l Conf. on Methadone Treatment* 1:1285-1288.

Smart, R.G., and Jackson, D. 1969. *A Preliminary Report on the Attitudes and Behavior of Toronto Students in Relation to Drugs.* Toronto: Addiction Research Foundation.

Smart, R.G. 1971. Illicit drug use in Canada: A review of current epidemiology with clues for prevention. *Int. J. Addict.* 6:383-405.

Smart, R.G., Fejer, D., and White, W.J. 1973. Trends in drug use among metropolitan Toronto high school students: 1968-1972. *Addictions* 20:62-72.

Smart, R.G., and Fejer, D. 1974. *Drug Education: Current Issues, Future Directions.* Toronto: Addiction Research Foundation of Ontario.

Smith, D.E., Linda, L., Loomis, S., Jacobs-White, L., Bricker, B., and Singleton, J. 1973. A community-based drug abuse rehabilitation program in the Haight-Ashbury. *Prev. Med.* 2:529-542.

Snowden, L., Wolf, K., and Panyard, C. 1973. Issues in developing useful screening indicators from variables which discriminate between successful and unsuccessful methadone treatment patient. *Proc. 5th Nat'l Conf. on Methadone Treatment* 1:169-172.

Swisher, J.D. 1974. The effectiveness of drug education: Conclusions based on experimental evaluations. In M. Goodstadt (ed.), *Research on Methods and Programs of Drug Education*. Toronto: Addiction Research Foundation of Ontario, pp. 147-160.

U.S. National Commission on Marihuana and Drug Abuse. 1973. *Drug Use in America: Problem in Perspective*, 2nd Report. Washington: U.S. Govt. Printing Office.

Whitehead, P.C., and Smart, R.G. 1972. Validity and reliability of self-reported drug use. *Can. J. Criminol. and Corrections* 14:1-7.

The Methodology of the National Youth Polydrug Study (NYPS)

Yoav Santo

In this book, the National Youth Polydrug Study (NYPS) serves as a common data base, one which is examined from several vantage points by various authors reporting about drug-abuse problems among youths admitted for treatment. Thus it is important to clarify how this data base was created; what its goals, limitations, and sampling procedures were; and how the data was collected, processed, and analyzed.

The Goals of the NYPS

At the inception of this project in mid-1976, the National Institute on Drug Abuse (NIDA) did not have a uniform data instrument for youths entering treatment for drug abuse. The existing national data bases–CODAP, DARP, and DAWN[1] –were not geared to examine issues and topics of specific relevance for youths. For example, the use of phencyclidine (PCP), which had become widespread among young people, is only partially reported in the DAWN system and is not mentioned in any of the other national data banks. A new data base was therefore planned, to be used in conjunction and in comparison with the present national data files; it would provide, it was hoped, more pertinent and comprehensive information concerning the problems of youths in treatment for drug abuse.

In order to provide a significant new source of information concerning youths in treatment, three goals were set for the data base. First, it should be a national study of youths in treatment for drug abuse. By *national,* the intent was to include youths from the various geographic regions of the continental United States as well as from urban, suburban, small town, and rural community population settings within these regions. Second, the study would sample from the different treatment modalities wherein youths are treated and served. Third, the sample would include adequate representation of the major racial and ethnic categories in each region. It should be noted that the study sampling method did not attempt to achieve either a strictly randomized sample of all youths in treatment or a stratified sample in which clients were admitted into the study in proportion to preset stratifying criteria. Hence, the sample cannot be regarded as representative of all youths in treatment for drug abuse, but only as a rough approximation of this population.

Sampling Procedures

There were three sampling stages in the NYPS data-collection process: (1) delineation of the population; (2) recruitment of drug treatment programs into the sample; and (3) administration of the client information form (CIF), a standardized intake interview schedule to clients in the recruited programs. The criteria for inclusion as an interviewee in the NYPS were that the client had to be between the ages of 12 and 18 (inclusive) at admission to treatment, have a history of drug abuse, and have been admitted to the treatment program within the 3-month period preceding the interview. All subjects were interviewed during the 6-month period from September 1976 to March 1977, except for a special group of 140 Native American clients who were interviewed in early 1976 and were included in the sample in order to achieve an adequate representation of minority youth. Since participation was voluntary, an additional criterion was the client's consent to be interviewed as a research subject. However, the participating programs reported no difficulty in obtaining the clients' consent. The time required to complete the interview ranged from 40 to 90 minutes.

Delineation of the Study Population

The continental United States was divided into the following seven regions for sampling and data-collection purposes: Region 1, the Northeast; Region 2, the Southeast; Region 3, the Great Lakes; Region 4, the Midwest; Region 5, the Southwest; Region 6, the West Coast; and Region 7, the Northwest. From the U.S. Census report for 1975, we computed the proportion of the total number of United States residents within each region. Next, using the National Directory of Drug Abuse Treatment programs, we estimated the proportion of the total number of drug treatment programs located within each region. Third, taking the admission records of CODAP for 1975, we computed the proportion of all clients 12 to 18.99 years of age admitted to CODAP. This yielded the overall description of the population to be sampled (see figure 6-1). The Northeast region includes 29 percent of the entire population; the highest proportion of drug treatment programs, 40 percent; and 37.2 percent of all youth admissions to CODAP during 1975. The Southeast and the Great Lakes regions have a similar population size (19 percent of the general population) and a similar proportion of drug treatment programs (about 14 percent each). However, the Southeast region includes 23.5 percent of all youth CODAP admissions as compared with only 9.9 percent of youth admissions from the Great Lakes region. This suggests that youths from the Great Lakes region were underrepresented in the 1975 CODAP admissions, compared to their proportion in the general population.

Youth admissions to CODAP in 1975 were approximately 27,000 clients;

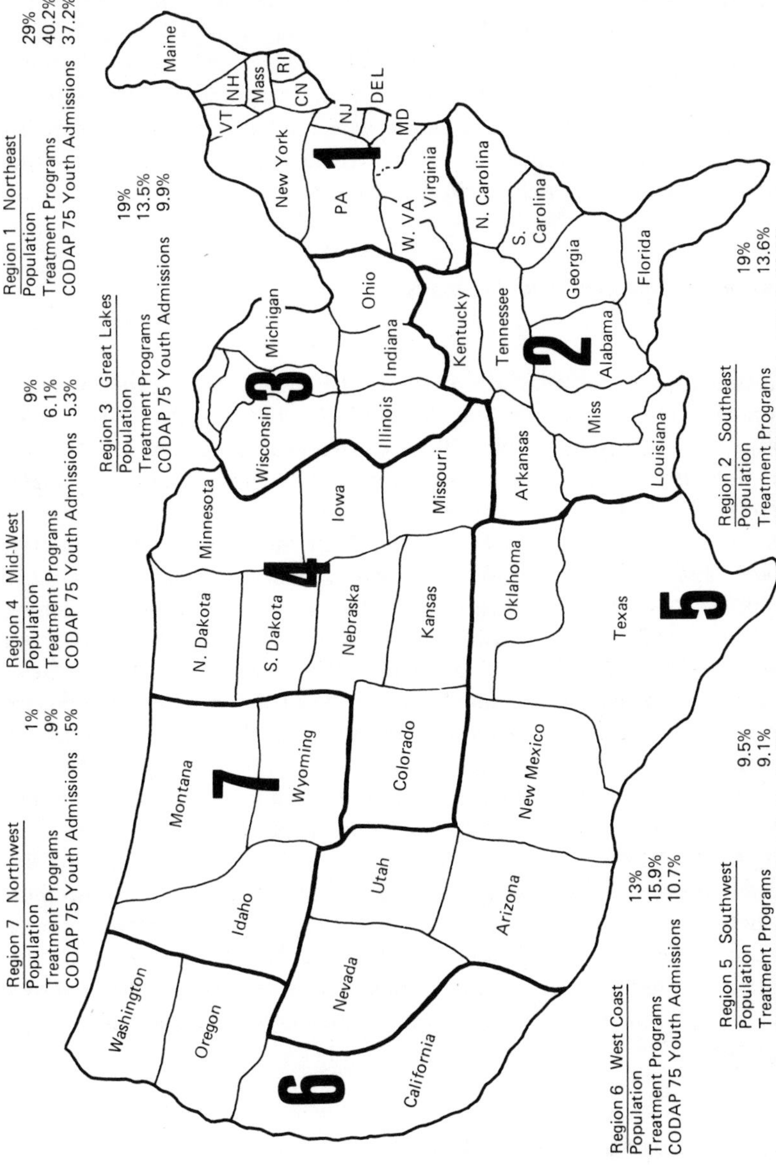
Region 1 Northeast
Population 29%
Treatment Programs 40.2%
CODAP 75 Youth Admissions 37.2%
Region 2 Southeast
Population 19%
Treatment Programs 13.6%
CODAP 75 Youth Admissions 23.5%
Region 3 Great Lakes
Population 19%
Treatment Programs 13.5%
CODAP 75 Youth Admissions 9.9%
Region 4 Mid-West
Population 9%
Treatment Programs 6.1%
CODAP 75 Youth Admissions 5.3%
Region 5 Southwest
Population 9.5%
Treatment Programs 9.1%
CODAP 75 Youth Admissions 12.9%
Region 6 West Coast
Population 13%
Treatment Programs 15.9%
CODAP 75 Youth Admissions 10.7%
Region 7 Northwest
Population 1%
Treatment Programs .9%
CODAP 75 Youth Admissions .5%
Maine
VT
NH
Mass
RI
CN
NJ
DEL
MD
New York
PA
W. VA
Virginia
N. Carolina
S. Carolina
Georgia
Florida
Ohio
Michigan
Indiana
Kentucky
Tennessee
Alabama
Miss
Illinois
Wisconsin
Louisiana
Arkansas
Missouri
Iowa
Minnesota
Oklahoma
Texas
Kansas
Nebraska
S. Dakota
N. Dakota
New Mexico
Colorado
Wyoming
Montana
Utah
Arizona
Idaho
Nevada
Washington
Oregon
California
1
2
3
4
5
6
7

Figure 6-1. The Description of the Population from Which the NYPS Sample Was Drawn.

and we planned our sample to be approximately one-tenth the size of the CODAP 1975 youth admissions. The total number of the NYPS was 2,750, but in several regions the proportion of CODAP admissions varied significantly from the proportion of the general population or from the proportion of treatment facilities in those states. In such instances, we admitted clients into the NYPS sample more nearly in proportion to the general population than in direct proportion to the number of clients in the CODAP system.

Recruitment of Drug Treatment Programs into the Sample

Drug treatment programs were recruited into the sample through the following three sources: (1) selection from the *NIDA Directory of Drug Abuse Treatment Programs* (the directory lists over 4,500 drug treatment programs, of which we estimated about 500[2] treated youths); (2) referral by single state agencies; and (3) referral by the NIDA project officers.

The drug treatment programs were contacted either by telephone, by letter, or by both, and the purpose of the study was explained. Programs with at least ten youth clients who were willing to participate in NYPS were sent a training client information form (CIF), a CIF manual instructing prospective interviewers how to complete the CIF, and a simulated tape-recorded CIF interview. Prospective interviewers were required to complete a CIF based on the responses given in the simulated taped interview. Thus, for example, if the interviewee in the simulated CIF interview said he was 17 years and 11 months old at the time of admission, the prospective interviewer was required to enter this information in its proper location on the training CIF. Completed training interviews were returned to the NYPS staff, who tallied the errors and gave feedback to the prospective interviewers regarding correct CIF administration. This procedure yielded both a standardized method of training the prospective interviewers and a means of estimating the reliability of the interviewers' processing of the information provided by the clients. (Training effectiveness will be reviewed later, based on data from 149 prospective interviewers who completed the training CIFs.)

Representativeness of the Programs Sampled: A Comparison of Drug Treatment Programs Participating in the NYPS and Those Declining Participation

In all, 97 drug programs completed this training procedure and contributed data on 2,750 newly admitted youth clients. A comparison of the drug programs participating in the sample with those which declined participation will provide information on whether there is any systemic bias in the selection of programs into the NYPS sample.

Contacts with all drug treatment programs solicited for participation in the NYPS included a brief review of the programs' characteristics. Nearly 500 such contacts were made, from which we obtained program characteristics on the 97 programs contributing data to the NYPS (participating programs) and on the 225 drug programs that declined to participate (nonparticipating). Each contacted program was requested to estimate the percentage distribution of clients along seven program characteristics. These responses were then averaged for the participating programs and for the nonparticipating programs (see table 6-1). The participating programs resembled the nonparticipating ones in the clients' distribution by sex, race, socioeconomic status, and treatment environment. The distribution of programs in urban, suburban, small town, and rural settings was also similar for participating and nonparticipating programs. The organizational context of the treatment programs (being a self-contained unit, a unit of a larger agency, or an agency subsuming smaller units) was not statistically different for participating and nonparticipating programs. The size of the treatment program was the only variable on which the participating and nonparticipating programs differed: participating programs tended to have a greater number of youth clients in treatment than nonparticipating programs. This was partially a self-imposed administrative bias, since programs treating less than ten youth clients were not selected for the sample.

Training of Interviewers and Reliability of Interview Data

The survey instrument, the CIF interview schedule, identified the items about which information was sought, but it did not provide the exact wording for each question. For example, the question "What is your age?" was not provided, but was indicated on the form as "age," the variable for which an answer was requested. It was left to the interviewer to formulate his or her own wording in presenting the question. The exact meaning of each item was presented in the interviewing manual. In addition, a standardized training process was developed in the effort to achieve uniform interviewing procedures and standardized interpretation of the meanings of items. This process was divided into two stages. The first included the self-learning by the prospective interviewer of the administration of the CIF through the use of the manual and the simulated tape-recorded interview. The second stage was composed of the evaluation of the effectiveness of the first stage and the provision for corrective feedback. An evaluation of the effectiveness of self-learning stage followed. We did not measure the effectiveness of the entire training process, but we estimated that the degree

Table 6-1
Characteristics of Programs Participating in the NYPS and Programs Not Included in the Sample

	Mean Percentages for Participating Programs (n = 97)	*Mean Percentages for Nonparticipating Programs (n = 225)*
1. Treatment Environment		
Outpatient	$\bar{X}$ = .69	$\bar{X}$ = .76
Daycare	$\bar{X}$ = .10	$\bar{X}$ = .03
Residential	$\bar{X}$ = .21	$\bar{X}$ = .21
2. Sex Distribution of Clients		
Male	$\bar{X}$ = .61	$\bar{X}$ = .63
Female	$\bar{X}$ = .39	$\bar{X}$ = .37
3. Race Distribution of Clients		
White	$\bar{X}$ = .70	$\bar{X}$ = .79
Black	$\bar{X}$ = .14	$\bar{X}$ = .12
Other	$\bar{X}$ = .16	$\bar{X}$ = .09
4. Socioeconomic Status of Clients		
Poor	$\bar{X}$ = .09	$\bar{X}$ = .11
Lower class	$\bar{X}$ = .48	$\bar{X}$ = .40
Middle class	$\bar{X}$ = .42	$\bar{X}$ = .48
Upper middle class	$\bar{X}$ = .01	$\bar{X}$ = .01
5. Program Setting		
Urban	$\bar{X}$ = .47	$\bar{X}$ = .42
Suburban	$\bar{X}$ = .25	$\bar{X}$ = .16
Rural	$\bar{X}$ = .09	$\bar{X}$ = .16
Small town	$\bar{X}$ = .15	$\bar{X}$ = .24
Other mixed	$\bar{X}$ = .04	$\bar{X}$ = .02
6. Organizational Context		
Subsumes smaller units	$\bar{X}$ = .11	$\bar{X}$ = .07
Unit of larger agency	$\bar{X}$ = .41	$\bar{X}$ = .51
Self-contained unit	$\bar{X}$ = .48	$\bar{X}$ = .42
7. Number of youth Clients on October 1, 1976		
10	$\bar{X}$ = .12	$\bar{X}$ = .29
11-20	$\bar{X}$ = .18	$\bar{X}$ = .26
21-40	$\bar{X}$ = .21	$\bar{X}$ = .14
41-60	$\bar{X}$ = .15	$\bar{X}$ = .08
61-100	$\bar{X}$ = .12	$\bar{X}$ = .13
>100	$\bar{X}$ = .22	$\bar{X}$ = .10

of uniformity achieved was higher than that achieved by the self-learning process alone.

Errors in the administration of the CIF were generally of two types: errors of omission, in which items were left unanswered, and errors of commission, in which responses were not consistent with the training instructions. The distribution of these two types of errors in demographic variables among the 149 training client information forms (CIF) submitted by prospective interviewers from participating programs is provided in table 6-2. Errors of omission occurred in more items, but at a low frequency, while errors of commission occurred in fewer items but with a higher frequency. Omissions averaged under 2 percent for the 513 distinct variables in the training CIF. Errors of commission occurred mainly in connection with multicomponent items involving write-in responses. When errors of commission were reviewed for the entire CIF, they were found to be averaging under 10 percent for write-in items and about 15 percent for a limited number of multicomponent items.

In summary, the interviewer training procedure provided a method for training interviewers, as well as a tool for assessing the accuracy and the reliability of the data recorded by the interviewers (based on the information which they received from the client subjects). The evaluation of the self-learning phase for prospective interviewers showed that, overall, the CIF was well understood and the interviewing guidelines yielded over 90 percent item uniformity. Several items were found to be more error prone, and they required additional attention before the actual interviewing was authorized.

It is not often that the reliability of an instrument is tested through a study of the training process of as many as 146 interviewers. On the whole, the reliability of the interviewers' input into the data was considered adequate for the statistical needs of the study. There was very little control, however, over the degree of accuracy of the reporting of information by the clients to the interviewers.

Data Processing

Completed CIF's were first screened by the NYPS staff for eligibility and for completion of key demographic information. In cases where demographic items were omitted, the interviewer was required to complete that information. The

Table 6-2
Prevalence of Errors in Training CIFs within Demographic Variables

	Number of Errors of Omission	*Number of Errors of Commission*	*Total n = 146*	*% of Total*
Age in Years	–	2	2	1.3
Age in Months	2	–	2	1.3
Sex	2	–	2	1.3
Race	4	1	5	3.4
Education	1	–	1	.7

coding of the CIF's entailed the entry of numerical codes for the few write-in questions and verification of each entry to be key-punched. Coding was in place—i.e., coders did not correct any CIF's, even in cases where there were apparent internal inconsistencies within the CIF. Coders used a uniform coding manual with specific coding instructions for each of the CIF items. Each coded CIF passed a final review to confirm that it was ready to be keypunched.

Keypunching was in a fixed-format key-to-tape process. Once the data were entered onto a magnetic tape, the error detection and correction procedure was initiated. There were two types of error detected: the identification of out-of-range or illegitimate entries and the identification of internal inconsistency within the CIF's. All out-of-range errors were reviewed and corrections were made whenever the original CIF provided the correct information. In cases where no determination was possible as to the correct response, information was coded as "missing data." In all, there were about 600 out-of-range corrections, or 0.04 percent error correction, considering that there were 513 items of information for each of the 2,750 questionnaires.

In addition to the detection and correction of out-of-range items, we examined the degree of internal consistency between items within a CIF. A pilot sample of fifty randomly selected CIF's was reviewed to identify the most frequent internal inconsistencies. Those inconsistencies were then examined for the entire sample by a computer program. Examples of internal inconsistencies were the indication of drug use on item 13 of the questionnaire and the omission of the same drug use in item 14, or an indication that the client's living arrangement prior to admission was inconsistent with his later responses describing present family status.

In reviewing the scope of internal inconsistency for the total sample, we found it was marginal and did not require any corrective action, such as case-by-case deletion of items found to be inconsistent.

Description of the Sample

The geographic distribution of the 97 drug treatment participating programs by region and state is given in table 6-3. Based on the location of the drug treatment programs, we ascertained which were in urban, suburban, or rural/small-town areas. Over 67 percent of the clients were receiving treatment in facilities located in areas classified as urban; 16.3 percent as suburban; and 16.4 percent as rural/small town.

Treatment Settings

The treatment programs were selected so that the various treatment environments and modalities characterizing drug-abuse treatment programs for youths

Table 6-3
Geographic Distribution of the 97 Drug Treatments Programs, by Region and State

Region	*States in which Programs Participated*	*Number of Participating Programs*
Northeast	Conn., Md., Mass., N.H., N.J., N.Y., Pa., Va., Vt.	26
Southeast	Ala., Ark., Fla., Ga., La., N.C., Tenn.	16
Great Lakes	Ill., Ind., Mich., Ohio, Wisc.	18
Midwest	Iowa, Kansas, Minn., Mo., N.D.	11
Southwest	Ariz., Nev., N.M., Okla., Texas, Utah	11
West Coast	Calif., Oregon, Wash.	12
Northwest	Idaho, Mont.	3
Totals	37 states	97 programs

be represented. The treatment environments included were inpatient (hospital), residential, daycare, and outpatient. The treatment modalities included detoxification with and without medication, counseling/psychotherapy, therapeutic communities, halfway houses, crisis centers, and methadone maintenance. The largest client group, comprising 63 percent of the total sample, was the outpatient group, which was being treated by the counseling and psychotherapy modality. The next largest category was the residential therapeutic community treatment group, which accounted for 12 percent of the subjects.

The Subjects

The demographic characteristics of clients in the NYPS are given in table 6-4.

Age. The mean age of the subjects was 16.4 years (S.D. = 1.7). Thirty-six percent of the sample was under 16; 65 percent were under seventeen; and 88 percent were under 18 years old.

Sex. Sixty-one percent of the subjects were male; 39 percent were female.

Race. The majority of the subjects were white, representing 70 percent of the sample. Fourteen percent were black, 7 percent Hispanic, and 5 percent Native American. Orientals and others accounted for the remaining 4 percent.

Education. The mean number of years of schooling completed by the subjects of the study was 9.1 (S.D. = 1.4), which is below the standard or norm that would be expected for a group with a mean age of 16.4. The calculation of the

Table 6-4
Demographic Characteristics of the NYPS Sample (n = 2,750)

		% of Subjects
Age Distribution	12.00-14.99	16
	15.00-15.99	20
	16.00-16.99	29
	17.00-17.99	23
	18.00-18.99	12
Mean Age	16.4 (S.D. = 1.7)	–
Sex	Males	61
	Females	39
Race	White	70
	Black	14
	Other	16
Education (Last Year of School Completed)	Less than 8	13
	8-9.99	47
	10-11.99	36
	12-13.99	4
Mean Years of School Completed	9.1 (S.D. = 1.4)	–
Marital Status	Single	98
	Married	1
	Separated or divorced	1
Religion	Protestant	34
	Catholic	34
	Jewish	2
	Other	2
	None/no response	28
Living Arrangements	At home	77
	With other relatives	5
	Group and foster homes	5
	Friends	3
	Alone	2
	Other	8

relationship between age and school grade attainment revealed that 54 percent of the total sample were retarded by at least one grade or were behind the expected appropriate grade level for their age. The percent of clients who were behind in their grade increased as age increased, with 73 percent of clients over 18 years of age having completed less than 12 years of school. There is a clear association between applying for treatment for drug abuse and being retarded in school attainment.

Twenty clients (0.7 percent) had, in the past, discontinued their education during grade school, 149 clients (5.4 percent) had, at one time, discontinued during junior high school, and 546 clients (19.8 percent) had discontinued, at least once, during high school. There were 1,984 clients (72.1 percent) who were currently enrolled in an educational program and 763 clients (27.7 percent) who could be considered school dropouts.

Marital Status. Ninety-eight percent of the subjects had never been married. Thirty-two (1 percent) were married; 22 (1 percent) were separated or divorced; and a single subject was widowed.

Religion. Of 2,636 subjects whose responses to this item were recorded, 34 percent identified themselves as Protestants, 34 percent as Catholics, and 2 percent as Jewish. Twenty-three percent stated that they identified with no religion. Other religious identifications, including American Indian and Islamic religions, were cited by 2 percent of the respondents; 5 percent declined to answer.

Parents' Religion. In general, the clients reported greater proportions of their parents to have religious affiliations than themselves. For example, the clients reported 37 percent of their fathers to be Protestant and 42.3 percent of their mothers to be Protestant compared with only 33.8 percent of themselves. Similarly, the clients reported 34.9 percent of their fathers to be Catholic and 38.8 percent of their mothers to be Catholic compared with 33.7 percent of themselves. The reverse was found for those who reported no religious affiliation. While there were 22.9 percent clients who reported no religious affiliation for themselves, only 16.5 percent reported their fathers to be without any religious affiliation. With regard to the client's evaluation of the importance of religion in his or her family, approximately one-quarter of the clients reported religion to have no importance in their families; nearly 30 percent indicated either minor or moderate importance; and 15.7 percent indicated great importance.

Living Arrangements. With regard to living arrangements at the time of entry into treatment, a large majority of respondents (77 percent) had been living at home with their parents. Another 5 percent had been living with other relatives, 3 percent in group homes, 3 percent with friends, 2 percent in foster homes, 2 percent had been living alone, and 8 percent in a variety of other settings.

Demographic Characteristics of Youth Clients in Four National Data Bases

Presently there are several large-scale national data bases which report about youths in treatment for drug abuse. This section will compare the demographic characteristics of youths in NYPS, CODAP, DAWN, and DARP. It should be noted that while CODAP and DAWN are mainly information systems designed for managerial purposes, DARP is primarily a research-oriented data base and in this respect resembles NYPS. The reader should also be alerted to the fact that the demographic data to be reported from CODAP refer to 1975, the data from DAWN refer to 1975-1976, the data from DARP to the period 1969-1973, and the data from the NYPS to the period of late 1976 and early 1977. When combined, these data bases reported on over 65,000 youths in treatment for drug abuse. The distribution of clients in these four national data bases by sex, race, and age is given in table 6-5. The total in each category is not always the value of *n* given, because of missing values.

A similar proportion of males was noted in NYPS and CODAP, 61.2 percent and 59.6 percent males, respectively. The proportion of males in DARP was higher than the proportion of males in NYPS and CODAP, 66 percent, while

Table 6-5
Comparison of NYPS, CODAP, DARP, and DAWN Data Bases on Sex, Race, and Age of Youth Clients

Characteristics	*NYPS (n = 2,750) 1976-1977*	*CODAP (n = 27,178) 1975*	*DARP (n = 6,259) 1969-1973*	*DAWN*[b] *(n = 30,858) 1975-1976*
Number of Clients:				
Sex				
Male	1,672	16,153	4,130	13,263
Female	1,061	10,942	2,129	17,575
Race				
White	1,852	19,060	3,762	21,650
Black	387	4,951	1,643	4,680
Other[a]	511	3,395	854	c
Age				
15	998	10,266	1,235	11,098
16-17	1,406	16,829	1,979	15,158
18	345	Not included	3,045	Not included
Percentage of Clients:				
Sex				
Male	61.2	59.6	66.0	43.0
Female	38.8	40.4	34.0	57.0
Race				
White	67.3	69.5	60.1	82.3
Black	14.1	18.1	26.3	17.7
Other	18.6	12.4	13.6	c
Age				
15	36.3	37.9	19.7	42.3
16-17	51.1	62.1	31.6	57.7
18	12.6	–	48.7	–

[a]Within all four data bases, the other category is mostly comprised of Hispanics.

[b]Emergency room and crisis center patients only (MEs excluded).

[c]Race percentages for DAWN are not calculated because the number in other racial category is not available.

DAWN had a much lower percentage of males (only 43 percent). It is noteworthy that DAWN is the only national data base showing females to be the majority of clients. The proponderance of women in DAWN may be related to the fact that women traditionally are reported to be more involved in the health care system, with more frequent contact with physicians and more frequent purchasing of prescriptions, especially tranquilizers. Many of these prescribed drugs are also the substances reported in DAWN as related to emergency room visits. Thus the population in DAWN probably represents, not the typical substance abuser who is being treated in traditional drug treatment programs, but rather the substance user who has accidently or willfully become involved in an overdose or in a drug-related emergency.

The comparison of the race distribution across the four data bases shows that the proportion of whites was similar in NYPS and CODAP, with 67.3 percent and 69.5 percent, respectively, and somewhat lower in DARP, which included 60.1 percent whites. The proportion of whites was the highest in DAWN, 82.3 percent. A distribution of other minority groups in the four data bases shows some marked differences. NYPS represents the lowest percentage of blacks compared with CODAP and DARP–14.1 percent blacks in NYPS compared with 18.1 percent and 26.3 percent in CODAP and DARP, respectively. This is probably the most significant characteristics in which NYPS differs from the other data bases, namely, it's lower percentage of blacks. To some degree this low proportion of blacks is explained by the high percentage of other minority groups, for example, Hispanic. NYPS contained 18.6 percent of "other" racial groups compared with 12.4 percent in CODAP and 13.6 percent in DARP. In DAWN, all racial groups other than whites were collapsed and represented 17.7 percent. In summary, the highest degree of similarity among the four national data bases is between NYPS and CODAP youth subsamples.

Additional Characteristics of NYPS Clients

Parents' Marital Status. The majority of clients (56.1 percent) reported their parents to be married; and 13.6 percent reported their parents to be separated, with the mean age of the clients when separation occurred of 8.9 years. Divorce of parents was reported by 28.8 percent of the clients, with the mean age of clients at the time of divorce at 7.8 years. The mortality rate of fathers was approximately twice as high as that of mothers, 8.1 percent versus 4.1 percent. Mean age of the clients when parental death occurred was 9.7 years. Remarriage of parents occurred at the rate of 10.8 percent for fathers and 13.5 percent for the mothers. Fathers remarried on the average when the clients were approximately 11 years old.

Occupational Status of Heads of Households. Households of clients were headed by the father in 49.3 percent of the cases, by the mother in 32.9 percent of the cases, and by a stepfather or a foster father in 7.1 percent of the cases. Fifty-seven clients, or 2.1 percent of the sample, reported themselves as being the head of the household. The occupational category of the heads of households is provided in the following breakdown: higher executive or major professional, 3.6 percent; business manager of large concerns, 7.7 percent; administrative personnel and small business owners, 9.8 percent; clerical, sales, and technical occupations, 12.5 percent; skilled manual employees, 12.8 percent; machine operators, 12.8 percent; unskilled employees, 13.5 percent; housewife, 8.1 percent; and 9.5 percent of the sample reported the head of the household to have no occupation. The remaining 9.7 percent of the sample did not respond to this item.

Socioeconomic Status. The socioeconomic status (SES) measure employed here was based on a formula especially developed for this study. It included the educational level of both parents rather than only that of the head of the household, as in the Hollingshead-Redlich formula, and it also included consideration of the subject's income and whether or not the family was on welfare. In addition, it included the occupational level of the head of the household. The distribution of one of the components of this measure, parents' education, for example, was as follows: father's highest grade completed: 16.6 percent completed or terminated at grades 1 through 8; 25.3 percent completed or terminated at grades 9 through 11; 37.8 percent completed high school; and 20.3 percent has some education beyond high school; for mothers: 13.3 percent completed or terminated at grades 1 through 8; 26.7 percent at grades 9 through 11; 43.6 percent completed high school; and 16.4 percent were reported as having some education beyond high school. The SES index developed here ranged in value from 2 (found among three clients) to a maximum of 86 (for one client). The mode was 48, and the mean was 42.4 (S.D. = 14.8).

Source of Clients' Financial Support. Clients were asked to check one to three sources of their financial and material support on a checklist that included seven types of sources of support. "Family" constituted 46.8 percent of all mentions of source of support and was followed by these other sources in rank order: "client's own earnings," 24.3 percent; welfare, 9.2 percent; illegal activities, 8.9 percent; and "friends," 6.6 percent. Within the illegal activities category, the drug-related illegal activities outnumbered other types of illegal activities in a ratio of almost 2 to 1.

Employment Status. At admission to treatment, 7.7 percent of this youthful sample reported that they were employed full time (at least 30 hours per week), 21.3 percent indicated part-time employment, and 71 percent were not employed.

Family Members' Problems. Information was obtained on whether other members of the client's immediate family had problems with drugs or alcohol, mental health problems, or problems with the law (arrests and convictions). Parental alcohol problem was the most frequent family member problem reported, with 454 of the clients (16.5 percent) reporting a father with an alcohol problem and 215 of the clients (8.0 percent) reporting mothers with the same problem. The next most frequent type of problem among parents was related to the mental health of the mothers (reported by 162 clients) and of the fathers (reported by 54 clients). Siblings of clients, as compared with parents, were characterized by a relatively higher proportion of drug problems than alcohol problems. There were 113 clients reporting older brothers as having a drug problem, 70 who reported their older brothers as having an alcohol problem, and 59 who reported older brothers with both an alcohol and a drug problem. Seventy-seven clients indicated that their elder sister(s) did have a drug problem, 34 an alcohol problem, and 26 both an alcohol and a drug problem. In regard to younger siblings, 42 younger brothers were reported with a drug problem, 15 with an alcohol problem, and 13 with both a drug and an alcohol problem. Thirty-two younger sisters were reported with a drug problem, and only 10 with an alcohol problem. Twenty-six percent (26.0 percent) of fathers, as compared with 19.9 percent of mothers, were reported with at least one of the types of problems listed.

While 52 percent of the young male drug-abuse clients indicated that none of their family members had any problems, a significantly lower percentage (42 percent) of females reported no problems for other family members. The mean number of family members with any problems as reported by the female clients is 1.1 (S.D. = 1.2), and only 0.8 (S.D. = 1.1) for males (t value = 6.4, $p \leqslant .01$). Stated differently, approximately equal percentages of male and female clients (28 percent each) reported one family member with a problem(s), but 30.7 percent of female clients reported two or more family members with problem(s) as compared with only 19.8 percent of male clients who reported the same.

As table 6-6 indicates, female clients report proportionately more of their parents with problem(s) then do male clients. It is interesting, as a side issue, to view this data in terms of the concept of identification with the parent of the

Table 6-6
Comparison between Male and Female Clients on Reported Parental Mental Health, Substance, and Legal Problems, by Sex of Parent

	Male Clients (% Reporting)	*Female Clients (% Reporting)*
Fathers with any problem(s)	23.1	30.5
Mothers with any problem(s)	15.8	26.3

same sex. While this rule is not clearly supported in our data, since more fathers than mothers had problems for female clients as well as for male clients, there is nevertheless a trend in the data to support this hypothesis: for male clients 7.3 percent more fathers than mothers had problems, while for female clients only 4.2 percent more fathers than mothers had problems. A similar finding was made at our center in a study on psychopathology, comparing parents of young male schizophrenics and parents of young female schizophrenics (Friedman and Friedman 1979).

Legal Status. Fifty-five percent of the entire sample reported having arrests for some type of offense. Twenty-eight percent of the clients reported arrests in only one offense category, and 27.3 percent reported arrests in two or more offense categories. The following is a rank ordering of percentages of the sample reporting one or more arrests in each of the eleven offense categories: for private property offenses, 12.8 percent; for alcohol use, 11.6 percent; for public property offenses, 11.6 percent; for violent victim offenses, 7 percent; for nonviolent victim offenses, 6.7 percent; for weapons offenses, 5.1 percent; and for drug sales, 3.9 percent. Less than 1 percent of the sample reported arrests for prostitution/procurement and for illicit alcohol sales. Approximately 9 percent of the sample reported arrests for other nonspecified types of offenses.

Overdosing, Suicide Attempts, and Previous Treatment History. Of the sample, 22.7 percent reported one or more drug overdoses, and 15.9 percent reported one or more suicide attempts. With regard to treatment history, 35.2 percent of the sample reported some type of previous treatment episode, either drug or alcohol treatment, drug- or alcohol-related hospitalizations, or mental health treatment episodes or hospitalization; 20.4 percent reported that they had had previous mental health treatment episodes; and 16.1 percent reported previous drug or alcohol treatment episodes.

Clients' Reasons for Contacting and Entering Treatment Programs. The abuse of drugs and alcohol was the single most frequent reason mentioned for contacting or entering the drug-abuse treatment programs, with 53.2 percent of the clients indicating it to be the reason for contact or entry. Following in order of their frequency of mentions were (1) family-related problems, reported by 48.5 percent clients; (2) school-related problems, reported by 39.5 percent clients; (3) legal problems (involvement in the criminal justice system), reported by 35.3 percent clients; and (4) emotional or psychiatric problems (need for counseling, etc.), reported by 27.7 percent clients. A closer examination of the more specific reasons indicates, for example, that among those reporting a substance-abuse problem, drug problems were reported by 45.5 percent of the cases, while alcohol problems were reported by 21.9 percent, and both types of abuse problems were reported by 14.1 percent. A breakdown of family-related problems indicates that conflict with the parents was reported by 37.8 percent clients, while family crisis and runaway were reported by 25.2 percent and 17.8 percent of the clients, respectively. A breakdown of legal problems indicate that the majority of them (20.0 percent of the total sample) were due to arrests, and 10 percent were due to court referrals to treatment. Need for counseling ("had no one to be counseled or advised by") was reported for 14.5 percent of the clients, and a similar need ("no one to talk to") was reported by 14.3 percent of the clients. Emotional disturbance was reported by 9.5 percent of the cases.

Primary Source of Referral. For the 2,296 cases in which the primary source of referral is indicated, the following list is a rank ordering of the primary sources: families, 14.9 percent; peers, 14.9 percent; parole officer, 14.8 percent; self, 14.5 percent; school, 9.9 percent; judge, 8.4 percent; social service agency, 8.4 percent; police, 4.7 percent; and drug or alcohol treatment program, 3.0 percent. The remaining 6.5 percent of cases reported a variety of other primary referral sources, including psychiatric hospital and neighbor.

So far, we have described some characteristics of the youths admitted to treatment for drug abuse without addressing their drug use patterns. What drugs were used by the NYPS clients, at what frequency, together with what other drugs, will be reported and examined in the following chapter.

Notes

1. CODAP: Client Oriented Data Acquisition Process; DARP: drug abuse Reporting Program; DAWN: Drug Abuse Warning Network.
2. This estimate is based on the inquiries that we directed to programs listed in the directory.

References

Friedman, A.S., and Friedman, C.J. 1979. Psychopathology of parents of male and female schizophrenics. *Archives of Gen. Psychiat.* (*in press*).

National Directory of Drug Abuse Treatment Programs. U.S. Department of Health, Education and Welfare, Public Health Service, Alcohol, Drug Abuse and Mental Health Administration, NIDA, 11400 Rockville Pike, Rockville, Maryland 20852, 1976.

U.S. Bureau of the Census. *Statistical Abstract of the United States.* U.S. Department of Commerce, Washington, D.C., 1975.

Part III
Issues and Aspects

7 Multiple Drug-Abuse Patterns of Youths in Treatment

Edward C. Farley,
Yoav Santo, and
David W. Speck

Introduction

During the past decade, while public attention was focused on heroin addiction, another drug problem, multiple substance use among youth populations in the United States, has been increasing and spreading (Carroll et al. 1977; Kaufman 1977). Previously confined to specific geographic areas and within special populations, multiple drug use among young people is now a common phenomenon in all sections of the country, from Native American reservations to urban ghettos. Adolescents in this society, both male and female, are experimenting with a variety of different substances unlike any other youth population in our history. The long list of illicit substances being used includes many nonnarcotic but potentially harmful drugs and substances as well as opiate substances including heroin.

Heroin is widely recognized as a serious national and international problem, with severe health and social consequences and a high cost to society. The word *heroin* evokes fear in individuals and communities. The media devote attention to drug concerns and events that are dramatic or sensational. However, the public does not seem to be aware of, or perceive the dangers associated with, multiple substance use. *Multiple substance use* in this chapter is defined as the use of a variety of substances (drugs) either concurrently or sequentially. The multiple-substance-use phenomenon is not easily recognized or understood because it is so complex. It involves the use of a number of substances by different types of individuals and groups in many different ways. The social cost of this phenomenon is neither obvious nor immediately apparent, particularly within youth populations.

Marihuana use began appearing in secondary schools in the sixties during a period of social crisis in this country. Since then, drug use has become so pervasive in our secondary schools that in some communities the schools are viewed as sanctuaries for drug users. School officials are often reluctant to acknowledge the extent to which drug use exists in their schools because of the harm that a reputation for having a drug problem can have on a school system.

Phencyclidine hydrochloride (PCP) is a prime example of a drug that has been rather widely used by young people in combination with or alternately with other illicit drugs over a period of nine years (1969 to 1977) without coming to the attention of the public—and without receiving adequate attention from those working on drug abuse problems. PCP finally received considerable publicity in the early part of 1978 as a result of the serious physical and mental effects reported by clinics, hospital emergency rooms, and patients themselves. Although this drug had been used by youngsters since the late sixties, it took a series of serious and dramatic incidents (deaths and accidents) to bring it to the attention of the public.

The abuse of more than one substance by youths is not a new phenomenon. Freedman and Brotman (1969) and Smith et al. (1970) commented on the trend in the late 1960s. Despite such early recognition of the problem, there is a paucity of information available on either the nature of the problem or the extent of multiple drug use among youths. Unfortunately, most national surveys report only on the prevalence of use in single drug categories and do not provide data on concurrent, sequential, or lifetime use by individuals.

A recent national youth survey (Johnston et al. 1977) produced some startling findings regarding prevalence, trends, and changing attitudes toward drug use. It was learned that six of every ten high school seniors (61.6 percent) had used illicit drugs at some time in their lives. During the year preceding the survey, 48 percent of these students reported they had used marihuana, 23 percent had used stimulants, 18 percent had used tranquilizers, 17 percent had used sedatives, 14 percent had used hallucinogens, and 11 percent reported using inhalants and cocaine. These prevalence rates indicate that high school seniors who used illicit drugs used an average of two different types of illicit drugs. While it is likely that a substantial percentage of these youngsters used only marihuana, there is undoubtedly a significant percentage of high school seniors who had used three or more different drugs.

It was also found that the percentage of the seniors who had used illicit drugs increased steadily over a three-year period, from 55 percent in 1975 to 62 percent in 1977. In surveying attitudes toward drugs, Johnston et al. (1977) found that only one in three (36 percent) of the students felt that regular use of marihuana "entailed great risk or harm." In addition, 88 percent stated that it was "very easy" or "fairly easy" to obtain marihuana.

Lipton et al. (1977) concluded from a survey of more than 1.5 million students in New York public high schools during 1974-1975 that "multiple substance use is not predominant among marihuana users, but is predominant among users of other substances." Single et al. (1974) found that 35 percent of the 8,206 high school students sampled in a New York survey reported illicit drug use. A majority of the drug users in this sample had used more than one type of drug. In fact, 19 percent had used three or more different substances during their lifetime. A study by Gould et al. (1977) of a random sample of

1,094 high school students found that the mean number of different drugs these students have ever used was 2.6, and that 1.4 drugs were currently being used.

The phenomenon of multiple substance abuse has been more thoroughly studied and documented among adults than it has been among youth. For example, Chambers and Moldestad (1970) reported that the proportion of opiate abusers who also abused sedative hypnotic drugs had increased from 8 percent of the admissions at the federal narcotics treatment program in Lexington, Kentucky in 1944 to 54 percent in 1966. Curtis and Simpson (1976) reported that for 11,380 clients admitted to drug treatment programs between 1969 and 1971, 29 percent had drug abuse patterns involving heroin with various combinations of cocaine, barbiturates, and marihuana, and 16 percent had patterns of polydrug abuse involving the use of three or more nonopiate drugs. Thus at least 45 percent of this treatment sample had used more than one type of illicit drug during their lifetime and could be characterized as being multiple drug abusers. In addition, of the 197,406 clients admitted to federally supported drug treatment centers in 1977, approximately 87 percent were adults. Forty-three percent reported having a problem with only one substance; 27 percent indicated having a problem with two types of drugs, and 30 percent reported having a problem with three or more drugs (NIDA Statistical Series 1977).

Studies of multiple drug abuse have frequently been designed to either confirm or refute the "stepping stone" hypothesis which holds that the use of soft drugs such as marihuana will progressively lead to the use of hard drugs such as heroin. One study presenting evidence for such progression of drug use among young people was conducted by Kandel (1975). Using longitudinal data, she concluded that there is a path of progressive drug use which generally begins with beer drinking, continues with cigarette smoking and the drinking of hard liquor, and then to the use of illicit drugs.

Findings: Extent of Multiple Drug Use

The major focus of this chapter is to report on the nature and extent of multiple drug abuse among young people in drug treatment programs. The differences in multiple drug abuse patterns between sex and racial groups are also examined.

An indicator of the extent of multiple drug abuse among youth admitted to federally funded drug treatment programs can be found in our analysis of the youth subsample in the Client Oriented Data Acquisition Process (CODAP). CODAP data is routinely provided by all federally funded drug treatment programs. Only a quarter of CODAP youth (18 years old and under) who were admitted to federally supported drug treatment programs during 1976-1977 reported having a problem with only one drug. Another third of the admissions indicated problems with two drugs, and about 44 percent reported having problems with at least three drugs. Data on 14,104 admissions show that, on the average, the CODAP youth clients reported use of 1.9 drugs at the time of admission to treatment.

The National Youth Polydrug Study (NYPS) is a recent national survey of youth 12 to 19 years of age admitted to treatment for drug abuse during the period of September 1976 to March 1977. The NYPS sample included 2,750 subjects with an average age of 16.4 years; the sample was drawn from admissions to 97 drug treatment programs specifically designed to serve young people. A detailed review of the research methodology employed in this survey and the demographic characteristics of the sample is provided in chapter 6.

Before reporting on the number of drugs used by NYPS clients, a note of explanation is in order regarding the 15 substance categories or drug types used in the survey instrument. To capture more clearly and completely the overall extent of multiple drug abuse among young drug clients, we listed marihuana and hashish as separate categories. PCP was already known to be a significant drug problem in its own right. The other opiates category included drugs such as Dilaudid and Demorol. The other sedatives category included non-barbiturate sedatives, hypnotics, and tranquilizers such as Valium and Librium. The over-the-counter category included many cough preparations. By providing the respondents with more opportunities to report their overall drug involvement, we were able to elicit more information about their multiple drug abuse patterns. Incidentally, the decision to report PCP separately had the fortuitous effect of providing the first (1977) systematic data available on the prevalence of use at a time when there was concern about the possibility of a spread of PCP use among young people of epidemic proportions.

Table 7-1 reports on the extent of multiple substance abuse occurring among the youths in the NYPS sample. Three different aspects of multiple substance abuse are measured and reported. The first, and most inclusive, reports on the number of psychoactive substances that each subject used at least once in his/her lifetime. The second, current use, is based on the number of drugs used during the three month period before admission. The last measure, regular lifetime use, refers only to those substances used with an average frequency of at least once per week over a period of at least one month. On the average, five different substance types were reported as ever being used by a client on a lifetime basis, while slightly more than three different substances were being used currently; almost four different substances had been used on a regular basis sometime during their young drug-using lives. Only 9 percent of the sample reported lifetime use of only one type of drug. (One percent of the clients who were participating in a prevention program reported no lifetime drug abuse experiences.) Only 19 percent of the sample reported current use of only one drug, or no current drug use. Lifetime regular abuse of less than two types of substances accounted for only 16 percent of the sample. These data suggest that multiple substance use is the predominant mode of drug use among young

Table 7-1
Multiple-Substance Abuse within the NYPS Sample (n = 2,750)

Number of Substances Used	*Any Lifetime Use*		*Any Current Use*[a]		*Regular Lifetime Use*[b]	
	n	*Col. %*	*n*	*Col. %*	*n*	*Col. %*
None	20	(1)	148	(5)	121	(4)
1	241	(9)	391	(14)	331	(12)
2	449	(16)	641	(23)	598	(22)
3	410	(15)	454	(17)	474	(17)
4	293	(11)	301	(11)	320	(12)
5	241	(9)	264	(10)	242	(9)
6	226	(8)	190	(7)	188	(7)
7	178	(6)	141	(5)	162	(6)
8	176	(6)	87	(3)	134	(5)
9	136	(5)	66	(2)	68	(2)
10	155	(6)	40	(2)	60	(2)
11	126	(5)	19	(1)	34	(1)
12 or more	99	(4)	8	(0)	18	(1)
Col. Totals	2,750	(100)	2,750	(100)	2,750	(100)
Mean Number of Substances:	5.1		3.5		3.8	
S.D.	3.2		2.5		2.6	

[a]During the 3-month period preceding admission to treatment.
[b]At least weekly for at least a 1-month period.

people in treatment. The average number of types of substances used varies from three to five, depending on the indicator used.

In addition to the number of drugs used, it is also of interest to know which drugs are associated with different drug use patterns. Table 7-2 presents this information for weekly or regular users only. Marihuana and alcohol are the two most regularly used substances (86 and 80 percent respectively). Regular users of either one of these two substances tend to use fewer additional substances than do the regular users of other types of drugs. Nevertheless, regular marihuana and alcohol users have also used, on the average, slightly more than three *other* substances on a regular basis.

The regular users of other opiates, over-the-counter drugs (principally cough syrup), cocaine, and illegal methadone report the highest extent of multiple substance abuse. On the average, the narcotic-abusing group used six other substances on a regular basis. Regular users of amphetamines, heroin, hashish, barbiturates, tranquilizers, hallucinogens and PCP, on the average, report having used approximately five other substances regularly.

Table 7-3 presents data pertaining to users who have ever used any of thirteen drugs and who have also used each of the other substances. Illegal

Table 7-2
Number of Additional Drugs Regularly Used by the Regular Users of Each Drug Category

Of Those Who Reported Regularly Using	*Number of Clients*	*% of the Sample*	*Have on the Average, also Regularly Used the Following Number of Other Drugs*
Marihuana	2,363	86	3.2
Alcohol	2,196	80	3.4
Inhalants	525	19	4.5
Other Drugs	28	1	4.7
Amphetamines	890	32	5.3
Heroin	215	8	5.4
Hashish	754	27	5.5
Barbiturates	811	29	5.5
Nonbarbiturate Sedatives (Tranquilizers)	581	21	5.8
Hallucinogens	656	24	5.8
PCP (Phencyclidine)	611	22	5.8
Cocaine	263	10	6.0
Over-the-Counter Drugs	136	5	6.2
Illegal Methadone	49	2	6.2
Other Opiates	397	14	6.3

Note: Regular use is defined as weekly or greater use for a period of at least 1 month.

methadone and other opiates are listed first because on the average the greatest proportions of these two groups had used all of the other substances. The other drugs are listed in rank order according to the extent to which the users of each of these drugs were involved in multiple drug abuse. It can be seen in table 7-3 that in addition to the almost certain use of marihuana and alcohol, at least three out of four of the users of illegal methadone have also used other opiates, cocaine, hallucinogens, hashish, and barbiturates. Further, tranquilizers, heroin, and PCP have been used by over half the users of illegal methadone. The drug profile for lifetime users of other opiates (that is, Dilaudid, Demerol, etc.) also indicates the extent of multiple drug use among "hard" drug users.

It is commonly believed, and in consonance with the stepping stone theory to assume that a heroin addict first tried many other drugs before settling on heroin. Indeed we found that involvement in heroin indicated a rather extensive multiple drug use history. However, users of illegal methadone, other opiates, cocaine, and tranquilizers all experienced, on the average, more extensive multiple drug use than did heroin users. Although the overall amount of multiple drug use is similar, there are marked differences between the drug profiles of those who have used heroin and the drug profiles of the nonnarcotic multiple drug abusers. By and large, users of nonnarcotic substances (PCP, hallucinogens, hashish, amphetamines, barbiturates, and sedatives) are substantially less likely to have used illegal methadone, other opiates, and cocaine when compared with users of heroin. On the other hand, users of heroin are substantially less likely to have used PCP, hashish, amphetamines, inhalants, marihuana, and alcohol. PCP and hallucinogen users have virtually identical lifetime drug use profiles. PCP users are somewhat more likely to have reported use of hashish, which like PCP, is a fairly potent psychoactive substance and can be smoked. PCP was found to have been used at least once by 32 percent of the total sample. This high prevalence rate found for PCP use by multiple drug users appears to have been the first nationwide data available on PCP prevalence and was somewhat of a surprise (Friedman et al. 1978).

Information was also obtained on the drugs that were most frequently used in combination with one another. The most prevalent currently used three-drug combinations were alcohol-marihuana-hashish, followed by alcohol-marihuana-amphetamines, and alcohol-marihuana-inhalants.

Illicit Drug Availability

How prevalent a drug is within a population and how frequently it is being used are assumed to bear some relationship to that population's ease of obtaining the drug and its availability in the community. This is one aspect of the time honored relationship of supply to demand. Figure 7-1 portrays the percentage of males and females who felt that it was easy to obtain the various illicit substances which they used.

As expected, marihuana is reported to be by far the most easily available illicit substance. Hashish (a cannabis derivative) and cocaine appear to be the two most difficult substances for youngsters to obtain. Only 22 percent of males who have ever used cocaine report that it is easy to obtain, compared with 86 percent for marihuana. The high price of cocaine must obviously be a factor in this difference. For nine of the eleven types of drugs, a higher proportion of females than males report that obtaining the drugs is easy. Part of the explanation for this may be found in the fact that a higher proportion of females than males report that they obtain these substances as gifts from friends.

Perhaps the most important finding from this data is that, for most drugs, the majority of users reported such little difficulty in obtaining the drug they use. It may be worthy of special note that a majority of users of heroin report little difficulty in obtaining that drug. Hashish was reported to be more difficult to obtain than illegal methadone, heroin, other opiates, PCP, sedatives, or hallucinogens, although it had actually been used by a greater number of the clients than the other substances.

The comparison of males and females on prevalence rates for each of the type of drug shows that proportionally, more males than females reported lifetime use of heroin, hallucinogens, hashish, and cocaine; and proportionally

Table 7-3
Percentage of Lifetime Users of Each of the Thirteen Drugs Who Used Each of the Other Drugs

Ranked by Overall Extent of Multiple Abuse	*Percent of Sample Lifetime Use*	*Number of Lifetime Users*	*Illegal Methadone*	*Other Opiates*	*Cocaine*	*Nonbarbiturate Sedatives (Tranquilizers)*	*Heroin*	*PCP (Phen-cyclidine)*
1 Illegal Methadone	4	107	–	78	80	65	63	64
2 Other Opiates	25	678	12	–	56	61	29	61
3 Cocaine	26	710	12	54	–	53	29	58
4 Nonbarbiturate sedatives	29	792	9	52	47	–	22	61
5 Heroin	12	343	20	57	61	50	–	51
6 PCP	32	875	8	47	47	56	20	–
7 Hallucinogens	40	1,098	8	46	49	51	21	57
8 Hashish	42	1,165	7	47	46	49	18	59
9 Barbiturates	40	1,096	8	44	46	50	21	54
10 Amphetamines	45	1,237	6	44	43	50	18	53
11 Inhalants	29	795	6	41	39	44	15	46
12 Marihuana	90	2,485	4	27	28	31	13	35
13 Alcohol	89	2,448	4	28	28	31	13	35

Ranked by Overall Extent Of Multiple Abuse	*Hallucinogens*	*Hashish*	*Barbiturates*	*Amphetamines*	*Inhalants*	*Marihuana*	*Alcohol*	
1 Illegal Methadone	78	80	79	74	46	100	100	1
2 Other Opiates	74	80	71	81	47	98	97	2
3 Cocaine	75	76	71	77	43	98	95	3
4 Nonbarbiturate Sedatives	71	73	69	79	44	98	96	4
5 Heroin	69	61	68	65	34	93	90	5
6 PCP	72	78	67	75	42	99	97	6

7 Hallucinogens	–	72	68	76	41	98	96	7
8 Hashish	68	–	62	73	41	99	97	8
9 Barbiturates	68	66	–	74	40	98	95	9
10 Amphetamines	68	69	65	–	39	98	96	10
11 Inhalants	57	61	56	61	–	92	92	11
12 Marihuana	43	47	43	49	30	–	91	12
13 Alcohol	43	46	43	49	30	92	–	12

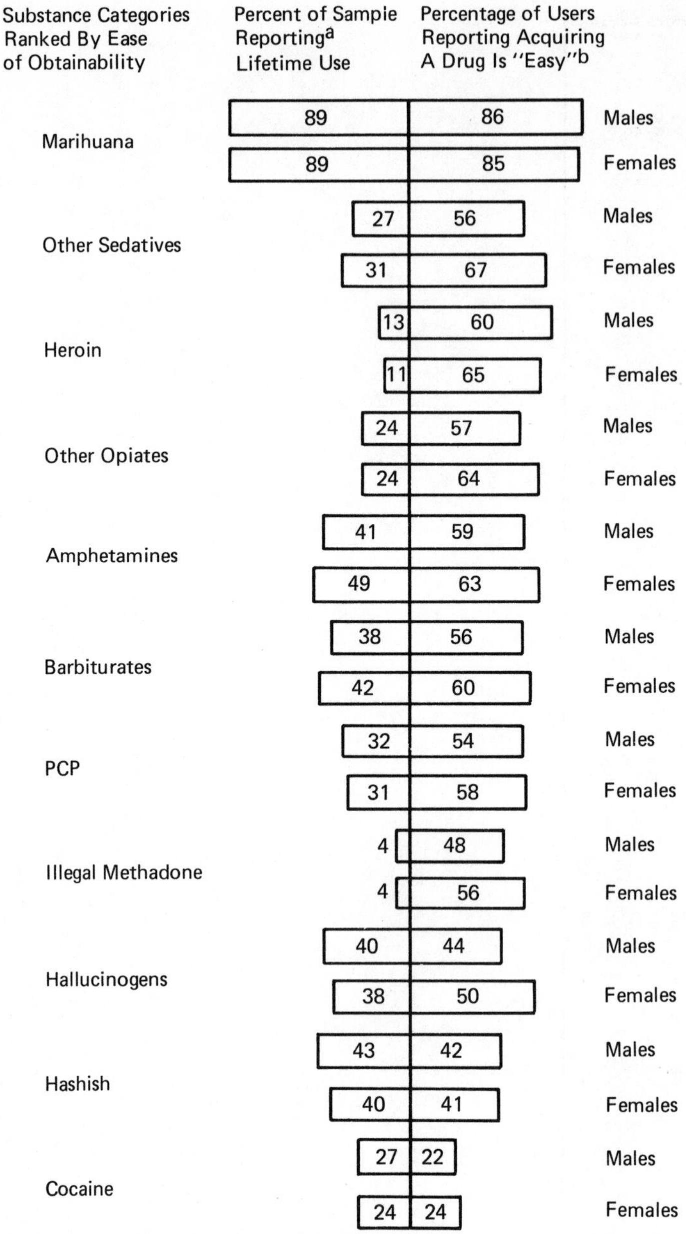

Substance Categories Ranked By Ease of Obtainability		Percent of Sample Reporting[a] Lifetime Use	Percentage of Users Reporting Acquiring A Drug Is "Easy"[b]
Marihuana	Males	89	86
	Females	89	85
Other Sedatives	Males	27	56
	Females	31	67
Heroin	Males	13	60
	Females	11	65
Other Opiates	Males	24	57
	Females	24	64
Amphetamines	Males	41	59
	Females	49	63
Barbiturates	Males	38	56
	Females	42	60
PCP	Males	32	54
	Females	31	58
Illegal Methadone	Males	4	48
	Females	4	56
Hallucinogens	Males	40	44
	Females	38	50
Hashish	Males	43	42
	Females	40	41
Cocaine	Males	27	22
	Females	24	24

[a]There are 1,672 males and 1,061 females in the sample.

[b]Response choices were: "Easy," "Available."

Figure 7-1. Comparison of Lifetime Use and Ease of Drug Obtainability for Male and Female Drug Users.

more females than males reported lifetime use of amphetamines, barbiturates and sedatives (tranquilizers). These findings and their implications are discussed in more detail in chapter 8, which is devoted to sex differences in adolescent drug abuse.

Johnston (1977) found even higher perceived illicit drug availability rates in his national survey of high school seniors. In the class of 1977, for instance, over 98 percent of recent marihuana users (within the past year) indicated that marihuana was "fairly easy" or "very easy" for them to obtain. The next substances rated most easily available among recent users were amphetamines (84.7 percent) and tranquilizers (84.4 percent). Of all the substances rated, heroin was reported to be the least available substance, yet slightly over half of the 27 seniors who reported using it within the past year indicated that it was at least fairly easy for them to obtain. These findings would be less startling if the surveys had been conducted only in Northeast or West Coast urban areas where illicit drugs are expected to be more readily available. However, these are national surveys and the findings suggest a common perception among young people throughout the United States that illicit drugs are indeed widely available.

Race and Drug Use

This section will present a comparison of drug use prevalence rates among three major race/ethnic groups (white, black, and Hispanic). The Hispanic group includes Puerto Ricans, Cubans, Mexican Americans, and those of other Hispanic origins. The total NYPS sample was 67 percent white, 14 percent black, and 11 percent Hispanic. The remaining 8 percent included Native Americans and Asians who will not be included in this comparison because of their small numbers. The white sample was 60 percent male and 40 percent female; blacks were 65 percent male and 35 percent female; and Hispanics were 74 percent male and 26 percent female. Thus there were proportionately more males within the minority samples than in the white majority sample. The mean age was 16.4 for the whites, 16.6 for the blacks, and 16.2 for the Hispanics. Statistically, the Hispanic group is significantly younger than both the white and the black groups. The difference in mean ages between the blacks and the whites was not statistically significant. The differences in drug use prevalence and frequency rates between the three race/ethnic groups are not likely attributable to the difference between the groups in regard to sex or age.

Table 7-4 presents the drug use prevalence and frequency rates for these race/ethnic groups. A higher proportion of the whites were found to have ever used each of twelve of the fourteen different types of drugs, and were also found to have used ten of these types of drugs on a more regular basis. Heroin and inhalants were the two exceptions, with a higher proportion of both minority

Table 7-4
Drug Use by Race

Substances Ranked by Prevalence of White Group	*Lifetime Prevalence — % Ever Use*			*Current Drug Use (Within 3 Months of Entry into Treatment) — % at Least Once a Month Use*			*Current Drug Use — % Weekly or More Use ("Regular" Use)*		
	White	*Black*	*Hispanic*	*White*	*Black*	*Hispanic*	*White*	*Black*	*Hispanic*
Marihuana	94	82	90	84	71	77	78	64	69
Alcohol	90	83	70	80	69	62	64	53	45
Amphetamines	58	16	20	30	8	10	18	7	4
Hashish	55	13	18	28	6	9	14	3	4
Hallucinogens	51	12	23	19	4	5	8	2	2
Barbiturates	49	22	21	26	10	15	16	9	9
Phencyclidine	42	8	9	23	3	5	14	1	2
Nonbarbiturate Sedatives (tranquilizers)	37	14	11	20	8	7	13	6	3
Other Opiates	31	10	10	12	4	4	7	3	2
Inhalants	30	16	31	7	11	17	4	11	14
Cocaine	29	19	24	9	8	10	5	6	4
Heroin	12	14	15	4	9	8	4	6	6
Over-the-Counter Drugs	11	5	2	3	2	1	1	0	1
Illegal Methadone	5	3	1	1	2	0	1	1	0

Note: All percents are calculated from the following *n*'s: whites = 1,850, blacks = 386, and Hispanics = 301.

groups reporting use of these drugs. It is clear that, overall, the white group in this national adolescent treatment sample has experimented with a greater variety of drugs and has also tended to use most of the drugs more frequently.

The comparison of the two minority groups with each other shows that proportionately more blacks (83 percent) than Hispanics (70 percent) had used alcohol, and proportionately more Hispanics (90 percent) than blacks (82 percent) had used marihuana. Other drugs in which the proportion of Hispanics exceeded the proportion of blacks in lifetime use to a substantial degree were amphetamines, hashish, hallucinogens, inhalants, and cocaine. A slightly higher proportion of blacks than Hispanics reported ever having used nonbarbiturate sedatives, illegal methadone, and over-the-counter preparations. Nearly equal percentages of blacks and Hispanics reported ever having used heroin. In regard to the overall lifetime pattern of drug use, the Hispanic use pattern resembled the white group pattern more so than did the black use pattern.

There is some evidence available which indicates that among youths who are not in treatment whites have a higher prevalence of illicit drug use than black or Hispanic youths. A recent national household survey of drug use (Abelson et al. 1977) reports that among white youths and among middle- to upper-middle-class youths, the use of some substances is somewhat more likely to be found than among their nonwhite counterparts. For instance, they found that white youths were twice as likely to have lifetime involvement with tranquilizers, and three times more likely than nonwhite youths to have used amphetamines. White youths were also reported to have more drinking and smoking experiences in the month prior to the survey. A survey of a nationwide stratified random sample of low-income youth in the Job Corps (Myers 1977) found that 65 percent of the white youths (17 years or younger) reported some lifetime use of at least one type of illicit drug (not including alcohol), compared with 54 percent of the black youths and 49 percent of the Chicano youths. Obviously, this particular finding cannot be explained by the readier access the white youths have to treatment resources, nor can it be assumed that this particular sample of white youths had more money with which to buy drugs.

In the NYPS sample, 67 percent of the clients were white, and in the CODAP youth subsample, 72 percent were white (Friedman (ed.) 1977). However, the Bureau of the Census reports that for 1976, whites composed 76 percent of the nation's 14 to 17 years olds (U.S. Bureau of the Census 1978). Thus minority youths enroll in government funded treatment programs in numbers greater than their proportion of the general population, but their degree of multiple nonnarcotic polydrug abuse is not as severe as it is for white youths in treatment. Some possible explanations for this over representation of minorities in publicly supported drug treatment programs include (1) the effect of special recruitment and outreach programs for minorities; (2) the fact that minority youths are more likely to be arrested and convicted on drug-related charges and mandated into treatment by court, probation, and parole authorities; and (3) the fact that minority youths are not as likely to have the money to pay for lawyers or to pay for private treatment services.

Table 7-4 also displays the prevalence of current regular use of each of the fifteen drug types. Current regular use in this study was defined as an average frequency of use of at least once per week during the three-month period preceding admission to treatment. Here it can be seen that there are conspicuous differences in the patterns of drug use between the white and minority samples. The percentage of whites surpassed the percentage of blacks to a substantial degree in current regular use of alcohol, marihuana, amphetamines, barbiturates, hashish, PCP, other sedatives, hallucinogens, and other opiates. Conversely, blacks and Hispanics were considerably more likely than whites to be current regular users of heroin, inhalants, and cocaine. The finding that proportionately more blacks (5.7 percent) than whites (3.5 percent) were using heroin on a regular basis is consistent with the findings of earlier drug addiction literature and suggests that heroin abuse is still a relatively greater youth drug abuse problem in the urban black community. The fact that 83.3 percent of the black subjects who reported ever using heroin also reported regular use, while the corresponding percentage for whites was only 53.5 percent, supports the idea that black youths tend to be more likely for whatever reasons to get addicted to, or seriously involved with heroin.

Several previous surveys of high school students showed that youthful drug users were more typically from higher socioeconomic classes than non drug users (Blum et al. 1969; Hager 1970; Gosset et al. 1971). In order to determine what effect socioeconomic status has on drug use rates, an analysis of covariance comparing the prevalence rates of three race/ethnic groups was conducted. The results showed, as expected, that the white group had significantly higher socioeconomic status (SES) scores than did either of the minority groups and that the white youths in treatment were still using significantly more drugs on a regular basis after taking into account differences in SES. Overall, 3.9 drugs were used regularly when all three race/ethnic groups were combined. Whites, however, even when the effect of SES was taken into account, reported using an average of 4.3 drugs regularly. Blacks and Hispanics both had significantly lower average regular drug use rates of 2.6 and 2.9, respectively.

The fact that a higher proportion of blacks (11.1 percent) were using inhalants on a regular basis than whites (4.2 percent) is also consistent with the lower socioeconomic status of blacks in the sample. A high prevalence rate of inhalant use has historically been related to lower SES minority groups. Inhalants are inexpensive and readily available to youths who do not possess the financial resources to obtain other drugs. The highest rate of current inhalant use within the entire sample was found among the Hispanic group, 13.6 percent of whom reported at least weekly use in the three months preceding admission to treatment. This finding does not appear to be unique to the NYPS sample. An analysis of the 1975 CODAP youth subsample data (clients between the ages of

12 and 17) showed that nearly 41 percent of all clients with inhalants listed as the primary drug problem were Hispanic, although Hispanics represented only 10 percent of all CODAP youth treatment admissions in 1975.

In summary, it appears clear that for this youth in treatment sample white youths were found to be more heavily involved in multiple drug use. The user's perception of ease of obtainability for each type of drug was examined separately for each race/ethnic group. We found that proportionately more minority drug users (blacks and Hispanics) reported that heroin, cocaine, and barbiturates were available or easy to obtain. On the other hand, proportionately more white treatment clients indicated that illegal methadone, other opiates, PCP, and hallucinogens were easy for them to obtain.

Initiation of Drug Use

Table 7-5 presents data on the average age of first drug use for each drug category. These data suggest that there is a sequential drug use onset pattern that started, on the average, at 12.2 years of age with alcohol and at 12.9 years of age with marihuana. On the average, clients began using inhalants and hashish when they were 13 years of age while use of other substances generally began when the clients were 14 years of age (except for illegal methadone, which was started at a mean age of 15.1). The majority of the clients in this survey started their drug careers before they reached 13 years of age (Santo 1978).

For the most part, the age of first regular or continuing use of a substance is reported to follow closely after its initial use. In this sample inhalants were

Table 7-5
Average Age of First Use and First Regular Use for Each Drug

	Age of First Use			*Age of First Regular Use*		
	$\bar{X}$	*S.D.*	*n*	$\bar{X}$	*S.D.*	*n*
Alcohol	12.2	2.6	2,449	13.8	1.8	2,117
Marihuana	12.9	1.9	2,486	13.6	1.7	2,330
Inhalants	13.2	2.0	795	13.1	2.2	495
Hashish	13.9	1.7	1,165	14.2	1.6	699
Amphetamines	14.1	1.5	1,237	14.5	1.7	848
Barbiturates	14.1	1.5	1,097	14.5	1.5	757
Nonbarbiturate Sedatives (Tranquilizers)	14.3	1.5	797	14.5	1.5	545
Other Opiates	14.4	1.7	678	14.7	1.7	346
PCP	14.6	1.4	875	14.8	1.4	579
Hallucinogens	14.8	1.4	1,098	14.6	1.6	632
Cocaine	14.8	2.4	710	15.2	1.6	336
Heroin	14.9	1.6	344	15.4	1.5	206
Illegal Methadone	15.1	1.6	108	15.7	1.5	47

found to have been used regularly at an earlier age than all other substances. Of the 795 clients who have used inhalants, only 62 percent of them continue to use them regularly. Curiously, the mean age of first use of inhalants was reported to be later than the mean age of first regular use; that is, the older first users of inhalants tend not to use inhalants regularly. Regular inhalant use appears to be a drug use pattern of choice only among very young drug users.

A Comparison of Drug Prevalences Between NYPS and Other National Data Bases of Youths in Treatment

In order to enable us to compare NYPS and CODAP prevalences of drug use more adequately, we first converted the CODAP data regarding primary, secondary, and tertiary drug problems into drug mentions. All CODAP cases that listed heroin as either a primary, secondary, or tertiary drug problem were summed, and this sum reflected the number of heroin mentions in the CODAP data base. This procedure was repeated for all drug categories in the CODAP system. Similarly, every instance of current use of all drug types reported by clients in the NYPS was also converted into mentions. By this method, a standard unit of measurement of drug use was obtained which could be utilized for both data bases. In addition to the use of the same unit of measurement to study drug prevalence, we also used the same period of admission to treatment, September 1976 to March 1977, for both data bases.

Figure 7-2 displays the most frequently abused substances being reported by youths as they enter our nation's drug treatment programs. The drug mentions for two national data bases, NYPS and CODAP, show comparable results. Marihuana, hashish, and alcohol are the most frequently mentioned substances in both data sources. Combined they account for over half the drug mentions in both NYPS (a 53.2 percent share) and CODAP (a 51.5 percent share).

Hallucinogens, amphetamines, and barbiturates, in that order, are the next most frequently mentioned substances within the NYPS sample. These same three substances are the next most prevalent group among CODAP youths, albeit in precisely the reverse order. Tranquilizers are ranked fifth in prevalence in both data systems. Inhalants are reported as mentions in 3.7 percent of both data bases. Heroin was among the substances least mentioned. CODAP youths reported 4 percent of the current drug mentions as heroin, compared with less than 2 percent in the NYPS sample. In a separate analysis of the 1976 Drug Abuse Warning Network (DAWN) youth drug mentions (Farley et al. 1977), we found that heroin accounted for only 2 percent of all DAWN drug mentions. These findings would indicate that among youths in treatment heroin is among the least popular substances. Most of these youngsters are in treatment not because of heroin abuse but because of problems associated with multiple drug abuse.

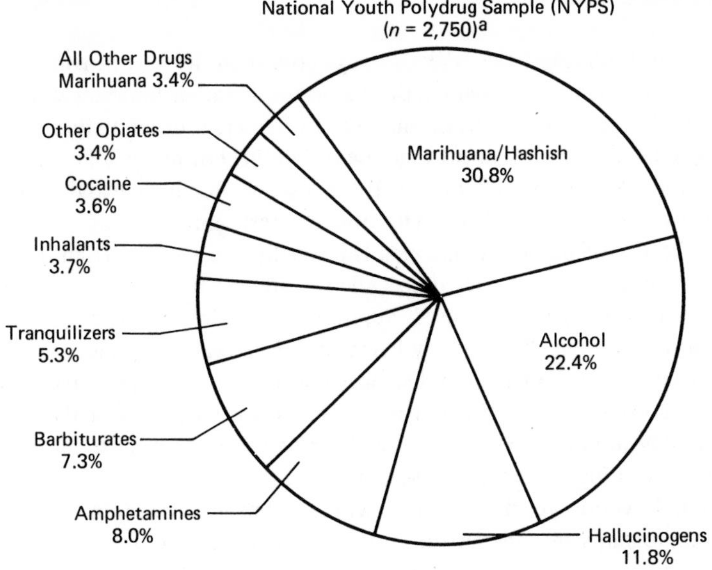

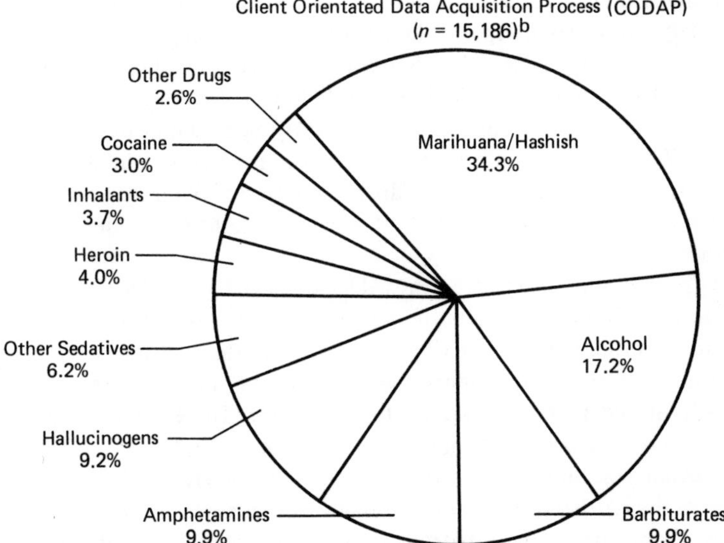

[a]Total mentions = 9,815, 1976-1977, under eighteen-year-old admissions.

[b]Total mentions = 30,698, October 1976 to March 1977, twelve- to eighteen-year-old non-prison admissions.

Figure 7-2. Comparison of Drug "Mentions" between Two National Samples of Youth in Drug Treatment Programs.

Summary and Conclusion

Based on the findings of the NYPS survey, youths in drug treatment programs across the country are best characterized as multiple rather than single substance abusers. Use of nonopiate drugs and types of opiates other than heroin was found to be much more prevalent than use of heroin. For nearly all of the clients the multiple abuse patterns included the use of marihuana and alcohol in addition to other drugs. Those with the severest multiple-drug involvement reported the use of illegal methadone. The startling conclusion from the data is that the average young drug abuse client (other than primary alcohol or marihuana users) regularly abused approximately five other drugs prior to coming into treatment. We are now living in a drug-oriented society in which a great variety of licit and illicit substances are readily available to most youths who are interested in using them. The youths in this study report that most of the drugs they use are easy to obtain, and young females appear to have an even easier time acquiring drugs than do young males.

Although white youths are somewhat underrepresented in public drug treatment programs in comparison to their numbers in the overall population, general drug abuse surveys as well as the NYPS's survey of youths in treatment find that the whites abuse more different types of drugs more frequently than their minority group counterparts. In regard to this finding in the high school surveys one could speculate that a disproportionate number of drug using minority youths drop out of school and are therefore underrepresented in these surveys. In the past social deprivation and poverty were implicated as causes of drug abuse. While this may still be somewhat true for heroin addiction, it does not appear to be true for the multiple drug use patterns found in the 1970s. It is clear that middle-class, suburban, and urban white youths represent a significant market for non-narcotic drugs.

Youngsters in our society are exposed to drugs and alcohol and their effects at an early age. The drug careers of the majority of adolescents in the NYPS survey started before they turned 13 years of age. Multiple substance use is not a problem that can be easily understood and treated, nor will the full consequences of multiple drug use be known for some time. There are many questions which need to be addressed and studied, for example:

Are certain multiple drug use patterns more likely to lead to future dependency than others? Is there a stepwise progression from one drug to another or from one drug-use pattern to another? What kinds of effects will various combinations of drugs have on youngsters in regard to their health, their social functioning, and their life adjustment? Will current multiple substance users become more dependent psychologically and/or physiologically on drugs later in their lives? How do various current combinations of drugs (taken simultaneously) affect a person's state of consciousness, perception, alertness, attentiveness, responsiveness, and ability to concentrate?

Up to this point in time, it has been relatively easy to classify and distinguish various drug use patterns. Public attention has been focused on the distinct patterns of drug use that have been publicized in the media. As a result, most people are now familiar with issues associated with the recreational use of marihuana, heroin addiction, and outbreaks of LSD and PCP use. However, multiple drug use in youthful populations is a relatively new phenomenon of previously unrecognized proportions. It will continue to increase in complexity and severity as different chemical compounds become available, as more youngsters become involved in using drugs, and as attitudes toward individual drugs and drug use in general change.

More important, it should be understood that we do not, as yet, know how to respond to this phenomenon. The problems associated with multiple drug use have not been adequately defined. We do not know why various combinations of drugs are consumed, how they are experienced psychologically and physically, nor the consequences of such use over time. We are, at this point, in no position to mount large education/prevention campaigns or to establish extensive treatment networks. We must first obtain a better understanding of multiple drug use—the nature, extent and patterns that have and will continue to occur.

Bibliography

Abelson, H.I., Fishburne, P.M., and Cisin, I. 1977. *National Survey on Drug Abuse 1977,* vol. 1; Main Findings. Rockville, Maryland, National Institute on Drug Abuse.

Blum, R.H., Aron, J., Tutko, T., Feinglass, S., and Fort, J. 1969. Drugs and high school students, In R.H. Blum and Associates (Eds.), *Students and Drugs,* Vol. 2. San Francisco: Josey-Bass.

Carroll, J.F.X., Malloy, T.E., Hannigan, P.C., Santo, Y. and Kenrick, F.N., 1977. The meaning and evolution of the term multiple substance abuse. *Contemporary Drug Problems* (Summer).

Chambers, C.D. and Moldestad, M. 1970. The evolution of concurrent opiate and sedatives addictions, In J.C. Ball and C.D. Chambers (Eds.), *The Epidemiology of Opiate Addiction in the United States,* Springfield, Ill.: Thomas.

Curtis, B., and Simpson, D.D. 1976. Demographic characteristics of groups classified by patterns of multiple drug abuse: A 1969-1971 sample. *International Journal of the Addictions* 11 (1):161-173.

Farley, E.C., Cohen, B.Z., Tirabassi, A., Friedman, A.S. and Shor, M.N. 1977. *DAWN IV: Statistical Report on Youth Sample.* Unpublished NIDA report. Philadelphia Psychiatric Center, Philadelphia, Pa.

Freedman, A.M., and Brotman, R.E. 1969. Multiple drug use among teenagers: Plans for action-research, J.R. Wittenborn et al (Eds.), in *Drugs and Youth.*

Proceedings of the Rutgers Symposium on Drug Abuse, Springfield, Ill.: Thomas.

Friedman, A.S., Farley, E.C., Santo, Y. and Speck, D. 1978. *Phencyclidine use among youths in drug abuse treatment.* NIDA Services Research Branch Newsletter, DHEW, U.S. Government Printing Office, Washington, D.C.

Friedman, A.S., (Ed.) 1977. *CODAP 1975: A Statistical Report on Youth Admitted to Treatment in Calendar Year 1975 from the Client Oriented Data Acquisition Process (CODAP) National Data File,* Unpublished NIDA report. Philadelphia Psychiatric Center, Philadelphia, Pa.

Gosset, J.T., Lewis, J.M., and Phillips, V.A. 1971. Extent and prevalence of illicit drug use as reported by 56,745 students. *JAMA* 216 (9):1464-1470.

Gould, L.C., Berberian, R.M. and Kasl, S.V. 1977. Sequential patterns of multiple-drug use among high school students. *Archives of General Psychiatry* 34 (2):216-222.

Hager, D.L. 1970. Adolescent Drug Use in Middle America: Social-Psychological Correlates. Unpublished Doctoral Dissertation, Michigan State University.

Johnston, L., Bachman, J.G., and O'Malley, P.M., 1971. Drug Use Among American High School Students 1975-1977. NIDA DHEW Publication No. (ADM) 78-619.

Kandel, D. 1975. Stages in adolescent involvement in drug use. *Science* 190 (November):912-914.

Kaufman, E. 1977. Polydrug abuse or multidrug misuse: It's here to stay. *British Journal of Addiction* 72 (4):339-347.

Lipton, D.S., Stephens, R.C., Babst, D.V., Dembo, R., Diamond, S.C., Spielman, C., Schmeidler, J., Berman, P.J. and Uppal G.S. 1977. A survey of substance use among junior and senior high school students in New York State, Winter 1974-75. *American Journal Drug Alcohol Abuse* 4 (2):153-164.

Myers, V. 1977. Drug use among minority youth. *Addictive Diseases* 3 (2):187-196.

National Institute on Drug Abuse Statistical Series, SMSA, 1977. Series E, Number 9, Rockville, Md.

Santo, Y. 1978. First drug use in relation to drug career among youth in treatment for drug abuse. Paper presented at the National Drug Abuse Conference, Seattle, Washington.

Single, E., Kandel, D., and Faust, R. 1974. Patterns of multiple drug use in high school. *Journal of Health Social Behavior* 15:344.

Smith, D.E., Gray, G.R., and Ramer, B.S. 1970. Adolescent heroin abuse in San Francisco. *Proceedings Third National Conference on Methadone Treatment,* NIMH, PHS Publication No. 2172.

U.S. Bureau of the Census, 1978. *Characteristics of American Children and Youth: 1976.* Current Population Reports, Series p-23, No. 66. Washington: U.S. Government Printing Office.

8 Female Adolescent Drug Use

George M. Beschner and
Kerry G. Treasure

Sugar and spice and everything nice—that's what little girls are made of.

As with most aspects of their lives, the drug-taking behavior of girls (and women) has been stereotyped. Girls have been cast in a paradoxical role: on the one hand, they are viewed as having a less serious drug problem than boys; on the other hand, a girl with a drug problem is considered to be sicker than her male counterpart. Researcher after researcher has noted surprise when the stereotype has not been supported by findings:

> Our study [of young people] did not produce the expected sex differences in marihuana use [Josephson 1971].
>
> Rates of exposure and current use are the same for females and males for most substances. This finding is of special interest inasmuch as previous surveys have indicated that males exceed females in terms of alcohol/drug exposure rates and extent of use [Pandina 1977].
>
> Contrary to recent published reports on student drug use in school populations, the overall use of the drugs studied in this investigation appears to be independent of sex [Wolfson et al. 1971].

There are hints of difference between girls and boys; these are seen in their drug preferences, their modes of initiation, their frequency of use, and their sources of drugs. This chapter will explore some of these differences. It is time to stop being surprised by the statistics that show that girls have serious drug problems, comparable with those of boys. In some ways, girls have achieved a dubious equality.

As a method of dispelling the stereotype of adolescent female drug use, it is helpful to explore the roots of the stereotyping. Rogers (1977) assessed the impact of polarized sex roles and concluded that the female adolescent is forced to cope with the unfounded notion that women are less stable and less responsible than men. She is taught to be passive and to concede positions of greater authority and significance in society to males.

The traditional feminine role includes such traits as dependence, passivity, concern about the family, avoidance of illegal and violent activities, responsiveness to peer and parental desires, lack of ambition, inability to make rational decisions, and a lack of worldliness. Certain of these traits have been viewed as buffers between girls and drug use (indeed, against all types of delinquency). The stereotype adopts a moralizing attitude toward girls and holds that those who use drugs and thus deviate from this role have wandered farther afield than boys who have been indoctrinated to another set of traits: independence, competitiveness, business skills, rationality, worldliness, ambition, self-confidence, and leadership ability. This is curious, at least from one perspective. Surely it can be reasoned that it is a greater leap from independence (masculine trait) to drug dependence than from dependence (feminine trait) to drug dependence. How can people be surprised when upon encouraging a girl to be passive and to lack ambition, she turns to drugs that encourage submission and squelch ambition?

Second, stereotypes thrive in the absence of reliable information. In the past, there has been pitifully little research about the extent and etiology of female—youth or adult—drug use. This deficiency has been commented on by Levy and Doyle (1974) and Schwartz (1977), but it continues to persist, perhaps because of the biases and attitudes of investigators. There is encouraging evidence that this oversight is being remedied and that the stereotype is beginning to fade. Pressure from the Women's Liberation movement and concern about the pregnant addict have combined to focus attention on female drug use, as has a much-publicized national study which stated that "current prevalence rates . . . (of psychotherapeutic drug use) are twice as high for women as for men. . . ."

What has been learned about the nature and extent of female adolescent drug use? What kinds of drugs do girls 18 years of age and under use? What are the forces that lead to drug use by adolescent females? How has society responded to this problem? And how can we improve this response? These questions are explored in the balance of the chapter.

The Nature and Extent of the Problem

The first step—recognition that girls do have a serious drug problem—must be followed by a concise specification of that problem. In describing the reported patterns of drug use by girls, comparisons between boys and girls cannot be avoided. These comparisons provide a point of reference, but excessive concern about the differences between boys and girls can also obscure the fact that the drug problem is serious for both sexes. The finding that x percent fewer girls than boys use drugs should not outweigh the finding that large proportions of both sexes are drug users.

To document the nature and extent of the problem, this chapter draws on data garnered from three sources: (1) household, community, and school surveys; (2) hospital emergency rooms, crisis centers, medical examiners, and inpatient units administered and cosponsored by the National Institute on Drug Abuse; and (3) data from treatment programs.

Household, Community, and School Surveys Demonstrate Relatively Consistent Drug Use Patterns for Girls and Boys

Household, community, and school surveys are subject to serious limitations. Most obviously, they rely on self-report by young people who may be motivated by peer pressure to overreport or by parental pressure to underreport. Cross-study comparisons are particularly difficult, since items are structured differently and studies vary in the rigor and precision of their design, the representativeness of their sample, the time periods considered, and the drugs studied. The picture is further clouded by the varying definitions of drug use. Researchers such as Elinson (1977) have studied, among other things, the following:

Prevalence, which measures the percentage of the population that has ever used a drug. This does not distinguish the casual from the serious user.

Incidence, which identifies the "... rates of *new* users within a specified time period" (Kandel et al. 1976). This indicates the current popularity of the drug.

Current user rates, which distinguish people who have used the drug within a recent time period from those who used the drug at some time in the more distant past. Current time periods and levels of use are variously defined by each researcher, for example, marihuana use five or more times during the past month, alcohol use once a week or more for 4 of the past 6 weeks.

Frequency of use, which rates acknowledged users according to their relative drug use, for example, less than once a week, one or two times a week, more than twice a week.

Retention rate, which determines the ratio of people who have tried the drug to those who continue to use it, for example, 57 percent of the sample who ever tried *x* drug continue to use it.

Several researchers have studied the most *recent time period* in which drug use has occurred.

Others have identified the *total number of times* the drug has been used, to distinguish heavy from light users.

Comparisons of survey results can be made only when the measurement of drug use is constant. Thus the dilemma for the analyst: reports of prevalence are the least enlightening but the most uniformly reported findings. Current use rates and frequency of use rates are slightly more meaningful indicators of drug problems, but often defy comparisons from one study to another. These two categories of data and miscellaneous findings from a number of studies make up the next sections.

Prevalence Studies. A review of the literature on prevalence studies (drug ever used) reveals mixed findings. Although generalizations are difficult, most researchers report that there are no glaring differences between girls and boys. The findings of the six following major and fairly recent prevalence studies are summarized in figure 8-1.

1. New York State survey of drug use among New York State high school students, conducted in 1971 (Kandel et al. 1976).
2. San Mateo County, California, survey of student drug use, conducted in 1977 (Blackford 1977).
3. Nationwide survey, conducted by Social Research Group, George Washington University, conducted in 1975-1976 (Abelson and Fishburne 1976).
4. Nationwide youth survey, conducted by Institute for Social Research, University of Michigan, conducted in 1976 (Johnston et al. 1977).
5. New Jersey adolescent alcohol/drug abuse survey, conducted in 1976 (Pandina 1977).
6. Survey of drug abuse in six New Jersey high schools, conducted in 1971 (Wolfson et al. 1971).

Highlights of these studies are expressed below:

Girls have had considerable experience with alcoholic beverages. In four of the five studies, beer, wine, and/or hard liquor consumption is reported by over 80 percent of the girls. When type of alcohol is specified, girls prefer (or have readier access to) beer and wine. Only small differences between girls and boys are noted, with the single exception of New York State findings, where 10 percent more boys than girls drink hard liquor.

Between 45 and 75 percent of the girls studied had tried cigarettes at one time or another. Although the studies vary considerably from each other, girls and boys are almost identical on prevalence *within* each study.

Reported use of marihuana and hashish varies considerably; from one-fifth to three-fifths of the girls report using marihuana, and slightly less have tried hashish. Girls report consistently lower use rates than boys (from 2 to 12 percentage points lower).

Use of LSD and other hallucinogens did not exceed 20 percent for either girls or boys, and as with marihuana, girls have a slightly lower usage rate than boys.

Amphetamines are used by both boys and girls more than any drug except the "common" drugs (alcohol, cigarettes, and cannabis). Exposure is remarkably similar for boys and girls, in contrast to the greatly different use rates found in adult males and females.[1]

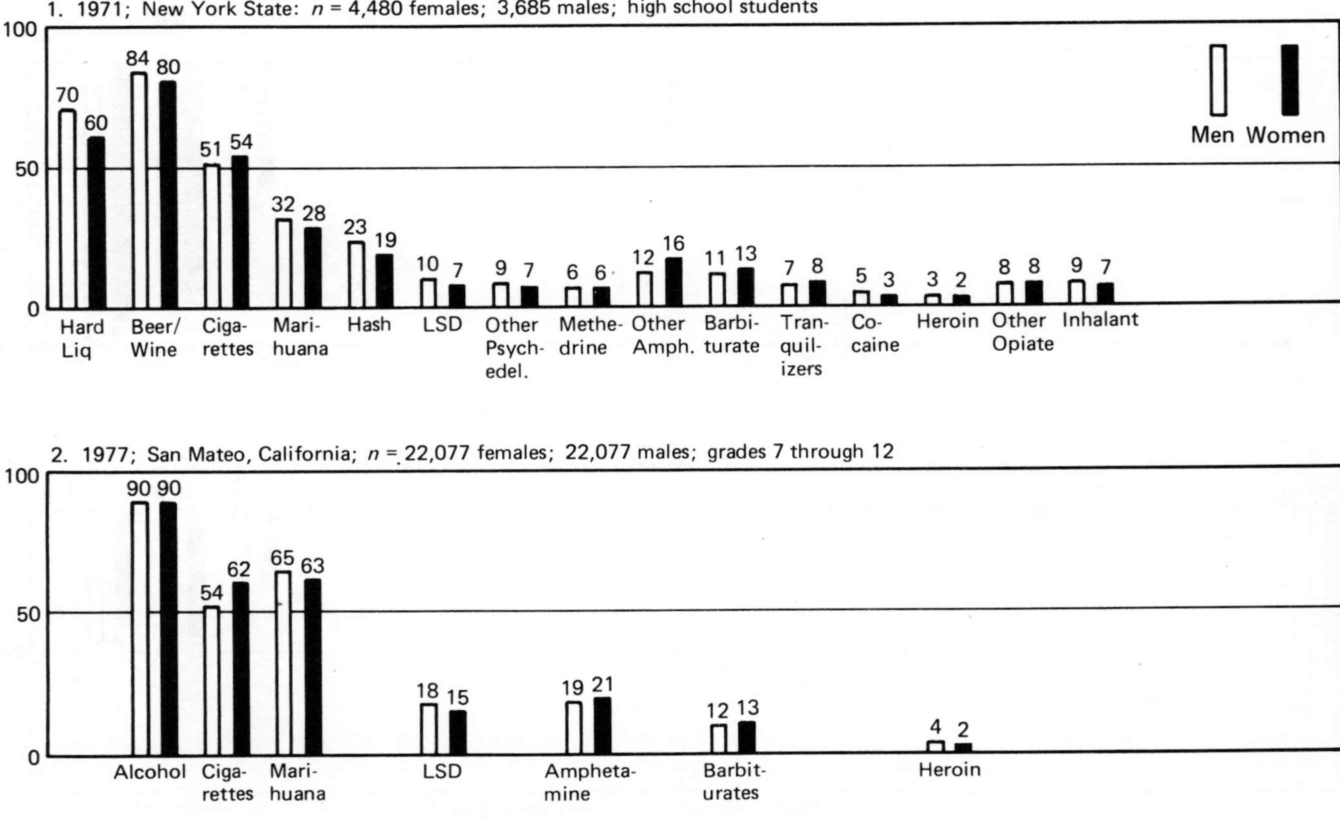

Figure 8-1. Percent Ever Used The Drug.

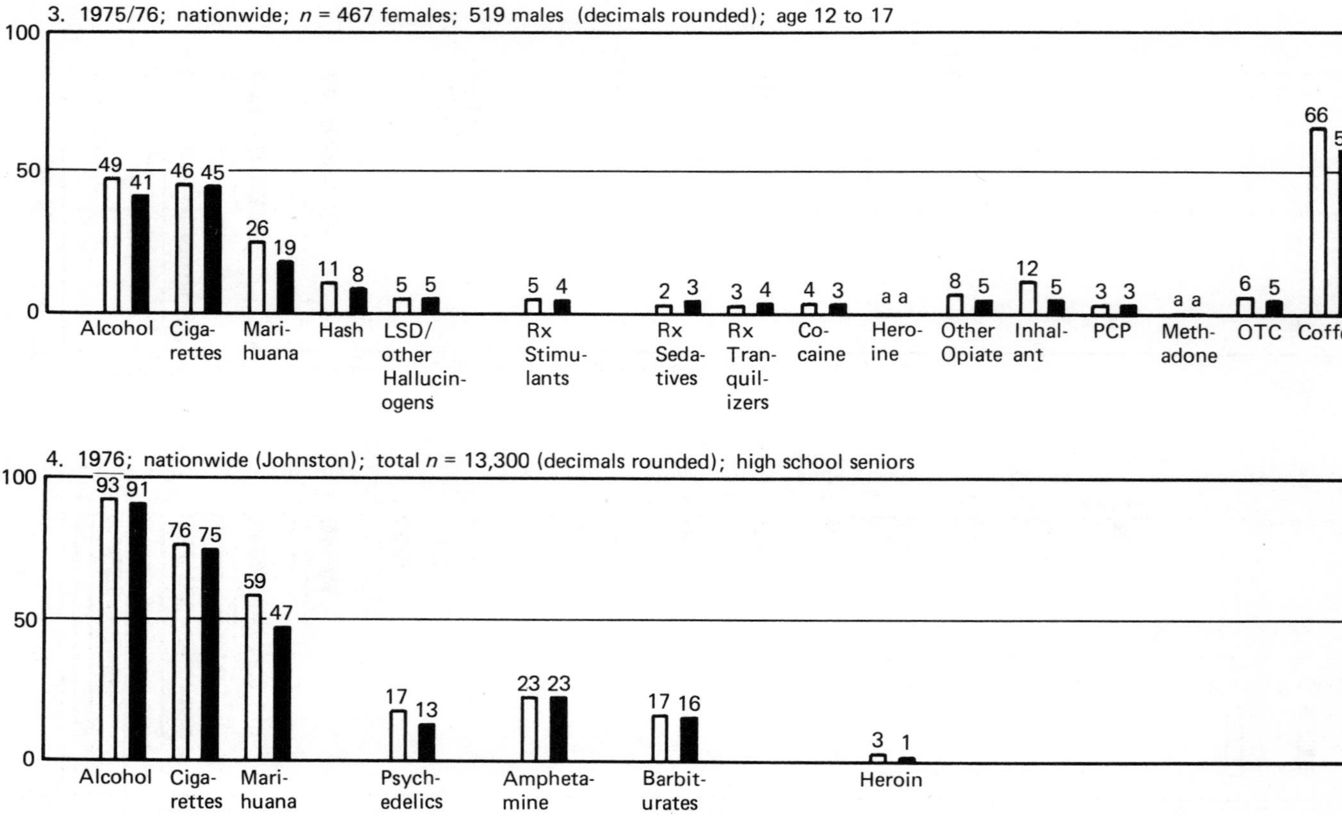

Figure 8-1 continued

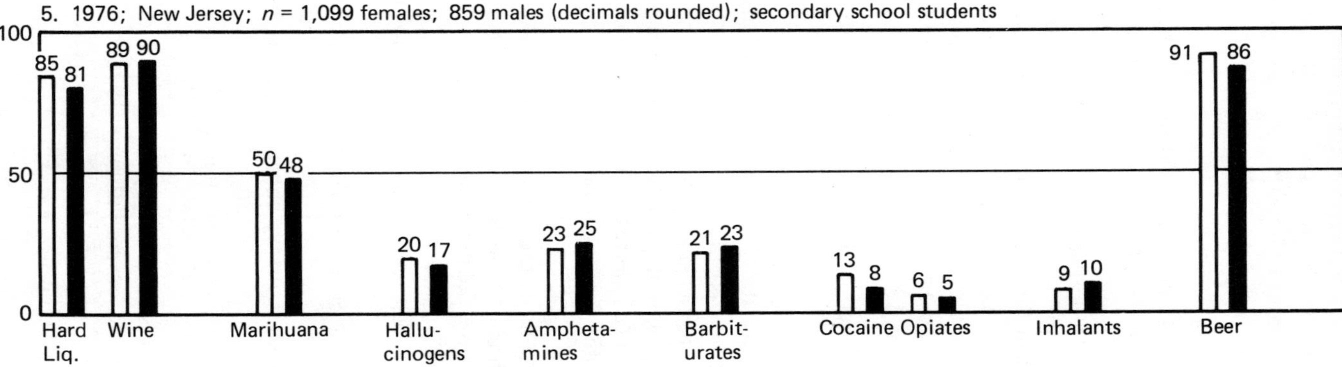
5. 1976; New Jersey; n = 1,099 females; 859 males (decimals rounded); secondary school students
100
50
0
85 81
Hard Liq.
89 90
Wine
50 48
Marihuana
20 17
Hallu- cinogens
23 25
Ampheta- mines
21 23
Barbit- urates
13 8
Cocaine
6 5
Opiates
9 10
Inhalants
91 86
Beer

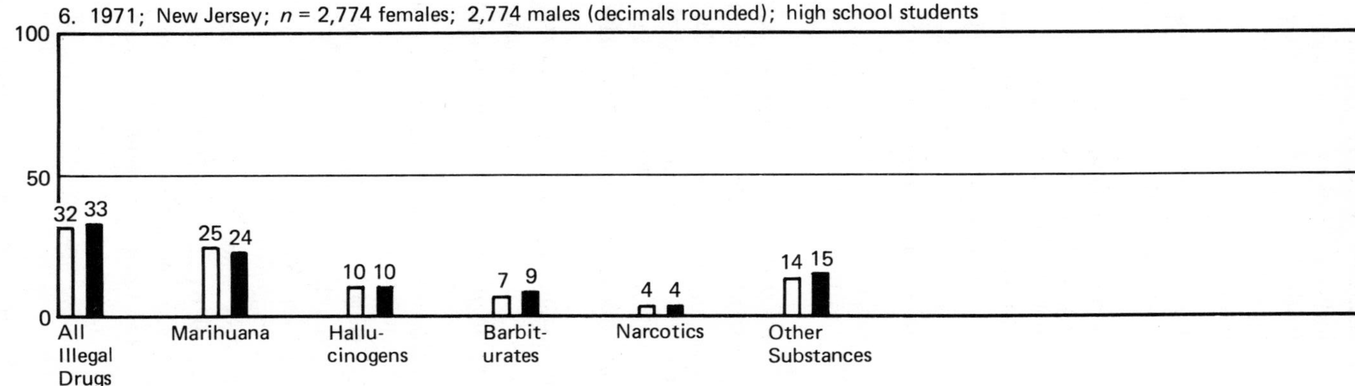
6. 1971; New Jersey; n = 2,774 females; 2,774 males (decimals rounded); high school students
100
50
0
32 33
All Illegal Drugs
25 24
Marihuana
10 10
Hallu- cinogens
7 9
Barbit- urates
4 4
Narcotics
14 15
Other Substances

Barbiturates are the only drug in which girls consistently report equal or higher rates of exposure than boys; moreover, the use rates for both sexes (with the exception of the George Washington University study) are quite high: between 9 and 23 percent for the girls and 9 and 21 percent for the boys.

Tranquilizers were included in only two of the six studies; girls and boys reported about the same use, with prevalence less than 8 percent in all cases.

In all six studies, heroin is among the least frequently (if not *the* least frequently) used drugs. In three studies, cocaine was reported to be used more frequently than the opiates; less than 5 percent of the girls (and only slightly more boys) had experience with any of the opiates, including heroin. This boy/girl ratio bears little resemblance to the reports of known heroin addicts, in which males generally outnumber females four or five to one (Suffet and Brotman 1976; Cuskey et al. 1972; Chein 1964).

Inhalants were studied by only two researchers, and prevalence ranged from 7 to 10 percent for girls and boys alike.

In general, the following pattern of prevalence of drug use is fairly consistent across all major surveys: relatively high use of alcohol, cigarettes, and cannabis; substantial use of hallucinogens, amphetamines, barbiturates, tranquilizers, and inhalants; and relatively limited (but not insignificant) exposure to narcotic drugs. Despite the variation in prevalence reported from study to study, girls and boys *within* each study have remarkably similar exposure rates.

Frequency and Currency of Use. Frequency and currency of use provide a more descriptive portrait of drug-use patterns than mere reports of ever used. Figure 8-2 summarizes currency and frequency data from the following six surveys.

1. Survey of drug abuse in six New Jersey high schools, conducted in 1971 (Wolfson et al. 1971).
2. Drugs in junior high school in the San Francisco area, conducted in 1972 (Linder et al. 1974).
3. New Jersey adolescent alcohol/drug abuse survey, conducted in 1976 (Pandina 1977).
4. San Mateo County, California, survey of student drug use, conducted in 1976 (Blackford 1977).
5. Nationwide survey, conducted by Social Research Group, George Washington University, conducted in 1975-1976 (Abelson and Fishburne 1976).
6. Nationwide youth survey, conducted by Institute for Social Research, University of Michigan, conducted in 1976 (Johnston et al. 1977).

Note that the top of each graph in figure 8-2 specifies the definition of current or frequent use. Although care must be taken in comparing these graphs, the general trends noted in the prevalence tables are repeated here. Girls and boys are:

About equally likely to have tried a drug without becoming a frequent or current user.

About equally likely to be frequent or current users of a given drug within a given survey.

More likely to be using cigarettes, alcohol, and cannabis; less likely to be using psychedelics, amphetamines, barbiturates, sedatives, and inhalants; and least likely to be using narcotic drugs.

Trends in Drug Use Over Time. The most coveted—and most rare—statistical information is that which sheds light on trends in drug use over a period of years. Precious little information exists about drug use by adolescent females over time. What information there is indicates, again, mixed results:

Four national household surveys conducted in 1971, 1972, 1974, and 1975-1976 found that after a rapid rise in marihuana use (from 14 percent to 21 percent between 1971 and 1974), girls dropped back to 19 percent in 1975-1976.[2] This reduction could be the result of a sampling difference or reflect a leveling off of marihuana use by girls. In contrast, boys experienced a steady rise in marihuana use over this period (from 14 to 26 percent). Rates of *current* use (that is, use during the past month) showed a similar but less marked trend; girls rose from 5 to 11 percent between 1971 and 1974 and then leveled off at 11 percent in 1975-1976. Current use by boys continued to rise unabated, from 7 percent in 1971 to 14 percent in 1975-1976 (Abelson and Fishburne 1976).

The same study reports a fairly stable prevalence rate for all youths regarding nonmedical use of prescription psychoactive drugs. A national survey conducted under the auspices of the National Institute on Alcohol Abuse and Alcoholism (NIAAA) found a clear pattern of increasing marihuana involvement for both males and females over time; approximately 5 percent of both sexes in the seventh grade reported using the drug, compared with 45 percent of the males and 38 percent of the females in the twelfth grade. The study also reports that boys generally showed a higher degree of involvement at all grade levels. These sex differences were quite small until the eleventh grade (Chase and Jessor 1977).

A 10-year longitudinal study of San Mateo high school students found that female students had increased their use (prevalence) of alcohol by a staggering 22 percent, marihuana by 31 percent, LSD by 5 percent, tobacco by 4 percent, and amphetamines by 3 percent. Barbiturate and heroin use both declined (by 2 and 1 percent, respectively). Patterns were identical for

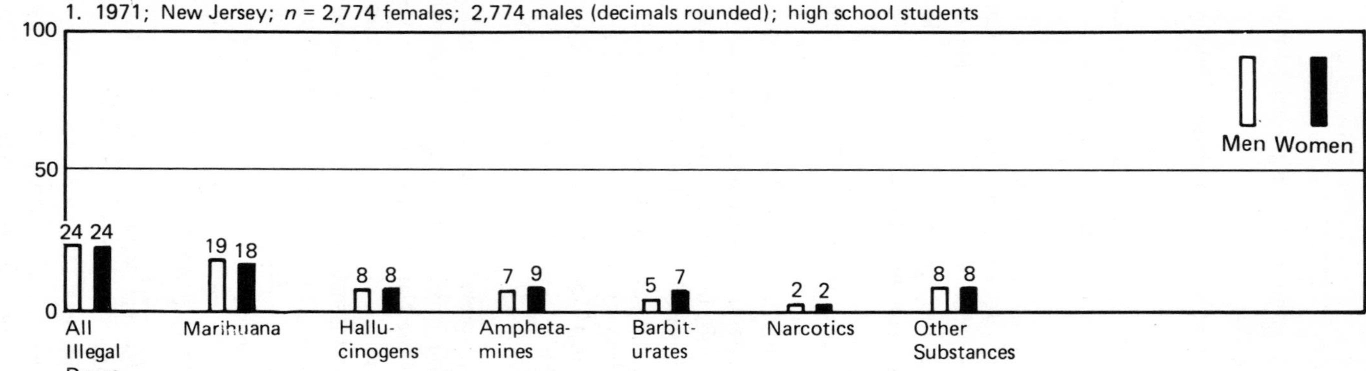

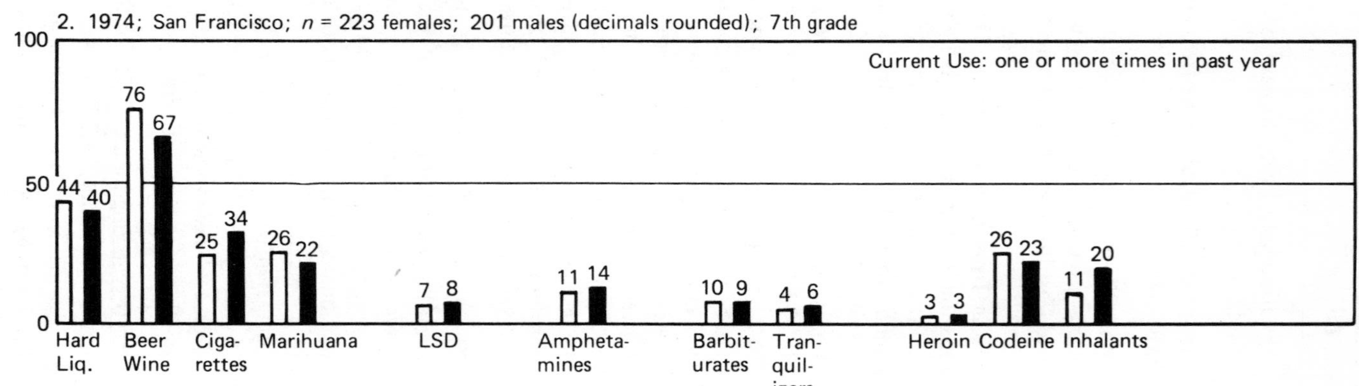

[a]Less than 1 percent.

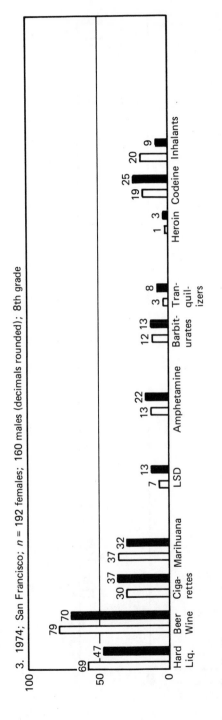

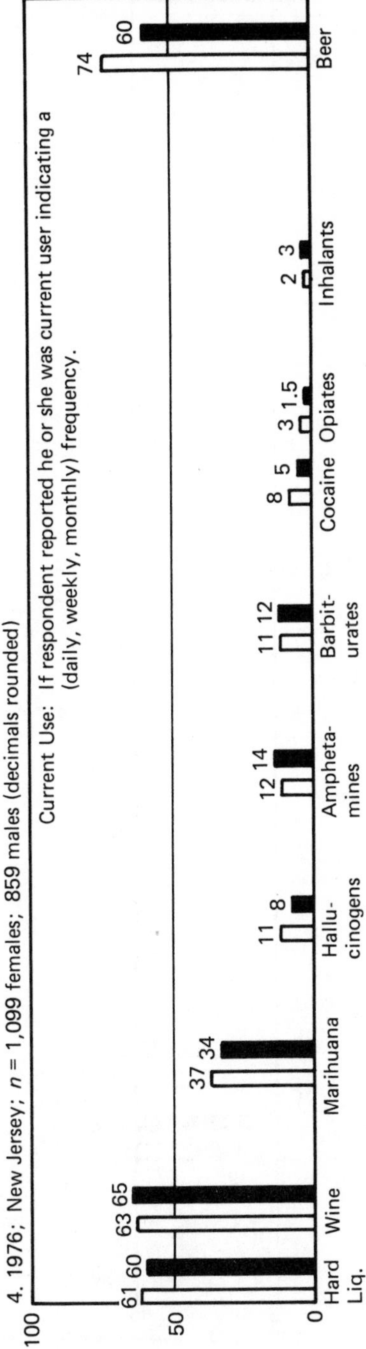
3. 1974; San Francisco; n = 192 females; 160 males (decimals rounded); 8th grade
100
50
0
69
47
79
70
30
37
37
32
7
13
13
22
12 13
3
8
1
3
19
25
20
9
Hard Liq.
Beer Wine
Ciga- rettes
Marihuana
LSD
Amphetamine
Barbit- urates
Tran- quil- izers
Heroin
Codeine
Inhalants
4. 1976; New Jersey; n = 1,099 females; 859 males (decimals rounded)
Current Use: If respondent reported he or she was current user indicating a (daily, weekly, monthly) frequency.
100
50
0
61
60
63
65
37
34
11
8
12
14
11
12
8
5
3
1.5
2
3
74
60
Hard Liq.
Wine
Marihuana
Hallu- cinogens
Ampheta- mines
Barbit- urates
Cocaine
Opiates
Inhalants
Beer

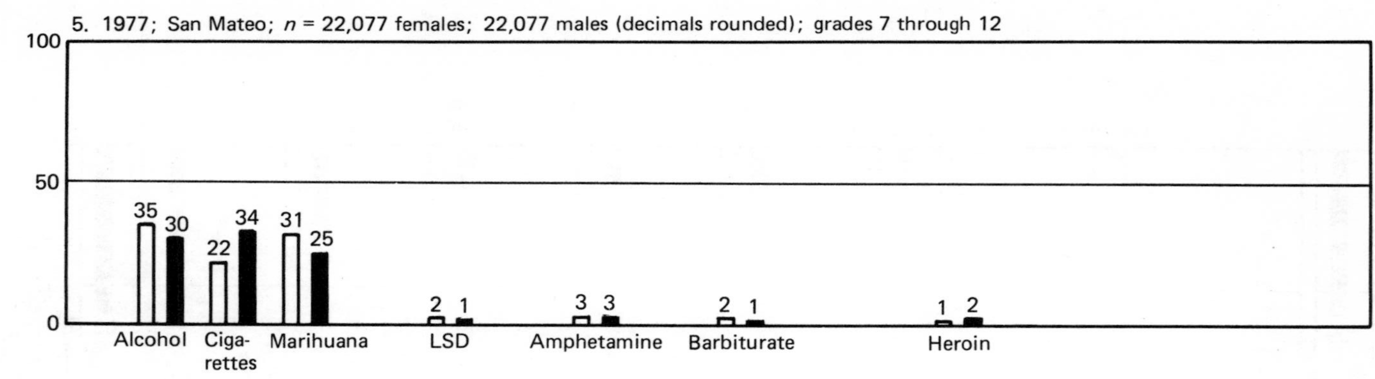

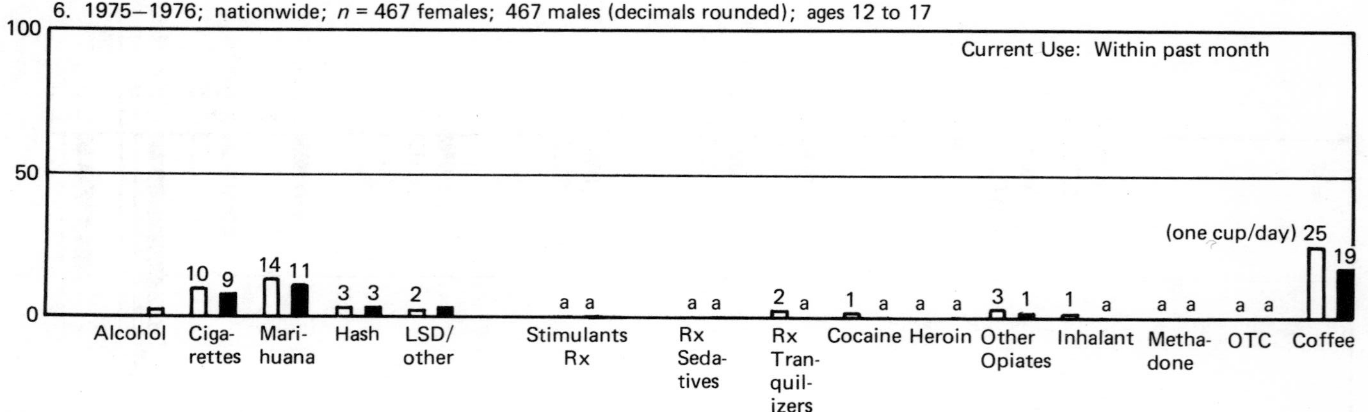

Figure 8-2 continued

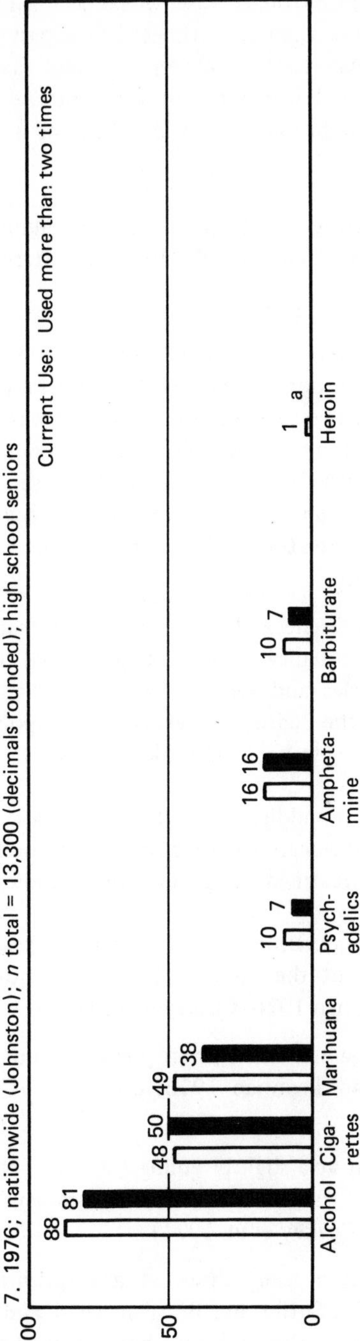
7. 1976; nationwide (Johnston); *n* total = 13,300 (decimals rounded); high school seniors
Current Use: Used more than two times
100
50
0
88
81
48
50
49
38
10
7
16 16
10
7
1
a
Alcohol
Ciga-
rettes
Marihuana
Psych-
edelics
Ampheta-
mine
Barbiturate
Heroin

> boys, with the sole exception of tobacco use, which declined slightly. Girls' reports of frequent use (more than fifty times) in the past year followed identical trends, except that LSD remained low—less than 1 percent. Interestingly, boys reported lower rates of frequent use in five drug categories: amphetamines, barbiturates, heroin, LSD, and tobacco (Blackford 1977).

Recent surveys concentrated in rural and urban communities have also reported trends in their findings of comparable drug-use patterns of girls and boys.

> A rural adolescent drug-use survey conducted in 1976 reported in chapter 16 of this book "supports the notion that sex differences are disappearing, if they have not already done so. When lifetime drug use was examined as a function of sex, males were found to be over-represented only in the use of beer. The notion that sex differences are disappearing is supported by the fact that when current drug and alcohol use rates were examined as a function of sex, *no* significant relationships were found" (Kirk 1978).
>
> The results of a recent (1975) teenage drug-use survey in an urban ghetto show no significant sex differences. It was speculated that "the recent general trend toward sexual equality among youngsters and the acceptance of similar standards for males and females has already had a significant impact on the drug scene in the Bedford Stuyvesant, Greenpoint and Crown Heights section of Brooklyn, New York" (Brook et al. 1977).

Miscellaneous Study Findings. In addition to the three national reporting systems, a number of independent researchers have commented on the characteristics of young women who seek treatment. In general, these studies report:

> Young women in treatment are using about the same types of drugs and drug combinations with about the same frequencies as boys (Levy and Doyle 1974; Suffet and Brotman 1976; Cuskey et al. 1972).
>
> In the treatment setting, female adolescents are greatly outnumbered by the male adolescents (Suffet and Brotman 1976; Cuskey et al. 1972; Chein 1964; Byrne et al. 1977).
>
> Girls tend to enter treatment at a slightly younger age than boys (Klinge et al. 1976; Cuskey et al. 1971) and have had a drug problem for a shorter time (Levy and Doyle 1974; Cuskey et al. 1971).
>
> The girls—like the boys—begin using drugs at a surprisingly early age (Abelson and Fishburne 1976; Suffet and Brotman 1976; and Cuskey et al. 1972). Most authors agree that girls and boys begin drug experimentation

and use at similar ages (Pandina 1977; Eldred and Washington 1977; Hindermarch 1971), and when age differences *are* noted, the girls have usually tried drugs at an earlier age than boys (Klinge et al. 1976; Burt et al. 1977; Pittel 1973).

In summary, the portrait of the female adolescent using drugs does not vary significantly, regardless of the source of information reviewed. It does, however, contrast significantly with the stereotype of the meek girl—the girl taking drugs only in the shadow of her male peers.

Having measured these girls with statistics, what else can be said about them? Aside from numbers and percentages, what kind of *girls* are they? What kind of problems have they experienced? From what kind of environments do they come? And what kinds of responses can we make to reduce their involvement with drugs?

Profile of the Adolescent Girl Drug User

Each one of them is unique. In practice, in teaching, in treatment, in child rearing, it is essential that this uniqueness be remembered: that is the marvel of the infinite variation among human beings never to be forgotten.

Gisela Konopka (1966) was referring to the adolescent female when she made this statement. She went on to conclude that whatever new knowledge may emerge to help us obtain a better understanding of all adolescents must be qualified by the awareness that each girl is different and that her plea not be "treated by the book" but heard.

Throughout the literature, various authors have proposed theories of etiology based on the pressures and forces that appear to move young people to drug use. But most writings center on a particular variable, claiming that "it's the family," "it's the sexual ambivalence," or "it's the school experience" that leads to drug abuse. Such narrow analyses will not present the whole story. In attempting to comprehend the "causes" of drug use among young women, we should first examine the very nature of adolescence: the relationships with family members and peers, the struggle between emerging feelings of independence and the safety of dependence, the search for meaning in life, the need for a career or a family of one's own, and the startling changes in a young woman's body, and sexuality.

Figure 8-3 illustrates the myriad pressures and forces that converge on young women during their adolescence. It could be hypothesized that no single force moves a girl to drug use, but rather combinations of these forces drive her to seek certain outlets and to mobilize her defenses. The more negative forces surrounding the girl, the less likely she is to have access to constructive outlets.

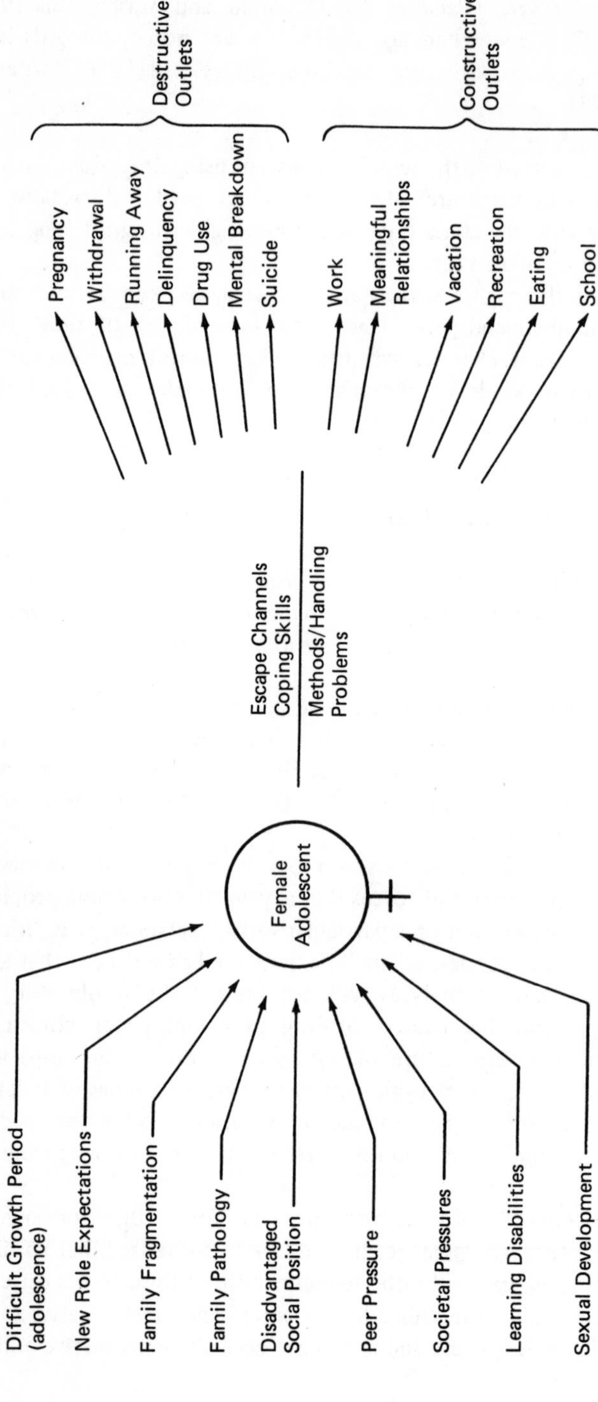

Figure 8-3. Constellation of Forces Operating during Female Adolescence.

For example, if she is experiencing difficulty with her parents, then the family may not be a constructive outlet for her energies.

Granted that all adolescents experience some trauma, why is it that some begin using drugs while others find more constructive methods of reacting to trauma and coping with new experiences and new feelings? A good starting point for examining motivations would be the "reasons" produced from surveys and investigations, for example:

> A survey of New Jersey high school students indicated that over 50 percent of the students used drugs (1) because it was pleasurable, (2) for kicks, (3) out of curiosity, or (4) for the experience itself (Wolfson et al. 1971).
>
> Drug users in Haight-Ashbury claimed that the drugs (mostly psychedelic) gave them feelings of relaxation, happiness, peace, and love. They believed that if more people used psychedelic drugs, the world would be a better place to live (Pittel 1973).
>
> A study of elementary school students found that most who used drugs did so to be part of the gang (58 percent), for kicks (30 percent), and out of curiosity (31 percent) (Lerner 1974).
>
> In *The Road to H,* Chein (1964) notes that the ostensible reason for first trying heroin is curiosity.

These stated reasons suggest that there are several significant avenues into drug use for female adolescents. Studies (references) have supported the hypotheses that a period of initial experimentation, followed by incremental increases in drug use, precedes addiction. However, each of these studies indicates that there were secondary forces supporting the movement into drug use and the subsequent addiction. These are discussed in the following sections.

Peer Relations: The Pressure to be Part of the Group

A major drive of the female adolescent is to gain independence from her parents and become an autonomous adult. It is during this same period that the adolescent girl must attempt to discover the limits of her own personality and achieve an identity. To ease the pain of separation from parents and acquire a real sense of self, most adolescents turn to their peers. It is with the peer group that they hope to find support and understanding. It is also through this group that they are likely to be introduced to drugs and with this group that they are likely to participate in drug-taking activities. For example:

> Students in New Jersey high schools reported that most of their drug experiences occurred during the school day. The authors concluded that the

entire school population was being exposed to a significant amount of drug-use (Pandina 1977).

Slightly more than half the young women in Chein's (1964) sample first took drugs with a person in their own age range.

A study of school-aged children in Denmark revealed that cannabis users tend to take the drug, as well as amphetamines and LSD, in either a large or small group. Solo drug taking was extremely rare (Hindermarch 1971).

In another study of Danish school children, the drug users were characterized as more sociable, and as visiting or being visited by friends more often than nonusers (Winslow 1971).

In fact, one researcher has noted that "if you are looking for a powerful predictor of drug use among adolescents, knowing what their friends do predicts as well as anything else, if not better" (Josephson 1977).

While peer pressure affects both girls and boys, it has a curious twist where girls are concerned. Both girls and boys can look forward to being influenced by members of the opposite sex throughout their lives, but in the case of girls and drug abuse, boys often provide a stimulus for initiation or maintenance of drug using behavior. Almost without exception, the literature reports that girls are introduced to drugs by boys (and sometimes men) and that the majority of their drug taking is done in groups that are dominated by males (Eldred and Washington 1977; Cuskey et al. 1972; Chein 1964; Wolfson et al. 1971; Suffet and Brotman 1976). One author even goes so far as to say 'that the greatest predisposing factor for female addiction—at least in an illicit opiate market—was the addicted male associate (Cuskey et al. 1972). One might well ask what predisposes a young woman to associate with an addict!

Family Pathology and Fragmentation

In our nuclear-family oriented society, there is a tendency to blame the family for problematic children. One wants to avoid obvious answers, but it is nonetheless difficult to avoid the conclusion that "malignant familial environments" (Cuskey et al. 1972) are fertile ground for nurturing drug-abusing children. Numerous authors (Pittel 1973; Winslow 1971; Klinge et al. 1976; Lavenhar et al. 1971; Patch 1973; Noble et al. 1972, Brook et al. 1976; Chein 1964) have commented on the importance of the family relationship. Female adolescents who use drugs heavily have often been reported to be members of families:

1. That are broken by divorce, desertion, or death (Noble et al. 1972; Brook et al. 1976; Cuskey et al. 1972, Patch 1973; Roth 1971).

2. In which the father was away for long periods of time during the girl's youth (Cuskey et al. 1972; Chein 1964).
3. In which the parental relationship is weak or troubled (Chein 1964; Patch 1973).
4. That have made frequent moves, resulting in a sense of rootlessness and instability (Pittel 1973; Brook et al. 1976).
5. With a family history of alcoholism, addiction, or nonmedical drug use (Cuskey et al. 1972; Chein 1964; Konopka 1966; Lavenhar et al. 1971).
6. That employed uneven and harsh disciplinary procedures (Chein 1964) and in which the parents have also used drugs. Surveys on drug use among adolescents and their parents have shown a positive association between reported drug use of parents and their adolescent children (Smart and Feger 1972).

Although most authors do not comment on the differences between the families of girls and boys, a few have noted such differences as the following:

1. A significant percentage of the female heroin addicts in treatment had been abused by their parents in their childhood. Densen-Gerber (1977) conducted an intensive sociological study into the backgrounds of 204 heroin-addicted women in Odyssey House treatment programs. Approximately 32 percent of the subjects in this study reported that they had been sexually abused by their parents. Only 17.6 percent of the subjects had positive memories of their parents.
2. Girls tend to be more sensitive and responsive to problems within the family. "Girls are more 'bound' to their families emotionally, cognitively, and behaviorally" than are boys (Klinge et al. 1976).
3. Chein (1964) noted that the family experiences of young men and women addicts were virtually identical, with the exception that the fathers of males tended to have unrealistically high or low aspirations for the boys early in childhood and that the mothers had unrealistic expectations (too high or too low) for the boys throughout their youth. Apparently, girls were not the victims of unrealistic expectations (Chein 1964).
4. Schwartz (1977) found that female addicts related better to fathers than to mothers. The mothers of the females tended to be distant, authoritarian, and cold, while the fathers were often indulgent and seductive.
5. It has been reported by Rado (1957) and Wishnie (1973) that the feelings of hopelessness and helplessness experienced by female addicts were often related to their unsatisfactory relationship with their mothers.
6. In Wolforf's (1973) sample, almost twice as many female addicts as male (46 percent compared with 26 percent) grew up in homes containing addicts or heavy drinkers. He concluded that "drug problems in families of women were much more prevalent than with men, and probably compounded the general family disorganization."

It is important to recognize that these familial traits are not the exclusive claim of low income groups. Only two studies noted correlations between poverty and addiction (Patch 1973; Cuskey et al. 1972). To the contrary, most authors stressed that these characteristics cut across the traditional socioeconomic strata (Pittel 1973).

Sexual Development and Sexuality

One of the most important—either terribly good or terribly bad—experiences of adolescence is sexual development, and girls have a particularly taxing adjustment to make. The physical changes experienced by girls are pronounced, and these, combined with contradictory social signals about sexuality, create confusion, guilt, and rebellion in many girls. For example:

> The onset of menstruation can resemble to a young girl physical injury and sickness (that is, bleeding). A surprising number of girls are unprepared for these bodily changes and suffer in silent shame or terror of their "unique" malady (Konopka 1966).
>
> Emergence of a womanly figure creates ambivalence in adults, particularly in adult males who are "allowed" to be attracted to young women. In turn, these mixed adult feelings create confusion in young women about appropriate sexual behavior.
>
> For girls, sexual relations represent a responsibility and a threat of danger or shame (that is, pregnancy or loss of virginity) that does not exist for boys.
>
> Girls tend to construct expectations and fantasies around love, sex, and romance that are stronger than those of boys and often lead to disappointment. Girls have more at stake in a sexual relationship and are therefore likely to have more emotion invested in the relationship. Early sex is often physically unsatisfying for girls—partly because they and their young male partners are inexperienced and inept lovers and, reportedly, because many women do not reach the height of sexual enjoyment until their late twenties and thirties.
>
> Girls get many confusing and contradictory messages about sexuality. Despite the attention in the popular press to sexual liberation (that is, coed dorms, the Pill, increased female aggressiveness and women's liberation) (Farnsworth 1972), most girls are still torn by a double standard. In many ways, sexual liberation does not represent personal liberation for young girls who can no longer delay their sexual initiation under the guise of "nice girls don't do it." Thus they may be pressured, again by peers (predominately male), to engage in sexual activity that is not personally comfortable.

In addition, there is much evidence that young women are ill prepared for these changes (Konopka 1966; Posner et al. 1977).

Loneliness and Rebellion Against the Adult World

In discussing the importance of family relationships to drug use, it was noted that the essence of adolescence is breaking dependent ties with the parents and accepting the responsibilities and privileges of adulthood. This process, while never easy, need not be destructive if supported by understanding adults, spurred by challenging and diverse adult role models, and accompanied with opportunities for friendships, hobbies, academic study, careers, or other meaningful activities. Unfortunately, many girls do not enter adolescence with these supports.

First, although the generation gap may be a cliché, it is true that many adolescent girls do not have adult friends with whom they can share the experiences of growing up. Both mothers and fathers find it difficult to talk frankly with young women about their sexual development and other powerful feelings. Outside the family, girls have few places to seek adult friendship. Thus loneliness emerges as a pervasive cry among young girls who use drugs or who act out through some other form of delinquent behavior.

> Drug users in Haight-Ashbury were characterized by their loneliness and profound sense of isolation from others—more a feeling of uniqueness than simple loneliness (Pittel 1973).
>
> A study of Canadian youths found significant relationships between normlessness scores and drug use of any kind. The study also found a relationship between overall alienation and use of all drugs except "speed" and between social isolation and all drugs except alcohol, tobacco, glue, barbiturates, and tranquilizers (Roth 1971).
>
> When adolescent heroin addicts were tested with the Minnesota Multiphasic Personality Inventory (MMPI), they showed high levels of isolation, alienation, and confusion (Patch 1973).
>
> In her study of delinquent girls, many of whom had experience with drugs, Konopka shares the desperate cries of a number of girls:
>
> > "There's nobody I can talk to, they don't understand."
> > "One expects parents to listen. Why don't they?"
> > "I felt so lonely."
> > "I am just terribly lonesome."
> > "People don't understand. Adults forget. Nothing helps me when I am homesick. Oh, I wish I were a child."

Konopka acknowledges that adolescent boys also feel lonely and struggle to find understanding. Yet her studies have convinced her that this search is not as central to the adolescent experience of boys as it is for girls. "While these girls also strive for independence, their need for dependence is unusually great—and almost completely overlooked and unfulfilled." Also, girls have less varied and dynamic role models to lure them into adulthood. Manhood is a status celebrated in our society, while womanhood suggests dubious and ambivalent rewards. Growing up, close to her mother, the adolescent girl becomes sensitive to some of the less attractive aspects of a woman's role, particularly the boredom and drudgery associated with housework and child care. This image of her mother's role, coupled with the traditionally greater acceptance of dependence by females, makes it more difficult for a girl to embrace the possibility of adulthood with enthusiasm.

If the parent does not make a good role model, where can the female adolescent turn? Female images portrayed on television and in school books are often limited to a few unflattering stereotypes. In television commercials women are depicted as homemakers obsessed with the cleanliness of kitchen floors and the family wash or overly concerned with apparel, cosmetics, personal hygiene, and other tasks that can help them express their traditional femininity.

Women in sports, academia, government, or business are still oddities, and suspicion about their ability to remain feminine in these nontraditional environments makes it difficult for girls to identify with them wholeheartedly. The use of drugs can offset some of the loneliness, ambivalence, and rebellion experienced by the female adolescent. She can become part of a subculture, less anonymous and less alone if not less lonely; she can transfer her need to be dependent from the adult world to drugs and flaunt the mores of the adult world; and she can mute the pain and anxiety of encroaching adulthood.

Personality and Psychological Characteristics: Cause and Effect?

To speak about the psychological characteristics of drug abusers is, almost by definition, to speak of deviance and maladjustments, for serious drug abuse, after all, deviates legally and statistically from the norm. One author cites "evidence that we are dealing with a psychological and social maladjustment that [simply] *expresses* itself in a form considered deviant. Addiction may be a form of adjustment to intolerable stress" (Cuskey 1972).

What is known about the psychological characteristics of young females with serious drug problems?

> In his intensive study of adolescent female heroin addicts, Chein (1964) noted that all were seriously maladjusted in at least one of three areas:

> family, school, or work. He classed the young women into four diagnostic categories: overt schizophrenia, borderline schizophrenia, inadequate personalities, and complex character disorders. Males demonstrated these characteristics with about the same frequency as females, but, noted Chein, the "gestalten of the character disorders was quite different."
>
> Drug users were found typically to (1) reject a social philosophy of rationality, restraint, moderation, and participation in the social life of the community; (2) reject the need for work, practicality, productivity, achievement; and (3) refuse to rely on the technical advances of society (Patch 1973).
>
> A study of adolescent girls sent to reform school in England found pronounced anxiety, mood swings, poor interpersonal relationships, and disturbed personality disorders in a large number of the girls. About 90 percent of the subsample that used narcotics manifested these characteristics, compared with 64 percent of the nonnarcotic drug abusers and 39 percent of the control group (delinquent girls who did not use drugs) (Noble et al. 1972).
>
> A study of young female "speed freaks" found that a great number were at odds with themselves, experienced superficial and impoverished interpersonal relationships, distrusted authority, and felt inadequate, inferior, and insecure. In general, the authors note, the "speed" users were more psychologically disturbed than their non-drug-using peers and the females "tended to be more psychologically disturbed than the males" (Brook et al. 1976).
>
> A study of the developmental histories of young female drug users found poorly developed "ego mechanisms of coping and defense" (Pittel 1973).

It is important to keep in mind that most of these findings pertain only to the drug users with the most serious problems. They do not address themselves to the personality characteristics of the occasional or recreational drug users.

Among the more interesting findings of the literature surveyed are two points upon which a surprising number of authors agreed. First, drug users are found to be of at least average, if not above average, intelligence (Cuskey et al. 1972; Noble et al. 1972; Brook et al. 1976; Pittel 1973). As might be expected, however, most studies found that—native intelligence notwithstanding—drug users tend to perform rather badly in school (Pittel 1973; Noble et al. 1972; Brook et al. 1976; Lavenhar et al. 1971; Roth 1971; Chein 1964). Second, there was considerable conformity among the findings that suggest that the psychological disturbances correlated with drug use predate the drug use (Chein 1964; Cuskey et al. 1972; Pittel 1973; Brook et al. 1976; Steffenhagen et al. 1971). Not a single author suggested that the personality disturbances or maladjustments were caused by or even postdated the drug use.

From the available general population survey and treatment data, it is known that significant numbers of female adolescents are now using drugs. It also appears that there has been a trend of increased drug use among young females and that their drug-use patterns are becoming more like those of their male counterparts.

This chapter has portrayed the vulnerabilities of the female adolescent in our complex society in order to highlight some of the underlying forces, pressures, and problems that may contribute to or sustain this trend. It has also brought to light some of the fundamental needs and problems to be considered in any serious attempt to develop treatment services for this population. This chapter now asks and discusses the following questions: What has been the response to these troubled adolescent girls? Who are the female adolescents that do get into treatment? How and when do they get into treatment? What type of treatment do they receive? What happens to them when they do enter treatment?

The Problem of Adolescent Female Drug Abuse Is Different When Viewed from Treatment Settings

Prevalence studies such as those presented earlier tap the general population and thus suggest the possible dimensions of the drug-abuse problem. Data collected from the treatment setting, on the other hand, define that portion of the drug-using population that enters into treatment. This subpopulation is probably not representative of the overall drug-using population, particularly where women and youths are concerned. The composition of the treatment population is influenced by the types of facilities available, their orientation and philosophy, their staffing patterns, their geographic location, and their referral sources. The treatment population therefore may not reflect the characteristics or size of the entire drug-using population.

Client-Oriented Data Acquisition Process (CODAP)

CODAP, a reporting system required of all federally funded drug-abuse treatment programs, is the largest available data base of drug clients in treatment. Of the approximately 224,000 admissions to CODAP participating programs in 1975, somewhat more than 27,000 (12 percent) cases were under 18 years of age. An examination of table 8-1 shows that females comprise 40.3 percent of the youth sample and males 59.7 percent. This 19 percent difference is greater than the differences generally found between the sexes in the prevalences of use of the various drugs in the high school and community surveys. Does this mean that more male drug users get into serious trouble with drugs and therefore require treatment? Or, are treatment programs not as responsive to the problems and needs of young females?

Table 8-1
Youth Clients (Under 18 Years of Age) in the CODAP System: Admissions during Calendar Year 1975, by Race and Sex

Race	*Males*	*%*	*Females*	*%*	*Total*	*%*
White	10,977	(66.4)	8,083	(72.4)	19,060	(68.9)
Black	3,016	(18.2)	1,935	(17.3)	4,951	(17.9)
Hispanic	1,825	(11.0)	731	(6.5)	2,556	(9.2)
Other	719	(4.4)	420	(3.8)	1,139	(4.1)
Total	16,537	(100)	11,169	(100)	27,706	(100)
	(59.7%)		(40.3)		(100.0%)	

The distribution of primary drug problems as shown in the CODAP youth subsample varied somewhat across sex groups, but there were, on the whole, no very large or striking differences between the two sexes (see table 8-2). Males reported a higher proportion of their primary drug problems within two drug categories: (1) the inhalant category (8 percent of youth males versus 3 percent of youth females), and (2) the marihuana/hashish category (52 percent of youth males versus 48 percent of youth females). Youth females reported a higher proportion of their primary drug problems within two categories: (1) the amphetamine category (9 percent of youth females compared with 5 percent of youth males), and (2) in the barbiturate category (10 percent of youth female compared with 8 percent of youth males). The fact that a higher proportion of females reported a problem with amphetamines is not an unexpected finding, although it was not found in the high school surveys of the nontreatment population summarized earlier. A possible explanation may be that females are more likely to get involved in amphetamine use for the purpose of losing weight; however, in the past, this has been considered a more likely explanation for an older age group of females who obtain their amphetamines by legal prescription.

With regard to both heroin use and alcohol use, while one might expect a larger proportion of males to have the problem, very similar proportions were reported for each sex.

The Drug Abuse Reporting Program (DARP)

The National Institute on Drug Abuse contracted with Texas Christian University's Institute of Behavioral Research to establish and maintain a patient-reporting system to be used as a data base for treatment outcome evaluation research. A computerized file of longitudinal records was established which includes records on 43,931 patients' treatment in federally supported drug treatment programs.

DARP collected information from fifty-two treatment programs over a 4-year period (June 1969 to March 1973). Of all youth admissions during this

Table 8-2
Primary Drug Problem by Sex: CODAP Youth Subsample Admissions during Calendar Year 1975

Drug	*Male*	*Female*	*Total*	*%*
Heroin	322 (3%)	397 (4%)	919	3.6
Illegal Methadone	14 (<1%)	18 (1%)	32	0.1
Other Opiates	144 (1%)	75 (1%)	219	0.9
Alcohol	1,389 (9%)	900 (9%)	2,289	9.0
Barbiturates	1,263 (8%)	1,048 (10%)	2,311	9.1
Sedative-Hypnotics	419 (3%)	447 (4%)	866	3.4
Amphetamines	752 (5%)	916 (9%)	1,668	6.5
Cocaine	164 (1%)	107 (1%)	271	1.1
Marihuana/Hashish	8,018 (52%)	4,865 (48%)	12,883	50.5
Hallucinogens	1,075 (7%)	797 (8%)	1,872	7.3
Inhalants	1,193 (8%)	305 (3%)	1,498	5.9
OTC	36 (<1%)	57 (1%)	93	0.4
Other	94 (1%)	65 (1%)	159	0.6
Prevention	226 (2%)	222 (2%)	448	1.8
Totals	15,309	10,219	25,528	
%	(60.0%)	(40.0%)		100.0%

time, 39 percent were females. Generally, the differences in the prevalence of drug use found between girls and boys in DARP were statistically significant for most substances, due to the large samples (see table 8-3). The difference between the proportion of male and female users for any one class of drugs was no greater than 5 percentage points for all drug classes except barbiturates: half the females under 18 in DARP reported current barbiturate use, while only 43 percent of the males reported current barbiturate use. In both sexes, the rank order of the drugs used is identical, with marihuana being the most often cited and illegal methadone the least.

Only a few differences in this overall pattern occurred when race was taken into consideration. Although more boys than girls overall used heroin, white and Mexican-American girls used heroin more than their same-race male counter-

Table 8-3
DARP Youth Admissions: Proportions of Male and Female Youths Using Each Substance

	Proportion of Males	*Proportion of Females*	*Chi-Square,* X^2
Marihuana	.78	.81	1.392
Barbiturates	.43	.50	2.279
Hallucinogens	.39	.43	1.778
Amphetamines	.28	.31	2.453
Heroin	.25	.22	6.092*
Cocaine	.17	.13	2.513
Other Opiates	.11	.10	0.778
Other Drugs	.10	.05	4.179*
Illegal Methadone	.07	.05	1.881

Note: X^2 for $p < .05 = 3.84$.
*Indicates a statistically significant difference at the .05 level of confidence.

parts. Similarly, for all races, more boys than girls reported cocaine use. However, when each race group is considered separately, this pattern is seen only in blacks; white, Puerto Rican and Mexican-American girls all use more cocaine than their same-race male counterparts.

The Drug Abuse Warning Network (DAWN)

DAWN is a nationwide information system established by the Drug Enforcement Administration and cosponsored by the National Institute on Drug Abuse to provide data on drug-abuse patterns in the United States. It derives its information from contact reports provided by selected hospital emergency rooms, inpatient units, medical examiners, and crises centers in twenty-nine standard metropolitan statistical areas (SMSA) scattered throughout the country.

Table 8-4 shows the distribution by sex and race of youth 12 to 18 years of age who were treated in the twenty-nine SMSA hospital emergency rooms between April 1975 and April 1976 for various drug emergencies. In table 8-4 it can be seen that many more white females relative to white males and black females relative to black males received hospital emergency room treatment for drug-related problems. The majority of the drug mentions for tranquilizers, barbiturates, and aspirin were by females (60 percent of tranquilizers, 57 percent of barbiturates, and 87 percent of aspirin mentions).[3] One of the main factors that accounts for these differences is suicide attempts and gestures. White girls reported three times as many suicide attempts as white boys, and black girls reported five times as many suicide attempts as black boys. For example, 56

Table 8-4
DAWN IV Emergency Room Mentions for Selected Drugs by Sex and Race (April 1975-April 1976), Ages 12 to 18

Race/Sex Groups	*Tranquilizers*[a]	*Drug Unknown*	*Aspirin*	*Alcohol in Combination*
White males	754 (15)	557 (11)	234 (4)	589 (11)
White females	1,144 (14)	753 (9)	917 (11)	567 (7)
Black males	213 (21.3)	184 (19)	66 (6.2)	104 (10)
Black females	423 (19)	281 (12)	291 (13)	101 (4.5)
Others	390 (12)	308 (9)	297 (9)	217 (7)
Totals	2,924 (15)	2,083 (10)	1,805 (9)	1,578 (8)

[a]Includes diazepam, chlordiazepoxide, chlorpromazine, thioridazine, meprobomate, perphenazine, amitrp.

[b]Includes secobarbital, amobarbital, barbiturate sedative, phenobarbital, pentobarbital.

[c]Includes amphetamine, "speed."

percent of all females in emergency rooms who mentioned tranquilizers as their drug problem indicated that a suicide attempt was the "motivation" for the drug use, while only 33 percent of males reported that suicide was the motivation in their tranquilizer mentions. To some extent, suicide rate differences between the sexes may also explain the higher percentages of girls relative to boys who came to hospital emergency rooms for problems associated with aspirin and barbiturates.

As can be seen in table 8-4, there are more drug mentions for white females for amphetamines and heroin, but the numbers of mentions are much too small to draw any conclusions. For heroin this averages out to less than ten emergency room cases identified in each SMSA over the period of 1 year.

DAWN crisis center mentions for leading drugs used by girls and boys is presented in table 8-5. There is only a relatively small difference (50 percent for males versus 47 percent for females) in crisis center drug mentions for all drugs. There are higher percentages of boys with marihuana, alcohol, and LSD mentions, while girls' mentions are more frequent for methaqualone and barbiturates. However, black females only comprise 5 percent of the total mentions in crisis centers and show much smaller percentages than black males in all the drug categories but barbiturate/sedatives and tranquilizers.

Much smaller percentages of suicide attempts and gestures for the different drug classes are reported in crisis centers where drug use appears to be associated more with other motivating factors, that is, psychic effects and dependence.

When one considers the fact that the data are collected from the largest cities in the nation, it is surprising that there were only 356 heroin mentions (or 3 percent of all 11,874 drug mentions) from the sixty-five crisis center facilities represented in DAWN IV. While tranquilizers were the type of drug most frequently mentioned in hospital emergency rooms, marihuana was, by far, the drug most frequently mentioned in crisis centers.

Barbitu-rates[b]	Marihuana	Ampheta-mines[c]	Heroin	All Other Drugs	Totals
367 (7)	243 (5)	112 (2)	61 (1)	2,258 (44)	5,175 (100)
502 (6)	194 (2)	127 (2)	66 (1)	4,052 (48)	8,322 (100)
67 (7)	47 (5)	5 (.5)	47 (5)	248 (25)	981 (100)
117 (5)	42 (2)	9 (.5)	30 (1)	963 (43)	2,257 (100)
130 (4)	97 (3)	32 (1)	22 (1)	1,783 (54)	3,276 (100)
1,183 (6)	623 (3)	285 (1)	226 (1)	9,304 (47)	20,011 (100)

In summary, the portrait of drug use for the young woman does not vary significantly from that of the young man, regardless of the source of information reviewed. It does appear, however, to vary significantly from the stereotype of the meek girl—the girl prohibited by social mores from engaging in illicit drug use, the girl taking drugs only in the shadow of her male peers.

The National Youth Polydrug Study (NYPS)

To enrich the data obtained from the CODAP, DARP, and DAWN report systems and to gain a better understanding of youth drug users in treatment, the National Institute on Drug Abuse (NIDA) initiated the National Youth Polydrug Study (NYPS). NYPS is a cross-sectional survey of 97 drug treatment programs providing admission data on 2,750 youth drug-abuse clients who entered treatment between late 1976 and early 1977.

The comparison of males and females in the NYPS sample on age, race, and education is provided in table 8-6. Females, on the average, were younger than males (mean age for females 15.8 and males 16.0, $t = 3.7, p < .01$), and females had completed slightly more years of school (9.2 for females and 9.1 for males). There were relatively more females in the white and American Indian groups and relatively fewer females in the black and Hispanic groups.

Table 8-7 compares males and females on lifetime prevalence (numbers and percentages of clients who ever used) for each of the fifteen types of drugs. Alcohol and marihuana use were almost universally reported by this in-treatment population by both males and females. Consistent with many indications in the literature, amphetamine use was reported by a significantly higher proportion of females (50.3 percent of females as compared with 42.3 percent of males). Similar trends were found also for other sedatives (32 percent of females versus

Table 8-5
DAWN IV Crisis Center Mentions for Selected Drugs by Sex and Race (April 1975-April 1976), Ages 12 to 18

Race/Sex Groups	*Marihuana*	*Barbiturates*[a]	*Alcohol in Combination*	*LSD*
White males	1,389 (32)	291 (7)	308 (7)	282 (6)
White females	1,198 (31)	366 (10)	190 (5)	225 (6)
Black males	338 (36)	71 (8)	86 (9)	52 (6)
Black females	131 (26)	79 (16)	40 (8)	33 (6)
Others	309 (24)	83 (6)	110 (8)	118 (9)
Totals	3,365 (31)	890 (8)	734 (7)	710 (7)

[a]Includes secobarbital, amobarbital, barbiturate sedatives, phenobarbital, pentobarbital.

[b]Includes amphetamine, "speed."

[c]Includes diazepam, chlordiazepoxide, chlorpromazine, thioridazine, meprobomate, perphenazine, amitrp.

27.5 percent of males), and for over-the-counter drugs (10.2 percent of females versus only 4 percent of males). Males, on the other hand, reported a higher lifetime prevalence in the use of two drug categories: inhalants (32.6 percent of males versus 24.2 percent of females) and cocaine (27.6 percent of males versus 23.6 percent of females). In all other drugs there were no statistically significant differences in lifetime prevalence across the sexes.

Females not only had a higher prevalence of ever having used amphetamines, sedatives, and over-the-counter drugs, but in addition, a relatively greater proportion of them who had ever used these substances used them regularly (at least once a week for a period of at least one month). For example, of the 524 females reporting ever having used amphetamines, 72 percent used them regularly, compared with 66 percent of the 688 males who had ever used amphetamines. Similarly, 72.1 percent of the females ever using barbiturates used them regularly, compared with 67 percent of the males. With over-the-counter drugs, 59.4 percent of the female users had used regularly, compared with 45 percent of the males.

The higher prevalence of use of certain drugs by females may be meaningfully related to the fact that females reported greater ease in obtaining these particular drugs. For example, 62.6 percent of all females described amphetamines as being easily obtainable, while only 58.7 percent of all males gave the same obtainability rating for amphetamines. The case was similar with over-the-counter drugs, in which 91.5 percent of females reported them as easy to obtain while only 87.2 percent of males so reported. Like trends exist for barbiturates and other opiate drugs.

The relationship between greater ease of obtaining drugs and higher prevalence of lifetime use holds also for males. For example, a higher proportion of males (32.61 versus 24.21 percent of the females) used inhalants. Concomi-

Amphetamines[b]	*Tranquilizers*[c]	*Methaqualone*	*Heroin*	*All Other Drugs*	*Totals*
197 (5)	154 (4)	165 (4)	87 (2)	1,442 (23)	4,315 (100)
248 (6)	188 (5)	193 (5)	72 (2)	1,137 (30)	3,817 (100)
46 (5)	5 (1)	17 (2)	96 (10)	216 (23)	927 (100)
26 (5)	17 (3)	12 (2)	51 (10)	122 (24)	511 (100)
57 (4)	64 (5)	33 (3)	50 (4)	480 (37)	1,304 (100)
574 (5)	428 (4)	420 (4)	356 (3)	3,397 (31)	11,874 (100)

tantly, a higher proportion of males reported inhalants as being easy to obtain (90.01 percent of males compared with 86.54 percent of females).

The greater ease of obtaining drugs for females is probably related in turn to the source of the drugs. For males, the street was the primary source for all the drugs they used, while for females, a gift from a friend (presumably a male friend) was the primary source for drugs. Street buys from a friend were the primary sources of drugs for 35 percent of the males, and another 24.3 percent of the males reported street buys from a dealer as their primary source of the drugs they used. On the other hand, the most frequent source mentioned by females was a gift from a friend, reported by 35.7 percent of the females, and the second most frequent source was a street buy from a friend. The tendency for males to acquire drugs primarily on the street, either from a friend or a dealer, and for females to obtain drugs as gifts may explain the easier obtainability of drugs for females as compared with males.

The two sex groups differed on the following personal and social history (see table 8-8) scales: male clients reported a more intensive involvement on ten measures of illegal and criminal justice system involvement (drug-use offenses, property offenses, violent offenses, being referred by the criminal justice system, etc.). Females reported more suicide attempts, more drug- or alcohol-related problems of their mothers, and more psychiatric, health, and personal problems with family listed as the reason for seeking treatment. It is interesting that while females more often report health problems as reasons for seeking treatment, males more often report physical (health) problems as being an obstacle to attending school.

Miscellaneous Study Findings

In addition to the three national reporting systems, a number of independent researchers have commented on the characteristics of young women who seek treatment. In general, these studies report the following:

Table 8-6
National Youth Polydrug Study Demographic Variables of Race, Age, and Education by Sex

	Male		Female		Total Sample	
	n	%	*n*	%	*n*	%
White	1,091	(67.5)	740	(72.3)	1,831	(69.3)
Black	246	(15.2)	133	(13.0)	379	(14.4)
American Indian	62	(3.8)	72	(7.0)	134	(5.1)
Hispanic	218	(13.5)	79	(7.7)	297	(11.2)
Total	1,617	(100%)	1,024	(100%)	2,641	(100%)
	(61.2%)		(38.8%)		(100%)	

	Male		Female		Total Sample		
	$\overline{X}$	*S.D.*	$\overline{X}$	*S.D.*	$\overline{X}$	*S.D.*	*t*
Age	16.0	1.39	15.8	1.35	15.9	1.38	3.1**
Education (Last grade completed)	9.1	1.52	9.2	1.44	9.1	1.46	−1.75

*$p < .05$.
**$p < .01$.

Young women in treatment are using about the same types of drugs and drug combinations with about the same frequencies as boys (Suffet and Brotman 1976; Klinge et al. 1976; Cuskey et al. 1972; Levy and Doyle 1974).

In the treatment setting, female adolescents are greatly outnumbered by male adolescents (Suffet and Brotman 1976; Cuskey et al. 1972; Chein 1964; Byrne et al. 1977).

Girls tend to enter treatment at a slightly younger age than boys (Klinge et al. 1976; Cuskey et al. 1971) and to have had a drug problem for a shorter period of time (Eldred and Washington 1977; Levy and Doyle 1974).

The girls—like the boys—begin using drugs at a very (even surprisingly) early age (Abelson and Fishburne 1976; Suffet and Brotman 1976; Cuskey et al. 1972). Most authors agree that girls and boys begin drug experimentation and use at similar ages (Eldred and Washington 1977; Pandina 1977; Cuskey et al. 1971); and when age differences *are* noted, the girls have usually tried drugs at an earlier age than boys (Burt et al. 1977; Klinge et al. 1976; Pittel 1973).

What Types of Treatment Do Young Women Receive?

When young women do decide to get help, where do they turn? A number of authors (for example, Brook et al. 1976; Roth 1971) have noted with despair

Table 8-7
National Youth Polydrug Study. Lifetime Prevalence of Drug Use by Sex (The Fifteen Drug Categories are Ranked According to Number of Female Users (n = 2,750)

	Females				Males				
	Ever Used		Never Used		Ever Used		Never Used		
	n	Females (%)	n	Females (%)	n	Males (%)	n	Males (%)	X^2
Alcohol	946	(91.0)	95	(9.0)	1,461	(89.0)	181	(11.0)	2.49
Marihuana	944	(90.4)	100	(9.6)	1,481	(90.5)	156	(9.5)	.001
Amphetamines	524	(50.3)	517	(49.7)	688	(41.1)	946	(57.9)	17.39*
Barbiturates	415	(42.8)	594	(57.2)	630	(38.6)	1,001	(61.4)	1.63
Hashish	420	(40.6)	614	(59.4)	717	(43.9)	917	(56.1)	2.75
Hallucinogens	402	(39.0)	630	(61.0)	668	(41.2)	954	(58.8)	1.30
Other Sedatives	333	(32.1)	703	(67.9)	448	(27.5)	1,180	(72.5)	6.53*
Phencyclidine	327	(31.6)	708	(68.4)	527	(32.3)	1,103	(67.7)	.16
Other Opiates	253	(24.6)	777	(75.4)	408	(25.1)	1,216	(74.9)	.11
Inhalants	250	(24.2)	781	(75.8)	528	(32.6)	1,090	(67.4)	21.34*
Cocaine	243	(23.6)	786	(76.4)	448	(27.6)	1,173	(72.4)	5.28*
Heroin	116	(11.3)	911	(88.7)	211	(13.0)	1,406	(87.0)	1.78
Over-the-Counter	105	(10.2)	924	(89.8)	60	(4.0)	1,499	(96.0)	41.92**
Illegal Methadone	36	(3.5)	993	(96.5)	70	(4.3)	1,552	(95.7)	
Other	12	(1.2)	1,017	(98.8)	32	(2.0)	1,590	(98.0)	

* = $p < .05$.
** = $p < .01$.

Table 8-8
National Youth Polydrug Study. Correlation of Background Variables by Sex (n = 2,750)

	Correlation Coefficient
A. Criminal Justice System and Legal Variables	
Number of alcohol and drug offenses	.33
Number of arrests for property offenses	.24
Number of times picked up by the police	.19
Number of public and private property offenses	.19
Legal problem as a reason for contacting the treatment program	.18
Number of arrests for violent offenses	.15
Number of arrests for substance-related offenses	.15
Referred by criminal justice system	.14
Adjudicated delinquent	.14
Public and private property convictions	.14
B. Other Background Variables	
Physical problems being the obstacle to school attendance	.17
Number of suicide attempts	−.15
Psychiatric problems being a reason for contacting the treatment program	−.15
Health problems being a reason for contacting the treatment program	−.15
Personal problems with family being a reason for contacting the treatment program	−.14
Mother having a drug/alcohol problem	−.12

Note: A positive correlation indicates a significantly greater association with being male.

that young people reject the established community channels for help—families, churches, schools, and physicians. Friends, drug treatment programs, and rap centers are the most frequently cited refuge, and young women most often seek drug-free outpatient treatment. The concept behind the outpatient service is to provide an environment in which clients can obtain some basic treatment services while remaining in the community. Although group counseling is available, the primary focus is on individual counseling in which short-term personal, family, and school problems can be discussed in relation to drug-use problems. Table 8-9 presents the sex distribution of clients across treatment environments and modalities based on the 1975 CODAP data. The outpatient environment is subdivided into the three treatment modalities: detoxification, maintenance, and drug free. There is a significantly greater proportion of young males in residential treatment than females (phi = .0349), and there is also a significantly greater proportion of male youths in daycare treatment than female youths (phi = .0241). This may, in part, be attributed to the fact that boys are more likely to have been referred by the criminal justice system and are generally required to remain in treatment for a predetermined period of time. It has also been reported that many of the traditional therapeutic communities

Table 8-9
Distribution of CODAP Youth Admissions by Modality/Environment and Sex in 1975

Modality/Environment	*n Males*	*Males (%)*	*n Females*	*Females (%)*
Detox outpatient	65	.4	47	.4
Maintenance outpatient	30	.2	23	.2
Drug-free outpatient	11,582	72.8	8,217	76.7
Drug-free daycare	1,433	9.0	818	7.6
Drug-free residential	2,426	15.2	1,366	12.6
Other	384	2.4	242	2.3
Column Totals	15,920	100.0	10,713	100.0

(residential programs) are inappropriate for girls because of the therapeutic approaches used (aggressive confrontation approach), the limitations in facilities and because they tend to be dominated by male clients and male staff (DeLeon and Beschner 1976).

The almost negligible number of female youths as well as male youths under 18 years of age in outpatient detoxification treatment and in outpatient methadone maintenance treatment can be explained by the fact that federal and state regulations discourage methadone treatment for patients under 18 years of age.

What Happens to Them When They Get into Treatment?

Very little is known about treatment outcomes for young women (or adult women, for that matter) who enter treatment. Scanty findings reported in the literature suggest that the differential status of females in general follows them into treatment. For example:

> At the root of many adolescent female drug problems lie anxiety, concern, ignorance, and ambivalence about sexuality and reproductive functioning. A large number of young drug users are struggling with fears about homosexuality. Female sexuality and physiology are little understood by most men (who dominate the treatment scene) (Levy and Doyle 1974), and thus little emotional or medical attention is given to these problems (Cuskey et al. 1972).
>
> Both female offenders and female addicts have been described in more negative terms than their male counterparts and have been widely presumed to be more difficult to treat (Eldred and Washington 1977; Kirsh 1974). Chein (1964) noted that the female addicts in treatment were similar to

males in that they made meager use of hospital resources (educational, recreational, psychotherapeutic), but unlike males, the young women had a high incidence of physical complaints without demonstrable physical pathology.

The female stereotype afflicts all girls in treatment in many subtle ways. The jobs assigned to female residents in therapeutic communities are sex typed: women wash dishes, cook, and clean; men make repairs, fix cars, etc. (DeLeon and Beschner 1976). The career development and vocational rehabilitation opportunities presented males and females differ along traditional lines (Levy and Doyle 1974; Schwartz 1977). Females are reportedly encouraged (if not required) to dress "appropriately," that is, to be feminine but not provocative (Schwartz 1977).

As a result of interviews with seventy female ex-clients of drug treatment programs, Schwartz developed a four-part typology that describes their perceptions of the attitudes of the treatment staff toward women in treatment. Women invariably reported being characterized as one or more of the following:

Slut/whore. This stereotype derives from the relationship between drug addiction and prostitution and creates a number of problems for women addicts. At the same time, in some places these women are expected (and in some cases forced) to engage in sexual relationships with the staff.

Intellectual junkie. Females who are too smart or too articulate (that is, those who can fight back or question staff discipline or interpretation) are put down. Apparently, intelligence and self-assertiveness—clearly not part of the female role constellation—are not part of the addict role either.

Abusive mother. Young females with children are automatically assumed to be uncaring, abusive mothers.

Hypochondriac. Treatment staff are reportedly unsympathetic to women's complaints about physical or health problems, and such complaints are more often diagnosed as mental in origin than physiological.

Other authors have found that treatment staff are surprisingly out of touch with or unsympathetic to their female client's problems. For example:

A study of adult women (mean age thirty-five) in treatment found that they felt that the most valuable aspect of drug-abuse treatment was the methadone itself, in contrast with the males who considered camaraderie and communication with the counselors the most important parts of the treatment experience (Byrne 1977).

> A study of attitudes toward women in a methadone program found vast discrepancies between staff and female client perceptions. Staff perceived that most of the females in the program "did nothing" for a living when, in fact, many were employed and fewer women than men in this sample were unemployed. Staff greatly underestimated the extent to which female clients (1) felt unable to express their feelings, (2) had bad feelings about their bodies, and (3) felt they were not smart enough or educated enough to get a good job (Levy and Doyle 1974). In a companion study of a residential treatment program, the same authors (Levy and Doyle) found that the staff misperceived women's (1) suicide tendencies, (2) concern about family relations, (3) willingness to help themselves, (4) bad feelings about their bodies, and (5) feelings of ignorance and stupidity.

Although these data do not constitute an indictment against all treatment centers, it is likely that the disadvantages and prejudices that all women suffer are carried into the treatment center.

This differential treatment, if it is widespread throughout the network, is not reflected in the available treatment outcome statistics (Rosenthal 1976). Based on partial sample of CODAP discharge reports (see table 8-10), it is known that:

> Women under 18 complete treatment at about the same rate as boys—27 percent for both, as shown in table 8-10.

Table 8-10
CODAP Treatment Outcomes by Sex: Comparison of Female and Male Adolescents

Treatment Outcome	*%Males (n = 906)*	*% Females (n = 906)*
Completed treatment	27	27
Transferred–referred	20	18
Noncompliance	9	6
Client left	42	48
Other	1	1
Total percentage	100	100

Note: The analysis was performed on a computer-generated random sample of the CODAP historical clients file consisting of 13,268 clients. Historical client file of CODAP, includes admission and discharge data on clients discharged from federally supported drug treatment programs during the first three quarters of 1975. Over one-half of all drug-abuse treatment programs in the United States are federally supported, and these programs account for approximately two-thirds of all clients in treatment.

Looking at the "split" rate (client left) for young males and females, it appears that the young women under 18 "split" more frequently than the young males—48 and 42 percent, respectively.

Both males and females are more likely to successfully complete treatment if they are employed, enrolled in an education program, or have a high school diploma.

Summary

The Nature and Extent of Drug Use

The drug-use patterns of girls and boys under 18 years of age are quite similar. Six youth surveys show similar patterns with such drugs as alcohol, hallucinogens, amphetamines, tranquilizers, and inhalants. According to the surveys, higher percentages of boys use marihuana, while higher percentages of girls use barbiturates. Heroin and cocaine are rarely used by youngsters under 18. The prevalence rates for marihuana and alcohol use have been increasing for both boys and girls, while these rates have stabilized for nonmedical use of prescription psychoactive drugs. There has not been much change in the prevalence rates for other drugs, and one study shows a small reduction over time in the use of barbiturates.

Of the boys and girls who entered treatment programs reporting to CODAP, there were only slight differences in the age of first use regarding thirteen drug categories. However, it was found that girls had progressed sooner to first continuous use in most of the categories.

DARP, another large treatment data base, shows only small differences (for most substances) in drug-use frequency for girls and boys.

The DAWN data indicate that drug mentions for hospital emergency rooms are not too different for girls and boys, once suicide attempts and gestures are identified and excluded. There were only slight differences in the alcohol in combination and marihuana mentions between white girls and boys and between black boys and girls. The DAWN crisis center data also show only slight differences in male and female drug mentions. Boys had slightly more marihuana, alcohol, and LSD mentions, while girls reported more frequent use of methaqualone and barbiturates.

What does all this mean? Besides showing that there are similarities in the drug-use patterns of girls and boys, we can also see that a substantial percentage of girls are involved in using drugs. We find that at an early age, girls are beginning to experiment with many different drugs, although hard drugs (heroin and cocaine) are used by only a small percentage of either girls or boys. It means that we should no longer view drug use as only a male problem, particularly with regard to those who are under 18 years of age.

It is quite clear that there are no simple explanations for or reasons why young girls begin using and/or abusing drugs. It is for this reason that the problem has been so elusive and difficult to address. Separate agencies, organizations, and programs are often established to treat the various aspects of drug abuse (for example, physical and psychological problems), yet we know that the underlying causality is complex and must be dealt with in a comprehensive fashion.

In this chapter we have tried to present a profile of the adolescent female drug user and the combination of forces that may be responsible for her drug-taking behavior. Peer relations, family pathology and fragmentation, sexual development and sexuality, loneliness and rebellion, and certain psychological characteristics may be considered some of the primary motivating factors in girls' involvement in drug use. These causes have been documented in the literature by those who have studied and/or treated female drug abusers. Often, these causative factors have been identified retrospectively after a woman has developed an addiction for drugs and required treatment. Certainly, these underlying factors should provide some clues for treatment and prevention strategies. Like all drug problems, there are other underlying problems that need to be diagnosed before any meaningful treatment attempt can be made. As Konopka stated so eloquently, "In attempting to treat girls, it is essential that their uniqueness be remembered."

Society's treatment response obviously needs more planning and organization. In a review of the CODAP data, it was seen that females comprised 40.3 percent of youth under 18 years of age in treatment in 1975 and only 4.9 percent of the total CODAP treatment population.

Drug-free outpatient programs are the predominant drug treatment modality serving girls, but as yet there is little information available on treatment outcomes from these modalities. However, it is known from the CODAP historical file that only 27 percent of the girls are considered to have actually completed treatment. There is little comfort to be found in the fact that these statistics are not much different for boys.

From the available literature it appears that girls who do enter treatment have to contend with a number of inequities, misperceptions, and biases. It is also becoming more apparent that many drug treatment programs are not adequately structured or equipped to address the special social, psychological, and medical needs of girls.

Several conclusions can be drawn from the material presented in this chapter. Unfortunately, a number of conclusions can also be drawn from information that is not included in this chapter or elsewhere in the literature of female adolescent drug abuse.

First, it must become commonly understood that young women have extensive and, in many cases, serious drug problems. Social services agencies, health care delivery organizations, law enforcement officials, schools, and parents must recognize that girls are as likely to experiment with and use drugs as boys. More important, all individuals and organizations concerned with the drug problems of young people must begin to understand the underlying problems that lead to or complicate the drug use of young *women.* Antidrug campaigns, law enforcement activities, and treatment based on stereotypes about boys, adolescents, or adults will not be adequate.

Any attempt to tailor a rational program of prevention and treatment for young women will be a difficult challenge. There is no single reason why young women turn to drugs, no single pattern of use, no predictable outcome of treatment. To comprehend the nature of the drug-use problem in this population, one must attempt to understand the motivational and behavioral factors that drive this population, and these are as complex as adolescence and as varied as the female population.

What is needed? First, as a matter of course, researchers must begin to include young women as a discernible subsample in study populations. The weight of existing evidence indicates that there are differences between girls and boys and that henceforth these differences cannot be masked or ignored in studies or attempts to define the problems of "adolescents." The body of knowledge about usage patterns, motivation, and treatment outcomes must be enhanced and continuously updated.

Second, public agencies entrusted with the responsibility for "solving" the drug problem and formulating public policy must begin to recognize young women as a distinct target population with priorities equal to that of other target populations. The evidence that young girls begin to use drugs at an early age suggests a need to emphasize prevention activities in this target group.

Third, treatment agencies and their staffs must become better prepared to deal with the emotional, political, and physical components of drug use by young women. By *emotional* we mean the particular psychology of female adolescence in general as well as the motivational factors related specifically to drug use. Much is known about the former, although the wealth of existing knowledge is largely untapped by the treatment community. Very little is known about the latter, and clinicians and researchers must therefore bear some responsibility for advancing the state of knowledge. By *political* we mean the particular abuses reportedly suffered by young women at the hands of insensitive treatment staff and male clients. That these abuses are unintentional consequences of subtle social prejudices is no excuse. Consciousness raising is an effective tool for educating staff as well as for treating clients.

And, fourth, clinicians who work with girls with drug problems must become more knowledgeable about the physical development and concomitant problems experienced by adolescent females. They must either develop informed resources in house or become sensitive to the need and establish appropriate liaison relationships with professionals in the medical and mental health fields.

This is a great challenge, but the evidence points to an ever-increasing drug problem among this population, and the time to respond is now. Despite the sugar and spice, everything is *not* nice. We must begin to deal with what girls are *really* made of.

Notes

1. A nationwide prevalence study of nonmedical use of prescription stimulants found that 10 percent of adult males and 6 percent of adult females had used prescription stimulants for nonmedical reasons. This pattern was accented by young adults 18 to 25, among whom 21 percent of the males and 13 percent of the females reported nonmedical use of prescription stimulants (Abelson and Fishburne 1976). This finding contrasts with a nationwide survey of *prescriptions* for psychotherapeutic drug use. Parry et al. (1973) reported that 8 percent of the women studied versus 1 percent of the men had received a prescription for stimulants.

2. Some data 1970 to 1977, other data from 1968 to 1977.

3. A drug mention represents an instance in which an individual interviewed at a reporting facility mentioned a substance which was related to the visit to that facility.

References

Abelson, N.I., and Fishburne, P.M. 1976. *Nonmedical Use of Psychoactive Substances.* 1975-1976 Nationwide Study Among Youth and Adults, The George Washington University for the National Institute on Drug Abuse, Division of Research, Behavioral and Social Sciences Branch, response analysis.

Blackford, L. 1977. *Summary Report–Surveys of Student Drug Use.* San Mateo, California, 1968-1977, funded by PHS Research Grant RO1-DA00094.

Brook, J., Lukoff, I.F., Whiteman, M., and Whiteman, G. 1977. Teenage Drug Use in an Urban Ghetto: Preliminary Findings. Support for study grant H81 DA 01103-01, NIDA.

Brook, R., Szandorowska, B., and Whitehead, P.C. 1976. Psychosocial dysfunction as precursors to amphetamine abuse among adolescents. *Addictive Diseases: An International Journal* 2 (3):465-478.

Burt, M.R., Glynn, T.J., Sowder, B., and Gilden, Z. 1977. *An Investigation of the Characteristics of Drug Abusing Women.* National Institute on Drug Abuse, Under contract number 271-76-4401. NIDA.

Byrne, R., 1977. Distinctive Problems of the Female Drug Addict: Experiences at the Illinois Drug Abuse Program (IDAP). Unpublished paper based on study conducted in 1972-1973.

Chase, J.A., and Jessor, R. 1977. A Social Psychological Analysis of Marihuana Involvement Among a National Sample of Adolescents. Report prepared under contract number ADM 281-75-0028, NIAAA.

Chein, I., Gerard, D.L., Lee, R.S., and Rosenfeld, E. 1964. *The Road to H: Narcotics, Delinquency, and Social Policy.* New York: Basic Books.

Cuskey, W.R., Premkumar, T., and Sigel, L. 1972. Survey of opiate addiction among females in the United States between 1850 and 1970. *Public Health Reviews* 1:5-41.

Cuskey, W.R., Moffett, A.D., and Clifford, H.B. 1971. Comparison of female opiate addicts admitted at Lexington Hospital in 1961 and 1967. *HSMA Health Reports,* 86 (4):332-340.

DeLeon, G., and Beschner, G. (eds.). 1976. The therapeutic community. *Proceedings of Therapeutic Communities of America Planning Conference, January 29, 1976.* NIDA Publication.

Densen-Gerber, J. 1977. *Sociological Autopsy, Odyssey House Parents Demonstration Program.* Report to NIDA, produced through grant H81 DA 01698.

Drug Abuse Warning Network (DAWN). 1977. *Report IV.* NIDA.

Eldred, C.A., and Washington, M.N. 1977. Female Heroin Addicts in a City Treatment Program: The Forgotten Minority Speaks Out. Unpublished paper.

Eldred, C.A., and Washington, M.N. 1977. *The Role of Social Relationships in Heroin Use by Men and Women.* Narcotics Treatment Administration, Washington, D.C.

Elinson, J. 1977. Status of operational definitions. *The Epidemiology of Drug Abuse, Current Issues.* Research Monograph Series 10, NIDA.

Farnsworth, D.L. 1972. The dilemma of the adolescent in a rapidly changing society. *Proceedings of the 105th Annual Meeting of the West Virginia State Medical Association.*

Hindermarch, T. 1971. Patterns of drug use and attitudes to drug users in a school aged population. *Proceedings of the First International Conference on Student Drug Surveys.* Baywood Publishing Co., Farmingdale, New York 11735.

Johnston, L., Backman, G., and O'Malley, P. 1977. Monitoring the Future: A Continuing Study of the Lifestyle and Values of Youth. U.S. Department of Health, Education, and Welfare, Rockville, Maryland.

Josephson, E., Haberman, P., Zanes, A., and Elinson, J. 1971. Adolescent marihuana use: Report on a national survey. *Proceedings of the First International Conference on Study Drug Surveys.* Baywood Publishing Co., Farmingdale, New York 11735.

Josephson, E. 1977. Surveys of special populations. *The Epidemiologies of Drug Abuse, Current Issues.* Research Monograph Series 10, NIDA.

Kandel, D., Single, E., and Kessler, R.C. 1976. The Epidemiology of drug use among New York State high school students: Distribution, trends and change in rates of use. *American Journal of Public Health* 66 (1).

Kirk, R.S. 1978. Alcohol and Drug Use Patterns and Correlates among High School Students in Vermont. Study produced through grant H81 DA 01545, NIDA.

Kirsh, B. 1974. Consciousness raising as therapy for women. In V. Franks and V. Burtle (eds.), *Women in Therapy.* New York: Brunner/Mazel, Inc.

Klinge, V., Vaziri, H., and Lennox, K. 1976. Comparison of psychiatric inpatient male and female adolescent drug abusers. *The International Journal of the Addictions* 11 (2):309-323.

Konopka, G. 1966. *The Adolescent Girl in Conflict.* Englewood Cliffs, N.J.: Prentice-Hall.

Lavenhar, M.A., Wolfson, E.A., Sheffet, A., Einstein, S., and Louria, D.B. 1971. Survey of drug abuse in six New Jersey high schools: II. Characteristics of drug users and non-users. *Proceedings of the First International Conference on Student Drug Surveys.* Baywood Publishing Co., Farmingdale, New York 11735.

Lerner, S.E. and Linder, R.L. 1974. Drugs in the elementary school. *Journal of Drug Education* 4 (3).

Levy, S., and Doyle, K. Attitudes toward women in a drug treatment program. *Journal of Drug Issues* 4 (4):428-434.

Linder, R.L., Lerner, S.E., and Burke, E.M. 1974. Drugs in the junior high school, Part I. *Journal of Psychedelic Drugs* 6 (1).

MacPherson, M. 1977. Blue collar women: The gap widens. *Washington Post,* June 19, 1977.

Noble, P., Hart, T. and Nation, R. 1972. Correlates and outcomes of illicit drug use by adolescent girls. *British Journal of Psychiatry* 120:497-504.

Pandina, R.J. 1977. New Jersey Survey of Alcohol and Drug Use Among Adolescents. Study produced through grant H81 DA 01702, NIDA.

Parry, H.J., Balter, M.B., Mellinger, G.D., Cisin, I.H., and Manheimer, D.I. 1973. National patterns of psychotherapeutic drug use. *Archives of General Psychiatry.* 28:769-783.

Patch, V.D. 1973. Public health aspects of adolescent drug use in America. *Problem in Perspective, Technical Papers of the Second Report of the National Commission on Marihuana and Drug Abuse,* Vol IV: Treatment and Rehabilitation.

Pittel, S.M. 1973. The etiology of youthful drug involvement in drug use in America. *Problem in Perspective, the Technical Papers of the Second Report of the National Commission on Marihuana and Drug Abuse,* Vol I: Patterns and Consequences of Drug Use, pp. 879-912.

Posner, L., Soler, E., and Abod, J. 1977. Women in treatment: Client self-report, a summary. *Women in Treatment: Issues and Approaches, Resource Manual.* National Drug Abuse Center for Training and Resource Development.

Rado, S. 1957. Narcotic bondage: A general theory of the dependence on narcotic drugs. *American Journal of Psychiatry* 1957:114, 165-171.

Rogers, D. 1977. *The Psychology of Adolescence.* Englewood Cliffs, N.J.: Prentice-Hall, p. 365.

Rosenthal, B.J. 1976. Drug Treatment Outcomes: Is Sex a Factor? Prepared for presentation at the National Drug Abuse Conference, March 28, 1976.

Roth, R. 1971. Student drug abuse in southeastern Michigan and profiles of the abusers. *Proceedings of the First International Conference on Student Drug Surveys.* Baywood Publishing Co., Farmingdale, New York 11735.

Schwartz, B. 1977. The female addict. *Women in Treatment: Issues and Approaches, Resource Manual.* National Drug Abuse Center for Training and Resource Development.

Smart, R., and Feger, D. 1972. Drug use among adolescents and their parents: Closing the generation gap in mood modification. *Journal of Abnormal Psychology* 79 (2):153-160.

Steffenhagen, R.A., Schmidt, F.E., and McAree, C.P. 1971. Emotional stability and student drug use. *Proceedings of the First International Conference on Student Drug Use.* Baywood Publishing Co., Farmingdale, New York 11735.

Suffet, F. and Brotman, R. 1976. Female drug use: Some observations. *International Journal of the Addictions* 11 (1):19-33.

U.S. Bureau of Census. 1976. *Statistical Abstract of the United States.* U.S. Department of Commerce, Washington, D.C.

Winslow, J. 1971. Drug trying/use and social participation. *Proceedings of the First International Conference on Student Drug Surveys.* Baywood Publishing Co., Farmingdale, New York 11735.

Wishnie, H. 1973. Opiate addiction: A masked depression. In S. Pesse (ed.), *A Masked Depression.* Boston: Little Brown.

Wolforf, D. 1973. *Careers in Dope.* Englewood Cliffs, N.J.: Prentice-Hall.

Wolfson, E.A., Lavenhar, M.A., Blum, R., Quinones, M.A., Einstein, S., and Louria, D.B. 1971. Survey of drug abuse in six New Jersey high schools: I. Methodology and general findings. *Proceedings of the First International Conference on Student Drug Surveys.* Baywood Publishing Co., Farmingdale, New York 11735.

9 Drug Abuse and Delinquency: A Study of Youths in Treatment

Carl G. Leukefeld and
Richard R. Clayton

Introduction

Delinquency in general and youthful drug abuse in particular are both extremely complex and urgent problems that touch many Americans in some negative way—be it the overburdened taxpayer, the burglarized homeowner, or the guilt-ridden parent. All this is in addition to the harmful effects that drug abuse and delinquent behavior bring to the youths involved.

These problems seem to be worsening. Reports from the FBI indicate that the juvenile crime rate is at record highs. There is alarm about the accelerating proportion of young people who are problem drinkers or who use and abuse illicit substances like marihuana and phencyclidine.

Tragic as the human costs are in wasted lives and destroyed families, these are only part of the picture. The social costs of continued public financing of just a small number of offenders' careers is staggering. One study conducted by the Department of Corrections in the District of Columbia in the late 1960s provided data on the costs generated by only 25 young men. During their "criminal history" each offender experienced approximately 25 correctional actions and the accompanying services. The costs ranged from over $13,000 to more than $68,000 per case. The study estimated that this one small cohort alone cost about $10 million in public tax money. Although quite startling, these statistics are nevertheless typical of costs incurred in servicing criminal careers within the criminal justice system.

From a historical perspective, youthful drug abuse is a relatively new phenomenon, and only recently has it been labeled as a social problem. It first gained public attention and generated concern during the mid-1960s, in connection with the so-called hippie movement and the Vietnam war. The roots of public concern about juvenile delinquency emerged much earlier, and for decades now, juvenile delinquency has constituted a viable substantive specialty in sociology and social work. However, quite recently the "linkage" and interaction between illicit drug abuse and delinquency has emerged as an important topical focus for research and policy.

The opinions expressed herein are those of the authors and do not represent the official policy of the National Institute on Drug Abuse or the Alcohol, Drug Abuse, and Mental Health Administration, Department of Health, Education and Welfare.

There are four major research questions that must eventually be resolved if we are fully to understand the relationship of drug use/abuse and delinquent/criminal behaviors among youths. They are:

1. What is the *degree of association* between illicit drug use and delinquency?
2. What is the usual *time order of occurrence*—does drug use usually precede delinquent behavior or vice versa?
3. What is the effect on the drug use/delinquency relationship when variables antecedent to both are statistically controlled (that is, *testing for spuriousness*)?
4. Can a meaningful typology of drug use and delinquency be developed, and then, can *effective predictors* of the types be discovered?

These are questions that from a policy and research perspective require a special type of data base. The National Youth Polydrug Study (NYPS) was designed to provide extensive information on the correlates of drug use/abuse among a sample of youthful drug users in treatment. The reader is reminded that the NYPS data are from a purposive sample. The study is not assumed to be representative of all treatment programs, youthful clients in treatment for drug abuse, or all youths who have abused drugs. Given these limitations, the NYPS data do provide valuable information about the drug use/delinquency relationship. This chapter will address, albeit tentatively, questions one and three above.

Sample

The respondents for this chapter are the 2,750 adolescents in the National Youth Polydrug Study sample. These data were collected by the Philadelphia Polydrug Research Project Survey in 1976-1977. The subjects were drawn from a national sample of 97 youth drug-abuse treatment programs from thirty-seven states. All subjects were 18 or younger. As noted earlier in chapter 6, the average age is 16.4, 61 percent are males, and 7 out of 10 are white.

This sample has several distinguishing characteristics. First, all the respondents are in treatment programs and thus have been labeled as drug users or abusers. A comparison of these youths with those identified through normal household sampling procedures (see Abelson et al. 1977) or in studies in which the primary sampling unit is the school reveals a considerable difference in reported drug use. This is most apparent with regard to the use of illicit substances "beyond" marihuana; for example, only 1 percent of youths 12 to 17 in the national household sample had ever used heroin compared to 12 percent from the NYPS group. The difference is also apparent with regard to marihuana: 23 percent of the national sample have used marihuana (ever), while 81 percent of the NYPS sample had used it within 3 months prior to entering treatment.

A second distinguishing characteristic is the degree of contact with officials of the criminal justice system, that is, police, judges, and corrections personnel. Only 28 percent of the sample reported never being picked up by the police. For the 72 percent that have been picked up, 46 percent of them reported five or less separate police contacts, the mode being 1. A total of 962 of the NYPS youths, 35 percent of the entire sample, had been incarcerated; the average age at first incarceration is 14.7. Respondents had an opportunity to indicate what pressures from the criminal justice system were among their reasons for contacting or entering the treatment program. Of the 35 percent (971) stating their reason to be for a legal problem, 21 percent (379) of them specified its nature to be for an arrest, while 10 percent (277) indicated an upcoming court date.

A final distinguishing characteristic of the sample is the racial distribution. As indicated earlier, the NYPS sample is predominantly white (70 percent). Data on race and ethnic distributions among those arrested, convicted, imprisoned, and released into the communities on probation or on parole are usually skewed toward the nonwhite population.

While different in the degree to which these subjects have been involved with drugs and the criminal justice system, this sample cannot be viewed as comprehensively deviant. While most subjects have had contact with the police, the modal number of times picked up is 1. Although the degree of drug use is high and all these respondents were "in treatment," only 16 percent of the sample had received prior treatment for drug abuse or alcohol use. These are not "street people." In fact, over two-thirds received treatment on an outpatient status and three-fourths indicated that they lived in their parents' homes.

Illicit Drug Use, Delinquency, and Criminal Justice Contacts

One of the primary concerns about youthful drug use is that it may be facilitative of serious involvement with criminal activities and that this crime/drug interaction often leads to serious confrontations with criminal justice authorities. This line of thought is, of course, the basis for legislative action which emphasizes early intervention strategies and techniques for "troubled" youths.

Some 1,035 of these youths (38 percent) reported at least one instance of a private property offense; 627 (23 percent) had been arrested at least once for this offense, while 377 (14 percent) had actually been convicted for a private property offense. It is thus safe to conclude that a substantial proportion of these youths have had more than a little contact with the criminal justice system concerning an offense usually associated with drug abusers. Data concerning the interaction of drug use, self-reported private property offenses, and contact with the criminal justice system (arrests, convictions) for these offenses appear in table 9-1. These variables were dichotomized.

As the data in table 9-1 indicate, those who have ever used the eight drug classes listed at the left of the table are much more likely to report involvement in private property offenses than those who have not used these substances. The strength of the association between drug use and crime is seen in the percentage differences—from a low of 19 percentage points difference for the heroin-use variable to a 26-point difference for amphetamines and hallucinogens. Those differences persist in the columns for arrests and convictions. For example, 27 percent—over 1 in 4 of those who have ever used heroin—have been convicted of a private property offense. This phenomenon would be even more dramatic if the heroin-use variable were spread out in a number of categories (for example, number of separate occasions of use, length of time used daily, etc.).

Data concerning other offenses (drug use and possession, drug sales, public

Table 9-1
Drug Use and Private Property Offenses

	Percent of Youths Reporting Private Property		
Drug Use (n in parentheses)	*Self-Reported Offenses*	*Arrests*	*Convictions*
Heroin			
Yes (344)	54	38	27
No (2,406)	35	21	12
Barbiturates			
Yes (1,100)	51	30	20
No (1,650)	29	18	9
Amphetamines			
Yes (1,238)	52	30	20
No (1,512)	26	17	9
Cocaine			
Yes (713)	53	31	21
No (2,037)	32	20	11
Marihuana			
Yes (2,491)	40	24	15
No (259)	16	12	7
Hallucinogens			
Yes (1,101)	53	32	23
No (1,649)	27	16	8
Inhalants			
Yes (797)	54	33	22
No (1,953)	31	19	11
Phencyclidine			
Yes (876)	52	31	20
No (1,874)	31	19	11

Note: The figures for self-report are: Yes = 1,035 (38%), No = 1,715 (62%); for arrested, Yes = 627 (23%), No = 2,133 (77%); for convicted, Yes = 377 (14%), No = 2,373 (86%).

property offenses) were also examined with regard to ever/never use of the eight drug classes. The results were virtually identical to those found in table 9-1. Regardless of offense, those who have ever used a substance seem to be considerably more likely to report involvement in the criminal behavior, arrest for it, and conviction. These data confirm the strong association between drug use and criminal activity often observed between narcotic use/addiction and crime (see Greenberg and Adler 1974), and for a youthful population and for use of a number of types of drugs other than opiates (see Voss 1976 for comparable data on young men 20 to 30 years old).

Additional Variables

A question arises as to the variables that might affect the crime/drug relationship. Three were available in the NYPS data file. The first is *sex as gender.* Historically, there has been a clear differentiation between men and women with regard to their involvement with both drugs and criminal justice systems. The second variable is *race/ethnicity.* In this study, race/ethnicity was divided into four categories: white, black, American Indian, and Hispanic. However, because of the small numbers of subjects in the latter two categories, data regarding these groups are not reported here. The third variable is a constructed index of the use of *marihuana/heroin.* This index is introduced to balance the skewed distributions obtained whenever use of heroin is used as a variable. It reflects the notion that there is a progression through stages of drug use—beginning with licit substances like tobacco and alcohol, with marihuana usually regarded as the drug of entry into patterns of illicit drug use. The marihuana/heroin variable reflects this progression assumption. Those younger individuals included in the marihuana category have never used heroin, although they may have used other drugs that are illicit. Those in the heroin category have used heroin, and it may be safely assumed that they have used other drugs as well, including marihuana. Use of heroin is thought to represent the most serious level of involvement in the drug culture and in most cases occurs later on in a drug career. Within the NYPS youthful sample, heroin users are indeed older than their nonusing counterparts.

In the NYPS interview schedule, under "legal history" the respondents were asked to indicate the number of times they had *ever* been involved in eight types of criminal offense, that is, alcohol use, drug use and possession, drug sales, public property offenses, private property offenses, nonviolent victim offenses, violent victim offenses, and weapons offenses. For each offense, the categories of response were (1) never; (2) rarely, once or twice; (3) occasionally, three to six times; (4) fairly often, seven to fifteen times; and (5) frequently, more than fifteen times. The respondents were then asked how many times they had been arrested and convicted for each offense in which there was self-reported involvement.

The data presented in table 9-2 reflect self-reported participation in eight criminal behaviors. Participation is assessed along two dimensions: ever and frequent (more than fifteen separate occasions). The data should be viewed with some caution for two reasons: (1) they are based on self-reports of delinquency from a population already labeled by the "Establishment" as deviant; and (2) there are no criteria for determining whether underreporting or overreporting has occurred.

With these limitations in mind, several consistencies in table 9-2 should be noted. First, among both males and females, higher percentages of whites report having ever or frequently engaged in the delinquent acts. For example, one in four white females and close to 40 percent of the white males report frequent participation in drug sales, compared with 13 and 18 percent for black females and males, respectively. Second, except for self-reported alcohol use and drug use/possession behaviors, a higher percentage of the males than females, regardless of race, report participation in the other delinquent activities. Third,

Table 9-2
Self-Reported Criminal Offenses, Ever and Frequently, by Race and Sex

Self-Reported Offenses, Ever/Frequently	*Males*		*Females*	
	White (%)	*Black (%)*	*White (%)*	*Black (%)*
Alcohol use				
Ever	87	69	86	71
Frequently	75	58	69	62
Drug use/possession				
Ever	87	70	89	71
Frequently	78	64	76	60
Drug sales				
Ever	62	29	48	24
Frequently	38	18	25	13
Public property				
Ever	52	33	29	17
Frequently	17	2	8	6
Private property				
Ever	63	43	39	25
Frequently	23	15	13	13
Nonviolent victim				
Ever	30	27	20	11
Frequently	10	8	8	1
Violent victim				
Ever	31	20	17	9
Frequently	8	4	4	1
Weapons				
Ever	37	31	17	16
Frequently	20	10	9	6

more than a negligible percentage of the males and females in this sample report involvement in private property offenses, a common source of income for adult drug abusers (see McGlothlin 1977; Stephens and Ellis 1975). Over six out of ten white males and 43 percent of black males have committed a burglary (private property offense) at least once, compared with 39 and 25 percent of the white and black females, respectively.

The drug progression hypothesis (see Kandel 1975; O'Donnell and Clayton 1978) would suggest that as drug involvement increases, the frequency of involvement in delinquent activities will increase. To test this hypothesis, three of the delinquent behaviors usually associated with drug use and abuse (that is, drug sales, public property offenses, and private property offenses) have been singled out for closer examination. The marihuana/heroin index has been introduced as an indicator of relative drug involvement. Although this index is rather crude, it is used here to achieve the purposes of this chapter. Those subjects who are included under the heroin category have used heroin at least once. It is likely that most have also used marihuana. Those in the marihuana category may have used other illicit drugs besides marihuana, but they have *never* used heroin.

Even a cursory examination of the data in table 9-3 reveals that those involved with heroin are more likely than those who have never used heroin to report *frequent* (fifteen or more separate occasions) participation in all three of the delinquent behaviors. The only exception occurs among black females. However, the size of *n* in the heroin group among black females is so small that the last column in table 9-3 should be viewed with caution.

The basic conclusion, then, is that type of drug use (heroin versus marihuana) is associated with frequency of participation in three types of delinquent behaviors: drug sales, public property offenses, and private property offenses. It should be noted that we are not suggesting that drug use "causes" delinquency, but that there is an identifiable association between the variables. To substantiate a conclusion of causality would require, in addition to the statistical association, that the temporal order among the events be established and that the relationship be tested for spuriousness. As Johnston (1976) has shown with a national sample of high school youths, there are complex methodological issues involved in unraveling the time order (that is, chicken and egg) question. Further, without longitudinal data or retrospective life-history data of prime quality, it is difficult to rule out spuriousness.

The data presented in tables 9-2 and 9-3 include self-reported frequency of participation in various delinquency behaviors. The NYPS respondents were also asked how many times they had been arrested for each of the eight types of delinquent behaviors in which they had participated. The data in table 9-4 represent the *mean number of self-reported arrests* by the categories of the marihuana/heroin index with sex and race controlled. The criminal behaviors included are arrests for drug use/possession, drug sales, public property offenses,

Table 9-3
Marihuana/Heroin Index and Extent of Involvement in Three Offenses, Race and Sex Controlled

Self-Reported Offenses (Frequency or Extent of)	Males				Females			
	Whites		Blacks		Whites		Blacks	
	Marihuana but Not Heroin	*Heroin Ever Use*	*Marihuana but Not Heroin*	*Heroin Ever Use*	*Marihuana but Not Heroin*	*Heroin Ever Use*	*Marihuana but Not Heroin*	*Heroin Ever Use*
Drug sales								
Never	39	18	70	41	55	17	81	56
Occasionally	27	13	11	22	26	15	8	22
Frequently	34	69	19	37	19	68	11	22
Total *n*	757	135	105	27	490	75	53	18
Public property								
Never	48	34	68	46	72	60	77	94
Occasionally	37	34	19	33	13	8	16	0
Frequently	15	32	13	21	15	32	7	6
Total *n*	737	134	102	24	468	70	56	17
Private property								
Never	38	26	55	39	62	48	69	88
Occasionally	41	34	30	25	27	22	14	6
Frequently	21	40	15	36	11	30	17	6
Total *n*	773	138	116	28	478	71	65	17

Table 9-4
Marihuana/Heroin Index by Mean Number of Arrests for Four Offenses, Race and Sex Controlled

	Males				*Females*			
	Whites		*Blacks*		*Whites*		*Blacks*	
Offenses Arrests	*Marihuana but Not Heroin*	*Heroin Ever Use*	*Marihuana but Not Heroin*	*Heroin Ever Use*	*Marihuana but Not Heroin*	*Heroin Ever Use*	*Marihuana but Not Heroin*	*Heroin Ever Use*
Drug use	0.61	1.69	0.70	0.84	0.20	1.07	0.11	1.04
Drug sales	0.06	0.63	0.01	0.13	0.01	0.11	0.04	0.65
Public property	0.22	0.64	0.29	0.65	0.04	0.09	0.12	0.39
Private property	0.67	1.86	0.44	1.06	0.17	0.63	0.18	0.26

and private property offenses. For both sexes, the data are quite clear: those with any contact with heroin are more likely than those in the marihuana category to have been arrested for these behaviors. However, there are no clear or consistent results when whites are compared with blacks within sex.

As mentioned earlier, those who have used heroin within the NYPS youth sample are, on the average, older when compared with clients who never have used heroin. One could reason that as drug users become older, the probability of criminal justice involvement would increase. Thus the importance of controlling for the effect of age becomes evident. The data in table 9-5 indicate that this was indeed the case even with the truncated age sample. Only 61 clients under 16 years of age have used heroin. When we look at the over-16-year-old category we find 213 clients have used heroin. Despite the fact that heroin use is skewed toward the older age groups, the crime/drug use relationship is still maintained. Within each age category, those who have ever used heroin report substantially more involvement with private property offenses. They also report more arrests and convictions as a consequence of these offenses.

We have examined the extent of criminal behavior associated with the use or nonuse of a particular drug. This approach has revealed a consistent trend of increased delinquency associated with the use of each particular substance when compared to the nonuse of the same substance. The marihuana/heroin index compared those who never used heroin but used marihuana and probably other substances with those who have used heroin probably in addition to marihuana and other substances. This index indicated that heroin use is associated more with delinquent behavior than marihuana use per se.

A possible problem with this approach is that the patterns of use are multiple rather than single. For instance, those who have used heroin have also

Table 9-5
Percentage of Clients Who Reported Private Property Offenses for Those Who Ever Used Heroin and Who Never Used Heroin, Controlling for Age at Admission

	Less than 16 Years Old		*16 Years Old*		*17 Years or Older*	
	Use of Heroin		*Use of Heroin*		*Use of Heroin*	
Private Property	*Yes (n = 61)*	*No (n = 929)*	*Yes (n = 66)*	*No (n = 710)*	*Yes (n = 213)*	*No (n = 746)*
Self-reported offenses	57.4	32.8	53.0	37.5	54.5	37.5
Arrests	27.4	17.8	39.4	21.5	41.1	23.3
Convictions	22.6	8.8	19.7	12.4	30.5	15.3

Note: The number in each cell is a percentage of the number of clients indicated at the top of the column for that cell.

used, on the average, 6½ substances regularly. This contrasts sharply with the 3½ average for those who have never used heroin.

To address this problem of multiple drug abuse, table 9-6 is presented. Here the marihuana-only group is composed of clients who have regularly used marihuana with no regular use of any other drug. Note the small number of clients in this select group. As reported earlier, the heroin-ever group is composed of clients who reported any lifetime use of heroin. This heterogeneous group has not been further refined because of the already demonstrated predictive power exhibited by heroin-ever use. The data indicate that when controlling for age, the group who used heroin are, on the average, four times more involved in delinquent behavior when compared with those who regularly use only marihuana. The three delinquency measures used are the number of arrests for substance-related offenses, a combination score of arrests for assaults and weapon offenses, and finally, arrests for offenses against public or private property.

The fact that the heroin group was arrested for more substance-related offenses reflects, in part, the use of more drugs by that group. This trend, however, extends to other offense categories which are non-substance-abuse related. Thus the relationship between delinquency and harder drug use appears to be confirmed in those data.

Criminal Justice Referral

The preceding analysis has confirmed the association between crime and drug use among youths and the connection between use of "harder" drugs and involvement with the criminal justice system. An important aspect of these findings from a policy and programmatic perspective has to do with the "linkage" between the criminal justice and drug treatment systems. Do criminal justice authorities recognize the effect of drug abuse on criminal actions? Are

Table 9-6
Multiple Classification Analysis of Delinquency Measures by Regular Marihuana-Only Use and Heroin Ever-Use Groups, Controlling for Age at Admission

	Mean Number of Arrests	
Delinquent Behavior Category	*Regular Use of Only Marihuana (n = 196)*	*Heroin Ever-Use (n = 342)*
Substance-related	.26	1.42
Assault or weapons	.13	.62
Property	.31	1.02

they willing to refer youthful addict-criminals to treatment rather than send them to jail or prison? Evidence germane to these questions can be seen by examining the referral source of NYPS clients.

Four sources of criminal justice referral were included in the NYPS interview schedule. They are parole-probation officer, judge, police and prison. As indicated in table 9-7, 890 subjects were referred to treatment by at least one of these criminal justice sources. This represents some 32 percent of the 2,750 NYPS subjects. As expected, over half ($n = 456$) the criminal justice referrals were from probation and parole officers—a figure which underscores the degree to which these youths have encountered law enforcement personnel.

This 32 percent criminal justice referral rate to treatment for the NYPS subjects is almost twice as great as that reported by the Client Oriented Data Acquisition Process (CODAP). CODAP is a data system which contains information on drug abusers admitted to and discharged from federally funded drug-abuse treatment programs. Approximately 1,700 clinics are involved in this reporting effort, with 245,105 admission forms and 248,256 discharge forms submitted in 1976. Taking into account all admissions to CODAP in 1976, 17.3 percent were nonvoluntary admissions (CODAP 1978). *Nonvoluntary admissions* are defined in CODAP as the type of legal coercion affecting a client's decision to enter treatment. In other words, 82.7 percent of the clients reported to CODAP in 1976 were voluntary admissions—they entered of their own free will and under no legal compulsion. A 17 to 18 percent nonvoluntary admission rate has been fairly uniform over the past several years. However, discussions with treatment program personnel and criminal justice system representatives indicate that this nonvoluntary referral rate is relatively low.

An examination of the Drug Abuse Reporting Program (DARP) data supports the hypothesis that the number of criminal justice referrals reported by CODAP may be low. Approximately 40 percent of the DARP admissions were on probation, on parole, awaiting trial, or had some other legal proceedings pending. Further, in a subsample of 3,214 DARP admissions under the age of 18, some 38.8 percent were nonvoluntary admissions (Sells 1977). Although the definitions of criminal justice referral and nonvoluntary admissions are different for the NYPS sample and the DARP youth sample, the overall percentages are comparable.

Table 9-7
Criminal Justice Sources of Referral for the NYPS Sample

Source of Referral	*Number*	*%*
Parole/probation officer	456	51.2
Judge	279	31.3
Police	145	16.4
Prison	10	1.1
Total	890	100.0

A comparison of drug use by source of referral—criminal justice versus voluntary—indicates that a greater percentage of youths referred by criminal justice system officials use drugs. This difference holds true for seven of the eight drug classes examined (see table 9-8). The only exception was with regard to marihuana, one that is understandable given the extent to which marihuana use is prevalent in this sample. Stated broadly, criminal justice referrals in the NYPS sample are more involved with drugs than those who entered treatment voluntarily, with about 50 percent of criminal justice referrals having used barbiturates, amphetamines, and hallucinogens.

Summary and Implications

Some 2,750 youths under 19 years of age from 97 drug-abuse treatment programs nationwide were interviewed as part of the National Youth Polydrug Study. Among the variables included in the interview schedule were those which measured drug use/abuse, source of referral to treatment, and involvement with criminal activities and criminal justice authorities. Several distinguishing characteristics of the subjects were noted: 73 percent had been picked up by the police; 36 percent had been incarcerated; and 32 percent were referred to treatment by the criminal justice system. Regardless of the criminal offense examined (that is, public or private property, drug use, possession, or drug sales), those youths who had used any of the substances examined were more likely to report involvement in criminal behaviors, arrest for that behavior, and conviction.

These findings, though tentative, do highlight two significant questions that have implications for both social policy and the delivery of services. The first question is, What should be done with these youths? There are at least two approaches to this question. One group would argue that these youths are

Table 9-8
Drug Use by Source of Referral

	Source of Referral	
Drug Types	*Voluntary Referral (% Users)*	*Criminal Justice Referral (% Users)*
Heroin	11	17
Barbiturates	36	48
Amphetamines	42	52
Cocaine	23	31
Marihuana	90	91
Hallucinogens	36	50
Inhalants	25	37
Phencyclidine	29	38

"rotten kids" and represent that proportion of every birth cohort that one might expect to make "trouble" for the system, those who have already jumped on a treadmill of failure. Those endorsing this interpretation often advocate treating these youths as if they were adults under the law. They say that the most appropriate response to illegal and deviant behavior is swift and certain punishment. Needless to say, this is a costly and pessimistic orientation.

There are others who would be willing to define these youths as currently delinquent and deviant but capable of change. Instead of labeling them as "trouble" for the system, those endorsing this second orientation would say these youths are "troubled" and in need of help. They see such youths as individuals involved in seemingly self-destructive types of behavior that are costly from a societal viewpoint. Those who adopt this second perspective would rephrase the question listed above to read, What can be done for these youths? There are a number of possible answers to this question. These youths can be provided with quality comprehensive treatment for their drug-dependence problems–treatment that would include such things as counseling, an opportunity to complete education through high school if such is not already accomplished, job training, and training that deals with such things as how to present oneself in a job interview. Another facet of intervention would be to further expand mechanisms by which criminal justice authorities would divert youths to treatment without prejudice, and for those youths convicted and sentenced under criminal statutes, an opportunity to avoid the prison system milieu.

The youths included in this study are not representative of all young people who have abused drugs and, fortunately, do not represent a significant proportion of all young people in these age categories. However, they do represent a population whose productive inputs to society over an entire life history will probably be curtailed, if not lost entirely. The challenge for members of the helping professions is to devise innovative and effective primary prevention, early identification, and intervention strategies. From a social policy standpoint, it is essential that individuals who are at risk of being costly to society be assisted in developing into productive citizens. From a humanistic perspective, these are people in need of therapeutic intervention.

References

Abelson, H.I., Fishburne, P.M., and Cisin, I. 1977. *National Survey on Drug Abuse: 1977,* Vol. I, Main Findings. Rockville, Maryland: National Institute on Drug Abuse.

CODAP 1978 *NIDA Statistical Series Annual Summary Report 1976*, Series E, Number 4 Rockville, Maryland.

Greenberg, S.W., and Adler, F. 1974. Crime and addiction: An empirical analysis of the literature, 1920-1973. *Contemporary Drug Problems* 3:221-270.

Johnston, L. 1976. Nonaddictive drug use and delinquency: A longitudinal analysis. In *Drug Use and Crime: Report of the Panel on Drug Use and Criminal Behavior.* Springfield, Virginia: National Technical Information Service.

Kandel, D. 1975. Stages in adolescent involvement in drug use. *Science* 190:912-914.

McGlothlin, W., Anglin, M.D., and Wilson, B.D. 1977. An Evaluation of the California Civil Addict Program. Rockville, Maryland: National Institute on Drug Abuse.

O'Donnell, J.A., and Clayton, R.R. 1978. The stepping-stone hypothesis—Marihuana, heroin, and causality. Paper read at meetings of the American Sociological Association, San Francisco, September 1978.

Sells, S.B. 1977. Reflections on the Epidemiology of Heroin and Narcotic Addiction from the Perspective of Treatment Data, in J.D. Rittenhouse (ed.) *The Epidemiology of Heroin and Other Narcotics* NIDA Research Monograph 16, Rockville, Maryland.

Stephens, R.C., and Ellis, R.D. 1975. Narcotic addicts and crime: Analysis of recent trends. *Criminology* 12:474-488.

Voss, H.L. 1976. Young men, drugs, and crime. In *Drug Use and Crime: Report of the Panel on Drug Use and Criminal Behavior.* Springfield, Virginia: National Technical Information Service.

10 Youth Drug Abuse and Education: Empirical and Theoretical Considerations

Allan Y. Cohen
and *Yoav Santo*

Among the special drug-abuse issues deserving attention is the relationship between drug use and the educational experience of youths, and the impact of each of these factors on the other. Education in the broadest sense, formal schooling and prevocational training, is a critical gateway between adolescent adjustment and adult maturity. Serious disruptions in youth educational experiences and opportunities are likely to decrease the future productivity of such youths. Further, school experiences, whether positive or negative, dominate much of the daily lives of young people involved with drugs.

The National Youth Polydrug Study (NYPS) offers a data base to examine some of the most salient considerations surrounding this issue, since these data provide an education profile of the young polydrug user in treatment and of the obstacles he or she experienced in attending school. One of the main purposes of the present chapter is to examine these new findings in the context of previous theory and empirical evidence and to consider their implications for the understanding of youth drug abuse and for treatment program planning.

The relationship between youthful drug use and educational experience has been examined previously from two distinctive causational (but not mutually exclusive) perspectives. The first is by far the more obvious: that drug abuse by the young significantly inhibits educational (and prevocational) performance, motivation, and adjustment. Adolescence is considered to be a crucial period in generating productive options for later life. Disruptions in adolescence, especially when they involve failure in the school or work setting, can create a vicious cycle of further disruption. With such problems, young people are less able to cope with the tasks of advancing age and of functional autonomy, and they are therefore more prone to further drug abuse, antisocial behavior, and personal ineffectuality. Older drug abusers who have completed their education and/or have developed marketable skills can more easily reenter a productive lifestyle after treatment. Young drug users who fail to take advantage of their early education opportunities because of severe chemical dependency may become so prematurely affected that there is very little to fall back on, even if treatment is effective at a later age.

Discovery of drug use by family or school often leads to suspension, other disciplinary action, or, at the least, negative labeling. These effects reduce the probability of successful educational development. Young drug users who become involved with the juvenile justice system are likely to be further handicapped by that association. Also, decreased motivation and performance on afterschool and summer jobs because of drug use can have a negative impact on vocational growth and development. If current drug use of a young employee becomes known to employers, career prospects are hardly enhanced.

School Performance and Youth Drug Abuse: Evidence

There is abundant empirical and clinical evidence of an association between drug use and various measures of school performance and attendance (Brook et al. 1976; Chein et al. 1964; Lavenhar et al. 1971; Noble et al. 1972; Patch 1973; Pittel 1973; Roth 1971). All such findings are consistent with the notion that drug use may be a significant predisposing factor in poor academic performance or attendance. (The alternate explanation–that poor academic performance can lead to drug use–will be considered in the next section.)

One of the more recent studies (Dembo et al. 1977) surveyed 1,045 junior high school students in an inner-city school during the winter of 1976. Primarily a study of the relationship between drug use and neighborhood and lifestyle variables, the study showed a strong correlation ($p < .001$) between extent of drug involvement and "missed school due to alcohol/drug use in last six months." Some of the other factors that were also found in this study to correlate highly with drug involvement, such as "participation in the drug/street culture" and "non-engagement in the print media and stay at home spare time activities," would seem to be precisely those which would tend to interfere with sound prevocational development.

Another of the more recent studies (C_2ODAC 1976) was commissioned by the staff of an innovative youth alternatives program in Boise, Idaho, involving a sample of 482 people residing in that city. An unexpectedly high level of drug experimentation was found among young people. One statistical comparison had relevant implications for educational achievement. In a subsample of students, only 3.75 percent with an A grade average were current users of marihuana, while 100 percent of those with a D average reported current marihuana use.

A longitudinal study (Jessor et al. 1973) found that low grade point average not only differentiated current marihuana users from current nonusers in high school, but also predicted the shift from nonuse to use 1 year later. Grade point average, however, was *not* found to predict subsequent marihuana use in college students.

It may be that the association between drug use and academic performance tends to break down in certain college populations. Mellinger et al. (1978) failed to find relationships between drug use and measures of academic performance in a student population at the University of California, Berkeley. The authors caution that this population was a select one, and that those adolescents who had initiated drugs in high school and been vulnerable to untoward effects (or to drug subculture participation) would not be highly represented as successful Berkeley admittees. Indeed, given the trend to earlier initiation of drug use and serious drug use, academic performance correlations should not be expected nearly as much at the college level as at the secondary level.

Complicating the relationship between youth drug use and educational attainment is the possible role of drug use as an adolescent "rite-of-passage." In a recent conference paper (1978), Jessor suggested that drug use, along with other health-threatening behavior, may represent means by which adolescents attempt to establish independence, autonomy, and control over the environment. A by-product of this behavioral complex (including proclivities toward alcohol, tobacco, and sexual experimentation) may be declining academic aspiration and achievement.

Another Perspective

Although not dominant in the literature, increased attention has been given to the impact of social institutions (such as school systems) on the attitudes of young people toward drug abuse. It is not valid to argue the existence of a "drug-dependent" personality that emerges from early childhood and inevitably erupts later in drug abuse or alcoholism almost irrespective of social or peer environment. Since the adolescent moves away from family and toward peers, the school, community environment, and workplace generally become more influential during this period.

Data from primary prevention and early intervention programs suggest that positive curricular and school climate can lessen predisposition to drug use. Some successful community-based programs have generated relevant vocational roles for the young, whether the programs are directly tied to a prevocational career track or are designed only to increase self-esteem and feelings of social competence and responsibility. Findings indicating that changes in the school curriculum or climate and in vocational opportunity may influence attitudes about drug use also demonstrate the linkage between educational experience and drug use.

Turning Off from Education: Evidence

It is frequently mentioned that public schools have been unable to assume the ever-increasing responsibility for developing socialization skills being delegated to them. The connection between failures in education and drug abuse have been highlighted in two studies. Schaps et al. (1975) comments, "Widespread abuse of psychoactive drugs is one indication, one loud and clear signal, that America is mis-educating her young. It is not that schools are doing a poorer job of what they have always done. . . rather, *how* teaching occurs, and what is *not* taught have become problematic." The authors suggest that failure in meeting affective as well as cognitive developmental needs of young people increases the probability of drug abuse. They associate drug experimentation with the failure of the school system to address the needs of the young for personal identity, self-esteem, and social competency. Phin et al. (1976) describe such internal problems in educational systems as "overcrowding, the need for students to conform or drop (or be thrown) out; entrenched resistance to change, and a chronic focus on quantity rather than quality." The authors also contend that today's educational system "has frequently failed to teach (coping) skills" and "has also begun to isolate its students from the adult society around him." It is concluded that deficiencies in school and community experience contribute to the negative forces that influence youngsters to use drugs.

An obvious corollary of this perspective is that some adolescents are particularly vulnerable to inadequacies in educational institutions. Such vulnerability, marked perhaps by deriving less that is positive and satisfying from other aspects of their lives (family, inner value systems, good peer relationships, etc.), would be reflected in a relatively high rate of drug abuse. The nature of educational deficiencies pertinent to drug use might well be more in the affective than cognitive domains. Lack of stimulation, boredom, irrelevance, and an overdetermined authority structure might impact most on students' overall negative reactions. Some of the statistical association between drug abuse and poor school performance could also be explained by the frustration and lowered self-esteem that results from poor school performance.

A number of research studies document the association between the students' attitudes toward school, or perceived nonfulfilling characteristics of school, and drug use in vulnerable youths. One such study involved a representative sample of 8,553 students in New York State public schools, seventh through twelth grade, surveyed during the winter of 1974-1975 (Babst et al. 1977). In general, it was found that the more students were involved in substance use, the greater their friends' substance use, the more favorable their attitudes toward risk taking and drug use, and the poorer their family and school adjustment. The survey included an index measuring students' interest in school. A cross-tabulation of the degree of school interest (high, moderate high, moderate low, and low) with the number of substance types ever used yielded striking results. Table 10-1 presents the extreme four categories from the study cross-tabulations, showing the obvious association between drug use and lack of interest in school. Causation should not be inferred from this association, since the association might be explained by other intervening variables (for example, the degree of association of drug use with "family affinity" found in this study was even more striking).

Table 10-1
Cross-Tabulations of Degree of School Interest and Number of Substances Ever Used*

		Percentage of Students and the Number of Substances They Ever Used	
Interest in School Index	*No. of Students*	*None (%)*	*Five to Seven Substances (%)*
High interest	1,392	28.7	1.9
Low interest	1,575	9.1	9.1

*Adapted from data presented in Babst et al. (1977), on 8,553 students in New York State public schools.

From the findings of a 1970-1971 survey of New York State rural and suburban high school students Babst et al. (1976) concluded that "the combined impact of peer, family and school factors is a more important predictor of attitudes toward drugs than the distinction between rural and suburban living." On the questionnaire was one item in which students were asked whether most classes were interesting or not interesting. Of those students (both rural and suburban) who had "used one or more drugs" for a "high" (n = 1,727), 24.9 percent found most classes interesting, compared with 46.5 percent who had *not* used one or more drugs for a "high" (n = 5,070).

A Synergistic Formulation

Our review of the literature seems to support a synergistic or interactive hypothesis: that drug abuse may lead to educational prevocational failure, and, at the same time that institutional deficiencies in the educational system together with student failures in school performance predispose toward drug use and abuse; and that drug use combined with limitations in educational opportunity can have more serious implications than either problem on its own. What is suggested is the possibility of a "vicious cycle" where, for example, a boring educational environment contributes to drug experimentation, drug use hinders successful student adjustment to school or job, increasing failure in school or job encourages deeper involvement in drugs, and so on. This cycle will undoubtedly also include family difficulties, peer difficulties or group isolation, and possibly confrontations with the juvenile justice system. While these youths may be tempted to "self-medicate" themselves with drugs for the tensions caused by the pressures or vacuums of adolescent life, in doing so they are likely to be adding to their problems and pressures.

To study this problem area, the National Youth Polydrug Study offers a rich base of interactive data. The data analyses, findings, and discussion that follow focus on specific educational variables (including some limited data on nonschool vocational activities). In reporting the associations derived from these data, one-way causational interpretations are discouraged. Naturally the reader must also be aware of the potential effects of other intervening variables, discussed at length in other chapters in this book.

Analysis of the CODAP Youth Subsample

The Client Oriented Data Acquisition Process (CODAP), the reporting system for drug programs that receive federal funding, also provides data on the educational levels of those youngsters who require treatment for drug abuse. The CODAP subsample (n = 27,000+) is comprised of clients 12 to 18 years of age admitted to treatment during the calendar year 1975. The demographics of CODAP subsample and the NYPS sample are highly similar (see chapter 6). Males outnumbered females approximately three to two, although the difference was smaller at ages 15 and under. White youths comprised nearly 68.9 percent of the sample; black youths, 17.9 percent; and Hispanics, 9.2 percent. About two-thirds (68 percent) of the CODAP youth sample, reported current enrollment in an education program at the time of admission to treatment, and 4.3 percent reported current enrollment in a skill-development program. An analysis of the number of grades completed in relation to chronological age uncovered an important discrepancy. In this analysis it was assumed that an "appropriate" grade level for one's age can be defined as one's age at time of study less 6 years. Thus students 17 to 18 years of age were expected to have completed the eleventh grade. Approximately 32 percent of the sample were between the ages of 17 and 18; but only 11.5 percent of the sample reported having completed grade eleven or twelve. The 20.5 percent discrepancy is assumed to represent both school dropouts and those who are still enrolled but are behind their expected grade level. This rate of discrepancy between age and educational attainment (70.1 percent of the sample of clients aged 17 were below their "expected" grade) is substantially greater than the national average for 17-year-olds in the general population.

Further analysis of the data into discrete cohorts for each age level showed a linear increase in those students below their appropriate grade level as age increases. There was a 5 to 10 percent increase in this rate for each cohort (ranging from 31.7 percent below appropriate grade level for 12-to 13-year-olds to the 70.1 percent described for 17-year-olds). These data need to be compared with similar calculations for the general school populations, for youths who are not drug abusers and not in treatment, and for the NYPS sample of youth in treatment. As this discussion moves to a description of NYPS, certain limitations of the data deserve mention. Because there were no control or comparison groups, only cross-tabulations and correlations between or among variables are available. Any statements made regarding cause-effect relationships can only be speculations.

The Education Data of the National Youth Polydrug Study

The methodology of the National Youth Polydrug Study (NYPS) has been described earlier in this book. NYPS involved a national sample of 2,750 males and females aged 12 to 19 who were admitted to one of 97 drug-abuse programs. Unless otherwise specified, hereafter *polydrug abusers* shall indicate those clients in the NYPS sample. The data were collected by interview through a semistructured client information form (CIF) from September 1976 to March 1977. The sample consisted of 61 percent males and 39 percent females; 70 percent were white, 14 percent black, 7 percent Hispanic, 5 percent American Indian, and 4 percent Asians and other racial groups. The mean age of the subjects was 15.9 years (S.D. = 1.7; 12 percent were 18 years old, 23 percent were 17, 29 percent were 16, and 36 percent were 15 years old and younger.

Educational Attainment of Clients:

Current Enrollments. There were 1,528 subjects, or 55.5 percent of the sample, currently enrolled in the public schools, either grade school (1.4 percent), junior high school (13.9 percent), or high school (40.2 percent); 9.1 percent were enrolled in alternative schools (alternative schools are generally set up for youngsters who experience difficulties or are not well served by the traditional public school system). Another 10.5 percent were currently enrolled in a variety of other educational settings, including private school, parochial school, boarding school, GED programs, vocational technical school, vocational training school, business school, college, or other educational programs. In addition, 1.4 percent were participating in other vocational training programs. (It should be noted that some of the categories—for example private school versus boarding school or alternative school versus high school—may not be mutually exclusive since coders were instructed to check all categories that applied.)

School Completion. Although completion of grade levels might not be the most accurate estimate of the educational attainment of the sample, it can be considered a conservative variable for assessing attainment and thus for speculating on the potential social costs of drug abuse. Grade level is likely to be less sensitive than other criteria of educational achievement, since many schools "pass" students exhibiting minimal academic performance and low motivation.

It was found that 92.6 percent of the sample had completed grade school, 73.2 percent had completed junior high school (note that junior high school comprises different grades in different school districts), and only 4.1 percent had completed high school. Twenty clients (0.7 percent) had discontinued their education during grade school, 149 (5.4 percent) had discontinued during junior high school, and 546 (19.8 percent) had already discontinued during high school.

These data suggest that approximately 26 percent of the sample might be considered school dropouts. Overall, the mean number of years of schooling completed by the NYPS subjects was 9.1 (S.D. = 1.4). The number of grades completed does not differ significantly for males (9.1) and females (9.2).

Grade Level Attainment and Age. A trend was noted previously in the 1975 CODAP youth subsample: drug users may be retarded in their educational attainment as measured by completion of grade levels. Using the same assumption as in the CODAP analysis, table 10-2 displays the relationship between age and education attainment for the NYPS sample. A close look at table 10-2 and the age cohorts shows that among clients who at admission were between 12 and 13, 65.4 percent were at an appropriate grade level and 34.6 percent were retarded in their grade relative to their age. The percentage of clients who were "behind" in their grade relative to their age increased as age increased, with 73.3 percent of clients who were over 18 not completing at least twelve years of schooling.

Breaking down the sample for sex, the data suggest a superior age/grade appropriateness for the female subjects. While 18.7 percent of the 16-year-old males have *not* completed the ninth grade, only 11.4 percent of the 16-year-old females have not reached that level. In the 17-year-old subgroup, expected to have completed the tenth grade, the comparison is 36.6 percent (males) not completed versus 19.7 percent (females). This finding of superior school grade attainment may apply to female students generally or may be specific to the females in the sample. It is generally easier for males to break from school, having more traditional access to constructive alternatives to school, for example, the work role, or destructive alternatives in the form of antisocial

Table 10-2
Distribution of the Number of School Years Completed, by Age, for the NYPS Sample

Age at Admission	*Appropriate Grade Level to Have Completed*	*At Appropriate or Advanced Grade Level for Age (%)*	*Behind Appropriate Grade Level for Age (%)*	*Total (%)*	*Total n*
12+	6	65.4	34.6	(100)	26
13+	7	65.2	34.8	(100)	112
14+	8	62.3	37.7	(100)	292
15+	9	59.1	40.9	(100)	562
16+	10	46.9	53.1	(100)	783
17+	11	36.0	64.0	(100)	623
18+	12	26.7	73.3	(100)	341
Total %		47.1	52.9	(100)	
Total *n*		(1,286)	(1,453)		(2,739)

activity. It may be that by tradition, families and society tend more to reinforce girls to maintain their studies.

Independent of whether the client "lagged" behind in his or her level of educational attainment relative to age, the relationship between the number of years of school completed and thirty-six other variables was examined also (see table 10-3). Correlations with grade completion may not be very meaningful

Table 10-3
Correlations of Selected Background and Drug-Use Variables with Number of School Years Completed

Description	*No. of School Years Completed* *r**
Female = (0); male = (1)	–.03
(0) = Nonwhite; (1) = white	.05
Sum of drugs used regularly	.13
(1) = Catholic; (0) = non-Catholic	–.03
Number of drug overdoses by client	.04
Number of suicide attempts reported by client	.03
(1) = No PCP use; (2) mild PCP use; (3) regular PCP use	.08
(0) = Never, (4) always	.05
Father or mother deceased = (1); not = (0)	.05
(0) = Intact family; (1) = broken family	–.07
(1) = Supported in part by family; (0) = not	–.05
(1) = Referred by criminal justice system; (0) = not	–.02
Total number of violent weapons arrests	.02
Total number of private property arrests	–.02
Number of times "picked up" by police	.00
Adjudicated delinquent (1) = yes; (0) = no	–.03
Adjudicated dependent (1) = yes; (0) = no	–.01
Outpatient (1) = yes; (0) = no	–.07
Total number of reasons for contacting agency	.03
(1) = Suburban; (0) = other residence	–.04
(1) = Rural; (0) = other residence	.01
Referred by self = (1); not = (0)	.07
Referred by family = (1); not = (0)	–.02
Referred by peers = (1); not = (0)	–.04
Referred by school = (1); not = (0)	.00
(1) Employed; (0) = unemployed	.07
Importance of religion in client's family (0) = no importance; (5) = great importance	–.01
Total no. of obstacles to school attendance	–.02
Use of drug combinations (1) = yes; (0) = no	.09
Index of socioeconomic status	.10
Age in years	.41
Total number of substance (sales or possession) arrests	.05
No. of months employed in last 2 years	.15

*Pearson r of .05 = $p < .01$.

since so many of the variables other than age are age sensitive. Easily seen in table 10-3 is the dominance of the correlation of grade completion with age (.41). The correlation would undoubtedly be stronger for those students still enrolled in school; most schools do not encourage a large disparity in age among students in a similar grade level. Further, those students kept back for more than 2 years are likely to become school dropouts. The second highest correlation (.15 with the number of months employed in last 2 years) is also mediated by age.

It may be of interest to comment on some of the other correlations at .05 level or higher. (With the sample of 2,707, statistically significant findings occur at relatively low correlational levels, for example, $r = .05$ represents the .01 level of significance.) There is a .10 correlation with an index of socioeconomic status. Given the ordinarily high relationship in America between affluence and children's completion of school, this finding is not unexpected.

Of most interest are the possible correlations with various measures of drug use. The highest correlation (.13) appears with the sum of types of drugs used with a frequency of once per week or more (in either the current or peak period of use). But here again, age is a likely mediating variable. The older the client, the more likely there was opportunity for exposure to different drugs, a longer drug history, and a tendency to have used more drugs in the past and to use more drugs currently. The use of drugs in combination ($r = .09$) is probably also mediated by age in the same way. Similar logic can be applied to the .08 correlation with PCP use; age is expected to account for some of the variance. Of some interest were the findings of a significant negative correlation (–.07) between grades completed by the client and his report of having a broken home.

Any effect of drug abuse on number of school years completed would be seen best in a longitudinal study and after the entire sample had become 22 years of age or so. This would allow much more of the effect to be seen. Since school attendance is more or less mandatory for many of the younger clients in the present sample, a profound effect is not likely.

Educational Attainment of Parents

For the purpose of this analysis, the educational attainment (in grades completed) of parents is considered to be an indicator of the family background of clients. It is a key indicator of parents' socioeconomic status and probably relates to the social and education opportunities available to clients.

Clients were asked to relate the highest grade that their fathers and mothers completed either in the United States or abroad. Nearly 89 percent of the clients reported their fathers to be educated in the United States, and 92 percent of the clients reported their mothers to be educated in the United States.

A correlational analysis of parents' educational attainment and client background demographic characteristics turned up relatively little that would be unexpected (see table 10-4). Fathers' and mothers' highest grade completed (in the United States, n = 2,500) were highly positively correlated (.65) with each other, and grades completed for both parents were significantly related (.30 and .32) to racial identification as Caucasians. There was also a tendency for client reports of good health to be positively correlated with number of grades completed by both parents.

There was a significant positive relationship between parent educational

Table 10-4
Correlations of Selected Background and Drug-Use Variables with Parents' Education
(Number of Years of Schooling Completed)

	Parents' U.S. Educational Attainment	
Client Support Sources and Employment History	*Father*	*Mother*
Proportion employed	.06	.07
Number of months employed past 2 years	.03	.02
Proportion of client support: Illegal	.00	−.00
Proportion of client support: Client Legal Earnings	.12	.13
Proportion of client support: Welfare	−.14	−.15
Summary Drug-Use Items		
Sum of all drugs ever reportedly used	.13	.13
Sum of all drugs used currently	.12	.11
Sum of all drugs ever reported used on a weekly basis	.08	.08
Months longest abstinence of all drugs	−.02	−.01
Months longest abstinence of all drugs except alcohol and marihuana	.05	.05
Individual Drug-Use Frequency within the Past 3 Months of Admission to the Drug Program		
Inhalants	−.08	−.09
Any opiates	−.03	−.02
Barbiturates and other sedatives	−.03	−.05
Amphetamines	.04	.03
Cocaine	.04	.01
Marihuana	.06	.07
Hashish	.06	.04
Hallucinogens	.04	.02
Phencyclidine (PCP)	.06	.04
Alcohol	.02	.02
Over-the-counter drugs	.03	−.01
Other substances	−.00	−.01

Note: A correlation (r value) of .05 or greater indicates a statistically significant association at the .05 level of confidence, or better. (Father n = 2,425; mother n = 2,560.)

attainment and clients' reports of being supported by their own earnings and a negative relationship with the clients' reports of receiving support from welfare. Again, these findings are consistent with the hypothesized impact of socioeconomic status reflected by parental educational attainment.

Of most interest are the significant positive correlations between parental educational attainment and the number of different drugs ever used, or used currently, at least once a week. The white, middle-class youths in this sample were found to use a larger number of drug types. The higher economic status of these families is probably the mediating factor in these interrelated findings, permitting these particular youths greater access to a variety of drugs.

Looking at frequency of use of individual drugs in relation to parent education attainment, the only significant finding shows a negative relationship between parents' educational attainment and the frequency of client use of inhalants during the 3 months prior to admission to the drug program. This is consistent with the findings of a negative relationship between socioeconomic status and the frequency of inhalant use—and was to be expected since the determination of the socioeconomic status of the parent was partially based on the number of years of school they completed. The use of inhalants and solvents has been observed to be more frequent among those of lower socioeconomic status in both the United States and Latin America. The relatively low cost of such substances and their relative ease of availability may be more attractive to children of families of lower socioeconomic status.

A somewhat similar hypothesis has been proposed by the authors, namely, that youths from poverty environments may prefer the "depressant" type drugs (for example, opiates, barbiturates, sedatives, inhalants) and that upper-middle-class youths may be more prone to stimulants and mind-altering substances (cannabis, hallucinogens, amphetamines, cocaine, PCP). To the extent that the family poverty versus affluence variable is assessed in these data, the directions of the correlations are consistent with this notion. The magnitude of the correlations in table 10-4, however, did not reach statistical significance, and this hypothesis was therefore not supported in this study.

Obstacles to School Attendance

A very important aspect of NYPS pertaining to educational issues involved the reporting of forty-five types of obstacles to school attendance. Clients affirmed or reported the obstacles experienced, either currently or when the client was last attending school. *Obstacles* were problems inside or outside the educational system which were reported by the client to make it difficult or impossible to attend school; thus they are indicators of educational problems. One can presume that obstacles are strongly related to attitudes regarding school, to performance in school, and to actual learning—yet such relationships are undoubtedly not perfect. An example of the weakness in this relationship is the student who finds few problems sufficient to get in the way of his or her attending school but finds the school experience hollow, frustrating, or boring.

Another limitation of the "obstacles" data is that categories of obstacles were not coded on *intensity,* or the relative power of any particular obstacle subcategory in preventing school attendance. For example, some students might have experienced relatively milder superficial but noticeable degrees of frustration or disturbance with several of the problem subcategories, but might be less prone to drug abuse than students who may have profound difficulties with just one or two problem subcategories.

However, there is no reason to believe that such limitations in the data skews the results to make "obstacles" a more powerful cluster than it really is. Indeed, considering the preceding factors "obstacles" is probably weakened as a measure of educational disruption. It thereby becomes a conservative measure; thus, if significant results are found, they must be carefully considered.

Table 10-5 displays the prevalence of clients identifying different factors as obstacles to school attendance. These obstacles were grouped into nine clusters, which were rank ordered in the table according to their frequency. Percentages are given for each problem cluster and for the specific items in that cluster. Perhaps initially most striking is the sheer number and frequencies of perceived obstacles mentioned by clients. Given the conservative nature of the measure, this group appears to be one widely beset with many school problems.

As can be seen in table 10-5, five clusters dominate the number of obstacles mentioned, ranging from educational problems in school (66.8 percent) to personal problems with peers (44.6 percent). The nine leading specific obstacles (items) out of the forty-five (included in the nine clusters) were the following:

Lack of motivation (school)	47.1 percent
Boring curriculum	46.7 percent
Drug use	45.2 percent
Suspensions and expulsions	40.5 percent
Arguments with teachers	37.8 percent
Alcohol use	27.9 percent
Runaway (from family)	23.8 percent
Family disruptions (chronic)	23.7 percent
Peer group pressures	23.0 percent

More clues to understanding the dynamics of the youth treatment population can be extracted by examining each cluster. For educational problems in school (cluster 1), obstacles relating to deficiencies in the physical, personnel, and curricular resources in school are far outweighed by the perceived nonstimulation of the curriculum and a general lack of motivation for the school experience.

Table 10-5
Prevalence of Obstacles to School Attendance

	%	Total %
1. Educational Problems in School		66.8
Lack of motivation	47.1	
Boring curriculum	46.7	
Overly large classes; poor student-to-teacher ratio	10.8	
Unavailability of needed programs	8.9	
Poor condition of school's environment	7.7	
Inadequate educational materials, supplies, and equipment	5.2	
Other	5.0	
2. Personal Problems with School or School Personnel		55.5
Suspensions and expulsions	40.5	
Arguments with teachers	37.8	
Fights with teachers	18.0	
Other	2.5	
Conflicts with dorm staff	1.8	
3. Personal Problems with Family		49.2
Runaway	23.8	
Family disruptions (chronic)	23.7	
Family crises (health, mental, death, etc.)	18.5	
Lack of family interest and support in schoolwork	13.4	
Family moves	7.1	
Family responsibilities	5.4	
Other	2.5	
4. Drug/Alcohol-Use Problems		48.5
Drug use	45.2	
Alcohol use	27.9	
Other	1.2	
5. Personal Problems with Peers		44.6
Peer group pressures	23.0	
Disruptions in the classrooms	18.3	
Participation in gang activity	11.2	
Fear of hostile gangs, gang threats, etc.	8.4	
Racial conflicts	7.9	
Distruct, shame, or guilt	7.2	
Other	2.0	
6. Physical Problems		13.8
Physical illness	7.6	
Physical appearance	2.9	
Pregnancy	2.9	
Other	1.6	
7. Economic Problems		12.5
Severe financial deprivation	8.3	
Transportation	5.6	
Other	.9	
8. Ethnocultural Considerations		8.1
Discrimination of client at school because of ethnicity or race	4.1	

Table 10-5 continued

	%	Total %
Strong cultural influence counter to culture of school	3.2	
Rejection of client because of ethnicity or race	2.8	
Language barriers	2.7	
Other	.4	
9. Others		5.1
Had to repeat grade	.9	
Legal trouble	.5	
Social life conflict	.4	

The striking finding in the second cluster (personal problems with school or school personnel) was that 40.5 percent of all clients had apparently experienced difficulty with suspensions and expulsions. Although some readers might not find this surprising (somehow the clients ended up in a drug treatment program), it characterizes almost half the sample as having had disciplinary problems and conflicts with the school system and with Establishment authority.

Personal problems with family was the third-ranking cluster. There were fewer mentions of critical family life events (family health crises, family moves, family responsibilities) than of personal conflict situations (family disruptions, runaways). An interesting finding is that almost one-fourth of the entire sample cited runaway phenomena as having interfered with their school attendance.

The appearance of drug/alcohol use problems as obstacles to school attendance (48.5 percent) corresponds with the expected primary reason for entry into a treatment program (53.2 percent of the clients cited drug abuse as the reason for contact or entry to the program). There may have been underreporting of drug use as a cause of school problems. For example, one youngster indicated that drugs were not a problem in attending school. He reported, "If I wasn't so stoned during school, I couldn't have stood it." Thus it is especially important that almost half saw their use of drugs and alcohol directly inhibiting their school attendance (and, by implication, their performance).

The cluster of personal problems with peers (cluster 5) was led by peer group pressures, a finding that was not unexpected. However, gang-related activity or fear was a factor with 19.6 percent of the clients, and classroom disruptions were cited by 18.3 percent. Certainly, it is expected that such phenomena would occur more in the urban areas and the inner cities; organized gangs and exposure to violence are generally considered to be much higher for the inner city environment and a less critical factor in the suburban and rural school systems.

The other four clusters were mentioned significantly less often and serve to point up the relative importance of the first five. It seems from the data that attitudinal, affective and psychological reasons blocking school attendance outweigh *external* or impersonal ones. Subcategories reflecting breakdowns in motivation or conflicts with authority generated more mention than the clusters of physical problems, economic problems, ethnocultural considerations, and others taken together. However, many of the attitudinal and affective responses may be due to deficiencies in the educational system itself, reflected perhaps by the reported inability of the school to interest or stimulate this group. The implications of such a possibility will be examined in the Discussion section later in this chapter.

For another analysis, a breakdown for only those clients who had cited school-related problems as primary reasons for their ultimate contact with the treatment program shows that 20.8 percent cited problems that occurred in school, 17.7 percent mentioned problems that impinged on school but that occurred outside of school, and 16.3 percent had problems associated with truancy.

Obstacles to School Attendance and Demographic Variables. Since the number of obstacles checked is the main summary score for educational problems used in this study, it may be useful to report the sex and race distributions of these scores. Table 10-6 shows a tendency for females to mention more obstacles.

Table 10-6
Obstacles to School Attendance by Sex and Race

	*Sex**			*Race***		
Number of Obstacles Mentioned	*Female (Column %)*	*Males (Column %)*	*Row Totals*	*White (Column %)*	*Non-White (Column %)*	*Row Totals*
0	78 (7)	162 (10)	240	128 (7)	113 (13)	241
1 to 5	286 (27)	491 (29)	777	498 (27)	283 (32)	781
6 to 10	324 (30)	542 (32)	866	624 (34)	247 (28)	871
11 to 15	211 (20)	314 (19)	525	376 (20)	153 (17)	529
16 to 20	110 (10)	130 (8)	240	164 (9)	78 (9)	242
More than 20	52 (5)	33 (2)	85	56 (4)	22 (2)	78
Column totals	1,061 (100)	1,672 (100)	2,733	1,848 (100)	896 (100)	2,742

*Chi-Square = 29.35, d.f. = 5, $p < .001$.
**Chi-Square = 38.12, d.f. 5, $p < .001$.

Since the males had been found to tend to lag more in their educational attainment relative to their age, one might consider the explanation of the sex difference on obstacles to be that females tended to be more verbal, responsive and/or more compliant than males in the interview situation.

Table 10-6 also displays a tendency for whites to mention more obstacles than nonwhites. Although the tendency is not pronounced at the high end of the scale (from sixteen mentions and above), it is a noticeable trend with fifteen obstacles and under. On some grounds this finding might be puzzling, since the white subsample generally completed more years of education than the non-whites and thus have experienced greater school attendance. This finding would have been less difficult to interpret if the factor of intensity (or degree of impact on the client) had been included. Apparently the impact of the obstacles to school attendance was de facto more powerful for non-whites, since their educational attainment (and dropout ratio) was higher. Also, the present finding could represent simply a response set or a greater degree of comfort with the interviewer. The result may also have been mediated by the extent that whites, who were of higher educational status, were more verbally facile, thus generating more mentions of different obstacles to school attendance.

Obstacles to School Attendance and Background Variables. Table 10-7 displays the bivariate correlations between obstacles (total number of obstacles mentioned in all clusters) and other client characteristics and dimensions measured in NYPS. It should be noted first that the correlation between obstacles and number of school years completed (–.02) suggests that they are unrelated variables.

No relationship is found between obstacles and geography of residence (urban versus rural and urban versus suburban). A statistically significant inverse (–.08) relationship is found with the index of socioeconomic status. It seems reasonable that students from lower socioeconomic homes would have a tendency to have more difficulties with school. This relationship was found to obtain overall, in spite of the fact that the white subsample had higher socioeconomic status and also had more mentions of obstacles, relative to the non-white subsample. Obviously some of these inter-relationships are complex.

Concerning the structure of the family, although there is no relationship between obstacles and the fact of a father or mother being deceased, there is a significant correlation (r = .11) with having a broken family. It is entirely understandable that family difficulties tend to be manifested more in broken families and that family difficulties tend to generalize in clients' lives to their school experience.

Obstacles and Employment Variables. The two correlations involving work status (current employment and history of employment) show no relationship to obstacles. There was a significant relationship (r = –.08) between obstacles and

Table 10-7
Correlations of Selected Background and Drug Use Variables with Total Reported Number of Obstacles to School Attendance (n = 2,707)

Description	*No. of Obstacles to School Attendance* r*
Female = (0); Male = (1)	–.10
(0) = Nonwhite; (1) = White	.07
Sum of drugs used regularly	.32
(1) = Catholic; (0) = non-Catholic	–.02
Number of drug overdoses by client	.12
Number of suicide attempts reported by client	.20
Frequency of PCP use	.17
Frequency of getting drunk	.21
Father or mother deceased = (1); not = (0)	.02
(0) = Intact family; (1) = broken family	.11
(1) = Supported in part by family; (0) = not	–.08
(1) = Referred by criminal justice system; (0) = not	.08
Total number of violent weapons arrests	.16
Total number of private property arrests	.14
Number of times "picked up" by police	.16
Adjudicated delinquent (1) = yes; (0) = no	.16
Adjudicated dependent (1) = yes; (0) = no	.14
Outpatient (1) = yes; (0) = no	–.09
Total number of reasons for contacting agency	.52
(1) = Suburban; (0) = urban	.03
(1) = Rural; (0) = urban	.02
Referred by self = (1); not = (0)	.07
Referred by family = (1); not = (0)	.04
Referred by peers = (1); not = (0)	–.04
Referred by school = (1); not = (0)	–.00
(1) Employed; (0) = Unemployed	.04
Importance of religion in client's family (0) = no importance; (5) = great importance	.06
Use of drug combinations (1) = yes; (0) = no	.17
Index of socioeconomic status	–.08
Age in years	–.02
Total no. of substance (sales or possession) arrests	.15
No. of months employed in last 2 years	.00

*Pearson r of .05 = $p < .01$.

clients not being supported financially, at least in part, by their families. Here lack of family support cannot be equated with client financial or vocational independence. Clients might be supported from welfare, residential programs, or illegal activities. Perhaps more relevant is the possibility that family disintegration may be related to the family not supporting the client (runaway phenomena, broken homes, etc.), and that both of these factors are involved in the number of obstacles to school attendance.

Obstacles and Religious Factors. There appears to be no association between obstacles and the fact of family Catholicism. Neither is there a significant correlation between obstacles and the perceived importance of religion in the family.

Obstacles and Criminal Justice System Involvement. The findings confirm a consistent positive relationship between obstacles and involvement with the criminal justice system. Four different variables (total number of violent and weapon arrests, private property arrests, substance arrests, and times picked up by police) each relates to obstacles to a similar degree (positive correlations from .14 to .16). The same level of positive relationship was found with whether the client had been adjudicated "delinquent" (r = .16) or "dependent" (r = .14). Ordinarily, one might suspect an automatic or artificial connection with these variables, since such legal trouble as arrests would be expected to interfere with school attendance, either from temporary confinement or perhaps because of suspension or expulsion. Interestingly, however, only 0.5 percent of the sample cited legal problems as an obstacle. It may also be that juvenile probation departments put an emphasis on school attendance as a criterion for successful probation.

At the very least, it is important to emphasize that the size of these correlations tends to be minimized among this rather homogeneous population with the high rate of illegal offenses. If the sample were extended to the rest of the teenage population, one might expect a much more dramatic relationship between attitudes, school adjustment, and involvement with the criminal justice system.

Obstacles and Program Variables. The highest correlation in table 10-7, but probably not the most meaningful, is the .52 relationship between obstacles and the total number of reasons given by the client for contacting the treatment agency. Over and above the potentially valid relationship between these variables, two kinds of artifacts may be distorting and increasing the size of the correlation: a response set and a halo effect. Some respondents may have had a response set for expanding on items that have multiple response options. Perhaps an even more powerful factor was a halo effect between items in the client information form pertaining to obstacles and those which later appeared in the reasons for referral section. There is more than a passing similarity between the subcategories of the former and the latter. If mentioned on the former, there would be a natural tendency to mention the subcategory when being questioned about referral factors.

It may be that multiple forces operate on clients to push them over the threshold for deciding to make program contact. Indeed, the data appear to reconfirm a tendency for a cluster of personal, interpersonal, educational, and social distresses to be operating in these clients. Thus the number of problems clients report experiencing in their school world may be reflected to some extent in the number of problems they report as salient to their program contact.

Interestingly, there are no significant correlations between obstacles and the source of referral to the program. Of some importance might be the "non-finding" ($r = -.00$) between the number of obstacles and referral by school. This seems to suggest again, as mentioned earlier in another connection, that the obstacles subcategories are not merely a reflection of trouble with school authorities and poor school conditions, but are much more likely a valid reflection of clients' internal perception.

Also found was a tendency for those clients reporting more obstacles to be in a residential program rather than in an outpatient program ($r = -.09$). Since obstacles are shown in table 10-7 to reflect a tendency toward greater severity in drug abuse (sum of drugs used regularly), and since residential program clients in this sample have relatively more severe drug abuse, these three variables are apparently interrelated.

Obstacles and Self-Destructive Behavior. Although this subsection discusses only two correlations, they involve variables of utmost seriousness—reports of life-threatening behavior. There is a statistically significant association ($r = +.12$) between obstacles and the number of drug overdoses reported by the client. Certainly, this finding could be mediated by the tendency of users of a greater number of different types of drugs, and of certain types of drugs, to be more likely to experience accidental overdose. Self-destructive tendencies, indicated by the total number of suicide attempts reported by the client, has an even higher correlation ($r = +.20$) with obstacles. This is the strongest evidence reported yet that establishes a link between problems surrounding the school experience and profound feelings of intra-psychic distress, in this group of young clients. It is less probable that the intensity of drug use, or the number of drugs used, accounts for most of the variance expressed by this correlation. Any such contaminating effect should have been stronger for the overdose variable than for the suicide attempt variable. There is evidence for this in the fact that the correlation between the number of O.D.'s and the number of types of drugs used (Regsum) is .37, while the correlation between the number of suicide attempts and Regsum is only .18.

Obstacles to School Attendance and Drug Use. The relationship between perceived obstacles and various measures of drug use among the sample are at the very heart of the present analysis. The findings reported thus far have given valuable background to this central question and should help with the interpretation of the explicitly drug-related data. The number of self-reported obstacles to school attendance is the best measure available in this study to relate educational problems and disturbance in school progress with drug use and abuse.

Referring once again to table 10-7, several disparate relationships all in a consistent direction are found. There is a relationship (r = +.21) between obstacles and the frequency with which the client gets drunk when he or she drinks alcohol which indicates that more immoderate drinking is associated with greater school related difficulties. A significant relationship (r = +.17) is also found between obstacles and the frequency of phencyclidine (PCP) use. A similar correlation (r = +.17) is found with a dichotomous variable reflecting whether the client uses two or more drugs together, in combination, to "boost or counterbalance" the effects of one or more of the drugs. The combination drug users (67.7 percent of the sample) are likely to report more school-related problems than those clients who do not follow such a practice. The second largest correlation in table 10-7 is also the most important one for this analysis: the total number of obstacles to school attendance mentioned is found to have a correlation of r = +.32 with the number of different types of psychoactive drugs that were used regularly (at least weekly for at least a month) by the key summary drug use index utilized in the NYPS analysis. This strong correlation with obstacles is particularly important, suggesting a direct and meaningful association between polydrug abuse and educational problems. Remembering that the sample, almost by definition, is already composed of serious drug users who required treatment, the association with severity of drug involvement is even more meaningful.

Types of Obstacles and Drug Use. Utilizing this same summary drug use measure or index, table 10-8 compares the mean number of drugs used regularly for clients who report obstacles with the mean number of drugs for clients who do not report obstacles in each of the 8 categories of obstacles to school attendance. It can be seen that these differences are statistically significant for all obstacle categories, with the exception of economic problems and ethno-cultural considerations, both of which were mentioned relatively rarely by the sample.

Thus, there is a clear tendency for clients who report obstacles to school attendance also to use significantly more types of drugs regularly, compared with clients who did not report any obstacles. Most impressive is the 1.4 mean difference in the drug alcohol use problem category. This relatively large difference would be expected and adds to the face validity of the categorical breakdown.

Discussion

In summary, the NYPS suggests a meaningful association between polydrug use and perceived obstacles to school attendance. Large proportions of the sample (table 10-5) report obstacles to school attendance and numerous problems relating to the school system, the family, peers, and drugs. The data suggest that

Table 10-8
Obstacles to School Attendance in Relationship to the Number of Drugs Used Regularly

	Mean Number of Drugs Used Regularly for Clients without *Obstacles in Each Category*			*Mean Number of Drugs Used Regularly for Clients* with *Obstacles in Each Category*				
Category of Obstacles	*Mean*	*S.D.*	*No. of Cases*	*Mean*	*S.D.*	*No. of Cases*	*Student's t Value*	*p**
Education Problems in School	3.4	2.3	849	4.3	2.6	1,901	9.2	<.001
Personal Problems with School or School Personnel	3.5	2.3	1,175	4.4	2.7	1,575	9.4	<.001
Personal Problems with Family	3.6	2.3	1,345	4.6	2.7	1,405	9.5	<.001
Drug/Alcohol-Use Problems	3.3	2.2	1,377	4.7	2.6	1,375	15.6	<.001
Personal Problems with Peers	3.7	2.4	1,469	4.3	2.6	1,281	6.0	<.001
Physical Problems	3.9	2.5	2,362	4.5	2.7	388	4.0	<.001
Economic Problems	4.0	2.5	2,383	4.3	2.9	367	1.8	N.S.
Ethnocultural Considerations	4.0	2.6	2,501	3.8	2.6	249	1.3	N.S.

Note: *Regular use* is defined as at least weekly use either currently or in the past over a period of at least one month.

*A t value of 3.3 with 2,748 degrees of freedom is significant at the .001 level.

the more severe the frequency of drug use, and the number of different drugs used, the more dominant are problems (obstacles) relating to school attendance (and vice versa). Since the data available from NYPS and CODAP indicates that the educational attainment of polydrug abusers suffers relative to the general youth population, it seems reasonable to anticipate that more perceived obstacles to school attendance will likely translate into more stunted educational attainment for that part of the sample also manifesting relative greater polydrug abuse.

Correlational analyses further suggest a cluster of associations between obstacles to school attendance, drug-use indexes, and other variables reflecting life problems (criminal justice involvement, suicidal attempts and deprivation in the socioeconomic area). Again, it is useful to emphasize that all these findings take on even more importance because they occur within a quasi-homogeneous population already requiring treatment for drug abuse.

Such educational problems as lack of motivation and boring curricula were frequently mentioned by this sample as the most prominent obstacles to school attendance, suggesting that the school program failed to interest these youngsters. Whatever the cause-effect sequence, the data, combined with previous work, make it difficult to overlook the powerful connection between young peoples' polydrug-use patterns and their perception of their educational experience and of their adjustment to school.

Need for Further Research

The data base of the National Youth Polydrug Study was sufficiently rewarding to stimulate researchers to become interested in expanding the scope of such studies. Clearly, questions could be asked in the future to test various hypotheses more specifically. Of highest priority would be a similar study with a comparison group of drug using youths not in treatment programs and a representative sample large enough to generate sufficient numbers of nonusers and users. Also of great value would be longitudinal studies of multiple drug users following parallel samples for 3 to 5 years, such as the study that Jessor et al. (1973) conducted with high school and college marihuana users. More attention might also be directed to the study of the possible effects of different levels (intensity) of drug use on school performance and educational attainment.

Implications for Program Policy and Planning

Certainly the NYPS data and previous studies suggest that there should be more emphasis on educational/vocational problems and programs in the rehabilitation, treatment, early intervention, and primary prevention of youthful drug users.

Treatment programs should be cognizant of the educational obstacles faced by the young and the needs of their young polydrug clients. Drug-abuse program counselors working in school systems should recognize the possible contribution of the educational system to drug-misuse vulnerability. Further, the data would seem to support an increase in school-based intervention/prevention programs and relevant vocational alternatives for adolescents. In the past, many school systems have been reluctant to get involved in the drug area, fearing the negative publicity that can result from exposing drug-use problems.

There are parallel but distinct strategies suggested for the early intervention and primary prevention stages. Early intervention presumes that clients have been identified, whether by self-referral or otherwise, as having some difficulty associated with drugs, directly or indirectly. Treatment programs must therefore assess the educational progress made by youngsters, encourage exposure to alternatives, help to solve problems, and attempt to improve attitudes, so that school or prevocational regimens become a constructive force in their lives.

Primary prevention programs are ordinarily not aimed at particular individuals but rather at groups of individuals. There is increasing evidence that well-planned and theoretically sound prevention programs may actually show measurable impact on drug attitudes, intentions, and self-reported use. A recent study of evaluations of prevention programs (Schaps et al. 1978) demonstrated that rigorous evaluations of programs featuring affective or "alternative" approaches show promising results. Basing many of these programs and strategies in the school setting makes practical and logistical sense. After all, it is within this setting that most young people are introduced to drugs. One possible strategy is to group or segregate students with serious drug-abuse problems into special classes that will receive affective education, special counseling, and alternative programs. The advantages and disadvantages of such a strategy need to be explored.

In summary, as youth drug use is tracked more accurately and studied more carefully in the educational setting, the critical interaction between drug-use patterns and the educational setting will be better understood. Such understanding can perhaps stimulate constructive changes and reforms in both drug-abuse programs and in those responsible for education and prevocational training so that the potentiality for both educational effectiveness and freedom from chemical reliance will be enhanced.

References

Babst, D.V., Miran, M., and Koval, M. 1976. The relationship between friends' marijuana use, family cohesion, school interest and drug abuse prevention. *Journal of Drug Education* 6(1):23-41.

Babst, D., Uppal, G.S., and Schmeidler, J. 1977. Relationship of youths' attitudes to substance abuse in New York State. *Journal of Alcohol and Drug Education (forthcoming)*.

Brook, R., Szandorowska, B., and Whitehead, P.C. 1976. Psychosocial dysfunction as precursors to amphetamine abuse among adolescents. *Addictive Diseases* 2(3):465-478.

Chase, J.A., and Jessor, R. 1977. A Social-Psychological Analysis of Marihuana Involvement Among a National Sample of Adolescents. University of Colorado Institute of Behavioral Science, prepared under contract ADM 281-75-0028 with NIDA.

Chein, I., Gerard, D.L., Lee, R.S. and Rosenield, E. 1964. *The Road to H: Narcotics, Delinquency, and Social Policy,* Chap. XII, The Female Addict. New York: Basic Books.

C_2ODAC. 1976. *Community Youth Development Survey (1975-1976).* Ft. Boise Community Center, Boise, Idaho.

Dembo, R., Burgos, W., Babst, D.V., Schmeidler, J., and LaGrand, L.E. 1977. Neighborhood Relationships and Drug Involvement Among Inner City Junior High School Youths: Implications for Drug Education and Prevention Programming. Unpublished paper.

Jessor, Richard. 1978. Adolescent Health and Behavior, paper presented at National Academy of Medicine Conference, reported in *Washington Drug Review,* Vol. II, No. 7 (July 14, 1978), page 4.

Jessor, R., Jessor, S.L., and Finney, J. 1973. A social psychology of marihuana use: Longitudinal studies of high school and college youth. *Journal of Personality and Social Psychology* 26(1):1-15.

Lavenhar, M.A., Wolfson, E.A., Sheffet, A., Einstein, S. and Louria, D.B. 1971. Survey of drug abuse in six New Jersey high schools. II. Characteristics of drug users and non-users. *Proceedings of the First International Conference on Student Drug Surveys.* Farmingdale, New York: Baywood Publishing Co.

Mellinger, G.D.; Somers, R.H.; Bazell, S.; Manheimer, D.I. 1978, in Kandel, D.B., ed. *Longitudinal Research on Drug Use,* Hemisphere Publishing Corp., Washington, D.C., pp. 157-176.

Noble, Peter, Hart, T. and Nation, R. 1972. Correlates and outcomes of illicit drug use by adolescent girls. *British Journal of Psychology* 120:497-504.

Patch, V.D. 1973. Public health aspects of adolescent drug use in America: Problem in perspective. *Technical Papers of the Second Report of the National Commission on Marijuana and Drug Abuse,* Vol. IV. Treatment and Rehabilitation.

Phin, J.G., Morein, M.J., Meltzer, R., and Snyder, J.F. 1976. *New Roles for an Old Institution: Preventing and Treating Substance Abuse in an Educational Milieu.* Philadelphia: Polydrug Research Project, Report to NIDA Services Research Branch, Grant H81-DAO1657.

Pittel, S.M. 1973. The etiology of youthful drug involvement in drug use in America: Problem in perspective. *The Technical Papers of the Second*

Report of the National Commission on Marijuana and Drug Abuse, Vol. II. Patterns and Consequences of Drug Use, pp. 879-912.

Polydrug Research Center. 1977. Report on Youth Admitted to Treatment in Calendar Year 1975. From the Client-Oriented Data Acquisition Process (CODAP) National Drug File. Philadelphia Psychiatric Center, Unpublished report to NIDA.

Roth, R. 1971. Student drug abuse in southeastern Michigan and profiles of the abusers. *Proceedings of the First International Conference on Student Drug Surveys.* Farmingdale, New York: Baywood Publishing Co.

Schaps, E., Cohen, A.Y., and Resnik, H.S. 1975. *Balancing Head and Heart: Sensible Ideas for the Prevention of Drug and Alcohol Abuse. Book 1: Prevention in Perspective.* Lafayette, California: Prevention Materials Institute.

Schaps, E., DiBartolo, R., Palley, C., and Churgin, S. 1978. *Primary Prevention Evaluation Research: A Review of 75 Program Impact Studies.* Rockville, Md.: PYRAMID Project, Prevention Branch, National Institute on Drug Abuse.

11 Pharmacological Aspects of Youth Drug Abuse

Sidney H. Schnoll

Introduction

The pharmacology of drugs that are abused is often misunderstood or totally ignored when drug abuse is studied, except for a listing of the drugs used. Over the years, prejudices have developed leading to a classification of drugs that tends to define them as either "good" or "bad." Drugs that have a high abuse potential are frequently considered bad or harmful, and those with a low abuse potential are considered good or beneficial. This approach to drugs of abuse may be helpful to some because of its simplicity, but it does not address the important issue of why certain drugs have a high potential for abuse.

In the determination of a drug's status, more than abuse potential should be considered. What are the toxicities of the drug? What are the chances of becoming dependent on the drug? Is dependency on a drug necessarily bad? Sometimes these questions are difficult to answer. Certainly, two of the most toxic drugs we know are alcohol and tobacco (nicotine). These drugs are sold legally, and in fact, state and federal governments benefit from the sale of these drugs by taxation. Dependency to both of these drugs develops, as it does to caffeine, which is found in varying doses in coffee, tea, cola drinks, and chocolate. Why are we so concerned about dependency on opiates and not caffeine? Heroin, if given in pure form for long periods of time, has few toxic effects. Because of some apparent inconsistencies between a drug's pharmacology and its legal status, it is important to become aware of our prejudices involving drugs and try to approach the pharmacology of drug abuse dispassionately.

It must be recognized that drugs are simply chemicals, and that the effect a specific drug has on a person can vary from individual to individual and these variations are based on the interaction between the person and the drug. Not only does a person's physical make-up influence the effect a drug might have, but many psychological factors are involved as well. What was the mood (set) of the person at the time the drug was taken? In what location (setting) was the person at the time the drug was taken? What expectations did the person have regarding the drug's actions (placebo effect)? A drug's effects are the interactions between the actions of the drug and the psychological and physical states of the person taking the drug.

Basically, the effects of drugs can be divided into three types: (1) the expected effect; (2) the toxic effect; and (3) the idiosyncratic reaction or the unexpected toxic effect. An example of an expected effect would be the relief of pain by aspirin. An example of a toxic effect would be the upset stomach frequently caused by aspirin. This type of toxic effect is well known, and it can be predicted that a certain percentage of individuals who take the drug will experience this effect. Toxic effects become more prevalent as the dose of the drug increases. An example of an idiosyncratic reaction or an unexpected toxic effect would be an allergic reaction to aspirin. This type of effect occurs rarely, and there is no way to predict its occurrence until after the person has taken the drug. Increased doses of a drug may increase the chances of an idiosyncratic reaction, but these reactions are frequently not dose dependent.

Although all drugs have toxic effects, if the drug is to be used for medical purposes, the beneficial effects should be greater than the toxic effects in the dose ranges normally used. To determine if the beneficial effects outweigh the toxic effects, a ratio has been developed called the therapeutic index (TI). The TI is the ratio of the dose of the drug that will cause lethality or death in 50 percent of the people who take it (LD_{50}) to the dose of the drug that will give the expected therapeutic effect in 50 percent of the people who take it (ED_{50}). This ratio is usually depicted as the LD_{50}/ED_{50}. The higher the TI, the safer the drug; the lower the TI, the greater the chances of a toxic or lethal reaction from the drug.

Looking at drugs of abuse from this point of view, most abused substances have a high therapeutic index. Not only are most abusable substances generally safe, but they also give the people who take them pleasurable experiences. It is important to remember that most people who abuse drugs feel that the beneficial effects they receive from the drugs outweigh the risks involved. The perceived beneficial or pleasurable effects may vary from user to user, and what is considered to be pleasurable by one user is not necessarily pleasurable to another. (One person's dysphoria may be another person's euphoria.)

It is frequently said that drugs (even those abused) are used to self-medicate some underlying problem. This assumption may be reasonable since drugs of abuse sedate, relieve pain, or stimulate. These effects are also the effects of some of the most commonly prescribed drugs. A tranquilizer, diazepam (Valium), is currently the most prescribed drug in the United States. It is usually prescribed to relieve anxiety through its sedating effect. It is also the fourth ranked drug of abuse in DAWN IV data for youths. Parents who receive prescriptions for diazepam and take it to relieve anxiety or assist in sleep may leave the unused portion of the prescription in the medicine cabinet, where the pills may be taken by their children. If the adolescent is found with the pills he or she may be classified as a drug abuser, even if the diazepam was taken for the same reason the parent took it. Thus a licit drug may also be an illicit drug depending on how, when, where, or by whom it is used.

Licit drugs may be purchased through a pharmacy or on the street. If the drug is purchased at the pharmacy, the buyer can be reasonably confident that the drug is what was written on the prescription, in the dose recommended, and without contaminants present. When an attempt is made to purchase the same drug on the street illicitly, the buyer can never have the same confidence in the quality of the drug. What is the situation when an illegal drug is purchased on the street? The study of illicitly purchased drugs has become known as "street drug" pharmacology. It takes into consideration all the vagaries and complications of illicitly purchased drugs, for the effects of these drugs may differ substantially from a pure substance being studied in a laboratory. Since the majority of drugs abused by young people are purchased illicitly, the emphasis in this chapter will be on street-drug pharmacology.

Street-Drug Pharmacology

Although most studies on drugs of abuse are carried out with pure substances of known dose, this is not the way drugs are most frequently taken in the streets. The users of illicitly purchased drugs are often totally unaware of the actual chemical substance, the dose being purchased, and the contaminants that may be present in the sample.

The analysis of street drugs has become a more common practice in recent years, and data are available to document the purity of various preparations sold illicitly. The data show that the degree of deceit in the illicit drug market varies depending on the drug and on the area of the country in which it is sold. There are numerous reasons for substituting one drug for another, but most relate to the availability of, and demand for, a particular drug.

In the early 1970s, mescaline was a popular drug among youthful drug users because it was considered to be "natural." LSD, on the other hand, was a synthetic material that had received extensive play in the press because it was alleged to cause chromosomal damage. For the time period 1970 to 1972, Brown and Malone (1975) found that mescaline was the drug most frequently submitted for analysis at the centers they surveyed. For the period from 1972 to 1974, it had fallen to third place among samples submitted for analysis. The Street Drug Identification Program at the Los Angeles County, University of Southern California Medical Center (LAC-USC) between 1971 and 1975 averaged almost eighty-six samples of mescaline a year. However, from 1976 to 1977, only twenty-three samples were received.

As the demand for mescaline declined, the relative purity increased, even though mescaline remains a very difficult drug to obtain in pure form. During the 1971-1975 time period, 97.1 percent of the samples contained no mescaline, compared with 82.7 percent containing no mescaline in 1976-1977. Of interest in this report is the presence of phencyclidine (PCP) in the mescaline samples. For the 1971-1975 time period, 26.3 percent of the mescaline samples contained

PCP, whereas in the 1976-1977 time period, only 8.6 percent of the samples contained PCP.

As the demand for PCP has increased in recent years, there has been a decrease in its appearance as a substitute for some other drugs. The LAC-USC reports show that not only has there been a decrease in the appearance of PCP in samples submitted as mescaline, but there has also been a decrease for other hallucinogens. Between 1971 and 1975, almost 10 percent of all samples submitted as hallucinogens contained some PCP. For the 1976-1977 time period, 2 percent of hallucinogens submitted for analysis contained PCP.

Despite its disappearance as a substitute for other drugs, the purity of PCP itself has also decreased as the demand has increased. In 1971-1975, 80 percent of all samples submitted as PCP contained some PCP. During 1976-1977, this fell to 60 percent in the LAC-USC analysis program. Demand for a drug may not change, but there may be a significant decrease in availability. In 1972, amphetamines were moved into Schedule II of the Controlled Substance Act. By being placed in Schedule II, the government could control the amount of amphetamine produced in the United States, and as a result production has decreased over 90 percent. For 1970-1972, Brown and Malone reported the misrepresentation rate for amphetamines to be 22.5 percent. For the 1972-1974 time period, the misrepresentation rate increased to 45.8 percent.

Based on the preceding information, the first major question that has to be answered with regard to street drugs is whether the individual has actually received the drug he thought he had purchased. This likelihood varies from drug to drug. For example, if an individual believes he or she has purchased tetrahydrocannabinol (THC) on the street, the chances of actually getting THC are almost zero. THC is a drug which is very difficult to manufacture, very expensive, and–if indeed someone did manufacture it or extract it from the plant–it rapidly oxydizes to inert cannabinols unless stored in a nitrogen atmosphere. For this reason, it is practically impossible to obtain THC on the street.

On the other hand, marihuana–which is the most frequently cited drug of abuse for youth populations in DAWN IV data–is almost always marihuana. Brown and Malone summarized the data from four centers that collectively analyzed 309 samples submitted as marihuana; 93 percent of the samples were indeed marihuana. In their data for heroin from the same centers, 63 percent of the samples contained some heroin. Weisman et al. 1973 analyzed twenty samples of heroin obtained from the police in Philadelphia and found that 100 percent of the samples contained heroin.

As can be seen from these figures, the deceit rate varies from drug to drug and from one area of the country to another. If the purchaser is fortunate enough to obtain the drug that he or she thinks was bought, the second important question to be answered is this: What was the dose of the drug in the sample purchased?

Doses can vary significantly. In the previously cited study of heroin samples from the Philadelphia area, samples varied from less than 1 mg to 17.5 mg. In similar studies, LSD samples have varied from material containing no LSD to material with over 1,000 mcg of LSD. These variations in doses are extremely important, since the user, not knowing what dose has been purchased, can inadvertantly overdose or develop a toxic reaction to a high dose of the drug when a lower dose was expected.

An example of this has occurred with cocaine, which at the present time on the East Coast is normally about 30 to 35 percent cocaine. Three regular users seen by the author had purchased cocaine that they suspected to be of 30 to 35 percent purity; it turned out to be pure cocaine. Using it at their normal rate, these individuals were now receiving three times the amount they were accustomed to taking. Over a period of an evening, all three of the users took sufficient quantities to develop psychotic behavior that had to be treated with medical attention.

A third question to be considered is the matter of the contaminants that may be present in samples purchased on the street. As was mentioned before, the actual amount of drug present and the percent of purity can vary greatly. If a drug sample contains only 20 percent of the ingredients for which it is purchased, 80 percent of the sample must contain something else. These other products can vary from other drugs to relatively inert substances. Table 11-1 is a breakdown of the contaminants found in samples of cocaine analyzed on the East Coast. As can be seen, many of the contaminants can produce toxic reactions in their own right. Even substances normally considered inert may produce toxic reactions. Talcum powder, for example, when suspended in water and then injected intravenously, can produce microemboli in the lungs and other blood vessels because the talc particles cannot pass through small capillaries. Unless there is complete knowledge of the contents of street drug samples, inaccurate information may appear in overdose reports generated from verbal reports of consumption. For example, one report of cocaine overdose on careful examination turned out to be an overdose of tetracaine. The person purchasing the sample believed he had purchased cocaine, and that was how the death was reported in the media. Only after careful analyses of blood samples were done was the real cause of the overdose determined.

As can be seen from these data, individuals purchasing drugs on the street may not know what they are getting, may have no idea of the purity of the drugs, and may be unaware of contaminants present. This brings into question much of the data based on self-reporting from patients in emergency rooms or people calling crisis centers. Unless the program either does hard-sample analysis (analysis of the material purchased) or takes blood or urine from the individual and analyzes it for a host of different drugs, the reported data can be highly inaccurate. A case in point occurred in a hospital where a young woman, claiming to have taken amphetamines, was brought following a seizure. Analysis of blood

Table 11-1
Adulterants Found in Illicit Cocaine Submitted for Analysis

Adulterant	*Number of Samples with Cocaine*	*Number of Samples without Cocaine*
Lidocaine	16	2
Procaine[a]	3	2
Lactose	2	–
Phencyclidine	4	1
Caffeine[b]	–	3
Diethylproprion[c]	1	–
Ephedrine	–	2
Phenylpropanolamine	–	2
Methamphetamine	–	1
Phenacetin[b]	–	1
Aminopyrine[b]	–	1
Antipyrine[d]	1	2
Salicylate[d]	–	1
Quinine[a]	–	1
Diphenhydramine	–	2
Magnesium Sulfate[c]	1	–

[a]Found in combination in one sample.
[b]Found in combination in one sample.
[c]Found in combination in one sample.
[d]Found in combination in one sample.

and urine in the hospital showed no amphetamine present, yet the woman was reported as an amphetamine overdose. On further toxicologic evaluation, it was discovered that the woman had taken phencyclidine (PCP) instead of amphetamine. The hospital lab routine did not contain an examination for phencyclidine, and it was only because this hospital was affiliated with a medical school where these further tests were available that the true nature of the woman's overdose was discovered. Because this information was not available until several weeks later, the report from the emergency room still is listed as amphetamine overdose.

Physicians who work in emergency rooms attempt to determine as accurately as possible the causative agent in drug overdoses or toxic reactions. However, studies have shown that even experienced physicians cannot always make an accurate clinical determination of what drug has been taken. Bellets et al. 1973 reported that rapid mass spectrometry of gastric contents confirmed the physician's diagnosis in 44 percent of the cases. This indicates that in over 50 percent of the cases, the physician was unable to make an accurate diagnosis. If analysis of stomach, urine, or blood samples is not available to the physician, then a decision as to the drug taken is based on clinical findings alone. The decision may be based on other factors: (1) what the patient or a friend of the patient says was taken; (2) what is being reported in the press, radio, or television as a popular drug; (3) what prejudices the physician has regarding certain drugs; and (4) the physician's expertise in diagnosing acute drug reactions.

The data available from DAWN is primarily self-reporting and is not usually substantiated by any hard-sample analysis or biological-fluid analysis. When the amount of deceit that is present in the street drug market is taken into consideration, one has to question very carefully the validity of these data. This is especially true among youthful drug users—the heaviest users of street drugs—who frequently have less money and are not tied in with the more established drug sales network. Because of this, they are frequently sold poorer quality materials.

It is certainly much more expensive to do urine, blood, and hard-sample analyses to collect the data than simply to accept verbal reports. However, if data are of questionable validity, then we must look at whether it is worthwhile to collect such data at all.

Drug Interactions and Multiple Substance Abuse

Drug interactions occur when two or more substances are taken at one time or within a sufficiently short time period so that the actions of the first drug have not worn off when the next drug is taken. It would be nice to be able to list all the drugs of abuse and their interactions with other drugs, but this is not possible. Drug interactions are usually not systematically studied and are reported only when the interaction is observed by a physician. Despite the lack of systematic investigation, some important general principles of drug interactions are known.

The interactions of drugs can be divided into several categories. First is the *additive effect,* when two or more drugs are taken which have similar actions, the effects of each drug adding to the effects of the other so that there is double, triple, or greater effect than the single drug has. The effects of these drugs add together in a direct 1 + 1 + 1 fashion depending on how many doses were taken. Second is the *synergistic effect,* when two or more drugs are taken together and the drugs have similar actions, but the effects are more than additive: 1 + 1 = 3 would represent this type of action. Third is the *potentiating effect,* when two or more drugs are taken that do not have similar actions, but one drug enhances an effect of the other. An example of this occurs when amphetamines are given with morphine. The amphetamine enhances the pain-killing action of the morphine—even though the amphetamine itself has no direct pain-killing action. Fourth is the *antagonistic effect,* when two or more drugs are taken together and one drug counteracts the effects of the other drug. Antagonism can occur in several different ways. One drug can block the effects of the other by competing for a cellular receptor site even though the blocking drug may not have action by itself. An example of this is heroin and naloxone. Naloxone has no effect of its own unless it is given in conjunction with an opiate. When this occurs, it blocks the effect of the opiate and can even reverse an opiate overdose. Another type of antagonism occurs when two drugs have opposite actions, such as stimulants and depressants. In this case, each drug modifies the effects of the other. The stimulant counteracts the depressant's effects and the person may not feel as drowsy, and the depressant counteracts the stimulant effect and the person may not feel as energized.

Drug abusers are usually aware of some of these drug interactions and will use one drug to modify the effects of another. Most people are aware of the additive and sometimes synergistic effects of all the depressant drugs (table 11-2). In addition to the drugs listed, alcohol also has additive or synergistic effects with these drugs. By taking more than one of these substances at a time, the drug abuser gets a greater effect than if one drug was taken alone. Sometimes the user is not aware that the effects of drugs are additive or synergistic; the user will take several different drugs in this group hoping not to take enough to overdose—but does take too much and does overdose.

When drug abusers take more than one drug at a time, they are called *polydrug abusers* or *multiple-substance abusers.* Multiple-substance abuse has become more common in recent years and can occur in several different ways. Often the abuser consciously takes two or more drugs together because the combined effect is enjoyed more than when a single drug is taken. Multiple-substance abuse can also occur when a combination drug is the preferred drug of abuse. This can occur when abusing cough syrup, which contains codeine. All these syrups contain large amounts of alcohol as well as codeine. Therefore, the abuser is taking codeine and alcohol, which becomes multiple-substance abuse.

Table 11-2
Sedative-Hypnotics

Barbiturates:
Seconal (secobarbital), Nembutal (pentobarbital), Amytal (amobarbital), Tuinal (secobarbital and amobarbital), Luminal (phenobarbital)

Sleeping Pills (Sedative-Hypnotics):
Chloral Hydrate, Quaalude (methaqualone), Placidyl (ethchlorvynol), Doriden (glutethimide), Noludar (methyprylon)

Minor Tranquilizers and Anxiolytics:
Equanil and Miltown (meprobamate), Valium (diazepam), Librium (Chlordiazepoxide), Serax (oxazepam)

Muscle Relaxants:
Soma (carisoprodol), Robaxin (methocarbamol)

Another form of multiple-substance abuse can occur when a user buys drugs on the street that contain a contaminant that is another drug. PCP, for example, has been mixed in with samples of LSD. If the user takes LSD that is mixed with PCP, this could be called "inadvertent" multiple-substance abuse. Even though the use of the adulterant is not the primary reason for taking the drug, the drug abuser may become introduced to a new drug in this way.

In some cases, when street-drug mixtures are analyzed, there appear to be logical reasons for the contaminant's presence. Lidocaine is used to cut cocaine because the lidocaine also has local anesthetic properties and therefore is difficult to distinguish from cocaine. Caffeine is used to cut amphetamine because it also has stimulant properties. However, in many instances it is difficult to tell why a particular drug was used in a street-drug sample. For example, the reason diphenhydramine (Benadryl) would be added to cocaine is difficult to determine; diphenhydramine is a antihistamine with some sedative properties, whereas cocaine is a stimulant. It seems likely that some contaminants are added because they are available, not because of any particular interaction with the primary substance.

Just as the contaminant drug can interact to enhance some actions of the primary drug, it can also have a toxic interaction. The drugs that are used in street-drug combination have not been studied in combinations for the most part. For example, the interaction of LSD and PCP has not been studied, even though this combination has been found for many years. If the user buys the LSD sample unaware that the PCP is present and has an adverse reaction, the reaction is reported as an LSD reaction because the buyer is unaware of the other drug's presence. How often adverse drug reactions seen in hospitals or crisis centers are really toxic interactions is difficult to say. In fact, it is impossible to say because the proper studies (blood, urine, and hard-sample analyses) are almost never done. This once again calls into question the verbal reports collected in centers. It may be that all the toxic reactions seen are not due to a single drug but are really drug interactions. This is highly unlikely, but the possibility must be further evaluated.

Even if the proper studies were done on all cases of toxic reactions, the question may not be answered. There are limits to the sensitivities of many analytical tests; the presence of a drug below the detection limits of the analytic equipment in combination with another drug may be sufficient to cause a toxic reaction.

As we become more aware of the problem of multiple-substance abuse, new techniques must be developed to assist in identifying when drug interactions are the cause of adverse drug reactions. Some initial steps are being undertaken in this area, but until well-documented data are available, we can only guess at the prevalence of multiple-substance abuse. For this reason the available data have to be taken for what they are worth—which may not be very much.

Cannabis and Its Products

Marihuana is one of the oldest drugs known to be used in medicine. In recent years, there has been a great deal of controversy regarding this drug. Numerous studies have been done and reports written regarding the effects of marihuana and other cannabis products. Often these reports are conflicting, making it quite difficult for the average person to understand what the effects of the drug really are.

The recent studies on marihuana have been well summarized in the yearly reports to Congress by the National Institute on Drug Abuse. In reading these reports it is apparent that marihuana is one of the most thoroughly studied drugs known. The effects of marihuana have been studied on most organ systems in the body, as well as its effects on psychological functioning. To date, there is no evidence that marihuana creates a physical dependency, and users have been able to stop the use of the drug even after using large quantities for long periods of time without any physical difficulties. However, psychological dependency can develop on marihuana, as it can for almost any other substance. The psychological dependency can, at times, be much more difficult to deal with than the physical dependency.

Recent evidence indicates that tolerance may develop to repeated high doses of Δ9 tetrahydrocannabinol (THC) administration. THC is the principal active ingredient in marihuana. Although tolerance develops, much has been said about the reverse tolerance seen with marihuana. Instead of requiring increasing doses to achieve the desired effect, the regular marihuana user requires smaller doses to achieve the desired effect.

Several factors may come into play in this apparent reverse tolerance. First is the expectation of the user. Once the user has become aware of the effects of the drug, a placebo effect may take place so that the user anticipates certain effects of the drug and therefore feels high when in fact the effects are not present. This placebo effect is seen with many different drugs and soon diminishes if there is not some reinforcement with a substance actually giving the user the desired effect. Therefore, the user of marihuana may anticipate the desired effects, feeling them earlier than when the drug's effects actually occur. This is a learned phenomenon. When the true drug effect occurs, this acts as reinforcement for the anticipated effect.

Second, the effects of marihuana are sometimes very subtle. The experienced user learns how to recognize these subtle effects and therefore may report being high before the inexperienced user reports being high. The inexperienced user will be unable to recognize these subtle effects of the drug.

Third, THC is a lipid-soluble substance taken up by the fat stores in the body and then slowly released over a long period of time, creating a long half-life for THC (approximately 3 days). The half-life of a drug is the time it takes for one-half of a given dose of the drug to be excreted from the body. Since THC has a long half-life, the regular user may still have a relatively high blood level the next time the drug is used. Therefore, less of the drug is required to achieve a dosage necessary to give the user the effects wanted. All these effects may come into play to produce the reverse tolerance described by the regular user of marihuana.

Considering the large number of users of marihuana at the present time, adverse effects are not frequently seen from use of the drug. However, there are two commonly seen adverse effects. The first is an acute paranoia, which occurs most often in the naive user during the first or second use of the drug. This paranoid reaction can last for several hours and then gradually subsides as the effects of the drug begin to wear off. It does not necessarily recur with subsequent use of the drug. The second adverse effect is one combination of hypotension and tachycardia sometimes seen with very potent forms of marihuana. The user becomes flushed, appears shaky, and may also develop nausea and vomiting. This effect may last for 45 minutes to an hour and also gradually subsides as the drug's effects wear off. Cases of allergic reactions to cannabis products have been reported, and the hypotensive episode may be an allergic type of reaction.

Some of the better-known effects of marihuana include its mild sedative action, disruption of recent memory, enhancement of appetite, and distortion of time. In high doses or with very potent marihuana products, hallucinations have been reported. This reaction is infrequently seen with the cannabis products sold normally in the United States. Marihuana has been reported to cause an amotivational syndrome leading an individual to drop out of normal activities, becoming extremely lethargic. This has been brought into question by studies done in Jamaica which have shown that users of marihuana tend to work harder in the fields than nonusers. The question to be answered is whether marihuana causes the amotivational syndrome or whether the individual has previously developed an amotivational behavior pattern and this in turn has led to marihuana use.

Recent studies have shown that marihuana lowers testosterone levels in the male. Upon cessation of use, the testosterone levels return to their preuse levels. In these studies, testosterone levels, even during heavy use, have remained within the normal range.

Marihuana has also been shown to cause alterations in the immune system of the user. Numerous studies have been reported that present conflicting data on the effects of marihuana on the immune system. At this time, it is difficult to determine precisely what the actions are. However, to date no one has determined the clinical significance of these alterations. As other drugs have begun to be studied with regard to their effects on the immune system, we have learned that many of them, including alcohol and aspirin, depress the actions of the immune system.

Bronchitis has been reported in heavy users of hashish, and there is some evidence that the organic byproducts produced when marihuana is burned may be carcinogenic.

Marihuana is available in many different dosage forms in the United States. The most common is the dried plant material that usually consists of the flowering tops, leaves, and stems of the plant. Contrary to common myth, both the male and the female plant contain THC, with the highest concentration being in the flowering tops of the plant. The reason the male plants are removed from the fields is that once the female plant is pollenated, the THC level of the male plant will drop. The THC content of the plant can range from 0 to 13 percent in the most potent forms. The average material sold in the United States has a THC content of between 1 percent and 2 percent.

Hashish is a resinous material gathered from the tops of the flowering plants and has an average THC content of about 5 to 8 percent. Various extracts of the plant have been produced, the most widely used being hash oil, which has been found to have a THC content as high as 60 percent. THC can be extracted from the plant or it can be synthesized. The THC crystals melt at approximately room temperature; they are not soluble in water but are soluble in alcohol. Once extracted or synthesized, THC is rapidly oxydized in the atmosphere to cannabinoid products incapable of producing the desired high.

Sedative-Hypnotic Drugs

The sedative-hypnotic drugs are the most widely prescribed and among the most widely abused drugs in the world. This group of drugs contains many substances we do not normally classify together. They all have similar actions and can frequently be substituted one for the other without the user knowing that the drug of choice is not being taken. One reason these drugs can be grouped together is that all of them show cross-tolerance with one another. This means that when tolerance develops to one drug in this group, any other drug in the group has to be given in a higher dose than normal in order to achieve the desired effect. Another reason is that cross-dependence occurs with all drugs in this group. Thus, if a person is physically dependent on any one drug in this category, any other drug in the category can be substituted to prevent the onset of a withdrawal syndrome. The presence of a cross-dependence and cross-tolerance indicates that these drugs have very similar actions. Drugs in this category include the minor tranquilizers, all the barbiturates, the prescription sleeping pills, sedative-hypnotics, muscle relaxants, and alcohol (table 11-2).

Table 11-3 lists the drugs in order of their dependence liability. Those drugs with the greatest dependence liability also have a short latency period, which means that the effects of the drug come on rather quickly. For the most part, drug abusers prefer drugs that have a short latency period because they do not want to delay gratification for 45 minutes to an hour.

Table 11-3
Dependency Liability of Sedative-Hypnotics

Drugs	*Onset of Action*	*Duration of Action*
Short-Acting Barbiturates (Seconal, Nembutal)	Minutes	4-8 Hours
Sleeping Pills (Doriden, Placidyl, Quaalude) (Alcohol falls in this category)	Minutes	4-8 Hours
Intermediate-Acting Barbiturates (Amytal, Butisol, Chloral Hydrate, Equanil)	1 Hour	6-8 Hours
Benzodiazepines (Valium, Librium, Tranxene, Serax, Dalmane)	Minutes	10-12 Hours
Phenobarbital	1+ Hours	10-12 Hours

Drugs with a short latency period frequently have a short duration of action. The short latency is due to rapid absorption into the blood stream, high lipid solubility, and the rich blood supply to the brain, which gets these drugs into the central nervous system very quickly. The drugs are then redistributed and may be taken up by the fat stores of the body where they are stored but are usually no longer active. As the latency of a drug gets longer, the duration of action usually gets longer and the abuse potential usually decreases, as does the dependency liability. The benzodiazepines, which have a low dependency liability, have a very short latency, and this may account for their high abuse potential. On the other hand, the benzodiazepines usually have a long duration of action, have a long half-life, and can accumulate in the body if taken for long periods of time.

Tolerance, as well as physical dependence, develops to all the drugs in this category. The withdrawal syndrome seen with the sedative-hypnotic drugs is the most severe of any group of drugs and can be life-threatening. Tremulousness, loss of sleep, nausea, and vomiting are frequently seen and can develop into seizures and status epilepticus, which is life-threatening if not treated. Also, as is sometimes seen in alcohol withdrawal, delirium tremens can develop with all drugs in this category. The rapidity with which the withdrawal syndrome develops, as well as the severity of the withdrawal syndrome, depends on the duration of action of the drug. With the shorter-acting drugs, the withdrawal syndrome can be seen within 24 hours after the drug is stopped and reaches its peak of severity within 2 or 3 days. When one is withdrawing from the longer-acting drugs, the appearance of a withdrawal syndrome may not occur until 7 to 10 days after the drug is withdrawn, and the peak is reached approximately 14 days after withdrawal. The severity of the withdrawal from the longest-acting drugs is not as great as with shorter-acting drugs. For this reason, the longer-acting drugs are usually used in the treatment of the withdrawal syndrome.

The primary effect of these drugs is to depress the entire central nervous system. This depression begins with the higher cortical centers; as the dose increases, more and more of the nervous system becomes depressed until, in high doses, the respiratory centers of the central nervous system are depressed leading to death. In low dosages, these drugs can be used for the treatment of anxiety and hypertension; higher doses are used as sleeping medication. Their actions as muscle relaxants stem from their ability to lower the tone of the nervous system, which in turn lowers muscle activity.

It is important to remember that all the drugs in this category are interchangeable, and that users will frequently change one "downer" with another, depending on what is available at any given time, even though they will have specific preferences as to their favorite drug. It is also important to remember that the effect of each of the drugs in this category is usually additive but may be synergistic, as seen in the combined use of alcohol and diazepam. Users are frequently not aware of this and feel that if they mix drugs they will not get into any trouble. Part of the problem stems from the different names used for the different drugs in this class, making people believe they are actually taking drugs that are unrelated.

Unique among the drugs in this category is alcohol. Very few drugs taken by individuals are as toxic to almost every organ in the body. Alcohol has toxic effects on the central and peripheral nervous systems, the liver, the GI tract, the heart, the blood, the bones, the skin, and the reproductive system. Because it is frequently discussed as a separate drug of abuse, its relationship to the other drugs in the sedative-hypnotic group is not widely appreciated.

Stimulants

The basic pharmacology of the stimulants is to produce effects that are just the opposite of the sedative-hypnotic drugs. The sedative-hypnotics depress the central nervous system, whereas the stimulants increase the activity of the central nervous system. The most frequently abused drugs in this category are the amphetamines and cocaine.

Up until the late 1960s, the amphetamines were among the most abundantly produced drugs in the United States. They were believed to be effective in the treatment of numerous disorders. However, with the realization of their high abuse potential they were placed in Schedule II of Controlled Substance Act of 1970, and the federal government curtailed the manufacture of amphetamines by over 90 percent. At the present time, these drugs are primarily used for the treatment of narcolepsy, hyperkinetic children, and obesity.

Amphetamines increase the activity of the central nervous system, allowing the user to remain awake for long periods of time. In low doses they tend to increase concentration. As the dose increases, the user may begin to perform repetitive activities like picking at the skin or trying to disassemble and reassemble objects such as radios or clocks. As the dose increases even further, seizures may develop. Other effects of amphetamines are elevation of blood pressure, tachycardia (rapid heart rate), difficulty urinating, and dilated pupils. When amphetamines are taken in high doses for long periods of time, a toxic psychosis can develop. This psychosis is indistinguishable from a psychosis that might occur naturally. It is normally a paranoid type of psychosis, and the person suffering from this toxic reaction can become violent. The expression "speed kills!" did not refer to the fact that high doses of amphetamines would kill the user, but that those who used high doses of amphetamines may violently strike out at those around them and kill. In order to treat the toxic psychosis, the important step is to remove the user from his or her source of amphetamine.

Amphetamines are most widely used for their control of appetite. In low doses, amphetamines will suppress the appetite center of the brain. However, tolerance develops to this effect over a period of 2 to 3 weeks, and in order to continue to achieve this appetite-suppressant effect, the dose of amphetamine must be increased. Many users of amphetamines have found that after starting their use of the drug for its appetite-suppresent effect, they were soon using it for relief of fatigue, depression, or to get high.

Amphetamines can be taken orally, "snorted," or injected. The most commonly used injectable form is methamphetamine, which, because of its rapid uptake into the brain, has an extremely high abuse potential. For many years it was believed that amphetamines did not cause dependency; therefore, there was not supposed to be a withdrawal syndrome upon cessation of amphetamine use. Recent evidence, however, indicates that this may be untrue and that a specific withdrawal syndrome may exist. Certainly, after prolonged use of amphetamines, the individual may sleep for many hours and have a severe depression for several weeks. In order to relieve the depression, amphetamine abuse may recur and this leads into a cycle of amphetamine abuse known as a "run."

Closely related to amphetamines because of its stimulant properties is cocaine. Cocaine is an alkaloid extracted from the coca plant, which grows in the Andes Mountains of South America. If the coca leaf is chewed, along with a basic substance in the mouth, a mild stimulation and feeling of general well-being develops in the user. However, once the cocaine is extracted from the plant, it is normally taken by insufflation ("snorting") or by IV injection.

The stimulating effects of cocaine are believed to be rather short acting, lasting approximately 20 minutes; however, recent studies indicate that the effects last about 2 hours. The effects of amphetamines can last from 4 to 6 hours.

Cocaine is also a potent local anesthetic that causes a numbness in the mucous membranes of the nose if it is "snorted" or in the areas around where it is injected if there is leakage into the tissues. Another of cocaine's properties is to constrict blood vessels. This particular effect can lead to consequences if cocaine is taken continuously over long periods of time. Individuals who "snort" large quantities of cocaine for long periods of time develop problems in the nasal mucosa because of vasoconstriction that results in death of the mucosal tissues.

Other stimulants with abuse potential include methylphenidate (Ritalin) and diet pills. All these drugs, when taken together can have additive properties with one another. Table 11-4 is a list of the commonly abused stimulants.

Hallucinogenics

The hallucinogenics, also known as psychotomimetics or psychedelics, have gone through waves of popularity. Although it was believed that these substances could cause psychotic reactions, it is presently conceded that the effects of the stimulants and not the hallucinogenics can mimic true psychotic reactions. The effects of the hallucinogenic drugs result in distortions of perception, but these are not similar to a psychosis.

The basic differences between the true psychotic reaction and the effects of the hallucinogenics are these: (1) in the psychotic reaction, the hallucinations are usually auditory, whereas with the hallucinogenic drugs the hallucinations are primarily visual; (2) the individual who is psychotic is not aware that the distortions of perception are not real, whereas the hallucinogenic drug user is frequently aware that the distortions are not real, merely alterations of perception. The primary differences among the hallucinogenic drugs are the amount of drug necessary to cause an effect and the duration of action of the drugs. The most familiar and widely studied of these drugs is lysergic acid diethylamide (LSD). LSD is one of the most potent drugs known, and approximately one microgram per kilogram of body weight is needed to cause the drug effect. The actions of LSD will last for approximately 12 hours, with the effects coming on in approximately 1 to 2 hours and peaking at 4 to 6 hours after the drug is taken.

The hallucinogenics are very closely related to the stimulant drugs. Figure 11-1 shows the similarity in the structure of amphetamine and mescaline. The actions of the hallucinogenics, other than the hallucinations, are similar to the

Table 11-4
Stimulants

Stimulants
Amphetamine (Benzedrine)
Methamphetamine (Methedrine)
Cocaine
Dextroamphetamine (Dexedrine)
Phenmetrazine (Preludin)
Phendimetrazine (Plegine)

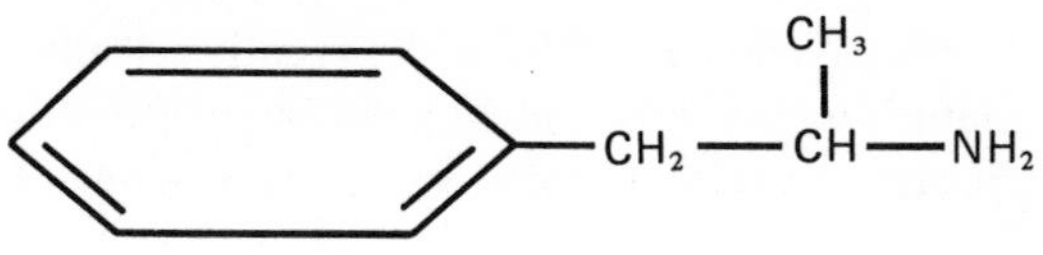

CH_3

$-CH_2-CH-NH_2$

Amphetamine

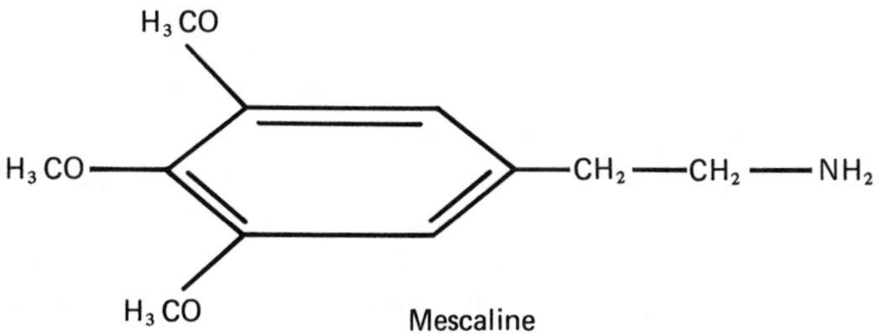

H_3CO

H_3CO- $-CH_2-CH_2-NH_2$

H_3CO Mescaline

Figure 11-1. Molecular Structure of Amphetamines and Mescaline.

stimulants: loss of appetite, increased blood pressure and heart rate, decreased fatigue, and seizures in high doses.

There has been much discussion in recent years about the effects of hallucinogenic drugs on the chromosomes. The evaluation of this data indicates that there is no hard evidence at this time indicating that any pure hallucinogenic drug causes chromosomal damage, nor is there any indication that these drugs cause permanent psychosis.

In recent years, the abuse of hallucinogenic drugs has decreased markedly, and very few toxic reactions are seen. Table 11-5 is a listing of the most commonly used hallucinogenic substances.

Table 11-5
Hallucinogenics

Lysergic acid diethylamide (LSD)
Mescaline
Methylenedioxyamphetamine (MDA)
2,5=Dimethoxy=4=methylamphetamine (DOM, STP)
Trimethoxyamphetamine (TMA)
N,N=dimethyltryptamine (DMT)
N,N=dimethyltryptamine (DMT)
N,N=diethyltryptamine
Cannabis and its products

Phencyclidine (PCP) is frequently classified as an hallucinogenic drug, although its properties are quite different from those of other hallucinogens. The properties of phencyclidine are discussed in chapter 13.

Solvents

Volatile solvents are the least expensive and most readily available of all the substances of abuse. Table 11-6 is a listing of some of the more common substances abused in this category; it can be seen that they are frequently substances that are readily available around the home, ranging from the propellants in aerosal sprays to gasoline. These substances for the most part are closely related to the general anesthetics such as ether and are usually general depressants of the central nervous system. Although there are numerous reports in the literature of toxic effects from abuse of these substances, most of the studies reported deal with animals that have been put in chambers where fairly high concentration of these substances are constantly in the atmosphere. This is certainly not the way these drugs are abused. The street user will take a high dose for a short period of time and then be drug free for a long period of time, allowing the substance to clear from the system. These substances are usually inhaled in a gaseous form, the onset of action occurs very quickly, and the drug is excreted very quickly, primarily through the lungs.

The most common toxic reactions seen in abusers are anoxia or the lack of oxygen that occurs as the drug is inhaled out of a sealed container. A common cause of death from abuse of these substances is anoxia.

Like the general anesthetics, these drugs also have an effect on the heart, which can lead to abnormal rhythms and cessation of an effective heartbeat. This has also been found to be a cause of death in abusers. The chronic toxic effects of these drugs are rarely seen in the adolescent drug user but have been seen in industrial workers who are around these substances in high concentrations for long periods of time. Some of the toxicities seen in these instances are liver damage and peripheral nerve damage. A more detailed discussion of the solvents is given in chapter 12.

Table 11-6
Solvents

Gasoline
Halogeneted hydrocarbons (Freon)
Nitrous Oxide
Toluene
Carbontetrachloride
Airplane glue

Opiates

In discussions of drug abuse, opiates tend to be the drugs that cause the greatest emotional response. They are among the oldest drugs known to humanity and have probably been abused since long before recorded history. Most of the opiates occurring naturally are extracted from the opium poppy, *Papaver somniferum.* Among its naturally occurring alkaloids are morphine and codeine. The semisynthetic opioids can be created by making additions to the naturally occurring opiates, and heroin is an example of this. Figure 11-2 shows the relationship of the structure of heroin to the structure of morphine.

Attempts to produce a drug that has the analgesic properties of opiates but lacks the dependency-producing potential have been going on for many years. From this research, numerous synthetic opioids have been developed. Table 11-7 is a list of the naturally occurring, semisynthetic, and synthetic opioids that are commonly abused.

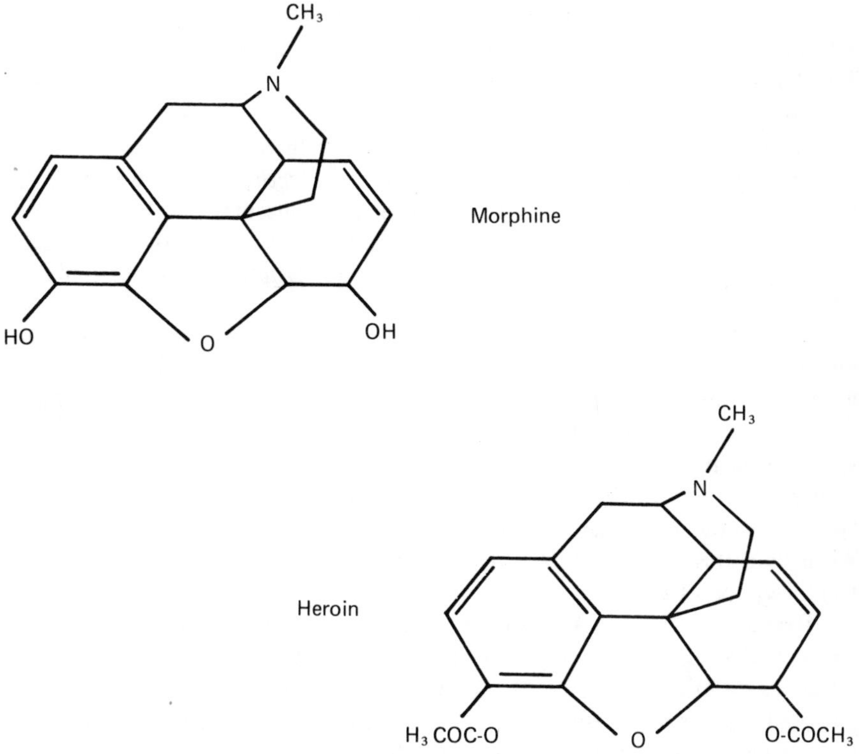

Figure 11-2. Molecular Structure of Morphine and Heroin.

Table 11-7
Opiates

Opium
Heroin
Morphine
Hydromorphone (Dilaudid)
Oxymorphone (Numorphan)
Codeine
Pentazocine (Talwin)
Methadone (Dolophine)
Propoxyphene (Darvon)
Meperidine (Demerol)

Opiates are the most potent analgesics known. Their action occurs in the central nervous system, and although they do not remove the sensation of pain like a local anesthetic, the individual taking the drug no longer has a reaction to the pain. Opiates also have sedative properties and produce a marked euphoria.

All the opiates have a high dependence liability and a rapid development of tolerance. Tolerance develops most rapidly to the euphoric action of the drug, and since this is one of the most desirable of its traits to the user, the dose taken escalates rapidly.

Because the effects of the drug when taken orally are either erratic or slow in onset, most opiate abusers take the drug by injection. This develops high levels in the blood stream rapidly and allows high concentrations to get to the central nervous system quickly, creating a rapid reaction or "rush." In high doses, opiates can cause seizures and, in overdoses, cessation of respiration and death.

Recently, much work is being done with derivatives of the opiate drugs that tend to block their actions. These drugs are called *narcotic antagonists.* The most widely used of these at this time are naloxone (Narcan) and naltrexone. When taken, these drugs can either reverse the effects of an opiate already in the system, thus making them useful for the treatment of overdoses, or precipitate withdrawal, to test whether an individual is indeed dependent on an opiate. Given chronically, the narcotic antagonists can block the effects of the opiate. When used this way, an individual who is taking a narcotic antagonist will not feel the effects of an opiate when it is taken.

Research to develop an opiate that will not produce dependency but will retain the analgesic properties has resulted in the discovery of the opiate receptor. With the discovery of the receptor, investigators then began to look for a naturally occurring substance which would bind this receptor. This has led to the discovery of the endorphins and enkephalins, which are naturally occurring opiate-like substances. Further research on these substances may go a long way to help us understand the nature of opiate addiction and develop drugs that will have beneficial properties without the addictive properties of the presently used opiates.

All the opiate drugs show cross-tolerance and cross-dependence with one another and can be used interchangeably. When taken together, their effects are additive.

References

Abelson, H.I., and Fishburne, P. 1976. *Nonmedical Use of Psychoactive Substances.* Nationwide Study Among Youth and Adults, Response Analysis Corp., Princeton, New Jersey.

Bellets, S., Canuth, J., Einolf, N., Ward, R., and Fenselan, C. 1973. Rapid identification of acute drug intoxications. *J. Hopkins Med. Journal* 133:148-155.

Brown, J.K., and Malone, M.H. 1975. *Pacific Information Service on Street Drugs* 4:2-6.

Hayes, S.L., Pablo, G., Radomski, T., and Palmer, R.F. 1977. Ethanol and oral diazepam absorption. *N. Engl. J. Med.* 296:186-189.

Inaba, D., Way, E.L., Blum, K., and Schnoll, S. 1978. Pharmacological and toxicological perspectives of commonly abused drugs. *NDAC, Medical Monograph Series* 1:5.

Jaffee, J. 1975. Drug addiction and drug abuse. In L.S. Goodman and A. Gilman (eds.), *The Pharmacological Basis of Therapeutics.* New York: MacMillan.

Los Angeles County–University of Southern California Street Drug Identification Program. Summary Report. 1971-1977.

Marijuana and Health. 1976. Sixth Annual Report to the U.S. Congress from the Secretary of Health, Education and Welfare.

Siegel, R.K. 1978. Street drugs 1977: Changing patterns of recreational use. *Drug Abuse and Alcoholism Review* 1:1-13.

Weisman, M., Lerner, N., Vogel, W.H., Banford, T., and Schnoll, S. 1973. Quality of street heroin. *N. Engl. J. Med.* 289:698-699.

Part IV
Special Problems

12 Marihuana: A Review of the Issues Regarding Decriminalization and Legalization

Robert L. DuPont

The marihuana plant—a weed actually—has a fascinating history. It has been used as fiber, food, and medicine. A botanist over 400 years ago noted that it will "kill every kind of vermin" and that it remedies horses with colic and gouty swellings. Hemp porridge was eaten in the monasteries in the Middle Ages, and in Russia, where cultivation has been traced to the seventh century B.C., marihuana seeds were thrown on hot stones and the vapors inhaled to alleviate toothaches. While these facts are interesting and the medical application of this plant is being explored actively in light of today's needs, it is also a fact that marihuana is used in this country as an intoxicant, not as fiber, food, or medicine. Thirty-six million Americans have used marihuana, and over 15 million are current users. The theme of this chapter is that decriminalization of marihuana possession makes sense on economic and humanitarian grounds. The nation is in midstride moving toward decriminalization of marihuana possession. What should the next step be?

Background

In 1972, when the National Commission on Marihuana and Drug Abuse recommended decriminalization, the public was startled by the proposals for reform. In the past few years, we have gone a long way toward clearing away the accumulated debris of misinformation that confused and distorted public attitudes about marihuana for 40 years. Thus 8 states have enacted "civil fine" penalties for possession of small amounts of marihuana. It appears that the changes in the rates of marihuana consumption in these 8 states have not differed from the pattern in the other 42 states. On the other hand, this new approach has minimized the injustices of the previous use of criminal sanctions and has conserved valuable criminal justice resources in a way that has received widespread public support.

While it is true that the decriminalization issue is now primarily an issue for

---

The contents of this chapter are based largely on a paper presented by Dr. DuPont on February 4, 1977, while he was serving as the Director of the National Institute on Drug Abuse.

state action, and while it is important for us to learn from and even encourage diversity in the states' approaches to the marihuana-possession offense, nevertheless some attention should be given to the need to enact decriminalization of marihuana possession at the federal level. There are sound reasons for decriminalization. First, it is *not* a health issue. Instead, the relevant question is the wisdom of using the criminal sanction as a means of discouraging consumption when considerably less costly avenues of discouragement are available. Second, decriminalization of the user is designed primarily to correct the mistakes of the past–to adjust our social policy to contemporary knowledge about the effects of the drug and to current social realities regarding its use. Third, decriminalization is not an irreversible reform. If research should uncover some unforeseen dread effect of use–and if the removal of criminal sanctions results in significant increases in consumption and therefore in the public health risk–there will be time enough to readjust our laws.

The basic principle is clear: the role of the legal system should be readjusted so that those who have chosen to use marihuana, despite efforts to discourage it and despite the efforts of law enforcement officials to restrict availability, are not unnecessarily punished for this choice. There are, of course, many subsidiary questions regarding the drafting of a decriminalization scheme. Many of these questions are technical. Certain issues, however, should be addressed. The first is the matter of the felonization of home cultivation.

Thus far the trend has been to decriminalize possession of small amounts (usually 1 ounce) and sometimes "casual" accommodation transfers between users. No state had decriminalized cultivation in the home for personal use–leaving the anomalous situation that this consumption-related behavior is, in most states, still a felony. Personal cultivation in the home can be considered the functional equivalent of private use. Home-grown marihuana will generally be less potent than much imported supply, and those who draw on their own supply will no longer be in constant contact with dealers who may offer other illicit items for sale. It is also unlikely that decriminalization of personal cultivation of small amounts will result in substantially increased use above and beyond any increases attributable to decriminalization of possession alone. For these reasons, it makes sense to reduce the penalty for cultivation of small amounts in the home to a civil fine or, at most, a misdeameanor punishable only by fine. These arguments are rooted in two principles: (1) marihuana use should be discouraged, and (2) the techniques used to discourage its use should themselves do as little harm as possible. The criminal law should therefore be used sparingly, and individual choice should be maximized. It does not make sense in the light of these principles that the individual who grows a few marihuana plants in his or her backyard should be penalized as a major trafficker by using felony penalties. On the other hand, lines must be drawn, and at the margins, these lines must be arbitrary. Large-scale cultivation–like large-scale trafficking in marihuana–is a serious crime and merits severe criminal sanctions.

A civil fine makes the point that home cultivation is prohibited behavior. The second such issue is the crucial distinction between public and private use. Using marihuana in public—or in places of public accommodation—is no more implicit in the concept of personal liberty than a similar use of alcohol or tobacco. A meaningful discouragement policy would be undermined if such behavior were to go unsanctioned. What is more important, social and legal sanctions for driving under the influence of any psychoactive substance, including marihuana and alcohol, are imperative.

Some consideration should also be given to the notion that marihuana should be rescheduled under federal law. As far as its scheduling for regulatory purposes is concerned, the key question is whether marihuana has an accepted medical use in the United States. If not, the basic structure of the Controlled Substances Act appropriately requires that its availability be limited only to research needs and therefore that it be classified in Schedule I together with other drugs that have no accepted medical use in the United States. Thus the real question here is whether marihuana should be available for the treatment of glaucoma, asthma, and the nausea and vomiting associated with anticancer chemotherapy and other illnesses. The National Institute on Drug Abuse is now funding investigations that will settle this question on scientific grounds over the next several years.

A primary concern about the move toward legalization of marihuana is based on the current experience with legalizing other psychotropic substances. Alcohol is legitimately available in the United States, its distribution being regulated in varying ways in each of the 50 states, and this legitimacy is invoked by those who wish to legitimate the use of marihuana. Recent data indicate that 32 percent of American teenagers and 59 percent of adults consider themselves to be current alcohol users. In addition, 4 percent of those aged 18 to 25 and 8 percent of Americans over the age of 26 drink alcohol *every day*. The National Institute on Alcohol Abuse and Alcoholism estimates that there are over 9 million alcohol-abusing men and women in the country today. Each year we count more than 25,000 alcohol-related traffic fatalities, 15,000 alcohol-related homicides and suicides, 20,000 deaths from alcohol-related disease, and 20,000 fatalities due to alcohol-related accidents on the job and in the home. The police record 2 million arrests each year for public drunkenness, and one out of every ten members of the nation's workforce is a serious alcohol abuser. Alcohol abuse not only brings suffering to individuals and families and wastes vast human potential, but it also exerts a heavy financial drain on the country's health and welfare resources, a drain recently estimated at some $25 billion a year.

Consider also the fact that 53 million Americans smoke tobacco, and while the number of teenage smokers is no longer increasing at the rate it was several years ago, there are still some 6 million teenage smokers. The American Cancer Society estimates the cost of tobacco smoking is now $17 billion each year. Cigarette smoking is responsible for nearly 70,000 cancer deaths a year, practically one in every five deaths from cancer in America. Coronary artery disease, emphysema, bronchitis, and many other diseases are strongly related to the use of tobacco. Women who smoke during pregnancy have a higher than average rate of newborn deaths and stillbirths. Thus the nation's experience with the consumption of psychoactive substances which are now legitimately available for "nonmedical" uses should raise a red flag in assessing the consequences of a legalized regulatory approach to the availability of marihuana.

Another argument for legalization—the "mafia fuel" argument—needs to be tempered by our recent experience with legalized gambling. Such arguments have been presented in that area as well as in the areas of prostitution and drug use. There is no evidence to show that legal gambling has eliminated or even reduced illegal gambling. In fact, it appears that a whole new group of gamblers use the legal gambling system. Thus, while legal gambling brings in government revenue, it has not eliminated criminal revenue from illegal gambling. Yet another problem with decriminalization is that the user is in a legal limbo which forces him into regular contact with criminals. Like the other arguments for legalized marihuana, it has merit, it does not produce costs that outweigh the benefits of discouragement of a decriminalized prohibition policy.

Unlike decriminalization, forging a legalized regulatory approach to marihuana is *not* a question amenable to easy resolution. Indeed, we have hardly begun to ask the right questions, much less formulate a consensus about the right answers. Unlike decriminalization, this *is* a public health issue. There should be some concern about the adverse social consequences of the rise in marihuana consumption that would surely result if availability were substantially increased. Mere speculation about a public health cost, such as has been documented for alcohol and tobacco, does not make the case for prohibition and against a legalized regulatory approach to marihuana. What makes the marihuana issue difficult is that the individual marihuana user claims that he benefits by using the intoxicant and wishes to be permitted to make his own choice. We may not be able to resolve the underlying dilemma, but we can call attention to the relevance of the aggregate public health concerns, the value on the *other* side of the equation that must be weighed against the society's general preference for individual choice.

One unanswered and perhaps unanswerable question that needs consideration is whether the population of daily users would be in addition to or substituted for the population of daily alcohol and tobacco users. It has been concluded, based on current patterns of drug use, that many of the regular cigarette smokers and regular alcohol drinkers would also become regular marihuana users. In addition, a substantial number of people who are neither daily alcohol drinkers nor daily cigarette smokers would become daily marihuana users. In the youth population, which now reports high rates of marihuana use, it is already clear that there has been no reduction in the number of regular smokers or regular drinkers in the last few years. On the basis of our current knowledge, it is clear that a rise in the daily use of marihuana would almost certainly not reduce our problems with alcohol and tobacco.

We have learned much about marihuana in recent years. It should, however, be emphasized that there is still much we do not know about the effects of chronic marihuana use—especially daily use—in American populations. All the unanswered questions about the possible adverse effects of marihuana on the body's immune response, basic cell metabolism, and other areas of functioning become vital here. So too do the continuing concerns about the impact of the use of the drug on reproductive functions. In addition, there are several other concerns. First, the data now indicate that some users are showing a preference for more potent preparations. It can be presumed that under any regulatory scheme, varying degrees of potency would be available; even if this is not true, we can assume that an illegal market in hashish or more potent preparations of marihuana will develop to supplement any legitimate available drug of low potency. It could be speculated that the risks to individual health and functioning will increase directly with the potency of the substance consumed.

A second concern relates to the types of people who become users. From a public health standpoint, we may be fortunate that marihuana users are now concentrated among young adults, a generally healthy subgroup of the population. The current data continually show that there is a precipitous drop in the rate of marihuana use in the over-30 generation, even among those who had tried this drug in their younger years. Undoubtedly, use would be distributed more evenly throughout the population under a legalized regulatory supply system, and the user population would include more individuals with already impaired physical or psychological functioning—for whom use, and particularly regular use, may have considerably different implications than does occasional use by those in fairly good health. The evidence on cardiac patients cited in the literature for several years now is but one example. Many patients with inadequate coronary arteries experience chest pains when they use marijuana. Similarly, the implications for use of marihuana by people having greater problems with coping or less skills for doing so may be quite different from those for the more competent, advantaged students who predominate in current-using populations.

Any legalized regulatory model also has the inevitable effect of increasing availability and consumption among young populations. Although the rate of teenage consumption even under the current prohibitory model is already high (12 percent of the 12 to 17 age group indicated current use of marihuana in the last national survey conducted by NIDA), this rate of use would be increased if the drug were legitimately available to their elders. Despite prohibitions against distribution of alcohol to teenagers, some 32 percent of the teenage population uses alcohol regularly. Similarly, some 23 percent of the teenage population are current smokers, and 4 percent smoke a pack or more of cigarettes per day despite prohibitions against distribution to minors. We can assume that under a regulatory approach, the proportion of teenagers who use marihuana at all would be in the range of 20 to 30 percent, and the proportion who use the drug every day would constitute at least 20 percent of the regular users. In the coming year, the federal government will be continuing its research into the health effects of marihuana use, concentrating specifically on those areas of greatest concern: endocrine functioning, the immune mechanism, bronchitis and possible cancer of the lung, and problems of daily use, particularly among the very young. Perhaps in the years ahead it will become clear that prohibition of marihuana is no longer a realistic alternative. Certainly that was the case for alcohol in 1933. But it is hoped that if prohibition proves infeasible or incompatible with important social values, we will have learned enough in the interim about the consequences of marihuana use and the efficacy of various noncriminal approaches to avoid the heavy social price exacted by alcohol and tobacco consumption in 1977.

13 Inhalants and Solvents

Sidney Cohen

Background, History, and Overview

The use of the respiratory tract and the lungs to absorb drugs and other substances must go back to primitive man and the discovery of fire. Aromatic, pungent, and intoxicating smokes, incenses, vapors, gases, and fumes have been inhaled since antiquity for hedonistic or therapeutic purposes or as rituals and *rites-de-passage* during religious or secular ceremonial activities. Hallucinogenic snuffs, opium, tobacco, cannabis, carbon dioxide, nitrous oxide, ether, and alcohol are only a partial list of the agents that have been or are being inhaled into the respiratory tract for their mind-altering qualities.

The advantage of the pulmonary transfer of consciousness-changing substances as opposed to the gastrointestinal route is that the material is delivered directly to the brain from the lungs through the left side of the heart. The pyschological effects appear more rapidly and are stronger, since the liver with its detoxifying enzymes is bypassed.

It was not predictable, however, that during the middle of the twentieth century, the intentional inhalation of an array of industrial solvents would become popular. These volatile solvents are ordinarily considered to be poisonous, and strenuous efforts are made to protect workers who must come into contact with them. Nevertheless, the deliberate sniffing of the glue from model airplanes sets and gasoline apparently began during the late 1940s in this country and has spread to a vast array of solvents and aerosols, and the practice has extended to every continent.

The industrial solvents have essentially no medical usefulness. They appear to act as central nervous system (CNS) depressants and, more specifically, as anesthetics when sniffed or huffed.[1] As with the more conventional anesthetics, a short initial period of psychic stimulation may precede the subsequent CNS depression of mental functioning. Depending on the dosage, this may vary from mild confusion, impaired judgment, and psychomotor clumsiness to stupor, coma, or death.

We do not know enough about the effects, long and short term, of these industrial solvents. With the introduction of new products and altered formulations of older, complex products (such as lacquer), with increasing polydrug abuse of different combinations and amounts of various psychochemicals, the problems of solvent inhalation become more complex and difficult to investigate and treat. The solvents of abuse differ from other substances of abuse (that is, the opiates, marihuana, barbiturates) in that they are not prepared or manufactured specifically for human consumption. They are almost entirely commercial products, some for use in the home and some for industrial use. The intoxicating substance may be only one component of the product, as with the aerosols, which contain intoxicating solvents and propellants in addition to the actual ingredients they deliver.

The Products Involved

Table 13-1 provides a classification of the major abused solvents. It is based on their chemical structure. Some general indications of their toxicity are included. The relative toxicity of these substances is by no means completely understood. Furthermore, two or more solvents that are of lesser toxicologic potential when inhaled separately can produce unexpected tissue damage when taken together.

The number and range of commercial products available are extensive, and only a partial listing is possible here. There are also dozens of aerosols that contain intoxicating solvents and propellants in addition to the ingredients they deliver. The ubiquitousness of the aerosol aggravates the situation further and has made solvent inhalation easier, more popular, and more dangerous.

To indicate the variety of inhalants, a sampling would include the liquid cements and plastic glues; inflammable substances like gasoline or lighter fluid; dry cleaning fluids and spot removers; paint and lacquer thinners and removers, including fingernail polish removers, wax strippers, refrigerants, and degreasers; and liquid shoeshine preparations. To illustrate the complexity of the problem, Prockop (1975) analyzed a marketed lacquer thinner and could identify eleven solvents. In addition, there were small amounts of impurities present that could not be identified.

At present the favorite solvents of abuse appear to be the aerosolized clear lacquers and the gold and bronze spray paints. Other sprays such as cooking oils, glass chillers, and furniture polishes are reported to be actively used. "Texas Shoeshine" is popular in the Southwest. Gasoline is fairly widely used, especially in rural areas and in urban ghettos. Transmission and brake fluids have been inhaled from time to time.

Technique of Usage

Several methods of inhaling solvents have been observed and described. Most commonly, the solvent is poured or sprayed onto a cloth or tissue and then placed in the mouth or around the nose and breathed in. Sometimes a plastic or paper bag is used to contain the solvent. Balloons have been used to receive the spray from an aerosol can. Warming the solvent, especially from aerosols, is occasionally practiced so that it will not chill the respiratory tract. However,

Table 13-1
A Classification of Abused Solvents

Volatile Solvent	*Physical Effects*
1. Aromatic hydrocarbons:	
Benzene	Bone marrow, liver, heart, adrenal and kidney impairment
Xylene	Bone marrow impairment
Toluene	Bone marrow, liver, kidney and CNS impairment
2. Aliphatic hydrocarbons:	
Hexane	Polyneuropathy
Naptha	Low toxicity
Petroleum distillates	Low toxicity
3. Halogenated hydrocarbons:	
Trichloroethylene	Cardiac arrhythmia, kidney and liver impairment
1,1,1=trichloroethane (methylchloroform)	CNS, lung, kidney, cardiac, and pancreas impairment
Carbon tetrachloride	Lung, liver, kidney and CNS impairment
Ethylene dichloride	Spleen, CNS, liver, and kidney impairment
Methylene chloride	CNS, liver, and kidney impairment
4. Freons:	
Trichlorofluoromethane (FC11)	Cardiac arrhythmia
Dichloroflouromethane (FC114)	Cardiac arrhythmia
Cryoflurane	Cardiac arrhythmia
Dichlorotetraflouromethane (FC12)	Cardiac arrhythmia
5. Ketones:	
Acetone	Low toxicity
Cyclohexanone	
Methylethylketone	Peripheral neuropathy, pulmonary hypertension
Methylisobutylketone	Peripheral neuropathy
Methylbutylketone	Peripheral neuropathy
Methylamylketone	Peripheral neuropathy
6. Esters:	
Ethyl acetate	Liver and kidney impairment
Amyl acetate	Low toxicity
Butyl acetate	Low toxicity
7. Alcohols:	
Methyl alcohol	Optic atrophy
Isopropyl alcohol	Low toxicity
8. Glycols:	
Methyl cellulose acetate	Liver and kidney impairment
Ethylene glycol	Liver, kidney, lung, and CNS impairment
9. Gasoline, leaded	Lung, bone marrow, liver, CNS, and peripheral nerve impairment

youngsters have been known to spray aerosols directly into the mouth. This could be particularly hazardous, leading to laryngospasm and bronchospasm. Another dangerous practice is the placing of a garment plastic bag over the head or entire body in order to increase the concentration of the solvent. Deaths due to asphyxiation have been reported from this method and also from inhaling in a closed space such as a sealed closet.

To point out how reckless some juvenile practices can be, isolated cases are known of juveniles inhaling the exhaust of automobile fumes. The practice is readily fatal if protracted, still it does not deter the young in mind from attempting this precarious activity.

Extent of the Problem

Less is known about the prevalence of solvent abuse than about other forms of substance abuse. Some surveys do not inquire about these materials (San Mateo Substance Abuse Survey 1975). In school surveys the prevalence is underreported because heavy inhalant users tend to be absent or drop out of school and are not captured in most of these surveys (tables 13-2 and 13-3). If data from juvenile halls are collected, the bias may be in the opposite direction, in that many youngsters under detention are there because of their dysfunctional behavior while using inhalants, or although they are under detention for other offenses, they often have been or are solvent users.

Until recently, the typical solvent abuser was reported to be between 10 and 17 years of age, predominantly male, with the Mexican-American or American Indian cultures overrepresented. These demographic characteristics are undergoing change at present. More people between 18 and 29 are being counted. Females are involved more frequently, and involvement of white, middle-class students seems to be increasing. Goldstein (1976) has reported on some New Mexico Indian tribes where two-thirds of the inhalant users were female. This unusual distribution apparently occurred because the young males had more ready access to alcohol and public drinking among women was taboo. In his sample, the gold spray paints were used almost exclusively.

Elinson (1975) has presented data that reflect some of the unusual aspects of the problem. Some 5.3 percent of seventh graders but only 1.3 percent of twelfth graders had used solvents during the 2 months preceding the survey. All drugs except inhalants showed an increase in incidence with increasing years in school. They also noted that of those who attended school regularly, 2 percent had used solvents in the past 2 months, while among absentees the figure was 5 percent. Mackie (1974) found that in grades 1 through 6, inhalants were the most frequently reported drug of abuse.

The New Hampshire Governor's Commission on Drug Abuse (1972) collected information comparing 10,258 urban and rural high school students. The

Table 13-2
Representative Surveys of Solvent Abuse

Population	*Number*	*Special Groups*	*Ever Used*	*Used Past Week*	*Occasional and Frequent Users*
1. Junior and senior high school students in West Virginia counties (Beal 1975)	1,333		8.0	1.0	
2. Grades 7 to 12 students in a Michigan school district (Harrison 1974)	7,420	Males Females	19.9 15.2		9.4 6.3
3. Grades 7 to 12 students in Houston, 1974 (Hays 1974) (see table 13-3)	5,755		11.4	2.7	
4. Grade 10 Maryland students (Maryland Dept. of Health 1973)	22,061		3.6	1.1	
5. Grades 4 to 6 in a suburban school in the San Francisco area (Lerner and Linder 1975)	194		15.7		10.6
6. Massachusetts high school students (Geleneau et al. 1973)	14,127		6.2		3.1
7. Grades 9 to 12 students in Gary, Indiana, (Hoock 1972)	6,572	Males Females	9.1 4.5		0.7 0.3
8. Grades 10 to 12 students in Monroe County, N.Y., 1972 (Yancy et al, 1972)	7,288		7.2	3.3	
9. National survey, (Abelson and Fishburne 1976)	986 882 1,708	12-17 18-25 26+	8.1 9.0 1.9		
10. Mexican-American children (Padilla et al. 1970)		25.0	13.1		
11. Junior and senior Indian high school students (Goldstein 1976)	1,844		17.2	13.9	

rural students exposed themselves to solvents approximately as much as the urbanites. Table 13-4 is based on that report.

The DAWN IV Data

The Drug Abuse Warning Network (Farley et al. 1977) data from May 1975 to April 1976 has been analyzed by extracting the youth subgroup (12 to 17 years of

Table 13-3
Solvent Use by Seventh through Twelfth Graders in Houston ($n = 5{,}755$)

Grade	*Sex*	*Ever Used*	*Past 6 Months*	*Past Week*
7	M	9.0	3.8	2.4
7	F	7.2	3.6	1.4
8	M	13.4	6.1	4.5
8	F	7.9	4.8	1.7
9	M	17.1	11.2	5.3
9	F	11.0	6.2	3.2
10	M	16.6	9.3	3.8
10	F	9.7	5.0	2.2
11	M	16.9	5.4	2.4
11	F	6.9	2.7	1.6
12	M	14.6	5.2	2.2
12	F	8.4	1.8	0.9
Overall		11.4	5.5	2.7

Source: Hays 1974.

age). A total of 31,049 "mentions" of abused substances were obtained from emergency rooms, crisis centers, and medical examiners' offices from 24 SMSAs around the country. Of these, 844 were for various solvents, or 2.7 percent of the total mentions.

The most frequently mentioned volatile substances in the DAWN data were the glues, with 300 or 36 percent of all solvent mentions. Glues ranked fourteenth in crisis center mentions, eighteenth in emergency rooms, and were unranked in medical examiner reports. The glues were the nineteenth most frequently mentioned substance overall. Interestingly, of the entire DAWN IV glue mentions, 61 percent were in the youth group. This was the highest for any abused drug, the second being marihuana, with 42 percent in the youth age range.

Transmission fluid was the second most frequently reported solvent, with 248 mentions or 29 percent of all solvent mentions. Other volatile substances were mentioned a total of 296 times, usually as solvents, petroleum, aerosols, and propellants. Those mentioned less than fifty times were paint, paint thinner, Pam, and "gas." A large number were named less than five times, including trichloroethylene, turpentine, hair spray, kerosene, formaldehyde, chloroform, furniture polish, nail polish remover, cologne, aerosol, wax remover, ether, brake fluid, benzine, propane, floor wax, and acrylics.

With specific reference to the youth sample (ages 12 to 17) in the DAWN data system, solvent mentions constituted 1.5 percent of all youth mentions but only 0.11 percent of all adult mentions. Inhalants, with 7.3 percent, are second only to propoxyphene (10.4 percent) in mentions by medical examiners in the 12 to 17 age group. Even more interesting is the comparison between medical

Table 13-4
Exposure of Urban and Rural Students to Solvents
Percentage

	1 to 2 Times Daily	*1 to 2 Times Weekly*	*1 to 2 Times Monthly*	*1 to 2 Times Yearly*	*Ever Used*
Urban	0.5	0.9	1.1	1.2	5.8
Rural	0.7	1.3	1.0	1.5	4.9

examiner reports for inhalants and the total number of inhalant mentions. The proportion of fatal inhalant incidents to the total number of mentions is 3.3 percent, making it the highest-risk category of all drugs.

The National Youth Polydrug Study (NYPS)

The NYPS (1977) collected data on 2,750 clients between the ages of 12 and 19 at 97 drug-abuse treatment programs during 1976-1977. The following statements summarize the inhalant-abuse information derived from the interviews.

1. Glue was the most common inhalant used (12 percent), with 6.6 percent reporting regular use.
2. Of all respondents, 13 percent (347) reported current use, with 3 percent (88) reporting daily use.
3. For inhalants, the age of first continuing use was 13.1 years (S.D. = 2.2). Of all fifteen drugs or drug groups inquired into, inhalants were used at an earlier age than all others. Marihuana was second (13.6), and alcohol third (13.8).
4. A higher percentage of males than females were involved in current use of inhalants (15.3 percent versus 9.6 percent). Males also reported current daily use of inhalants more often than females (13 percent versus 8 percent).
5. Hispanics were found to currently use inhalants more frequently than any other race (p = .01). Blacks were more involved than whites in inhalant abuse. Hispanics, who accounted for 10.1 percent of the sample, account for 15 percent of the regular inhalant users.
6. Inhalants were the only one of the fifteen types of substances for which there was found a greater number of daily users within the outpatient group than the average for the total sample.

Almost every country that has looked for the problem has found it. At a conference on inhalants sponsored by the Mexican authorities in 1976 reports ranged from an epidemic of gasoline sniffing among the young people of an isolated Indian village in Manitoba, Canada (Boeckx and Coodin 1976) to a number of reports from rural and urban communities in the United States and Mexico. Representatives from Argentina, Ecuador, and Japan spoke of the situation in their lands. In fact, this listing does not even begin to exhaust the extent of solvent abuse in other countries.

Inhalants have an importance beyond the numbers involved and the dangers to which developing individuals are exposed. They are often the first socially unacceptable and harmful drugs to be consumed (Glenn and Richards 1974). As such, they can represent an entry into a career of illicit drug use. In some studies, inhalants have been found to be the most frequently used drugs by minors if alcohol and tobacco are excluded.

Causative Factors

Before the antecedent causes of chronic inhalant misuse are examined, the three degrees of abuse should be described (Cohen 1973). The largest number of those who try solvents are the experimenters. These are the young people who sample some solvent once or a very few times and then discontinue the practice. Either the experience was unpleasant, or they found it enjoyable but insufficiently reinforcing to persist in the practice. Some experimenters have sniffed just to be able to say to their peers that they had done so. When this group is examined psychologically, they show no particular differences from a matched group of nonusers.

A second type of inhalant abusers are the occasional or social users. These are the people who use infrequently, perhaps once a month, when the situation is conducive, but do not make a career of the practice. These individuals either eventually stop employing solvents and go on to become social or habitual users or other intoxicants or they evolve into frequent, heavy users of inhalants.

The third type are the "heads," the people who use daily, some of them spending a good part of their waking day inebriated by huffing some volatile substance. They can be said to be suffering from solventism analagous to alcoholism in the degree of dependence and disability sustained. These are the ones at greatest risk of sustaining temporary or permanent damage to various organs. On psychological testing they will score more poorly than a comparable nonusing group. Apparently, the reason why this group shows more psychopathology is that those in psychic distress obtain the most relief from the intoxicated state and the results of prolonged, intense sniffing appear to be CNS impairment. The following discussion of causative factors refers to this third group.

In reviewing the literature on chronic abuse of volatile materials, there is general agreement that the causes are found to relate to a disorganized existence.

Whatever disagreement exists lies in the sources of that disorganization. Certain observers regard the primary disturbance as personality-based, indicating that the solvent "heads" include large numbers of sociopaths, borderline or overt schizophrenics, or individuals who are overwhelmed with anxiety, depression, or both. They assert that the inhalants are employed in a desperate effort at self-treatment, to relieve distressing emotional, interpersonal, and intrapsychic disturbances.

Other authors place heaviest emphasis on the massive familial disruption common in the homes of these individuals. They point out the high incidence of broken homes, of hostile, uncaring parents in the families still intact, and of the lifelong emotional deprivations sustained by these young people. They note that these children have had no healthy role model to emulate. Instead, a large proportion of the parents are either drug or alcohol abusers themselves. The fathers, in particular, are seen by the children as cruel, unjust, unapproachable, and uncaring, so that if they finally abandon their family, the situation is improved rather than worsened. Under such conditions, the youngster escapes to street life as soon as he can.

Sociologists in particular have emphasized social disorganization as the reason for the high incidence of solvent abuse in minority ghetto dwellers (Carroll 1977). The filth, misery, and hopelessness of the inner city provide little alternative, constructive activity for children. The social condition is perceived as a strong etiological factor in the flight into inhalants.

The school experience as a part of the demoralizing social system is believed to represent a factor of some weight in solventism. Repeated school failure and a dismal school experience are regarded as important precipitating factors. Whether poor school performance and a lack of rewarding school experiences are cause or effect of inhalant abuse is not easy to sort out.

The pervasiveness of the volatiles and their easy availability to youths are surely factors in their usage. The fact that the intoxication is achieved quickly must act as a rewarding element. They are probably the most cost-effective of all intoxicants. In certain communities they may be illegal to sell to minors, but they are not illegal to possess or use. Whether grade school craft activities utilizing plastic cements adds to the experimentation with solvents has not been established. At any rate, nonintoxicating glues are now available for classroom use.

One further causative factor is believed to be as important or more important than any of those previously mentioned. This is the solvent usage of the peer group, and especially of its leaders. Children with rather intact personalities from stable, loving homes, living in comfortable surroundings have become heavy users by being introduced into solvent usage by their friends. In addition, the continuation of the practice is frequently reinforced. What is more probable than any single theory of causation is that all the elements previously mentioned are operant to varying degrees in each young person who makes a career of solvent usage.

Chronic solventism itself produces a number of consequences that can only be described as disorganizing, so that if the lifestyle was not chaotic before solvent abuse began, it will become so after protracted usage. The psychophysiological results of chronic use include accident proneness, functional or organic tissue damage, developmental arrest psychologically, and graduation to other dangerous drug usage. The family of a severe solvent abuser is disturbed by his presence. He may "turn on" his younger siblings. He steals from the family to obtain funds. His aberrant behavior is difficult to live with. The scholastic consequences are many and disruptive. School failures, truancy, and eventual dropout occur. Eventually, theft, shoplifting, and other delinquent activities become a way of life. Violence is quite possible during the early stage of intoxication or during recovery from the effects.

Pharmacology

The inhalants gain access to the systemic circulation through the respiratory tract, the bulk being transported across the alveolar-pulmonary capillary membrane. Tissues with high lipid levels receive increased amounts because of the affinity of the solvents for lipids. The brain and spinal cord probably preferentially acquire higher concentrations than other organs, although these data are not yet available. Major portions of the absorbed volatile solvents are excreted unchanged through the lungs and expired air. As much as 50 percent of inhaled benzene has been measured in expired air. It is for this reason that solvent vapor can be smelled on the breath for hours following inhalation. Much of the residual solvent is metabolized in the liver and excreted in the urine either unchanged or conjugated as sulfates or glycuronides. Urine testing within 24 hours can reflect the type of solvent used and its metabolic products.

Tolerance to the intoxicating effects of inhalants does develop. Large daily amounts will induce tolerance in a week; lesser amounts require longer exposures. Tolerance development has been observed after 3 months following the first exposure of once-weekly usage of unspecified amounts of model airplane cement. The degree of tolerance can be impressive. One user had less effects from eight tubes of plastic cement than he obtained from a single tube 3 years earlier (Press and Done 1967). Another claimed to inhale twenty-five tubes of airplane glue (21 ml each) daily.

Psychological dependence certainly occurs in daily users (Nylander 1962). It is impressive how confirmed users will relapse back into solvent inhalation in spite of evident physical damage due to the solvent, repeated incarcerations, and the threat of further punishment. Some of the Indian youths reported by Boeckx and Coodin (1976) who had to be hospitalized for their lead neuropathy and encephalopathy relapsed back into gasoline sniffing upon return to their village. The dependence is on the intoxicated state, not to any specific chemical. Deprived of their favorite solvent, abusers will use any other intoxicating solvent available (Cohen 1973).

The evidence for physical dependence is much less convincing. There are reports of tremulousness, irritability, loss of appetite, and insomnia following the abrupt discontinuance of the practice. Such reactions may be nonspecific resurgent anxiety effects. However, they could represent minor abstinence symptoms, and major symptoms like withdrawal delirium or convulsions are not seen because the time-dose quantity of the absorbed material was insufficient to evoke them. Actually, delirium-tremens-like symptoms without the delusional component have been described following withdrawal from toluene. However, such observations are rare. Instead, reports of transient tingling and cramps of the hands and feet on cessation of glue sniffing are reported (Lindstrom 1960). Complaints of anxiety, irritability, vertigo, nausea, paresthesias, insomnia, and anorexia are mentioned in connection with toluene (Satran and Dodson 1963) and lighter fluid (Ackerly and Gibson 1964). It could be concluded that if physical dependence does develop from intentional inhalant use, it is mild in nature. Equally frequent are reports of improved mood and feelings of well-being on cessation of the sniffing habit. These can be understood as releasing effects from chronic use of CNS depressants.

Signs and Symptoms of Inhalant Intoxication

The signs and symptoms of solvent inebriation consist of an initial stimulation followed by a progressive and generalized CNS depression of varying intensity. The early manifestations of stimulation result from cortical disinhibition due to depression of the inhibitory neuronal tracts. This is analagous to the early phase of alcohol intoxication or the second stage of anesthesia and might include impulsiveness, excitement, hyperactivity, and exhileration. Feelings of numbness and weightlessness have been described. During the excited period, feelings of recklessness or omnipotence might occur. It is during this phase that the solvent inhaler is dangerous to himself and others. Accidental deaths have been reported following the jumping off a roof in an effort to fly. Others have lacerated their hands by putting them through glass windows through misjudgment or misperception. As the intoxication deepens, the clinical picture resembles that of a delirium. Mental confusion, psychomotor clumsiness, emotional disinhibition, and impairment of perceptual and cognitive skills are observed. Some of the developing symptoms consist of dizziness, slurred speech, staggering gait, drowsiness, drunkenness, and a dreamy, euphoric reverie. As the intoxication continues to develop, illusions, hallucinations, and delusional thinking can be identified. The hallucinated material is vivid, colorful, and usually pleasant. A further deepening of the state consists of increasing somnolence or stupor, sometimes culminating in coma. If the solvent exposure should continue, respiratory depression or arrest may occur.

Dizziness of some degree is almost invariable along with feelings of numbness and floating sensations. Some abusers have described sensations of being "blank" or "dead," or of floating or spinning in space. Another common report is of "buzzing." This may either be a sound heard or a feeling of vibration.

The monitoring function of the ego is impaired, and this results in two conditions: emotional dyscontrol and behavioral dyscontrol. Loss of emotional control may simply be a matter of uncontrollable laughter (the laughing jag) or tears, but on rare occasions it results in a profound depression. Behavioral dyscontrol results from a loss of ability to monitor one's thinking and in defective judgment. This can result in a flood of speech, an aggressive outburst, accident proneness, and on rare occasions, homicidal behavior. When group sniffing is practiced, "horse play," roughhousing, fighting, or homosexual practices may take place.

The period of intoxication is relatively brief lasting for a few minutes to an hour or two. This quick, short drunk makes it preferred to alcohol by a few users because they can get "high" and recover a number of times a day. Inhalant abusers who have experience with alcohol believe that inhalants provide more euphoria, feelings of power, and perceptual distortions. The hangover is said to be less troublesome.

The euphoriant effects are apparent during the active sniffing period and for 15 to 45 minutes thereafter. Then they are followed by a period of sleep or stupor. The CNS depressant effects wear off and the subject recovers. Amnesia may be complete for the intoxicated period. The sniffer will wake up feeling fairly alert or slightly dulled. If a hangover occurs, it consists of a headache, nausea, and some nondescript aches in the extremities.

Side Effects

A number of unpleasant effects have been described during solvent use and for variable periods thereafter. These include the irritant effect of the solvent on the eyes, including tearing, photophobia, and conjunctival injection. Loss of appetite, nausea, vomiting, and diarrhea also have been noted. Ringing in the ears, chest pain, and musculoskeletal aches and pains are sometimes complained of. During the intoxicated period, respirations may be depressed, the heart rate increased, and the pupils somewhat dilated.

Certain residual symptoms occur in chronic users. A chronic cough due to tracheobronchial irritation is a possibility. Loss of appetite and of weight is a fairly consistent finding. Sometimes a fine tremor or an unsteady gait may persist after the acute intoxication. The glue sniffer's rash is a dermatitis found around the mouth and nose due to the direct irritant effects of the solvent.

Acute Complications

In listing the personal dangers of the various drugs of abuse Irwin (1970) places the volatile solvents first above all other kinds of drugs. He considers them "highest in hazard to the individual because of rapid loss of control and consciousness leading to possible overdosage and death from respiratory arrest, and to their ability to produce irreversible damage to brain and body tissue."

Only partial documentation of these dangers is available. The acute adverse effects are more obvious than the chronic impact on the various organs. One hundred and four people died from acute solvent poisoning in Japan during 1968.[2] Bass had no difficulty finding 110 cases of sudden sniffing death in the United States, cases not caused by plastic bag suffocation (Bass 1970). The majority of these were due to aerosol abuse. Cleveland (1975) collected 156 aerosol deaths between 1967 and 1973. He estimates that there were 125 in 1975 alone. The most popular aerosols misused were vegetable oil, antiseptic, deodorant, and glass chiller sprays. Death from overdosage had been thought to be caused by a depression of the respiratory center with consequent apnea and anoxia. This is not considered likely at present because death is so sudden and the amount of solvent inhaled so small that death is now believed to be more frequently due to a major cardiac arrhythmia. At autopsy little is found except for pulmonary edema. It is hypothesized (Taylor and Harris 1970) that the terminal aberrant cardiac rhythm was precipitated by the overexcitement of a light-plane anesthesia or a hyperadrenergic crisis that potentiated the direct irritant effects of the solvent upon an hypoxic heart conduction system. The assumption that the volatile hydrocarbons sensitize the heart to asphyxia which then induces heart block has received support in studies in mice. The terminal arrhythmia was either an atrioventricular block or a sinoatrial arrest.

In another animal study (Reinhardt et al. 1973), it was found that toluene sensitizes the cardiac pacemaker to decreases in the oxygen content of the blood. The mice that inhaled toluene vapor under conditions of anoxia developed atrioventricular block. This could also be true for other solvents. Cardiac arrhythmias and cardiac arrest seem to be the most frequent cause of acute death.

Taylor et al. (1971) demonstrated that the inhalation of fluoroalkane gases by monkeys induced ventricular premature beats, bigeminy, and a sinus tachycardia. Aerosol propellants were also shown to sensitize the canine heart to epinephrine and cause serious arrhythmias (Reinhardt et al. 1971). It is true that acute cardiovascular death is more common among those inhaling aerosols than among those who inhale glue or paint products (Reinhardt et al. 1973). The recent work of Flowers and Horan (1972) suggests that neither anoxia nor the potentiation of epinephrine is necessarily the basis of the experimental arrhythmias. They demonstrated that during exposure to fluorinated hydrocarbons a pattern of rhythm disturbance consisting mainly of a slowing of the rate of the sinoatrial pacemaker occurred with a resultant junctional or ventricular fibrillation. The sinoatrial node appears to be particularly sensitive to the Freons. Once the sinoatrial slowing began in their experimental animals, "there was a relentless progression to a fatal conclusion."

Another not uncommon cause of death during acute exposure is suffocation. The user may lose consciousness and fall on the rag containing the evaporating material. He continues to breathe the vapor until the respiratory center fails, or his nose and mouth may be occluded by the rag or other substance. A fairly common alternative possibility is that the user covers his head or entire body in a plastic bag while inhaling. After losing consciousness, he exhausts the oxygen remaining in the bag and asphyxiates.

The acute hazards of the aerosols include the possibility of laryngospasm or airway freezing (Chapel and Thomas 1970) due to the very rapid vaporization, and such events will occlude the airway. Another possibility is for the Freons to obstruct the passage of oxygen across the alveolar-capillary membrane by mechanically preventing oxygen diffusion (Baselt and Cravey 1968). Baselt and Cravey, in fact, wonder whether the mechanism of the aerosol "high" is not simply an interference with oxygen transfer resulting in cerebran anoxia.

Another acute cause of death may be the toxic ingredients absorbed along with the aerosol solvents. Insecticide sprays have been occasionally used by youths in their search for intoxication. Accidental death is a further possible cause of acute sniffing death. The recklessness, poor judgment, and grandiosity of some sniffers have already been mentioned. These, plus the visual distortions, can cause a gross miscalculation of the environment, and this has led to serious auto accidents and other kinds of severe injuries.

The DAWN data system previously mentioned (Farley et al. 1977) makes an impressive case for the lethality of youthful solvent abuse. For every mention of a solvent from emergency rooms, crisis centers, and medical examiner's offices, inhalants had the highest percentage of medical examiner's mentions (3.3 percent). This lethality ratio makes its lesser incidence of use in comparison with other drugs like marihuana not as significant as its lethal potential.

Chronic Toxicity

Our knowledge of the long-term pathological effects of the volatile substance is based on case reports of abusers, information from factory workers who were exposed to low concentrations for prolonged periods, and information from animal studies simulating the industrial type of exposure. Only recently have animal studies been initiated that mimic the inhalant-abuse problem: young animals exposed to very high concentrations intermittently (Peterson and Buckner 1976).

The evaluation of the literature is difficult, and it does not lead to many definite conclusions about chronic organ damage. The following represents the toxic manifestations observed in abusers or deduced from appropriate animal experiments (Browning 1965; Casarett and Daull 1975; Hofman 1975).

Benzene

Benzene is a definite and markedly toxic substance with sufficient exposure resulting first in leucocytosis and anemia and eventually pancytopenia (Louria 1969), myeloid leukemia (Vigliani 1976), or aplastic anemia. Other toxic effects include fatty degeneration of the liver, necrosis of the liver, and eventually yellow atrophy of the liver. Some of the gastrointestinal effects include gastric pain, anorexia, dyspepsia, and chronic gastritis. The CNS effects may be relatively mild and include headache, drowsiness, and irritability. Benzene is also capable of causing chromosomal abnormalities. It has been barred for public sale in many countries because of its severe toxicity.

Toluene

Reports of chronic toxic effects of toluene on a variety of organ systems are to be found in the literature. Gastrointestinal reactions include nausea, epigastric discomfort, anorexia, jaundice, and hepatomegaly apparently from a fatty liver. Neurological reactions include mental dulling, tremors, emotional lability, nystagmus, cerebellar ataxia (Kelly 1975; Grabski 1961), polyneuropathies (Casarett and Duall 1975), and permanent encephalopathies (Knox and Nelson 1966). The urinary tract may be involved with pyuria, hematuria, and proteinuria (O'Brien et al. 1971), and renal tubular necrosis (Taher 1974) is a possibility. Hematopoetic abnormalities that have been described involve a reversible anemia (Vigliani 1976), with leucocytosis, reticulocytopenia, thrombocytopenia, leucopenia, and eosinophilia. There is a report that chromosomal damage can occur (Forni et al. 1971).

Hexane

Anemia and a sensorimotor polyneuropathy are mentioned in connection with hexane exposure (Taher et al. 1974). The latter consisted of muscle weakness, hypesthesias, paresthesias, muscle atrophy, and slowed nerve conduction times. An animal study revealed central and peripheral nerve degeneration (Shaumberg and Spencer 1976).

Xylene

Xylene is supposed to be one of the safer solvents. Mucous membrane irritation has been noted. Lead is sometimes found in xylene, and this contaminant has caused poisoning.

Gasoline

Toxic effects from exposure to gasoline tend not to be severe. However, very-high-level exposure may cause some toxicity. Usually it is the additives, tetraethyl lead, benzene, and other substances, that cause health problems. The following pathology has been described following gasoline sniffing itself. Neurological effects dominate, including confusion, tremor, ataxia, paresthesias, neuritis, and peripheral nerve and cranial nerve paralyses. Gastrointestinal effects including nausea, vomiting, anorexia, abdominal pain, and weight loss. Other symptoms occasionally reported include anemia, muscle weakness, and fatigue. The presence of lead can lead to plumbism and its associated anemia and encephalopathy (Durden and Chipman 1967; Law and Nelson 1968; Beattie et al. 1972). Patients with lead poisoning have been successfully treated with edetate calcium disodium (EDTA).

Naphtha

Reports on naphtha toxicity have been rare. Emotional lability and fainting have been mentioned, but no major organic disturbances have been noted.

Carbon Tetrachloride

Carbon tetrachloride is a highly toxic solvent, and its use in spot removers and dry cleaners has been discontinued. Gastrointestinal symptoms include nausea, vomiting, loss of appetite, abdominal pain, and weight loss. The more ominous indications are of renal and hepatic failure, including anuria, jaundice, and retention of products ordinarily excreted by the liver and kidney. Anemia and convulsions accompany the uremia (Durden and Chipman 1967). Deaths have occurred following exposure to modest amounts of carbon tetrachloride in an unventilated space. Alcoholics are particularly prone to hepatorenal damage. It has been postulated that alcohol interferes with the metabolism of carbon tetrachloride.

Trichloroethylene

Trichloroethylene has been claimed to cause liver cell dysfunction in the form of centrilobular necrosis. The possibility of optic trigeminal and other cranial nerve damage has been raised (Hasser et al. 1973). Renal tubular necrosis has been reported (Shaumberg and Spencer 1976), and these instances terminated in renal failure.

Ketones

The ketones have usually been considered relatively safe solvents until recently when a number of cases of peripheral neuropathies with demonstrable neuronal pathology have occurred (Allen et al. 1975). Clinical peripheral neuropathies have been induced in rats, cats, and chickens exposed to methylbutylketone or to lesser concentrations of methylbutylketone in the presence of methylethylketone (Couri 1976). Quinby (1975) states that methyl *n*-butylketone, even when present as an impurity, can be neurotoxic. Methylamylketone or its oxidation product is probably also a cause of polyneuritis. The presence of alcohol contributes to the neurotoxicity of these ketones. A sensorimotor neuritis with impotence and anosmia is the clinical finding.

Methyethylketone and methylbutylketone in combination are believed to cause a peripheral neuropathy that can be ascending and involve the nerves of respiration. Permanent paralyses have resulted (Couri 1975). Axonal swelling and demyelinization are found at biopsy (Saida et al. 1976). A case of retrobulbar neuritis has been attributed to methylethylketone.

Solvent Mixtures

As an example of the difficulties involved in ascribing chronic damage to a specific solvent, Prockop (1974) reported on a small "epidemic" of an ascending neuropathy. Seven white males in the Tampa area who had been huffing a lacquer thinner suddenly developed weakness and numbness of the extremities that ascended and progressed after the use of the solvent had stopped. Four of the patients had diffuse, severe muscle weakness, sensory loss, and areflexia. The four were confined to wheelchairs. Two others had bulbar paralysis and required respirators. One patient died of pulmonary complications.

The onset of the symptoms occurred during February and March of 1974. It was at this time that the manufacturer had changed the formulation of the lacquer thinner because of increased costs of some of the constituents. One and a half years later some functional improvement was noted in the patients, but one still required a wheelchair. The formulation consisted of eleven compounds, and the paralysis was apparently due to the interaction of two or more of the chemicals. Motor nerve conduction velocities were markedly slowed and showed a loss of myelinization. Central chromotalysis of anterior horn cells and axonal swelling in the fasciculus gracillis were found at autopsy (Means et al. 1976).

On the other hand, the Comstocks (1976) examined eight solvent abusers from their polydrug program. They had been inhaling for 4 months to 11 years using a variety of products including plastic acrylic sprays, thinner, "Texas Shoeshine," and gold paint spray. The physical and laboratory examintions were negative. Although they had been admitted with a diagnosis of acute brain syndrome, this rapidly subsided. Their only chronic symptoms were cough, chest pain, and some hemoptysis.

Brain Damage

The question of whether permanent brain damage occurs is a difficult one to answer. Much depends on the constituents of the product inhaled. Model airplane glue has been reported to cause fatigue, attentional difficulties and memory gaps (Wyse 1973), tremors, gait disturbances and amnesias (Massingale et al. 1963), abnormal EEGs (Glaser and Massingale 1962), elevated cerebral spinal fluid pressures (Tolan and Lingle 1964), cerebral edema (Winek et al. 1973), encephalopathies (Knox and Nelson 1966), and an acute brain syndrome (Comstock and Comstock 1976). Most of these are effects that recede over time.

Anatomic lesions in the brains of animals exposed to a variety of organic solvents were reported by Baker and Tichy (1953). Neuronal swelling, perinuclear chromatolysis, hyperchromaticity, pyknosis, shrinkage, and fragmentation were seen. The myelin sheaths were also grossly affected.

Although many authors imply that the inhalation of solvents is capable of producing permanent brain damage, the evidence remains incomplete. Toluene has been implicated by a number of authors (Grabski 1961; Kelly 1975; Knox and Nelson 1966). Chronic solvent sniffers are usually described as having low-normal intelligence test scores. On the other hand, Dodds and Santostefano (1964) found no significant difference between glue sniffers and a control group in tests of cognitive functioning. Massingale et al. (1963) reported that the EEGs of habitual glue sniffers were normal during the interval between inhaling. Andersen and Kaada (1953) also found no significant change in the EEGs of those exposed to a butylacetate and toluene lacquer thinner.

Among the first of the thorough evaluations of the mental status of solvent abusers was the study by Berry (1976). Berry thoroughly examined thirty-seven young people who had been abusing a variety of solvents for periods of from 1.5 to 17 years (mean of 5.5 years). Their ages ranged from 14 to 29 years, with a mean of 18.3 years. They usually gave a history of having been started on the solvent career by their peers. Ordinarily, they used the inhalants infrequently during the first 3 to 6 months, later increasing their use. Eventually, they inhaled an average of 3.7 times daily with an average frequency of 7,428 total exposures.

Alcohol had usually been the first drug used, then solvents were tried. Still later, marihuana was added, but other drugs were used minimally. The preferred solvents at the time of examination were the metallic paint sprays, the clear paint sprays, and the varnishes.

The following demographic data were provided. The male/female ratio was 33:4. Mexican-Americans constituted 62 percent; Anglos, 27 percent; and Indians, 11 percent. Blacks were not represented. The group had an average of 9.7 years of schooling. Only 16 percent were attending school or employed at the time of the study. A third of the fathers had abused alcohol. The subjects had been arrested an average of five times in the past 2 years and had received convictions an average of 2.3 times.

A control group was matched for age, sex, ethnicity, educational level, socioeconomic, and cultural backgrounds and was compared with the solvent abusers. Both groups were tested with an expanded Halstead-Reitan neuropsychological test battery, a well-validated test of multiple brain functions. The complete series of tests measured personality, intelligence, attention, cognitive functioning, motor proficiency, sensoriperceptual functions, aphasia, verbal learning, and memory.

In general, the solvent group showed more severe psychopathology than the control group. They were more depressed, dysphoric, and schizoid and revealed greater social alienation. On the Weschler Adult Intelligence Scale (WAIS) scales, the solvent group scored lower throughout with significant differences on the comprehension subtest and on the verbal and full-scale IQs. On the neuropsychological test battery, the solvent-group scores were also worse than the controls in every instance, with significant differences in tactual performance test time, block and memory scores, tactile form recognition, hand dynamometer, and maze coordination. Learning efficiency and delayed memory scores were significantly worse. The neuropsychological summary scores were also significantly worse. Fifteen of the thirty-seven inhalant users scored in the range considered to indicate probable brain damage, and no control subject scored in the brain damaged range.

Berry (1976) points out that these results are preliminary, and that pathology existing prior to the inhalant abuse could account for some of these differences. Further studies may provide a more definitive answer to the nature and degree of brain damage in chronic solvent abusers.

Korman et al. (1976) studied three groups of ninety-one inhalant abusers, ninety-one polydrug abusers, and ninety-one nondrug users that were matched for sex, age, and ethnicity. These were all patients at a psychiatric emergency clinic at a county hospital in Dallas. The inhalant group received the highest mean severity scores on a majority of clinical-problem variables. The fourteen variables found to be significantly worse for the inhalant group were poor hygiene, trouble with the law, family discord, school problems, abstraction deficit, insight deficit, judgment deficit, other cognitive difficulties, phobias, increased weight, potential danger to self and others, other self-destructive behavior, and other externally directed destructive behavior.

Only on five items did the polydrug group demonstrate the severest pathology, but the inhalant group also exceeded the control group on these. They were anxious and fearful behavior, loss of immediate recall, employment problems, initial sleep disturbance, and thoughts of suicide. Estimated IQ was not significantly different between the inhalant and control groups.

When an attempt was made to differentiate the inhalant abusers by their degree of usage, the heavy and moderate users significantly exceeded the light users in poor hygiene, inappropriate dress, flat and blunted affect, and soft and monotonic speech.

This study made two additional points not sufficiently emphasized in the literature: (1) sniffing behavior does not necessarily cease as youngsters reach 17, and (2) only a 3:1 ratio of males to females was found. The overrepresentation of Mexican-Americans and underrepresentation of blacks were confirmed, but the differences were not great.

Implications for Society

The social costs of the abuse of inhalants are not in its widespread use. From recent surveys it appears that 10 to 15 percent of all school children have tried a commercial solvent for recreational purposes at least once and 1 or 2 percent are current users. What the percentages for school dropouts are is uncertain, but it is probably higher. The fact that epidemics of this practice take place from time to time is disturbing, but the solvent-abuse problem remains numerically less prevalent than the opiate, cannabis, sedative, and stimulant problems.

But significant solvent-abuse issues do exist. The fact that these substances often are the first socially unacceptable agent to be used implies that if their use could be reduced, perhaps subsequent illicit drug use might also be avoided. Another problem of some consequence is the morbidity and mortality associated with the intentional use of solvents. Deaths from acute cardiac arrest, asphyxiation, accidents, and organ failure are sufficiently frequent to constitute serious hazards. Beyond the matter of lethality are the numbers of young people who survive but remain impaired because of permanent injury to the liver, kidney, bone marrow, lungs, or nervous system. Of special concern are the recent preliminary findings by Berry indicating a wide range of mental impairments.

The impact of youthful intoxication at frequent intervals, whether it be due to some vapor inhaled, some liquid drunk, or some pills swallowed, is certain to have its impact on a social system. Now that multiple drug usage is the mode, the special consequences of some single substance becomes more difficult to evaluate. As many as 70 percent of the NYPS (1977) survey reported the current use of more than one drug. Heavy solvent users with or without concurrent use of many other mind-altering drugs are unable to acquire the information and values that would enable them to become productive citizens. They become a burden to their families, the rehabilitative and social services, and the criminal justice system. Their unpredictable and sometimes bizarre behavior makes them a hazard to themselves and those in their vicinity.

Costs to the Individual

In addition to the obvious costs to the solvent-using individual already described, there are further considerations that impact on him. If the use is repeated daily, the time available to learn from life experience is abbreviated. The sniffer does not acquire techniques for coping with conflict and frustration, nor does he develop personality resiliency. He never learns the strategies for dealing with other people and remains psychologically immature developmentally.

It is well known that the growing brain is more sensitive to the effect of psychochemicals than the adult central nervous system. Since the users of inhalants are among the youngest people who abuse drugs, the possibility of a functional impairment of CNS metabolic activity during the developmental period is a further cause for concern. Those young people who had borderline personality development before they entered into their sniffing careers are in double jeopardy, since the impairment caused by extensive solventism can only add to their marginal adjustment.

Treatment

Acute Toxicity

The emergency room of a hospital does not see large numbers of acutely intoxicated solvent abusers. The condition is self-limiting and ordinarily so brief that recovery is the rule by the time the patient arrives at the hospital. He may still be delirious and ataxic, but the vital signs will be approaching normal levels. When cardiac arrest has occurred, death is often rapid. However, instances of such critical cardiac emergencies have arrived at emergency services. When they do, assisted respiration, cardiac massage and defibrillation, oxygen, treatment for vascular collapse, and related emergency procedures may be necessary.

If an acute delirium exists, its management is the same as for other delirial states. The patient should be kept under observation by a member of the family or one of the hospital staff. The room should be quiet and well lit. If possible, restraints and sedative medication ought to be withheld. Vital signs are taken at frequent intervals and recorded. For hyperactivity that does not respond to reassurance, soft restraints can be employed. If a sedative must be administered, it should be one that has minimal depressant effects on the cardiopulmonary system. The benzodiazepines are preferred in such instances.

Sometimes, the characteristic odor of some solvent will obscure a more complicated clinical problem. Simply smelling the solvent on the breath is insufficient reason to halt further diagnostic procedures. The fashion these days is polydrug consumption, and other chemicals may be as important or more important in making a complete diagnosis. Further history and drug-screening tests may clarify the picture and make more understandable the actual extent of the drug problem.

Chronic Toxicity

The management of the effects of the protracted use of inhalants will vary depending on which organ system is involved. It is important to establish a complete and accurate diagnosis by examining all the organ functions likely to be affected. Multiple diagnoses are the rule. A complete history, including a detailed drug-intake history, a thorough physical, and neurologic examination and psychiatric evaluation, is indicated. The routine laboratory studies should include a chest film, EEG, blood chemistries, complete blood count, and urine analysis. Depending on the findings, an electromyogram, nerve conduction velocities, bone marrow biopsy, panels of liver and kidney function tests, tests for lead and copper, and special pulmonary and cardiodynamic studies will be required. The testing of the mental status for objective evidence of organic brain impairment is necessary. In addition to the routine intelligence and personality tests, a neuropsychological battery like the Halstead-Reitan test will assist in picking up deficits not clinically apparent.

The treatment of solvent-induced anemias, neuropathies, encephalopathies, and liver or kidney dysfunctions is no different from the management of other toxic disorders of the organs involved. The baseline tests taken after admission to the hospital will help serve as indicators of whether the dysfunction is progressing or improving. It must be remembered that in addition to the solvents, other potent contaminating chemicals could be involved. For example, chelating agents may be required if exposure to leaded gasoline or the copper in gold spray paints was considerable. The hope is that during outpatient treatment for the residuals of chronic solvent toxicity, further exposure to the causative agent will not take place. Unfortunately, this cannot always be assumed.

Rehabilitation

Experience with attempts to rehabilitate the chronic user of solvents is sparse. Some drug-free clinics have worked with these clients, and recently clinics in Denver and Houston have been established to deal specifically with the problem of intentional inhalation of aerosols and solvents. The general opinion is that rehabilitation is difficult and marked by intermittent relapses. Relapse should not be considered a failure, rather it represents a temporary setback in a chronic, recurrent illness.

The most promising programs utilize an eclectic approach to the problem. The client's history is evaluated to determine which elements have contributed to the inhalant-seeking behavior. If it is a personality defect, a chaotic family situation, a demoralizing social situation, a series of failures at school, or an overwhelming pressure from the peer group, these factors must be analyzed and an attempt at correction made. It is necessary to involve the family, the school, and the peers in the treatment planning. School failure and truancy are frequent among inhalant abusers, and negative school experiences are simply one more reason to obliterate one's frustrations and negative self-image with the intoxicant at hand. Therefore the school situation requires careful attention. Special classes or tutoring may help improve the student's performance. It is possible that success at school may reinforce abstinent behavior; and less failures would reduce the compulsion to intoxicate oneself.

The family must be involved in the rehabilitative effort. If the family is antitherapeutic and completely disorganized, a foster family or other removal from the home environment is a reasonable approach.

It may be possible to involve the entire peer group in some recreational or athletic activity, thereby providing an entry into the group and an altering of its drug-taking behavior. At times, this may be the only way to impact on the situation.

Individual therapy has hardly been used and is unlikely to give results superior to group psychotherapy. In a group of solvent abusers it is desirable to have as a cotherapist a former abuser who can serve as the role model of one who has succeeded. He will also be able to identify all the con games that sniffers play and will be able to avoid being manipulated by them.

It will be a major problem to retain the client in any sort of remedial therapy. Unless it is a condition of probation, clients tend to drop out of treatment early. Legal coercion is a poor substitute for the motivation to stop using, but it may serve to hold the unwilling youngster in the treatment situation until the therapist can generate the motivation to change.

The therapeutic goal is to achieve a new, less-destructive lifestyle, probably one with new friends and perhaps with foster parents. It should provide alternative activities that are more rewarding than the sniffing of toxic materials. Just what these alternative activities will consist of will vary with the interests and abilities of each individual. Somehow ordinary consciousness must come to be appreciated as more gratifying and less destructive than the changed consciousness provided by solvent inhalation.

There is one special consideration that must be remembered in evaluating the possibilities of rehabilitation. If the recent work indicating that long-term cognitive defects occur in connection with long-standing use of solvents is correct, then the question of the user's ability to understand and cooperate in his treatment arises. At least it indicates that therapeutic explanations and suggestions must be simplified and repeated if they are to be understood.

Prevention

To reduce the numbers of young people who will expose themselves to exotic chemicals like the solvents, health education will have to begin at a preschool age. The first lesson would be "There are many things in the kitchen, the laundry, the garage, and the medicine cabinet that you must not put in your mouth or breathe in. They are too dangerous." It is natural for an infant to explore his environment, tasting and smelling the strange new items he can reach. It is a general rule of preventive medicine to keep all medicines and poisons secure from the exploratory hands of the very young.

School education about solvents and other drugs of abuse should occur in the context of general health education matters. It has been found that newspapers or other media reports on solvents, especially sensational stories, produce a subsequent increase rather than the expected decrease in usage.

It is a personal and societal responsibility to make physical access to solvents as difficult, not as easy, as possible. Increasing the difficulty of access will predictably reduce usage. Gasoline tanks should be locked. Packaged solvents and aerosols in retail shops ought to be kept out of the reach of youthful shoplifters. Deterrant additives like allylisothiocyanate designed to make the sniffing of airplane glue, but not its use in model airplanes, nauseating may be helpful. Another manufacturer claims that the plastic cement put out by that firm is not intoxicating. Certainly, very toxic products like carbon tetrachloride and benzene must be eliminated as consumer items. Whether methanol also requires such controls is a matter for further discussion. Community efforts to regulate the sale of airplane glue to unaccompanied minors may not have achieved too much. It is true that airplane glue is not used much at present, but indications are that youngsters have switched to more readily available items like thinner and aerosols.

It is possible that developments outside the field of substance abuse may help the volatile-solvent situation in time to come. The concern about fluorocarbon aerosols injuring the ozone layer in the trophosphere might accomplish their abolition as intoxicating agents. Similarly, the move to remove lead from gasoline for environmental reasons will help to eliminate instances of lead poisoning in our gasoline sniffers.

Juvenile solvent abuse appears to spread along characteristic epidemiologic lines. A single individual or small number of individuals introduce the practice into a community, and it disseminates outward by peer group contacts. Utilizing the communicable disease model, prevention would consist of immediately identifying the focus of infection and quickly eliminating access to the substance. Those already exposed should be isolated and treated. Then the involvement of new cases can be avoided. This procedure is difficult, but if we had an alert early warning system, it might work.

A more definitive approach will come when we understand the factors that impel a young person to continue to use these substances for their mental effects. We still do not know the underlying reasons why certain young people do this to themselves, nor do we know how to teach them not to. A fundamental solution will consist of corrective family and social experiences that will make solvent use irrelevant. At the same time, the self-image of these young people will have to be enhanced. Somehow they must mature to the point where their own internal motivations and controls will terminate their solvent abuse.

Conclusions

Inhalant abuse, a youthful substance-abuse problem of the past quarter century, is difficult for many adults to understand. When perceived from the perspective of the youths who tend to mimic the behavior of their peers, it becomes more comprehensible. The solvents are among the most available, inexpensive, and convenient of the intoxicants. They are effective in quickly producing the desired state of transforming or obliterating sober consciousness. The fact that their dangers are either hardly studied or actually known to be serious deter few youthful consumers who indulge because they seem to be more now oriented rather than future oriented. Information about the dangers of the practice are unlikely to persuade many to desist.

The person who experiments once or twice with some industrial solvent may simply be manifesting the natural curiosity or the mimicking behavior of the young. No particular treatment is needed for such individuals. It is the consistent consumer who is liable to the possible illnesses, injuries, and even fatalities associated with inhaling these intoxicants that were never meant to be consumed by man or beast. The unknown composition and multiplicity of the products used make treatment difficult when such people appear at a medical facility. The management of the psychic and somatic disabilities is complicated, and rehabilitation is unpredictable. It is in preventive measures that the greatest hope of making a real impact on the problem exists. Future strategies should focus on early, primary preventive efforts. However, it is acknowledged that these are the most challenging and most difficult to achieve.

Notes

1. *Sniffing* refers to inhalation through the nose; *huffing* consists of inhalation through the mouth. Both methods might be employed simultaneously.

2. T. Takayama, Abuse of solvents by adolescents, personal communication.

References

Abelson, H., and Fishburne, P. 1976. Non-Medical Use of Substances. Response Analysis Corp., Princeton, NJ.

Ackerly, W.C., and Gibson, G. 1964. Lighter fluid sniffing. *Am. J. Psychiat.* 120:1056.

Allen, N., J. Mendell, D. Billmaier, R. Fontaine, and J. O'Neill. 1975. Toxic polyneuropathy due to methyl n-butyl ketone. *Arch. Neurol.* 32:209.

Andersen, P., and Kaada, B.R. 1953. The electro-encephalogram in poisoning by lacquer thinner (Butyl acetate and toluene). *Acta Pharmacol. et Toxicol.* 9:125-130.

Baerg, R., and D. Kimberg. 1970. Centrilobular hepatic necrosis and acute renal failure in "solvent sniffers." *Ann. Int. Med.* 73:713-720.

Baker, A.B., and Tichy, F.Y. 1953. Effects of organic solvents and industrial poisonings on central nervous system. *Proc. A. Res. Nerv. Ment. Dis.* 32:475.

Baselt, J.T., and Cravey, R.H. 1968. A fatal case involving trichlormonofluronmethane and dichlordifluoromethane. *J. Forensic Sci.* 13:407.

Bass, M. 1970. Sudden sniffing death. *JAMA* 121:2075.

Beal, L. 1975. Results of a Drug Survey in Cahell, Lincoln, Mason and Wayne Cos., West Virginia, Dec., 1974. Community Mental Health Center, Region II, Huntington, W. Va.

Beattie, A.D., Moore, M.R. and Goldberg, A. 1972. Tetraethyl-lead poisoning. *Lancet.* 2:12-15.

Berry, G.J. 1976. Neuropsychological Assessment of Chronic Inhalant Abusers: A Preliminary Report. Presented at the First International Symposium on Deliberate Inhalation of Industrial Solvents, Mexico City.

Boeckx, R., and Coodin, F.J. 1976. An Epidemic of Gasoline Sniffing. Presented at the First International Symposium on the Deliberate Inhalation of Industrial Solvents, Mexico City.

Browning, E. 1965. *Toxicity and Metabolism of Industrial Solvents.* New York: Elsevier.

Carroll, E. 1977. Notes on the epidemiology of inhalants. In C.W. Sharp and M.L. Brehm (eds.), Review of Inhalants: From Euphoria to Dysfunction. Research Monograph, NIDA.

Casarett, L.J., and Daull, J. (eds.). 1975. *Toxicology: The Basic Science of Poisons.* New York: MacMillan.

Chapel, J.L., and Thomas, G. 1970. Aerosol inhalation for kicks. *Mo. Med.* 67:378.

Cleveland, F.P. 1975. Deaths From Abuse of Aerosols, Presented at the Second Technical Review on Inhalant Abuse, NIDA, Rockville, Md. 20852.

Cohen, S. 1973. The volatile solvents. *Public Health Reviews* 2:185-214.

Comstock, E.G., and Comstock, B.S. 1976. Medical Effects of Inhalant Abuse. Presented at the First International Symposium on the Deliberate Inhalation of Industrial Solvents, Mexico City.

Couri, D. 1975. Ketone Toxicities. Presented at the First Technical Review on Inhalant Abuse. NIDA, Rockville, Md. 20852.

Couri, D. 1976. Toxicological Evaluation on Intentionally Inhaled Industrial Solvents. Presented at the First International Symposium on the Deliberate Inhalation of Industrial Solvents, Mexico City.

Dodds, J., and Santostefano, S. 1964. A comparison of the cognitive functioning of glue sniffers and nonsniffers. *J. Pediatr.* 64:565-570.

Durden, W.D., and Chipman, D.W. 1967. Gasoline sniffing complicated by acute carbon tetrachloride poisoning. *Arch. Int. Med.* 119:371-374.

Elinson, J., 1975. A Study of Teenage Drug Behavior. Presented at the Second Technical Review on Inhalant Abuse. NIDA, Rockville, Md. 20852.

Farley, E.C., Cohen, B.Z., Tirabassi, A., Friedman, A.S. and Shor, M.H. 1977. DAWN IV Statistical Report on Youth sample, Services Research Branch report, unpublished, Rockville, Md.

Flowers, N.C., and Horan, L.G. 1972. Nonanoxic aerosol arrhythmias. *JAMA* 219:33-37.

Forni, A.M., Cappellini, A., Pacifico, E. and Vigliana, E.C. 1971 Chromosome changes and their evolution in subjects with past exposure to benzene. *Arch. Environ. Health* 23:385-391.

Gelineau, V.A., Johnson, M., and Pearsall, D. 1973. A survey of adolescent drug use patterns. *Mass J. Mental Health* 3:30-40.

Glaser, H.H., and Massingale, O.N. 1962. Glue sniffing in children–deliberate inhalation of vaporized plastic cements. *JAMA* 181:300.

Glenn, W.A., and Richards, L.G. 1974. Recent Surveys of Nonmedical Drug Use: A Compendium of Abstracts. NIDA, Rockville, Md. 20852.

Goldstein, G.S. 1976. Inhalant Abuse among the Pueblo Tribes of New Mexico. Presented at the First International Symposium on the Deliberate Inhalation of Industrial Solvents, Mexico City.

Governor's Conference on Drug Abuse, 1972. Montpelier, New Hampshire.

Grabski, D.A. 1961. Toluene sniffing produces cerebellar degeneration. *Am. J. Psychiat.* 118:461.

Harrer, G., Kisser, W., Pilz P., Sorgo, G. and Wolkart, N. 1973. Three cases of trichloreothylene and carbon tetrachloride sniffing with lethal outcome. *Nervenarzt* 44:645-647.

Harrison, J.A. 1974. Results of Administration of a Substance Abuse Questionnaire. Commission of Alcohol and Drug Education, Shiawasser Co., Corunna, Michigan 48817.

Hayes, J.R. 1973. Final Report: Psychological Communication Barriers in Drug Abusers. TRIMS, Houston.

Hays, J.R. 1974. The incidence of drug abuse among secondary school students in Houston, 1973. *St. Josephs Hospital Medical Surgical Journal* 9:12-17.

Hofmann, F.G. 1975. *A Handbook on Drug and Alcohol Abuse: The Biomedical Aspects.* New York: Oxford Univ. Press.

Hoock, W.C. 1972. Senior High School Drug Use Survey. Special services and instruction departments, City Schools of Gary, Ind.

Irwin, W. 1970. Drugs of Abuse (pamphlet). Student assoc. for the study of hallucinogens, Beloit, Wis. 53511.

I Simposio International sobre la Inhalacion Deliberada de Disolventes Industriales. 1976. Centro Mexicano de Estudies en Farmacodependencia, Mexico City. June 21-24.

Kelly, T.W. 1975. Prolonged cerebellar dysfunction associated with paint sniffing. *Pediatrics* 56:605-606.

Knox, J., and Nelson, J. 1966. Permanent encephalopathy from toluene inhalation. *New Engl. J. Med.* 275:194.

Korman, M., Timboli, F., and Semler, I. 1976. A Psychiatric Emergency Room Study of Inhalant Abuse. Presented at the First International Symposium on the Deliberate Inhalation of Industrial Solvents, Mexico City.

Law, W.R., and Nelson, E.R. 1968. Gasoline sniffing by an adult: Report of a case with unusual complications of lead encephalopathy. *JAMA* 204:1002.

Lerner, S.E., and Linder, R.L. 1975. Drugs in the elementary school. *J. Drug Educat.* 4:317-322.

Lindstrom, F. 1960. Delirium tremens som abstinenssymtom vis thinner sniffing. *Sevensk Lakastidn* 57:2214.

Louria, D.B. 1969. Medical complications of pleasure giving drugs. *Arch. Intern. Med.* 123:82.

Makie, L.J. 1974. Extent of Drug Use among an Arrested Population. Unpublished data.

Maryland Dept. Health and Mental Hygiene, Drug Abuse Administration. 1973. Survey of Drug Abuse Among Adolescents. First general report.

Massingale, O.N., Glasser, H.H., LeLievre, R.E., Dodds, J.B. and Klock, M.E. 1963. Physical and psychologic factors in glue sniffing. *New Engl. J. Med.* 269:1340-1344.

Massingale, O.N., Glasser, H.H. and LeLievre. 1963. Glue sniffing: A juvenile problem of increasing magnitude. *J. Pediatr.* 63:872.

Means, E., Prockop, L. and Hooper, G. 1976. Pathology of lacquer thinner induced neuropathy. *Am. Clin. Lab. Sci.* 6:240-250.

National Youth Polydrug Study (NYDS). 1977. Polydrug Research Center, Unit of the Philadelphia Psychiatric Center, Philadelphia, Pa. 19131.

Nylander, I. 1962. "Thinner" addiction in children and adolescents. *Acta Paedosphychait* 29:273.

O'Brien, E., Yeoman, W. and Hobby, J. 1971. Hepatorenal damage from toluene in a "glue sniffer." *Br. Med. J.* 2:29-30.

Padilla, E., Padilla, A., and Ramirez, A. 1970. Inhalants, Marihuana and Alcohol Use among Barrio Children and Adolescents. Unpublished paper.

Peterson, R.G., and Bruckner, J.V. 1976. Measurement of Toluene Levels in Animal Tissues. Presented at the First International Symposium on the Deliberate Inhalation of Industrial Solvents, Mexico City.

Press, E., and Done, A.K. 1967. Physiologic effects and community control measures for intoxication from intentional inhalation of organic solvents. *Pediatrics* 39:451.

Prockop, L., Alt, M. and Tison, J. 1974. "Huffer's neuropathy." *JAMA* 229:1083-1084.

Prockop, L.D. 1975. "Huffer's" Neuropathy: Seven Cases of Peripheral Nerve Damage Induced by Inhalation Abuse. Presented at the First Technical Review on Inhalant Abuse. NIDA, Rockville 20852.

Quinby, G. 1975. Solvents as a Cause of Polyneuritis. Presented at the Second Technical Review on Inhalant Abuse. NIDA, Rockville, Md. 20852.

Reinhardt, C., Azar, A., Maxfield, M., Smith, Jr., P., and Mullin, L. 1971. Cardiac arrhythmias and aerosol "sniffing." *Arch. Environ. Health.* 22:265-279.

Reinhardt, C.F., Mullin, L., and Maxfield, M. 1973. Epinephrine-induced cardiac arrhythmias and aerosol sniffing. *J. Occup. Med.* 15:953-955.

Saida, K., Mendell, J., and Weiss, H. 1975. Peripheral nerve changes induced by methyl *n*-butyl ketone and potentiation by methyl ethyl ketone. *J. Neuropathol. Exp. Neurol.* 35:207-225.

San Mateo Drug Use Surveys. 1976. San Mateo Co. Dept. of Public Health and Welfare, 225 37th Avenue, San Mateo, Ca. 94403.

Satran, R., and Dodson, V.N., "Toluene Habituation: Report of a Case," *New Engl. J. Med.* 268:719-721 (1963).

Shaumberg, H.H., and Spencer, P.S. 1976. Degeneration in central and peripheral nervous system produced by pure *n*-hexane. *Brain* 99:183-192.

Taher, S., Anderson, R., McCartney, R., Popovitzer, M., and Schrier, R. 1974. Renal tubular acidosis associated with toluene sniffing. *New Engl. J. Med.* 290:765-768.

Taylor, G.S., and Harris, W.S. 1970. Cardiac toxicity of aerosol propellants. *JAMA* 214:81.

Taylor, G.S., and Harris, W.S. 1970. Glue sniffing causes heart block in mice. *Science* 170:866.

Taylor, G., Harris, W., and Bogdonoff, M. 1971. Ventricular arrhythmias induced in monkeys by the inhalation of aerosol propellants. *J. Clin. Invest.* 50:1546-1550.

Tolan, E.J., and Lingle, F.A. 1964. Model psychosis produced by inhalation of gasoline fumes. *Am. J. Psychiat.* 120:757.

Towfighi, J., Gonatas, N., Pleasure, D., Cooper, H., and McCree, L. 1976. Glue sniffer's neuropathy. *Neurology* 26:238-243.

Vigliani, E. 1976. Leukemia associated with benzene exposure. *Ann. N.Y. Acad. Sci.* 271:143-151.

Winek, C., Collom, W., and Davis, E. 1973. Accidental solvent fatality. *Clin. Toxicol.* 6:23-27.

Wyse, D.G. 1973. Deliberate inhalation of volatile hydrocarbons: A review. *Canad. Med. Assn. J.* 108:71-74.

Yancy, W.S., Nader, P.R., and Burnham, K.L. 1972. Drug use and attitudes of high school students. *Pediatrics* 50:739-745.

14 Youthful Phencyclidine (PCP) Users

Steven E. Lerner and
R. Stanley Burns

In the youth culture, patterns of drug use are constantly changing. Multiple drug use has become a more common practice, youngsters are beginning to experiment with drugs at earlier ages and some "fad" drugs have become dangerous and harmful drugs of abuse. One of the most startling occurrences in recent years has been the rapid proliferation of the use of what appears to be a very dangerous drug, phencyclidine (PCP).

The growing popularity of phencyclidine in youth populations throughout the United States parallels the early histories of LSD and marihuana. The first reports of individuals experimenting with phencyclidine came from the West Coast in 1965. Initially the drug developed a bad street reputation, which was attributed to the method of use, a lack of experience with the drug, and unpleasant side effects and adverse reactions. However, during the past 3 years, its popularity has rapidly increased among youth populations in all sections of the country. The National Institute on Drug Abuse (NIDA) estimated that by the end of 1977, the drug had been used by more than 6 million people in the United States. The drug was associated with at least 80 deaths and over 4,000 emergency room visits in 1977.[1]

The medical problems emerging from the illicit use of this entirely new class of psychoactive drugs are severe. With the advent of the polydrug-abuse phenomenon, the widespread experimental and long-term use of phencyclidine has expanded at an alarming rate. The large quantities of phencyclidine that have been recently confiscated by law enforcement officials in California alone, which are commensurate with the reported Drug Abuse Warning Network "mentions" and associated deaths, are convincing indicators of a new major drug problem.

In this chapter, we will provide an overview of the pharmacology of phencyclidine and its effects on humans as well as the history of its illicit use and factors related to its increasing popularity. Data from three major federal sources are analyzed alone with the results of our hospital-based youth study. The increased problems and deaths seen in a community where PCP has been continuously available are presented and discussed. Our profile of chronic phencyclidine use includes a description of the patterns of use, the phencyclidine experience, tolerance, psychological dependence and side effects, chronic toxicity, and laboratory and neurological findings. A review of the acute intoxicated state caused by phencyclidine encompasses the clinical picture and of course, laboratory and toxicological findings, diagnosis, management, and treatment.

The Pharmacology of Phencyclidine and its Effects on Humans

Phencyclidine hydrochloride (in solution) was legally manufactured by Parke, Davis and Company for use in humans as a short-acting analgesic and for general anesthesia under the name Sernyl. In 1967 the patent was changed to permit the manufacture by Philips Roxane of the drug in solution as an anaesthetic for monkeys and other primates under the trade name Sernylan. The comprehensive Drug Abuse Prevention and Control Act of 1970 classified phencyclidine with the barbiturates and LSD in Section 202(c), Schedule III(b)(7) as "having a depressant effect on the central nervous system" [1].

Phencyclidine and its better-known derivative Ketamine belong to the arylcycloakylamine group and have a similar spectrum of activity. Administered to animals in increasing doses, these drugs produce excitation, ataxia, catalepsy, general anesthesia, and convulsions. The characteristic autonomic actions of these agents, hypertension and tachycardia, appear to be due to central sympathetic stimulation [2].

The degree of central nervous system stimulation and depression and the anesthetic potency of the drug vary among the species [2,3,4]. Based on behavioral criteria, phencyclidine and Ketamine act primarily as central nervous system depressants in both humans and monkeys. Immediate excitation does not usually occur, while surgical anesthesia is more readily induced in humans than in other species [2,4]. Ketamine is less potent, has a shorter duration of action, and produces convulsions less frequently [3,5,6].

Phencyclidine is active orally as well as parenterally (IM,IV) in humans [7,8]. In several studies involving normal subjects, comparable subanesthetic doses of phencyclidine of 0.1 mg/kg given intravenously over 2 to 12 minutes or 7.5 mg orally consistently produced decreased touch, pain, and position sense associated with nystagmus, ataxia, and hyperreflexia [8,9,10].

Impairment or increased threshold of audiometry, perimetry, visual acuity, and taste is seen [8]. Touch sense and two-point discrimination were found to be the earliest, most pronounced, and persistent sensory effects in one study. Changes in muscle tone ranging from a slight increase to catatonia and rhythmic motor behavior have been reported [9]. An increase in the diastolic blood pressure of less than 10 mm with an increase in pulse rate of generally 20 to 30 beats per minute was also noted. Side effects included nausea with repeated vomiting, vertigo, ptosis, and diplopia.

With intravenous administration over 5 minutes, the onset is immediate, with prominent symptoms lasting 1 to 2 hours [9]. Following oral administration, subjects have reported changes in their physical or psychological state within 45 minutes, with maximum effects at 90 minutes [11]. In a similar study of five obsessional patients given 5 to 10 mg phencyclidine orally, the point of onset at 30 to 60 minutes and a duration of 1 to 3 hours were reported [12].

Given intravenously in anesthetic doses of 0.25 mg/kg (or a total dose of 17.5 mg) over 35 minutes, phencyclidine increases the minute volume, rate, and depth of respirations of low order. A mean increase in minute volume of 1140 cc was measured in seven normal patients. Their tidal volume and respiratory rates increased a mean of 15.3 and 2.57 cc, respectively. A consistent and significant mean increase of 26 mm Hg in systolic and 19 mm Hg in diastolic pressure were observed. The pulse-rate change was significantly increased in three subjects and decreased in three subjects [13].

In surgical patients given 20 mg of phencyclidine intravenously following premedication with pethidine and atropine, no response to pain appeared after a few minutes, and most patients were completely unresponsive for periods of up to 90 minutes without respiratory depression [13]. Intravenous doses of 0.275 to 0.44 mg/kg produced anesthesia for an average of 25 minutes in 735 patients. The duration of surgical anesthesia with 0.5 to 0.75 mg/kg of Ketamine is less than 5 minutes, with recovery in ½ to 1 hour [14].

In subanesthetic doses there is general impairment of sensory function, with a decrease in the appreciation of touch (and pain), the earliest and most pronounced effects. Subjects are awake and able to communicate with movement preserved and impaired only by ataxia and occasional catatonia until consciousness is lost when higher anesthetic doses are administered. Dissociation between sensory and motor functioning at subanesthetic doses, implying a disturbance of sensorimotor coordination, appears to occur.

In humans, phencyclidine has psychotomimetic properties. The toxic psychosis induced by low doses is characterized more by the overt symptoms of schizophrenia than by hallucinations. Reproducing more of the primary symptoms than other drug models, the psychosis produced in normal volunteers is difficult to distinguish from schizophrenia [7,15,16]. Extreme exacerbation of existing psychoses followed the administration of phencyclidine to chronic schizophrenic patients [15,16]. The drug intensified disorders in thought processes and stimulated considerable affect. Patients acted out sexually and became more active, assertive, and hostile. These behavioral changes continued for 1 month [9].

Phencyclidine produces unique and profound alterations of thought, perception, and mood in subanesthetic doses. The mental effects in normal volunteers include changes in body image, loss of ego boundary, and depersonalization associated with feelings of estrangement, isolation, and dependency [9,10].

Affectively charged experiences are often evoked, and some subjects exhibit negativism and hostility or apathy [9,10]. Thinking is slowed, with disruption of attention span, inability to sustain organized directed thought [10], and impairment of learning. Time appreciation is disturbed, with underestimation of time intervals. Echolalia, neologism, and word salad may be observed with a loss of time "boundness." Some subjects manifest echopraxia and repetitive motor behavior [9]. Reaction time, tapping speed, rotatory pursuit performance, and weight discrimination have been reported to be impaired [12].

The oral "sedative" dose for humans is considered to be between 1 and 5 mg. Following oral administration of a subanesthetic dose of 7.5 mg, subjects report changes in their psychological or physical state within 45 minutes and maximum effects at 90 minutes [11].

Following anesthetic doses of phencyclidine, patients were amnesic for both surgery and the recovery period. The psychomimetic effects of phencyclidine are most apparent following administration of low doses. The anesthetic properties of the drug associated with changes in the level of consciousness predominate after high doses.

Profound behavioral effects are seen in several species following phencyclidine administration [17]. In the monkey, reinforcing properties have been demonstrated by the initiation and maintenance of lever pressing for injections of phencyclidine. The drug is self-administered in amounts producing a state resembling general anesthesia [17,18]. It is the only "hallucinogen" reliably self-administered by monkeys, which suggests a potential for abuse [7,9,17].

It has been reported that infants born to mothers who ingested phencyclidine prior to conception or during the first trimester had increased rates of limb reduction defects and tripoloidy. Users of phencyclidine had an increased rate of fetal loss, decreased fertility, chromosome breakage, and an additional F-like chromosome.

Several of our female patients have by history used phencyclidine regularly preceding and during pregnancy with their infants being in apparent good health. However one infant born to a mother who used phencyclidine regularly just prior to delivery exhibited poor feeding, a poor sucking reflex, and irritability.

Phencyclidine can be detected in concentrations of 1:1000 after extraction with an organic solvent from an aqueous solution by a color reaction with gold bromide or potassium permanganate [1]. The drug has been identified and quantitatively determined in extracts of body fluid (blood, urine, cerebral spinal fluid) and tissues by thin-layer chromatography, gas liquid chromatography with flame ionization detection, and gas chromatography/chemical ionization mass spectrometry [22,23,24].

The History of Illicit Phencyclidine Use

Street preparations of phencyclidine have continuously changed by name, physical form, and content. Phencyclidine is sold on the West Coast by such labels as angel dust, cannabinol, crystal, PCP, and THC [25,26,27,28,29]. In the

Midwest, among its street names are dust, TAC, and TIC [30]. On the East Coast, phencyclidine is sold as angel dust, erth, green, KW, and sheets. Recently, phencyclidine has been identified as being present in samples sold under fifty different names (see table 14-1). Many of these street nomenclatures are regional, while others are national in scope. Although phencyclidine is represented under a multitude of names, the most consistent misrepresentation is THC [28,29,31,32]. When sold as THC in tablet or powder form, the color may be beige, brown, blue, green, orange, pink, red, strawberry, white, or yellow. Phencyclidine sold as PCP usually appears beige, gray, brown, orange, speckled pink, tan, white, white gray, or white yellow in color.

Phencyclidine has appeared on the illicit market as a powder, a tablet, a leaf mixture, a liquid, and as 1-gram "rock" crystals. The crystalline or granular form is found most frequently in capsules. Phencyclidine found on parsley mint, oregano, or other leaves is usually in the form of a joint. Most street preparations contain the hydrochloride salt, although phencyclidine as the free base has been seen [33]. The crystalline or granular powder form is found most frequently as crystal or angel dust, which usually contains 50 to 100 percent phencyclidine. Found under other names, the purity drops to a range of 10 to 30 percent. Most tablets contain approximately 5 mg and tend to range from 1 to 6 mg [25,26,34]. Leaf mixtures have been found to contain between 0.24 and 7.9 percent phencyclidine, averaging 1 mg phencyclidine per 150 mg leaves [25]. Phencyclidine is taken orally, by inhalation (smoking), insufflation (snorting), injection, and infrequently by drops into the eye.

Analyzed street samples have contained phencyclidine in combination with other drugs (barbiturates, ethyl alcohol, heroin, cocaine, amphetamine, Quaalude, LSD, mescaline, procaine). Combination preparations that contained phencyclidine (phencyclidine-procaine, phencyclidine-marihuana, phencyclidine-caffeine, phencyclidine-cocaine, phencyclidine-doxepin, phencyclidine-LSD, phencyclidine-LSD-mescaline, phencyclidine-LSD-aspirin, phencyclidine-LSD-procaine, and some four to five other drug combinations) have also appeared on the illicit market. In addition the presence of PCC (1-piperidinocyclohenonecarbonitrile) has been detected as a contaminant in some illicit phencyclidine preparations [35].

Since 1975, only 25 percent of the street-drug samples containing phencyclidine contained additional drugs, a smaller percentage than found in street samples in earlier years. In 1971 to 1974, other drugs were found in 40 to 60 percent of street samples analyzed at the Street Drug Information Program at the University of Southern California School of Medicine. LSD was present in 86 percent of all combination preparations, with the "-caine" drugs accounting for another 4 percent. Phencyclidine was mixed with marihuana in only 2 of 317 samples [25]. This trend has also been reflected in other street-drug analysis programs across the United States.

The information needed for the preparation of phencyclidine was reported

Table 14-1
Names Given for Material Containing PCP-TCP

Name
Amphetamine
Angel dust
Bellodonna
Cocaine
Cadillac
Cannabinol
Crystal
Cyclones
Detroit pink
DMT (N,*n*-dimethyltryptamine)
Dust
Elephant tranquilizer
Erth
Goon
Green
Hashish
Hog
Horse tranquilizer
Killerweed
Kools
KJ crystal
KW
Lovely
LSD (lysergic acid diethylamide)
Marihuana
MDA (3,4-methylenedlaxyamphetamine)
Mescaline
Mintweed
Mist
Monkey dust
PCPA (*para*-chlorophenylalamine)
PeaCe Pill
Peaceweed
Peyote
Psilocybin
Rocket fuel
Scuffle
Sheets
Shermans
Snorts
Soma
STP (3-methyl-2,6-dimethoxyamphetamine)
Superweed
Surfer
T
TAC
THC (tetrahydrocannabinol)
TIC
TT-1
Wack-wack

over fifty years ago, with descriptions of the reaction of 1-piperidinoclohexane-carbonitrile (PCC) with Grignard reagents [33]. The majority of the illicitly synthesized phencyclidine is prepared according to the general directions of Kalir and modified in details as required by the availability of chemicals and equipment. Until recently, most batch operations were limited by the amount of piperidine to be used (usually a maximum of 500 g) and would produce on a 3- to 5-mole scale [33].

Piperidine was felt to be the most guarded reagent and the easiest to trace, and for these reasons manufacturers would pay as much as $1,000 per kilogram for a nontraceable bottle. Now piperidine is no longer the "limiting step," since it has become readily available or unlimited in its availability, leading to the manufacture of larger quantities. In addition, a new solvent for distillation that should prevent fires and explosions is now available. Manufacturing is now done in larger, better-equipped laboratories that are capable of producing great quantities of phencyclidine. Illegal laboratories containing as much as $35 million worth of phencyclidine have been raided. A seizure (in the Los Angeles area) of an illicit laboratory in 1977 yielded 900 pounds of phencyclidine.

During the summer of 1977, Drug Enforcement Administration agents raided an illegal laboratory in Michigan. Officials estimated that the $200 investment in chemicals could produce phencyclidine worth approximately $200,000 on the street. Major production centers have been discovered in Washington, D.C., Detroit, San Francisco, and Los Angeles. In the city of Los Angeles, 253,000 dosage units of phencyclidine were seized in 1974. By 1976, the number had jumped to 4,706,000 units. During 1977, over 5 million dosage units were seized.

Juvenile phencyclidine arrests in the city of Los Angeles also are on the increase. In 1976, 142 juveniles were arrested for possession of phencyclidine. The following year, 443 juvenile arrests were made. During 1976, 24 juveniles were arrested for possession for sale and sales. In 1977, juvenile arrests for possession for sale and sales had increased to 115. The same criminal elements that are selling opiates are now also selling phencyclidine. Phencyclidine sold as THC or angel dust is usually worth from $25 to $200 per gram and upwards of $1,000 per ounce. Individual phencyclidine joints vary from $1 to $20 or more.

Various patterns of phencyclidine use have emerged over the past several years. It is reported that first-time users unknowingly or in an experimental fashion smoke cigarettes containing phencyclidine. Although the occasional- or recreational-use pattern is seen, its development is mediated by an initial experience of unexpected and unpleasant effects [28,36]. In areas where the drug has been continuously available, it has gained a preferred-drug status with small cluster groups of individuals who use it on a chronic, daily basis for periods of 6 months to 6 years. Requests for our consultation services reveal chronic users in California, the District of Columbia, Hawaii, Illinois, Kansas, Kentucky, Maryland, Nevada, Pennsylvania, and Washington.

In the San Francisco area, chronic users purchase phencyclidine in gram amounts ranging from $85 to $125 per gram. Money for the purchase of phencyclidine is generally provided by a partner, through dealing, hustling, or Social Security Insurance (SSI).

Phencyclidine sold as angel dust in the Los Angeles area is packaged in foil bindles and Zip-Lock Baggies. In bulk form it generally sells for $125 an ounce. The more common foil bindles sell for roughly $10 and weigh approximately 1 gram. Tablets, infrequently seen, sell for $2 to $4 each. Liquid phencyclidine is generally a clear liquid found in 1-pint glass jars which sell for $800 to $1,100. In addition, phencyclidine has been used to adulterate commercially manufactured cigarettes by dipping the cigarettes in liquid phencyclidine. These cigarettes are sold for as much as $20 each.

Factors Related to Increased Phencyclidine Popularity and Use

When phencyclidine made its illicit debut in 1965, it was marketed as a mild psychedelic. Dealers described this new drug as a little stronger than marihuana and sold it in tablet and capsule form. The effects were often unexpected. Since the dosage could not be titrated, users often experienced adverse reactions. Hence, phencyclidine gained a bad reputation and subsequently was not seen on the streets.

By 1972, a change was observed in both the method of use and the attitude of users about the drug. A conversion had taken place from using phencyclidine orally in tablet or capsules to smoking it on leaf material. By this newly discovered method the user was able to more effectively control the dosage, thus decreasing the chance of overdose. Experienced users for the first time were able to inform new users about how to take the drug effectively and describe what the effects would be like. Because first-time users were now being prepared for this unique experience and because there were better methods of controlling the dosage, the popularity of phencyclidine spread rapidly. Illicit laboratories increased in proportion to the new demand for material.

With phencyclidine being easily manufactured in clandestine laboratories, its availability has dramatically increased. Young people are now using phencyclidine in social settings in a similar fashion to marihuana. While other drugs of abuse become difficult to obtain, phencyclidine in many areas is continuously available. Hence, groups of users are likely to select phencyclidine as their drug of choice and share it with their friends.

Due in part to the lack of information about the effects and dangers associated with phencyclidine, the drug continues to expand in popularity among young people. Young users who were questioned about the differences between LSD and phencyclidine uniformly responded that LSD was a much more dangerous drug and would not use it. However, phencyclidine does not have this connotation. Unless this attitude is changed, it would appear that usage will continue to expand.

The abuse of phencyclidine and other arylcyclohexylamines has emerged over the past 13 years. Phencyclidine was first seen illicitly in Los Angeles in 1965 [37]. Two years later it appeared in San Francisco under the guise of the "pea-ce pill" [28]. Marketed as a mild psychedelic, one step up from marihuana, it quickly gained a bad street reputation since users were primarily taking it orally and experiencing adverse reactions. In addition, the naive users were unaware and unprepared for the nature and length of the intoxication.

With media coverage of the adverse effects, phencyclidine disappeared from the street scene in the San Francisco area in 1968, at which time it surfaced on the East Coast as "hog." Since then it has been seen with increasing frequency throughout the United States.

In 1969, the *n*-ethyl analogue of phencyclidine, PCE (cyclohexamine) appeared on the streets in Los Angeles [36]. By 1972, as a result of the "ripple effect," phencyclidine appeared in five states from California to New York (see table 14-2). It should be noted that the PharmChem Research Foundation, from which these data were gathered, is only one of many street-drug analysis programs operating in the United States. Therefore, the epidemiology of its abuse is not necessarily reflected by these figures. Louisville, Kentucky and Eugene, Oregon represented the greatest increases in street samples containing phencyclidine.

In 1974, the thiophene analogue of phencyclidine, TCP, was first identified in Hawaii. That same year phencyclidine had spread into another four states. By 1975, the use of both phencyclidine and TCP had spread to twenty-two states. TCP was sold on the West Coast in Los Angeles, Newport Beach, Santa Cruz, and Sacramento. Outside of California, TCP was sold in Eugene and Coos Bay, Oregon and Seattle and Tacoma, Washington.

In 1976, phencyclidine appeared in another two states. The use of TCP decreased slightly, although it remained popular in Oregon and Washington. During 1977, phencyclidine was identified in twenty-nine states, exceeding all prior years. For the first time, samples of phencyclidine were received from Indiana, Kansas, and Nevada. Since these samples were in the powder form, the possibility of sophisticated chronic use was evident. Although they were PharmChem's first samples from these states, it is unlikely that phencyclidine had not been available previously.

Recently, PHP (pyrrolidine) was identified on autopsy in the body of an individual who was shot and killed by a police officer in Los Angeles. This was the first documented street appearance of this analogue.

Demography and Epidemiology of Illicit Use

A dearth of literature exists on the nature and extent of use of phencyclidine and its more than thirty analogues. The major federal sources for determining

Table 14-2
Distribution of PCP-TCP by State

State	*1972*	*1973*	*1974*	*1975*	*1976*	*1977*	*1978*[a]
Alabama				X	X		
Alaska			X		X		X
Arizona		X		X	X	X	
Arkansas							
California	X	X	X	X	X	X	X
Colorado	X	X	X	X	X	X	
Connecticut					X	X	
Delaware							
District of Columbia					X	X	
Florida	X	X	X	X	X	X	
Georgia		X	X	X	X	X	
Hawaii			X	X		X	
Idaho							
Illinois		X	X	X		X	X
Indiana			X	X	X	X	
Iowa			X		X	X	
Kansas						X	
Kentucky		X	X	X	X	X	
Louisiana						X	
Maine	X						
Maryland					X	X	
Massachusetts		X			X	X	X
Michigan		X	X	X	X	X	
Minnesota			X				
Mississippi							
Missouri							
Montana		X		X			
Nebraska							
Nevada						X	X
New Hampshire				X		X	
New Jersey				X	X	X	
New Mexico							
New York	X	X	X	X	X	X	X
North Carolina		X					
North Dakota							
Ohio		X	X	X	X	X	X
Oklahoma			X	X	X	X	
Oregon		X	X	X	X	X	
Pennsylvania			X	X	X	X	X
South Carolina							
South Dakota							
Tennessee			X			X	
Texas		X	X	X	X	X	X
Utah					X	X	
Vermont							
Virginia			X	X			
Washington		X	X	X	X	X	
West Virginia							
Wisconsin		X					
Wyoming							
Total states	5	17	21	22	24	29	9

Note: As confirmed by street-drug analysis.
[a]Analysis thru April 1978.

changes in emerging drug trends are the Client Oriented Data Acquisition Process (CODAP), the Drug Abuse Warning Network (DAWN), and the National Youth Polydrug Study (NYPS). The CODAP system provides the largest available national data base of patients in treatment. All drug-abuse treatment and rehabilitation programs receiving federal funds are required to collect and report data.

In the CODAP system, drugs of abuse are divided into fourteen categories. Phencyclidine is classified (incorrectly) as a hallucinogen with LSD, mescaline, MDA, DMT, mushrooms, peyote, and other drugs. Since CODAP has no flexibility in identifying and analyzing phencyclidine independently from the other drugs, this data source is not useful for our purposes.

The DAWN system has been in operation since spring 1973. Hospital emergency rooms and inpatient units, crisis centers, and medical examiners (coroners) in twenty-four selected standard metropolitan statistical areas (SMSAs) are contracted to report incidents of adverse drug reactions to the DAWN central office. In each report, the victim's age, sex, race, and employment and treatment status are noted, as well as the drug used, the route of administration, the source of the drug, and the form in which it was acquired. DAWN data, however, do not include all phencyclidine users, but only a sample of those who had adverse reactions that required agency intervention. Also, another limitation in the DAWN system is that the data are collected only in the major SMSAs. As an example, in California, DAWN data are collected only for the Los Angeles, San Francisco/Oakland, and San Diego areas. Data are not available from fifty-one of California's fifty-eight counties. Even within these reporting counties, the DAWN reporting system—emergency rooms, inpatient units, and crisis centers—is not complete: that is, within these communities, many phencyclidine-related problems are treated that are never reported to DAWN.

Those phencyclidine cases which do get reported often lack complete information. The victims are often not in sufficiently stable condition to properly respond to questions and are not commonly reinterviewed upon recovery.

From September 1972 through March 1973, phencyclidine was ranked as the twenty-third most abused drug in the DAWN system. During the period from April 1973 through March 1974, the use rose to the twenty-first position. By the following year (April 1974 through April 1975), phencyclidine use had increased to the fifth position. For the reporting period from May 1975 through April 1976, phencyclidine continued to rank overall as the sixteenth most frequently abused drug. However, for the youth population it was in tenth place for those between 12 and 18 years of age.

DAWN data reveal almost equal numbers of youthful phencyclidine patients seen in emergency rooms and crisis centers (see table 14-3). White males are twice as likely (61 percent) to report to DAWN emergency rooms than white females (32 percent). For crisis centers, the percentage of white female mentions is higher with approximately 48 percent for white females and 45 percent for

Table 14-3
Drug Abuse Warning Network. PCP Mentions, February to May 1976–Youth 12 to 17 Years

	Emergency Rooms		*Crisis Centers*	
Race and Sex	*Mentions*	*%*	*Mentions*	*%*
White males	186	61	146	45
White females	98	32	158	48
Black males	15	5	14	4
Black females	5	2	8	2
Totals	304	100	326	100

white males. The use of phencyclidine by blacks accounts for only 6 percent of the mentions from crisis centers and 7 percent from emergency rooms. For this youth population between February and May of 1976, there were 304 patients treated in emergency rooms, 326 patients seen in crisis centers, and 2 patients seen by coroners. During the same period, phencyclidine ranked as the eleventh most frequently abused drug in Philadelphia and Washington, D.C., seventh in Chicago and Cleveland, fifth in Minneapolis and Los Angeles, fourth in Detroit, and first in the San Francisco/Oakland area.

Ninety percent of phencyclidine users seen in crisis centers reported their source as a "street buy," whereas with emergency rooms only 48 percent reported "street buys" as their source (see table 14-4). The prime motivation for phencyclidine use among patients seen in both crisis centers and emergency rooms is for the "psychic effects," which account for 73 percent of the mentions (see table 14-5). Phencyclidine users from the crisis centers are much more prone (22 percent) to report dependence as their motivation than are the users from emergency rooms (2 percent).

Table 14-4
Drug Abuse Warning Network. Reported Patient PCP Sources, February to May 1976–Youth 12 to 17 Years

	Emergency Rooms			*Crisis Centers*		
Race and Sex	*Street Buy*	*Gift*	*Unknown/ Other*	*Street Buy*	*Gift*	*Unknown/ Other*
White males	98	5	83	133	6	7
White females	41	8	49	144	9	5
Black males	8	0	7	11	3	0
Black females	1	1	3	7	0	1
Totals	148 48%	14 5%	142 47%	295 90%	18 6%	13 4%

Table 14-5
Drug Abuse Warning Network. Reported Motivations for PCP Mentions, February to May 1976–Youth 12 to 17 Years

	Emergency Rooms				*Crisis Centers*			
Race and Sex	*Psychic Effects*	*Dependence*	*Suicide Attempt or Gesture*	*All Others*	*Psychic Effects*	*Dependence*	*Suicide Attempt or Gesture*	*All Others*
White males	140	5	7	34	96	45	0	5
White females	66	2	5	25	123	28	1	6
Black males	13	0	0	2	13	0	1	0
Black females	4	0	0	1	6	0	2	0
Totals	223 73%	7 2%	12 4%	62 21%	238 73%	73 22%	4 1%	11 4%

Crisis centers data indicate that the age group of 12 to 13 years for white females seems to be at particularly high risk. Furthermore, 42 percent of the phencyclidine mentions in this age group reported dependence as their prime motivation for use.

National Youth Polydrug Study Findings Regarding PCP Use

From September 1976 to March 1977, youths from 12 to 18 years of age were interviewed on admission for drug treatment as part of the National Youth Polydrug Study (NYPS). In all, 2,750 patients from 97 treatment programs in thirty-seven states participated in this study. These patients represented a national sample of youths in treatment from all religions and from the major treatment modalities and were sampled selectively for sex, race, and ethnic grouping by geographic region. Information contained in this new data base is the most comprehensive data available on youthful abusers.

Of the 2,750 clients under 19 years of age in the NYPS sample, 875 youths (31.8 percent) reported to have ever used PCP, with 561 reporting the use of PCP during the 3 months prior to admission (see chapter 6). The prevalence of PCP in this sample is the highest reported in any previous national sample for adults or for youths. As shown in table 14-6, PCP ranked seventh in prevalence among the fourteen types of drugs in the sample, and it was abused more frequently than many other well-known substances such as inhalants (abused by 28.9 percent of the sample), other sedatives (abused by 28.8 percent), or cocaine

Table 14-6
National Youth Polydrug Study. Use of 15 Drug Types for Youths in Treatment (N = 2,750)

Drug Type	*N*	*%*
Marihuana	2,486	90.4
Alcohol	2,449	89.1
Amphetamines	1,237	45.0
Hashish	1,165	42.4
Hallucinogens	1,098	40.0
Barbiturates	1,097	39.9
Phencyclidine	875	31.8
Inhalants	795	28.8
Cocaine	710	25.8
Other opiates	678	24.7
Heroin	344	12.5
Over-the-counter	232	8.4
Illegal methadone	108	3.9
Other	44	1.6

(abused by 25.8 percent). A comparison of PCP users with clients who never used PCP (see table 14-7) indicates that similar proportion of both males and females use PCP (32 percent), that proportionately more whites use it compared with other racial groups (42 percent of whites compared with 8 percent of blacks, 13 percent of American Indians, and 9 percent of Hispanics), that PCP use is more frequent in the suburbs (44.1 percent of all suburban clients compared with about 30 percent of urban and rural setting), that PCP users are slightly older at admission to treatment programs, that they average more years of education and have a higher socioeconomic status.[2]

Frequency of Use of PCP. Among the 561 current users of PCP (see table 14-8), approximately 50 percent were found to be using it on an average frequency of at least once per week during the 3 months prior to admission.

The Onset of PCP Use. The mean age of first PCP use was 14.6 years, and the mean age of first continuous use was 14.8 years (see table 14-9). Females reported the earlier mean age of first use for PCP, 14.4 years, compared with 14.7 years for males. This finding is consistent with most other drug types in this study (except alcohol, marihuana, and inhalants).

In the comparison of age of first use of PCP across race, American Indians were noted to have the earliest mean of first use (13.89 years), closely followed

Table 14-7
National Youth Polydrug Study. Comparison of Subjects Who "Ever Used" with Those Who "Never Used" Phencyclidine

	Never Used Phencyclidine		*Ever Used Phencyclidine*	
Characteristic	*N*	*%*	*N*	*%*
Sex				
Male	1,138	61.1	534	61.4
Female	725	38.9	336	38.6
Race				
White	1,068	58.8	784	90.5
Black	354	19.5	33	3.8
American-Indian	116	6.4	18	2.1
Oriental	3	.2	4	.5
Hispanic	274	15.1	27	3.1
Age (at admission)				
<12 years	31	1.8	1	.1
13	94	5.0	18	2.1
14	228	12.2	64	7.3
15	389	20.8	173	19.8
16	507	27.1	276	31.6
17	398	21.3	225	25.7
18	224	12.0	117	13.4

Table 14-8
National Youth Polydrug Study. Frequency of Phencyclidine Use by Subjects Currently Using Phencyclidine[a]

	n	%
Less than once a month	97	17.3
Once a month	69	12.3
Two to three times a month	112	20.0
Once a week	83	14.8
Two to three times a week	99	17.6
Four to six times a week	28	5.0
Daily	41	7.3
Twice a day	12	2.1
Three or more times a day	20	3.6
Total	561	100.0

[a]Frequency of use was assessed for the three month period preceding admission.

by Hispanics (14.00 years). (The number of PCP users in these two race groups, however, was too small to draw any inference.) Whites reported the third earliest age of PCP use, with a mean of 14.58 years, and blacks were the oldest (15.25 years).

Regional Distribution of PCP Use. The NYPS divided the United States into seven sampling regions (see table 14-10). It should be stated that the sample was not stratified by region, which means the proportion of the youth population in treatment in each region was not a criterion for inclusion in the sample. It may be that certain states are overrepresented in proportion to their relative population, for example, the relatively large number of cases in the sample from Illinois and Florida. Conversely, we know from the DAWN system that the San Francisco Bay area is one of the centers of PCP use, and it is underrepresented in this sample.

The regional prevalence of PCP in the NYPS sample indicates that the Great Lakes and the Midwest regions show the highest rate of PCP use, with 46.6 percent ($n = 270$) and 46.4 percent ($n = 116$) of each region's clients ever using PCP. Since the number of clients from these regions is fairly large and these clients were admitted to twenty-nine different treatment programs, these data seem to be a valid representation of PCP use in this region. They exceed the rates reported in DAWN and probably reflect upon the increased trend of PCP use among young people during the past 2 years. Other regions show PCP to be used by 31.5 percent of the clients from the Southeast ($n = 153$), 27.2 percent of the clients from the West Coast, 24.2 percent of the clients from the Northeast, and 23.8 percent of the clients from the Southwest.

The PCP User versus the Nonuser. Perhaps one of the most notable differences between those who ever used PCP and those who did not is in their involvement in polydrug use. The PCP users reported using twice as many substances as the nonuser of PCP, with PCP users reporting a mean of 6.0 substances ever used (S.D. = 2.6), while nonusers of PCP reported a mean of 2.8 substances ever used (S.D. = 1.8, $t = 33.4$, $p < .0001$). PCP users also reported a higher mean number of drugs used during the 3 months prior to admission to treatment: 5.8 substances (S.D. = 2.6) compared with a mean of 2.6 substances (S.D. = 1.8) for nonusers of PCP ($t = 28.1$, $p < .0001$). Thus, it is clear that for this youth population seeking treatment for drug abuse, PCP use is an integral part of a larger polydrug-abuse problem, and that is a more serious and complex problem than for the nonuser of PCP.

It is of particular interest that not a single subject who used PCP in this study used only this substance. All PCP users used other substances either at other times or concurrently with PCP. Almost all the PCP users used marihuana (99.5 percent). Other drugs reported used by PCP users were alcohol (by 97.7 percent of PCP users), hashish (by 77.8 percent of PCP users), amphetamines (75.8 percent), and hallucinogenics (72.2 percent). Aside from alcohol and marihuana (which are almost universally used in this sample) and hashish, PCP is next most often used by users of amphetamines and hallucinogens.

When looking at the cross use of the drugs from a different perspective, we find that the users of other sedatives (61.7 percent), over-the-counter drugs (61.6 percent), and other opiates (61.1 percent) were most likely to also have ever used PCP.

A Profile of the PCP User. Correlational profile of the PCP user was developed from analysis in which PCP use was correlated with each of thirty-three demographic, social history, and background variables. A 3-point scale measure was utilized for PCP use as follows: a score of 1 was assigned for no PCP use, a score of 2 for irregular PCP use, and a score of 3 for regular PCP use. A profile of the PCP users (compared with the nonuser of PCP) was derived from an analysis of eighteen variables from among the thirty-three variables that had a bi-variate correlational value of ±.10 or greater with PCP use. The following is a list of the descriptors in rank order of magnitude of the correlation: (1) regularly used a greater number of different drugs, (2) was white, (3) more often took more than one drug at a time (in combination) "to boost, balance, or counteract the effects" of one drug, (4) became drunk from drinking alcohol more often, (5) had more arrests for substance-related offenses, (6) was picked up more times by the police, (7) had more overdose episodes (ODs), (8) reported more obstacles to school attendance, (9) had more arrests for violent and weapons offenses, (10) listed more types of problems as reasons for contacting a treatment program, (11) had more arrests for property offenses, (12) had higher socioeconomic status, (13) was older, (14) was adjudicated delinquent, (15) tended to reside in suburbia, (16) more often was admitted to treatment in hospitals and residential settings than to outpatient settings, (17) more often made suicidal attempts, and (18) less often was referred to treatment by peers.

Table 14-9
National Youth Polydrug Study. Mean Age of First Drug Use and First Continuing Drug Use by Sex

		Males			Females			t	t
		X	S.D.	N	X	S.D.	N	Age 1st Use	Age 1st Continuing Use
Heroin	A_1	15.0	1.6	219	14.7	1.6	119	1.65	1.31
	A_2	15.5	1.5	130	15.2	1.6	73		
Illegal Methadone	A_1	15.1	1.7	70	15.0	1.3	37	.34	
	A_2	15.7	1.5	30	15.6	1.5	17		.22
Other Opiates	A_1	14.5	1.7	413	14.2	1.8	257	2.14*	
	A_2	14.8	1.9	207	14.7	1.5	135		.54
Alcohol	A_1	12.0	2.7	1468	12.4	2.5	952	−3.73**	
	A_2	13.9	1.8	1284	13.8	1.7	807		1.28
Barbiturates	A_1	14.2	1.6	633	14.0	1.4	447	2.18*	
	A_2	14.7	1.5	423	14.4	1.4	323		2.81*
Other Sedatives	A_1	14.4	1.5	449	14.0	1.6	332	3.60**	
	A_2	14.7	1.5	304	14.4	1.5	230		2.29*
Amphetamines	A_1	14.2	1.6	696	14.0	1.4	528	2.33*	
	A_2	14.6	1.7	461	14.3	1.5	378		2.71*
Cocaine	A_1	15.1	1.5	450	14.8	1.6	253	2.44*	
	A_2	15.3	1.7	216	15.0	1.4	118		0.0
Marihuana	A_1	12.8	2.0	1501	13.1	1.7	951	−3.97**	
	A_2	13.6	1.8	1416	13.6	1.6	884		0.0
Hashish	A_1	14.0	1.8	722	13.9	1.5	428	1.01	
	A_2	14.4	1.6	457	14.0	1.6	236		3.12*
Hallucinogens	A_1	14.5	1.6	678	14.2	1.4	409	3.24**	
	A_2	14.8	1.5	379	14.4	1.5	248		3.27**
Inhalants	A_1	13.0	2.1	534	13.3	1.9	253	−0.67	
	A_2	13.1	2.2	354	13.0	2.2	137		.45

Over-the-Counter	A_1	14.1	2.0	122	14.0	2.2	106	.36	
	A_2	14.6	1.6	55	14.3	2.3	63		.83
Phencyclidine	A_1	14.7	1.5	530	14.4	1.4	332	2.98**	
	A_2	14.9	1.4	356	14.8	1.4	216		.83
Other	A_1	14.0	3.0	32	13.3	4.0	11	.53	
	A_2	14.8	3.3	20	14.3	1.4	6		.54

$-t$ = earlier age of first use by males
$+t$ = earlier age of first use by females
* = significant at .05 level of confidence
** = significant at .01 level of confidence
A_1 = Age of first use
A_2 = Age of first continuing use

Table 14-10
National Youth Polydrug Study. Phencyclidine Use by Region

	Ever Used Phencyclidine		*Never Used Phencyclidine*		*Row*	*Total*
Region	*n*	*Row %*	*n*	*Row %*	*n*	*Col. %*
Great Lakes	270	(46.6)	309	(53.4)	579	(21.1)
Midwest	116	(46.4)	134	(53.6)	250	(9.1)
Southeast	153	(31.5)	333	(68.5)	486	(17.7)
West Coast	67	(27.2)	179	(72.8)	246	(8.9)
Northeast	191	(24.2)	599	(75.8)	790	(28.7)
Southwest	72	(23.8)	230	(76.2)	302	(11.0)
Northwest	7	(7.2)	90	(92.8)	97	(3.5)
Totals	876	(31.9)	1,874	(68.1)	2,750	(100)

Predicting Regular Use of PCP. The variables employed in constructing the profile of the PCP users were also used to predict regular use of PCP. Clients were divided into two groups: regular PCP users (those using PCP at least once a week for a period of at least 1 month) and those who did not use PCP at all. Clients who had used PCP minimally but never at a frequency of at least once per week for a period of 1 month were excluded from this analysis. The analysis is composed of two steps: the first is a bivariate correlation of all the variables included in the analysis, and the second is a step-wise multiple regression in which the dependent variable is the regular use of PCP and the independent variables are a subset of the variables appearing in the correlation.

The bivariate correlation of the variables employed to predict regular PCP use showed that the strongest association between regular use of PCP is with the number of substances regularly used ("Regsum"), $r = .63$. Since it seems reasonable to consider the relationship of demographic and other variables to PCP use separately from the question of how many other drugs the subject has used, we did not include this variable, "Regsum," in the equation of the step-wise multiple regression. The other background variables accounted for 16.8 percent of the variance in the differentiation of the regular PCP users from the nonusers. It might therefore be said that it provides only one-sixth of the information that would be needed to predict accurately to regular PCP use. The rank order of these variables, according to their relative abilities to predict to regular PCP use, is as follows: (1) race, (being white) accounts for 9.1 percent of the variance; (2) the number of times the client got drunk was the next variable in the equation, and it added 2.5 percent to the explained variance after controlling for race; (3) the number of ODs added 2.0 percent to the explained variance after controlling for the two previously indicated variables; (4) the number of obstacles to school attendance added 1.2 percent to the explained variance after controlling for the previously listed variables; (5) age added 1 percent; (6) suburban residence (versus living in an urban or rural location) added 0.4 percent.

The variables that did not enter into the equation to a statistically significant degree in explaining or predicting regular PCP use were sex, socioeconomic status, education, the number of months employed in the last 2 years, intactness of the family, and the number of suicide attempts. Some of these variables did not enter into the equation since they are significantly correlated with variables that had already been entered into the regression equation. For example, SES and employment are related to being white (race) and living in the suburbs (residence). Suicide attempts may have been excluded from the equation since they are correlated with ODs ($r = .15$). Education, which is highly related to age, was not included in the regression for the same reason. However, the sex variable was excluded from the regression equation because it was not associated with regular use of PCP. There is no difference between the sexes in their predisposition to be regular users of PCP.

The PCP User in the NYPS: A Summary. The preceding review of PCP use in the NYPS indicates that the spread of this substance into the youth population occurs primarily among the white suburban population and that PCP has not as yet reached the same level of use within the inner city or among the underprivileged minorities. PCP is being added to an already existing pattern of multiple-substance use and is not used by youths who do not use other drugs.

Two thirds of those young clients in the NYPS who ever tried PCP used it at least weekly. PCP is more likely to be used by clients who have a previous history of treatment either for substance use or emotional problems. Self-destructive behavior is also much more prevalent among PCP users as compared with nonusers. The PCP users were also found to have a more extensive involvement in the criminal justice system and more dysfunction in the education system. Finally, the PCP users were found to be characterized by their low level of heroin use. Whether the dependence of adults on heroin is also associated with a lower prevalence of PCP, as found among youths, is yet to be determined.

Hospital-Based Youth Study

We conducted a study of 179 youthful (aged 12 to 18 years) phencyclidine users seen at one county hospital in the San Francisco Oakland area between 1968 and 1976. During the 8-year period, the majority of these patients (76.3 percent) were males with a mean age of 16.8 years. The races represented were 96.1 percent Caucasian, 2.8 percent black, and 0.6 percent were Asian. A large portion of these patients were transported to the hospital by public transportation. The majority were brought to the emergency room by police vehicle (43.0

percent) or ambulance (31.8 percent). In most cases these patients were accompanied by police (39.1 percent), emergency service attendants (32.4 percent), parents (11.7 percent), friends (5.0 percent), and rarely by drug treatment staff (2.8 percent).

Reasons for hospital contact were primarily treatment (75.4 percent), a medical check for juvenile hall (12.3 percent), public service evaluation (4.5 percent), or a medical check for police (3.9 percent). In most cases these phencyclidine users were retained for observation (43.6 percent), admitted to the emergency room (35.2 percent), or admitted to a service (2.2 percent). Only 16.8 percent of these patients were immediately checked and released. At the time of hospital contact, 49.2 percent of the patients were disoriented, 31.8 percent were uncooperative, and 26.8 percent were either awake with decreased consciousness or stuporous or comatose.

The majority of these patients (80.4 percent) had taken only phencyclidine prior to hospital presentation. The most popular substance taken in combination with phencyclidine was alcohol (15.1 percent), followed by barbiturates (1.1 percent).

Among this youthful population, forty-three (24.0 percent) were chronic users of phencyclidine. These patients qualified as chronic users by having taken phencyclidine on a regular basis for greater than a 6-month period with multiple hospital admissions for phencyclidine-related problems. The youngest chronic user was a 15-year-old female.

Similarities in Drug Study Findings

A number of consistent patterns appear from an analysis of the data from the DAWN, NYPS, and our studies on phencyclidine. First, there is an overrepresentation of Caucasian phencyclidine users, with Caucasians accounting for more than 90 percent of all identified patients. This trend is observed in all the major data sources. However, it should be noted that in certain geographic areas, phencyclidine use appears to be limited to specific groups such as blacks (Washington, D.C. and Watts) and Mexican Americans (San Jose).

The majority of the individuals report the "psychic effects" as their primary reason for continued use of phencyclidine. Among all individuals exposed to this drug, approximately 23 percent become chronic users. Males represent the highest number of chronic users as well as hospital room emergency room contacts for problems related to phencyclidine. Phencyclidine users utilize and apparently need more medical treatment services than other drug users.

Problems Seen Where Phencyclidine is Continuously Available

As the availability of phencyclidine increases in a community, there is a direct relationship between the number of emergency room contacts and community problems, such as driving under the influence and violent and bizarre behavior—behavioral toxicity.

In San Jose, California, the police department has gathered data on phencyclidine seizures for the past 3 years. During the first quarter of 1975 (January-March), 69.7 grams of phencyclidine were confiscated. The following year during the same period, 125.1 grams of illegal material were collected. For the first quarter of 1977, 3,951 grams of phencyclidine have been recovered. In 1976 for the first quarter, there were 69 patients treated for phencyclidine-related problems, whereas in 1977, 100 patients were seen during this same period.

New problems have surfaced in communities (Alameda, Santa Clara, and Los Angeles) in direct proportion to the frequency and regularity of phencyclidine abuse. Violent and bizarre behavior is seen in the home, in public places, and in schools, often disrupting education. Young people exhibit unexplained speech problems, memory loss, thinking disorders, personality changes, anxiety, severe depression, and suicidal and homicidal tendencies. An increasing number of young people appearing violent, bizarre, unresponsive, extremely confused, or acutely psychotic are being seen in local emergency rooms. With increased use of phencyclidine an upsurge in violent crimes that culminate in homicide are observed.

Police report erratic driving and inappropriate behavior following automobile accidents in individuals who have no apparent evidence of alcohol or sedative-hypnotic ingestion. On toxicological examination, only the isolated presence of phencyclidine is often discovered. Young people who are observed to be highly intoxicated in public are often arrested for sale, possession, and being under the influence of phencyclidine. In addition, an increasing number of referrals by family, friends, and the criminal justice system are made to community drug-abuse programs in an effort to deal with this new drug problem.

The following are typical cases that illustrate the problems seen in youths on phencyclidine.

Case 1

A 15-year-old Caucasian male was found by police in a field with no clothes on, hanging on to a barbed-wire fence. He was distorted and incoherent upon questioning. A physical examination revealed a confused, disoriented youth with inflamed eyes, bloody mouth with an upper incisor missing, multiple scratches of the trunk, and scratches and lacerations of extremities. Fluctuations in orientation were observed over the next 7 hours ranging from cooperative and alert to unarousable. Prior to being discharged the patient stated that he "smoked some phencyclidine and got awfully stoned."

Case 2

A 17-year-old Caucasion male arrested by police who had allegedly ingested several phencyclidine joints and over a 1-hour-and-45-minute period became progressively uncommunicative and withdrawn. The youth was transported from jail to a local emergency room. On admission he was observed lying quietly, eyes wide open with a broad smile on his face. Although responsive to commands, he was only able to mouth words rather than speak. When ipecaced he vomited green parsley flakes. Over the next 6 hours he alternated between quietly staring at the ceiling to being abusive, agitated, combative, and fighting restraints. Upon regaining normal orientation, he was observed for an additional 2 hours and released.

Case 3

An 18-year-old Caucasian male ingested tablets and capsules in his possession prior to a police traffic stop. Immediately after the officers departed he was driven to an apartment where the other occupants of the automobile induced vomiting of what they believed was all the ingested material. Later he began screaming and having convulsions. He was driven to a local hospital where he was pronounced dead on arrival. The coroner ruled that death was caused by aspiration of gastric contents due to phencyclidine ingestion. Phencyclidine was the only drug found on toxicological examination.

Case 4

A 15-year-old Caucasian male reported to be "out of hand" was seen earlier in the month at a local medical center for bizarre behavior. He had been involved with drugs and talked about "getting it all over." He was found hanging by an electrical cord from a beam in his garage. Toxicological examination revealed a phencyclidine blood level of 0.10 μg/ml. No other drugs were detected.

Case 5

During the summer, a youth gave a pool party while his parents were away on vacation. A 17-year-old Caucasian female guest was discovered at the bottom of the swimming pool. Postmortem examination revealed no head or neck trauma and the isolated presence of phencyclidine in the urine (0.5 μg/ml).

Case 6

Distressed over a college setback, a 17-year-old Caucasian male snorted phencyclidine for the first time with friends. He lost consciousness became apneic and cyanotic. On admission to the emergency room, this semiconscious patient was agitated, had writhing movements of all extremities, vomited, and had copious nasal and oral secretions. Within 3 hours he appeared alert; 3 hours later he was cooperative and completely oriented.

Case 7

A 16-year-old Caucasian female smoked "a crystal joint" while at school and began acting bizarre. School authorities notified her mother, who brought her to a local hospital. On admission she was dazed and unable to recall who gave her the drug or how much she had taken. The patient was oriented to person and place. A blood sample taken on admission was negative for sedative-hypnotics. Urine obtained at the same time for toxicology was positive only for phencyclidine, with a value of 0.5 μg/ml. The patient became fully oriented 2½ hours later and was discharged.

Case 8

A 16-year-old male, acting belligerent and combative, was brought to the hospital from a party where he had smoked "crystal" and drank beer. On admission he was drowsy but responsive to verbal stimuli. There was an abrasion on his right arm and face. Over the next 3 hours he became verbally abusive, belligerent, and uncooperative and was transferred to the county hospital. Initially violent, he alternated between periods of sleep to moaning. Toxicology screen obtained at this time revealed a phencyclidine urine value of 1.1 μg/ml. Over the next 15½ hours the patient became alert and oriented and was subsequently discharged.

In addition to hospital presentations for complications related to phencyclidine intoxication, there recently have been several homicides committed by youths in which phencyclidine was implicated (San Jose and Los Angeles, California; Las Vegas, Nevada; Kansas City, Kansas). The defense attorneys in the majority of cases claim that their clients were not guilty either by diminished capacity or by reason of insanity (drug-induced psychoses). With bizarre and violent behavior and with defendants claiming amnesia to the event—given the unique properties of phencyclidine and the circumstances of many of these deaths—it appears that the legal issues raised will require further debate and study.

Deaths

A large number of deaths have occurred in association with phencyclidine intoxication. In the majority of cases the immediate cause of death was asphyxia by drowning or trauma, circumstantial evidence suggesting that death was secondary to the "behavioral toxicity" of phencyclidine. The user could not indicate where his limbs were in relation to three-dimensional space or could not respond appropriately to imminent danger. Other individuals have been found dead from no apparent cause, the presence of phencyclidine in high concentrations constituting the only positive finding. The most probable cause of death in high-dose phencyclidine intoxication is primarily respiratory depression.

Phencyclidine users report going swimming while intoxicated because they experience an unusual but pleasant sensation from the water. Sensory disturbances, incoordination, and muscle rigidity resulting from "street" doses of phencyclidine may seriously interfere with the user's ability to swim, drive, climb at heights, and flee from a fire or sense imminent danger.

Suicide by self-inflicted trauma or a massive oral overdose of phencyclidine has occurred in the chronic user who became moody or severely depressed. It is the chronic user who is in possession of large amounts of phencyclidine. Threatening behavior or violence has resulted in provoked homicide.

Blood levels of phencyclidine as low as .10 μg/ml may be associated with behavioral effects leading to death by injury or trauma. Levels greater than 1.0 μg/ml are associated in most individuals with coma and may result in death secondary to medical complications or respiratory depression and seizures. Doses of 2.0 to 2.5 μg/ml and greater are probably uniformly fatal, producing primary respiratory depression and seizures.

Phencyclidine deaths nationally appear to be on the increase. In Los Angeles alone the coroner's office reported twenty phencyclidine-related deaths during 1976 and sixty-six deaths during 1977.

Chronic Phencyclidine Use

A study of phencyclidine use designed to describe *chronic use patterns* and to determine evidence of chronic toxicity was carried out by the authors in the San Francisco Bay area in February 1975. Individuals who had been treated on several occasions for phencyclidine "overdose" at music concerts were invited to participate. They in turn brought other known phencyclidine users into the study and, in particular, friends who had used the excessive amounts over the longest period of time. The final study group of twenty had used phencyclidine regularly (3 or more days per week) over a period greater than 6 months without concurrent, heavy, extensive use of other drugs. Phencyclidine was present in the urine samples obtained both on the initial and follow-up visits. The fifteen male and five female chronic users ranged in age from 20 to 43 years old, with a mean age of twenty-five. All were Caucasian. Eighteen (90 percent) were single and nineteen (95 percent) had a heterosexual preference.

The mean age at first use was 19.2 years, with ten (50 percent) individuals 18 years or younger. The majority (80 percent) had first used phencyclidine between 1967 and 1970 at 15 to 21 years of age, with a second group (20 percent) starting in 1972 and 1973.

Most users were introduced to phencyclidine by friends (85 percent) in a social setting, and took the drug out of curiosity (55 percent) or to get "high" (45 percent). Within 1 year, ten (50 percent) were using phencyclidine regularly, 3 or more days per week—and by 3 years, 75 percent used phencyclidine regularly.

The cumulative period of regular use from first exposure to the time of the study ranged from 6 months to 5½ years, with a mean of 27½ months. The longest period of daily or almost daily use (5 or more days per week) averaged 10.3 months, and maximum abstinence averaged 5.9 months. The period of recent uninterrupted use of phencyclidine prior to the study averaged 9.9 months. Two to four times per month, users would go on 2- to 3-day "runs," taking phencyclidine repeatedly without sleeping. Seventy percent continued to use marihuana, and 50 percent used alcohol on a regular basis during their use of phencyclidine.

By 1972, the availability on the illicit market in amounts of 1 gram or more of nearly pure phencyclidine allowed for the individual preparation of joints of chosen strength, guaranteeing a more long-term or continual supply for the user. With possession of large amounts of phencyclidine, users started taking the drug on a regular basis.

The razor shavings from the "rock" crystal or the powder are sprinkled on parsley and smoked in the form of a joint. The amount of street-purchased material used in the preparation of one joint varies from 50 mg for a "street" joint to about 100 mg for a "regular" or "good" joint. Up to ¼ gram was used in a "killer-diller," "heavy," or "party" joint which is often shared by many people. The primary mode of taking phencyclidine was by smoking (90 percent) or snorting (10 percent). All the chronic users had taken phencyclidine at least once by smoking. The majority had also snorted it (75 percent) and taken it by mouth (60 percent). Only six (30 percent) individuals had used phencyclidine intravenously. Five of the six used it intravenously not more than five times.

Smokers reported using the equivalent of one to two street joints or about 80 mg of street-purchased material two to three times per day. The average daily intake was about 216 mg by smoking. The reported maximum amounts used in a 24-hour period ranged from ¼ to 1 gram and averaged 500 mg. The two individuals who regularly snorted phencyclidine estimated the two "lines" dose to be about 5 mg of street-purchased material. They would snort the drug four to six times per day. These two individuals toward the end of a prolonged period of daily use of phencyclidine would place amounts of up to ¼ gram of powder layered with parsley, or as a crystal in a pipe, and smoke it in one sitting.

Phencyclidine users reported that the subjective effects "come on" within 1 to 5 minutes of smoking a typical "street" joint and reach a "peak" or a "plateau" over a 5- to 30-minute period. They report staying "loaded" or "high" for 4 to 6 hours, followed by the "come-down" which lasts 6 to 24 hours after taking the drug. Following a 2- to 3-day "run," the time required before the user felt normal again took approximately 48 hours to 1 week. A more rapid onset of 30 seconds to 1 minute followed insufflation of a "street" dose of the powdered form. The time course of the subjective effects otherwise did not appear to differ.

The Phencyclidine Experience and Why It Is Repeated

Eighty percent of the chronic users considered their first phencyclidine experience to be pleasant and wanted to take the drug again. They found it "fun" or "exhilarating" and felt "happy" or "euphoric." It seemed to be a "perfect escape" or a "dream world." Fifteen percent disliked their first experience, feeling "scared" or finding it "terrible," while one individual (5 percent) characterized the experience as "strange" and "weird, but interesting." In 95 percent of the cases, first use occurred in a social setting, with 70 percent smoking and sharing a joint at a party or with a small group of friends (mean of five) at someone's house. Four users (20 percent) related minor injuries, repeated vomiting, or arrests by the police as problems occurring with the first use. Three of these individuals had either snorted phencyclidine or taken it by mouth.

The phencyclidine "high" was reported to be very intense, several times stronger than marihuana, and comparable to LSD but shorter in duration. Most individuals compared it with LSD, but insisted that it was different or "in a class by itself." The drug had a pronounced effect on the subject's thinking, time perception, and sense of reality and mood. Thinking was described as "speeded" or "wired," the mind going faster while time was slowed down, with "no more reality." Everything was reported as being different, in another dimension, and seen from a new point of view. Life was dramatized as a fantasy world where "you don't have to dream, your wishes are fulfilled," and "what you want to happen comes true."

Everything was felt to be complete and make more sense. The mind could focus on one thing and see beauty in the smallest thing. A sense of community, a oneness with others and animals, was reported. Religious thoughts and the experience of death were frequently mentioned. Mood states were also intensified, with users in most cases feeling happy or euphoric, although everyone had also experienced severe depression and had recognized the drug's potential for bringing one to either "the heights or the depths of their being." Music was "absorbed," light was "felt," and space and depth were "distorted," "seen in 2-D." Frequently users reported feeling like they were "floating." Rarely did they relate visual hallucinations.

Users also experienced a feeling of strength and endurance. They described feeling "powerful," "superior," "arrogant," with "bursts of energy," "like God was with you, and you could move mountains." There was also a loss of inhibitions. It was felt to be difficult to do things, one had "to think about moving or talking." In addition, they described feeling restless and nervous.

Chronic use of phencyclidine took place in a social setting with the sharing of joints. Individuals would go to a friend's house, join in with two to five others, or stay at home. The membership of a group who shared in the use of phencyclidine remained quite stable over long periods of regular use. They would listen to music, talk, dance, and enjoy sex together while "high." Less often, they would go to a rock concert or out in public. They took phencyclidine as frequently during the daytime as in the evening.

The majority (60 percent) continued to use phencyclidine because they enjoyed or liked the "high." Frequently, all their friends used phencyclidine and "it had become a lifestyle." At times the availability of phencyclidine or making money from phencyclidine sales played a role. For 80 percent of the users, phencyclidine was their drug of choice. Three individuals preferred heroin, and one preferred Seconal. Nonavailability, incarceration, or hospitalization were the major factors interrupting the regular use of phencyclidine. Participation in a drug treatment program or moving out of the area program also interrupted the pattern of phencyclidine use.

Tolerance, Psychological Dependence, and Side Effects

Tolerance to the psychic effects of phencyclidine was reported by chronic users. Initially they would get "high" after two or three puffs on a phencyclidine joint; following a 1-week period of daily use, they required one-half to one joint. After smoking for a period of 2 to 6 weeks, most individuals used one or two joints at a time. Some users reported being able to smoke up to ¼ gram of street-purchased material at one sitting, following several months of regular, daily use. Psychological dependence, described as craving, was noted by chronic users, but no withdrawal symptoms were reported.

Phencyclidine taken in typical "street" doses was reported to prevent sleep for 8 to 12 hours, decrease appetite, and cause constipation and urinary hesitancy. Chronic users averaged one meal or less per day and lost 10 to 35 pounds of body weight during periods of regular use.

Chronic Toxicity

Chronic phencyclidine users reported persistent problems with memory and speech and difficulty with thinking following long periods of regular use of the drug. Recent memory capability appears to be primarily affected. Users complain of stuttering, inability to speak, or blocking, and difficulty with articulation. Speech and memory difficulties lasted as long as 6 months to 1 year following prolonged daily use of large doses of phencyclidine.

Several chronic users complained of anxiety or nervousness during and following periods of regular phencyclidine use and sought psychiatric care. Some individuals became severely depressed and attempted suicide on repeated occasions after chronic exposure to phencyclidine. Chronic users reported personality change, social withdrawal, social isolation, and divorce from their use of phencyclidine. In some cases violent behavior was one of the effects.

Employment has been lost and education disrupted as a result of the effects of the drug with chronic patterns of phencyclidine use. Frequent arrests for being under the influence of phencyclidine or in possession result in a criminal status.

Chronic phencyclidine use has culminated in a picture of violent and aggressive behavior, paranoia, delusional thinking, and auditory hallucinations. In most cases, no known behavioral disturbance or psychiatric problems preceded phencyclidine use. The individual had used phencyclidine over several months or a few years with the same group of friends. For no apparent reason a sudden development of paranoia and auditory hallucinations were accompanied by violent, unpredictable behavior. Friends and family often became fearful and brought the user to medical attention.

The Acute States of Phencyclidine Intoxication

History and Presentation

The spectrum of signs and symptoms and the pattern of recovery in acute intoxication with phencyclidine varies with the dose and route of administration. Individuals are most frequently brought to a hospital emergency room when found unresponsive or when exhibiting bizarre or violent behavior. Others are brought in after having been observed to be grossly incoordinated, driving erratically, or acting inappropriately after an automobile accident. Some individuals present with minor or major trauma.

Clinical Picture and Course

A confusional-state delirium lasting less than 8 hours appears to follow a typical street dose after smoking one "joint." Individuals who either smoke greater amounts or take a higher dose orally or by snorting may present in stupor or coma. This initial state lasts less than 3 hours in most cases and a confusional dose-related state follows for 24 to 72 hours. Massive oral "overdose" involving up to 1 gram of street-purchased material have resulted in periods of stupor or coma of several hours to 2 weeks in duration. This initial stage is followed by a prolonged recovery with a confusional state persisting for up to 2 weeks.

The confusional-state delirium induced by phencyclidine is characterized by immobility and a "blank stare" appearance in a patient who is noncommunicative. The patient is disoriented and apprehensive, becoming easily agitated or excited. These patients are grossly ataxic and exhibit horizontal and vertical nystagmus and catalepsy on testing. Muscle rigidity may be present. Most patients are communicative within 1 to 2 hours and appear alert, oriented, and exhibit normal behavior within 5 hours of admission to the emergency room.

In phencyclidine stupor or coma, the eyes may remain open, although the patient is responsive only to deep pain. Hypertension and tachycardia are present, and in all but the more massive oral "overdoses," respiration is normal. The pupils are initially miotic but reactive to light. Spontaneous nystagmus, "purposeless" movements, facial grimacing, and muscle rigidity on stimulation are characteristic findings. Repeated episodes of vomiting, increased bronchial and oral secretions, and profuse diaphoreses are frequently observed. An initial stage of stupor or coma lasting less than 4 hours may be followed by a period of confusion or delirium lasting up to 2½ days.

Massive oral "overdoses" involving up to 1 gram of street-purchased material have resulted in periods of coma of 6 hours to 5 days in duration. Delayed and prolonged hypoventilation associated with irregular respirations or apnea requiring ventilatory assistance may occur. Generalized motor seizures may be seen early or a few days after admission and are preceded by muscle tremors, muscle twitching, decerebrate rigidity, and opisthotonic posturing.

These cases are also marked by sustained hypertension and tachycardia. Coma and stupor are characteristically followed by a prolonged recovery period lasting up to 2 weeks, marked by a fluctuating confusion, disorientation, apprehension, agitation, and anarthria. The patient may be alert and oriented at one moment and difficult to arouse several minutes later.

Persistent irritability, emotional lability, hostility, and depression following the confusional phase of acute phencyclidine intoxication have necessitated psychiatric care in many cases. A persistent psychosis manifested by either paranoia with aggressive and violent behavior or severe depression with suicidal ideation has required extended psychiatric hospitalization for up to several weeks in some cases. The persistent phencyclidine psychosis is not accompanied by hypertension, tachycardia, ataxia, or nystagmus. In most cases the persistent psychosis followed initial recovery from a large oral "overdose."

Clinical problems associated with acute phencyclidine intoxication include respiratory depression, aspiration pneumonitis, generalized motor seizures, hypertensive crisis, hyperpyrexia, and myoglobinuria resulting in renal failure.

Laboratory and Toxicological Findings

Laboratory screening frequently reveals an increased white blood count (up to 20,000) an elevated CPK (up to 20,000 units +), and the presence of ketones in the urine. The electroencephalogram may reveal diffuse theta or, in some cases, theta and delta slowing.

Serum levels of 54 to 230 mg/ml have been found in six acutely confused patients who by history smoked parsley "joints" containing phencyclidine within 6 hours. In four cases of acute intoxication with a confusional state on admission and a history of smoking one joint, urine phencyclidine levels of 0.4 to 2.1 μg/ml were found in samples obtained within 4 hours of admission.

Coma with mild respiratory depression has been associated with plasma concentrations of phencyclidine between 190 and 220 mg/ml. Patients in coma with severe respiratory depression and seizures who eventually recovered have been associated with phencyclidine serum or blood levels of 340 to 530 μg/ml.

Urine phencyclidine levels of 26.2 to 151.9 μg/ml were found in samples collected within 12 hours of admission in four patients who remained in coma for longer than 6 hours and required between 7 and 15 days for recovery to normal. Status epilepticus followed by cardiopulmonary arrest without recovery has been reported with a blood phencyclidine level of 7.0 g/ml.

Diagnosis

Drug use is frequently considered to be the etiology when a young person presents acutely confused or delirious with no focal neurological findings. But encephalitis, head injury, postictal state, and metabolic causes must not be ruled out. The "blank stare" appearance and catatonia/catalepsy appear to be unique to phencyclidine as effects of commonly abused drugs. The absence of mydriases and the presence of ataxia and nystagmus rule out the central nervous system stimulants and LSD when considering the acutely excited and confused patient.

In coma with or without respiratory depression, hypertension and hyperreflexia differentiate phencyclidine intoxication from a sedative-hypnotic overdose. If, in addition, decerebrate posturing or repetitive generalized seizure activity is observed, phencyclidine intoxication should be suspected—although other serious causes producing a similar clinical picture must not be ruled out. Cases involving the ingestion of large doses of phencyclidine present with coma, which may last several hours or days. The prolonged recovery with a confusional state lasting up to 2 weeks is characteristic of phencyclidine intoxication. If persistent paranoid or depressive psychosis follows recovery, phencyclidine intoxication should be suspected.

In combined intoxications involving phencyclidine and barbiturates, normal or low blood pressure, hyporeflexia, and respiratory depression may be observed.

Management

The acutely confused patient is best managed by sensory isolation with observation at a distance. Minimizing verbal and tactile stimulation does not preclude the monitoring of vital signs. Important functions to monitor are respiration, blood pressure, muscle tone and activity, renal function, and temperature. Ideally, the patient would be placed on a cushioned floor in a "quiet room" with a monitor present. In most settings, protection of the patient and staff necessitates the use of restraints.

The early management of the stuporous or comatose patient involves gastric aspiration-lavage and nasopharyngeal suctioning. In view of the recovery of large amounts of phencyclidine from the stomach contents in fatal overdoses, gastric lavage is indicated in oral ingestions.

Intubation is often difficult because of increased muscle tone. Larygeal reflexes are maintained and active, and attempted endotracheal intubation may precipitate laryngospasm. More responsive patients fight intubation by biting the tube off or spitting it out. However, respiratory depression may be delayed in appearance and necessitate a prolonged period of ventilatory assistance. Positioning and intermittent suctioning will preclude respiratory distress secondary to secretions in the posterior pharnyx.

Urine and blood samples should be collected at the time of admission and screened for phencyclidine, sedative-hypnotics, ethyl alcohol, opiates, and amphetamines. Urine samples should be capped to prevent loss of phencyclidine, which is volatile.

The Recovery Phase

Most acutely confused patients are communicative within 1 to 2 hours and alert and oriented within 6 to 8 hours of admission after ingesting the usual street dose. After they are alert and oriented, patients should be monitored for a minimum of 2 hours. Patients who remain oriented and alert and exhibit normal behavior can be discharged. If a patient remains stuporous or comatose, responding only to deep pain for greater than 2 hours, a minimal observation period of 24 hours is indicated. The recovery phase may vary from several hours to days depending on the route and the dose ingested.

Suicide has been reported during the "come down" period, from 6 to 24 hours after taking phencyclidine. Patients should be informed about depression, irritability, and the feelings of isolation and nervousness that often accompany this period and last up to 48 hours.

All patients in whom coma is followed by a prolonged period of confusion should have a psychiatric evaluation prior to discharge. Persistent paranoia or depression may require transfer to a psychiatric unit.

Treatment

No agent is known to be specific for antagonizing the toxic effects of phencyclidine. However, some experience has been gained in the symptomatic treatment of seizures, hypertensive crises, and aggressive and violent behavior.

Intravenous diazepam (Valium) in doses of 10 to 15 mg, followed by intravenous diphenylhydanton (Dilantin), has been effective in the control of seizures. In some cases it has been necessary to give an acutely confused patient 10 to 20 mg of Valium orally to prevent injury to both the patient and staff. During the confusional phase of the prolonged recovery period, some patients have received repeated doses of 10 to 15 mg of Valium to control motor restlessness and agitation. These therapeutic doses of sedative-hypnotic agents do not appear to produce significant respiratory depression in phencyclidine intoxication.

Diazoxide (Hyperstat) has been used to reduce blood pressure during a hypertensive crisis associated with acute phencyclidine intoxication. Hydralazine hydrochloride (Apresoline) has also been suggested as a possible substitute agent. In addition, recently, severely overdosed patients have been successfully treated utilizing ion trapping by continuous gastric suctioning and acidification of urine and/or blood with ammonium chloride [38,39,30].

Phenothiazines are contraindicated in acute phencyclidine intoxication where a confusional state is associated with hypertension, tachycardia, ataxia, and nystagmus. It has not been demonstrated that phenothiazines shorten the recovery phase or antagonize the behavioral effects of phencyclidine. In some cases they have produced prolonged severe hypotension.

In a relatively short period of time phencyclidine hydrochloride (PCP) has become a popular illicit street drug in the United States despite the fact that there are serious physiological and psychological dangers associated with its use, for example, acute behavioral toxicity, an anesthetized state, thought disorder, confusion, psychiatric emergency reactions, paranoia, violent outbursts, accidents, etc. First identified on the illicit market in 1965, PCP did not achieve notoriety until the midseventies, when it had spread to communities throughout the country. PCP is not readily classified as either an "upper" or a "downer," or as being a hallucinogen like LSD. It produces a different kind of "high" in those people in whom it does produce a high.

There is much to be learned from this short history of PCP and the spread of its use. We are living in a scientific age in which more and more chemical substances are being produced. Drug use has been spreading downward in age, and more people are becoming involved in multiple-substance-use patterns. Given the right set of circumstances, it is possible for any drug to find its way into the illicit market. The right circumstances did exist for PCP to become one of the most widely used drugs in our society. The National Institute on Drug Abuse estimated that in 1978, PCP had been used by more than 7 million people in the United States. The drug was associated with at least 100 deaths and over 4,000 hospital emergency room visits in 1977.

Obviously, a combination of factors contributed to the spread of PCP, including the following:

It is easily manufactured.

Manufacturing PCP can be very profitable.

It is readily available in many communities.

It is inexpensive.

There are large markets for the drug.

Users have gained experience with PCP and have learned to control the dosage.

Experienced users teach others to use it.

The dangers were largely unrecognized.

The drug produced a desirable effect for most users (80 percent of chronic users reported a pleasant first experience in one report).

PCP is used in social settings and encouraged by peers.

It is clear that our society was not prepared for the onset of PCP use and the problems associated with such use. Although we have gained considerable knowledge recently about PCP and how it is used, there is still much to be learned about the drug. The PCP phenomenon has demonstrated that there is a need for a better understanding of such substances in order to be able to predict how they can be used and how such use can spread. Communities must be prepared to respond to new drug problems and trends in a timely and appropriate manner based on knowledge and understanding, and to develop appropriate prevention and intervention strategies.

These are not easy problems to solve, but it is hoped that something useful can be applied from the experience with PCP to the problem presented by the spread of use of any new substance in the future.

Notes

1. NIDA Capsules, issued by NIDA Press Office, February 1978, C78-4.

2. The SES measure employed in this analysis was based on a formula which was especially developed for this analysis and which was found to be more discriminating than the Hollingshead-Redlich formula. It included the educational level of both parents rather than only that of the head of the household, and it also included consideration of the subject's income, and whether or not the family was on welfare, in addition to the occupational level of the head of the household.

References

[1] J.C. Munch. Phencyclidine: Pharmacology and toxicology. *Bulletin on Narcotics* 26(4), October-December 1974.

[2] G.M. Chen and J.K. Weston. The analgesic and anesthetic effect of 1-(1-phenyl-cyclohexyl)piperidine HCL on the monkey. *Anesth. Anag., Current Res.* 39(2):132, 1960.

[3] G. Chen, C.R. Ensor, D. Russell, and B. Bohner. The pharmacology of 1-1(phenylcyclohexyl)piperidine HCL. *J. Pharm. Exptl. Therap.* 127:241, 1959.

[4] G. Chen. "Evaluation of phencyclidine-type cataleptic activity. *Arch. Int. Pharmacodyn.* 157(1):193-201, 1965.

[5] E.F. Domino, P. Chodoff, and G. Corssen. Pharmacologic effects of CI-581, a new dissociative anesthetic in man. *Clin. Pharm. and Therapeutics* 6(3):279-291, 1965.

[6] G. Corssen and E.F. Domino. Dissociative anesthesia: Further pharmacologic studies and first clinical experience with the phencyclidine derivative CI-581. *Anesth. Analg., Current Res.* 45:29-40, 1966.

[7] E.F. Domino and E.D. Luby. Abnormal mental states induced by PCP as a model for schizophrenia. In J.O. Cole, A.M. Freedman, and A.J. Friedhoff (eds.), *Psychopathology and Psychopharmacology*, Baltimore, Md.: Johns Hopkins Univ. Press, 1972, pp. 37-50.

[8] E.F. Domino. Neurobiology of PCP (sernyl), a drug with an unusual spectrum of pharmacological activity. *Int. Rev. Neurobiol.*, 6:303, 1964.
[9] E.D. Luby, B.D. Cohen, G. Rosenbaum, J.S. Gottlieb, and R. Kelly. Study of a new schizophrenomimetic drug–sernyl. *Archives of Neurology and Psychiatry* 81:363-369, March 1959.
[10] B.M. Davies and H.R. Beech. The effect of 1-arylcyclohexylamine (sernyl) on twelve normal volunteers. *Journal of Mental Science* 106:912-924, July 1960.
[11] H.R. Beech, B.M. Davies, and F.S. Morgenstern. Preliminary investigations of the effects of sernyl upon cognitive and sensory processes. *Journal of Mental Science*, 107:509-513, May 1961.
[12] B.M. Davies. Oral sernyl in obsessive states. *Journal of Mental Science*, 107:109-114, January 1961.
[13] F.E. Greifenstein, J. Yoshitake, M. DeVault, and J.E. Gajewski. A study of 1-aryl cyclo hexyl amine for anesthesia. *Anesth. and Analg., Current Res.* 37(5):283, 1958.
[14] C. Chen, C.R. Ensor, and B. Bohner. The neuropharmacology of 2-(0-chlorohphnyl)-2-methylamino-cyclohexanone hydrochloride. *J. Pharmacol. Exp. Ther.* 152:332, 1966.
[15] V.J. Collins, C.A. Gorospe, and E.A. Rovenstine. Intravenous nonbarbiturate, nonnarcotic analgesics: Preliminary studies. 1. Cyclohexylamines. *Anest. Analg. Current Res.* 39, 302-306, 1960.
[16] P. Luisada and C. Reddick. An Epidemic of Drug-Induced Schizophrenia. wPaper presented at the 128th Annual Meeting of the American Psychiatric Association, Anaheim, California, May 5-9, 1975.
[17] R.L. Balster and L.D. Chait. The behavioral pharmacology of phencyclidine. *Clinical Toxicology* 9(4):513-528, 1976.
[18] R.L. Balster. Personal communication.
[19] R.E. Ober, G.W. Gwynn, D.A. McCarthy, and A.J. Glazko. Metabolism of 1-(1-phenylcyclohexyl)piperidine(sernyl). *Federation Proceedings* 22(2):539, 1963.
[20] A.J. Glazko. Identification of chloramphenicol metabolites and some factors affecting metabolic disposition. *Antimicrobial Agents Chemotherapy–1966.* American Society for Microbiology, pp. 660-661, 1967.
[21] D.C. Lin, A.F. Fentiman, R.L. Foltz, R.D. Forney, and I. Sunshine. Quantification of phencyclidine in body fluids by gas chromatography chemical ionization mass spectrometry and identification of two metabolites. *Biomedical Mass Spectrometry* 2:206-214, 1975.
[22] S.H. James and S.H. Schnoll. Phencyclidine: Issue distribution in the rat. *Clinical Toxicology* 9(4):573-582, 1976.
[23] P.C. Reynolds. Clinical and forensic experiences with phencyclidine. *Clinical Toxicology* 9(4):547-552, 1976.
[24] W.D. MacLeod, Jr., D.E. Green, and E. Seet. Automated analysis of phencyclidine in urine by probability based matching gc/ms. *Clinical Toxicology* 9(4):561-572, 1976.

[25] G.D. Lundberg, R.C. Gupta, and S.H. Montgomery. Phencyclidine: Patterns seen in street-drug analysis. *Clinical Toxicology* 9(4):503-511, 1976.

[26] B. Radcliff. Personal communication.

[27] D.C. Perry. PCP revisited. *PharmChem Newsletter* 4(9):1-7, 1975.

[28] R.S. Burns, S.E. Lerner, R. Corrado, S.H. James, and S.H. Schnoll. Phencyclidine–States of acute intoxication and fatalities. *The Western Journal of Medicine* 123(5):345-349, November 1975.

[29] R.S. Burns and S.E. Lerner. Perspectives: Acute phencyclidine intoxication. *Proceedings of the 38th Annual Scientific Meeting, Committee on Problems of Drug Dependence.* National Academy of Sciences, Richmond, Virginia, 1976, pp. 552-574.

[30] A.K. Done, R. Aronow, and J.N. Micelli. Diagnosis and management of phencyclidine toxicity. *Emergency Medicine,* 10:180-181, May 1978.

[31] R.S. Burns and S.E. Lerner. Management and treatment of acute phencyclidine intoxications. In P.E. Bourne (ed.), *Acute Drug Abuse Emergencies: A Treatment Manual.* New York: Academic, 1976, pp. 297-305.

[32] S.E. Lerner and R.S. Burns. Phencyclidine returns. In K. Blum, S.J. Feinglass, A.H. Briggs, et al. (eds.), *The Social Meaning of Drugs: Principles of Social Pharmacology*, New York: Harper and Row (*in press*).

[33] A.T. Shulgin and D. MacLean. Illicit synthesis of phencyclidine (PCP) and several of its analogs. *Clinical Toxicology* 9(4):553-560, 1976.

[34] Drug Enforcement Administration. Personal communication, June 5, 1975.

[35] C. Helisten and A.T. Shulgin. The detection of 1-piperidino-cyclohexanecarbonitrile (PCC) contamination in illicit preparations of PCP (1-(1-phenylcyclohexyl)-piperidine) and TCP (1-(2-thienyl)-cyclohexyl)-piperidine). *J. Chromatogr.* 117:232, 1976.

[36] R.S. Burns and S.E. Lerner, The Crystal People: Chronic Daily Users of Phencyclidine. (*In preparation.*)

[37] D. MacLean. Personal communication.

[38] R. Aranow, J.N. Micelli, and A.K. Done. Clinical observations during phencyclidine intoxication and treatment based on ion trapping. In R. Peterson and R. Stillman (eds.), *Phencyclidine (PCP) Abuse: An Appraisal.* National Institute on Drug Abuse Monograph 21, DHEW Publication No. (ADM)78-728, Washington, D.C., U.S. Government Printing Office, 1978.

[39] A.K. Done, R. Aronow, and J.N. Miceli. Pharmacokinetics of phencyclidine (PCP) in overdosage and its treatment. In R. Peterson and R. Stillman (eds.), *Phencyclidine (PCP) Abuse: An Appraisal.* National Institute on Drug Abuse Monograph 21, DHEW Publication No. (ADM)78-728, Washington, D.C., U.S. Government Printing Office, 1978.

15 Youth Opiate Use

Clyde McCoy,
Duane C. McBride,
Brian R. Ruse,
J. Bryan Page, and
Richard R. Clayton

Introduction

Recent epidemiological studies indicate that the problem of heroin abuse in this country has stabilized after peaking in the late sixties. Although these studies provide some estimate on the level of heroin use, they have serious limitations. Heroin use is a complex phenomenon. We still know little about the characteristics of heroin users, the developmental processes leading to the use of heroin, and how to identify populations at risk.

The heroin epidemic that occurred in the United States from the mid-1960s to the mid-1970s has been examined from a variety of perspectives. Numerous factors have been cited as contributing to the epidemic and the increased use of heroin by the younger white youths in our society. The Vietnam war certainly had some impact on the changing drug scene. In addition to the rapid increase in heroin addiction within the military force, the war led to social unrest in the United States. At the same time, the opium growing countries of the world continued to increase the supply of opium to the United States, which had the greatest concentration of heroin addicts in the world (estimated at 560,000 in 1971) and the most lucrative market for all kinds of opiates.[1]

Another factor often cited is the so-called generation gap—the schism between the more conservative, status quo values of adults and the anti-Establishment values of young people including the desire to escape from a materialistic reality into a state of altered consciousness. Still another factor, the impact of the post-World War II "baby boom" has generally been ignored. The postwar birth cohorts were disproportionately large and therefore account for some of the increased drug use during the epidemic, particularly among the younger cohorts.

In contrast to the earlier epidemic years, there has actually been little change in the number of heroin addicts in this country during the past several years. The latest government estimates on the number of heroin addicts in the United States (Greenwood and Crider 1978) for the years 1974 to 1977 are as follows:

Year	*Estimate*
1974	558,000
1975	546,000
1976	546,000
1977	559,000

It should be recognized that during this period (1974 to 1977), there have been a combination of forces at work at the federal, state, and local levels to reduce the supply of heroin and expand the health delivery system. There was an intensified and coordinated international drug control effort initiated in August 1971 with the establishment of the Cabinet Committee on International Narcotics Control. Supply-reduction activities were coordinated under the Drug Enforcement Administration (DEA) in July 1973. These activities included law enforcement efforts to cut off the supply of heroin to the consumer and international cooperative agreements aimed at reducing the production and processing of opium abroad.[2]

In recent years, a new trend seems to be developing: the intense societal focus on youthful heroin abuse so apparent during the epidemic period of the late sixties and early seventies has subsided. Why the dimunition of interest? Is it a result of a change in youthful drug-taking behavior? Has the average age of heroin users been increasing? If so, what accounts for this change in drug-taking behavior?

The primary purpose of this chapter is to examine these issues utilizing data produced in a study of heroin users in treatment in the Dade County, Florida area, and data pertaining to heroin-related deaths. In addition, the data will be used to assess trends in heroin-use prevalence rates, consider reasons for the changes, and explore methods of identifying populations at risk. Study of heroin use in the adolescent age group is most likely to yield clues regarding future trends in heroin use.

Sources of Data

The data presented in this chapter were collected in the city of Miami, Dade County, Florida. Miami holds a median rank in comparison to other large metropolitan areas vis-à-vis the "heroin problem index" (see Person et al 1976) and is often identified as a major port of entry for illicit drugs. The analysis will focus on the *age distribution of heroin users* in three salient populations:

1. Heroin-related admissions to drug treatment in Dade County, 1972-1977.
2. Heroin-related emergency room appearances at the Jackson Memorial Hospital, the county hospital affiliated with the University of Miami Medical Center, 1972-1976.

3. Heroin-related deaths from records of the Dade County Medical Examiner's Office, 1972-1975.

In Dade County drug treatment programs are organized under a single administrative umbrella called the Comprehensive Drug Program (CDP). Admissions to treatment are coordinated through a central medical intake facility (Weppner and McBride 1975). Information on heroin-related deaths was collected by examining records in the medical examiner's files for each year from 1972 through 1975. Emergency room data were collected by abstracting pertinent drug-use and sociodemographic information from patient records *if* the attending physician had concluded that the emergency room visit was due to use of heroin. Inciardi et al. (1978) reported that the Jackson Memorial Hospital emergency rooms accounted for about 70 percent of all heroin-related emergency room appearances in the Miami area. The data on heroin users in treatment were obtained by interviews conducted by Dade County Comprehensive Drug Program staff. The data from each of these three sources are part of the research data bank at the Center for Drug Research in the Division of Addiction Sciences at the University of Miami.

Age and Admission to Treatment for Heroin Use

A central focus of the federal response to drug abuse has been demand reduction, that is, the provision of treatment services for those who desire them or who are willing to be diverted from criminal justice systems into treatment program. More than a little of the impetus to field a nationwide treatment effort stemmed from a widely held fear that far too many American youths were abusing drugs. This fear was no doubt fueled in part by the reported accounts of heroin use among servicemen in Vietnam, the growing market for opium in the United States, and the increase in drug-related criminal activity. In fact, there was a heroin "epidemic" in the United States beginning around 1965 and continuing through 1972 (Dupont and Greene 1973; O'Donnell et al. 1976). The epidemic was more visible than it otherwise might have been because of the sheer number of young people in society relative to those in older age categories.

The data in table 15-1 show the ages of people admitted to treatment for heroin problems from 1972 through June 1977 in Dade County. The high watermark for young people was 1973 when almost one in three admissions were under the age of 21. In 1974, youth heroin admissions had dropped to a little more than one in four; in 1975, it was one in five; and by the end of the first 6 months of 1977, only 12 percent of heroin treatment admissions were under 21 years old. These figures for 1972 and before, 1973, and 1974 are not much different from those found for the 1969-1970, 1970-1971, 1971-1972, and 1972-1973 admissions reported to the Drug Abuse Reporting Program (DARP).[3] Respectively, the percentages of total DARP admissions for those

Table 15-1
Age Structure Trends in Opiate Treatment Admissions: Dade County, Florida, 1972 to June 1977

	Year of Admission											
	1972 or before *(n = 195)*		*1973* *(n = 282)*		*1974* *(n = 1,883)*		*1975* *(n = 2,924)*		*1976* *(n = 2,769)*		*Jan.-June 1977* *(n = 944)*	
16 or younger	10.8		1.8		6.5		3.8		2.2		1.9	
17-18	3.1	27.2%	10.3	32.0%	8.9	25.8%	5.1	20.2%	3.4	15.5%	2.8	12.2%
19-20	13.3		19.9		10.4		11.3		9.9		7.5	
21-24	31.8		34.4		33.8		33.3		34.5		32.7	
25-33	25.1		28.0		33.6		38.4		40.6		46.7	
34 or older	15.9		5.7		6.9		8.0		9.4		8.4	
Mean Age	22		23		23		23		24		26	
Modal Age Category	21-24		21-24		21-24		25-33		25-33		25-33	

under 21 years of age were 18, 23, 29 and 36 (Sells 1977). The average percentage for the four cohorts in DARP was 30 percent; and for the 1972, 1973, and 1974 Dade County cohorts, the overall figure was 28.8 percent under 21 years old.

The data in table 15-1 indicate quite clearly an aging of the heroin treatment population. This is seen in the reduction of the proportion of that population under 21 and in the progressive increase for those ages 25 to 33, from 25.1 percent of admissions in 1972 to 46.7 percent in 1977. It is also seen in an increase in the median age of admissions from 22 in 1972 to 26 in 1977. There are several factors that may account for the aging of the heroin treatment population in Dade County as well as in other areas of the country. First, the baby boom cohorts (born between 1946 when the boom started through 1957 when it peaked) who became heroin addicts are beginning to experience the "maturing out" phenomenon (Winick 1962). In 1977 the baby boom people would have been between the ages of 20 and 31. These age categories represent over 75 percent of the admissions in the first 6 months of 1977.

A second factor accounting for the aging of the heroin treatment population is the apparent neutralization, albeit partial, of the "classic" epidemiological process. The addicts in Miami have not been able to "infect" enough new young users to keep the median age of the treatment population stable and low. Instead, the median age of those in treatment has increased rather dramatically. In Dade County the percentage of all heroin treatment admissions with prior treatment experience has risen from 33 percent in 1974 to 71 percent in 1978. A similar trend is revealed in the data from the Client Oriented Data Acquisition Process (CODAP), the federal reporting system for drug treatment programs. From April 1973 through September 1974, the largest age category of heroin users in treatment was 21 to 25 years. For the period April through June 1977, the largest age category of heroin users in treatment was 26 to 30; more than 60 percent were 25 years of age or older (NIDA Statistical Series 1976, 1977).

School and community surveys of adolescents who are not in treatment show a similar downward trend during recent years in prevalence rates of heroin use (see chap. 2). It appears that youngsters 18 years and under are now less inclined to use heroin but more likely to be experimenting with and using a variety of other substances. Actually, increased proportions of the adolescent population are now using drugs and are starting to use them at an earlier age. Based on a national survey conducted in 1977, it was reported that 28 percent of youths aged 12 to 17 had tried marihuana, 9 percent had used inhalants, 4.6 percent hallucinogens, 5 percent stimulants, 3 percent sedatives, and 4 percent tranquilizers. Only 1 percent of the youngsters aged 12 to 17 reported ever having used heroin (Abelson et al. 1977). There are some indications that earlier prevalence rates for heroin use among school youths were higher. Among the high school seniors studied by Johnston and Bachman (1977), only 1.8 percent of the 1977 cohort had ever used heroin, compared with the same percent for the 1976 seniors and 2.2 percent for the 1975 seniors. The New York State survey of 8,206 high school students, administered in 1971-1972, yielded a heroin-use prevalence rate of 2.8 percent (Kandel et al. 1976).

The age distribution at admission to treatment and the heroin-use prevalence rates found in school and community surveys are, of course, not the only methods of determining trends in heroin use. The typical or model sequence followed in the development of heroin addiction is (1) experimental use (onset of heroin use), (2) first "continuous" use (often defined as regular use at least once per week over a period of several months), (3) daily use, or addiction, and (4) entry into treatment. For all Dade County heroin clients (June 1973 through June 1976), 34.3 percent were less than 18 years old at age of first "continuing" use, while 23.6 percent were either 19 or 20 years old. The figures for heroin arrestees in Dade County show a somewhat earlier average age of first continuing use; 57.9 percent initiated continuous use of heroin before age 19, with 16.1 percent beginning continuous use at 19 or 20 years of age.

Data from CODAP (NIDA Statistical Series 1976) and other sources indicate that a hiatus usually occurs between first continuous use of heroin and entry into treatment, a hiatus that ranges from a period of several months to as many as eight years. A relationship can be found between age at first continuing use of heroin and entry into treatment: the earlier first continuous use occurs, the longer the hiatus before entry into treatment.

Age and Treatment History of Heroin Users in Dade County

Almost 9,000 *opiate* users have been processed by the Dade County CDP for entry into treatment since the early 1970s, and for most of these (8,175), the primary drug of abuse was heroin. These heroin users account for over 60 percent of *all* clients ever in drug treatment in Miami from 1972 to 1977. As noted earlier, the ratio of *readmissions* to all admissions increased substantially—from 33 percent in 1974 to 71 percent in 1978. It is thus important that readmissions be dealt with separately from first admissions in examining how the age structure affects treatment admissions for heroin abuse. This can be seen in table 15-2.

Of the 8,175 admissions to treatment for heroin abuse in Dade County, only 4,300 (52.6 percent) are *first* admissions, meaning an average of 1.9 treatment experiences per heroin-abusing client. An examination of the percentage columns for first admissions indicates that 769 or 17.9 percent of all first admissions to heroin treatment were under 21 years old. The center percentage column indicates that only 44 percent of all who said they were 16 or younger at treatment intake for heroin abuse were *first* admissions. The percentages for first admissions vis-à-vis all admissions by age category are: 17 to 18 years old, 63.8

Table 15-2
First Admissions into Treatment for Heroin Abuse versus All Admissions for Heroin by Age

Age	*First Admissions n (%)*	*Percent First Admissions of All Admissions (%)*	*All Admissions (n)*
16 or younger	59 (1.4)	(44.0)	134
17-18	210 (4.9)	(63.8)	329
19-20	500 (11.6)	(59.5)	841
21-24	1,585 (36.9)	(55.6)	2,853
25-34	1,670 (38.8)	(49.1)	3,401
35 or older	276 (6.4)	(45.1)	612
Totals	4,300 100		8,175

percent; 19 to 20 years old, 59.5 percent; 21 to 24 years old, 55.6 percent; 25 to 34 years old, 49.1 percent; and 35 years old or older, 45.1 percent. The high percent of readmissions (66 percent) in the 16 and younger category reflects the impact of heavy drug involvement and the daily "hustle" on those who enter a deviant career early. The steady decline in percentages of first admissions for each age group over 17 to 18 years of age probably indicates that the longer one has been using heroin, the more likely it is that one has already had a prior treatment experience.

Sex and Age at First Admission to Treatment

In most treatment programs across the country, males substantially outnumber the females. In this sample from Miami the same is true. Males constitute 71.2 percent of all admissions to treatment for heroin use and 72.5 percent of the 4,300 first admissions.

The data in table 15-3 indicate that only 39.4 percent of all males 16 years of age or younger at admission to treatment were there for the first time; over six out of ten were readmissions. Almost half (49.2 percent) the females admitted at 16 years of age or younger did *not* have prior treatment experience. An examination of the other percentage figures in table 15-3 indicates that for all five other age categories, males are less likely to have had a prior treatment experience. This suggests two possibilities. First, the smaller pool of female than male heroin addicts in Miami tends to be "recycled" more often through the treatment system. It may also reflect a tendency of female addicts to move into the male heroin network and to limit their associations to other addicts, primarily male. Second, there is a quicker movement into treatment among male

Table 15-3
Age at Admission to Treatment for Heroin Abuse by Sex: First Admissions versus All Heroin Admissions

	Males			*Females*		
Age	*First Admissions (n)*	*Percent First Admissions of All Admissions (%)*	*All Admissions (n)*	*First Admissions (n)*	*Percent First Admissions of All Admissions (%)*	*All Admissions (n)*
16 or younger	28	(39.4)	71	31	(49.2)	63
17-18	127	(65.5)	194	83	(61.5)	135
19-20	343	(63.3)	542	157	(52.5)	299
21-24	1,125	(56.2)	2,003	460	(54.1)	850
25-34	1,257	(50.2)	2,503	413	(46.0)	898
35 or older	238	(46.9)	507	38	(36.2)	105
Totals	3,118	(53.5)	5,823	1,182	(50.3)	2,352

heroin users and addicts since larger proportions of admissions in each age category are first admissions. This latter possibility could be explained by the fact that male heroin users are more likely to get into the criminal justice system and thus be mandated into treatment. One of the first indications of the beginning of another epidemic would be an upsurge in young (16 or younger) female admissions to treatment for heroin.

The data in table 15-4 concern *only* first admissions to treatment for heroin abuse by sex and age at admission. An examination of the column percentages reveals a slight though consistent tendency for females to enter treatment earlier than males. For example, 22.9 percent of all females ever in treatment entered prior to age 21, while the comparable figure for males is 16 percent. By age 24, the respective cumulative percentages are 61.8 for females and 52.1 for males.

The row percentages in table 15-4 indicate the proportion of first admission to treatment for heroin abuse within age categories that were male or female. Females constitute a majority *only* in the 16 or younger category. The male proportion increases from 60.5 percent in the 17 to 18 age range to 82.6 percent in the 35 years old and older category. This means that over three out of four heroin users who first enter treatment at age 25 or later are male.

If the current state of affairs in heroin supply (that is, low heroin purity, relatively low supply of heroin, relatively high price, and relatively high costs in terms of the arrest rate) continues for an extended period, it is possible that the heroin problem will follow the down phase of the "classic" epidemiological curve. Without new and younger users attracted into addiction, the pool of addicts could get older as well as smaller because of mortality, treatment effects, and the "maturing out" phenomenon. However, given the difficulties and costs inherent in patroling a state like Florida for supply-reduction purposes, the influx of a relatively large supply of heroin with lower prices and somewhat higher purity could easily produce another generation of young heroin addicts.

Table 15-4
Heroin Users in Treatment in Dade County: Age at First Admission to Treatment by Sex

	Male			*Female*			*Total*	
Age	*Row %*	*(n)*	*Col. %*	*Row %*	*(n)*	*Col. %*	*(n)*	*Col. %*
16 or less	(47.5)	28	(0.9)	(52.5)	31	(2.6)	59	(1.4)
17-18	(60.5)	127	(4.1)	(39.5)	83	(7.0)	210	(4.9)
19-20	(68.6)	343	(11.0)	(31.4)	157	(13.3)	500	(11.6)
21-24	(71.0)	1,125	(36.1)	(29.0)	460	(38.9)	1,585	(36.9)
25-34	(75.3)	1,257	(40.3)	(24.7)	413	(34.9)	1,670	(38.8)
35 or more	(86.2)	238	(7.6)	(13.8)	38	(3.2)	276	(6.4)
Totals		3,118	(100.0)		1,182	(99.9)	4,300	(100.0)

Note: The data contain only first admissions by age and sex; readmissions have been deleted.

Race/Ethnicity and Age at First Admission to Treatment

It is not feasible to examine the relationship of race/ethnicity to age of first admission to treatment for heroin abuse without first eliminating the readmission data. These data are presented in table 15-5 for whites, blacks, and Hispanics. Several findings in table 15-5 deserve special emphasis. First, in every age category whites have the *lowest figure* for proportion of first treatment admissions. Stated differently, for every age category, white heroin users entering treatment are less likely to be first admissions than are blacks. In each age category, blacks and Hispanics are more likely by 10 to 25 percent to be first admissions. Overall, 44.3 percent of white heroin admissions were seeking treatment for the first time compared with 59.2 percent of the blacks and 55.4 percent of the Hispanics. Hispanics generally fall between whites and blacks on the ratio of first admissions to all admissions. These data imply that, compared to blacks and Hispanics, white heroin users seeking treatment are more likely to be recycled from a previous treatment population. For blacks and Hispanics in every age category (except blacks 35 and over), the majority of clients seeking treatment were entering for the first time. The data suggest that either the pool of new white heroin addicts is relatively small compared with their proportion in the general population or the recruitment of white heroin users into treatment has been relatively less successful.

It is apparent that black heroin addicts entering treatment in Dade County are more likely than their white counterparts to be first admissions. This finding may have some implications for the delivery of heroin treatment services; 57.4 percent (2,469 of over 4,300) of all first admissions were black and slightly over half of all heroin admissions and readmissions were black. An examination of the race/ethnic breakdown for first admissions under the age of 21 reveals that 58.5 percent were black, 35.4 percent were white, and 6.1 percent were Hispanic. Those figures are markedly different from the race/ethnic characteristics of youth heroin abusers in the National Youth Polydrug Sample (see chap. 7), where 68.7 percent were white, 16.3 percent were black, and 13.5 percent were Hispanic. The race/ethnic composition differences between the NYPS sample and the Dade County youth heroin abusers in treatment can possibly be attributed to regional factors and to the fact that Dade County has a central medical intake facility, while the NYPS sampled mostly treatment programs oriented toward serving youth populations.

A third finding worthy of note in table 15-5 is that 61.1 percent of all Hispanic heroin treatment admissions in the 35 years old or older category were *first* admissions. This is considerably higher than comparable figures for whites (35.9 percent) and blacks (48 percent). This suggests that Hispanics with a heroin problem may seek "public" and Anglo-dominated treatment as a last resort—something to be tried only if the Hispanic *clinicas* services were not successful. As Derbyshire (1972) has noted, immigrant populations generally are not knowledgeable about the host culture's health care system and are hostile to

Table 15-5
Race/Ethnicity and Age at Admission to Treatment: Heroin Users in Dade County, Florida, 1972-1977

	White			*Black*			*Hispanic*[a]		
	First Admissions (n)	*First Admissions of All Admissions (%)*	*All Admissions (n)*	*First Admissions (n)*	*First Admissions of All Admissions (5)*	*All Admissions (n)*	*First Admissions (n)*	*First Admissions of All Admissions (%)*	*All Admissions (n)*
16 or younger	19	(31.1)	61	36	(55.4)	65	4	(50.0)	8
17-18	65	(51.2)	127	131	(72.0)	182	14	(70.0)	20
19-20	188	(52.8)	356	282	(64.8)	435	29	(58.0)	50
21-24	564	(46.5)	1,214	911	(62.9)	1,448	109	(57.7)	189
25-34	627	(41.7)	1,505	942	(55.7)	1,692	101	(50.0)	202
35 or older	75	(35.9)	209	167	(48.0)	348	33	(61.1)	54
Totals	1,538	(44.3)	3,472	2,469	(59.2)	4,170	290	(55.4)	523

Note: The total for all admissions in this table is 8,165. A total of three whites and two blacks for whom age at admissions was unknown were dropped, as were five individuals classified as "other" in the race/ethnicity question.

[a]In the Hispanic category 148 or 51 percent are Cuban, 10.6 percent or 31 are Puerto Rican, 2 or 1 percent are Mexican, and the remainder, 109 or 37.6 percent are other Hispanic (see First Admissions column).

and suspicious of these institutions. Derbyshire found that Mexican immigrants in California were much more likely to use non-Anglo health care resources in their own communities than the Anglo institutions.

An examination of the column percentages in table 15-6 reveals only slight differences by race/ethnicity in the distribution of first admissions across the age categories. For example, 16.2 percent of Hispanic, 17.6 percent of whites, and 18.2 percent of black first admissions occur prior to age 21. Approximately three-fourths of all first admissions for heroin treatment occur between the ages of 21 and 35 for all three race/ethnic groups (77.5, 75.1, and 72.4 percent for whites, blacks, and Hispanics, respectively).

The row percentages in table 15-6 confirm that between 56.4 and 62.3 percent of first admissions in the various age categories are black. The whites account for between 27.3 and 37.7 percent of first admissions in the various age groups. The comparable percentages for Hispanics are all near 6 percent, except for the 35 and older category where they account for 12 percent of first admissions.

Age Distribution of Heroin-Related Emergency Room Appearances in Dade County, Florida, 1972-1976

One situation in which the relationship of drug use patterns and age might be most apparent is in acute adverse reaction to a drug requiring immediate medical attention in hospital emergency room settings. In this section, heroin-related emergency room appearances at Jackson Memorial Hospital from 1972 to 1976 will be examined with regard to the age of the patients. Unlike the CDP treatment data reported above, the number and percentage of heroin-related emergency room reappearances are too small to have any effect on the age variable.

The data presented in table 15-7 on age and heroin-related emergency room appearances are similar to the data on age and heroin treatment admissions. The mean age of those experiencing acute adverse reactions to heroin requiring emergency room treatment has risen from 21 in 1972 to 24 in 1975 and 1976. In 1972-1974 the modal age category (largest number) of people appearing at emergency rooms because of heroin was 21 to 24 years. In 1975 and 1976, the modal age category was 25 to 34 years.

There has been a steady decline since 1972 in the percentage of heroin-related emergency room cases under 21 years of age. In 1972, some 37 percent were under 21 years old. For the years 1973-1976, the respective percentages under 21 years old were 30, 22, 19, and 16. It should be noted, however, that at least six out of ten of those under 21 in each year were either 19 or 20. This is not surprising since the average age at onset of heroin use was found to be 19 or 20 in a number of studies (see, in particular, Nurco et al. 1977; McGlothlin, et

Table 15-6
Heroin Users in Treatment in Dade County, Florida: Age at First Treatment by Race/Ethnicity

	White			Black			Hispanic[a]			Total
Age	*Row %*	*(n)*	*Col. %*	*Row %*	*(n)*	*Col. %*	*Row %*	*(n)*	*Col. %*	*(n)*
16 or less	(32.2)	19	(1.2)	(61.0)	36	(1.5)	(6.8)	4	(1.4)	59
17-18	(31.0)	65	(4.2)	(62.3)	131	(5.3)	(6.7)	14	(4.8)	210
19-20	(37.7)	188	(12.2)	(56.5)	282	(11.4)	(5.8)	29	(10.0)	499
21-24	(35.6)	564	(36.7)	(57.5)	911	(36.9)	(6.9)	109	(37.6)	1,584
25-34	(37.5)	627	(40.8)	(56.4)	942	(38.2)	(6.0)	101	(34.8)	1,670
35 or more	(27.3)	75	(4.9)	(60.7)	167	(6.8)	(12.0)	33	(11.4)	275
Totals		1,538	(100.0)		2,469	(100.1)		290	(100.0)	4,297

Note: The data contain only first admission by age and race/ethnicity; readmissions have been deleted.

[a]In the Latin column, 148 or 51 percent are Cuban, 10.6 percent or 31 are Puerto Rican, 2 or 1 percent are Mexican, and the remainder, 109 or 37.6 percent are other Hispanic.

Table 15-7
Age and Heroin-Related Emergency Room Appearances: Dade County, Florida, 1972-1976

	1972		1973		1974		1975		1976	
	(n)	*(%)*	*(n)*	*(%)*	*(n)*	*(%)*	*(n)*	*(%)*	*(n)*	*(%)*
16 or younger	8	(4.9)	3	(1.8)	3	(1.5)	4	(1.1)	4	(1.1)
17-18	15	(9.1)	16	(9.8)	16	(7.9)	22	(5.9)	17	(4.5)
19-20	37	(22.6)	30	(18.4)	26	(12.8)	46	(12.4)	40	(10.7)
21-24	59	(36.0)	67	(41.1)	81	(39.9)	115	(31.0)	129	(34.4)
25-34	38	(23.2)	39	(23.9)	64	(31.5)	146	(39.4)	149	(39.7)
35 or older	7	(4.3)	8	(4.9)	13	(6.4)	38	(10.2)	36	(9.6)
Totals	164	(100.1)	163	(99.9)	203	(100.0)	371	(100.0)	375	(100.0)
Mean Age	21		22		23		24		24	
Modal Age Category	21-24		21-24		21-24		25-34		25-34	

al. 1978). Thus it is apparent that the aging of the heroin population in treatment has also occurred among those experiencing a heroin-related emergency room episode.

The Jackson Memorial Hospital data are similar to those from the nationwide DAWN statistics in that the majority of the youthful heroin users appearing in the emergency room were female (53.8 percent). However, unlike the DAWN data, over two-thirds (67.6 percent) of the Jackson Memorial youths were black, with whites representing 29.7 percent and Hispanics only 2.7 percent. In the DAWN emergency room data, most youthful heroin patients were white.

The problem most commonly encountered by emergency room staff treating heroin-using youths is the withdrawal syndrome (37.5 percent). It is striking that although many of these patients are under 20 years of age, they have already been using heroin long enough to experience the withdrawal symptoms of physical addiction. The next largest problem at admission is overdosage of heroin (31.9 percent). Third on the list of complaints is infections associated with intravenous use of narcotics (18.7 percent), a common side effect of frequent heroin use. The remaining youthful heroin-related emergency room patients entered with complaints associated with heroin use, for example, drug-precipitated psychosis, allergic reactions, and a need for psychiatric evaluation (13.7 percent).

Although close to one-third of these youths entered the emergency room as a result of heroin overdose, only 5.5 percent, or one in twenty, were unconscious at the time of their treatment in the hospital. It should also be noted that there were no deaths from heroin overdose in this emergency room group. In fact, almost six out of ten of the youthful heroin users entering the emergency room for services were both conscious and coherent. It is well known that heroin does not affect mental functioning to the degree barbiturates and some other illicit drugs do.

The youthful heroin users appearing for emergency room treatment at Jackson Memorial Hospital are not unlike their counterparts anywhere in the United States—they use and abuse a variety of drugs, often simultaneously. The most commonly cited other drugs used by 182 youthful heroin users requiring emergency treatment were barbiturates (28.3 percent), nonbarbiturate sedatives (15 percent), major hallucinogens (11.7 percent), and cocaine (11.7 percent).

An examination of referral sources shows that about three out of ten clients (29.7 percent) were referred by their family or friends, 12.2 percent came in by themselves, and 28.6 percent were referred by criminal justice agencies (police, the Public Safety Department, the Corrections and Rehabilitation Department). Finally, the fire and rescue and ambulance services accounted for 14.8 percent of the referrals, with the source of referral for the remainder (14.8 percent) being unknown.

Age and Heroin-Related Deaths

During the 20-year period between 1955 and 1975, a total of 233 deaths were recorded in the Dade County Medical Examiner's Office as related to *opiate* use. Of these, fifty individuals under 21 years of age died in connection with heroin use, while fourteen individuals under 21 died as a result of the use of other opiates. Most of the heroin-related deaths for youths under 21 have occurred since 1970, with the peak year being 1971. This is consistent with the reports of the drug epidemic in the late 1960s and early 1970s. It is worth noting that there were no reported deaths involving individuals under 21 years of age in connection with heroin or other opiate use before 1968.

The heroin-related youth deaths in Dade County have occurred primarily among white, single males, over four out of ten of whom were students at the time. A large majority of the youthful heroin-related deaths were reported to be accidental rather than resulting from suicide or homicide.

The aging of the heroin-using population is also reflected in mortality data (table 15-8). From 1971 through 1975, the mean age increased from 21 to 25, while the percentages of heroin-related mortalities under 21 decreased and the percentages of those 25 years and older increased. As the current heroin-using population grows older, there may be a larger number of deaths resulting from long term drug use. Heroin addicts live relatively short lives anyway, given the toll from the daily "hustle," poor nutrition, and other adverse health effects of addict lifestyles. However, it is unlikely that deaths among addicts and former addicts resulting from such things as kidney failure at age 40 to 45 will be classified as drug-related. Heroin-related deaths also reflect changes in the availability of heroin and its purity. It is possible that with both increased availability and purity, heroin deaths in Miami could climb quickly again to the level reached in 1971.

The estimate of the social costs of heroin addiction soars when the costs of the medical complications resulting from addict lifestyles and the costs of the lack of economic productivity are considered. It is quite possible that many addicts "mature out" of the drug treatment programs and emergency room episodes and "mature into" long-term inpatient or outpatient medical status, requiring expensive medical care and becoming long-term recipients of social transfer services like food stamps and welfare. The aging of the heroin population in Dade County may signal more of a beginning than an end of the costs of the drug problem.

Implications

The data from Dade County indicate quite clearly an aging of the current known heroin-using population. In recent years, smaller proportions of users utilizing

Table 15-8
Heroin-Related Deaths by Age: Dade County, Florida, 1971-1975

	1971		*1972*		*1973*		*1974*		*1975*	
Age	*(n)*	*(%)*	*(n)*	*(%)*	*(n)*	*(%)*	*(n)*	*(%)*	*(n)*	*(%)*
16 or younger	1	(2.8)	–		–		–		–	
17-18	5	(13.8)	3	(11.5)	2	(16.7)	3	(15.0)	–	
19-20	9	(25.0)	6	(23.1)	3	(25.0)	–		3	(13.6)
21-24	10	(27.8)	9	(34.6)	4	(33.0)	4	(20.0)	8	(36.2)
25-34	8	(22.2)	6	(22.8)	2	(16.7)	13	(65.0)	10	(45.7)
35 or older	3	(8.3)	2	(7.7)	1	(8.3)	–		1	(4.5)
Totals	36	(99.9)	26	(99.7)	12	(99.7)	20	(100.0)	22	(100.0)
Mean Age	21		21		22		25		25	
Modal Age Category	21-24		21-24		21-24		25-34		25-34	

treatment programs and emergency room facilities for heroin-related problems are under 20 years old. This suggests that the spread of heroin use has slowed down. Data from other sources, including high school surveys, seem to support this conclusion.

There are methodological limitations in both the national survey and high school senior data that may mask a potential pool of heroin addicts. First, the sampling designs are geared toward the people least likely to be heavily involved in deviant activities (that is, those found in residential households and attending high school in their senior year). Thus the prevalence figures reported above are surely underestimates for the youthful population as a whole. Second, because the studies are designed primarily for descriptive purposes, information relevant for understanding causes of drug use and changes in age at onset of drug use is not readily available.

Because of these limitations, the national survey and high school senior data and the data presented in this chapter do not provide a clear picture of the extent of the heroin risk pool. The data presented and referred to generally indicate that the heroin epidemic cohort is aging and that the heroin-use problem is stabilizing. However, before drawing the implied conclusion that the heroin problem is ending, other types of data should be examined to determine if there might possibly be a hidden prevalence and the potential for a new epidemic cohort. One suggestion that there might be such a "hidden prevalence" problem can be seen in data from the treatment population in the National Youth Polydrug Study. Some 12.5 percent had used heroin and 24.7 percent had used other opiates. Forty-four percent of those who had ever used heroin had used it daily or more frequently. This degree of frequency is usually considered a reliable indication of dependence or addiction. The NYPS sample included youths in treatment, not necessarily youths from known high-drug-use areas.

In a study in 1974 of 294 men whose names were drawn from Selective Service files in areas in Manhattan where heroin use was endemic, 25.5 percent of the 20- to 30-year-old men reported that they had used heroin, and 75 percent of the heroin users had been addicted (see chap. 4). In another study reported by Brunswick in chap. 18, 15 percent of youths 18 to 23 years of age in the Harlem, New York community were found in 1975-1976 to have used heroin at least once; 13 percent were found to have used heroin at least three times. Thus prevalence takes on different meanings when one moves from national household to treatment to "normal" populations from high drug availability areas.

There may be a substantial proportion of youths in the population who have tried heroin and are not currently using it but who may be "at risk" for further heroin use should an appropriate situation arise. Such a situation might develop if a new purer supply of heroin becomes available. We simply do not know the true parameters of the youthful population that might be at risk for heroin use because of prior contact with heroin.

Let us assume for the moment that the limited supply of heroin currently available and the current low level of heroin purity remain constant for an appreciable period of time. The data from Miami, supported by the examination of other data sets, would forecast an increasingly older treatment population, constantly being recycled through the treatment system. Considerable attrition would occur as the older addicts mature out of heroin use or involuntarily leave the scene because of incarceration or death. Some others would probably move away from heroin treatment and into treatment for alcohol (Preble and Miller 1977). The most important policy consideration centers around social costs attributable to those remaining. Long-range maintenance of addicts on methadone is expensive and would essentially constitute acute nursing care on a regular outpatient basis. Even more costly would be the acute secondary medical complications of heroin abuse, particularly such things as kidney failure and the need for renal dialysis. The costs of providing health care services to an aging user population over many years could be astronomical. This is one policy implication that deserves attention in deliberations on national health insurance.

Now let us assume that supply-reduction efforts temporarily break down in the face of a massive infusion of high-purity, relatively low-cost heroin into the American market from the Golden Triangle, the Middle East, and Mexico. It is possible that we could witness an epidemic that would make the one that occurred in the midsixties to early seventies seem mild. All those with previous extensive marihuana experience in the "susceptible" category and a large pool of individuals who have only experimented thus far with heroin, as well as those in the prime years for introduction to heroin use, particularly inner-city black males 15 to 19 and 20 to 24 years of age, would be at risk. As the data in table 15-9 indicate, in 1960 only 13.3 percent of all white males were either 15 to 19

Table 15-9
Youth Birth Cohorts and Percent of All People Comprising the 15 to 19 Age Cohort by Race and Sex

			All People in These Race-Sex Categories Who Are 15 to 19 Years Old for Various Years (%)			
Birth Years for 20- to 24-Year-Olds	*Birth Years for 15- to 19-Year-Olds*	*Year of Census*	*White Males*	*Black Males*	*White Females*	*Black Females*
1916-1920	1921-1925	1940	17.9	18.8	18.2	20.2
1926-1930	1931-1935	1950	14.5	16.0	14.4	17.0
1936-1940	1941-1945	1960	13.3	14.3	13.2	14.4
1946-1950	1951-1955	1970	17.6	19.0	17.0	18.5
1952-1956	1957-1961	1976	18.6	21.3	18.0	20.7
1956-1960	1961-1965	1980	18.3	22.3	17.7	20.8
1966-1970	1971-1975	1990	14.2	18.2	13.2	16.9

or 20 to 24 years old, and the percentage for black males, white females, and black females were equally low. By 1976, over one in five black males and females were in these drug-prone years, as were over 18 percent of white males and females—a reflection of the impact of the baby boom. The inference is that we perhaps have not seen the last of the baby-boom cohorts who are now in the age range susceptible to drug abuse. We should not assume that another epidemic could not occur. Such an epidemic could be composed of individuals who have experimented with heroin and those who have been heavily involved in the use of other illicit drugs. The pool of potential heroin users is probably as large now as it has ever been, and that pool could be stirred to activity given favorable supply, purity, and price conditions.

Conclusion

The coordinated federal program to solve the heroin problem by both supply- and demand-reduction efforts seems to have borne fruit. The data presented in this chapter quite clearly indicate an aging of the known heroin-using population seen in drug treatment facilities, emergency rooms, and the county morgue in Miami. This aging phenomenon probably reflects various factors, including the advancing age of the post-World War II baby-boom cohorts. However, it would not be prudent to suggest that we have again "turned the corner" on heroin abuse in the United States. Considerable evidence exists to suggest that another heroin epidemic could occur given the emergence of certain conditions, primarily at the supply end of the continuum. Continued restriction of supplies of heroin should be coupled with a continued commitment to the delivery of quality treatment and auxiliary services. The bottom line, though, for youthful heroin abuse should be prevention. It is essential that (1) the research literature on "predictors" of youthful abuse of heroin be thoroughly searched for consistency and consensus; (2) these "predictors" be assembled and disseminated to people in various agencies that deal with young people for the purpose of "flagging" those youths who may be on the road to drug abuse; (3) programs be developed to offer "early intervention" for these youths; and (4) the great cost to the individual of moving into heroin use be made so clear that only foolhardy youths would risk such action.

Notes

1. Federal Drug Abuse Programs, a report prepared by the Task Force on Federal Heroin Addiction Programs for the Drug Abuse Council, 1972, Library of Congress Card Catalog Number: 72-95470.

2. Federal Strategy for Drug Abuse and Drug Traffic Prevention, 1975, U.S. Government Printing Office, 1975, 631-061/268-31.

3. The Drug Abuse Reporting Program (DARP) is a national data base for treatment outcome evaluation research administered for the federal government by the Institute of Behavioral Research of Texas Christian University.

Bibliography

Abelson, H.I., Fishburne, P.M., and Cisin, I. 1977. National Survey on Drug Abuse. A Nationwide Study—Youth, Young Adults and Older People. Vol. I, DHEW Publication No. (ADM)78-618.

Ball, J.C. 1965. Two patterns of narcotic drug addiction in the United States. *Journal of Criminal Law, Criminology, and Police Science* 56:203-211.

Ball, J.C., Thompson, W.O., and Allen, D.M. 1970. Readmission rates at Lexington Hospital for 43,215 narcotic drug addicts. *Public Health Reports* 85 (July):610-616.

Blackford, L. 1977. Student Drug Use Surveys, San Mateo County, California, 1968-1977. San Mateo Department of Public Health and Welfare.

Brown, L.P. 1915. Enforcement of the Tennessee anti-narcotic laws. *American Journal of Public Health* 5 (April):323-333.

Chitwood, D.D., McBride, C., McCoy, C.B. 1975. The Extent of Substance Use Among Miami Springs High School Students. Coral Gables, Florida: Center for Social Research on Drug Abuse.

Cisin, I.H., and Moss, A.R. 1975. Comparison of Drug Use Estimates from Sample Surveys. Technical Report 75-4. Washington, D.C.: George Washington Univ. Social Research Group.

Cisin, I.H., and Parry, H.J. 1975. Sensitivity of Survey Techniques in Measuring Illicit Drug Use. Technical Report 75-1. Washington, D.C.: George Washington Univ. Social Research Group.

Derbyshire, R.L. 1972. Adaptation of adolescent Mexican Americans to United States society. In Eugene B. Brody (ed.), *Behavior in New Environments.* Beverly Hills, Calif.: Sage.

Drug Abuse Warning Network (DAWN I Analysis and Later Reports). 1973. 1977. Drug Enforcemnt Administration, U.S. Department of Justice, Washington, D.C.

Dupont, R.L., and Greene, M.H. 1973. The dynamics of a heroin addiction epidemic. *Science* 181:716-722.

Elliott, D., and Voss, H.L. 1974. *Delinquency and Dropout.* Lexington, Mass.: Lexington Books, D.C. Heath.

Greenwood, J., and Crider, R. 1978. Estimated Number of Heroin Addicts: 1977. Forecasting Branch Report, National Institute on Drug Abuse, DHEW.

Hunt, L.G. 1977. Incidence of first use of a drug: Significance and interpretations. *Addictive Diseases* 3(2):177-186.

Hunt, L.G. 1973. *Heroin Epidemics: A Quantitative Study of Current Empirical Data.* Washington, D.C.: Drug Abuse Council, 1973.

Hunt, L.G., and Chambers, C.D. 1976. *The Heroin Epidemics: A Study of Heroin Use in the U.S., 1965-1975.* Holliswood, New York: Spectrum.

Inciardi, J.A., McBride, D.C., Russe, B.R., Wells, K.S., Siegal, H.A., Chitwood, D.D., and Pottieger, A.E. 1977. *The Acute Drug Reactions.* Project Report to the National Institute on Drug Abuse.

Inciardi, J.A., McBride, D.C., and Pottieger, A.E. 1978. Drugs and death. In D.J. Lettieri (ed.), *When Coping Strategies Fail: Drugs, Alcohol and Suicide*, Vol. 2. Beverly Hills, Calif.: Sage.

Jaffe, J. 1973. A conversation with Jerome Jaffe conducted by T.G. Harns. *Psychology Today* 7:68-79.

Johnston, L.D., and Bachman, J.G. 1977. *Monitoring the Future: A Continuing Study of the Lifestyles and Values of Youth.* Descriptive brochure. Ann Arbor, Michigan: Institute for Social Research.

Kandel, D., Single, E., and Kessler, R.C. 1976. The epidemiology of drug use among New York State high school students: Distribution, trends, and change in rates of use. *AJPH* 66(1).

Lichtenstein, P.M. 1914. Narcotic addiction. *New York Medical Journal* 100 (November):962-966.

Marshall, O. 1878. The opium habit in Michigan. *Annual Report, Michigan State Board of Health* 6:63-73.

McBride, D.C. 1976. Social Control and Adolescent Drug Use Patterns. Ph.D. dissertation, University of Kentucky, Department of Sociology, Lexington, Kentucky.

McGlothlin, W.H., Anglin, M.D., and Wilson, B.D. 1978. Narcotic addiction and crime. *Criminology* (in press).

National Commission on Marihuana and Drug Abuse. 1972. *Marihuana: A Signal of Misunderstanding.* Washington, D.C.: Government Printing Office.

National Commission on Marihuana and Drug Abuse. 1973. *Drug Use in America: The Problem in Perspective.* Washington, D.C.: Government Printing Office, 1973.

National Institute on Drug Abuse. 1975. *Research Issues II.* Predicting Adolescent Drug Abuse: A Review of Issues, Methods and Correlates.

National Institute on Drug Abuse. 1976. Statistical Series–CODAP Data April 1973-September 1974. Supplemental Report.

National Institute on Drug Abuse. 1977. Statistical Series Quarterly Report. April-June.

Nurco, D.N., and DuPont, R.L. 1977. A preliminary report on crime and addiction within a community-wide population of narcotic addicts. *Drug and Alcohol Dependence* 2:109-121.

O'Donnell, J.A. 1969. *Narcotic Addicts in Kentucky.* Washington, D.C.: U.S. Government Printing Office.

O'Donnell, J.A., Voss, H.L., Clayton, R.R., Slatin, G.T., and Room, R.G.W. 1976. *Young Men and Drugs–A Nationwide Survey.* National Institute on Drug Abuse Research Monograph 5.

Person, P.H., Retka, R.L., and Woodward, J.A. 1976. *Toward a Heroin Problem Index: An Analytical Model for Drug Abuse Indicators.* National Institute on Drug Abuse Technical Paper.

Preble, E., and Miller, T. 1977. Methadone, wine and welfare. In *Stout Ethnograph*. Beverly Hills, Calif.: Sage.

Sells, S.B. 1977. Reflections on the epidemiology of heroin and narcotic addiction from the perspective of treatment data. In J.D. Rittenhouse (ed.), *The Epidemiology of Heroin and Other Narcotics.* National Institute on Drug Abuse Research Monograph 16.

Weppner, S.; McBride, D.C. 1975. Comprehensive drug programs: The Dade County example. *American Journal of Psychiatry* (July):132-137.

Winick, D. 1962. Maturing out of narcotic addiction. *Bulletin on Narcotics* 14 (January-March):1-7.

Part V
Special Youth Populations

16 Drug Use Among Rural Youth

Raymond S. Kirk

A search of the psychological and sociological literature for information regarding rural adolescent drug use reveals little substantive information. Researchers (Adler and Lotecka 1973; Blumberg 1975; Marden and Kolodner 1977; Kandel et al. 1976; Tec 1972) are in general agreement that our present knowledge of the incidence and prevalence of drug use by American youths is quite limited, and that within our limited knowledge we know the least about drug use in rural settings.

Possible differences between the drug-use patterns of urban, suburban, and rural youths is of increasing concern since it has implications for the reformulation of policies and the planning of treatment programs for different types of settings. Some researchers (Kandel et al. 1976) have conducted parallel studies in three settings–urban, suburban, and rural–and some have conducted studies that have included all three settings (Rachal et al. 1975). These and other studies indicate that there is considerable drug use in rural communities, but the results differ greatly from study to study. It appears clear, however, that rural drug use patterns differ from those of urban and suburban samples. Heiligman (1973), for example, found that only 10 to 15 percent of tenth through twelfth graders sampled in a rural Minnesota town had ever tried a nonmedically approved drug. Of those who had, marihuana was the drug of choice. In contrast, Tolone and Dermott (1975) found that 30 percent of ninth through twelfth graders sampled in a northern Illinois community had at least experimented with marihuana and 15 percent had used hard drugs such as amphetamines and hallucinogens.

The nationwide alcohol survey conducted by Rachal et al. in 1975 did include some rural settings, but their method of partitioning by population allowed "only a gross measure of urbanization to use in looking at various drinking levels" (p. 74). With regard to alcohol only, they found a slightly higher abstainer rate in nonmetropolitan areas than in metropolitan ones, with all other drinking-level categories being roughly equal.

Kandel et al. (1976) sampled six New York City communities, six suburban New York communities, and six rural New York communities, and their data indicate that there are marked differences between the various community types with regard to both total numbers of users and drug categories. The suburbs had the highest alcohol rates, followed by the rural and city samples, respectively.

Some of the research discussed in this chapter was funded by the National Institute on Drug Abuse, Grant No. 5H81DAO1545-03.

With regard to illegal drug use (not including heroin), the suburbs led again (41 percent), followed by the cities (38 percent) and trailed by the rural communities (28 percent). When heroin was examined, the city samples led with 5 percent "tried," followed by the suburbs with 2 percent. Heroin had not been used to a measurable degree in the rural communities.

Studies that have included alcohol (Adler and Lotecka 1973; Calhoun 1975; Kandel et al. 1976; Rootman 1972) have demonstrated that it is the drug of choice among teenagers. Kandel et al. (1976), for example, reported that by the end of their senior year, 82 percent of all high school students in their sample had at least tried alcohol, as compared with 41 percent for marihuana. Adler and Lotecka (1973) found that 69 percent of the tenth through twelfth graders in their sample had tried alcohol, compared with 23 percent for marihuana. Calhoun (1975) reported that 85 percent of his high school sample ($n = 73$) and 81 percent of his junior high school sample ($n = 117$) had consumed alcohol, with regular users accounting for 78 and 67 percent, respectively.

One of the few nationwide attempts to specifically investigate rural-urban differences and to include alcohol as a drug category is a recently released Services Research Report compiled by the National Institute on Drug Abuse (USDHEW 1977). The report is based on CODAP (Client Oriented Data Acquisition Process) data and includes both youth and adult clients in treatment. Whereas 65.7 percent of the urban clients reported opiates to be the primary drug of use, only 8.1 percent of the rural clients did so. On the other hand, 30.7 percent of the rural clients reported marihuana to be the primary drug of use, compared with 10.7 percent of the urban clients. Rural and urban clients reporting alcohol as their primary drug problem were quite few in number relative to other drugs, due mainly to the fact that NIDA-supported programs are usually not supposed to provide service to those whose primary problem is alcohol abuse. Even so, rural clients reporting alcohol as a primary drug of choice outnumbered urban alcohol clients by a ratio of almost three to two (5.7 percent rural, 3.8 percent urban). Regarding age, it was reported that 62.2 percent of all the rural clients were under 21 years of age, whereas only 18.5 percent of the urban clients were under 21. This is a very large age difference, and the fact that age is highly correlated with different stages and types of drug use may account for the major portion of the differences in the drug use prevalence rates previously reported. Legal restrictions on the provision of methadone maintenance treatment to clients under 18 will also tend to decrease the number of younger clients seeking treatment for opiate abuse.

The preceding comparisons indicate that there are differences between urban and rural populations of drug users who are in treatment. The literature also suggests that there are differences in drug use patterns between urban and rural youths in the general population as well as across the various rural settings that have been studied.

The Washington County Drug Study

In order to better understand rural adolescent drug use the Washington County Youth Service Bureau of Montpelier, Vermont conducted in late 1976 a broad-based survey of drug use by high school youths in rural Washington County, Vermont. The remainder of this chapter will be devoted to a report of this study. The selection of variables to include in the survey was problematic, because of the lack of agreement among researchers as to operational definitions and the wide range of potential etiological factors. This was particularly true in the area of clinical or personality factors. For example, in a major review of numerous American drug-use surveys Blumberg (1975) stated that "no one seems to have identified any personality correlates that transcend both specific drugs and populations." The literature reviewed suggested that the list of variables should include age and sex (Blumberg 1975; Schumann and Polkowski 1975; Blackford 1977; Marden and Kolodner 1977), academic standing (Carlin and Post 1974; Annis and Watson 1975; Finnell and Jones 1975; Jessor and Jessor 1975), employment history (Carlin and Post 1974), influence of peers (Tec 1972; Linder et al. 1974; Tolone and Dermott 1975; Smart 1976; Sorosiak et al. 1976), family relationships (Streit and Oliver 1972; Graham 1973; Streit et al. 1974; Tolone and Dermott 1975; Battegay et al. 1976), religiosity (Adler and Lotecka 1973; Smart 1976; Marden and Kolodner 1977), curiosity (Tec 1972; Annis 1975; Schumann and Polkowski 1975), and the other traditional demographic and socioeconomic indicators. While relationships between these variables and drug use are largely correlational, they may provide information from which testable hypotheses can be derived.

Though infrequently included in past research, self-disclosed reasons for using or not using drugs are also relevant since it may be found that individual reasons for using drugs correlate highly with different family types or various combinations of demographic variables. At the very least they provide anecdotal information that can be used to direct the analysis of other variables whose relationships might not be immediately apparent.

Washington County is located in the central part of Vermont and has an economy based on farming (dairy), granite quarrying, and the tourist industry (skiing). The population of the entire county is about 50,000, more than half of whom live in rural settings in the rugged Green Mountains. Most of the remainder of the inhabitants live in four towns, all with populations less than 10,000. Montpelier, the state's capital, is one of those towns.

The Research Instrument[1]

The research instrument employed in this study emanated from the Rutgers University Medical School and the Center for Alcohol Studies at Rutgers

University. It was chosen as the most appropriate model because of its inclusion of the following.

Demographic Variables. Included in this section were questions relating to age, sex, weight, race, academic performance, future employment aspirations, place of birth, living arrangements (including the number of times the family had moved and sibling position), religious affiliation of respondent and parents, respondent's employment history, and the employment history of parents, including the length of employment and the job type.

Streit-Schaefer Family Perception Inventory. The Streit-Schaefer is a 78-item forced-choice questionnaire based on the assumption that a child's perception of parental behavior can be measured as a function of two orthogonal dimensions: love versus hostility, and autonomy versus control (Schaefer 1965). This two-dimensional model is schematically represented in figure 16-1.

A series of statements depicting parental behavior defined by each of the axes and quadrants in figure 16-1 are presented to the child, who indicates that statement which describes the behavior of the mother, the father, both, or neither. Scores are then obtained by summing the positive responses to questions from each category. In the present study, the scores for mother, father, and both

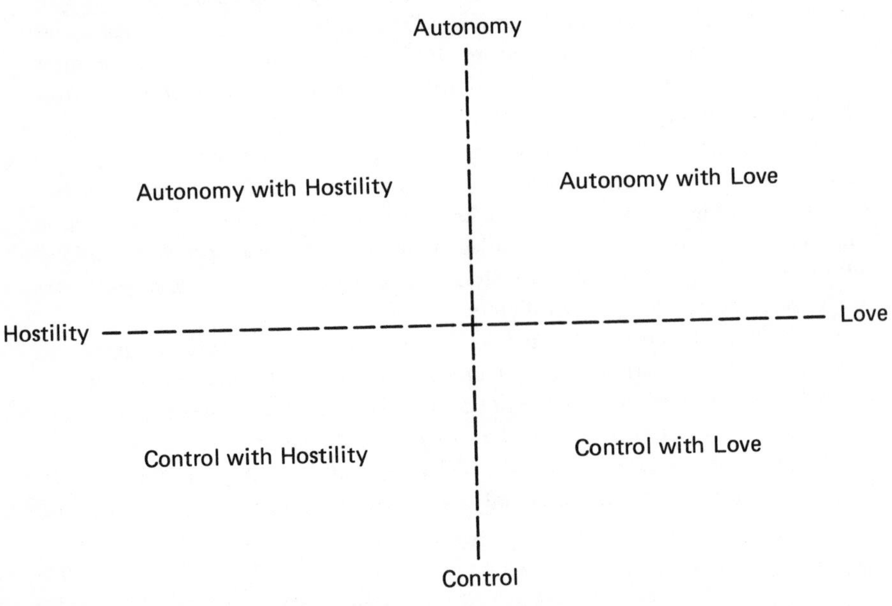

Source: Schaefer 1965. © The Society for Research in Child Development.

Figure 16-1. Schematic Conceptualization of Two-Dimensional Model of Children's Perception of Parental Behavior.

parents were summed, yielding a total of eight scores describing the parents' behaviors toward the respondent. While some discriminatory power was undoubtedly lost by collapsing the three parent scores into a single score for each axis and quadrant, it was regretfully necessary because of computer limitations.

Drug-Use History Questions. The drug-use history section contained an extensive item pool designed to assess lifetime use, age at first use, drug source at time of first use, present drug source, preferred time of use, present frequency of use, changes in use frequency over the last 2 years, last time of use, ease of access to drugs, and quantities of alcohol consumed. This information was gathered on the following drug categories: beer, wine, liquor, hallucinogens, amphetamines, opiates, barbiturates, inhalants, cocaine, marihuana, and other (over-the-counter or unknown) drugs.

Self-Disclosure Item. This section included a lengthy checklist by which the respondent could indicate any of a number of reasons for starting, continuing, stopping, or never trying drugs. It also contained a checklist of items which describe various drug or alcohol experiences and some general interest questions concerning drug and alcohol counseling and sources of knowledge about drugs and alcohol.

Because of the requirements of the present research setting, the Rutgers survey was extensively modified. It was necessary to reduce the time required to complete the survey to that of a normal classroom period (45 to 50 minutes); and it was felt desirable to eliminate redundant or unnecessary items, to make the survey easier to read, and to make the directions easier to follow. To this end, the survey was modified as follows.

All drug-information questions were changed from question-and-answer format to matrix-scoring format, which increased the ease and decreased the time of administration. Redundant items were eliminated, as were the SCL-90 and Piers-Harris scales. The final version of the survey instrument took between 40 and 50 minutes to complete.

The Survey Sample

Permission was obtained from five of the six union district high schools in the county (only one very small town in Washington County maintains its own high school) to administer the questionnaire during the school day. A total of 500 questionnaires was administered, with the number of questionnaires administered in each of the five schools being in proportion to the school's population. The sample thus reflects county-wide representation. Of the 500 questionnaires administered, 413 were included in the final data analysis. (The balance was excluded following internal consistency checks for being incomplete, or for containing obvious fallacious answer patterns.) The final number of surveys represented approximately 10 percent of all Washington County youths between 12 and 18 years of age, although the major portion of respondents were between 14 and 18 years of age (see table 16-1).

Within each school, selection of subjects was random, in line with the

Table 16-1
Demographic Descriptors of the Survey Sample

Sex:	Male	Female
n	182	231
%*n*	44.1	55.9

n = 413

Age	12	13	14	15	16	17	18+
n	11	34	73	118	78	84	15
%*n*	2.7	8.2	17.7	28.6	18.9	20.3	3.6

n = 413

School Grade Distribution:	7th	8th	9th	10th	11th	12th
n	6	36	77	126	58	110
%*n*	1.4	8.7	18.6	30.5	14.0	26.6

n = 413

Grade Average Distribution:	A	B	C	D	F
n	49	179	163	17	5
%*n*	11.9	43.3	39.5	4.1	1.2

n = 413

Number of Times Family Had Moved:	0	1	2-3	4-5	6-7	8-9	10+
n	105	83	111	66	28	10	10
%*n*	25.4	20.1	26.9	16.0	6.8	2.4	2.4

n = 413

Sibling Position:	Only child	Youngest child	Middle or one of Middle	Oldest child
n	8	115	172	118
%*n*	1.9	27.8	41.6	28.6

n = 413

	Catholic	Protestant	Jewish	No religion
n	192	151	4	51
%*n*	46.5	36.6	1.0	12.3

n = 398

request to provide as broad a representation of students as possible. In all cases, participation in the study was voluntary, anonymity of respondents was assured, and respondents were aware that they could stop at any time, whether they had completed the questionnaire or not. A summary of the more common demographic descriptors of the survey sample is presented in table 16-1. It can be seen that there was a fairly even distribution of respondents across age, school grade, sex, and grade average.

Several demographic variables not represented in table 16-1 are noteworthy, in some cases because of the lack of distribution of possible responses. For example, racial representation within Washington County can certainly be said to be limited, with 99 percent of the respondents being white, 0.2 percent black, 0.2 percent Oriental, and 0.5 percent undeclared. The sample was also overwhelmingly indigenous, with 68.3 percent of the respondents being native-born Vermonters. Of the remaining, 11.4 percent were born in either Connecticut, Massachusetts, or New Hampshire, so that 79.7 percent of the sample were native-born New Englanders. In addition to a high percentage of native respondents, native-born parents of respondents were also highly represented. Fully 59.1 percent of the fathers of respondents and 56.7 percent of the mothers of respondents were native-born Vermonters.

Degree of family intactness was quite high among the sample, with 76.3 percent of the respondents living with both of their parents. Those living with the mother only accounted for 9.9 percent of the sample, and 9.2 percent of the sample lived with one natural and one stepparent. Only 1 percent of the sample lived with adoptive parents, and all other categories were represented by less than 0.5 percent of the sample.

When employment history of the respondents was examined, the sample was found to be quite industrious: 34.4 percent of the sample held at least a part-time job during the school year, and the majority of the sample (62.5 percent) held summer jobs during the previous summer. Employment of respondents' parents was also quite high: 93.5 percent of the respondents reported that either one or both of their parents had been steadily employed over the last 5 years. Unemployment of respondents' fathers was quite low (4.8 percent) and employment was high (85.5 percent). Of the remaining 9.7 percent of fathers, the majority were either retired, disabled, or deceased. The type of employment of fathers of respondents was widely distributed over possible categories: 15.7 percent of respondents reported that their fathers were laborers, 12.8 percent held clerical jobs, 23 percent were craftsmen, 11.1 percent were proprietors, and 23.2 percent held professional jobs. Of the mothers, 63.9 percent were employed at the time of the study and 29.8 percent were unemployed. Of the mothers who were employed outside of the home, 15.5 percent were reported to be laborers, 33.9 percent held clerical jobs, 2.9 percent were craftsmen, 3.6 percent were proprietresses, and 17.7 percent were professionals.

Since Washington County contains agrarian-, rural-industrial, and tourist-based economic subdivisions, it can be viewed as fairly typical of the entire state of Vermont. It can be noted that the largest city in Vermont (Burlington) has a population of less than 50,000, making Vermont one of the most rural states in the nation.

Results

Drug-Use History. A summary of lifetime drug use, collapsed across ages and sex, is presented in table 16-2. When lifetime substance use was examined, alcohol (especially beer) was found to be the most frequently used drug. As shown in table 16-2, 31 percent of the sample had drunk beer more than fifty times in their lifetime. When this category is added to "20 to 50 times lifetime use," a cumulative percentage of 51 percent results, indicating that more than half the sample had had considerable experience with alcohol. Only 5.3 percent of the sample reported having never drunk beer. While a similarly small percentage (8.5 percent) of the sample reported having never tried wine, the overall frequency of use was much lower, with a cumulative percentage of only 21.1 percent having used wine twenty times or more. Only a small number of respondents (6.8 percent) reported drinking wine more than fifty times. Liquor was the least popular form of alcohol among the sample but was by no means without representation. A cumulative percentage of 20.8 percent had drunk liquor more than twenty times in their lifetime, but only 8.5 percent had drunk liquor more than fifty times. Only 15 percent of the sample reported having never drunk liquor.

At the time of the survey, use of hard drugs in Washington County was very low when compared with alcohol. It can be seen in table 16-2 that between 85 and 96 percent of the sample had never tried hallucinogens, amphetamines, opiates, barbiturates, or cocaine, and of the few who had tried them, the majority had used them only once or twice.

It appears, therefore, that for drugs other than alcohol, marihuana was the drug of choice among teenagers in Washington County. Of the sample in this study, only 39 percent had never used marihuana. Conversely, a cumulative percentage of 33.6 percent had used marihuana more than twenty times, and a very large proportion (23.7 percent) had used it more than fifty times. A summary of lifetime drug use reveals that marihuana was second only to beer in frequency of use, surpassing even wine and liquor.

Use of all drugs other than those listed above also appears to be low in Washington County. This final category includes such substances as medicines, cough syrups, over-the-counter (OTC) drugs, and drugs which the respondents may have tried but did not know what they were at the time of use. Fully 61.7 percent of the sample said they had never used drugs in this manner, and only 15.3 percent of the sample reported using drugs in this manner more than twenty times.

Table 16-2
Frequency of Life Drug Use. Distribution of Respondents for Each Drug Type, Expressed as Percentages of the Total Sample ($n = 413$)

Drug Type	*Lifetime Frequency of Use*					
	Never Tried	*1-2 Times*	*3-9 Times*	*10-19 Times*	*20-50 Times*	*50+ Times*
Beer	5.3	11.6	16.9	15.5	19.1	31.0
Wine	8.5	24.2	25.7	19.6	14.3	6.8
Liquor	15.0	19.6	24.7	18.9	12.3	8.5
Hallucinogens	87.9	6.8	2.7	0.2	1.0	0.2
Amphetamines	86.2	6.5	3.6	1.0	1.7	0.2
Opiates	96.1	1.5	1.0	0.2	0.0	0.0
Barbiturates	85.2	8.2	4.4	0.5	0.5	0.2
Inhalants	91.8	4.8	1.5	0.5	0.2	0.2
Cocaine	91.5	4.4	1.2	0.2	0.2	1.2
Marihuana	39.0	10.7	7.0	8.7	9.9	23.7
OTC or Unknown	61.7	10.4	5.3	6.1	6.1	9.2

Drug Use and Client Characteristics

When the relationship of lifetime use of drugs with various demographic variables was examined, several significant relationships were observed. A summary of these relationships is presented in table 16-3.

Age. Lifetime alcohol use was found to be significantly associated with age, with the association being strongest for beer ($\chi_2 = 99.41, p < .001$). While this relationship was not surprising, it was also found that some very young respondents were represented in the high-frequency categories. For example, among the 13-year-olds, 20.5 percent had consumed beer on more than twenty occasions. The largest increase occurred between age 15 and 16, by which age 67.6 percent had drunk beer on more than twenty occasions. By age 18, not only were there no abstainers, but the larger majority (66.7 percent) had drunk beer more than fifty times.

When wine was examined along the age dimension, the relationship was again significant ($\chi^2 = 72.53, p < .001$). However, even among the older subjects, wine did not appear to be as popular a drug as beer. Only 20 percent of the sample in the 18 year and older category reported using wine more than twenty times in their lifetime. However, as with beer, the very young were found in relatively high frequency of consumption categories. By the age of 15, this figure increased to 51.7 percent and by the age of 16, it had reached 65.2 percent of the total sample.

Liquor was the least used of the alcohol beverages, although the relationship between age and lifetime consumption remained significant (χ^2 at 36df = 79.37, $p < .001$). The differences between liquor and wine were very small. In the 18

Table 16-3
Association between Frequency of Lifetime Drug Use and Various Demographic Variables

	Age	*Sex*	*Scholastic Achievement*	*Religious Affiliation*	*Employment History*
Beer	*	*	**	***	***
Wine	*	N.S.	N.S.	N.S.	***
Liquor	*	N.S.	N.S.	***	N.S.
Barbiturates	*	N.S.	N.S.	N.S.	N.S.
Marihuana	*	N.S.	$p = .07$	N.S.	**

*$p < .001$.
**$p < .01$.
***$p < .05$.
N.S. Not Significant.
Note: Lifetime frequency of hallucinogenics, amphetamines, opiates, inhalants, cocaine and O-T-C or other drugs did show any significant association with any of the demographic variables.

year and older category there were no abstainers, although a relatively high percentage (60 percent) had used liquor only nine times or less. Only 33.3 percent had used liquor more than twenty times, slightly more than wine but considerably less than beer. As with beer and wine, youthful consumption of liquor was surprising. By age 14, 16.7 percent of the sample had drunk liquor more than ten times; 51.3 percent had done so by age 15; and 75.7 percent had done so by age 16.

Because of the limited total numbers of people using drugs in the various hard-drug categories, statistical associations based on chi square (χ^2) may be somewhat misleading. With regard to age, no significant relationships were found between age and lifetime use of hallucinogens, amphetamines, opiates, inhalants, cocaine, or the drug category which includes cough syrups and medicines. However, age was found to be associated with barbiturate use ($\chi^2 = 59.6$, $p < .001$), the data indicating that almost all barbiturate use occurs at or above 15 years of age.

Regarding marihuana, increasing age was found to be strongly related to use ($\chi^2 = 83.9$, $p < .001$), but marihuana use was much higher than expected among the youngest respondents. For example, 26.4 percent of all 13-year-olds in the sample had at least tried marihuana once or twice, and 14.6 percent of all 13-year-olds had used marihuana twenty times or more. By the age of 14, 54.2 percent of all respondents had at least tried marihuana. However, the bulk of this increase occurred in the "one to two times" or "three to nine times" categories, with only slightly higher extensive use among 14-year-olds than 13-year-olds. Beyond 15 years, the relative percentages of abstainers remained approximately constant–though for users, lifetime frequency of use increased dramatically. By age 17, more than 50 percent of the respondents had used marihuana over twenty times, with 35.7 percent having used it over fifty times.

Sex. When lifetime alcohol use was examined in relation to gender, it was found to be significantly related only to beer (χ^2 at 5df $= 23.39$, $p < .001$) (see table 16-3). Furthermore, this relationship occurred in the highest consumption category; that is, 42.8 percent of all males in the sample had consumed beer more than fifty times, whereas only 22 percent of all females had done so. In all other frequency of use categories the relationship was not a strong one, although there were twice as many female abstainers (6.9 percent) as male abstainers (3.3 percent). For both wine and liquor, partitioning by sex did not reveal any significant relationships.

Unlike beer, when all other drug categories were related to sex, no significant relationships were found (see table 16-3). There did exist a slight trend indicating a male preference for marihuana, although the test did not reach significance ($\chi^2 = 6.8$, $p = .23$).

Scholastic Achievement. Beer use was found to be significantly negatively related to scholastic achievement ($\chi^2 = 44.24$, $p < .01$), although this relationship did not obtain for either wine or liquor (see table 16-3). With the two highest beer consumption categories combined, it was found that 36.6 percent of all A students had consumed beer more than twenty times, 48.8 percent of B students, 54.9 percent of C students, and 64.6 percent of D students. When only the category of "over fifty times" lifetime use was examined, this relationship was even more robust. Only 14.3 percent of all A students in the sample had consumed beer more than fifty times in their lifetime, whereas 27.5, 38.9, and 52.9 percent of the B, C, and D students, respectively, fit this category.

No significant relationships were found between scholastic achievement and use of any nonalcohol drug categories, although the relationship for marihuana did closely approach significance ($\chi^2 = 36.03$, $p = .07$). Of interest is the increasing number of marihuana abstainers as grade average increased: 57.1 percent of all A students had not tried marihuana, whereas 39.9 percent of B students, 35.6 percent of C students, and only 17.7 percent of D students were abstainers.

Family Intactness. One of the earliest hypotheses formulated during this study was that children from broken homes or single-parent families would be overrepresented as drug users. However, when lifetime alcohol consumption was examined as a function of these variables, no significant relationships were observed. Similarly, these variables were not associated with the use of any of the nonalcohol drug categories.

Religious Affiliation. Religious affiliation of the respondents was significantly related to lifetime beer consumption ($\chi^2 = 28.71, p < .02$). It was observed that 38.2 percent of all Catholics in the sample had consumed beer more than fifty times in their lifetime, whereas only 27.8 percent of Protestants had done so. Interestingly, only 18 percent of those who declared no religious affiliation were found in the "over fifty times" category. This relationship was also found for lifetime liquor consumption ($\chi^2 = 30.87, p < .05$). Catholics accounted for 12.1 percent of the "over fifty times" category, compared with 5.3 percent of the Protestants. Religious affiliation was not associated with the use of any drug category other than beer and liquor (see table 16-3).

Employment History. Employment history of the respondents was significantly related to beer and wine use but not liquor use. The relationship between present employment and lifetime beer consumption was significant ($\chi^2 = 11.44$, $p < .05$) (see table 16-3). A cumulative percentage of 59.5 percent of all those "working now" had tried beer at least twenty times, with 36.9 percent having consumed beer more than fifty times. Among those who were not working at the time the survey was taken, a cumulative percentage of 45.4 percent had consumed beer over twenty times. For wine this relationship was also significant ($\chi^2 = 14.7$, $p < .05$), with employed respondents accumulating to 27.3 percent in the "over twenty times" category versus 17.8 percent of the unemployed respondents. For liquor consumption, the relationship was not significant, although the trends were the same.

Current employment of the respondents was not related to the use of any nonalcohol drug category except marihuana (χ^2 at 9df = 22.89, $p < .01$). Of these respondents employed during the school year, 41.3 percent had used marihuana more than twenty times. Of those who did not have a job during the current school year, only 29.9 percent had used marihuana over twenty times. With regard to abstainers, 31 percent of the employed respondents were abstainers as compared with 43.7 percent of those unemployed. Parental employment history was not associated with the use of any drug category.

Ages and Sources of Introduction

Results of this study indicate that children in Washington County are introduced to alcohol at a very young age. For example, 76.4 percent of the sample had been introduced to beer by the age of 13, almost half (45.9 percent) had been introduced to wine by that age, and more than a quarter (26.6 percent) had been introduced to liquor at that age.

In general, nonalcoholic drugs were not experienced until much later. Specifically, for all nonalcohol drug categories except inhalants, marihuana, and "other," less than 1 percent of the sample had tried these drugs prior to age 13, and for inhalants only 2.5 percent had had experience prior to age 13. Regarding the "other" category, it should be remembered that this category included medicines (both prescribed and otherwise), OTC drugs, and unknown drugs and therefore is not a "clean" category from which interpretive judgments should be made. For marihuana, it can be noted that 8.3 percent had at least tried the drug prior to age 13. Dramatic increases occur at this age, with 15.5 percent of the sample being introduced to marihuana during their thirteenth year, 16.7 percent during their fourteenth year, and 11.6 percent during their fifteenth year. Therefore, while the age of introduction to marihuana is the early teen years, it is considerably later than the age of introduction to alcohol.

Regarding sources of drugs, it was found that more respondents were introduced to alcohol in their families (44.3 percent) than anywhere else. However, a large number (30.3 percent) did obtain their first alcoholic drink from a friend outside the family, and an additional 10 percent had someone of legal age purchase alcohol beverages for them.

For drugs other than alcohol, the majority of respondents who had tried them indicated "friends" as their source at the time of first use. However, for all nonalcoholic drugs except marihuana, the total number of users was so small as to obviate meaningful interpretation of the data.

For marihuana, the source of introduction was much different than that of alcohol. Of the slightly more than 60 percent who had tried marihuana, the large majority (45.8 percent) were introduced by a friend. Only 5.1 percent obtained it from a family member, and 1 percent said they took it from someone without their knowledge. The balance (about 8 percent) obtained their first marihuana from someone outside the circle of family or friends.

Current Drug Use

Many respondents who had experimented with drugs or who had even used drugs for some period of time were found to be no longer using them at the time of the survey. For example, 95.2 percent of the sample had experience with beer, but 15.8 percent had either never tried or no longer used beer at the time of the survey. The combined nonuse categories, as well as other "present frequency of use" categories, are presented in table 16-4.

It can be seen in table 16-4 that only alcohol and marihuana had large numbers of users at the time of the survey. Analysis of "current sources" data revealed that the overwhelming majority of respondents reported multiple sources for both drugs, but that "multiple sources" consisted primarily of friends and family members for marihuana and friends and legal outlets for alcohol.

Consumption Patterns

For drugs other than alcohol and marihuana, the low frequency of current users obviated reporting preferred-use patterns. However, alcohol and marihuana were used by large numbers of people, and while there was some overlap of use patterns, the patterns were basically different.

The majority of beer drinkers (45.8 percent of the total sample) reported that most often they drank on weekend nights. An additional 21.5 percent reported multiple-use patterns that included weekend nights. For wine and liquor, the overall frequencies were lower, reflecting the lower numbers of current users, but the ratios of "weekend" drinkers to "multiple time" drinkers were similar to that of beer.

Consumption patterns for marihuana differed considerably from that of alcohol. The majority of marihuana users (24.7 percent of the total sample) reported "multiple time of use" patterns, and an additional 13 percent reported using marihuana primarily on weekend nights.

Discussion

The present study has demonstrated that alcohol and marihuana use among adolescents in rural Vermont is exceedingly high, whereas hard-drug use

Table 16-4
Present Frequency of Use: Distribution of Respondents in Each Frequency Category and Drug Type, Expressed as a Percentage of the Total Sample ($n = 413$)

	Frequency						
Drug Type	*Never Tried or No Longer Use*	*Less than Once per Month*	*Once per Month*	*2-3 Times per Month*	*Once per Week*	*Several Times per Week*	*Daily*
Beer	18.2	12.3	10.4	22.3	23.7	11.1	1.2
Wine	31.7	23.5	11.9	14.8	11.4	4.1	1.5
Liquor	30.1	22.5	12.3	15.3	13.1	3.9	1.2
Hallucinogens	88.4	5.8	2.7	1.2	1.0	0.2	0.2
Amphetamines	92.5	2.7	1.2	2.4	0.5	0.2	0.0
Opiates	97.6	0.7	0.2	0.0	0.5	0.2	0.0
Barbiturates	94.4	1.9	0.5	1.5	0.5	0.5	0.0
Inhalants	96.8	0.2	0.2	1.0	0.7	0.0	0.0
Cocaine	94.9	2.2	0.0	1.2	0.7	0.2	0.2
Marihuana	54.0	4.8	2.7	7.0	8.0	16.2	5.1
OTC or Unknown	74.8	13.3	2.4	4.4	1.2	0.2	0.7

(amphetamines, barbiturates, heroin, etc.) is very low when compared with other studies. Results indicate that 95 percent of all people in the sample have drunk beer (91 percent for wine, 85 percent for liquor) and 60 percent have tried marihuana. Fifty-eight percent show regular beer-drinking patterns (two to three times or more per month), and 36 percent use marihuana in a similar manner. Conversely, only 11 to 14 percent of the sample had ever used hallucinogens, barbiturates, or amphetamines, and less than 3 percent had ever tried opiates. Only 1 to 2 percent of the sample used hard drugs regularly.

While other studies (Strimbu and Sims 1974; Smart 1976) predicted that alcohol and marihuana would be the drugs of choice, they did not suggest these use patterns. Heiligman (1973) found only a 10 to 15 percent *exposure* rate of tenth through twelfth graders in rural Minnesota to all "nonmedically approved drugs," including marihuana. Tolone and Dermott (1975) found that only 30 percent of rural Illinois high school students had tried marihuana, although his hard drug experimenter rate (15 percent) was comparable to the present study. All other studies (Kandel et al. 1976; Calhoun 1975; Sorosiak et al. 1976; Rachal et al. 1975) observed much lower exposure and use rates. It may be that marihuana prevalence has increased over the past 2 years, but the rates are still markedly different. Furthermore, alcohol use rates were also elevated relative to other studies. The study by Rachal et al. (1975) of nationwide alcohol-use patterns reported a 13 percent regular use rate (three to four times per month) for beer, compared with 58 percent in the present study who drink beer two to three times per month. Only Wechsler and McFadden (1976) found alcohol exposure rates above 90 percent (among 1,737 high school students in Massachusetts), but their data suggest lower regular use rates.

It becomes apparent, therefore, that even in very rural areas the potential for drug abuse exists, even though that abuse involves mainly alcohol and marihuana and not hard drugs such as has been the case in many urban and urban-rural comparison studies (Kandel et al. 1976; Blumberg 1975).

The respondents in the present study represented the general school population; that is, they were a nontreatment sample. However, a recent study released by the Services Research Branch of the National Institute on Drug Abuse has found that even the nonurban treatment client is different from his or her urban counterpart (USDHEW 1978). That study was conducted during 1976, the data being collected from fifty-nine nonurban drug treatment programs (that is, programs located in communities of 25,000 or less), representing all the major geographic areas of the United States. The study found that clients of nonurban treatment programs are typically quite young (62 percent were under 21 years of age), and that marihuana, amphetamine, and alcohol use problems predominated. The relative youth of these clients contrasts sharply with CODAP admissions for 1976, only 22 percent of whom were under 21 years of age (NIDA 1978).

The majority of programs in nonurban areas are outpatient and drug free (forty-five out of fifty-nine surveyed). Residential and methadone maintenance programs are rare in comparison with urban treatment programs. This reflects both the relative youth of clients in nonurban treatment programs and the lower prevalence rates of heroin use, which is probably related to the low degree of availability of heroin in rural communities.

There is a high degree of concordance between the prevalence rates of various drugs as found in the National Youth Polydrug Study (NYPS) rural treatment sample and the rates of "primary drug" problems presented in the recent NIDA survey of nonurban treatment programs. (The NIDA study was able to link age of the clients and primary drug of abuse in only eight of the fifty-nine nonurban treatment programs studied.) The rank order of prevalence of "primary drugs" of abuse for clients under 19 years of age in the eight programs ($n = 336$) were marihuana (24 percent), amphetamines (21 percent), barbiturates (9 percent), inhalants (6.5 percent), and other sedatives (4 percent). Heroin and other opiates were reported by a combined 7 percent of the clients. The vast majority of the clients in the NIDA survey, as well as in the NYPS, were multiple-substance users, rarely confining their use to a single substance.

The rank order of prevalence rates of the various drugs in the NYPS rural sample ($n = 443$) is very similar to that of the "primary drug" rates of the NIDA survey, with the exception of alcohol and other sedatives. The rank order of the "ever used" rates (excluding alcohol, which was reported by 94 percent of the NYPS rural treatment sample) in the NYPS were marihuana (90 percent), amphetamines, (52 percent), hallucinogens (42 percent), barbiturates (39 percent), inhalants (34 percent), other opiates (33 percent), other sedatives (28 percent), cocaine (25 percent), and heroin (8 percent).

The fact that the rates for the NYPS sample are so much higher than for the NIDA sample (for example, 90 percent compared with 24 percent for marihuana) is primarily due to the fact that only those clients for whom marihuana was the main or most severe drug problem ("primary drug problem") were counted for marihuana in the NIDA sample, whereas all cases who used marihuana were counted for the NYPS sample regardless of how many other "harder" drugs they used.

The very low percentage who had alcohol as their primary substance of abuse in the NIDA sample is explained by the fact that NIDA-supported programs are not permitted to accept clients whose primary problem is alcohol; such clients are supposed to be treated in programs funded by NIAAA.

It is noteworthy that the NYPS and the NIDA survey of nonurban drug programs found primarily alcohol and marihuana abuse, and that among the nontreatment sample from the Washington County study, alcohol and marihuana use were pervasive.

While the overall exposure and use rates for Washington County youth are very high, results of partitionary drug use by sex, age, etc. appear to be in line with past research and current trends. Many studies (Linder et al. 1974; Sorosiak

1976; Rachal et al. 1975; Marden and Kolodner 1977) have reported positive correlations between age and drug and/or alcohol use. The only study cited which found no relationship between increased age and increased drug use is Tolone and Dermott (1975), although their sample was small (n = 136) and their overall use rates relatively low. Significant relationships were found in the present study between age and use for all alcoholic drugs, as well as for barbiturates and marihuana.

The modal ages of introduction indicate that alcohol is first used during the very early teen years, and in a large number of cases in the preteen years. Marihuana is generally first experienced in the early teen years. After about age 15, the number of marihuana abstainers remains relatively constant, and for those who have made the decision to use marihuana, the frequency of use tends to increase. Hard drugs, on the other hand, are rarely used prior to age 15 and in the present study at least are used only rarely and by few people.

Although the literature addressing the issue of sex differences and drug use remains equivocal, several major reviews (Marden and Kolodner 1977; Blumberg 1975) and many studies (Kandel et al. 1976; Wechsler and McFadden, 1976; Tolone and Dermott 1975; Adler and Lotecka 1973) have found that traditional sex differences are either waning or did not obtain at all. Those which did report differences (Sorosiak et al. 1976) revealed that differences were small, and in some cases the differences were in a direction opposite than that expected. Kandel et al. (1976), for example, found that 4 percent more girls than boys used amphetamines, barbiturates, and tranquilizers. Although significance levels are unknown, examination of Blackford's (1977) data indicate that while males are consistently overrepresented as marihuana users, those differences appear to become large only in the highest use-rate categories.

Results of the present study support the notion that sex differences are disappearing, if they have not already done so. When lifetime drug use was examined in relation to gender, males were found to be overrepresented only for beer. This relationship did not obtain for any other alcoholic beverage or other drug category, including marihuana. Furthermore, the major portion of the sex-by-lifetime-beer-use difference was accounted for by the highest consumption category. By the time the respondents in the present study reached the age of 18, moreover, 100 percent of both sexes had consumed beer ten times or more—that is, there were no sex differences.

Academic performance had been generally negatively associated with drug use (Jessor and Jessor 1975; Carlin and Post 1974; Smart 1976), although the relationship is not clear. Jessor, et al. (1968), for example, have recognized the negative correlation but postulate that it is academic failure that leads to problem drinking. The present study confirmed statistically the negative relationship between alcohol and academic performance and closely approached making the same relationship for marihuana. For alcohol, only 14.3 percent of A students had consumed beer more than fifty times, whereas 52.9 percent of D students had ($p < .01$). The relationship for these categories and all between is approximately monotonic. For marihuana, an identical number (14.3 percent) of A students had used the drug more than fifty times, whereas 41.2 percent of D students had done so.

Employment history was also found to be significantly related to drug use, but not in a beneficial or ameliorative manner. For both alcohol and marihuana, employment was positively associated with drug use. This disagrees with some previous research (for example, Carlin and Post 1974) although much previous research has dealt with hard-drug addicts. It may be speculated that where softer drugs (alcohol and marihuana) are concerned, employment simply provides money for the purchase of drugs.

Religion was another variable that produced unexpected results. Whereas most of the literature (Smart 1976; Marden and Kolodner 1977; Adler and Lotecka 1973) has found religiosity to be negatively related with drug use, results from the present study do not agree. However, this interpretation does require some qualification. In the present study, respondents were asked to declare their religious affiliation but were not asked questions about church attendance or degree of religious involvement. Nevertheless, those respondents who declared no religious affiliation (15.9 percent) were consistently significantly underrepresented in the various alcohol-use categories. Furthermore, they also represented, proportionally, the most abstainers. For those who did declare a religious affiliation, Catholics were consistently overrepresented vis-à-vis Protestants in the alcohol-use categories. Religious affiliation did not predict use of any drugs other than beer or liquor. It was speculated that religious affiliation in this sample might have been correlated with various socioeconomic indicators that were covariate with drug use. However, a post hoc analysis of religion and various socioeconomic indicators failed to reveal any significant relationships, and therefore it must be assumed that the statistical overrepresentation of Catholics in the alcohol consumption categories is not artifactual, but real and significant.

Self-Disclosed Reasons for Drug Use

Self-disclosed reasons for drug use vary widely, but a few seem to prevail. The two reasons most often stated by respondents for trying alcohol or other drugs were curiosity and peer pressure. For continuance of drug use, peer pressure remained, but curiosity was replaced by thrill seeking. This refutes some studies (Smart 1976; Marden and Kolodner 1977), but is congruent with the majority of them (Annis 1975; Sorosiak et al. 1976; Tec 1972; Tolone and Dermott 1975; Adler and Lotecka 1973). Other studies have found both peer pressure and thrill seeking to be important (Schumann and Polkowski 1975), and Linder et al. (1974) concurred on all three (that is, peer pressure, "kicks," and curiosity).

Samuels and Samuels (1974) report even higher attribution rates to these variables than were obtained in this study, although their subjects were in a drug rehabilitation center, indicating much heavier drug involvement than was found in the high school population in Washington County.

Among the stated reasons for drug use, there was very little evidence to support some of the clinical literature. For example, rebelliousness (Davidson 1973) and inferred antisocial behavior (Rosenberg 1969) could only be attributed to about 3 to 4 percent of the present sample. There was, however, support for the notion that drugs are used to alleviate stress, anxiety, and depression (Dohner 1972; Rause and Ewing 1973). In the present study, 23.1 percent of the respondents said they drank alcohol, and 14.6 percent said they used other drugs for these reasons.

Prediction and Etiology

Rural drug users from Washington County have demonstrated their preference for alcohol and marihuana over other drugs and have indicated several reasons for beginning drug use (curiosity, peer pressure) and continuing drug use (peer pressure, thrill seeking, relief from stress). However, these are general notions that may or may not apply to small groups of users of drugs other than but not necessarily to the exclusion of alcohol and marihuana. It would be naive to assume that all drug users differ from nonusers in the same direction on various predictor variables.

This section will present evidence that different types of family interaction histories not only contribute to the use of various drug types but can be used to predict that use. The results of the Streit-Schaefer family perceptions inventory, various demographic variables, and drug-use histories can be combined into fairly powerful predictive models. While the present data and models developed from them apply to the rural Washington County sample, their theoretical underpinnings are not limited to rural applications.

The pooled family perceptions data (that is, collapsed across mother, father, and both parents) and lifetime drug-use histories were factor analyzed, and the results strongly supported both the theoretical constructs of the Streit-Schaefer and the notion of distinctly different drug-use categories. The factor analysis resulted in six distinct factors: three represented family perception and three represented drug categories.

For family perception data, the first factor represented the love-hostility dimension of the Streit-Schaefer, accounted for 36.8 percent of the total variance, and was distinctly bipolar. The factor score for love was −.83, and for hostility +.76. Autonomy was also represented on this factor, but only when coupled with love (−.65) or hostility (+.68).

Whereas the love-hostility dimension was represented on a single, bipolar factor, the control-autonomy dimension was represented on two unipolar factors and therefore did not yield the continuous dimension expected. However, they each loaded quite independently. The control factor accounted for 10.9 percent of the total variance, with the factor score for control being .70, although love and hostility were also represented on this factor when coupled with control (factor scores .59 and .60, respectively). The autonomy factor accounted for only 5.5 percent of the total variance, yet autonomy alone loaded on this factor with a score of .58.

The category loadings of the three drug factors were quite distinct. The first drug factor represented alcohol and marihuana to the exclusion of all other drugs. It accounted for 27.9 percent of the total variance and contained the following factor scores: beer = .83, wine = .70, liquor = .80, and marihuana = .63. There was some slight contamination of this factor by barbiturates (factor score = .29). The second drug factor represented almost the total accountable variance of hallucinogens (factor score = .82) and accounted for 12.3 percent of total variance. There was some contamination of this factor by opiates (factor score = .36) and barbiturates (factor score = .35), although their contributions to the factor were small. The third drug factor represented opiates (factor score = .44) and cocaine (factor score = .58). This was the least "clean" of the drug factors, being contaminated by barbiturates (factor score = .32) and "other" drugs (factor score = .36), which, it will be recalled, was the catch-all category for OTC and unknown drugs. This third drug factor accounted for only 6.6 percent of the total variance, but it should be remembered that use of opiates and cocaine was very slight relative to other drugs.

Taken as a whole, the factor analysis just described suggests distinct groupings of drugs that are not related to legality or medical definition. Rather, it is speculated that they are categorized according to user perceptions. Marihuana, for example, is considered by users to be in the same general category as alcohol, despite its illegality and slightly lower use rates. Hallucinogen and amphetamine (and some barbiturate) use, on the other hand, probably reflect the recreational and/or experimental use of hard drugs by those willing to go beyond the use of alcohol and marihuana. It is expected that this type of user differs from the users responsible for the alcohol-marihuana factor in kind, not just in degree. The third drug factor, while accounting for a relatively small portion of total variance, reflects use of the hardest drugs (opiates, cocaine, and some barbiturates), and again it is hypothesized that these users also differ in kind from users in the other two categories.

The distribution of barbiturate variance across all three drug factors and the loading of the "other" category on the same factor as opiates and cocaine may at first appear to be random or error variance. However, if, as has been speculated, the three drug factors represent distinct user types and not simply the progression of softer drugs to harder drugs, then this apparent error variance may be explicable. Specifically, it will be recalled that the "other" drug category not only represented OTC drugs but also drugs of any kind that the user may have tried not knowing what they were. It may be argued that this type of drug use is the most desperate and pathogenic type, not surprisingly found in the same category as opiates (heroin) and cocaine.

Similarly, the behavioral effects of heavy barbiturate use would also suggest that some of its use variance would be found in this category. The behavioral and psychological effects of hallucinogens and amphetamines do not suggest that they would fall into this category, being excitatory and mind-expanding rather than sedating. However, mild barbiturate use is disinhibitory and relaxing without necessarily being sedating to the point of debilitation, and therefore some of its use variance might also be expected to load onto the second drug factor with hallucinogens and amphetamines. The very small amount of barbiturate variance that loaded onto the first drug factor (alcohol and marihuana) may be explained by its mild use as a social facilitator-disinhibitor. Alcohol, after all, is also a CNS depressant and is disinhibitory. Furthermore, barbiturates are perhaps the drug most abused by adults (parents) with medical prescriptions and therefore may be viewed as more like alcohol and marihuana than other drugs by some respondents.

In order to determine whether the family perception and demographic data could predict the use of various drugs, these variables were employed to derive discriminant function equations for lifetime drug use of all drug categories. Included in the analyses were the eight pooled family perception variables and seven demographic variables (age, sex, grade average, Catholicism, Protestantism, and types of employment of mothers and fathers). The list of demographic variables was the result of a stepwise elimination of variables that failed to contribute to the discriminant function of at least one drug type. It should be noted that in other research settings, or with other samples, some variables might remain that were eliminated from this analysis, and vice versa.

The results of the discriminant function analysis are presented in table 16-5 and are expressed as standardized discriminant function coefficients for all significant predictor equations. Examination of the coefficients in table 16-5 verifies some of the relationships between drug categories and various demographic variables and reveals the reasons for the drug loadings that emerged during factor analysis.

The very strong contribution of age to the functions for all three alcohol categories and marihuana reaffirms the importance of this variable to the particular age range of the respondents in the sample. Similarly, sex contributed significantly to the function of beer but for no other drugs, reaffirming the waning of traditional sex differences between drug users. The contribution of Catholicism to alcohol prediction was also obtained, being strongly manifested in the alcohol categories.

Regarding the family perception data, the similarities of contributing variables to the drugs that loaded on common factors is striking. For example, it

Table 16-5
Discriminant Function Coefficients (Standardized) of Significant Functions for Each Variable in the Combined Demographic and Family Perception Equations Predicting Lifetime Drug Use

	Drug Type[a]							
Variable	*Beer*	*Wine*	*Liquor*	*Amphetamines*	*Opiates*	*Barbiturates*	*Inhalants*	*Marihuana*
Age	–.674*	–.620*	–.655*	–.179*	.262	–.184	.314	–.639*
Sex	.355*	.133	.003	.168	.266	.059	–.050	.187
Grade average	–.163	–.024	–.027	–.118	–.172	–.297*	–.037	–.386*
Catholic	–.417*	–.499*	–.577*	–.490	–.379	–.506	–.151	–.371
Protestant	–.180	–.084*	–.343	–.206	–.368	–.337	.026	–.243
Fathers employment	–.159	.065	.072	–.134	.186	.187	.195	–.037
Mothers employment	–.078	–.085	–.029	.135	–.056	.194	–.517*	–.018
Autonomy	–.167*	.011*	–.113*	.221*	–.160*	–.200	–.096	–.004*
Autonomy with love	–.070	–.312*	–.240	–.053	.110*	.208*	–.154	–.113
Love	–.078	–.020*	.056*	.336*	.260*	–.059*	.808*	–.055
Love with control	.158*	.034*	.090*	.367*	.570*	.128	.162*	.293*
Control	.186	.406*	.225	.371*	.230*	.647	.073	.257
Control with hostility	–.065	–.030*	.049	.221*	.340*	.160	–.444*	.035
Hostility	–.186	–.138*	–.205*	–.350	–.229	–.515*	.405	–.202
Hostility with autonomy	–.126*	–.421*	–.386*	.037	.175	–.297*	–.055*	–.244*

[a]Equations for prediction of lifetime use of hallucinogens, cocaine, and "other" drugs were not significant and are not included in the table. There was, however, strong evidence suggesting that increased *n*'s would provide significance.

*Variables contributing significantly to function, based on univariate *F*ratio, $p < .05$ or less.

will be recalled that the first drug factor represented beer, wine, liquor, and marihuana. Family perceptions associated with increased use of all four drugs were increasing autonomy, decreasing love with control, and increasing hostility with autonomy.

The second drug factor represented hallucinogens and amphetamines. Only the discriminant function for amphetamines was significant, yet the similarities between variables contributing to each equation (amphetamines and hallucinogens) are again striking. Increasing use of both amphetamines and hallucinogens was associated with decreasing perceptions of autonomy, love, love with control, control, and control with hostility.

The third drug factor (representing opiates and cocaine) was not as concisely reflected in the family perception data as were the first two factors. In fact, the loading of the major portion of cocaine variance upon the third factor is inexplicable using family perception data, and the discriminant function for cocaine was insignificant.

The hypotheses suggested by the factor analysis (that is, three classes of users differing in kind and not just degree) is supported in the case of the first two drug groups, but the model weakens when the third group (factor) is considered. Even though the discriminant function for opiates was significant, the following interpretations are made guardedly because of the small number of opiates users.

Opiates users are similar to the users of hallucinogens and amphetamines to the extent that increased opiates use was associated with decreasing perceptions of love, love with control, control, and control with hostility. However, compared with hallucinogens and amphetamines, the decreases in these perceptions associated with opiates were precipitous. To this extent opiates users differ in degree from users of hallucinogens and amphetamines. However, there is also evidence that they differ in kind, since increased use of amphetamines was associated with decreasing perception of autonomy, and opiates use was associated with increased perceptions of autonomy.

The distribution of barbiturate use across the three drug factors was also reflected in the family perception data. Increased use of barbiturates was associated with decreasing perceptions of love (similar to amphetamines and opiates) and with increasing perceptions of hostility and hostility with autonomy (similar to alcohol). Furthermore, the decrease in perceptions of love and love with control in the highest barbiturate-use category were almost as precipitous as the opiate users. Barbiturates users were the only group to score very high on perceptions of hostility, and to this extent they are unique.

The following summarizes the drug group differences on the family perception data. The discriminant function coefficients for each of those variables can be observed in table 16-5: (1) users of all drugs, including alcohol, scored lower on perceptions of parental love and love with control than nondrug users; (2) users of alcohol and marihuana scored higher on hostility with autonomy than users of other drugs, and scores were also elevated on perceptions of autonomy; (3) users of hallucinogens and amphetamines scored lower on control and control with hostility than alcohol and marihuana users, but the major change was the decrease, rather than the increase, in perceptions of autonomy; (4) users of opiates scored even lower on perceptions of control and control with hostility than hallucinogen and amphetamine users but unlike them scored very high on perceptions of autonomy; (5) the distribution of barbiturate use across the more distinct group of users of other drugs is reflected in the direction of score changes on autonomy with love, love, and hostility with autonomy and are unique in the very high scores on perceptions of hostility. Although their study did not include alcohol, the findings of Streit et al. (1974) are in general agreement with those of the present study.

Much more data are needed, particularly data on hard-drug users, to further develop these notions. It is clear, however, that family interaction histories as perceived by the child (and measured by instruments such as the Streit-Schaefer family perceptions inventory) contain etiological importance and potential for prediction.

There are undoubtedly many variables that contribute to drug use that were not employed in the present study. Reliance solely on demographic variables and family histories would be too simplistic. Indeed, for even the most powerfully predictive variables described above, the canonical correlation of variables was not exceedingly high (ranging from .293 for opiates to .463 for beer), indicating that functions were moderately but not highly correlated with the drug group centroids. However, the variables included in the factor and discriminate function analyses do not provide for decisionmaking on the part of the respondents. The decision making type of data was ascertained in the Washington County sample by the analysis of self-disclosed reasons for drug use or nonuse. Self-disclosed reasons constitute a class of variables quite different from demographic and family history variables in that they relate, at the conscious level of the respondent, directly to drug use.

In order to detect possible differences among self-disclosed reasons for use of different drugs, and thereby detect different types of users, respondents were categorized as being either nonusers, alcohol users, marihuana users, or hard-drug users. These categories were dictated to a large extent by the distribution of user types within the Washington County sample and the assumptions of the statistical analysis employed.

Alcohol users were operationally defined as those who had used either beer, wine, or liquor more than twenty times but who had used no other drugs more than twice (*no* use of opiates was allowed for this group). Marihuana users were defined as those who had smoked marihuana more than twenty times but who had used no harder drugs more than twice (opiates use was again disallowed, and alcohol use was disregarded). Hard-drug users were defined as those who had used any opiates more than twice or who had used other hard drugs ten times or more. Alcohol and marihuana use were disregarded for the classification of hard-drug users. Significant differences were found among these groups as a function of their self-disclosed reasons for drug use.

In general, alcohol drinkers tended to be nonresponsive, if not defensive, about their drug-taking practices. Compared with the other groups, very few alcohol users declared positive or goal-oriented reasons for beginning drug use (alcohol) and denied that they continued to drink in order to get "high," "wasted," or simply drunk ($\chi^2 = 14.72, p < .001$). On the contrary, those who had progressed to marihuana use had begun using alcohol and then marihuana for different reasons than the alcohol-only group. They appeared to be more hedonistically oriented, claiming curiosity ($\chi^2 = 11.82, p < .01$) and the desire to get "high" (χ^2 at 2df = 9.44, $p < .01$) as reasons for beginning alcohol use and thrill seeking as a reason for continued alcohol use ($\chi^2 = 6.58, p < .05$).

Subtle distinctions between the marihuana users and the hard-drug users are also evident along this dimension. More marihuana users admitted to curiosity ($\chi^2 = 7.85, p < .01$) and thrill seeking ($\chi^2 = 4.50, p < .05$) as reasons for the use of drugs other than alcohol than did the hard-drug users. Indeed, the hard-drug users stood alone in admitting that they used drugs (including alcohol and marihuana) simply to feel better ($\chi^2 = 6.85$, $p < .05$). While not reaching statistical significance, response frequencies to several other questions were strongly suggestive that those who had progressed beyond marihuana use were trying to relieve psychological stress (that is, to feel less tense or nervous, to feel happier, to forget problems, etc.).

While there was considerable variance among the preceding etiological factors, the evidence is compelling that different drugs were used for different reasons at the conscious level (self-disclosure), either by different types of adolescents or by adolescents in different psychological states. Certainly, the preceding comparisons are not inflexible. They do not, for example, preclude the possibility of an increase in psychological stress contributing to the decision of an alcohol user to turn to hard drugs. On the contrary, they would suggest such a decision. However, the obvious importance of certain demographic variables, and of a youth's family interaction history in affecting the decision of whether or not to use drugs, indicates the necessity of a multivariate approach in determining whether or not drug use will occur under a given set of circumstances.

In conclusion, the present study has demonstrated that the potential exists for high drug-use rates among rural youths, but that alcohol and marihuana are the drugs of choice, almost to the exclusion of other drugs. Urban youths, on the other hand, have been found in most studies to have much higher exposure rates to hard drugs than rural youths, although the most prevalent drugs used are still marihuana and alcohol. Results of the NYPS and NIDA survey suggest that rural and urban youths *in treatment* also differ along the same dimension. Since analysis of self-disclosed reasons for drug use in the present study indicate that those youths who progress to hard drugs are trying to relieve psychological stress, it is suggested that the generally lower hard-drug use rates observed among rural youths may be due in part to the less stressful conditions of rural living. On the other hand, the isolation and frequent boredom experienced by youths living in rural areas may contribute to the "thrill-seeking" type of drug use found to be so prevalent in Washington County. Similarly, the divorce rate of a given area may indicate the degree of supportive and fulfilling family relationships—relationships that exist, and may therefore be a powerful predictor of prevalence of drug use. Within the Washington County sample the divorce rate was found to be much lower than the national average.

It has not been the intent of this chapter to place value judgments upon rural or urban living but rather to suggest that by noting the differences in drug-taking behaviors of youths from the different rural and urban settings, it is possible to gain a clearer understanding of adolescent drug use in general and to suggest that future prevention and treatment programs may require fundamentally different approaches for the differing regions.

Note

1. Copies of the research instrument are available from the author on request.

References

Adler, P.T., and Lotecka, L. 1973. Drug use among high school students: Patterns and correlates. *The International Journal of Addictions*, 8(3):537-548.

Annis, H.M. 1975. Adol-scent drug use: The role of peer groups and parental example. *Ontario Psychologist* 7(4):7-9.

Annis, H.M., and Watson, C. 1975. Drug use and school dropout: A longitudinal study. *Canadian Counsellor* 9(3-4):155-162.

Battegay, R., Ladewig, D., Mühlemann, R., and Weidman, M. 1976. The culture of youth and drug abuse in some European countries. *The International Journal of Addictions* 11(2):245-261.

Blackford, L.St.C. 1977. *Summary Report–Surveys of Student Drug Use, San Mateo County, California.* Department of Health and Welfare, San Mateo County, California.

Blumberg, H.H. 1975. Surveys of drug use among young people. *The International Journal of Addictions* 10(4):699-719.

Calhoun, J.F. 1975. An examination of patterns of drug use in six suburban groups. *The International Journal of Addictions* 10:521-538.

Carlin, A.S., and Post, R.D. 1974. Drug use and achievement. *The International Journal of Addictions* 9(3):401-410.

Davidson, S. 1973. Types and treatments of adolescent drug abusers in Israel. *Israel Annals of Psychiatry and Related Disciplines* 11(3):210-218.

Dohner, V.A. 1972. Motives for drug use: Adult and adolescent. *Psychosomatics* 13(5):317-324.

Finnell, W.S., Jr., and Jones, J.D. 1975. Marijuana, alcohol and academic performance. *Journal of Drug Education* 5:13-21.

Graham, D.L. 1973. Attitudinal variable associated with adolescent drug use at the secondary level. *Dissertation Abstracts International* 34(3a):1080.

Heiligman, A. 1973. A survey of drug use in a rural Minnesota senior high school. *Drug Forum* 2(2):173-177.

Jessor, R., Garman, R.S., and Grossman, P.H. 1968. Expectations for need satisfaction and drinking of college students. *Quarterly Journal of Studies on Alcohol* 29:101-116.

Jessor, R., and Jessor, S.L. 1975. Adolescent development and the onset of drinking. *Journal of Studies on Alcohol* 36:27-51.

Kandel, D., Single, E., and Kessler, R. 1976. The epidemiology of drug use among New York State high school students: Distribution trends, and changes in rates of use. *American Journal of Public Health* 66(1):43-53.

Linder, R.L., Lerner, S.E., and Burke, E. 1974. Drugs in the junior high school. *Journal of Psychedelic Drugs* 6(1):43-49.

Marden, P.G., and Kolodner, D. 1977. Alcohol Use and Abuse Among Adolescents. NCAI, 026533.

NIDA. 1978. Annual Summary Report 1976: Data from the Client Oriented Data Acquisition Process.

Rachal, J.V., Williams, J.R., Brehm, M.L., Cavanaugh, B., Moore, R.P., and Eckerman, W.C. 1975. A National Study of Adolescent Drinking Behavior, Attitudes, and Correlates. NIAAA Report PB-246-002.

Rause, B.A., and Ewing, J.A. 1973. Marijuana and other drug use by women college students: Associated risk taking and coping activities. *American Journal of Psychiatry* 130(4):480-491.

Rootman, I. 1972. Drug use among rural students in Alberta. *Canada's Mental Health* 20(6):9-14.

Rosenberg, C.M. 1969. Young drug addicts: Background and personality. *Journal of Nervous and Mental Disease* 148:65-73.

Samuels, D.J., and Samuels, M. 1974. Low self-concept as a cause of drug abuse. *Journal of Drug Education* 4:421-438.

Schaefer, E.S. 1965. Children's reports of parental behavior: An inventory. *Child Development* 36:413-424.

Schumann, S.H., and Polkowski, J. 1975. Drug and risk perceptions of 9th grade students: Sex differences and similarities. *Community Mental Health Journal* 11(2):184-194.

Smart, R.G. 1976. *The New Drinkers: Teenage Use and Abuse of Alcohol.* Addiction Research Foundation of Ontario, Toronto.

Sorosiak, F., Thomas, L.E., and Balet, F.N. 1976. Adolescent drug use, on analysis. *Psychological Reports* 38(1):211-221.

Streit, F., Halstead, D., and Pascale, P. 1974. Differences among youthful users and nonusers of drugs based on their perceptions of parental behavior. *The International Journal of Addictions* 9(5):749-755.

Streit, F., and Oliver, H.G. 1972. The child's perception of his family and its relationship to drug use. *Drug Forum* 1(3):282-289.

Strimbu, J.L., and Sims, O.S. 1974. A university system drug profile. *The International Journal of Addictions* 9(4):569-583.

Tec, N. 1972. Differential involvement with marijuana and its sociocultural context: A study of suburban youths. *The International Journal of Addictions* 7(4):655-669.

Tolone, W., and Dermott, D. 1975. Some correlates of drug use among high school youth in a Midwestern rural community. *The International Journal of Addictions* 7(4):655-669.

USDHEW: NIDA-DHEW. 1977. *Services Research Report: An Investigation of Selected Rural Drug Abuse Programs.* Publication No. (ADM) 77-451.

USDHEW: NIDA-DHEW. 1978. *Services Research Report: Nonurban Drug Abuse Programs: A Descriptive Study.* Publication No. (ADM) 78-636.

Wechsler, H., and McFadden, M. 1976. Sex differences in adolescent alcohol and drug use: A disappearing phenomenon. *Journal of Studies on Alcohol* 37:1291-1301.

17 Drug Use Among Native American Adolescents

E.R. Oetting, and
George S. Goldstein

Reports of drug problems are not unique to Native American youths. Adolescents in all subcultures are involved with drugs to some extent; it is a problem of national scope. While there is considerable survey information about the use of drugs in most youth populations, surveys have for the most part excluded representative samples of Native Americans because these youths tend to be in separate schools and in isolated locations. It has also been difficult to collect data on drug use from the reservations where Native Americans reside because of difficulty in establishing anonymity. There is also an unwritten norm among Native American groups that problems are not shared with outsiders.

In this chapter we will provide epidemiological data collected in 1975 (Oetting and Goldstein 1975) on a large sample of young Native Americans. The data will confirm what has been found in subsamples of major surveys and in other small studies of Native Americans: that young Native Americans are more heavily involved in drug use than other adolescent populations. In order to provide some perspective, we will begin by describing our observations of some of the unique problems that Native American adolescents face, problems that result in personal and social stresses and ultimately lead to drug involvement. We will then note the information about Native American drug use from other studies and report in detail on our own investigation. Our concern has not only been with epidemiology, but also with developing measures of underlying correlates of drug use. The final section of the chapter discusses those results.

Growing Up Indian

It would not be possible in a single chapter to describe the problems of the many different groups of Native American children. Each tribe, and indeed each community, would require its own volume. There are, however, some common types of problems that occur for nearly all these young people.

In areas far away from reservations, Native Americans may be accepted and there may even be some pride in claiming a bit of Indian ancestry on the part of Anglos. In the towns next to the reservations, however, there is considerable prejudice, and the young people from the reservations must be prepared to face biases and injustice directly. The adolescent, in an age group in which drug use spreads rapidly, is particularly sensitive to rejection. To be rejected for your race, something you cannot do anything about, attacks your very foundations and thus your concept of yourself as a person.

In addition, Native Americans must face poverty as a fact of life. Their average income is far below the rest of the nation. A report of the Bureau of Indian Affairs (1974) states that "in 1970, 38 percent of all Indians were considered to be living on incomes that were below what was then considered to be the 'poverty level.' " In 1977 about 40 percent of the potential Native American labor force was not employed, which is substantially higher than the national unemployment rate of about 7 percent in 1977. An Indian born today can expect to live to age 64.9; the average life expectancy for the total U.S. population is estimated to be 70.9. The incidence rate for tuberculosis (TB) among Indians is 6.5 times as high as the rate among the U.S. all-races population. The age-adjusted death rate from TB among Indians and Alaskan natives is 7.6 times as high as the rate of TB deaths among the general population.

This poverty is further emphasized by isolation, limiting the available activities for young people. With no money and many miles to the nearest town, it is difficult to meet new friends, buy a magazine, or see a movie. In addition, prices in the local trading posts, which have little variety in merchandise, tend to be much higher than those in town, making one even poorer.

The federal government may have also played a part in making it more difficult for the Native American adolescent to develop adequately. Townsley and Goldstein (1977) point out that Native Americans have been entrenched in a way of life where being passive, dependent receivers of government services is rewarded rather than the development of initiative or autonomous thought. This position in which the Native Americans find themselves inhibits growth and restricts the opportunities for leadership and advancement in a growing society.

The Native American child lives in two societies, and the task of growing up can become immensely more difficult when you are caught between two cultures. There is more opportunity for rejection, rebellion, and alienation. The conflict is made worse because the societies themselves have conflicting values and beliefs. To accept one is to reject the other; to act right in one is to act wrong in the other. There are two languages. Often, the grandparents speak only the native language, while the parents, raised in an Indian culture but having been required to use English in school, tend to have poor language development in both the native language and English. Today many children use both the native language and English in school, making it even more confusing for their parents. Many of the parents, in fact, have felt so punished for being Indian that they would prefer it if their children spoke only English.

The language that is used has other implications as well. To identify oneself as a Native American implies using the native language. Outside the local area, however, that language is useless, even with other Native Americans. The local area is usually small and impoverished, but moving away to better economic opportunities requires using English. The choice is at least partly, then, between one's identity as a Native American and opportunity.

Breakdown in family structure is much more frequent among some Native American tribes than in the general population. There are more divorces, separations, and single-parent homes; and even where the formal family structure is intact, there may be more than the usual problems in adjusting to family life. The family may be separated for part of the year while the father, mother, or both work somewhere else. Many children are further separated from their families by having to attend boarding schools, often beginning as early as age 6, and live in dormitories with dozens of other children.

There are many conflicts in values. In school the Anglo teachers emphasize competition in sports and classes. At home the elders teach "do not push ahead, do not seek power or prestige." School lessons include heroes who are different and unique. At home the lesson of the coyote or raven tale may be "do not be different." In Anglo culture, medicine and religion and church and state are clearly separated, while in many Native American cultures medicine, religion, and law are one. Anglo teachers tell children not to be superstitious, but in folk medicine there may be both natural and supernatural cause for disease. Tribal ceremonies, a rich part of life, mark the changes of the year, bring people together, and serve as carnival and cure, but they are often laughed at or viewed as quaint oddities by Anglo teachers, bosses, and even friends.

These conflicts are difficult enough for an adult to handle. The adolescent wants things to be right. He is not a relativist. Things are black or white, right or wrong. There is the "Indian" way and there is the white American way, two sets of rights and two sets of wrongs, and he is trapped between them. He must choose teachers or parents, support Indian movements, be Indian, or move away and be like other Americans. It is little wonder that Bryde (1970) found that eighth grade Native American children felt more rejected, depressed, paranoid, withdrawn, and alienated than their Anglo counterparts.

The forces operating on the child are not all negative. Where the family is intact, for example, there is often a very strong love for the children. At the same time, children are not overprotected and are often given greater freedom of choice about their own behavior than is typical in Anglo families. Families want their children to be better off than they are and will work to help them. There is, however, a tendency in the older people to want their children to have Anglo benefits. They may want them to be Indian, but they also want them to have jobs, money, cars, televisions, and education.

There are positive values within the tribes as well. Children are usually taught values that support being strong, self-controlled, and self-disciplined. Overuse of alcohol or use of drugs would be against these values, and there often are strong sanctions against the use of these substances.

Within many Native American tribes there are also ways of helping people deal with problems that are not available to Anglos. In the tribes we studied, for example, there are ceremonies that help a person who has had dreams or has been frightened by something that happened (for example, nearly struck by lightning). There are, in addition, very specific ceremonies that deal with death, which are extremely helpful.

Perhaps the greatest asset that Native Americans have is that most of them are still living in a community where people know each other intimately. It is not necessary to ask what problems someone is having. Family, friends, and neighbors usually know what the problem is and sometimes know how to help.

Unfortunately, even these positive forces can create problems for some adolescents. The strong tribal social sanctions against drug use come up against the peer pressure to experiment with drugs. There may be help available for some problems through old ceremonies, but there is also pressure, sometimes from both peers and families, to avoid involvement in Indian things, to be successful by being like white Americans. There may even be counterpressures within the same family, with old members valuing Indian ways but seeing them as quiet, contemplative methods for personal peace, young adults also pressuring for the Indian movement but seeing it as an active, aggressive social force, and the middle-aged seeking identification with white American culture as a way out of poverty and prejudice.

The nature of the small community, while it offers strong social supports, also prevents privacy and is a hotbed of gossip. In addition, within most of the communities there are constant long-term feuds. Clans or families may be in conflict, political groups are involved in infighting, and different religious groups view each other negatively. Thus the problems facing Native American children are severe. They include the usual problems of growing up in any society and the additional problems that grow out of living in a minority culture in a state of transition. It is not hard to understand why some would turn to drugs either as a release or as a form of rebellion.

Studies of Drug Use Among Native Americans

There are almost no basic data on the epidemiology of drug use among Native Americans. Strimbu et al. (1973) identified a total of seventy-six Native Americans among over 20,000 college students. Obviously a group of this size cannot be construed as representative of all Native Americans. These students were a very special group who had (1) left the reservation, (2) chosen to attend college, and (3) were living as a very small minority among a very large majority. They were, however, the group with the highest use of drugs, and this is at least suggestive that young Native Americans may have special problems with drugs. Cockerham et al. (1976) compared Native Americans with other students in a high school near the Wind River Reservation. They found that the Native

Americans had a more positive attitude toward drugs and tended to experiment more with them. They also interpret their data as indicating that young Native Americans did not continue to use drugs more than other students. Their own data, as reported in the article, however, suggest the opposite. Twelve percent of the Native Americans reported that they were presently using a drug other than marihuana, while only 3 percent of the other students reported such drug use.

Survey Methodology

The questionnaire for this survey was tested on about 300 students in a pilot study. The pilot study analyses were used to (1) evaluate the questions for internal consistency and completeness, (2) develop and test a method for identifying and selecting groups of adolescents who have highly similar patterns of drug use, and (3) test whether the social and personal questions are relevant to drug use in Native Americans by determining whether they are significantly related to the drug-use patterns.

For most drugs, the three questions that clustered together were: how often they had used the drug in the last 2 months, when they used it, and whether they saw themselves as a user. The item asking whether the person had ever used the drug did not cluster with these three items, and probably does not indicate established use of a particular drug. For most of the drugs, therefore, the three listed items were used together to indicate extent of use.

The survey was structured to include as many adolescents as possible from each of five tribes. Eleven junior and senior high schools were surveyed, including the nine junior and senior high schools used by these tribes. The two schools were added because a significant number of young people from one or more of these tribes were attending them. In addition, lists of those adolescents who were no longer in school were obtained from the five tribes and as many of these young people as could be found were also surveyed.

The survey was administered anonymously to 1,918 seventh through twelfth graders from five different but culturally related Native American tribes in the Southwest. The tribes used in our study differ in degree of isolation, but all are somewhat remote. The least remote is over 40 miles from an urban community but approximately 1 mile from a rural, nonnative American community. Income level is low, but the people are not subject to extreme economic deprivation. Social and religious organizational structures are still retained, but culturally the tribes are clearly in a transition state with considerable modification of traditional institutions. Approximately 52 percent of all the adolescent sample still carried on the tribal roles. The previous description of stresses faced by young Native Americans would be applicable to these tribes.

All the students attending these schools on the day of testing were included in the survey. Where there was evidence of unreliability, exaggeration, endorsing use of fake drugs, or gross inconsistencies in marking items, questionnaires were eliminated. The final sample included 939 males and 905 females between the ages of 12 and 18.

Reliability and Validity

Generally, three items prove to be of use in assessing the extent of involvement with a particular drug: (1) frequency of use in the last 2 months, (2) when the drug is used (weekends, during the week, or daily), and (3) the self-rating as a user of the drug. The items that clustered also had high internal consistency reliability for almost every drug, including the three forms of alcohol. The reliabilities range from 0.84 to 0.94 for different drugs.

There is internal evidence to indicate whether the instrument has discriminant validity across different drugs; that is, whether it shows differences between drugs. A second source of evidence for internal consistency is whether the content of the items that cluster together is meaningfully interrelated. The planned content was established before the cluster analysis was performed. Therefore, if items planned to assess the use of the same drug appear in the same cluster, they provide further evidence for internal validity. In general, the items planned to assess use of a particular drug cluster together, providing evidence of discriminant validity.

Comparison of Native American Drug Use with a National Sample

In order to give some perspective to our findings of drug use, we compared our group with a more broadly based sample of adolescents taken from the large-scale study done at Columbia University (Elinson et al. 1973). Their sample of approximately 32,000 students (grades 7 to 12) was selected from both large and small cities, upper- and lower-middle-class school areas, and black and white neighborhoods in four different regions of the United States.

The general format of the drug-use sections of the questionnaire is similar to that used by Elinson et al. (1973), but questions were modified to make them easier to read and fewer alternative responses were provided. For comparison, the groups were broken up into three subgroups: seventh and eighth graders, ninth and tenth graders, and eleventh and twelfth graders.

Table 17-1 presents the comparison of the drug-use prevalence findings of the two studies. A significantly greater proportion of the young people in the Native American sample in all three grade groups reported having tried alcohol, glue or other inhalants, and marihuana. A significantly greater proportion ($p <$

Table 17-1
Columbia-Native American Comparison: Percentage of Adolescents Reporting Having Tried Drugs

	Columbia Sample			*Native American Sample*			*Technical Institute*
Grades:	*7 and 8* $n = 2{,}412$	*9 and 10* $n = 14{,}074$	*11 and 12* $n = 12{,}553$	*7 and 8* $n = 683$	*9 and 10* $n = 607$	*11 and 12* $n = 454$	$n = 276$
Inhalants	9.97	11.69	11.13	15.37*	18.90*	17.36*	30.30
Cocaine	4.51	7.51	11.03	3.37	7.41	8.11	15.20
Amphetamines	6.46	15.12	21.29	5.57	14.40	20.93	35.70
Heroin	2.73	3.46	4.21	2.34	3.13	3.08	5.40
Barbiturates	7.07*	16.80*	22.97*	3.65	9.21	12.97	23.70
Hallucinogens	2.92	8.08	12.35	3.51	6.26	12.50	22.50
Marihuana	17.68	41.55	55.84	27.31*	52.89*	61.76**	69.50
Alcohol	47.40	68.80	78.80	61.80*	82.10*	89.10*	94.90

Note: The technique of differences between proportions of two samples from binomial distributions was used to analyze differences because it is a highly reliable technique sensitive to real differences when the two sample sizes differ greatly.

*Significantly greater, $p < .001$.
**Significantly greater, $p < .01$.

.001) of the young children in the Columbia sample, on the other hand, reported having tried barbiturates. There were no statistically significant differences in the proportions of adolescents in the two samples who had tried cocaine, amphetamines, heroin, or LSD.

Experimentation with other drugs is at about the same level as that of young people in the national sample. This level of use, however, occurs despite the relative isolation of these tribes and is a sign that drugs are available throughout our society if young people want them.

Alcohol is the drug of preference among American Indian youths, with almost 90 percent having at least tried it by twelfth grade. For both the national sample and the Native American sample, alcohol use is prevalent by the seventh grade. There is another large increase in both samples by the ninth grade, and another increase, but not quite so large, by the eleventh. At every grade level, the Native American sample is higher than the Columbia national sample by approximately the same percentage.

Marihuana is the second drug of preference, with 62 percent of the Indians having tried it by the twelfth grade, with a pattern similar to that of alcohol use. There is considerable use by the seventh and eighth grades (about 18 percent), a very large increase in the ninth and tenth, and some further increase in the eleventh and twelfth. Again, in the seventh and eighth grades, Native American marihuana use is higher, and it stays higher by about the same percentage.

Inhalant use shows a somewhat different pattern. It is already present at close to its highest level by the seventh and eighth grades, increases slightly during the next couple of years, and then stabilizes. Inhalant use is known to be a drug of choice primarily of the very young, with older ages more likely to be involved with marihuana, alcohol, or other drugs. Again, however, inhalant use is higher in the Native American sample at all grade levels. (About 18 percent of the sample had used inhalants.)

One difference that is not noted in table 17-1 is that while the proportion using hallucinogens is about the same in both the Columbia and the Native American samples, the actual drug used may be different. Peyote is often the hallucinogen that is used in the Native American sample, since it is more readily available in their area. This availability, however, does not increase the overall use of hallucinogens. About the same number of Native Americans and other adolescents seem to develop an interest and involvement with hallucinogens, whether it be peyote among Native Americans or LSD, the most frequently encountered hallucinogen in other groups.

Among the very young Native Americans there is a higher involvement with alcohol, marihuana, and inhalants, which are the drugs that youngsters on a reservation are likely to find most available. Although alcohol is banned in many of these communities and it is sometimes 30 miles to the nearest bar, it is nevertheless readily available to children. Marihuana can be grown in open fields and is available in most locations. Other drugs are obviously available also but probably are too expensive and less familiar to the younger children in these areas. Once children are aware of inhalants and their effect, it seems to be almost impossible to keep them from experimenting with these substances. Local stores in some study areas had already controlled and limited the sale of airplane glue, but as has happened in other communities, the Native American children soon discovered other sources of inhalants (paint, gasoline, ink markers, etc.) and started using them, many even before entering the seventh grade.

Ethnographic studies have shown that alcoholism among adult Native Americans (Heath 1975) can present special problems. Levy and Kunitz (1974) found that there is also some evidence that alcohol use has different patterns among Native Americans. There is an Indian way of drinking, a social pattern that dictates the way alcohol is often used. It consists of binge drinking of large amounts with long periods of abstinence. Certain special situations call for this type of drinking in many cultures, but it is a more typical way of drinking among Native Americans. The danger involved is reflected in the large number of accidents and injuries among Native American adolescents. There is also an exceptional number of "unexplained" deaths among adolescents, particularly in some communities, and there have been epidemics of suicides in some places. While these cannot be tied directly to drug or alcohol use, there have been local reports that they are drug-related. The Bureau of Indian Affairs reported (1974) that in 1973, the age-adjusted suicide death rate for Indians and Alaskan natives was more than twice the rate for the total U.S. population, that accidents were the leading cause of death among Native Americans, and that cirrhosis of the liver was the fourth most frequent cause of death.

The Continuation of Drug Use Among Young Native American Adults

The curves in figure 17-1 show that prevalence of drug use continues to increase through the twelfth grade. Does this trend continue into adulthood? We do not have evidence of increased rates from the communities involved in this study, since adults were not sampled. We did, however, obtain data on drug use from an older group of Native Americans (Goldstein et al. *in press*) in pretesting the questionnaire used in this study. This pretest was conducted at an urban technical institute, a post-high-school institution which provides training in arts and technical skills for students from various reservations throughout the country.

We surveyed 127 male and 149 female students with a mean age of 21, of whom 90 percent were between ages 18 and 27. Higher percentages of this older (young adult) sample were found to have used *all* types of drugs, compared with the high school students (see table 17-1). Since the group at the technical institute is older than the high school students, they have had more time to expand their

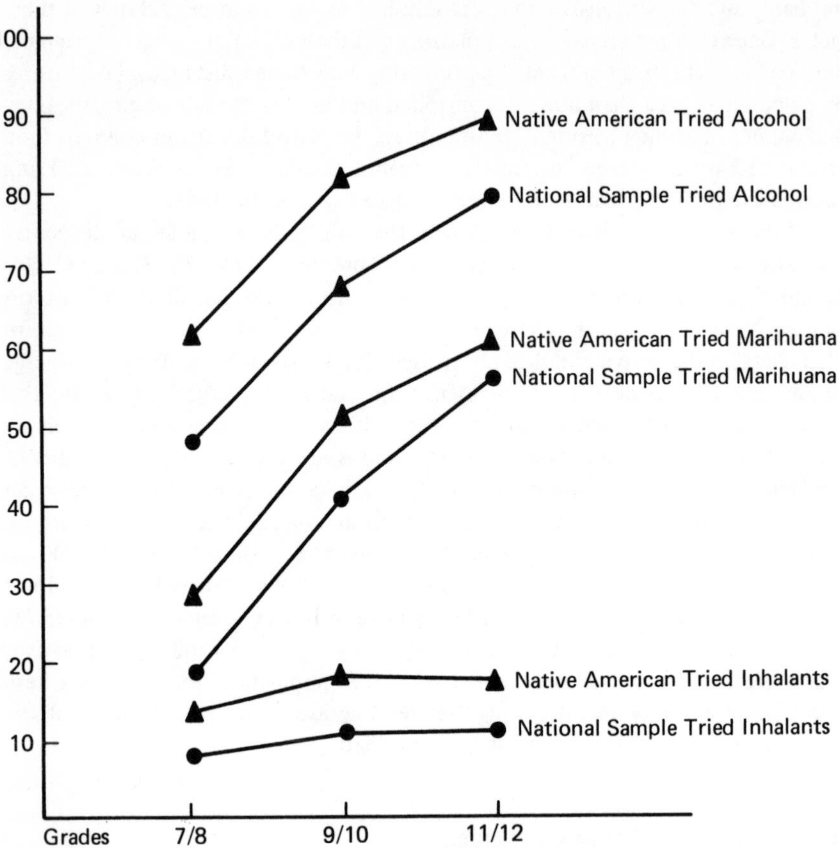

Figure 17-1. Comparison of Native American and National Samples.

lifetime drug experiences, particularly with inhalants, cocaine, heroin, barbiturates, and hallucinogens. The percentages of prevalence found in this sample (amphetamines, barbiturates, inhalants, heroin, and cocaine) are among the highest reported for nontreatment populations sampled anywhere in the country. In assessing the drugs they had used during the last 2 months before the survey, it was found that there was no greater prevalence of current use of drugs such as heroin and cocaine among the technical institute students than among the high school students. More of them had experimented with various drugs, but it had not led to greater current involvement.

There was, however, a higher prevalence rate of current use of alcohol, amphetamines, and marihuana in the older technical school students. Some of these differences may be due to greater availability of drugs in the urban setting.

Since we have little data on such young-adult Native Americans, it may be that the increasing prevalence of use of these drugs with age which we saw in high school continues into young adulthood. At least, this appears to be true for alcohol and marihuana, the drugs of choice for Native American youths. Considering what has already been known about the susceptibility among Native Americans to alcoholism, this increase in the rate of drug use, in combination with alcohol use, could indicate a potentially dangerous situation.

The increasing rate of amphetamine use at the technical institute is disturbing. Occasional mild use may do little harm, but heavy prolonged use, or use to the point of psychological dependency, or use in conjunction with alcohol, can be a serious problem. It may be, however, that the high prevalence rate at the technical institute is not representative of that age group of Native Americans in general. Perhaps these students initiate use of stimulants when studying long hours for examinations, or amphetamine use may be part of the social culture, the "in" thing to use at this one particular school.

This situation may nevertheless point to a more fundamental problem: it may show what happens when young Native Americans leave their relatively isolated tribal and school settings and come to a large urban center where drugs of many kinds are more readily available.

Types of Drug Use Among Native American Adolescents

The previous information shows how much experimentation has occurred with drugs but does not tell us much about how young Native Americans actually use drugs. For example, two young people may both have tried marihuana, but one of them now smokes it occasionally and the other smokes everyday and uses amphetamines and barbiturates as well. They are clearly very different types of drug users. Calling them both marihuana users would not be an adequate description of their drug-use patterns.

First, we developed an overall score indicating the degree of involvement with each drug. This was based on three questionnaire items: (1) the total number of times the substance was used during the past 2 months, (2) whether the substance was used only on weekends or on weekdays, daily, etc., and (3) the subject's self-rating on a 6-point rating scale of how "light" or "heavy" a user he or she is. Cluster analysis (Tryon and Bailey 1970) was used to determine which rating scale points in each of the three items grouped together to indicate the following levels of use of each drug: (1) nonuser, (2) light, (3) moderate, and (4) heavy.

On the basis of this information, we were able to assess the different patterns of drug use found among young Native Americans. Only 12 persons out of almost 1800 were considered to be addicted or drug dependent; 3 used

Table 17-2
Proportion of Young Native Americans in Each Drug-Use Type

Drug Use Group (In order of risk)	*Grade in School*		
	7th and 8th	*9th and 10th*	*11th and 12th*
Heavy use dangerous drugs	21.7	39.1	29.1
Use of several dangerous drugs	10.0	40.0	50.0
Inhalant use	37.0	44.4	18.5
Hallucinogens use	20.0	40.0	40.0
Heavy marihuana use	13.7	43.8	42.5
Heavy alcohol use	19.6	37.5	42.9
Light inhalant use	37.6	35.6	26.7
Light hallucinogens use	30.8	38.5	30.8
Light marihuana use and experimentation	25.0	33.3	41.7
Light marihuana use	29.3	35.9	34.8
Moderate alcohol use	29.5	40.9	29.5
Tried a drug	32.3	36.2	29.5
Very light use	46.1	35.1	18.8
Never used a drug	63.4	24.7	11.9

amphetamines daily; 2 used barbiturates daily; and 7 were heavy and daily users of alcohol. The remaining subjects in the sample were classified in the drug-use categories listed in table 17-2 in order of risk. The determination of the degree of risk for different substances is based on our own judgment. For example, inhalant use is ranked highest, while heavy marihuana use is considered more serious than heavy alcohol use. Table 17-2 lists the proportions of the young Native American sample in each drug-use group. The sections which follow describe each of these drug-use groups and the characteristic patterns of behavior of the subjects.

Heavy Use of Several Dangerous Drugs

This represents a group of young people heavily involved with drugs. They are not addicted or dependent, but are probably in grave danger of becoming addicts. They consume a variety of drugs, such as "uppers" and "downers," marihuana, and hallucinogens. About 1 percent of young Native Americans sampled were heavily involved with several dangerous drugs. Table 17-3 shows what drugs they were using and the extent of their use. About half the young people in this group had ever used heroin. All subjects in the group used multiple drugs, with one or more drugs being used quite heavily. The specific effect of the drug does not seem to be as important to the users as the use of drugs within the social structure of the group and the general interest in achieving a "high" state.

Table 17-3
Percent of Young Native Americans Using Each of Four Drugs, in Degree of Use within the Subsample Heavily Involved with Dangerous Drugs (Group I) ($N = 23$)

	No Use (%)	*Light Use (%)*	*Moderate Use (%)*	*Heavy Use (%)*
Heroin	47.8	21.7	8.7	21.7
Amphetamines	–	26.1	56.5	17.4
Cocaine	26.1	43.5	8.7	21.7
Barbiturates	–	43.5	47.8	8.7

Use of Several Dangerous Drugs

This second group, presented in table 17-4, has a similar pattern to the first group, in that they use the same drugs, but not as heavily or as often. Members of this group take a variety of drugs, and all use at least one and generally more than one of the drugs that are high on the danger hierarchy. The drug that is most often associated with multiple-drug involvement is amphetamines, and 90 percent of this group used amphetamines. Heroin use is rare in this group, but cocaine or barbiturate use is common. Avoiding heroin while being willing to use several other hard drugs may be the clearest differentiating characteristic of this group. Heroin still has the reputation as the most serious of drugs.

Inhalant Use

Some of the young people in the previous two groups use inhalants occasionally, but their overall pattern indicates that inhalants are only one more drug in a long shopping list, not their drug of choice. This third group uses three drugs almost exclusively: inhalants, alcohol, and marihuana. All of them either used inhalants

Table 17-4
Percent of Young Native Americans Using Each of Four Drugs, in Degree of Use within the Subsample Using Multiple Drugs (Group II)

	No Use (%)	*Light Use (%)*	*Moderate Use (%)*	*Heavy Use (%)*
Heroin	93.3	6.7	–	–
Amphetamines	–	66.7	33.3	–
Cocaine	–	80.0	20.0	–
Barbiturates	–	76.7	20.0	3.3

more than three times in the 2 months, used them during the week, and/or rated themselves as heavy users. They are thus not just experimenting with inhalants. Nearly all of them drank beer as well, and three-fourths of them used marihuana.

Hallucinogen Use

There are two separate groups whose drug use centers on hallucinogens. The only hallucinogen that the first group uses is peyote, the sacrament of the Native American Church, but they use it outside the church just to get "high." The other group uses LSD or other hallucinogens, with a few using peyote as well. Both groups tend to use marihuana heavily and alcohol moderately, but other drug use in the two groups is quite different: those who use LSD are also likely to have used some amphetamines or barbiturates and a few have used cocaine and are thus more involved in multiple-drug use and more into the drug culture.

Those who use peyote but not LSD show a considerably different pattern. There is little use of amphetamines, barbiturates, or cocaine. This contrast is striking. It suggests that peyote is not viewed by these young Native Americans as merely another hallucinogen like LSD. It is likely that they have seen adults use the drug legitimately and may therefore have less fear of its effects.

Heavy Use of Marihuana

Nearly all of this group rate themselves as "moderate" to "heavy" users of marihuana and as having used it more than ten times during the past 2 months. A few use it daily, although most of the daily marihuana users were involved with other drugs as well and were classified in one of the previous groups.

There is considerable variation in the use of alcohol by heavy marihuana users. Almost all use it to some extent, but only about 1 percent of the total sample use both alcohol and marihuana heavily. The rest of this group tend to use alcohol moderately, although they frequently use alcohol and marihuana together. They are much more likely to use marihuana during the week than they are to use alcohol. Marihuana is probably their drug of choice.

Heavy Alcohol Use

Alcohol is still the most frequently used drug by young Native Americans, and this subgroup uses it quite heavily. They drink during the week as well as on weekends and rank themselves as "moderate" to "heavy" users. They use beer mainly, with liquor and wine being used primarily on weekends and holidays. Adequate data on the amount they use at any one time is not available, but this group is reported to have a very high rate of getting drunk and blacking out from alcohol. While the heavy use of alcohol distinguishes the group, about half of them do use some marihuana as well.

Most of the young people for whom drugs represent a clear and present danger are accounted for in the categories listed above. The rest of the young people used drugs infrequently or not at all. It must be noted, however, that the average age of these youngsters is quite young, and some increase in their drug use is to be expected as they get older.

Light Marihuana and Light Drug Experimentation

Quite a few young people use marihuana occasionally and are experimenting with other drugs as well. (See table 17-5.) Members of this group tend to be quite young, and most are found in the earlier grade levels.

Light Marihuana Use

The young people in this group use marihuana primarily on weekends and holidays and use no other drugs. Few have used marihuana more than nine times in the past 2 months, and most have used it only once or twice. Most also use beer, and some use liquor, moderately or lightly. This is quite a large group, about 15 percent of the total sample. They appear to use both alcohol and marihuana as social drugs, and usually in social settings when they are out with their friends. By the twelfth grade, well over half this total sample of Native Americans, and somewhat over half of the national sample, had tried marihuana (see figure 17-1). The prevalence, or extent, of its use as a social drug seems to be approaching that of alcohol.

Table 17-5
Percent of Total Sample Who Tried One or More of Each of the Listed Drugs Only Once or Twice

Inhalants	27.9
Cocaine	2.3
Amphetamines	9.0
Heroin	3.2
Barbiturates	6.3
LSD	6.3
Marihuana	67.1

Never Tried a Drug or Alcohol

There are still quite a few in this young Native American sample who have never even tried alcohol. For the most part they are very young and can be expected to follow the pattern of alcohol use of the older Native American students, since alcohol use has been part of their culture. By the time they are in the twelfth grade, 90 percent of young Native Americans will have tried alcohol.

Characteristics of Sample: Age

Drug use spreads over the entire age range of the survey youth population, but the higher-risk drug users were usually the older adolescents (see table 17-6). Inhalant users were the one exception, since inhalants were primarily used by younger children. Table 17-6 suggests that drug use gets heavier or more severe with increasing age, and that some of those now using drugs lightly will end up using them heavily. Previously reported data on technical college students suggest that this trend does not end with high school.

Half of those who had used beer and half of those who used inhalants first tried these two substances before they were thirteen. The median age for first trying other drugs, including marihuana, is over fourteen. Alcohol and inhalants are more available and are used earlier than other drugs. The percent of seventh and eighth graders who tried inhalants is almost as large as the percent of inhalant use in the eleventh and twelfth grades. Either the rate of inhalant use is increasing (youngsters stop using inhalants after a certain age), or the children are beginning to use inhalants at a younger age. Those who became users or

Table 17-6
Average Age and Sex Distribution of Drug-Use-Type Groups

Average Age	*Drug-Use Group*	*Males (%)*	*Females (%)*
15.7	Heavy use of several dangerous drugs	54.5	45.5
16.2	Use of several dangerous drugs	43.3	56.7
14.6	Inhalant use	33.3	66.7
15.8	Hallucinogen use	100.0	–
15.8	Heavy use of marihuana	64.0	36.0
15.5	Heavy alcohol use	53.7	46.3
14.2	Light inhalant use	52.0	48.0
15.9	Light hallucinogen use	46.2	53.8
15.5	Light marihuana and drug experimentation	41.7	58.3
15.2	Light marihuana use	48.8	50.8
14.6	Moderate alcohol use	56.8	43.2
14.9	Tried a drug once or twice	55.0	45.0
14.4	Very light alcohol use	49.4	50.6
13.7	Never tried a drug or alcohol	34.8	65.2

heavy users of dangerous drugs started with drug use earlier than the average. Not all of them had used inhalants, but of those who did, half began using them before they were eleven years of age.

Sex

More boys than girls had tried or used alcohol, had tried or used marihuana, and had tried inhalants (table 17-6). In fact, only one-third of those who had never tried alcohol or any drug were boys. Native American boys are encouraged to be more adventurous and to "act out" more than girls, and an indirect effect of this may be more drug and alcohol experimenting as well. Despite the greater tendency for boys to experiment with alcohol and marihuana, the heavy-drug-use groups include equal numbers of boys and girls. The groups using alcohol heavily, both marihuana and alcohol heavily, and the groups using several dangerous drugs were about equally divided between the sexes.

While more boys than girls experimented with inhalants, or used them lightly, the inhalant group that used inhalants moderately to heavily was about two-thirds girls. The very young children who use inhalants heavily seem to feel isolated and without opportunity. Perhaps more Native American girls have these feelings than boys and turn to inhalants as a way of escaping these feelings.

Personal and Social Characteristics Related to Drug Use

As part of the plan of this study we had tried to develop measures of demographic, personal, and social characteristics that might be associated with drug use among young Native Americans. We have a number of different hypotheses, partly derived from the literature and partly from our own observations. These data were then analyzed using a cluster analysis technique.

Tribe Characteristics

We do not know yet what it is about a tribe that prevents or encourages drug use, partly because the tribes are different in so many ways. Isolation could prove to be a factor. There was slightly less drug use found in the more isolated tribes, perhaps because it was harder to get drugs. Even in the most isolated of the tribes studied, however, some individuals had been able to acquire almost any type of drug.

The more isolated tribes with less drug use also tended to have more traditional values and attitudes. The people and tribal leaders had more negative attitudes toward drug use, which may have helped discourage such use. We found, however, that the tribe in which the tribal leaders punished children most severely for drug use had the *highest* percentage of very heavy drug users. The severe punishment may have developed because the tribe had so many drug-related problems. On the other hand, the pattern of punishing severely may have preceded and may have been one of the causes of the more severe drug use by making some of the punished children feel rejected by and alienated from adults. In response they could have gone on to use drugs even more heavily.

Traditional Native American values did not appear to be related to drug use among the young people themselves. Those who felt it was quite important to speak a Native American language, learn legends or tribal stories, and take part in traditional practices were as likely to use drugs as those who felt it was unimportant.

Tribes that had more alternative activities for young people reported less use of the most dangerous drugs. They did not, however, use less alcohol and marihuana. Slightly under half the drug users in the sample said that one reason they used drugs was that there was "nothing else to do around here."

The Family

In the tribes surveyed, 33 percent of the fathers and 10 percent of the mothers were not living at home. In the families of the young people who used dangerous drugs heavily, 56 percent of the fathers and 44 percent of the mothers were not at home. If the family is broken, and particularly if the mother is not living at home, it appears that children are more likely to be involved in drug use. Among young people who do not use drugs or who only use alcohol moderately, 75 percent have married parents, while only 50 percent of those who use dangerous drugs have married parents.

Those young people who perceived their families as being somewhat more successful "in the Indian way" also felt that they, personally, would be more successful "in the Indian way" and were less likely to use drugs. (See figure 17-2.) The children who were most heavily involved in drugs felt their families were less successful "in the Indian way." It is not just the overall success of the family that counts. Success "in the white American way" did not appear to be associated with drug use in the same way. It seems likely that where there is a strong intact family which has good traditional values and plays an important part in tribal affairs, the children are less likely to use dangerous drugs.

The feeling that the family cared about the children and about their using drugs was also related to drug use. When asked what their parents' feelings were about drugs, most of those who used drugs said "They don't care what I do." This may have been partly because many of these children came from broken

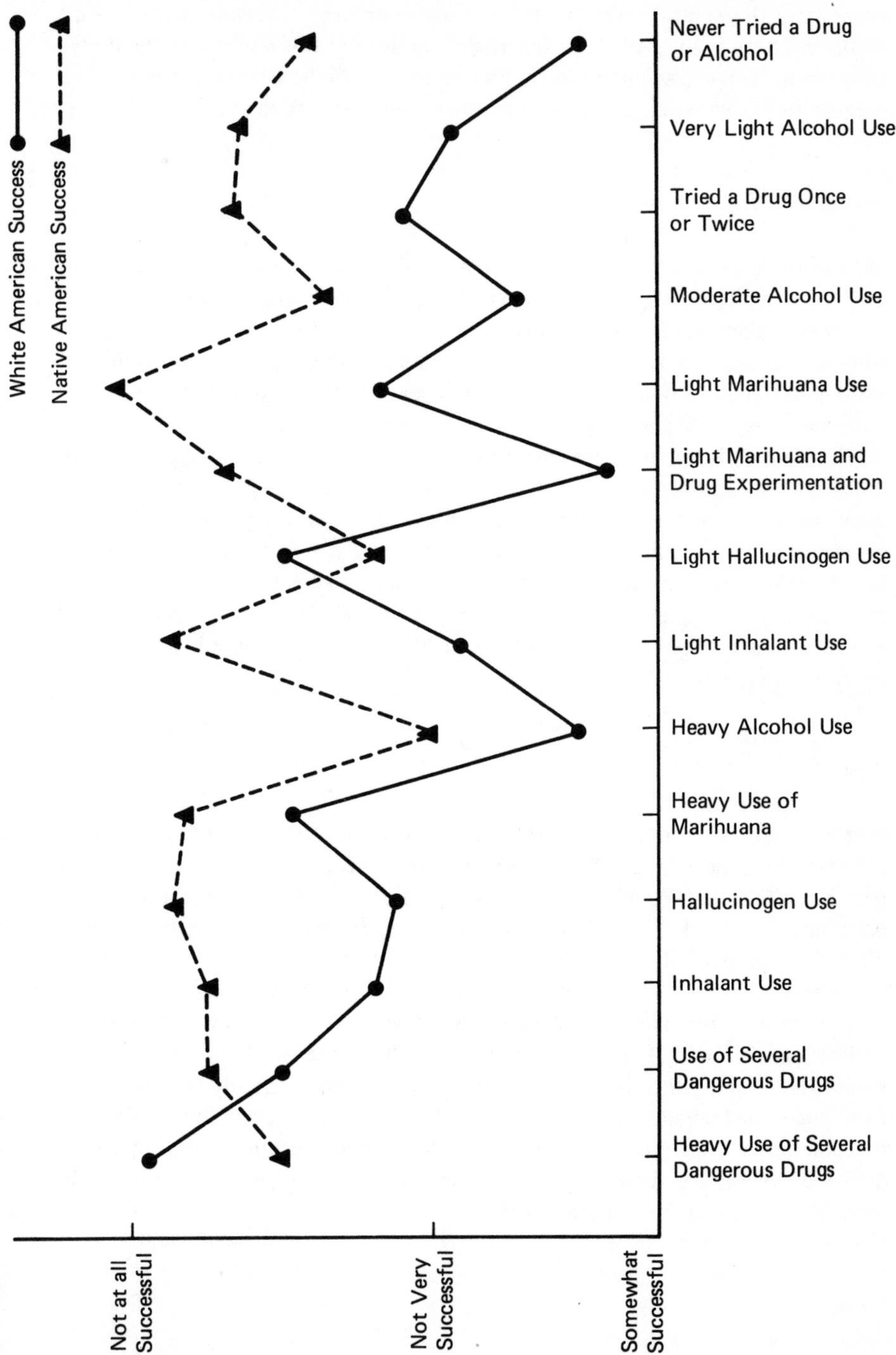

Figure 17-2. Native American Success versus White American Success.

homes and the parents were not there to care for them; or it may be that some of the children who used drugs felt their families did not really care; or it may have been, in part, an attitude that some of the children projected onto their parents, or exaggerated, by way of justifying their own drug use behavior.

School

Most of the drug and alcohol users were not failing in school, and many even had very good grades. Generally, however, the more involved with drugs they got, the poorer their grades were likely to be. Unexpectedly, some of the students who were most heavily involved with drugs had good grades. It is possible that many poor students who were heavily into drugs dropped out, leaving only those who were able to do good school work despite heavy drug involvement.

Students who were more involved with drugs had a lower expectancy of doing well in school, and inhalant users had the lowest expectancy of all, the least chance to access academic goals. This agrees with other information that suggests the young inhalant users may have already given up, feeling that the future holds little in store for them. (See figure 17-3.) There is also some evidence that young drug users are more distant from their teachers in the school and feel their teacher's advice is less "valuable" than young people who did not use drugs. (See figure 17-4.)

Peers

Peer attitudes are dramatically related to drug use. Figure 17-5 shows peer influence on drug-taking behavior, while figure 17-6 shows the mean scores for peer sanctions: (1) Would your friends try to do something to make you stop using drugs or alcohol? (2) Would you do something to make your friends stop using drugs or alcohol?

The peer group is a potent force for young Native Americans. Friends of drug users are also likely to be users, encourage use, and apply few sanctions against use. Friends of nonusers are likely to be nonusers, discourage use, and apply sanctions against use. Two different factors are probably involved here. First, the young person in a particular social group is under considerable pressure to conform to that group's attitudes and behaviors, including those related to drug use. Second, the young person interested in drug involvement is more likely to seek friends who share those attitudes.

Social Respect

Two survey items ask how important it is to be a "good person" or a "good student." The items were meant to assess how much the young person wants the

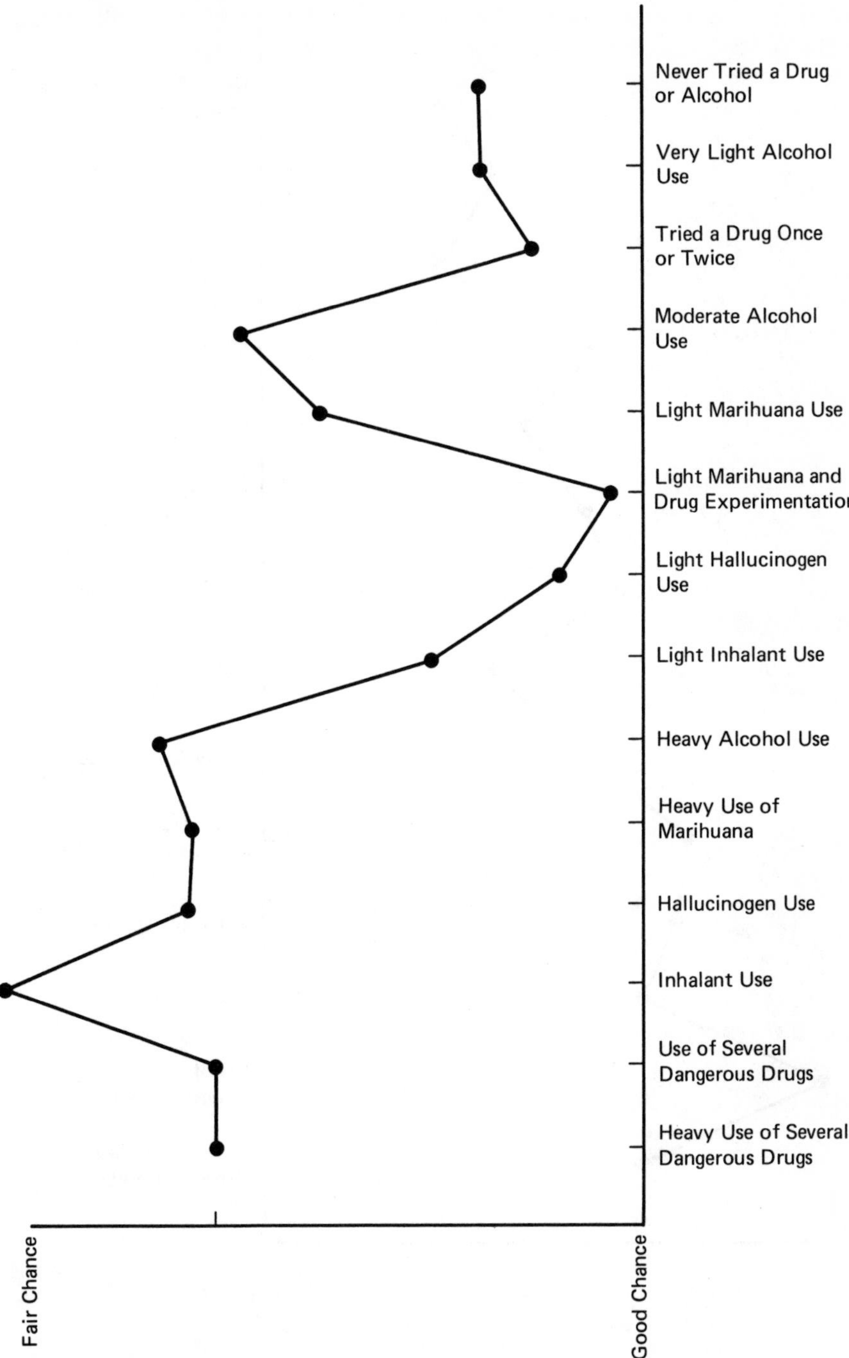

Figure 17-3. Access to Goals (Academic).

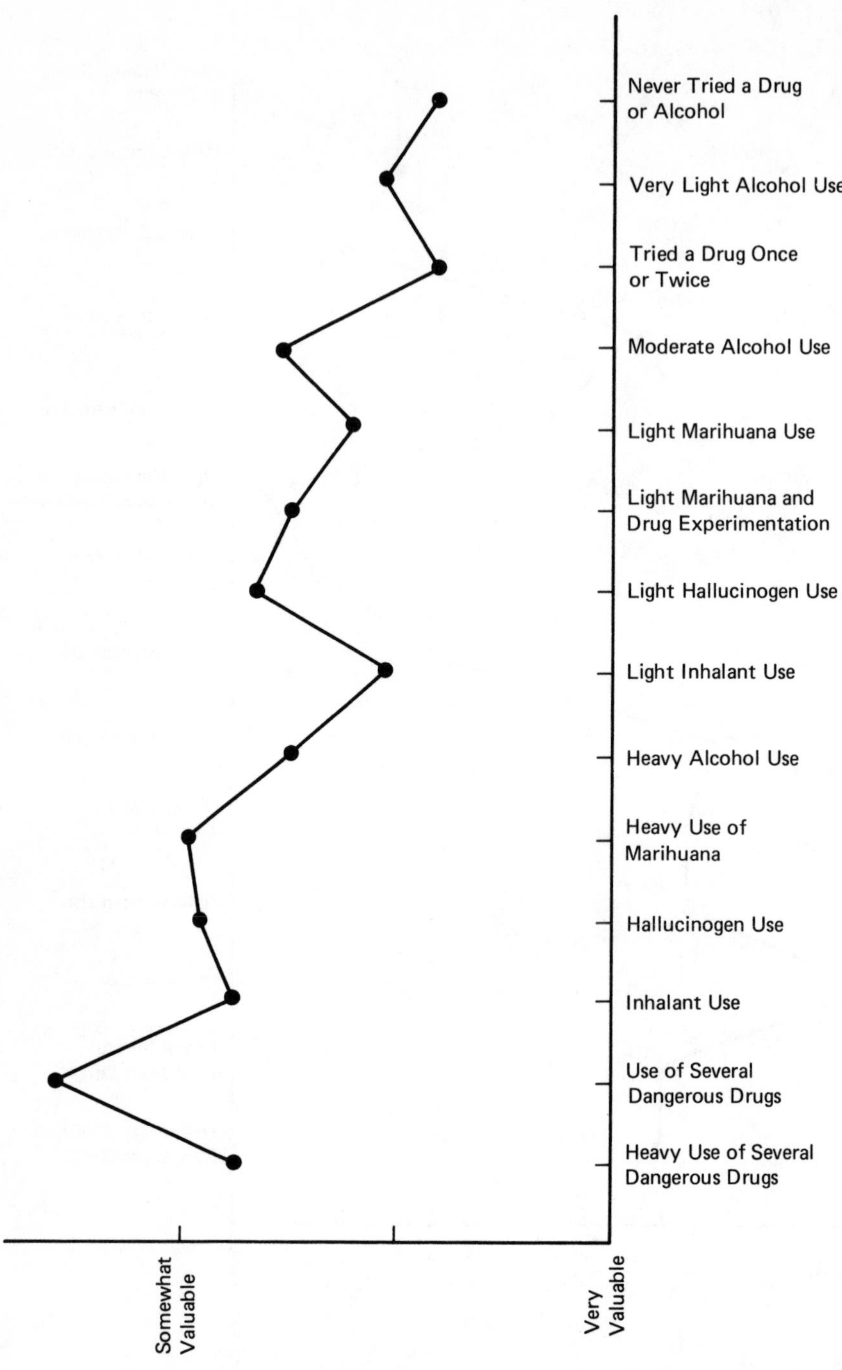

Figure 17-4. Teacher Advice.

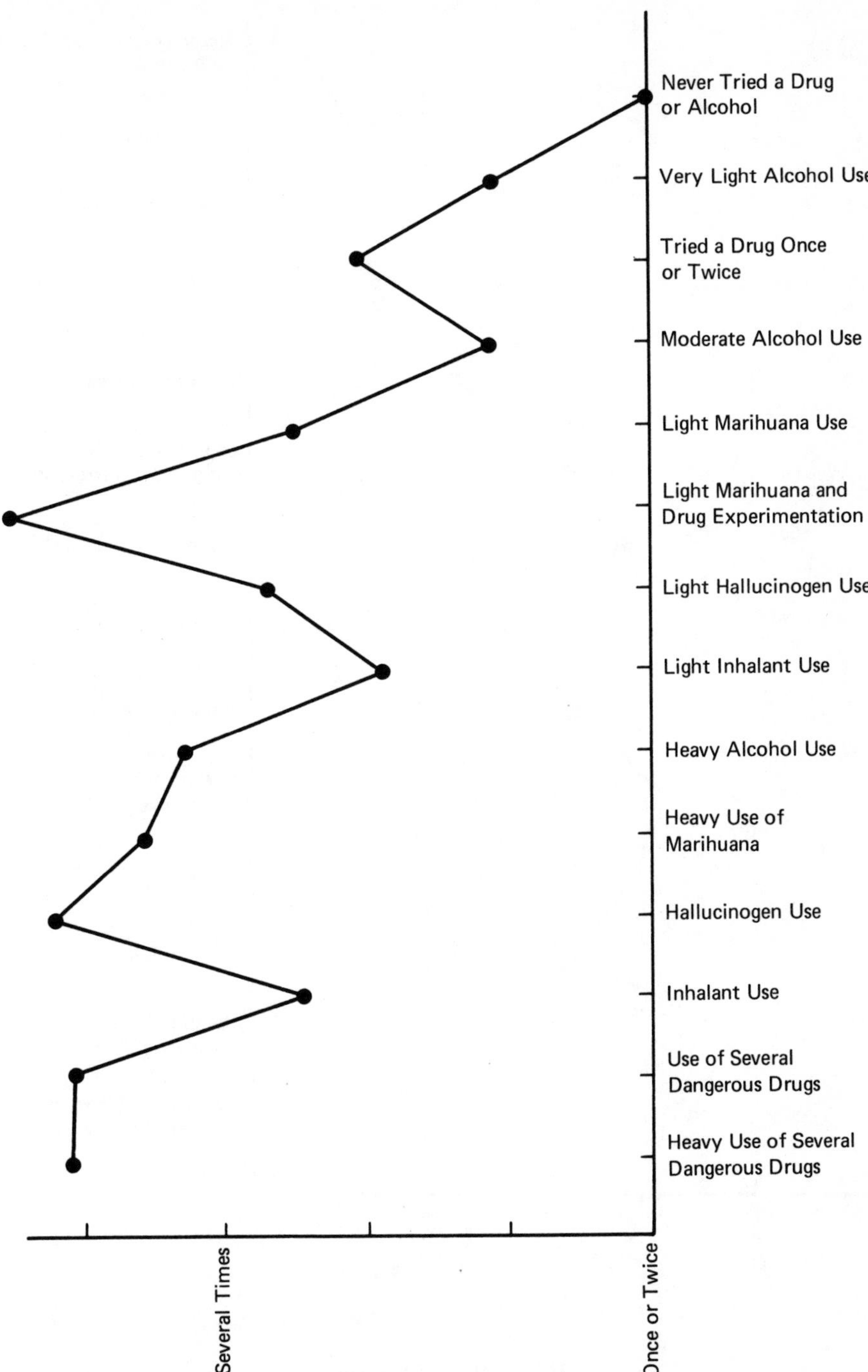

Figure 17-5. Peer Encouragement to Use Drugs.

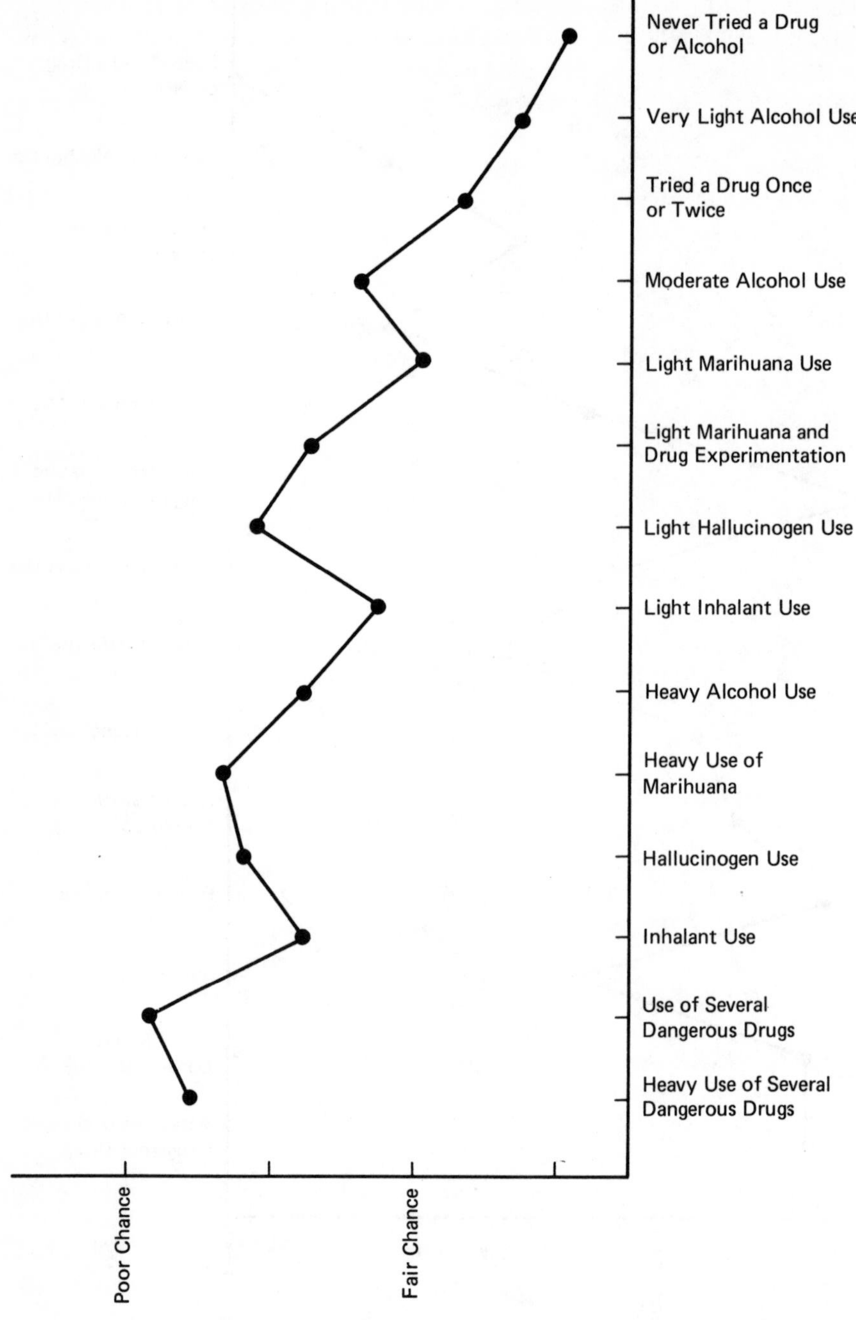

Figure 17-6. Peer Sanctions.

respect of others. It was interesting to find that the desire to be seen as a good person is highly related to the desire to be seen as a good student, although there is slightly more desire to be a good person. For the nonusing part of the sample, there may, in fact, be an overemphasis on school work as a basis for valuing a person.

Questions in the same cluster asked how important it is to their parents and to their friends that they be a "good person" and a "good student." For subjects not involved in drugs or alcohol, the person's own need to be a good person or good student was found to be more closely related to family attitudes than to the attitudes of their friends, while this was not true for the users. This could be a very meaningful finding, suggesting the possibility that family influence can be used to prevent drug use, at least to some extent. The students who use drugs or alcohol did not report as much need for social respect. (See figure 17-7.) They apparently felt less pressure from their families to be good students or good persons. It was still somewhat important to them, but not nearly as important as it was for those students who did not use drugs or alcohol.

Religion

The young people who attend religious ceremonies regularly or often and perceive themselves as being religious were less involved with drugs. The strength of the religious identification and the practice of religion were more highly correlated (negatively) with drug use than was the particular type of religion or church. It is conceivable that there is a causal relationship, and that a strong religious identification and practice is an important factor in prevention of drug use and abuse.

Attitudes toward Deviant Behavior

It was found that young Native Americans from these tribes have strong negative expressed attitudes toward socially unacceptable or deviant behavior. They say it is wrong to lie, steal, or skip school. Those more heavily involved with drugs, however, tend to express somewhat higher tolerance of deviance. (See figure 17-8.) The students who use drugs, compared with those who do not, were also more likely to have talked back to their teachers, cheated on tests, or damaged property on purpose. (See figure 17-9.) Almost half of those who used no drugs, however, said they had damaged property at one time or another, and talking back and cheating on tests happened even more frequently. The amount of this unacceptable behavior is thus highly inconsistent with the attitudes expressed toward this type of behavior.

The groups with the heaviest involvement with drugs had lower expectation

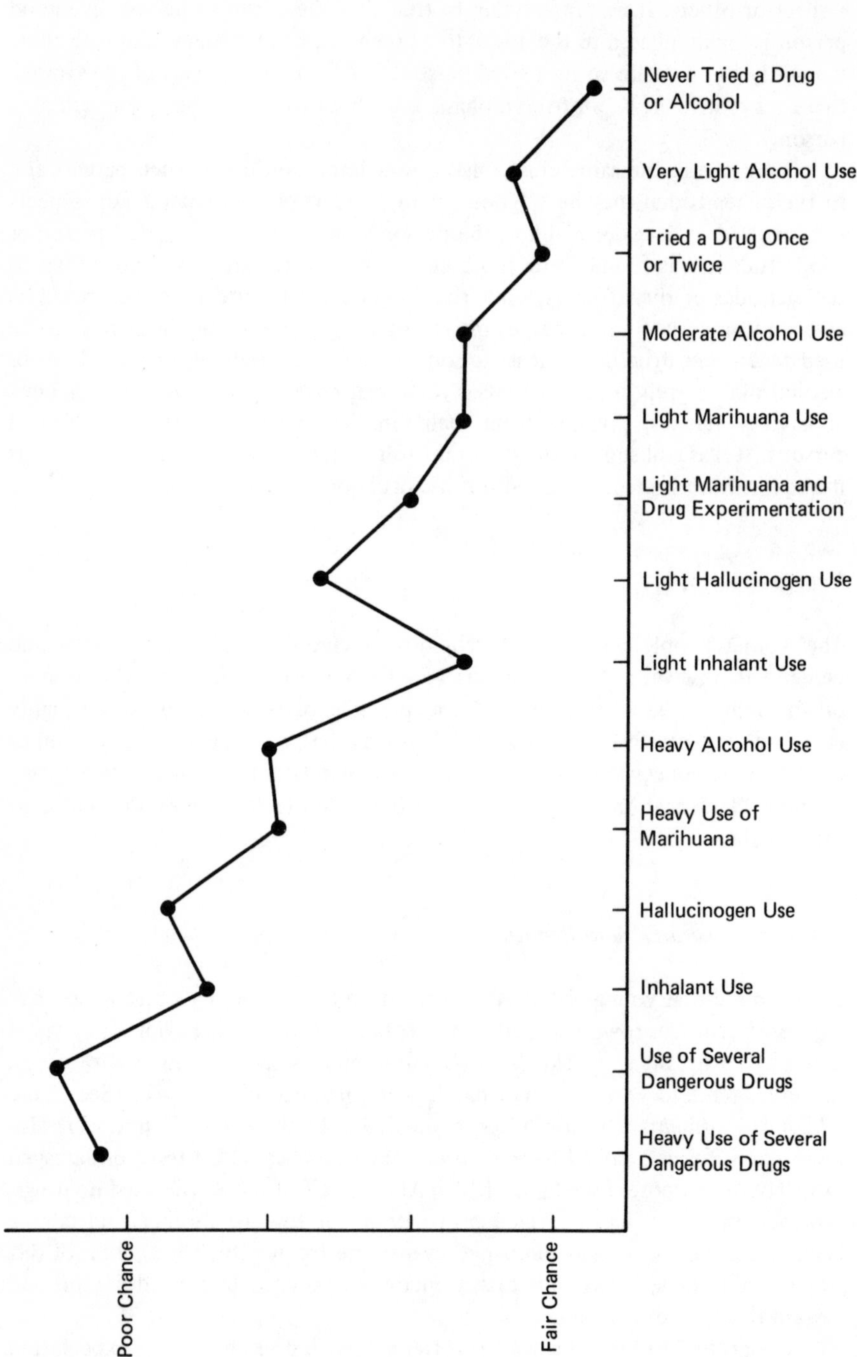

Figure 17-7. Importance of Respect.

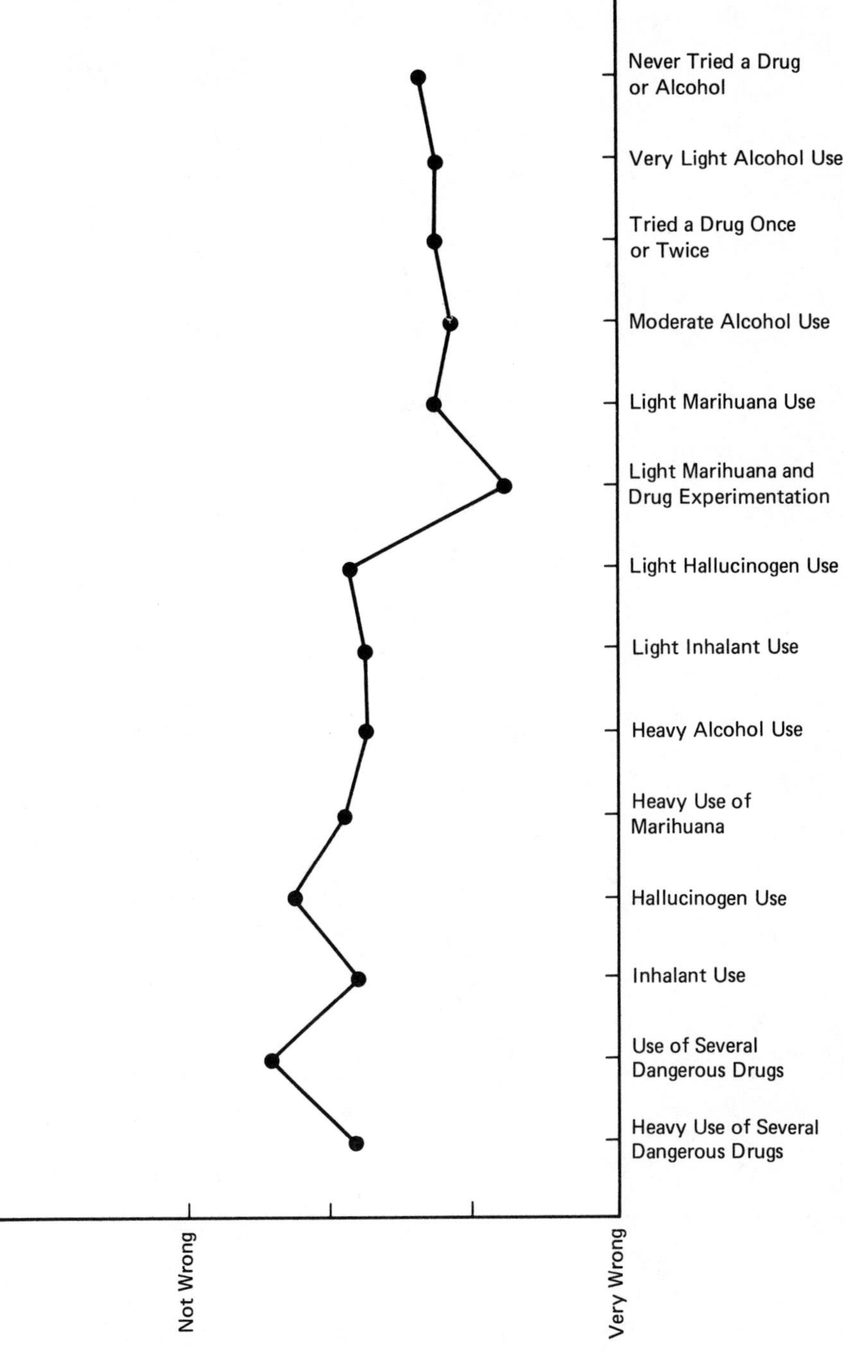

Figure 17-8. Attitudes toward Deviance.

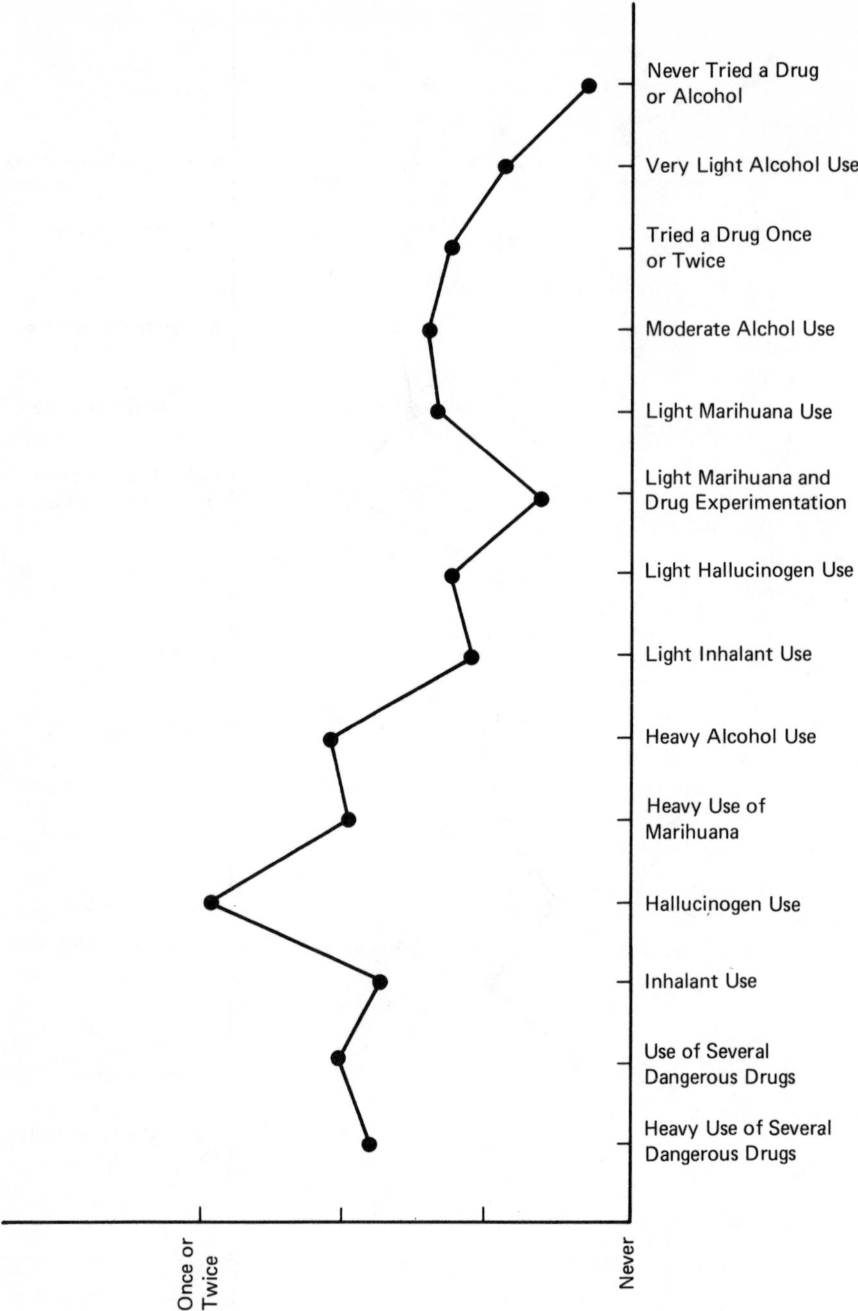

Figure 17-9. Deviant Behavior.

of achieving their life goals. They felt that there was less chance of earning a good living and/or of being respected by others. The young people who used inhalants had the lowest expectancy of all, suggesting a high degree of discouragement among them. At age 14, many felt that they were already failures and had already given up on life. (See figure 17-10.)

Summary

There is evidence that social surroundings, family conditions, and personal attitudes are all related to drug use, but additional information is needed to clarify these relationships. First, the broken family, a common condition among Native Americans, is an important factor in very heavy drug involvement. About 500 of the approximately 1,500 families in this sample did not have fathers living at home. Most of the young people from these homes did not end up using drugs heavily, but a disproportionate number did. If the mother is not living at home, the child is more likely to be involved in heavy drug use. Heavy and self-destructive drug abuse is a multiply determined problem, and no one factor, such as coming from a broken home, is sufficient to explain it.

Hallucinogen use is of particular interest in this group because of the use of peyote as a religious sacrament. It was learned that children of the Native American church used peyote to get "high" (not in church ceremonies) slightly more often than children of other religions, but in general, the greater the identification with religion, including the Native American Church, the less drug use. Peyote users tend to limit themselves to peyote and marihuana, while LSD users tend to experiment with other drugs much more often.

The young Native Americans who use drugs are more likely than nonusers to be somewhat alienated from both the Indian and the white American culture. They have less contact with the social institutions which discourage drug use. Their families are less successful in the "Indian way." They are less religious and have less respect for their teachers' advice. Those with a history of involvement in several dangerous drugs also expressed less need for the respect of others, further reducing the possible effect of social influence. They engage in more deviant behaviors and think that some deviant behaviors are less "wrong" than do nonusers.

While alienated from major social systems and institutions, the drug users are not alienated from their peers. The close match of peer attitudes with drug use indicates that the user either selects friends with similar attitudes and interests or responds to peer pressures.

There is little evidence from this study that a specific type of drug use is related to any specific social or personal characteristic. However, it appears that greater use of drugs is associated with greater social-personal problems. Thus drug use by these adolescents may be one facet of a general response to an

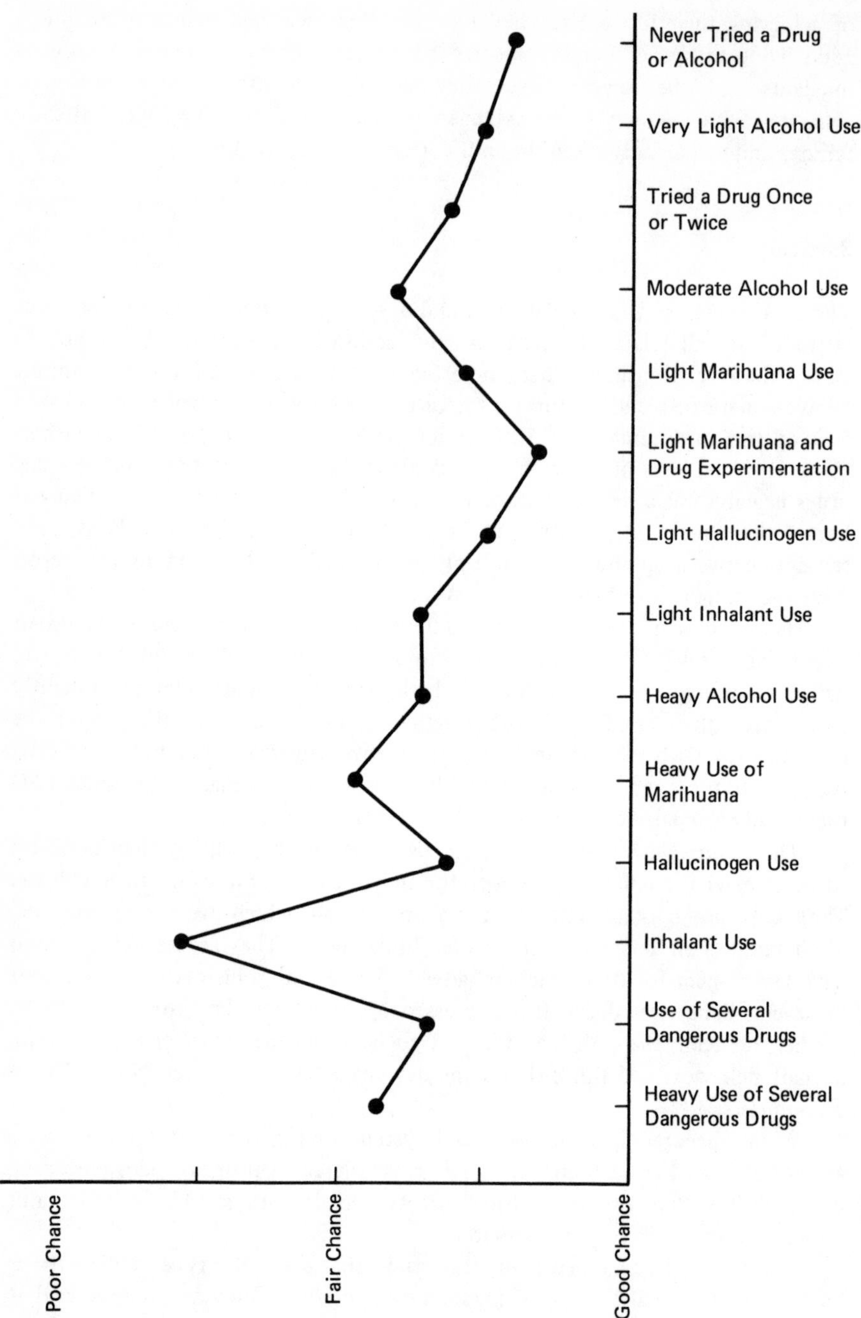

Figure 17-10. Expect to Meet Life Goals.

underlying social and personal malaise. The other alternative, that the drug use leads to alienation, is also possible, or both may be true.

Inhalant Use: A Special Problem

Young people who are heavily involved with inhalants appear to have special problems and needs. Many of them end up heavily involved with drugs, and they have a low expectancy of achieving any satisfactory life goals. Why does this early feeling of failure develop? Is it one of the prime causes of inhalant use? There have been reports of coma and death resulting from inhalant use. Bass (1970) reported over 100 deaths in the 10-year period of the sixties from solvent sniffing. Others have challenged this report (Brecher 1972; Silberberg and Silberberg 1974), suggesting that the danger from inhalant abuse is much overrated. Despite these challenges, inhalant abuse needs to be considered as a major health problem. In the sixties, abuse was most often of toluene, the classic airplane glue. There is now more control of these substances, but we are increasingly hearing about paint thinners, pan sprays, gasoline, Magic Marker pens, and an endless list of new substances being used by Native Americans and other populations, some of which are far more toxic than toluene (see chap. 12).

The other reason for deep concern with inhalants is the young age of the children who use these substances. Linder and Lerner (1974) found that 25 percent of the fourth graders in their study in San Francisco had tried inhalants. Elinson et al. (1973), for example, report about 11 percent use of inhalants among young people in the Columbia national sample. Children of this age are not knowledgeable enough to protect themselves from the severe consequences. Recently there have been reports of lead poisoning from sniffing gasoline among Shamattawa Indian children (Heidenriech 1976). There have been reports from reservations of children smothering in plastic bags, being burned badly from lighting a match near the fumes, and having accidents resulting from lack of coordination or passing out. The data indicate that about 18 percent of young Native Americans in these tribes had used inhalants, a percentage significantly higher than that reported in the Columbia national sample.

Conclusion

Although the data are still limited, it appears that drug use among Native American adolescents is a serious problem. There is a need, of course, to conduct more intensive studies to determine the extent of drug use in other Native American populations and the underlying causes for such use. The apparent association between early inhalant abuse and later heavy drug involvement reinforces the need for early intervention efforts with young Native American children. Education, prevention, and remedial programs should be planned and tested in practical settings to make sure they are effective with Native Americans.

As studies identify locations with particularly virulent drug problems, local tribes and the Indian Mental Health Service should be encouraged to develop programs to respond to these problems. It is clear from our study that drug use is not an isolated phenomenon, and therefore it cannot be treated as such. Programs should make every effort to seek out and find the roots of the problem, for it is only with this knowledge that they will have capacity to address the complex issues and needs.

Bibliography

Bass, M. 1970. Sudden sniffing death. *JAMA* 212(12):2075-2079.

Brecher, E.M., and the Editors of Consumer Reports. 1972. *Licit and Illicit Drugs.* Boston, Mass.: Little, Brown, pp. 322-323.

Bureau of Indian Affairs. 1974. *The American Indians: Answers to 101 Questions.* Washington: U.S. Govt. Printing Office.

Bryde, J.F. 1970. *The Indian Student: A Study of Scholastic Failure and Personality Conflict.* Vermillion, South Dakota: Dakota Press.

Cockerham, W.C., Forslund, M.A., and Raboin, R.M. 1976. Drug use among white and american indian high school youth. *The International Journal of the Addictions* 11(2):209-220.

Elinson, J., Josephson, E., Zanes, A., Haberman, P.W. 1973. *A Study of Teen-Age Drug Behavior.* Conducted at Columbia University School of Public Health, supported by NIDA grant 2-R01-DA-00043.

Goldstein, G.S., Oetting, E.R., Garcia-Mason, M.A., and Edwards, R. *In press.* Drug use among Native American young adults. *International Journal of Addiction.*

Heath, D.B. 1975. A critical review of ethnographic studies of alcohol use. In R.J. Gibbin, Y. Israel, H. Kalant, R.E. Pophan, W. Schmidt, and R.G. Smart (eds.), *Research Advances in Alcohol and Drug Problems*, Vol. 2. New York: Wiley.

Heidenreich, C.A. 1976. Alcohol and drug use and abuse among Indian-Americans: A review of issues and sources. *Journal of Drug Issues* 6(3):256-272.

The Journal. August 1, 1976, Toronto.

Levy, J.E., and Kunitz, S.J. 1974. *Indian Drinking.* New York: Wiley.

Linder, R.L., Lerner, S.E., and Wesson, D.R. 1974. Solvent sniffing: A continuing problem among youth. *Journal of Drug Education* 4(4):469-473.

Oetting, E.R., and Goldstein, G.S. 1975. *Final Report: Drug Abuse Among American Indian Adolescents.* NIDA, Rockville, Maryland.

Oetting, E.R., Edwards, R., Goldstein, G.S., and Garcia-Mason, V. *In press.* Drug use among adolescents of five Southwestern Native American Tribes. *International Journal of Addiction.*

Silberberg, N.E., and Silberberg, M.C. 1974. Glue sniffing in children—A position paper. *Journal of Drug Education* 4(3):301-307.

Strimbu, J.L., Schoenfeldt, L.F., and Suthern, S.O. 1973. Drug usage in college students as a function of racial classification and minority group status. *Research in Higher Education* 1(3):263-272.

Townsley, H.C., and Goldstein, G.S. *In press.* One view of the etiology of depression in the American Indian. *Public Health Journal.*

Tryon, R.C., and Bailey, D.E. 1970. *Cluster Analysis.* New York: McGraw-Hill.

18 Black Youths and Drug-Use Behavior

Ann F. Brunswick

Introduction

Reported here are data concerning nonmedical substance use taken from a longitudinal study of black youths from the Harlem section of New York City. The purpose of this report is to describe—from an epidemiologic or population perspective—the extent and nature of drug use and characteristics of different drug users in an inner-city black youth population. The rationale for what is reported here is based on a simple but often overlooked premise: all behavior has meaning—for the individual actor and for the people and institutions with whom he interacts. The first step toward better understanding behavior and hence clarification of its meaning is careful and accurate observation and report—the assumed task of the research reported here. Attention can then be focused on rational treatment of that behavior.

A further premise is that illicit drug use, given its current magnitude, is a phenomenon with social as well as individual determinants. Both aspects need to be clarified. The population studied here, black youths, and the methodological approach, epidemiological, are well suited to contribute to such clarification.

Black youths, historically and currently, are known to be at high risk for illicit drug use. Indeed, as will be seen shortly, the at risk age for heroin use began at age 13 and was almost completed by age 18 in this population-representative inner-city black youth sample. Why this should be so may be related, in part, to the ambiguity and marginality of the life situation of youth generally. The dubious access the black youth of this study have to the opportunity structure (educational and occupational advance) of society is probably an additional significant factor. These elements thus offer the possibility of shedding some light on two associated issues, namely, the intragroup socioeconomic and sociocultural factors which are related to drug use.

One circumstance that sets this study population apart is its accessibility to illicit drugs ("the heroin capitol of the world") (Waldorf 1973). This may be changing, as shown by one study which found availability distinctions lessening between black and white youths (O'Donnell et al. 1976).

The study questions addressed below are: (1) What is the extent and pattern

The research on which this chapter is based was supported by the National Institute on Drug Abuse Research Grant 5 R01 DA 00852-03. The author also receives partial support from the Center for Socio-Cultural Research on Drug Use, Columbia University.

of nonmedical drug use in a representative sample of inner-city black youths? (2) In what ways do different drugs used nonmedically vary in respect to their patterns of use and in the personal attributes of their users? Out of this broader approach, attention will be focused more specifically on the drug with which greatest social pathology has been linked—heroin. After comparing the characteristics of use and users of heroin with those of other drugs, analysis will be concerned with the question: (3) Who comes into treatment and how do they differ from comparable other young people who have used the same drug (heroin) but have not sought or required treatment? Concommitant with the objective of clarifying the meaning of drug use by comparing use and users across various drugs, a question which has been studied surprisingly little prior to this study will be posed: (4) What are the extent and nature of *sex* differences in prevalence and types of drugs used, in personal correlates of use of various drugs, in the utilization of treatment services, and in the characteristics distinguishing those who are and are not treated?

The analysis undertaken here has eschewed a single-drug approach or even a hierarchical classification of individuals according to their "hardest" or "heaviest" drug use. Instead, it is based on overlapping groups of young people, sorted according to each drug they have used. Thus it portrays drug users as they occur naturally in their natural population, which includes their polydrug interactions (Rittenhouse 1976).

Related Research

Most of what we know about drug use has come from studies of special groups of users (for example, treated populations) and/or from ethnographic community investigations. The limited epidemiologic work that has been produced has come mostly from studies of high school populations which report relatively little information on use of heroin.

Epidemiologic data based on community-representative samples of young people are limited and rarely include longitudinal data. Prior research already reported by the author include a small selected subgroup of drug users drawn from the first wave of this longitudinal study of Harlem youths. That analysis suggested that the attributes which distinguished hard-drug users in this population were similar to what distinguished youthful and predominantly white marihuana users from their peers (Brunswick 1977). Studies of inner-city minority populations have been conducted by Kellam in the Woodlawn section of Chicago (Kellam et al. 1977) and by Lukoff, Kleinman, and Brook in and around the Bedford-Stuyvesant area of Brooklyn, New York (Kleinman and Lukoff 1975; Kleinman and Lukoff 1978; Brook et al. 1977) and have found lower rates of illicit drug use than in the study presented below.

Another epidemiologic study that included drug use among black youth populations was the O'Donnell et al. (1976) hallmark study of male Selective Service registrants between the ages of 20 and 30. It included comparative national white and black samples. Of particular interest were the increasingly similar illicit-drug-use rates among successively younger cohorts of white and black males. Meyers' study of Job Corps youths includes females as well as males and provides comparative data on black, Hispanic, and white youths; male and female drug-use rates were more nearly similar among black youths than others (Meyers 1977).

Jessop, Kandel, and Lukoff (unpublished) have compared findings on drug use among black youths from their school- and community-based investigations, respectively. Findings were consistent with those from the present study in relation to the dominant types of drugs used, but reported rates of use were considerably lower.

Robins has contributed perhaps the earliest longitudinal data based on a community sample of black males who were followed over time from their initial selection in elementary school and demonstrated both the feasibility and validity of retrospective self-reports of drug-use behavior (Robins and Murphy 1967; Robins et al. 1970).

The national survey conducted for the National Commission on Marihuana (Abelson and Fishburne 1976) concluded that the representation of blacks in this national sample was too small for race-specific estimates. Others have noted the limitations of a national sampling frame in rendering adequate estimates of such an unevenly distributed event as "hard-drug" use (Johnston 1976; Lukoff 1976; O'Donnell 1976; Robins et al. 1977). This points to the value of community studies, particularly in those areas known to have high drug-use rates (Brunswick et al. *in press*; Kellam et al. 1977; Lukoff 1976), in enabling comparative analysis with sufficient numbers of drug users *from the same community* so that correlates of use (predictors, concommitants, and/or consequences) can be compared to those of nonuse. And just as important, such area studies provide subsamples for analyzing the correlates of natural cessation of use. More and more investigators are concluding that a substantial portion of drug use, even heavy use, subsides without intervention (Boyle and Brunswick 1978).

Furthermore, drug-use behavior varies from community to community and among different segments (age, sex, ethnic, income) of the same community—in respect both to the extent of use and the drugs of choice. The ultimate utility, therefore, of analyzing prevalence and patterns of drug use in a single high-risk area is to provide a data base for formulating community-appropriate preventive and treatment strategies for specific subgroups (based on age, ethnic, and sex criteria).

Methods of Data

How Data Were Collected

The data for this chapter came from the second wave of a prospective longitudinal health study of urban black adolescents ages 12 to 17 at time of first study.[1] The study group was drawn in the late 1960s on the basis of a stratified community probability sample of households located in a single inner-city health district, Central Harlem, New York City. The initial sample was drawn over two consecutive years with a sampling ratio, each year, of one in twenty-five households. The follow-up was conducted in 1975-1976. At this point the study group included 536 young people 18 to 23 years of age, or 80 percent of the entire initial sample. This actually represented 89 percent of those who were still alive and located in the metropolitan New York City area.

Males and females are represented in the restudy in about equal proportions: males number 277, or 52 percent; females number 259, or 48 percent. Data were obtained through personal interviews conducted at home by ethnically and gender-matched interviewers. As part of a feasibility study, the first 87 of these follow-up interviews were conducted with the oldest panel members between April and September 1975. The remaining 449 interviews (84 percent) were conducted between April and September 1976.[2]

There was no bias or differential sample loss from first to second interviews on the basis of socioeconomic background, health status, or other of more than twenty variables tested. Sample losses due to death (2 percent) and nonlocation (6 percent), which might be expected to affect the least advantaged disproportionately, were offset by young men's recruitment into the Armed Forces and young women's migration south–presumably experienced by the more advantaged in this population. The single variable on which the reinterviewed and nonreinterviewed differed beyond what could be attributed to chance sampling fluctuations was whether or not they had participated in the initial free medical examination: more of the reinterviewed had *not* been examined and, conversely, more of those who had initially come in to medical examinations were lost to reinterview. This runs against what logically might have been expected, and seems indicative of the retained representativeness of the sample, especially of those most likely to have been lost without the thorough follow-up procedures employed to relocate the sample. Interview completion rates are given in table 18-1. Completion rates for males and females were quite similar.[3]

Quality of the Data

Reliability of drug reports on personal interview has been adequately established (Ball 1967; O'Donnell 1976; Robins 1973; Robins and Murphy 1967; Robins et al. 1974; Single et al. 1974; Stephens 1972; Whitehead and Smart 1972). Indeed, O'Donnell has produced evidence to show that opiate users and/or addicts are more likely than others to be candid about socially disapproved behaviors. Generally, there is a tendency to underreport drug use, including current use and lifetime prevalence ("ever use"), and underreporting will be greater for heroin than for marihuana use. Reliability tests of this study's data were consistent with these findings.[4]

Table 18-1
Reinterview Field Completions: Follow-up Study of Harlem Youths 6 to 8 Years Later[a]

Total Sample Listed for Location and Reinterview	*Total (n = 668)*		*Male (n = 351)*		*Female (n = 317)*	
Reinterview completed[b]	80%	(536)[e]	79%	(277)	82%	(259)
	Col. %	(*n*)	Col. %	(*n*)	Col. %	(*n*)
Deceased	2	(11)	3	(9)	1	(2)
Out of metropolitan N.Y. Area						
Address known[c]	6	(44)	8	(29)	5	(15)
No known address	2	(12)	1	(5)	2	(7)
Not located	6	(39)	6	(19)	6	(20)
Nomadic[d]	2	(11)	2	(8)	1	(3)
Refused	2	(15)	1	(4)	3	(11)

[a]Limited to black youths not from Hispanic backgrounds.

[b]Only 63 percent of the reinterviewed were still living in Central Harlem.

[c]"Out of the metropolitan area" includes eighteen currently in the Armed Forces.

[d]"Nomadic" refers to a group who eluded interview even though direct contact was established with the family. The family relayed study messages to respondent. Only two people in this group actually lived at the family address but were never at home despite repeated callbacks; the remaining nine had no address known to their families where they could be contacted.

[e]*n*'s or numbers in parentheses represent actual unweighted counts.

The Sample

At restudy as at initial study, the sample was 52 percent male and 48 percent female. The age, sex, and location distributions of the sample are shown in table 18-2. Just under two-thirds of both males and females (63 and 62 percent, respectively) at follow-up had maintained residences in Central Harlem.

Background characteristics are discussed in greater detail, by sex and by type of drug used, in a later section. Briefly, about one third of the sample had not completed high school, one third had completed high school and gone no further, and one third had some schooling beyond high school.

A quarter of the sample (24 percent) was attending school full time, and another 7 percent were attending part time. Slightly more than one third of the sample had jobs (three-quarters of which were full time). Not surprisingly, more men than women were working: of males, 44 percent (including 13 percent who were also attending school) had jobs; among females, 31 percent were working (including 7 percent who were also attending school). Four percent of the males were in jail when interviewed and 2 percent were in the Armed Services. Almost one fifth of the females were married (18 percent), compared with only 4 percent of the males. Half the females (52 percent) and one quarter of the males (28 percent) had at least one child. Almost three-quarters either were themselves born in the southern United States or had a mother who had been born there.

Table 18-2
Total Sample Characteristics: Age and Location by Sex

Years of Ages	*Male* (*n* = 277)		*Female* (*n* = 258)	
18	(25)	9%	(15)	6%
19	(44)	16	(36)	14
20	(51)	18	(46)	18
21	(73)	26	(63)	24
22	(57)	21	(60)	23
23	(27)	10	(38)	15
Location of Current Residence				
Central Harlem	63%		62%	
Other Manhattan	13		12	
Bronx	17		19	
Other Metro. Area	7		7	

Findings: Prevalence and Patterns of Nonmedical Drug Use

Extent and Type of Drug Use

Table 18-3 presents rates of lifetime experience for nine drugs or drug categories (plus tobacco) by sex and type of drug use (experimental versus nonexperimental users). The data for total "ever used" are included to facilitate comparison with other studies, even though subsequent analysis will focus on nonexperimental use.

Surprisingly, the rate of marihuana use (past month) was about the same as that reported for current cigarette smoking: 57 percent who smoked cigarettes versus 56 percent who smoked marihuana. Furthermore, the marihuana rates were only slightly less than the rate of current (past month) alochol drinking (63 percent).[5]

Table 18-3 shows that rates for males were generally higher than for females on all illicit drugs. An exception was that females reported considerably more experimentation with marihuana and the same percentage of methadone use. These data differ from other study and survey data (see chapter 8), which show that young females are using drugs at the same rate as males. It should be remembered that this study focuses on a special population—an inner-city black population somewhat older than the subjects reported on in other chapters in this book.

The overall prevalence rate of psychedelics use in the Harlem community sample was higher than expected based on data for black youths reported elsewhere (Abelson and Fishburne 1976; Kandel 1976).

Table 18-3
Lifetime Prevalence

	Percentage Reporting Use		
	Male *(n = 277)*	*Female* *(n = 258)*	*Total* *(n = 535)*
Tobacco, cigarettes[a]	57	62	59
Alcohol			
(Once or twice)	3	5	4
(More than)	85	81	83
Marihuana			
(Experimental = 1-2 times)	6	12	9
(User = 3 or more times)	80	58	69
Cocaine			
(Experimental = 1-2 times)	10	6	8
(User = 3 or more times)	32	19	25
Heroin			
(Experimental = 1-2 times)	2	2	2
(User = 3 or more times)	16	10	13
Methadone[b]			
(Experimental = 1-2 times)	4	1	3
(User = 3 or more times)	5	5	5
Psychedelics (acid)			
(Experimental = 1-2 times)	13	5	10
(User = 3 or more times)	12	5	8
Amphetamines			
(Experiemtnal = 1-2 times)	5	2	3
(User = 3 or more times)	7	4	6
Barbiturates, sedatives			
(Experimental = 1-2 times)	5	3	4
(User = 3 or more times)	6	4	5
Glue/other inhalants			
(Experimental = 1-2 times)	4	1	3
(User = 3 or more times)	3	1	2

[a]Inquired about elsewhere in the interview and in terms of current use only. Percentages for all other drugs were based on lifetime experience, i.e., former and/or current use.

[b]Includes both therapeutic and nontherapeutic use. Proportions for all other drugs refer to nontherapeutic use. Analysis of methadone rates suggest that use was restricted to those who had been in methadone treatment, although whether their use was restricted to therapeutic periods and amounts cannot be determined from these data.

Another way of portraying drug experience is by comparing intensity or number of uses of the various illicit drugs. Estimates for this were computed in the Harlem data by multiplying the reported usual frequency of use per year by the number of years used (table 18-4). Examining the mean number of uses *among nonexperimental users* of each drug (table 18-5) provides a perspective on "heaviness" of use by those who used different drugs and highlights some notable distinctions between men and women: the two drugs men used most heavily were marihuana, first, and then heroin, with methadone a distant third; among women, the most heavily used drug was heroin, with methadone and

Table 18-4
Lifetime Drug Use, by Drug, for a Sample of Young Black Men and Women, Aged 18 to 23

	Males (n = 277)		*Females (n = 258)*		*Total (n = 535)*	
	Mean	*S.D.*	*Mean*	*S.D.*	*Mean*	*S.D.*
Marihuana	794	1011	397	693	599	891
Heroin	140	495	100	394	121	449
Cocaine	108	312	29	94	70	237
Methadone	23	135	33	179	28	158
Psychedelics	25	124	7	42	16	94
Downers	8	47	6	48	7	47
Uppers	13	93	3	19	8	68
Glue	3	26	4	40	4	33

Note: Number of uses computed as number of times used per year multiplied by number of years used (less than a year average at half a year).

marihuana following with about equivalent scores. (Note the wide dispersion of scores, denoted by the standard deviations, so that small mean differences are unimportant.)

Evaluation of intensity of drug experiences among cocaine users provides a perspective on how the drug is used. Although cocaine was second to marihuana in terms of prevalence among the illicit drugs, the extent or intensity of its use was of a different and considerably lower order.

Not unexpectedly, rates of use of illicit drugs in this low-income, black

Table 18-5
Mean Lifetime Use (Number of Uses) Averaged Over Nonexperimental Users of Each Drug

	Male			*Female*			*Total*		
	Mean	*S.D.*	*n*	*Mean*	*S.D.*	*n*	*Mean*	*S.D.*	*n*
Heroin	897	950	(43)	1010	816	(26)	939	898	(69)
Marihuana	998	1041	(213)	685	795	(150)	869	958	(362)[a]
Methadone	451	420	(14)	640	505	(13)	542	464	(27)[a]
Cocaine	341	481	(86)	160	169	(46)	278	410	(133)[a]
Psychedelics	211	310	(32)	137	146	(12)	190	274	(44)
Uppers	171	307	(20)	74	71	(9)	142	261	(29)
Downers	135	148	(16)	136	202	(11)	136	168	(27)
Glue	111	126	(7)	326	171	(3)	179	169	(10)

Note: Number of uses computed as number of times used per year multiplied by number of years used (less than a year averaged at half a year).

[a]Total number of cases may be greater or less than the sum of male and female frequencies because of fractional weighting and rounding.

community sample were higher than those reported in studies based on a general population (see, for example, Abelson and Fishburne 1976). An interesting comparison can be made with findings from the recent national survey of men ages 20 to 30 (O'Donnell et al. 1976). Table 18-6 indicates that there was a much higher prevalence of marihuana, heroin, and cocaine use in the Harlem sample than in the national survey.[6]

Comparing black males only, in Harlem and national (O'Donnell et al. 1976) surveys, the difference was smaller but still notable, especially considering the younger age of the Harlem sample. Black males in the national survey had higher rates of alcohol and cigarette use, a similar rate of psychedelic use, and lower rates in other drug categories.

Finally, a comparison of lifetime use and past-year use in this sample (tables 18-7 and 18-8) shows that not all who begin drug use continue it. Particularly in the cases of marihuana and heroin, once a user does not mean always a user (Johnson 1976; Kleinman and Lukoff 1978; and, of course, Winick 1962). Whether reduction in prevalence means interrupted use or permanent termination cannot be determined (see Boyle and Brunswick 1978).

Patterns of Drug Use

As noted earlier, the five drugs (other than cigarettes) of widest nonmedical use in this sample were alcohol, marihuana, heroin, cocaine, and psychedelics. Dominant characteristics of the use of each of these substances (when and where initiated, frequency, recency, duration of use, and mode of administration) reported by nonexperimental users are presented below.

Table 18-6
Prevalence Comparison of Community Survey Black Males Aged 18 to 23 in 1975-1976 and National Sample of Males Aged 20 to 30 in 1975
(In Percents)

	Lifetime Use		
	Harlem	*National Black*	*National All Males*
Cigarettes (current)	57	66	60
Alcohol	88	94	97
Marihuana	86	65	55
Heroin	18	14	6
Cocaine	42	24	14
Psychedelics (acid)	25	25	22
Stimulants	12	25	27
Sedatives	10	24	20

Note: National data from O'Donnell et al. 1975.

Table 18-7
Number of Drugs Used Nonexperimentally (Including Alcohol)

	Lifetime Use			*Current Use (Past Year)*		
Number of Drugs Used	*Total (n = 535)*	*Male (n = 277)*	*Female (n = 258)*	*Total (n = 535)*	*Male (n = 277)*	*Female (n = 258)*
None	9%	8%	11%	15%	12%	18%
One	26	17	35	33	28	39
Two	37	40	35	34	38	29
Three	11	14	8	12	14	9
Four	9	12	5	5	6	4
Five	3	2	4	1	2	1
Six	3	4	1	*	1	–
Seven	2	2	2	*	*	*
Eight	1	1	–	–	–	–
Median	1.4	1.6	1.1	1.1	1.3	.8

Note: Respondents were questioned about nine specific drugs (or kinds of drugs): alcohol, marihuana, cocaine, heroin, hallucinogens (acid), amphetamines (uppers), barbiturates (downers), methadone, inhalants (glue), and an additional "any other drugs" which yielded "other opiates." Consequently, the maximum number of drugs which could be used was ten. This may understate the actual number of drugs used if more than one drug was used from a class.

*Indicates less than 0.5 percent.

Alcohol. Not unexpectedly, alcohol was the drug used earliest. One in five male users reported first use by age 10 (table 18-9). By age 14, half of male drinkers and almost that proportion of females had had experience with alcohol. The modal frequency of alcohol use was daily and/or several times a week for males and slightly less often for females (table 18-10). By time of interview, three-quarters of the alcohol users had been drinking for at least 5 years (table 18-11), and a similar proportion had taken at least one drink within the past month (table 18-12).

Table 18-8
Nonexperimental Use of Five Drugs: Lifetime versus Current (Past Year) Use
(In Percents of Entire Sample)

	Male (n = 277)		*Female (n = 258)*		*Total (n = 535)*	
	Lifetime	*Past Year*	*Lifetime*	*Past Year*	*Lifetime*	*Past Year*
Alcohol	85	81	81	75	83	78
Marihuana	80	66	58	44	70	55
Heroin	16	3	10	3	13	3
Cocaine	32	22	18	14	25	19
Psychedelics (acid)	12	7	5	3	8	5

Table 18-9
Age at First Use
(In Cumulative Percents Based on All "Ever" Using Five Drugs)

	Alcohol		*Marihuana*		*Heroin*		*Cocaine*		*Psychedelic*	
	Male (n = 244)	*Female (n = 219)*	*Male (n = 236)*	*Female (n = 182)*	*Male (n = 49)*	*Female (n = 31)*	*Male (n = 113)*	*Female (n = 61)*	*Male (n = 69)*	*Female (n = 27)*
10 years or less	20	8	3	–	–	–	–	–	–	–
11	25	9	7	1	–	3	–	–	–	–
12	35	19	13	2	–	–	–	–	–	–
13	45	31	21	9	18	10	4	2	1	–
14	51	45	36	21	29	26	7	5	4	–
15	67	60	53	35	47	35	17	6	14	11
16	83	79	68	59	63	71	26	26	20	30
17	94	89	82	74	78	77	43	38	38	44
18	98	96	94	84	86	90	76	64	56	70
19	98	99	96	92	92	97	86	80	82	78
20	100	99	97	96	96	100	95	93	94	85
21	–	–	99	99	100	–	98	98	98	–
22	–	100	100	–	–	99	100	100	100	92
23	–	–	–	100	–	–	100	–	–	100

Table 18-10
Usual Frequency Used

	Alcohol		*Marihuana*		*Heroin*		*Cocaine*		*Psychedelic*	
	Male (*n* = 235)	*Female* (*n* = 209)	*Male* (*n* = 221)	*Female* (*n* = 150)	*Male* (*n* = 42)	*Female* (*n* = 25)	*Male* (*n* = 87)	*Female* (*n* = 48)	*Male* (*n* = 32)	*Female* (*n* = 13)
Daily or few times a week	47%	26%	25%	21%	48%	60%	6%	–	6%	–
Once or twice a week	27	26	43	31	29	28	23	15%	16	15%
Few times a month	14	23	17	27	9	12	30	31	19	23
Once a month	6	9	9	8	5	–	19	23	12	15
Few times a year	6	15	6	13	9	–	22	31	47	46

Note: Based on those who used more than once or twice (nonexperimenters); tables do not always add up to 100 percent because of weighting and rounding.

Table 18-11
How Long Used Drug (Duration)

	Alcohol		*Marihuana*		*Heroin*		*Cocaine*		*Psychedelics (Acid)*	
	Male (*n* = 235)	*Female* (*n* = 209)	*Male* (*n* = 220)	*Female* (*n* = 150)	*Male* (*n* = 43)	*Female* (*n* = 26)	*Male* (*n* = 87)	*Female* (*n* = 46)	*Male* (*n* = 32)	*Female* (*n* = 12)
Less than 1 year	1%	2%	1%	5%	16%	13%	7%	7%	22%	7%
1 to 2 years	1	4	4	8	20	13	16	17	31	40
2 to 3 years	7	4	10	15	10	13	21	26	8	7
3 to 5 years	15	16	26	25	25	29	34	24	31	47
5 years or more	76	74	60	47	29	33	21	26	8	–
Mean no. years used ($\overline{X}$)	7.2	6.3	5.4	4.3	3.1	3.5	3.2	3.1	2.0	2.0
S.D.	4.0	3.2	2.7	2.4	2.5	2.3	2.1	2.1	1.5	1.3

Note: Based on those who used more than once or twice (nonexperimenters); tables do not always add up to 100 percent because of weighting and rounding.

Table 18-12
How Long Ago Last Used

	Alcohol		*Marihuana*		*Heroin*		*Cocaine*		*Psychedelic*	
	Male (*n* = 233)	*Female* (*n* = 208)	*Male* (*n* = 216)	*Female* (*n* = 150)	*Male* (*n* = 43)	*Female* (*n* = 26)	*Male* (*n* = 86)	*Female* (*n* = 46)	*Male* (*n* = 32)	*Female* (*n* = 12)
Less than 1 month	74%	74%	71%	63%	6%	10%	39%	34%	11%	7%
1, less than 2 months	8	7	3	4	–	3	6	12	11	7
2, less than 3 months	5	6	5	2	4	–	5	9	8	–
3 months, less than 1 year	8	6	4	7	8	13	22	23	22	47
About a year ago	3	2	9	4	8	3	14	4	11	13
More than 1 year ago	3	5	7	19	74	71	14	18	36	27

Note: Based on those who used more than once or twice (nonexperimenters); tables do not always add up to 100 percent because of weighting and rounding.

Marihuana. On the average, use of marihuana began later than alcohol. The mean age of onset for males was almost 2 years after alcohol (table 18-13). Half of all the males in the sample had smoked marihuana by 15.4 years of age, and half of all females by 16.8 years. Four in five males and three-quarters of females who used marihuana began by age 17. Few males began to use marihuana past age 18, and few females after age 20 (table 18-9). Reflecting this age distribution, five in six who have used marihuana reported that they were attending school when they began using this drug (table 18-14).

Modal frequency of marihuana use was a few times a week. Three-quarters of male users and half of female users smoked at least this often (table 18-10). Three in five males and almost half the females had smoked marihuana for at least 5 years by time of interview (table 18-11).

Heroin. On the average, heroin was the third drug used by males, beginning after alcohol and marihuana. It was the second drug used by females (table 18-13). Use generally began at age 13, by which time a fifth of male and a tenth of female users had initiated. Three-quarters of heroin users began by age 17. Most began using while still attending school (68 percent of males, 83 percent of females). About one in eight males reported first use when working (table 18-14).

Not surprisingly, modal frequency of use was daily (six to seven times a week), reported by about half of male users and three in five female users (table 18-10). More than half the males and three in five females had used heroin for upwards of 3 years; about one-third had used for five years or more (table 18-11). Few, however, reported that they were currently using heroin: four-fifths of male users (82 percent) and three-quarters of females (74 percent) reported that they had *not* used heroin within the year prior to interview (table 18-12).

Cocaine. On the average, cocaine use began later than the three drugs discussed above. Male users' mean age of onset was about 1½ years and females' about 2 years after heroin (table 18-13). By age 17, almost one-fifth of the male sample (18 percent) and nearly one-tenth of the females (9 percent) had started cocaine use. Both median and modal age of onset was between ages 17 and 18. Most began using while attending school (54 percent of males, 57 percent of females); others began while working (23 percent of males, 20 percent of females) or when "doing nothing" (19 percent of males, 16 percent of females). Modal frequency of use was a few times a month among males (30 percent) and either a few times a month or a few times a year for females (31 percent each) (table 18-10). About half the users had used it for between 2 and 5 years (table 18-11), and three-quarters reported using it within the year prior to interview (table 18-12).

Table 18-13
Reported Age at First Use (Alcohol and Four Illicit Drugs)

	Alcohol		*Marihuana*		*Heroin*		*Cocaine*		*Psychedelics (Acid)*	
	Male	*Female*	*Male*	*Female*	*Male*	*Female*	*Male*	*Female*	*Male*	*Female*
All "ever" users	(244)	(219)	(234)	(182)	(49)	(30)	(115)	(62)	(70)	(26)
Median age	13.8	14.3	14.8	15.6	15.2	15.4	17.2	17.5	17.7	17.2
Mean age	13.2	14.5	15.3	16.2	15.9	15.9	17.5	17.9	17.9	17.9
Used more than 1 to 2 times	(235)	(209)	(216)	(150)	(44)	(26)	(87)	(46)	(32)	(12)
Median age	13.7	14.1	14.6	15.5	14.9	15.4	16.9	17.2	17.1	17.8
Mean age	13.2	14.4	15.1	16.2	15.7	15.8	17.1	17.7	17.5	18.9

Note: Figures in parentheses are numerical frequencies on which medians and means are based; tables do not always add to 100 percent because of weighting and rounding.

Table 18-14
Usual Activity When First Used

	Marihuana		*Heroin*		*Cocaine*		*Psychedelic*	
	Male (*n* = 238)	*Female* (*n* = 182)	*Male* (*n* = 49)	*Female* (*n* = 30)	*Male* (*n* = 114)	*Female* (*n* = 61)	*Male* (*n* = 69)	*Female* (*n* = 26)
Going to school	85%	84%	68%	83%	54%	57%	52%	77%
School work	5	4	8	–	3	2	7	3
Work	5	5	12	3	23	20	22	11
Armed Forces	–	–	6	–	3	–	4	–
Something else (includes housework, traveling)	3	2	–	7	1	5	3	3
Nothing	3	5	6	7	17	16	12	7

Note: Tables do not always add up to 100 percent because of weighting and rounding.

Psychedelics. Psychedelic drugs, as noted earlier, showed a higher ratio of experimental to nonexperimental use than did any other drug. Indeed, the number of nonexperimental female acid users was exceedingly small ($N = 12$), and therefore, these estimates are likely to show considerable sampling fluctuation. Psychedelic drug use began much later than alcohol, marihuana, or heroin use (table 18-13). By age 17, almost 10 percent of males and half as many females had started using psychedelic drugs. School was still the most frequently cited activity at time of onset (table 18-14). Almost half of those who went beyond experimentation with psychedelics used them only a few times a year (table 18-10). Few had used psychedelics for as long as 5 years (table 18-12). Since it is a more recent drug of use, having arrived later on the scene, two-thirds of male's and three-quarters of female's last use was within a year of interview.

Summary of Patterns of Drug Use

The following summarizes what was found concerning patterns of nonmedical drug use across the five specified drugs.

1. Alcohol was generally the *first drug used* by this population. For males, it preceded marihuana use by a year on the average (median). For females, the interval between alcohol and initiation of the next drug—likely to be heroin—was slightly more than a year. Psychedelics were the last drug to be used and were most likely to be used on an experimental basis. Cocaine use also started later than marihuana and heroin use; its lifetime prevalence (not intensity or frequency) of use was second only to marihuana among illicit drugs.

2. *Major life activity* at time of initiation of each drug was "going to school." This may reflect the fact that school was the single most common activity available to all or most of the sample at any time.

3. Heroin was used with *greatest frequency,* followed by alcohol and then marihuana. Only a small number of the cocaine or psychedelic users took those substances on a weekly basis. Of the five drugs, psychedelics were the least likely to be used frequently.

4. *Length of time used* was congruent with earliness of onset. Alcohol and marihuana were the longest-used drugs, heroin third, while psychedelics had been used over the shortest period of time. Data regarding *recency* of last use indicated that a larger percentage (77 percent) of the subjects had stopped using heroin (no use in the past year).

Some Relationships Between Different Measures of Drug Use

In this section an attempt will be made to address several questions:

> Is earlier use of licit substance (alcohol) linked to greater likelihood of illicit drug use?

Is earlier onset linked to heavier use?

Is there a relationship between heavier (more frequent) use and longer use?

Another basic question which cannot be tested with the present data set because of the limited age range is whether earlier use leads to longer use.

To test early onset of licit drug use as an indicator of likelihood of subsequent illicit drug use, earliest reported use of alcohol (multiple categories) was compared to nonexperimental use of the four major illicit drugs studied for both males and females.[7]

In every case but one (the very small group of female psychedelic users), relationships were significant at least at $p < .05$. Surprisingly, perhaps, the only sizable relationship was between early age of alcohol onset and male cocaine use ($tau_c = .29$). (Other associations ranged from between .07 and .14, which are minor even if statistically reliable.) Thus one can only conclude from this data that there is, in this population, a general but weak association between early alcohol drinking and use of illicit drugs.

The next question, whether early onset of use of a substance was related to how frequently it was used (daily, weekly, etc.), showed fewer significant relationships but stronger ones. (Psychedelic use was not tested because of the limited variance in age at onset as well as the small number of cases.) The strongest association, for both males and females, was that between early onset and frequent heroin use (males, $tau_c = .42$, $p < .001$; females, $tau_c = .27$, $p < .05$).

Early marihuana use was also related to more frequent use (for males, $tau_c = .28$, $p < .0001$; for females, $tau_c = .22$, $p < .001$). The relationship for alcohol was weak but significant for males ($tau_c = .11$, $p < .05$) but not for females. We conclude that primarily for heroin and to a lesser extent marihuana, there is some increased likelihood of heavier use with earlier onset.

The final question, whether heavy (frequent) use was linked to longer use, showed a clear relationship in only three of the eight tests: the more frequently men used heroin, the longer they used it ($tau_c = .44, p < .0005$). (The analogous relationship was .15 among females and *not* significant.) Frequent marihuana use was related to long use over time (for males, $tau_c = .22, p < .0001$; for females, $tau_c = .25$, $p < .0005$). A weak but significant association was observed for alcohol use among women ($tau_c = .15, p < .002$) but not men.

Polydrug Use

Prevalence. Discussion thus far has been focused on the five most used drugs. It is also important to examine the patterns of multiple-drug use, since the majority of youths in the sample had used more than one drug (three or more times). Three-quarters of males and just over half of females had used at least two drugs. In terms of current (past year) use, about four in ten females and half the males used two or more drugs (see table 18-7). The most common two-drug combination was alcohol/marihuana, followed in frequency by marihuana/cocaine and alcohol/cocaine (table 18-15).

Combinations of three or more drugs were reported by a third of the males and half that many females, the dominant three-drug combination being alcohol/marihuana/cocaine. Lifetime experience with four or all five of the predominant drugs was reported by one in six males and half that number of females. The dominant four-drug use patterns were alcohol/marihuana/heroin/cocaine or, alternatively, alcohol/marihuana/cocaine/acid. Table 18-15 shows the extent and types of nonexperimental polydrug use of the five predominant drugs.

Other findings particularly worthy of note are: (1) females were twice as likely as males to use just one drug; (2) there was not much difference in the proportions of males and females who used two drugs; (3) males were twice as likely as females to use as many as three, four, or all five of the drugs; and (4) psychedelics were used mostly in combination with another drug and mostly in combinations with large numbers of drugs. Psychedelics were used most frequently in the four-way combination of all the major drugs, exclusive of heroin.

Alcohol and Illicit Drug Use. Another important aspect of polydrug use concerns the amount of alcohol consumed in relation to illicit drug use. As previously noted, almost three-quarters (72 percent) of males and half of females in this sample used both alcohol and marihuana nonexperimentally. Another point of interest is the link between frequency of alcohol consumption and use of illicit drugs (table 18-16). Heavy alcohol use increased with hard-drug use. Heroin users of both sexes were the heaviest drinkers.

Perspectives on Polydrug Risk. Robins' (1970) analysis of probabilities of marihuana use followed by hard drug use utilizing different sample bases (total group, alcohol drinkers, marihuana smokers, etc.) suggested the transitions and the likelihood of transitions from use of one drug to another. Analysis along similar lines was performed using the data from the Harlem study in order to address the following question:[8] does use of one drug increase the likelihood of using another? If so, which drugs are related to a progression toward hard drug use?

Findings from this analysis are presented in table 18-17, with the important qualification that temporal sequence has *not* entered into the analysis. The data are based solely on the conjoint use or link of any two drugs, disregarding which came first. Drugs have been presented in the sequence which analysis of age of onset indicated was the most usual one. The number of nonexperimental psychedelic users was considered too small to use as a base drug in this analysis, nor would it be meaningful, since acid was the drug experienced last as well as least.

Table 18-15
Number and Types of Polydrug Use
(In Percents)

Used	*Total* (535 = 100%)		*Male* (277 = 100%)		*Female* (258 = 100%)	
None of five	9%		8%		11%	
One (only)	26		18		35	
Alcohol		21		13		29
Marihuana		5		5		6
Cocaine		*		*		–
Two (only)	38		40		37	
Alcohol and Marihuana		36		38		33
Alcohol and Cocaine		*		–		1
Alcohol and Heroin		1		–		1
Marihuana and Heroin		*		–		*
Marihuana and Cocaine		1		1		*
Marihuana and Psychedelic		*		*		–
Three (only)	13		17		9	
Alcohol, Marihuana, Heroin		2		3		*
Alcohol, Marihuana, Cocaine		9		11		7
Alcohol, Marihuana, Psychedelic		1		2		–
Alcohol, Heroin, Cocaine		*		–		*
Marihuana, Heroin, Cocaine		1		*		1
Four (only)	11		15		7	
Alcohol, Marihuana, Heroin, Coke		6		9		4
Alcohol, Marihuana, Coke, Psychedelic		5		7		3
Five (all)	2		2		1	

Note: Proportions refer to nonexperimental use of five most prevalent drugs.
*Less than half of one percent.

Table 18-16
Frequency of Five or More Drinks in a Day by Type of Nonexperimental Drug Use

	Male					*Female*				
	Total *(n = 244)*	*Marihuana* *(n = 203)*	*Heroin* *(n = 41)*	*Coke* *(n = 81)*	*Psychedelics* *(Acid)* *(n = 32)*	*Total* *(n = 219)*	*Marihuana* *(n = 130)*	*Heroin* *(n = 20)*	*Coke* *(n = 44)*	*Psychedelics* *(Acid)* *(n = 12)*
Three or more times each a week	9%	10%	28%	16%	11%	6%	8%	29%	23%	27%
Once or twice a week	6	7	11	9	14	6	4	17	4	13
One to three times a month	15	15	9	17	25	10	15	17	17	33
Few times a year	15	16	17	13	8	20	18	17	13	13
Hardly ever or never	55	52	35	45	42	58	55	21	43	13

Note: Tables do not always add up to 100 percent because of weighting and rounding.
χ^2, 4 d.f., between nonexperimental users *versus* nonusers (including experimenter only):

	Male	*Female*
Marihuana	8.492, $p < .08$	13.377, $p < .02$
Heroin	28.097, $p < .0001$	33.897, $p < .0001$
Coke	12.069, $p < .02$	35.939, $p < .0001$
Acid	8.208, $p < .08$	23.903, $p < .0001$

Table 18-18
Personal Characteristics of Drug-User Groups (Age and Education)

	Male						Female					
Characteristic	*Total (n = 277)*	*Alcohol (n = 235)*	*Marihuana (n = 216)*	*Heroin (n = 43)*	*Cocaine (n = 87)*	*Acid (n = 32)*	*Total (n = 258)*	*Alcohol (n = 209)*	*Marihuana (n = 150)*	*Heroin (n = 26)*	*Cocaine (n = 48)*	*Acid (n = 12)*
Age												
18	9%	9%	8%	5%	5%	9%	6%	5%	4%	–	2%	–
19	16	16	15	7	13	19	14	15	13	–	12	15%
20	18	20	20	7	22	16	18	18	20	8%	14	15
21	26	25	27	36	36	28	24	25	24	15	18	15
22	21	21	21	34	20	16	23	23	24	50	33	–
23	10	9	9	11	5	12	15	14	15	27	20	54
Education												
Incomplete H.S.	36	35	39	55	40	39	31	29	35	71	43	27
Complete H.S.	28	30	28	22	25	19	31	32	26	16	26	27
Post H.S.	36	35	32	22	34	42	38	39	38	13	31	46

Note: Drug-use groups are not exclusive, e.g., heroin users are in the alcohol group, etc.; tables do not always add up to 100 percent because of weighting and rounding.

What table 18-17 shows is that alcohol use only slightly increased the probability of harder-drug use. Marihuana also had slight effect on enhancing proportions of heroin users, but had a somewhat greater effect on increasing the probability of cocaine use, and, for males, marihuana greatly increased the likelihood of acid use. Perhaps the most striking finding was that marihuana was the only one of the illicit drugs analyzed where the majority of users—whether they used in addition to alcohol (as in most cases) or alone (as in the case of 5 percent of males and 6 percent of females)—did not progress to using any harder drug.

The preceding observation not withstanding, use of heroin had a dramatic impact on rates of marihuana use—all males and six in seven females who used heroin also smoked marihuana. Heroin use greatly enhanced the likelihood of cocaine use—at least three-quarters of all heroin users also used cocaine. In contrast, the impact on male psychedelic use was relatively minor. Psychedelic-use rates increased considerably, however, among women who used heroin.

Like heroin users, cocaine users almost always were marihuana users. Using cocaine more than doubled (compared with the total sample) the probability of a male being a heroin user and quadrupled this probability among females. In addition, cocaine was associated with use of psychedelics.

In sum, a considerable amount of polydrug use is evident from the data. Marihuana use does not seem to increase the probability of hard-drug use. Heroin and cocaine users, on the other hand, tend to use other illicit drugs.

Findings: Personal and Background Characteristics of Users of Five Drugs

Characteristics of users (past and current, nonexperimental) of each of the five drugs most widely used in the black youth sample will be discussed, in bivariate relationship, in this section. The various groups of drug users will be compared with respect to age, educational attainment, current major life activity, marital status, parenthood status (number of children), and proportion of drug-using friends (tables 18-18 through 18-25). (In other studies, this last variable has been found to be an important predictor of drug use; for example, Jessor et al. 1973; Kandel 1973, 1974*a, b.*) All comparative analyses of the groups are sex-specific.

Age

The most notable difference with regard to age was the substantially greater use of all drugs among the older (22- and 23-year-old) females relative to younger women (these were the female cohorts of 1952-1954). This disparity was evident in alcohol and marihuana use, was more extreme among cocaine users (just over half of whom were in these cohorts), and appeared most extreme among female heroin users, three-quarters of whom were of these older ages.

Males did not show such a great differential in age distribution according to drug use. The most notable difference was the substantial concentration of heroin users among the next to oldest cohorts (the 21- and 22-year-olds, born 1953-1955), and the underrepresentation of heroin users among males in the youngest cohorts (as had also been the case among females).[9] Male cocaine users were overrepresented in the middle age range. Generally, the male age distribution in heroin and cocaine groups peaked a year earlier than the female. Acid, marihuana, and alcohol age distributions among males followed quite closely the way that age distributed in the total male sample (table 18-18).

Educational Attainment

Heroin users among both males and females completed less education than the other groups. Even though this was a reliable difference for both sexes, the females' educational status was considerably more affected than the males': 71 percent of females had not completed high school in comparison with 55 percent of the male heroin users (table 18-18). Distribution of education levels among the other groups showed patterns which were similar to that of the total sample.

Current Major Life Activity

Notable differences in current life activity clustered chiefly around heroin use. Male heroin users were less likely to be working, more were in jail, and slightly more were looking for work–relative to the distribution of the total male sample. Still, about one-third of male heroin users reported that they were working and about one-eighth indicated that they were attending school without working. This differed considerably from the total sample, as well as from the other drug-use groups (table 18-19).

Among female heroin users, only one in twenty was employed, and even fewer (3 percent) were attending school. One in six (considerably more than in the sample as a whole) reported that she was just staying home (16 percent), and almost half (42 percent) said that they were housewives at home. The other drug-use groups approximated the female sample as a whole in their distribution. Various differences between the sexes should be noted particularly for the heroin group, as well as for the total samples (table 18-19).

Marital Status

Overall, the rate of marriage among males was 4 percent, with no variation by drug use. Married females numbered almost one in five (18 percent) in the total

Table 18-17
Drug-Use Rates for Differing Drug-Use Samples (Nonexperimental Use Only)
(In Percents)

	Total Sample		*Alcohol Users*		*Marihuana Users*		*Heroin Users*		*Cocaine Users*	
Proportion Who Have Used	*Male (n = 277)*	*Female (n = 258)*	*Male (n = 235)*	*Female (n = 209)*	*Male (n = 220)*	*Female (n = 150)*	*Male (n = 43)*	*Female (n = 26)*	*Male (n = 87)*	*Female (n = 48)*
No drug	8	11	–	–	–	–	–	–	–	–
No other drug	–	–	15	36	6	10	–	–	–	0
Alcohol	85	81	100	100	89	85	95	77	92	92
Marihuana	80	58	85	61	100	100	100	84	99	94
Heroin	16	10	18	10	20	14	100	100	40	40
Cocaine	32	18	32	21	40	30	80	76	100	100
Psychedelics (Acid)	12	5	13	6	14	8	18	20	30	25

Note: The percentages listed in the table represent the percentages of the category of users listed at the head of the column who also had used the row category or type of drug. For example, 100 percent of male heroin users also used marihuana, but only 20 percent of the male marihuana users also used heroin.

sample, but significantly more of the heroin using females (39 percent) reported that they were married[10] (table 18-20).

Fertility Status

Considerably more young people in this sample had children than were married. Even so, parenthood status was highly associated with heroin use for *both* men and women. About half the male heroin users (49 percent) and three-quarters of females (74 percent) reported having one or more children (table 18-20).

Household Size

Despite the relatively high parenthood rate among heroin users, variations observed in household size among the drug groups were neither substantial nor consistent. There was little difference according to drug use. Female heroin users more often resided in households of seven or more people (19 percent) than did the female group as a whole (11 percent). With respect to the total sample, females exceeded males in percentage residing in households of just two people, and males exceeded females residing in households of seven or more (table 18-21).

Household Income

Most notable in the data on household income was the high "refused" or "don't know" category among both males (53 percent) and females (35 percent). About one quarter of the sample reported household incomes below $7,000, and fewer than one in seven reported incomes of $10,000 or more (table 18-22).

Geographic Origin

Differences in drug use have been linked to migration status (Brunswick 1977; Kleinman and Lukoff 1978). Cross-classifying the sample according to maternal and own birthplace provided three generational status groups (table 18-23): (1) recent first-generation migrants (mother and study respondent both born in southern United States, identified as So.-So.; (2) second-generation migrants (mother was Southern born but respondent was born outside the South, identified as So.-No.); and (3) three or more generations outside the South (identified as No.-No.).

For males, migration generational status showed no variation among drug-use groups. Female hard-drug users, consistent with Kleinman and Lukoff's (1978) findings, were *less* often first-generation migrants.

Table 18-19
Personal Characteristics of Drug-User Groups (Life Activity)

	Male				
Characteristic	*Total (n = 277)*	*Alcohol (n = 235)*	*Marihuana (n = 220)*	*Heroin (n = 43)*	*Cocaine (n = 87)*
Current major life activity					
Work; work and school	44%	47%	46%	33%	38%
School only	20	17	16	12	16
Looking for work only	22	23	23	31	26
In jail	4	3	4	12	7
In Armed Forces	2	3	2	–	1
Housewife	–	–	–	–	–
Nothing, staying home	8	8	8	12	11

Note: Because of weighting and rounding, percentages do not always total exactly 100 percent.
[a]Half of 1 percent or less.

Mother's Education

Maternal education status was generally below the twelfth grade level. Moreover, the drug-use groups, both male and female, were remarkably homogeneous with respect to mothers' completed education (table 18-23).

Number of Drug-Using Friends

A consistent finding among marihuana researchers has been the concordance of own drug-use patterns with peer or friends' behavior (Jessor et al. 1972; Kandel 1974). Generally, hard-drug users in this sample tended to have more drug-using friends[11] (table 18-24). A notable exception to this pattern was among the females who used heroin, whose proportions of drug-using friends were similar to the alcohol and marihuana groups.

Summary of Personal Characteristics of Users of Different Drugs

What was learned about variations in personal characteristics among different drug users, chiefly heroin, may be summed as follows:

1. Regarding age, the oldest female cohorts (born 1952-1954), relative to other females in the study, evidenced heavier use of all drugs. The association was sharpest for heroin users—three-quarters of whom were in the oldest group,

Male	*Female*					
Acid (n = 32)	*Total (n = 258)*	*Alcohol (n = 209)*	*Marihuana (n = 150)*	*Heroin (n = 26)*	*Cocaine (n = 48)*	*Acid (n = 12)*
47%	33%	32%	32%	6%	21%	27%
14	22	21	20	3	17	27
28	16	19	20	32	31	33
6	a	a	a	–	–	–
3	a	–	–	–	–	–
–	24	23	23	42	24	7
3	6	5	4	16	7	7

aged 22 and 23. For males, the only drug-use group with a skewed age distribution was the heroin-use group, who were concentrated among 21- and 22-year-olds.

2. The heroin-use group deviated from the rest of the sample on just about all other studied characteristics. They had the lowest educational achievement, a deficit even greater among female users than male.

3. Heroin users were less often employed (one-third of the heroin-using males were employed, contrasted with 44 percent of all males). Again, the disparity was greater for female than male heroin users. Almost six in ten women who had used heroin were staying home (as housewives or "doing nothing"), compared with three in ten in the total sample of women.

4. Considerably more female heroin users were married than in the rest of the sample. About three-quarters of them were mothers, compared with half of all the women. Although male heroin users did not have a higher marriage rate than other males, they were more likely to have a child.

5. Regarding reports of household income, there was a more frequent absence of these reports among heroin users, and especially males.

6. Geographic origin, perhaps not surprisingly, given the relatively homogeneous population that this sample represented, did not show much variation. More female heroin users were Northern born, and fewer were Southern born.

7. Maternal school attainment was generally below the high school completion level for all the drug-user groups.

8. There was a relationship between perceived peer group behavior and "own" drug-use patterns. One notable and unanticipated exception was the pattern of the female heroin users. Unlike other hard-drug users of both sexes, they did *not* report that "most" of their friends used drugs.

Table 18-20
Personal Characteristics of Drug-User Groups (Marital and Fertility Status)

	Male				
Characteristic	*Total (n = 277)*	*Alcohol (n = 235)*	*Marihuana (n = 220)*	*Heroin (n = 43)*	*Cocaine (n = 87)*
Married					
Yes	4%	4%	4%	4%	3%
No	96	96	96	96	97
Fertility status					
No children	73%	71%	69%	51%	61%
One child	18	19	20	35	30
Two children	8	9	10	14	9
Three or more children	2	2	1	–	–

Findings: Reported Problems and Treatment for Drug Use

The preceding sections provide an epidemiological perspective on drugs used and their uses. Findings will now be presented on (1) problems experienced with drug use, (2) rates and types of treatment experiences, and (3) differences between treated and not treated heroin users.

Drug and Drinking Problems

Approximately one in five (21 percent) of the males and females in this sample who either drank or used an illicit drug reported on interview that they had experienced some problem from use of one or another of these substances.[12] Problems of mentation or thinking, perception (including hallucinations), and/or emotional problems (in their own words—"depression," "paranoia") were cited by at least half of those who said they experienced any problem. Alcohol was the drug most often cited as resulting in problems (by 33 percent of males who had had a problem and 44 percent of females); heroin was the runner-up, cited by about one in five of each sex (19 percent).

Treatment Experiences

Treatment rates based on the full sample of males and females showed that one in eleven males (9 percent) and slightly fewer females (7 percent) reported

Male	*Female*					
Acid (n = 32)	*Total (n = 258)*	*Alcohol (n = 207)*	*Marihuana (n = 150)*	*Heroin (n = 26)*	*Cocaine (n = 48)*	*Acid (n = 12)*
3%	18%	18%	20%	39%	19%	–
97	82	82	80	61	81	100%
66%	48%	51%	49%	26%	46%	83%
28	36	34	32	44	33	17
6	14	13	17	22	21	–
–	2	1	3	7	–	–

having been in treatment for heroin at least once. An additional 3 percent of both males and females said they had thought about getting treatment but had never been treated.

Approximately half of all those who had *ever* used heroin (45 percent of male users and 53 percent of female users) had been treated. Focusing only on the group of nonexperimental heroin users, the treatment rates were 51 percent for males and 62 percent for females. Females were much more likely than males to be in treatment at time of interview: of those who had ever been treated, 56 percent of females and 18 percent of males were currently in a treatment program.

About three in five (62 percent) of both males and females who had ever been treated for heroin had been in treatment just once; about a quarter had been in treatment twice (29 percent of treated males and 25 percent of treated females); and 10 and 12 percent, respectively, of treated males and females reported three or more treatment experiences. Males reported shorter treatment episodes, mentioning more treatment periods of 1 month or less. More females than males reported total treatment durations in excess of 1 year. In short, female heroin users were more likely to find their way into treatment and to remain in treatment for longer periods.

Treated male and female heroin users also were compared on the time interval between reported onset of heroin use and entry into treatment. Particularly notable is the finding that females used heroin for longer periods prior to beginning treatment; for almost three-quarters (72 percent) of the treated female heroin users, 4 or more years elapsed between their first use of heroin and their entering treatment. Almost one-third (29 percent) of treated male heroin users indicated that treatment began within a year of their first

Table 18-21
Personal Characteristics of Drug-User Groups (Household Size)

	Male						*Female*					
Characteristic	*Total (n = 277)*	*Alcohol (n = 235)*	*Marihuana (n = 220)*	*Heroin (n = 43)*	*Cocaine (n = 87)*	*Acid (n = 32)*	*Total (n = 258)*	*Alcohol (n = 209)*	*Marihuana (n = 150)*	*Heroin (n = 26)*	*Cocaine (n = 48)*	*Acid (n = 12)*
Household size												
Live alone	8%	9%	9%	6%	6%	6%	5%	6%	7%	6%	7%	13%
Two in household	13	12	13	15	16	17	18	20	20	16	16	20
Three or four	39	38	38	34	40	40	43	43	43	39	48	40
Five or six	23	22	22	28	22	26	23	21	19	19	16	13
Seven or more	18	19	18	17	16	11	11	10	11	19	14	13

heroin use; another third entered treatment from 1 to 2 years after onset of use; and only one quarter of males (24 percent) waited as long as 4 years.

Most explained their reasons for entry into treatment as "wanting it";[13] more females answered this way than males (78 and 48 percent, respectively). Unexpectedly, "to please others" was a frequent reason among males (for 30 percent of their treatment episodes). Few subjects entered into treatment because they had "no choice" (18 percent of males and 9 percent of females).

Those who had been in treatment were asked to identify the type of program in which they received treatment.[14] Males and females differed substantially in the extent to which they had used methadone clinics: 61 percent of females were treated at methadone clinics, but only 23 percent of males. About one-third of both sexes (32 percent male, 30 percent female) had some experience in residential treatment. About one in five males were treated in a clinic or hospital other than a methadone center, compared with one in eleven among females. Moreover, one in eight of males were treated in prison and about one in twenty in a military clinic or hospital (table 18-25).

Consistent with the preceding, analysis of services provided to males and females in treatment showed the largest difference to be in the proportion receiving methadone therapy. Approximately three-quarters of the treatment experiences of females (74 percent) involved methadone; the corresponding figure for males was 50 percent[15] (table 18-25). Personal therapy was the second most frequently cited service (57 percent females and 44 percent males). Males reported more treatment episodes in a residential center (males 31 percent and females 22 percent) and with "encounter" type therapy (19 percent males and 22 percent females). Females reported more treatment which included job help than did males (30 and 3 percent, respectively). Finally, only one in ten treatment episodes took place in a drug-free environment (12 percent males and 9 percent females).[16]

Patterns of Use Among Treated and Not Treated Heroin Users

Table 18-26 presents findings on patterns of heroin use, comparing treated and not treated heroin users among males and females. The single aspect on which they differed, for both sexes, was in duration or length of time they used heroin: treated samples had used longer than not treated (see O'Donnell et al. 1976, for the same finding). Differences were slight in relation to age of onset, frequency, and recency of use. Intensity of involvement, denoted by the estimated mean number of uses, reflected the noted difference in duration of use. Correspondingly, treated users' scores were larger than those not treated. Furthermore, the previously observed higher female heroin mean-use score, relative to males, can now be traced entirely to the group of treated females. (Not treated males and not treated females showed remarkably similar scores.) This corroborates the earlier finding as to longer use of heroin, prior to treatment, among young women than men.

Table 18-22
Personal Characteristics of Drug-User Groups (Household Income)

	Male				
	Total (*n* = 277)	*Alcohol* (*n* = 234)	*Marihuana* (*n* = 220)	*Heroin* (*n* = 43)	*Cocaine* (*n* = 87)
Household income					
None	a	a	–	–	–
Under 3,000	4%	4%	5%	6%	9%
3,000 to 4,999	7	7	6	4	3
5,000 to 6,999	10	8	10	14	9
7,000 to 9,999	12	12	11	2	8
10,000 or more	13	14	13	8	10
Refused or did not know	53	54	56	65	61

[a]Half of 1 percent or less.

Patterns with regard to use of drugs other than heroin generally showed minor differences among treated and not treated, but in contrary directions for men and women. Among men, differences tended in the direction of less involvement in other drugs on the part of the not treated. Among females, to the contrary, the not treated heroin users had greater polydrug experience. They also started drinking and using drugs other than heroin earlier and used more frequently.

These results are useful despite their small numbers, particularly in view of the scarcity of data from representative community samples dealing with sex-controlled comparisons of treated versus not treated heroin users. The consistency of the findings regarding longer female heroin use prior to treatment certainly warrants further investigation.

Personal and Background Characteristics of Treated and Not Treated

Examination of the extensive array of data on the background characteristics of treated and untreated heroin users showed relatively few differences of a magnitude worthy of note. In terms of education, for both males and females, the treated groups completed less education (females, 89 percent who did not complete high school, males, 67 percent) than the not treated (females, 42 percent who did not complete high school, males, 44 percent). With regard to current life activity, not treated males and females were more likely to be working than those who had been treated. Among females, 17 percent of the not treated were working, none who had been treated had jobs; treated females were

Male	*Female*					
Acid (n = 32)	*Total (n = 258)*	*Alcohol (n = 209)*	*Marihuana (n = 150)*	*Heroin (n = 26)*	*Cocaine (n = 48)*	*Acid (n = 12)*
–	2%	2%	2%	6%	3%	7%
6%	11	12	12	16	21	–
3	18	17	20	13	21	13
8	8	9	7	7	4	13
14	12	10	13	13	14	13
19	14	13	14	–	9	7
50	35	37	33	45	29	47

primarily "housewifes" (53 percent). Among males, 44 percent of the not treated were working compared with 21 percent of treated males; the latter primarily reported "looking for work" (54 percent).

Again, the finding of greatest heuristic interest related to a sizable *age* difference between treated and not treated women heroin users where there was no such difference for men. Congruent with what has already been reported about young women's delay in entering treatment, treated women were considerably older than those who used heroin but had not been treated: median age of 22.7 years for treated compared with the not treated's median of 21 years.

One further question intended to delineate this age relationship was put to the data: could the greater age of treated females be accounted for by their having completed their heroin careers–stopped using–whereas those untreated might be ongoing users who had not yet reached the age for therapy and cessation of use? This was tested by controlling whether women were current users (used within past year) or not current users and then comparing treated and not treated for their age at last use. Past, but not current users ($N = 19$) differed little in their age at last use, regardless of whether they had been treated or ceased use without treatment. (Treated past users' median age of last use was 18, not treated was 17.6 years.)

Among the small group of women ($N = 7$) who had used heroin within a year of their interviews, the median age at last use among the treated was 22.8 years, among the not treated it was 20 years, showing as clearly as this small number of cases could that treated and not treated really differed in age, not merely in stage of their heroin careers.

Analyzing the relation between current heroin use and treatment showed

Table 18-23
Personal Characteristics of Drug-User Groups (Geographic Origin)

	Male						*Female*					
Characteristic	*Total (n = 277)*	*Alcohol (n = 235)*	*Marihuana (n = 215)*	*Heroin (n = 43)*	*Cocaine (n = 87)*	*Acid (n = 32)*	*Total (n = 258)*	*Alcohol (n = 209)*	*Marihuana (n = 145)*	*Heroin (n = 25)*	*Cocaine (n = 46)*	*Acid (n = 12)*
Geographic origin or migration generation												
So.-So.[a]	18%	19%	21%	18%	20%	17%	20%	19%	18%	4%	5%	7%
So.-No.[b]	55	53	53	59	53	61	49	50	49	58	55	73
No.-No.	26	27	25	23	27	22	29	29	31	38	39	20
No.-So.	1	1	1	–	–	–	2	2	2	–	–	–
					(Mother's Education)							
Mother's education												
Incomplete HS	69%	72%	72%	81%	76%	64%	70%	70%	71%	79%	65%	72%
Complete HS	25	22	23	17	22	36	26	24	23	21	29	21
Post HS	6	6	6	2	2	–	4	5	6	–	6	7

[a]Denotes birthplace of mother and of respondent, respectively.
[b]Labeled North to summarize all birthplaces outside the South.

that a quarter of both males and females who had been treated fit our definition of "current" user—had used heroin within the year prior to interview. Viewed from the perspective of who comprised the group of "current" users, two-thirds had reported some treatment experience (67 percent of the men and 62 percent of the women). This corroborates the earlier finding regarding longer use among treated relative to not treated users, and also the observation that black youths using heroin at the time of study (1975-1976) were disproportionately from birth cohorts of the early 1950s (see also Boyle and Brunswick 1978).

Summary and Conclusion

Data for this study were derived from an area-representative sample of the single largest black community in the United States (Central Harlem Health District in New York City). Such a community-representative study enables analysis of the natural life history of drug use, thus supplementing what can be learned about drug behavior and its correlates from studies of treated populations alone.

This chapter has examined three major dimensions of the drug-use behavior of black youths: prevalence of nonmedical drug use, patterns of use and characteristics of users compared across the five major drugs of use, treatment experiences, patterns of use, and life situations characteristic of treated heroin users compared with the nontreated. Running through all these analyses has been the search for the differential patterns and meaning of drug use for black males and females. This interest stems both from postulated sex differences in life roles and social expectations of youths (for example, behavior norms), and also because relatively little research has been directly concerned with learning about the drug experiences of females, although there has been considerable concern about the effects of heroin and methadone on female fertility experiences and infants born of addicted mothers (Ferguson et al. 1974). Analysis has focused primarily on nonexperimental user groups, excluding those who reported using a substance only once or twice. Consistent with concern about describing use patterns, no attempt has been made to classify "addicted" or "dependent" use as such. Rather than attempt to summarize the many findings that have been presented in text and tables, this section will be more in the nature of "highlights" of the findings with discussion of some of their suggested implications.

Considering first prevalence, not unexpectedly, reported rates of use of illicit drugs were higher in this urban black youth sample than for black subsamples in national or student surveys. Findings from this sample were consistent with what others have found about the relatively low rates of "pill" use ("uppers" and/or "downers") by black youths, with the major illicit drugs of choice being marihuana, heroin, and cocaine, *in that order.* Indeed, for males, *current* (past month) use rates showed only a slightly higher rate for alcohol than for tobacco and marihuana. The similarity in males' rates of use of these three drugs suggests that marihuana is not considered to be more harmful than

Table 18-24
Personal Characteristics of Drug-User Groups (Number of Drug-Using Friends)

	Male				
Characteristic	*Total (n = 277)*	*Alcohol (n = 234)*	*Marihuana (n = 220)*	*Heroin (n = 43)*	*Cocaine (n = 87)*
No. of drug-using friends					
Almost all	39%	42%	47%	55%	59%
Most	12	11	12	2	8
About half	10	10	10	10	11
Just a few	23	23	19	22	15
None	16	13	12	10	7

alcohol or tobacco. Some survey respondents' direct comments to interviewers reflected this sentiment.

Psychedelics were more widely used here than has been found in other studies based on black samples. A considerable proportion of this use was "experimental" (tried just once or twice). Psychedelic drugs were the latest drugs to be initiated in this population. Whether these findings portend a potential increase in use of psychedelics by ghetto populations cannot be reliably inferred, but the data suggest this possibility. It may also be that other drugs, such as PCP, are being mistaken for psychedelics.

Interestingly, not only did males' rates of illicit drug use exceed the rates exhibited by females, but, except for marihuana, there was more experimental or exploratory use—consistent with more generalized exploratory and risk-taking behavior usually associated with young males. Within the ghetto and increasingly outside of it, illicit drugs serve as a vehicle for expressing this generally accepted phenomenon, which was earlier referred to as "sowing wild oats." An implication to be drawn from this is that one important approach to the reduction of illicit drug behavior is to provide socially desirable alternative situations for expanding opportunities for growth and mobility in relation to occupational and other psychosocial skills for young black males and other youths.

Patterns of use of different drugs showed considerable variation as to frequency and duration of use. As noted, females had lower rates of use of illicit drugs than males; on all drugs except heroin, females who used illicit drugs reported lesser frequencies of use. As to licit drugs, while slightly more females than males smoked cigarettes, males showed heavier drinking patterns than females. This is congruent with an observed positive correlation between heavy drinking and illicit drug use. The latter finding that heavier drinking is associated with use of other drugs, with heroin users comprising the heaviest drinkers, is an important one. Its implication is that treatment should not be drug-specific but, to be effective, needs to reach some more basic level—be it bio, psycho, social, or a combination of the three.

Male	*Female*					
Acid (n = 32)	*Total (n = 258)*	*Alcohol (n = 207)*	*Marihuana (n = 150)*	*Heroin (n = 26)*	*Cocaine (n = 48)*	*Acid (n = 12)*
64%	24%	29%	35%	29%	45%	73%
22	9	9	12	13	16	27
8	7	7	10	19	17	–
–	33	32	30	26	17	–
6	27	23	13	13	5	–

The difference between lifetime and current use was least for marihuana and cocaine, indicating those as drugs of more enduring use. The difference was greatest in the case of heroin, showing that a greater proportion of people had stopped using it (as indicated by no use in the past year). Generally these findings on past versus current use indicated that, to some extent, there are developmental phases associated with hard-drug use in an inner-city black youth population. This is truer for males than females and can be discerned particularly in relation to termination of heroin use. In this regard, the comparison of treated and not treated heroin users showed that the not treated males resembled nonusers in terms of current life activity, income reporting, etc. Yet the only clear distinction in use patterns between the treated and not treated was duration or length of time they used heroin, and not in the frequency of use. These findings are consistent with a view that initiating heroin use is not in itself predictive of deviancy within this population. However, its continued use, which reflects the absence of social supports for terminating use, predictive of deviancy. Another finding that was congruent with this interpretation (as to social support systems enabling termination of drug use) was the proportion of males (but not females) who cited entering treatment "to please others."

The finding in the present study of spontaneous stopping is consistent with research based on male adult addict (Kleinman and Lukoff 1975; Nurco 1975; Winick 1962) and nonaddict populations (Robins and Murphy 1967; Robins et al. 1977). Accordingly, a substantial amount of heroin use in a normal population of black youths, particularly males, which starts in adolescence terminates by the early twenties. This poses an important research challenge–to investigate the environmental, demographic, and/or psychosocial factors which support or encourage youngsters to discontinue heroin use. An equally important and challenging objective is to attempt to distinguish what accounts for the apparent greater resiliency in males who start using hard drugs compared with females.

Polydrug use was another aspect of drug behavior considered in this report.

Table 18-25
Experiences in Treatment

	Male (*n* = 32)	*Female* (*n* = 23)
Type of treatment place		
Residential	32%	30%
Methadone clinic	23	61
Other clinic or hospital	19	9
Prison	13	–
Military clinic or hospital	6	–
Other place	6	–
Kinds of services offered		
Methadone	50%	74%
Drug-free environment	12	9
Residential program	31	22
Detoxification	28	30
Personal therapy	44	57
Encounter group	19	22
Other group therapy	19	26
Job help	3	30

Note: Percentages are based on number of treatment episodes.

Given the high rates of alcohol and marihuana use, it was not surprising to observe that a majority of youths have used more than one drug, not that males used a greater number of drugs than females. Alcohol and marihuana were by far the most prevalent drug combinations (the two drugs were taken by two in five males and one in five females), followed by marihuana and cocaine, with alcohol and cocaine just behind. A third of males and half as many females had experience with three of the five studied drugs. Psychedelics were most often used by multiple-drug users who used as many as three or four other drugs; relatively few psychedelic users had experience with only a few drugs.

Analysis of different probabilities of using harder drugs based on softer-drug use indicated that marihuana use, rather than being a "stepping stone" to hard-drug use, hardly increased the probabilities of using harder drugs over what they were when youths were classified by alcohol use. Congruent with other findings, the majority of marihuana users did *not* become users of other illicit drugs. This analysis suggests strongly that, rather than a linear progression in drug use from alcohol, to marihuana, to heroin, cocaine, and acid, which implies some interval measurement, the transition or "jump" from marihuana use to using harder drugs is of a different order and magnitude than is usually assumed in a linear model.

When personal characteristics of different drug users were analyzed, heroin users were the only drug-use group which showed consistent differences from the total samples of males and females. Differences were greater for females than for males. Particularly notable were the deficits in educational attainment; the

Table 18-26
Treated versus Not Treated Heroin Users: Patterns of Use

	Male		*Female*	
	Treated (n = 21)	*Not Treated (n = 22)*	*Treated (n = 16)*	*Not Treated (n = 10)*
Age onset heroin				
Median	15	14.9	15.2	15
Mean	15.7	15.8	15.7	16
Usual frequency				
Daily or near daily	58%	48%	79%	50
Few times a week	25	24	10	33
Few times a month	4	16	10	17
Once a month	4	–	–	–
Few times a year	8	12	–	–
Duration of use				
Less than 1 year	8%	24%	16%	8
About 1 year	12	28	5	25
2 years	8	12	–	33
3 to 5 years	33	16	37	17
5 years or more	38	20	42	17
Recency of last use				
Less than 1 month ago	8%	4%	11%	8
1, less than 2 months ago	–	–	5	–
2, less than 3 months ago	8	–	–	–
3 months, less than 1 year ago	8	8	11	17
About 1 year ago	–	16	5	–
More than 1 year ago	75	72	68	75
Mean no. of heroin users				
Mean	1,109	678	1,227	668
S.D.	1,034	848	796	761
No. of other drugs used (in cumulative percents)				
Seven	12	–	–	–
Six	21	8	–	50
Five	29	40	10	58
Four	46	52	42	58
Three	88	88	74	83
Two	100	100	84	83
One	–	–	100	100

Note: Tables do not always add up to 100 percent because of weighting and rounding; nonexperimental users only; excludes those who have used only once or twice.

increased numbers who were staying at home and/or not employed; the fact that more females, but not more males, were second- or later-generation in the North; that more heroin-using females were married; that heroin users, both males and females, were more likely to have children; and that females evidenced an unexpected decrease in perceived friends' drug use.

Regarding treatment experiences, somewhat more women who used heroin than men entered treatment; more men terminated use without treatment.

Women spent longer periods in treatment than men, and there was a longer lapse between females' onset of heroin use and their entering treatment. Consequently, females in treatment were older than males in treatment. Comparison between treated and not treated in patterns of heroin use showed no significant differences with respect to frequency, recency, and age at onset. The chief difference between them was in how long they used heroin.

Already cited was the finding that some men, but not women, reported that they entered treatment to "please someone else." This, combined with earlier treatment and the smaller social deficit suffered by males relative to females who used heroin, implies a relatively greater lack of social supports and alternatives for women. Males seem also to have more "resiliency" and supports, both internal and/or external, for terminating use. But the findings from comparing current social roles of treated and not treated users strongly point to the implication for both sexes that, once in treatment, the social prognosis is less hopeful than what it is when heroin use is terminated without treatment.

Summing up what was learned about the treated compared to not treated subsamples:

1. Treated were notably "worse off" than not treated. This probably reflects less on the effects of treatment per se than on the selectivity of who goes into treatment and the severity of the problems experienced by those who require treatment. This is true for heroin users of both sexes. Concluding that those who need treatment have fewer social supports and role alternatives is consistent with the findings from this study.
2. Treated users were also older than not treated users.
3. Those who continued using heroin were more likely to be treated users.

The differences between treated and not treated heroin users emerged even more clearly than might have been expected in the normal population sample with its small numbers of treated heroin users. The differences were similar across sexes. They were congruent also with the only available comparable findings, those from the O'Donnell et al. (1976) national survey of young men drawn from Selective Service registration lists. There too, shorter duration of drug use was the chief distinction between treated and not treated heroin users, with current users more likely to be drawn from the treated subsample. This congruence adds assurance as to the reliability of these findings despite the small numbers of cases involved.

Because this study of a normal population of urban black youths was able to examine differences between male and female drug users, the concluding remarks will emphasize some of the implications of those differences for treatment as well as for prevention programs. Illicit drug use is (statistically) more norm violating for young women than for young men. Following from this, and not unlike more generalized patterns of difference arising from male and female socialization experiences, women in this sample who used heroin had a longer commitment to its use with more serious life outcomes. We might hypothesize that just as medical care in general serves many functions (see, for example, Shuval 1970), so too drug treatment may provide certain compensatory social functions. Such a hypothesis fits with the observed longer periods of treatment young women reported. Further investigation along these lines might add meaningfully to our understanding of treatment processes and treatment outcomes.

Generally, the need for more sex-specific investigations which include females as well as males seems clear. Clear also is the need for recognizing these sex differences when formulating policies and programs for drug prevention and treatment.

Notes

1. The initial study was conducted under funds granted by Maternal and Child Health Services, HEW. The restudy has been funded by the National Institute on Drug Abuse, ADAMA, HEW.

2. In the first study year, interviewing was supervised out of the project director's office. In the second and larger study year, interviewing was subcontracted to the National Opinion Research Center, University of Chicago (New York Office), which followed the same procedures developed in the feasibility study a year earlier. Respondents were paid $10 for their time in interview, and confidentiality of report was stressed. It is likely that this remuneration, along with participation in interview and medical examination as part of the original study 6 to 8 years earlier, increased cooperation in the reinterview. In all, only 2 percent of the sample refused interview, and only 6 percent of the original sample were not located. Analysis showed no evidence of sample bias by demographic characteristics. Interview completion rate was slightly lower among the older than younger sample members, reflecting greater moveout rates on the part of older females and a higher deathrate on the part of older males. Two percent of the original sample had died by the time of reinterview.

3. The small excess in female completions based on the full initial sample was reversed when rates were recalculated without those who had died and without those who were in the Armed Forces and/or out of town—the uninterviewable. Of the potentially interviewable, 90 percent of the males completed reinterviews, compared with 88 percent of females. Note, too, the higher refusal rate for females, for which there is no single or simple explanation. Also of interest is the small group of "nomads," those whose families could not refer us to an address where we might find them because they had none. We assume that they contribute to the census undercount of young black males.

4. In the community survey to be reported here procedures for estimating

reliability in response included repeated questions on alcohol drinking in different parts of the interview, which produced but three instances of inconsistency (about one-half of 1 percent). In following up replies of thirteen survivors in the restudy among seventeen drug users who had been identified at initial interview (two had died, the other two had moved out of the area), ten or 77 percent gave dates of onset which were consistent with our initial findings. The reply of one of these respondents differed by 1 year and another by 2 years. All but one corroborated earlier report of use. Additionally, the research relied on techniques in data collection that would enhance the quality, viz. reliability, of the data: (1) it built on cooperation obtained in the first wave of this broad ranging health study, which at that time included a free medical examination (the reported findings from the study contributed to the initiation of an adolescent service at the municipal hospital cooperating in the study); (2) respondents were paid $10 for their time in the reinterview; (3) interviewers were matched to respondents for race and sex and were recruited through local agencies and newspapers; (4) guarantees of confidentiality and anonymity included the Department of Justice Assurance of Confidentiality; and (5) extensive training of interviewers along with ongoing checks of reliability and "validation" of their interviews was conducted.

5. No distinction has been made in this analysis between type of alcohol consumed—beer, wine, or liquor. Controls on amount used were exercised by unit of measurement, that is, can of beer, "glass" of wine, "shot" of liquor, each of which constituted one drink. Analysis of frequency of heavy use which appears later in this chapter used the criterion of five or more drinks in a day.

6. Editor's note: This finding is somewhat different than findings in other chapters in this book, but again, it should be recognized that this is a special population that includes older (18 to 23 years of age) inner-city black youths. Carlisi (chapter 19) makes some comparisons between black youths and white ethnic groups living within the same inner-city communities.

7. Tau_c was used as the ordinal measure of association, given an unequal number of categories in the two variables.

8. In no way is this intended to lend credence to a "stepping-stone" theory of drugs, implying that use of one drug automatically leads to use of the next.

9. Analysis to be reported elsewhere tested developmental age separately from chronological year in relation to onset of drug use. Findings from that analysis demonstrate that these differences in heroin prevalence observed among cohorts are *not* a function of age at onset but did reflect changing patterns in drug choice (Brunswick and Boyle *in manuscript*).

10. Marital status was ascertained by the question: "Are you married?" If "No," "Have you ever been married?" Former and current married have been grouped for the "Yes" category in table 18-22. No further questions were asked as to whether the marriage was formalized or common-law. The higher marriage

rate among female heroin users, not among male, cannot be explained from data at hand.

11. The question was "About how many of your friends use drugs? Would you say almost all, most, about half, just a few or none?" It was asked toward the end of the questions concerning drug use (question 70), and respondents interpreted the term "drugs" within their own frame of reference, without its being specified further in the question wording.

12. Question 59 asked: "Have you ever had any problems or trouble as a result of drinking or taking drugs?" If "yes," "What was the trouble? Which drug(s) mostly caused the trouble?"

13. Question 63 asked: "Did you yourself *want* treatment (that time), did you want to *please* someone else, did you just want to *stay out of trouble,* or *didn't* you have any choice?"

14. Question 62a asked: "Which one of these places best describes where you were treated (the first/second/etc. time)—a live-in treatment center, a methadone clinic, some other clinic or hospital, a prison, or a military clinic or hospital?"

15. Question 64 asked: "What kinds of services did the program include (that time)? Anything else?" This was a field-coded question in which alternatives were not read to the respondent.

16. Note that the numbers on which these percentages were based are small: 32 treatment periods for males, 23 for females.

References

Abelson, H., and Fishburne, P. 1976. *Nonmedical Use of Psychoactive Substances.* Princeton, N.J.: Response Analysis Corp.

Ball, J.C. 1967. The reliability and validity of interview data obtained from 59 narcotic drug addicts. *American Journal of Sociology* 72:650-654.

Boyle, J.M., and Brunswick, A.F. 1978. What Happened in Harlem? Analysis of a Decline in Heroin Use among a Generation Unit of Urban Black Youth. Paper prepared at the Conference on the Utilization of Research in Drug Policy Making, Washington, D.C., May 3-5, 1978.

Brook, J.S., Lukoff, I.F., and Whiteman, M. 1977. Peer, family, and personality domains as related to adolescents' drug behavior. *Psychological Reports* 41:1095-1102.

Brunswick, A.F. 1977. Health and drug behavior: A study of urban black adolescents. *Addictive Diseases* 3 (2):197-214.

Brunswick, A.F., and Josephson, E. 1972. Adolescent health in Harlem. *Supplement to AJPH* 62 (1):62pp.

Brunswick, A.F., and Boyle, J.B. 1977. Patterns of Drug Use: Influence of Developmental Age and Chronological Year on Time of Onset. Unpublished manuscript.

Brunswick, A.F., Boyle, J.B., and Tarica, C. *In press.* Who Sees the Doctor? A Study of Urban Black Adolescents. Paper presented at Fifth International Conference on Social Science and Medicine, Nairobi, Kenya, August 1977.

Elinson, J. 1977. Status of operational definitions. *The Epidemiology of Drug Abuse: Current Issues.* NIDA Monograph No. 10. Rockville, Md.: NIDA.

Elinson, J., and Nurco, D. (eds.). 1975. Operational definitions in socio-behavioral drug use research. *National Institute on Drug Abuse Research.* NIDA Monograph No. 2. Rockville, Md.: NIDA.

Ferguson, P., Lenox, T., and Lettieri, D.J. 1974. *Drugs and Pregnancy.* Rockville, Md.: NIDA.

Jessop, D., Kandel, D., and Lukoff, I. 1976. *Comparative Analyses of Stages of Drug Use in Different Ethnic Groups: Center Cross Study I.* Center for Socio-Cultural Research on Drug Use, Columbia University.

Jessor, R., Jessor, S., and Finney, J. 1973. A social psychology of marihuana use: Longitudinal studies of high school and college youth. *Journal of Personality and Social Psychology* 26 (1):1-15.

Johnson, B.J. 1976. The race, class and irreversibility hypotheses: Myths and research about heroin. In J.D. Rittenhouse (ed.), *The Epidemiology of Heroin and Other Narcotics.* Rockville, Md.: NIDA.

Johnston, L.D. 1976. Survey data as contributors to estimation. In J.D. Rittenhouse (ed.), *The Epidemiology of Heroin and Other Narcotics.* Rockville, Md.: NIDA.

Kandel, D. 1973. Adolescent marihuana use: Role of parents and peers. *Science* 181:1067-1070.

Kandel, D. 1974*a.* Inter and intragenerational influences on adolescent marihuana use. *Journal of Social Issues* 30 (2):107-135.

Kandel, D. 1974*b.* Interpersonal influences on adolescent illegal drug use. In E. Josephson and E. Carroll (eds.), *Drug Use: Epidemiological and Sociological Approaches.* Washington, D.C.: Hemisphere Press.

Kandel, D. 1976. Convergences in Prospective Longitudinal Surveys of Drug Use in Normal Populations. Paper presented at the Society for Life History Research in Psychopathology, Fort Worth, Texas. October 1976 (mimeo).

Kellam, S.G., Ensminger, M.E., and Simon, M.B. 1977. First Grade Mental Health and Teenage Drug Use: Early Social Adaptation and Psychological Well-Being and Drug Use 10 Years Later. Unpublished manuscript, Social Psychiatry Study Center, Chicago, Ill.

Kleinman, P., and Lukoff, I.F. 1975. *Drug Use in a Ghetto Community: Ethnic Group, Generational Status and Friendship Networks.* Final project report to Nat. Inst. on Drug Abuse.

Kleinman, P., and Lukoff, I.F. 1978. Ethnic differences in factors related to drug use. *Journal of Health and Social Behavior* 19 (2):190-199.

Lukoff, I.F. 1976. Consequences of use: Heroin and other narcotics. In J.D. Rittenhouse (ed.), *The Epidemiology of Heroin and Other Narcotics.* Rockville, Md.: NIDA.

Lukoff, I.F., and Kleinman, P. 1977. The addict life cycle and problems in treatment evaluation. In A. Schecter (ed.), *Rehabilitation Aspects of Drug Dependence.* Cleveland, Ohio: CRC Press.

Myers, V. 1977. Drug use among minority youth. *Addictive Diseases* 3 (2):187-196.

Nurco, D. 1975. Studying addicts over time. *American Journal of Drug and Alcohol Abuse* 2 (2):183.

Office of Drug Abuse Services. 1977. *New York State Drug Abuse Program: State Plan Update.*

O'Donnell, J.A. 1976. Comments on Hunt's estimation procedures. In J.D. Rittenhouse, (ed.), *The Epidemiology of Heroin and Other Narcotics.* Rockville, Md.: NIDA.

O'Donnell, J.A., Voss, H.L., Clayton, R.R., Slatin, G.T., and Room, R.G.W. 1976. Young Men and Drugs: A Nationwide Survey. NIDA Research Monograph Series No. 5. Rockville, Md.: NIDA.

Richards, L.G., and Blevens, L.B. 1977. The Epidemiology of Drug Use: Current Issues. NIDA Monograph No. 10. Rockville, Md.: NIDA.

Rittenhouse, J.D. 1976. *Introduction to The Epidemiology of Heroin and Other Narcotics.* Rockville, Md.: NIDA.

Robins, L.N. 1973. *A Follow-up of Vietnam Drug Users.* Washington, D.C.: Special Action Office for Drug Abuse Prevention.

Robins, L.N. 1976. Estimating addiction rates and locating target populations: How decomposition into stages helps. *The Epidemiology of Heroin and Other Narcotics.* Rockville, Md.: NIDA.

Robins, L.N., and Murphy, G. 1967. Drug use in a normal population of young Negro men. *American Journal of Public Health* 57 (9):1580-1596.

Robins, L.N., Darvish, H.S., and Murphy, E.G. 1970. The Long-term outcome for adolescent drug users: A follow-up study of 76 users and 146 nonusers, *The Psychopathology of Adolescence.* J. Zubin and A. Freedmand, eds. London: Grune and Stratton.

Robins, L.N., Davis, D.H., and Nurco, D.N. 1974. How permanent was Vietnam drug addiction? *American Journal of Public Health* 64:38-44.

Robins, L.N., Davis, D., and Wish, E. 1977. Detecting predictors of rare events: Demographic, family and personal deviance as predictors of stages in the progression toward narcotic addiction. In J.S. Strauss, H.M. Babigan, and M. Roff (eds.), *The Origins and Course of Psychopathology.* New York: Plenum.

Shuval, J.T., Antonovsky, A., and Davies, A.M. 1970. *Social Functions of Medical Practice.* San Francisco: Jossey-Bass.

Single, E., Kandel, D., and Faust, R. 1974. Patterns of multiple drug use in high school. *J. of Health and Social Behavior* 15:344-357.

Smart, R. 1974. Addiction, dependency, abuse or use: Which are we studying with epidemiology? In E. Josephson and E. Carroll (eds.), *Drug Use: Epidemiological and Sociological Approaches.* Washington, D.C.: Hemisphere.

Stephens, R. 1972. The truthfulness of addict respondents in research projects. *International Journal of Addictions* 7:549-558.

Waldorf, D. 1973. *Careers in Dope.* Englewood Cliffs, N.J.: Prentice-Hall.

Whitehead, P.C., and Smart, R.G. 1972. Validity and reliability of self reported drug use. *Canadian J. of Criminology and Corrections* 14:1-8.

Winick, C. 1962. Maturing of narcotic addiction. *Bulletin on Narcotics* 14 (1):1-7.

Appendix 18A
Methodological Note

As indicated earlier, the purposes of this presentation were essentially descriptive and hypothesis generating rather than explanatory or confirmatory—to illuminate the extent (prevalence) and characteristics of drug use and drug users within a single area-representative sample of urban black youths. Consistent with its descriptive (as opposed to explanatory) intention, findings presented in percentage cross-tabulation have been tested to determine whether observed differences were within or beyond what might be expected from chance sampling fluctuation of observations in probability samples of the indicated sizes.

Table 18A-1 below provides the band or range in error of the estimate within which percentages observed at different levels might be expected to vary. The table has been set up according to the major drug-use groups, separately by sex. It shows, for example, that in comparing alcohol and marihuana user characteristics, if 30 percent of male alcohol users have a given quality and 50 percent of cocaine users do, this is not a chance sampling variation. The normal sampling variability for the alcohol group, expected in 95 samples out of 100, is within (plus or minus) 6 percentage points and thus would not extend to the cocaine observation at 50 percent. Similarly, the variability band for the cocaine group at the observed 50 percent level is within (plus or minus) 11 percentage points; the lower limit, which is 39 percent, is still out of range of the observation for the alcohol group.

Such comparisons are somewhat more complex because the drug-use groups are not discrete. Almost everybody in each of the illicit drug groups is also in the alcohol group, half of the cocaine group is in the heroin group, and so on. This is so because we have not attempted a unique classification but a natural one. To the degree that there is overlap, differences will be minimized or understated relative to what might be observed were the drug-use groups discrete. What is being analyzed, therefore, is not the significance of the difference between two percentages, but rather whether an observation for one group falls within or beyond the expected range of variation of another.

Table 18A-1
Guidelines for Estimating Statistical Confidence ($p < .05$)

Group	*Male*					*Female*				
		50%	*30%*	*10%*	*5%*		*50%*	*30%*	*10%*	*5%*
Total	(n = 277)	±6	±6	±4	±3	(n = 258)	±6	±6	±4	±3
Alcohol	(n = 235)	±7	±6	±4	±3	(n = 209)	±7	±6	±4	±3
Marihuana	(n = 220)	±7	±6	±4	±3	(n = 150)	±8	±7	±5	±4
Heroin	(n = 43)	±15	±14	±9	±7	(n = 26)	±20	±18	±12	±9
Cocaine	(n = 87)	±11	±10	±6	±5	(n = 48)	±14	±13	±9	±6
Psychedelics	(n = 32)	±18	±16	±11	±8	(n = 12)	±29	±26	±17	±13
Treated heroin user	(n = 21)	±22	±20	±13	±10	(n = 16)	±25	±23	±15	±11

19 Youth Drug Abuse and Subjective Distress in a Hispanic Population

Jose Szapocnik,
Robert A. Ladner, and
Mercedes A. Scopetta

Introduction

This chapter explores the specific factors associated with adolescence and acculturation and their subsequent impact on the drug-taking behavior of adolescent and young-adult second-generation Cuban immigrants. Research on the abuse of drugs among second-generation Cuban immigrant adolescents and young adults has recently been conducted in Miami, Florida. This study population is somewhat unique in that it represents the infusion and acculturation of a second-generation Hispanic society into the American culture and reveals some strengths and problems specific to the acculturation process. This chapter attempts to review some of these strengths and problems as they relate to the abuse of drugs and how this information may be generalizable to other host/migrant cultures.

Our conceptualization of causes or factors contributing to adolescent drug abuse among these second-generation immigrants emphasizes the role of the processes of maturation and acculturation, which are considered to interact to intensify the problems typically faced by adolescents. The stormy adolescent developmental period is complicated for these youths by a number of additional factors which increase the likelihood of deviant behavior and the use of drugs. The acculturation problems which are encountered by this population include: (1) a range of difficulties experienced in trying to adapt to a new culture, including problems with mobility (transportation), employment, and education (or the lack of it); and (2) generational and family differences and conflicts resulting from differing levels of acculturation among family members. These difficulties can produce friction and conflict between the first-generation immigrant adults and their second-generation children, which exceed the problems ordinarily experienced within the majority same-culture families and tend to promote dependence on the peer group as a source for self-identity and support. The peer group, in turn, requires a commitment to a different level of value achievement, placing more emphasis on self-expression and the freedom to pursue individual interests.

On Adolescence

Aside from the "storm and stress' associated with adolescence, there are several aspects of adolescent behavior of concern to individuals involved in the study of adolescent substance abuse. One such aspect is the segregation of adolescents from the adult population. Because of the development of consolidated school systems and the increase in the proportions of working parents of both sexes, adolescents spend increasing amounts of their time with people their same age. Since many of the socialization processes of American youths (education, recreation, interpersonal development) have been institutionalized outside of the family context, the average adolescent either needs or appears to need less contact with his or her parents for successful socialization. An increasing proportion of leisure-time activities is spent in commercial and public places, away from the control of family and other adults. As a result, adolescents spend an increasing proportion of their early life with peers, frequently segregated and unsupervised by adults.

It is normal to expect that there will be conflicts between the emerging values of the adolescent and the values of his or her parents. Differences between generations are most noticeable with respect to preferences in hair length, taste in clothes and music, and in sexual/moral values. In particular, adolescents tend to seek greater freedom at a time when adult pressure is directed toward molding them into responsible, independently acting, rule-conscious adults. When conflicts occur, there are several alternative courses of action open to the adolescent, ranging (as Merton first outlined in 1957) from ritualistic obedience to open rebellion.

Musgrove (1964) and Coleman (1961) highlight some of the effects of age segregation on the development of deviant behavior. Youngsters in particular age groups develop distinct cliques, each a variant of a general adolescent subculture. In immigrant cultures, where the adolescent role conflict is further intensified by cultural differences between the host culture and the migrant culture, as it is with Cubans in the Miami metropolitan area, the pressure to form separate peer groups as an insulation against cultural conflict is increased. The cliques based on age and social differences are likely to impose even stricter behavioral expectations and normative standards. For this reason, we see more social cohesion manifested among certain immigrant school aged groups, as illustrated by the development of alternative newspapers and school clubs, street gangs, and drug-using groups. This social isolation from adults and the concomitant adherence to an adolescent subculture fosters what Merton referred to as the resolution of role conflict through social support in adapting to an unintegrated role set (Merton 1975, p. 377).

Social support systems of peers have been described in the delinquency literature as "peer pressure" systems. These systems force the adolescent to comply with delinquent group norms in order to gain social acceptance (see

Erickson and Jensen 1977, for a review of this literature). This coercive model of adolescent subculture development has been challenged by researchers in adolescent behavior. In effect, adolescent culture is seen not only as a delinquent culture, but also as a vehicle for making a social adjustment, for status attainment and for the development of social competence. As the adolescent matures, those aspects of adolescent activities which are found to be rewarding are often carried forward into adult activities, albeit often without the rebellious anti-Establishment or self-defeating overtones that may have characterized the former behavior (Matza 1961).

Acculturation as a Special Problem in Adolescent Adjustment

In the case of the adolescent children of Hispanic immigrant families, the difficulty of adapting to host-culture values as well as adolescent-culture values, creates special problems for the young people and their families. Many studies have documented the high rates of behavioral disorders among immigrants. Tyhurst (1951) suggested that disorders may result from the stress in migrating and adapting to a new culture. More recently, increased attention has been given to the psychosocial factors which lead to family disruption (Berry and Annis 1974; Mezey 1960; Naditch and Morrisey 1976; Padilla and Ruiz 1974). Among the factors that induce stress, Berry and Annis (1974) include cultural change, the breakdown of family ties, abrupt change in environment, language barriers, and discrimination.

Our own clinical experience with the Hispanic immigrant community in Dade County indicates that the acculturation process results in a disruption of the family. This process is exacerbated by intergenerational differences in acculturation, since youngsters acculturate more rapidly than their parents. In our work with this population, we developed a psychosocial method to study the impact of acculturation (Szapocznik et al. *in press*). The methodology was designed to assess the occurrence of intergenerational/acculturational differences and the family disruption that results from these differences. *Acculturation* refers to the adjustment process—the borrowing, acquiring, and adopting of cultural traits from a host society by people who migrated from another society. Acculturation is, to a large extent, based on the amount of time a person has been exposed to the host culture. Moreover, the rate at which the acculturation process takes place is a complex function of the age and sex of the individual, with younger people acculturating more rapidly than older and males of some immigrant groups acculturating more rapidly than females. Research findings suggest that in attempts to understand the acculturation processes, values and behavior must be considered separately. Changes in values occur more slowly and are often of greater concern to immigrant families, while behavioral changes occur rapidly and are the most evident source of family conflict.

Acculturation and Drug Use

Acculturation was one of the sources of conflict and family disruption experienced by Cuban immigrants in Dade County. There were intergenerational differences in behavior within the traditionally closely knit nuclear family. Research findings at the Spanish Family Guidance Clinic, a community mental health program supported by the University of Miami Medical School, indicate that these intergenerational differences were associated with different types of drug-use behavior in the Cuban population (Szapocznik et al. *in press*).

As an outgrowth of the family conflict, there was an increased tendency for youngsters to participate in social support networks involved in antisocial and drug-using behavior. These groups were influential in the young alienated family member's choice of antisocial activities, which included drug abuse and other delinquent activity.

In the face of typical adolescent pressures and the conflicts between parental Hispanic values and those of American culture, peers provided an important source of social support for the Cuban youngster. In any attempt to understand the drug-taking behavior of Cuban youths it is therefore important to consider the influence of peers.

Given the desire of people of all ages to use drugs and alcohol to relax and facilitate social behavior, the choice of the substance reflects to some extent an identification with the values of the group. For many adolescents, marihuana use serves as a means of generating cohesion, although with reduced drinking ages in many states, alcohol is rapidly supplanting this drug. During adulthood, the social drug of choice is still most often alcohol.

Normally, support for drug-taking behavior is relatively constant throughout a given culture and is articulated in age-specific, situation-specific, and substance-specific ways. The "pot" parties among young white Americans, the earlier heroin-use habits of inner-city young black males, and the middle-age "Cuban overutilization" of sedatives and minor tranquilizers (Ladner and Page *in press*) are all examples of this phenomenon.

The Community Setting of the Study

The city of Miami is located at the southern tip of Florida in Dade County. The county has seen enormous growth over the past two decades, resulting in massive suburbanization and extensive intramural migration. The current population estimate for Dade County is 1.5 million, fully three times the population size 25 years ago.

In the decade of the 1960s, there was a significant addition to the population influx. After Fidel Castro came to power in Cuba in 1959, more than 400,000 refugees entered the United States through Miami; this represented almost 5 percent of the entire population of Cuba. Many of these people remained in Dade County: the 1970 Census lists the Cuban population at 218,000 people, fully 73 percent of Dade County's Spanish population. The primary effect was the "Latinization" of large areas of the county–predominantly in Central Miami and Hialeah. In addition, massive immigration was accompanied by suburbanization, as thousands of non-Latin whites left Miami and settled elsewhere in the county.

The name "Little Havana" was created by the Anglo community when a very heavy influx of Latins, predominantly Cubans, settled in the southeast section of Miami. This first group of Cuban immigrants belonged predominantly to the middle and high socioeconomic classes of Cuba. Many of these families achieved upward mobility rapidly and moved farther west into new areas of the city.

Political circumstances stagnated the Cuban exodus between 1962 and 1965, but a second major wave of Cuban immigration has occurred since 1966. This second wave of Cuban immigrants was composed primarily of less-affluent, semiskilled, and unskilled urban workers. As the more affluent Cuban immigrants moved out to new sections of the city, the poorer immigrants took their places and continued to concentrate in the "Little Havana" area.

A significant characteristic of the present inhabitants of the "Little Havana" section is their lack of knowledge of the English language. Although the first wave of Cuban immigrants included many families fluent in English and familiar with the American culture, the second wave was under a greater handicap, and assimilation to the American culture posed greater problems.

Wynwood, a very poor community, is located in the northwest section of the city of Miami in the midst of industrial and commercial sections. Wynwood is made up of approximately one-half Cuban immigrants and one-half other Latins, especially Puerto Ricans. The community has high rates of crime and drug abuse.

Study Population: Demography and Methodology

Since early 1973, the Spanish Family Guidance Clinic has provided direct counseling services to Hispanic drug abusers and their families in Dade County. These clients were, for the most part, first- and second-generation Cuban refugees and low-income Puerto Ricans. The Cubans resided primarily in a transitional neighborhood in the central city, nicknamed *La Pequena Habana* (Little Havana) by its residents, and the Puerto Ricans resided in the Wynwood section of Miami, a poverty area in the northeast section of the city.

Because the Cuban refugees acculturated more quickly than the Puerto Ricans, the Cuban refugee clients presented an appropriate population for study of the effects of acculturation. Although the Spanish Family Guidance Clinic had been organized to reach and serve "hard-core" drug users, particularly heroin addicts, it quickly became apparent that while there were other patterns of drug use, there was relatively little heroin use in the population that came for treatment. For example:

> Narcotic users, although highly visible, represented a very small minority of Cuban drug users. The majority of the Cuban drug-using population tended to be involved with marihuana, prescription sedatives, and tranquilizers.
>
> Cuban patients in treatment exhibited patterns of drug abuse that were unlike those conventionally reported in the drug-abuse literature. There were numerous cases of medication misuse among older members of the family, possibly an outgrowth of a cultural tendency toward self-medication which was characteristic of these people in Cuba.
>
> Cuban patients in treatment were reluctant to talk about their drug abuse, often resisting inquiry about drug-taking activity until well into a therapeutic relationship.

Some of these impressions of drug-use patterns gained from ongoing therapy with Cuban drug abusers and their families are consistent with data from the Client Oriented Data Acquisition Process (CODAP), the federal reporting system for drug treatment programs, but only in the sense that the Cuban prevalence rate of opiate use is smaller than the rates for other Hispanic groups. Table 19-1 shows the comparative drug involvement of the total population of Cuban,

Table 19-1
Comparison of Cuban, Puerto Rican, and Mexican Drug Abusers Admitted to Federally Funded Programs, CODAP Report, April-June 1976

	Hispanic-American Group				
Primary Drug Problem	*Cuban (n = 139)*	*Puerto Rican (n = 2,483)*	*Mexican (n = 3,862)*	*All Hispanic (n = 6,484)*	*All Non-Hispanic (n = 48,636)*
Heroin/Opiates	42.4	77.1	81.3	78.6	62.7
Alcohol	4.3	2.3	1.9	1.9	7.8
Marijuana	23.7	7.9	5.4	6.5	9.2
Barbiturates/Sedatives	12.9	2.5	2.4	2.5	5.0
Amphetamines/Cocaine	6.5	2.3	1.9	3.5	6.1
Inhalants	2.2	1.8	4.6	3.3	.9
Other	9.9	6.1	2.6	3.9	8.1
% of All Spanish	2.14	38.29	59.56	99.9	

Source: NIDA Statistical Series, Quarterly Report, April-June 1976, CODAP (Series 5), data from table 2-2.

Puerto Rican, Mexican-American, and non-Hispanics in drug-abuse treatment programs in the United States during April-June 1976. Note that while heroin and other illegal opiates constitute a large majority of drug-related treatment admissions for all non-Cuban Hispanic and all non-Hispanic drug patients, these drugs accounted for less than 43 percent of the admissions for Cubans. By contrast, Cubans were proportionately more involved with amphetamines/cocaine, marihuana, and barbiturate-sedative drugs than the other groups, and their involvement with alcohol was proportionately the highest for all Hispanic groups. Nevertheless, table 19-1 indicates the highest prevalence rate of reported drug problems for any type of drug was heroin-opiates, even among the Cubans in the CODAP sample. (It will be shown later that for the Cuban youth sample in treatment in the Spanish Family Guidance Clinic, the prevalence rate of heroin use was much smaller.)

The Spanish Family Guidance Clinic study of Hispanic drug use, which was conducted in the period from 1973 to 1977, included 273 clients of whom 160 were adolescents between 11 and 19 years of age (about 59 percent) and 113 were between 20 and 29 (about 41 percent), all of whom were admitted during the 1974-1976 program years. The sex breakdowns between the two age groups were not identical: the adolescent clinic population numbered 110 males to 50 females, a ratio of about 2 to 1. Within the population of postadolescents, the ratio was 55 males to 58 females, a ratio of about 1 to 1. It was determined that overrepresentation of males in the adolescent population reflected the more severe acculturation conflicts experienced by males, as well as the tendency for the acting-out behavior of male adolescents to be identified and labeled as deviant by schools, parents, and police. The majority of the Cuban patients (254) were Caucasian, representing 93 percent of the population. This latter figure is consistent with the racial composition of the Hispanic population in Miami: although blacks comprised about 25 percent of the population of Cuba at the time of revolution, the proportion of blacks among the exiles was slightly less than 4 percent in 1967 (Thomas and Huyck 1967, cited in Portes 1969). Since Cubans in Miami comprise about 85 percent of the Hispanic population (Ladner et al. 1976), the low proportion of blacks is consistent with the overall Hispanic demography as well as with the population of Cubans.

The ethnic breakdown of the Hispanic patients in treatment is shown in table 19-2. Note that there is a substantial difference in the proportions of Cubans in treatment: within the adolescent group, Cubans accounted for 89 percent of the client population, but they accounted for only 66 percent of the postadolescent group. These differences are statistically significant ($\chi^2 = 16.04$; df = 2; $p < .01$). The greater percentages of Cuban adolescents in treatment might possibly be explained by the preponderance of generational and cultural conflicts among Cuban families with adolescent children (see, for example, Szapocznik et al. *in press*).

In this report, data from two major research instruments will be reported:

Table 19-2
Ethnic Composition of Spanish Adolescent and Postadolescent Clients Treated by the Spanish Family Guidance Clinic

	Age Group			
Ethnic Group	*11 to 19*		*20 to 29*	
Puerto Rican	15	10%	17	16%
Cuban	126	89%	69	66%
Other Hispanic	6	1%	18	18%
Totals	147	100%	104	100%
Missing data	13			

x^2 (ethnicity by age) = 16.04; df = 2; $p < .01$.

the client information form (CIF) of the National Youth Polydrug Study (NYPS), a drug-abuse and psychosocial history form administered to all clients at the time of admission to treatment, and the psychiatric status schedule (PSS), administered to the patients at admission and termination. The PSS was developed in the early 1960s to augment the research value of traditional psychiatric-impairment assessment practices (Spitzer et al. 1970). The PSS also contains items dealing with leisure-time activities, adequacy of family role performance, substance abuse, alcoholism, and impairment in interpersonal activities, as well as the major psychopathological elements.

The analyses presented here are primarily concerned with the macro-level indicators of psychopathology obtained from the PSS. The macro-level scores are derived from a varimax principal components factor analysis of the entire 321-item test, resulting in four principal elements: subjective distress, behavioral disturbance, impulse-control disturbance, and reality-testing disturbance.

Subjective distress (SD) sums scores across five major subscales: anxiety and depression, impairment in everyday activities, social isolation, self-mutilation/suicide, and somatic preoccupation. *Behavioral disturbance* (BD) refers to manifested behavior and sums scores across six major subscales: speech disorganization, inappropriate affect, agitation, interview belligerence, disorientation, and affective retardation. *Impulse-control disturbance* (ICD) sums scores for antisocial impulses or acts, drug abuse, and reported overt anger. *Reality-testing disturbance* (RID) sums two subscales for grandiosity and paranoia/persecution/hallucination. The impulse-control disturbance (ICD) was omitted from this study because it had been found to have a rather strong correlation with drug abuse.

Not all clients at the Spanish Family Guidance Clinic were assessed with all PSS scales, since it was often necessary to facilitate the intake procedures for families in crisis and there were attendant difficulties in completing detailed forms. For this reason, missing data are included in tabular presentation (see table 19-2) to account for differences in population bases from table to table.

Results

Table 19-3 shows a comparison of the distribution of self-reported primary drug problems at admission among the adolescent and postadolescent drug users in treatment at the Spanish Family Guidance Clinic. Primary drug was identified by the client, reviewed at intake, and recorded on the interview form. (Note that in a number of instances drug abuse was not reported by the clients at the time of admission.)

Several aspects of this table are noteworthy. First, the distribution of primary drugs reported differs between the adolescent and the older age group (20 to 29 years of age). Second, there are also many differences between the predominantly Cuban Spanish Family Guidance Clinic population and the national CODAP sample of adolescent Spanish drug abusers in treatment in

Table 19-3
Comparison of Primary Drugs in Hispanic Adolescent and Postadolescent Populations in Treatment for Drug Abuse, Spanish Family Guidance Clinic and National CODAP Sample

	Age Groups (Spanish Family Guidance Clinic)		*Hispanic CODAP, 1975*
Drug	*11 to 19*[a] *(n = 101)*	*20 to 29 (n = 82)*	*10 to 18*[b] *(n = 2,687)*
Alcohol	4%	6%	7%
Barbiturates	4%	6%	5%
Sedatives, tranquilizers	20%	29%	2%
Marihuana and hallucinogens	59%	33%	49%
Inhalants	6%	0	24%
Amphetamine, cocaine	0	8%	4%
Heroin	0	2%	7%
Other	7%	15%	0
	100%	99%	98%
No drug reported, missing data:	59	31	169

χ^2 (adolescent versus postadolescent) = 27.65; df = 7; $p < .01$.

χ^2 (pooled Spanish Family Guidance Clinic clients versus CODAP clients) = 191.88; df = 7; $p < .01$.

[a]Mostly Cubans in this sample.

[b]Mostly non-Cuban Hispanics in this sample.

1975. Clearly, the Miami population of refugee-family adolescents represents a special population not representative of the Hispanic drug-abusing population in treatment nationwide.[1] Nevertheless, the predominantly Cuban Miami adolescent group appears to be fairly similar to the national adolescent group in the percentage who have reported marihuana and hallucinogens as their primary drug of use.

The proportion of marihuana users drops from 59 percent of the primary drug mentions in the under-20 population to 33 percent in the 20 to 29 age group; similarly, adolescent reporting of inhalants as a primary drug problem disappears entirely in the older group, and primary problems with minor tranquilizers and nonbarbiturate sedatives rises from 20 percent in the adolescent population to 29 percent in the 20 to 29 age population. We have pointed out elsewhere (Scopetta and Ladner 1977) that marihuana-using Hispanic adults over 40, particularly women, showed the highest distress levels of any drug-abusing subgroup of adults. Women using tranquilizers, which are more widely accepted in the Cuban culture, were found, on the other hand, to have the lowest stress levels of the adults in treatment. Hispanic adolescents using marihuana have low subjective distress. Thus it is interesting to speculate that the peer-group support for the particular type of drug use from the same-age cohort may be a factor in lessening the amount of stress subjectively experienced, in addition to the direct effect that tranquilizers and marihuana might have in lessening stress.

When primary drug use is examined in adolescent and postadolescent males and females (see table 19-4), it is noticed that among the adolescents, marihuana and hallucinogen use is more common among males (69 percent) as compared with females (37 percent). Nonbarbiturate sedatives and tranquilizers rank with marihuana among females (37 percent). Inhalants are used predominantly by males, as is alcohol.

Within the postadolescent population, however, the difference between the sexes is even more pronounced. Marihuana is still predominant among males, and sedatives and tranquilizers predominate among females. Males are proportionately more heavily involved with alcohol, amphetamine/cocaine, and heroin; females are proportionately more heavily involved with barbiturate-sedatives and other miscellaneous substances. It is evident from the data in this table that although the female postadolescent population is largely involved with the more "culturally acceptable" drugs, the male population in their twenties tend to use the illicit drugs typically used by the adolescent group. This group, however, shows evidence of involvement with heroin and stimulant drugs that were entirely absent in the adolescent population.

There is evidence from the CODAP national data file that the same tendency is found among drug treatment clients generally, regardless of ethnic origin: approximately five times as many female clients, proportionately, as male clients over 25 years of age have licit sedatives and over-the-counter drugs as

Table 19-4
Comparative Distribution of Primary Drugs, Adolescent and Postadolescent Male and Female Hispanic Drug Abusers in Treatment, Spanish Family Guidance Clinic

	11 to 19		*20 to 29*	
Drug	*Male (n = 71)*	*Female (n = 30)*	*Male (n = 40)*	*Female (n = 42)*
Alcohol	6%	0	10%	2%
Barbiturates	3%	7%	2%	9%
Sedatives, tranquilizers	13%	37%	18%	40%
Marihuana and hallucinogens	69%	37%	50%	17%
Inhalants	7%	3%	0	0
Amphetamine, cocaine	0	0	10%	7%
Heroin	0	0	5%	0
Other	3%	16%	5%	24%
	101%	100%	100%	99%
Missing data	9	20	15	16

χ^2 (male/female, 11 to 19 years) = 18.96; df = 5; $p < .01$.
χ^2 (male/female, 20 to 29 years) = 23.44; df = 6; $p < .01$.

their "primary drug problem." (However, this sex-differential issue is more important for the Miami Cuban sample, since the licit type of drug abuse only applies to 6.6 percent of the females and 1.1 percent of the males in the CODAP national sample.) Data from other studies (see, for example, Szapocznik et al. *in press*) suggest that females acculturate less quickly than males, and this difference is more marked in actual behavior.

To compare Hispanics with other ethnic groups, data were obtained on all patients admitted to the Jackson Memorial Hospital emergency room and the psychiatric crisis intervention center with drug-related problems in 1973 (see table 19-5). The highest percentage of acute drug reactions involving heroin occurred in the black sample, while the Hispanic sample (mixed Puerto Rican and Cuban) was found to have the lowest percentages involving heroin. We can see that Hispanics have a higher percentage of acute reactions resulting from sedative/tranquilizers than both the black and white hospital patients. Although the actual numbers are small, it was surprising to find that the younger (under 18 years of age) Hispanics atypically had a higher percentage of sedative/tranquilizer adverse reactions than the older Hispanics.

Drug-abusing clients in the Spanish Family Guidance Clinic were separated according to their levels of "impairment," as measured by the drug-abuse subscale of the Psychiatric Status Schedule (PSS). This subscale comprises a set of items relating to the aggregate quantity and frequency of drug use and its

Table 19-5
Emergency Room and Crises Intervention Data on Acute Drug Reactions for 1973 by Drug Type and Ethnic Group
(Percentages)

	Black		*Hispanic*		*Anglo-American*		*Total*	
Drug	*Under 18 (n = 91)*	*18 to 29 (n = 319)*	*Under 18 (n = 28)*	*18 to 29 (n = 97)*	*Under 18 (n = 99)*	*18 to 29 (n = 638)*	*Under 18 (n = 218)*	*18 to 29 (n = 1,066)*
Barbiturates	14	16	32	28	39	34	28	29
Sedatives/tranquilizers	24	19	32	30	14	24	21	23
Marihuana and other hallucinogens	10	4	7	10	19	10	14	8
Inhalants	3	1	11	1	0	1	3	1
Amphetamine/cocaine	2	4	0	7	9	6	5	6
Heroin	7	33	0	11	6	18	6	22
Prescription medicine	40	23	18	12	12	7	24	12
	100	100	100	99	99	100	101	101

interference with everyday life. Clients with no drug-abuse-related pathology were classed as "no pathology." Clients scoring below the fiftieth percentile of the ranked drug-abuse pathology scores were classed as "low pathology," and clients above the fiftieth percentile were classed as "high pathology." The relative "impairment" levels due to the drug abuse by age and sex among adolescent and postadolescent Hispanic drug abusers in treatment are presented in table 19-6.

Among adolescents, the drug-abuse behavior of slightly more than half of each sex group was considered to be "nonpathological," or unimpaired by drug use (53 percent male, 54 percent female). By contrast, there are substantial sex differences in the postadolescent group: more females are "nonpathological" (52 percent compared with 33 percent), and more males have "high pathology" (42 percent compared with 21 percent). These differences are statistically significant ($\chi^2 = 6.52$; df = 2; $p < .05$).

Within the two populations, the general trend is for the older drug-using clients to be more pathological. (Fifty-three percent of the adolescents are "nonpathological" compared with only 42 percent of the older group. Conversely, only 22 percent of the adolescents are in the "high pathology" group compared with 31 percent of the postadolescent group. This trend is found not be statistically significant.)

One may speculate about the greater drug use and more severe drug-related "pathology" in the postadolescent male population in terms of Wiley's (1967) concept of the "mobility trap." Deviant behavior which is tolerated in adolescence may have more profound consequences for the individual if the behavior is brought to the attention of labeling authorities; school expulsion and a criminal record contribute to reduced postadolescent mobility. This "secondary deviance" is sometimes a major factor in the individual remaining involved in a

Table 19-6
Level of Impairment (PSS Scores) by Sex and Age Groups in Spanish Drug-Abusing Clients
(Percentages)

	11 to 19[a]		*20 to 29*[b]		*Total*[c]	
Level of Impairment	*Male (n = 110)*	*Female (n = 50)*	*Male (n = 55)*	*Female (n = 58)*	*All 11 to 19*	*All 20 to 29*
None	53	54	33	52	53	42
Low	23	30	25	28	25	27
High	24	16	42	21	22	31
	100	100	100	101	100	100

[a]$\chi^2 = 1.88$, df = 2, p not significant.
[b]$\chi^2 = 6.52$, df = 2, $p < .05$.
[c]$\chi^2 = 3.69$, df = 2, p not significant.

deviant career beyond the time when such a career might have been a passing phase. This may be one of the reasons why, although some drug users may "mature out" of their drug behavior, a core of young adults remain involved in the drug-abusing lifestyle.

Subjective Distress and Drug-Related Impairment

Table 19-7 presents the comparative mean levels of "subjective distress" as measured by the PSS (depression/anxiety, guilt, somatic symptoms) at admission, for the adolescent and postadolescent age groups (A) and sex (S) groups, and for levels of drug-related impairment, as measured by the PSS (D). There are significant relationships between both age and subjective distress and drug-related impairment and subjective distress; adolescent clients show less subjective distress at admission than postadolescents, and there is a monotonic relationship between distress and the three levels of drug impairment. It is important to note that the effects of age and drug pathology on subjective distress are independent: the *F* ratio of the A × D interaction is not significant.

Table 19-7
Comparative Mean Levels of Subjective Distress in Hispanic Clients by Age Group, Sex, and Drug-Use Level

Source	*ss*	*df*	*ms*	*f*
Age (A)	4,622.0	1	4,622.0	46.4***
Sex (S)	256.5	1	256.5	2.6
Drug (D)	1,122.3	2	561.1	5.6**
A × S	71.2	1	71.2	0.7
A × D	281.0	2	140.5	1.4
S × D	399.7	2	199.8	2.0
A × S × D	116.2	2	58.1	0.6
Error	25,998.6	261	99.6	
Total	34,107.0	272	125.4	

	Mean Subjective Distress Levels
Age	
11 to 19 years	40.06
20 to 29 years	49.58
Sex	
Male	42.68
Female	46.01
Drug pathology	
None	41.74
Low	44.65
High	47.64

$^{**}p < .01$.
$^{***}p < .001$.

The importance of the nonsignificant interaction can be emphasized by summarizing the findings in table 19-7 in two statements:

1. The adolescents in treatment presented less subjective distress than the postadolescents, regardless of their level of drug pathology.
2. There is a positive association between levels of drug pathology and the levels of subjective distress at admission, when controlling for age groups.

The findings related to differences between adolescents and postadolescents in degree of subjective distress are not surprising, given our increased understanding of the supportive role of the peer adolescent subculture in mediating cultural and intergenerational conflicts and the tendency of adolescents to underreport distress in general. Some parents also may be more supportive and tolerant of problem behavior in adolescent offspring than in young-adult offspring. The postadolescent and young-adult drug users may not have support systems to enable them to maintain their drug-using life without stress. They are also confronted at this period of their lives with the often unsettling challenges of getting a job, becoming more self-sufficient and self-supporting, moving away from parents, etc.

It is important to bear in mind, however, that these findings are obtained from a population of people in treatment and, as such, do not reflect the relative levels of distress in the general population of Cuban adolescents and postadolescents. Therefore, generalization of these findings to acculturational issues in the population at large would be inappropriate.

Table 19-8 illustrates the comparative levels of reality-testing disturbance, as measured by the PSS, controlling for age (A), sex (S), and drugs (D) in the same way as was done in table 19-7. Again, there was a significant increment in the degree of reality-testing disturbance found in the postadolescent client population as compared with the adolescents. There were no significant differences for sex in levels of reality testing. Age and degree of drug-use impairment were significantly related to degree of reality testing.

Summary of Findings and Discussion

Data presented in this chapter indicate that a smaller percentage of Cuban youths in Miami are involved with heroin and opiates than other Hispanic or non-Hispanic groups. At the same time, there appears to be a higher prevalence rate of use of marihuana and sedatives among Miami Cubans compared with other Hispanic and non-Hispanic groups. Also, the Cuban prevalence rate of amphetamine use is higher than that of other Hispanic groups but resembles that of the non-Hispanic groups.

A comparison of drug-use patterns between youth and young-adult clients admitted to the Spanish Family Guidance Clinic (the majority of whom are

Table 19-8
Comparative Mean Levels of Reality-Testing Disturbance in Hispanic Clients by Age Groups, Sex, and Drug-Use Level

Source	*ss*	*df*	*ms*	*f*
Age (A)	578.1	1	578.1	9.0**
Sex (S)	78.1	1	78.1	1.2
Drugs (D)	76.1	2	38.0	0.6
A X S	185.1	1	185.1	2.9
A X D	103.0	2	51.5	0
S X D	468.0	2	234.0	3.6*
A X S X D	101.8	2	50.9	0.8
Error	16,799.0	261	64.4	
Total	18,434.1	272	67.8	

	Mean Reality-Testing Disturbance Levels
Age	
11 to 19 years	47.31
20 to 29 years	50.23
Sex	
Male	48.78
Female	48.13
Drug pathology	
None	48.15
Low	47.97
High	49.78

*$p < .01$.
**$p < .01$.

Cuban) indicates that fewer young adults use marihuana as compared with youths; young adults do not use inhalants, but more of them use heroin, sedatives and tranquilizers, alcohol, and barbiturates. A comparison of drug-use patterns by sex for both youth and for young-adult clients, shows that more females use tranquilizers, barbiturates, and "other" drugs compared with males, and fewer females use marihuana compared with males.

With regard to degree of psychic impairment and distress, male young adults were found to have a higher degree of impairment than female young adults. Level of impairment was also positively associated with age among both males and females, with older clients manifesting higher levels of impairment.

Some of the preceding findings were examined and interpreted in light of two factors in the life of the study sample: the second-generation Cuban adolescent has double identity crises as an effect of living in two contrasting cultures, and is subject to a sense of fragmentation, confusion, alienation, and anomie. The intergenerational (parent versus adolescent) and acculturational (Cuban versus American) value conflicts are perceived as etiological factors in adolescent drug abuse. During this period, the temporary shelter of a peer culture provides some support to the individual in his or her efforts to cope with the problems of adolescence and the pressures that result from living in two contrasting cultures. The peer group may assume more than the usual importance in filling the existing vacuum.

The Spanish Family Guidance Clinic has attempted to assess the impact of the growing estrangement of Cuban and other Hispanic children from the values of their parents, both in terms of the adolescent versus parent conflict anticipated during maturation and in terms of their acculturation to American social and behavioral standards. In the case of parents who are members of the host culture, the conventional wisdom of childrearing assures them that eventually their children will realign themselves with some of their basic values. Parents who are immigrants have no such reassurances, and the excessive concern and overprotectiveness of Hispanic parents toward their "deviant" children is a simultaneous expression of concern for the child and for the integrity of their own culture.

The emerging Hispanic adolescent experiences the same multiple stresses that face dominant-culture adolescents in a society with pluralistic values and standards of behavior. Is this drug-abusing Hispanic adolescent rebelling against specific conditions within his family and facets of his own upbringing and seeking to identify with and attain status in an alternative peer group? Or is he only "acculturating" by means of using marihuana or other drugs, and thus taking a behavioral stand against some aspects of his parents' culture without at the same time accepting the values of the alternative host (adult Establishment) system?

Although we have postulated that adolescents tend to feel less ashamed or guilty about their involvement with drugs than older age groups, and we have argued that one of the functions of adolescent culture is to insulate the individual from censure of the activity by adult authority, the data reported here show that the distress of the identified drug-abusing adolescent client does, nevertheless, increase as a function of drug use. These findings might be taken to suggest that although the adolescent may outwardly reject the values of parent culture, he or she still recognizes the moral validity of the normative system (see, for example, King et al. 1976), or at least has some doubts about the matter. It is also possible, however, that most of the subjective distress found in these adolescent clients derives from sources other than drug use and cannot be taken as indication of the adolescents' attitudes toward drug use. The drug use could, in fact, be a manifestation, or a symptom, of the other types or sources of stress.

The use and abuse of drugs may be conceptualized as a means of coping with and externalizing the conflicts experienced by the acculturating adolescent. For some, drugs may provide a source of escape, while for others it may help them identify with and become part of a peer group.

Many other immigrant populations have experienced and will continue to experience problems (distress) in the process of moving from one culture to another. American Indians, Mexican-Americans, and Asian populations have recently experienced problems associated with acculturation in the United States. The problems that result from the acculturation process are manifested in many ways. Drug use and abuse are two of the potential outcomes, particularly when many difficulties are experienced in the transition. We need to continue to study this phenomenon (acculturation) so that we are better able to understand the dynamics and address the problems that emerge.

Note

1. In an earlier report to the National Institute on Drug Abuse, we pointed out that Cuban refugee drug patients in treatment throughout the United States were not characteristic of the total population of Hispanic drug abusers (Ladner et al. 1977). Cuban-American drug patients represent a small proportion of the Hispanic patients in treatment, and the characteristics of the Hispanic ethnic/language group are determined predominantly by the large proportion of Chicano and Puerto Rican drug patients in treatment.

References

Berry, J., and Annis, R. 1974. Acculturative stress: The role of ecology, culture and differentiation. *Journal of Cross-Cultural Psychology* 5 (4):382-406.

Coleman, J. 1961. *The Adolescent Society*. New York: Free Press.

Erickson, M.L., and Jensen, G.F. 1977. Delinquency is still group behavior: Toward revitalizing the group premise in the sociology of deviance. *Journal of Criminal Law and Criminology* 68 (2):262-273.

King, O., Scopetta, M., and Szapocznik, J. 1976. Acculturation and Incidences of Drug Abuse in Cuban-Americans. Final report. Research contract 271-75-4136, National Institute on Drug Abuse, July 1976.

Ladner, R. 1977. Context, drug culture and language response: An analysis of responses to ambiguous drug-related homographs. *International Journal of the Addictions* 12 (4):529-540.

Ladner, R., et al. 1976. Social Service Needs and Resources of the City of Miami. Comprehensive Neighborhood Development Plan, Technical Appendix, October 1976.

Ladner R., King, O., and Janik, S. 1977. Drug Abuse and Family Mental Health Needs in a Cuban Clinical Population. Report to the National Institute on Drug Abuse, September 1977.

Ladner, R., and Page, W. *In press. Epidemiology and Service Utilization Patterns for Drug Abusers in an Emergency Ward Setting*. Cambridge, Mass.: Ballinger.

Matza, D. 1964. *Delinquency and Drift.* New York: Wiley.

McGrath, J., and Scarpitti, F. 1970. *Youth and Drugs: Perspectives on a Social Problem.* Glenview, Ill.: Scott, Foresman.

Merton, R. 1957. *Social Theory and Social Structure.* New York: Free Press.

Mezey, A. 1960. Psychiatric aspects of human migrations. *International Journal of Social Psychiatry* 5 (4):245-260.

Musgrove, F. 1964. *Youth and Social Order.* London: Routledge and Kegan Paul.

Naditch, M., and Morrisey, R. 1976. Role stress, personality and psychology in a group of immigrant adolescents. *Journal of Abnormal Psychology* 1976:113-118.

Padilla, A., and Ruiz, R. 1974. Latino Mental Health: A Review of the Literature. Washington, D.C.: U.S. Government Printing Office, 1724-00317.

Portes, A. 1969. Dilemmas of a golden exile: Integration of Cuban refugee families in Milwaukee. *American Sociological Review* 34 (4):505-518.

Report of the Subpanel on Hispanics of the Special Populations Task Force to the President's Commission on Mental Health. 1978. Washington, D.C.: The White House.

Scopetta, M., and Ladner, R. 1977. *Psychological and Social Predictors of Drug Abuse in Spanish Clinical Population: A Multiple Risk-Factor Analysis.* Report to the National Institute on Drug Abuse, July 1977.

Spitzer, R., Fleiss, J., and Burdock, E. 1964. The mental status schedule: Rationale, reliability, validity. *Comprehensive Psychiatry* 5:384-395.

Spitzer, R., Endicott, J., Fleiss, J., and Cohen, J. 1970. The psychiatric status schedule: A technique for evaluating psychopathology and impairment in role functioning. *Archives of General Psychiatry* 23:41-55.

Szapocznik, J., Daruna, P., Scopetta, M., and Arnalde, M. *In press.* Cuban immigrant inhalant abusers. *American Journal of Alcohol and Drug Abuse.*

Szapocznik, J., Scopetta, M., and King, O. *In press.* Theory and practice in matching treatment to the characteristics of Cuban immigrants *Journal of Community Psychology.*

Szapocznik, J., Scopetta, M. Kurtines, W., and Aranalde, M. *In press.* Theory and measurement of acculturation. *Interamerican Journal of Psychology.*

Szapocznik, J., Tillman, W., and Scopetta, M. *In press.* What changes and what stays the same in Cuban immigrant families. In M.C. Herrera, J. Szapocznik, and J. Rasgo (eds.), *Los Cubanos en los Estados Unidos* (Cubans in the United States). Miami: Editora Universal.

Tyhurst, L. 1951. Displacement and migration. *American Journal of Psychiatry* (8):561-568.

Wiley, N. 1967. The ethnic mobility trap and stratification theory. *Social Problems* 15 (fall):147-259.

20 Unique Aspects of White Ethnic Drug Use

John A. Carlisi

Introduction

Adolescent drug abuse has traditionally been viewed as a problem of inner-city minority youths who come from an environment of severe economic and social deprivation. It has been concluded that heroin use, which is suspected of being more prevalent in ghetto communities, has resulted in great costs to society. Therefore, a considerable amount of money has been spent over the past few years to establish programs that are specifically designed to address the drug-related problems of inner-city minority populations, but not for youths under 18 years of age.

Yet, secure in the feeling that they had identified the major drug users, the policymakers have ignored an important phenomenon—the emergence of the white, inner-city, ethnic, adolescent drug user. This chapter will examine drug use among white ethnic populations, explore some possible causes, and make recommendations for appropriate prevention and treatment services.

The national Center for Urban Ethnic Affairs (NCUEA), founded in 1970 and located in Washington, D.C., is a nonprofit organization that works with community residents to develop better living conditions in the older industrial cities. During the past 8 years, NCUEA has invested more than $6 million in supporting community organizations and community-development activities in ninety ethnic neighborhoods located within fifty-five cities. This work has been based on the concept that through a sense of ethnic identity, people in ethnic communities can be motivated to work together to address common problems. NCUEA has therefore concentrated on forming ethnic neighborhood groups into local coalitions and viable community organizations. Focusing on ethnic identification within neighborhoods where groups of predominantly Southern and Eastern European origin reside, NCUEA has had considerable success in helping ethnic groups organize around mutual concerns and interests.

NCUEA-sponsored conferences held over the last several years have elicited increasing concern from residents about drug use in their neighborhoods. The study to be described in this chapter was undertaken to assess the nature and extent of this problem in specific ethnic communities.

In recent years, there has been an increase in research on drug abuse among "special" populations. Such studies have attempted to assess both the influence of ethnic/cultural factors on drug use and the special treatment needs of these different populations. These studies have focused primarily on black, Hispanic, American Indian, and, to some extent, Oriental populations, but have almost totally ignored the inner-city, white, ethnic populations. Many ethnic/cultural studies indicate that a wide range of factors influence the drug-taking behaviors of different populations. NCUEA therefore hypothesized in this study that there would be a similar diversity of factors which influence the drug-taking behaviors of adolescents residing in white, ethnic communities. Similarly, it was felt that these sociocultural factors must be understood in order to establish more appropriate prevention, intervention, and treatment services in these communities.

Several investigators have reported finding relationships between the ethnic/cultural factors and problem drinking (Pittman and Snyder 1962; MacAndrew and Edgerton 1969) and have postulated that alcoholism problems develop differently in each ethnic group. Examining first- and second-generation Irish, Italian, Jewish, Swedish, and English male populations, Greeley (1978) examined the effects of parental role models in different ethnic groups. He focused on mothers' drinking patterns, levels of positive self-perception, attitudes toward authority, and individual achievement. The fact that Greeley found different factors at work within each ethnic group encourages the supposition that it should be possible to differentiate drug use patterns in ethnic populations. The plan of this chapter therefore is to review the concept of ethnicity and its relationship to mental health; describe some of the unique sociocultural characteristics found in inner-city, white, ethnic communities; assess the findings from health studies which are even marginally related to drug-taking behavior in ethnic communities; assess the data from a national youth drug study which differentiated among adolescent drug users by race and ethnicity; and finally, describe the results of the ethnic drug study conducted by the National Center for Urban Ethnic Affairs (NCUEA).

Ethnicity

The concepts of ethnicity and ethnic identity have been analyzed extensively by social scientists and community activists over the past decade and defined as "the organization of plural persons into distinctive groups, and second, of solidarity and the loyalties of individual members to such groups." Factors integral to a sense of ethnicity, according to Parsons (1967), include racial homogeneity within the particular group, a certain degree of religious uniformity, linguistic conformity, and a common cultural tradition. One area of divergence may be class, because major socioeconomic stratifications within ethnic groups can be found. Parsons describes an ethnic group as "a group, the members of which have, both with respect to their own sentiments and those of non-members, a distinctive identity which is rooted in some kind of a distinctive sense of its own history." Parsons further states, "American society, on the one hand by virtue of its political constitution, on the other hand by virtue of the history of immigration, pioneered in the establishment of a multi-ethnic society. If there is a single formula for ethnic identity in the American population, probably the conception of 'national origin' is the most accurate designation for most groups."

Glazer and Moynihan (1974) have compared the impact of ethnic awareness on group identity to that of the industrial revolution and assert that "there has been a pronounced and sudden increase in many countries and in many circumstances to insist on the significance of their group distinctiveness and identity and on new rights that derive from their group character."

In addition to being a source of group and individual identity, ethnicity has also become a major organizing principle, more powerful possibly than class. Glazer and Moynihan (1974) point out, "Different groups *do* have different norms. In the most natural way the unsuccessful group has the best chance of changing the system if it behaves as a group. It is as a group that its struggles become not merely against the norms of some other groups, but in favor of the already established norms of its own."

Ethnicity as a Factor in Mental Health

There is a paucity of literature relating to ethnicity, social class, and drug abuse per se. However, the link between drug abuse and mental health problems has been firmly established (Krug and Henry 1974; Rosencrans and Birgnet 1972). Poor self-image and low self-esteem are factors frequently cited in cases of drug abuse (Dodson et al. 1971; Levy 1972; Yankelovich, Skelly and White, Inc. 1975). The relationship between mental health and ethnicity is pointed out by Opler (1967) in his review of the work of Mead, Benedict, Kluckholn, Sullivan, Horney, Ferenczi, and Kardiner, all of whom stressed the influence of social and cultural environment on both normal and deviant behavior. The work of Koloday (1969), Spiegal (1965), Barrabe and Von Mering (1953), and Zborowski (1964) stresses that various ethnic groups differ in their responses to health, illness, and treatment. However, Kolm (1973) indicates that there is a lack of evidence linking treatment-utilization patterns to ethnic variation.

The classic work of Hollingshead and Redlich (1958) demonstrated a relationship between mental health and class status, and showed that a patient's position in the status system affects the type of treatment he or she receives. One conclusion they drew from their study was that occupation is a potent force in determining a person's general adjustments to life and ways of coping with problems. This conclusion is also supported by Srole's Midtown Manhattan study (1962), the Gurin et al. (1958) nationwide survey of 2,460 adults, and the work of Kornhauser (1962), Mills (1951), and Fromm (1955).

Giordano's (1973) review of the literature suggests that the influence of ethnicity becomes particularly significant in those studies where social class is held constant. This is particularly relevant here because all the neighborhoods in the NCUEA study are both ethnic and working class. Giordano notes that while professional or socioeconomic status is frequently isolated as an influential variable, ethnic variation is still often ignored, or worse, denied outright.

Giordano (1974) summarized some of the issues regarding ethnicity in the mental health field including the following:

> Ethnicity and ethnic identity have been generally ignored as having significant influence on the mental health of Americans.
>
> There are marked differences in how various groups perceive and use mental health services.
>
> When mental health practitioners are unaware of the difference in emotional language, family symbolism, and variation of family roles, the quality of treatment is likely to suffer.
>
> The type and quality of mental health services differ, depending on class or ethnic differences.
>
> Numerous studies have shown that working-class, ethnic communities are underserved in terms of their mental health needs.
>
> Mental health service systems in ethnic communities are fragmented and uncoordinated, resulting in duplication and gaps in needed services.

Ethnicity is, both directly and indirectly, a powerful determinant in the development of the individual. This fact alone should make it a significant consideration in treatment. But based on the lack of published treatment and research data which differentiate according to specific ethnic groups, we must conclude that it is ignored by most professionals.

Characteristics of Inner-City Ethnics

Despite the fact that many young professionals are moving back into the city, the core populations in most cities today are predominantly black, Hispanic, and white ethnic groups from the lower and lower-middle socioeconomic strata (Green and Baroni 1976). Each of these groups tends to live in its own geographically and culturally defined area, although they are often in close proximity to one another.

American Catholic ethnic populations are generally concentrated in the Northeast, Mid-Atlantic, and Midwest areas. Eighty percent of the nation's French Canadians, 88 percent of the nation's Italians, 87 percent of the Poles, and 84 percent of the Irish Catholics reside in these regions (Green and Baroni 1976).

The neighborhoods in which the Southern and Eastern European populations live are generally characterized by the following (all figures based on the 1970 census unless otherwise noted):

A high rate of religious homogeneity compared with surrounding areas.

Concentrations of white ethnic groups of different religions, primarily Roman Catholic, Eastern, Russian, and Greek Orthodox, Jewish (in some areas), and in recent years, large numbers of white Appalachian Baptist.

Cultural linkages to the religion, values, and mores of the original immigrant stock.

Close proximity to the inner-city black neighborhoods.

A level of income averaging 15.3 percent below that of the standard metropolitan statistical areas (SMSA) in which they are located but 34.5 percent above the adjacent black areas.

A median education level of 10.4 years compared with 11.9 for the SMSA and 9.6 for the adjacent black population.

A 43.4 percent rate of owner-occupied housing compared with 57.4 percent for the SMSA and 27.8 percent for the nearby black population.

Neighborhood stability as evidenced by the high percentage of people residing in their neighborhood since 1949 or earlier and a high rate of elderly, widowed, or divorced individuals.

High rates of blue-collar and low rates of white-collar and government employment.

While there are many similarities, such as lower socioeconomic status, among inner-city, white ethnic communities, characteristics which are quite unique to each specific ethnic group can also be found. For example, past NCUEA experience has yielded the following profiles of Polish and Italian neighborhoods.

Polish	*Italian*
Patriarchal family structure	Matriarchal family structure
Strong church affiliation	Moderate church affiliation
Predominantly blue-collar workers	Predominantly blue-collar workers
Presence of foreign language	Presence of foreign language
Modest family income	Modest family income
Average family laborforce	High female laborforce
High nonpublic school enrollment	Low nonpublic school enrollment
High owner-occupied housing	Low owner-occupied housing
High residential stability	High residential stability

While occupational identity, use of foreign language, family income, and residential stability are characteristics which are common to both communities, attitudes toward neighborhood institutions (primarily educational and religious), patterns of authority, home ownership, and female employment distinguish the Polish and Italian populations from one another.

Racial Differences in Drug Use

Several studies have explored the relationship between race and drug use, although the degree to which racial and other sociodemographic variables have been successfully differentiated is not always clear. A study conducted by Vaillant (1966) found that black and Hispanic minority-group membership correlated with probability of hospitalization for addiction, and that the highest risk was among the first generation of children of minority immigrants, not among the immigrants themselves. However in recent years, race-related (black-white) differences in prevalence of drug use among adolescents appear to have diminished or, in some cases, reversed. A study conducted 10 years after Vaillant's findings were published (O'Donnell et al. 1976) found that white youths born in 1953-1954 reported higher rates than blacks in use of sedatives, stimulants, psychedelics, and heroin, reversing earlier reported ratios. Fifty-one percent of the young black men, and 49 percent of the young white men surveyed reported current marihuana use as contrasted with 39 and 21 percent, respectively, for black and white men born about 20 years earlier. Similarly, the number of youths, both black and white who had ever used marihuana (lifetime prevalence) was equivalent among youths born in 1953-1954, but was considerably higher for blacks among older groups of men. In the youngest age cohort, white youths were 10 percent more likely than blacks to have used sedatives, whereas there was no race-related difference in sedative use among the oldest men sampled (O'Donnell et al. 1976).

Kandel's (1976) study among high school students in New York State showed that whites were more likely than blacks to have tried alcoholic beverages, marihuana, barbiturates, amphetamines, psychedelics, and inhalants, but less likely to have tried cocaine or heroin. These data further suggest that black youths begin experimenting with drugs at older ages than white youths. This pattern does not hold for other racial minority populations.

Although Native American students constituted only a small subsample in the Kandel study, the results bear noting. Members of this group were more likely, often by large percentage differentials, to have tried all psychoactive drugs except heroin. Orientals have consistently shown lower rates of drug use compared with all other racial groups (Seltzer et al. 1974).

Specific ethnic groups are rarely distinguished, even in larger studies, beyond a perfunctory designation of "race."

Very often American blacks and West Indian blacks will be subsumed under the single category of "black," although the two cultures are quite dissimilar. Further, under the category of "Hispanic" or "Spanish-American," many researchers include Puerto Ricans, Mexicans, and Chicanos, again three groups with quite different cultures. Valuable information which is relevant to treatment is frequently lost when this is done.

National Youth Polydrug Study (NYPS)

The National Youth Polydrug Study (1977), conducted by the Philadelphia Psychiatric Center in 1976 and 1977 collected data relating to white ethnicity. This national study of adolescent (18 years or younger) drug use surveyed youths who had been admitted to treatment in facilities throughout the United States. An open-ended question concerning ethnicity was posed in the demographic section of the questionnaire: "What ethnic group do you identify with?" Not surprisingly, many of the respondents chose not to answer the question or gave answers that were not specific: "white," "American," "North American," etc. Nevertheless, the question was answered often enough to permit analysis of the data provided.

The NYPS white, ethnic sample was composed of 287 respondents, 40 percent of whom were German, 34 percent Irish, and 26 percent Italian. The other white ethnic populations mentioned were too small to be included in this analysis. Of those white ethnics who could be studied, 98 percent had never been married, 64 percent were currently unemployed, 28 percent had part-time work, and 75 percent lived with their parents. In response to a question regarding occupation of the head of the household, one-third of the sample answered semiskilled or unskilled; over 60 percent reported skilled, clerical/technical, or administrative/manager type employment; and 5 percent cited executive or professional as an occupation. The German group tended to be predominantly Protestant, while the Italians and Irish were predominantly Catholic. Approximately one-quarter of the sample reported no religious preference. Further information indicated that this sample was composed of lower-middle- and middle-class adolescents who had close ties to their family and were largely unemployed.

To measure the extent of drug use in this population, regular/heavy substance use (defined as three times or more weekly for at least a 1-month period) was analyzed. These data are shown in table 20-1. The substance most extensively used on a regular basis is marihuana/hashish, followed by alcohol. It should be remembered that these youngsters were being treated in programs designed for drug abusers. Other data from this study indicate that alcohol is the most frequently used substance in this 18 and under population. Marihuana and alcohol use are followed with decreasing frequency by barbiturates, ampheta-

Table 20-1
Regular/Heavy Drug Abuse by White Ethnic Groups, NYPS Sample
(Percent of Respondents)

Substance	*Italians*	*Irish*	*Germans*	*Total White*
Alcohol	23.7	12.4	17.5	18.5
Marihuana/hashish	38.2	44.3	48.2	46.6
Barbiturates	7.9	7.2	4.4	6.3
Amphetamines	3.9	5.2	2.6	5.1
Heroin/other opiates	11.8	5.2	0.9	4.2
Illegal methadone	2.6	0	1.8	0.7
Inhalants	1.3	3.1	0	1.5
Tranquilizers/sedatives	7.9	6.2	2.6	4.9
Hallucinogens	1.4	3.1	0.9	1.5

mines, tranquilizers, heroin, and lastly, inhalants, hallucinogens, and illegal methadone.

Although these data come from a general treatment population, it is possible to distinguish the drug-use patterns of different ethnic groups.

While reporting the second highest rate of regular alcohol use and the lowest rate for marihuana/hashish use, the Italian adolescents reported the highest rates of use for barbiturates, heroin/opiates, illegal methadone, and tranquilizers—all depressants. The German youth group reported the lowest overall rates of use for barbiturates, amphetamines, tranquilizers, hallucinogens, and heroin, but reported highest rates of marihuana use. These differing drug-use patterns help to support the premise that sociocultural factors influence different youth populations. Since the numbers in each white ethnic subsample are quite small however, the results can only be considered as suggestive.

The NCUEA Ethnic Drug Study

One of the main purposes of the NCUEA study was to report on differences in drug-use patterns between various white, ethnic minority groups. It should be clearly understood, however, that the findings presented here are based on limited samples which are not adequately representative of the spceific urban ethnic groups studied and should therefore be perceived as a descriptive or exploratory study, intended to elicit hypotheses regarding drug use among white, minority, ethnic groups rather than as a definitive statement.

Method

NCUEA developed a 196-term questionnaire to assess ethnicity, drug use, and related attitudes. The instrument was field tested in August and September of

Table 20-2
Age Distribution of NCUEA Sample by City
(n = 1400)

	Youth (18 or less)		*Young Adults (19 to 22)*			
Cities	*Number*	*%*	*Number*	*%*	*% of Total Sample*	*Average Age*
Baltimore	311	74.1	109	25.9	30	17.4
Cincinnati	115	63	67	37.0	13	16.9
Detroit	530	86.2	86	13.8	14	17.9
Providence	125	68.6	57	31.4	13	17.5
Totals	1081	77.2	319	22.8	100	17.3

1975 and revised and administered the following month. Inner-city communities in four cities—Baltimore, Detroit, Cincinnati, and Providence—were chosen because of high concentrations of white ethnic groups. Local public and private high schools cooperated in Baltimore and Detroit, allowing students to complete the questionnaire anonymously during their homeroom periods. Since local high schools and boards of education were unwilling to cooperate in Cincinnati and Providence, an extensive outreach effort was organized to reach neighborhood youths in these cities. Conducting the survey in various community settings rather than in school homerooms proved to be less efficient and resulted in smaller sample sizes.

Demographic Characteristics of the Sample

Age Distribution. Two age groups are distinguished in this study—the adolescent, 15 to 18 years of age, and the young adult, 19 to 22 years of age. Seventy-seven percent of the sample were adolescents (see table 20-2).

Table 20-3 displays the sex distribution by city and type of setting for the

Table 20-3
Sex Distribution of NCUEA Youth "Sample" by City and Collection Method (n = 915)

	Youth Subsample by Sex	
	% Male	*% Female*
High school homeroom setting		
Baltimore	62	38
Detroit	48	52
Community setting		
Cincinnati	54	46
Providence	58	42
Total %	54	46

youths under 19 years of age. The sex distribution of 54 percent males and 46 percent females among the adolescents is typical of the overall sample, where males comprised 55 percent.

Several additional demographic characteristics were revealed. Over three-quarters of the adolescents were in grades 9 through 11. Nineteen percent did not currently attend school. Concerning parental occupation, 36 percent of the subjects' fathers worked as mechanics and skilled laborers, while 8 percent were small business owners. Another 19 percent worked as manual laborers or held clerical positions; 35 percent of the respondents, an unexpectedly large percentage, reported the father as having no occupation. Respondents were also asked to specify the ethnicity of each parent and six distinct parental ethnic group patterns were reported. Table 20-4 shows the number of youths in each of the six groups identified. Five of the white ethnic groups had parents with the *same* ethnicity. Most of the respondents within the other white category were from Anglican, Slavic, or Greek descent. The sixth group is composed of white parents with *mixed* ethnic backgrounds (for example, German mother and Irish father).

The NCUEA sample included a substantial number of nonwhites. These minority subjects were categorized into four additional groups accounting for a 35 percent share of the total sample. Blacks were the most predominant, followed by the mixed racial group, composed of subjects whose parents were from different white and nonwhite racial/ethnic backgrounds. The Native American group was third in size, followed by Hispanics.

Table 20-4
Age Distribution from NCUEA's High School/Community Sample by Ethnic/Race Groups

	Contribution of Each Group to Total Sample		*Amount of Youth–18 Yrs. or Younger within Each Group*	
Cultural Groupings	*%*	*n*	*%*	*n*
Six ethnic white groups				
Polish	18	203	84	170
Other white–same parents	22	251	78	195
White–different	8	96	74	71
Italian	9	98	74	72
Irish	4	46	63	29
German	4	43	54	23
Subtotal		737		560
Four nonwhite ethnic groups				
Black	15	177	91	161
Mixed racial	7	84	76	64
Native American	7	83	81	67
Hispanic	6	70	89	62
Subtotal		414		354
Totals		1151		915

Because of sampling as well as actual neighborhood variations, ethnic-group contributions to the study were distributed unevenly among the four communities. Detroit has the highest concentrations of Polish, black, and Hispanic parents, while the Cincinnati sample was composed primarily of Native Americans and white parents of different (other than Polish, Irish, Italian, and German) ethnicities.

Prevalence Rates in the NCUEA White Ethnic 18 and Younger Sample

In assessing the 18 and younger sample, the drug-use-prevalence indicators showed different patterns among the NCUEA ethnic groups. The data show that, in the particular communities studied, the drug use rates among the white ethnic youths and nonwhite groups differ. For example, the Irish and white-same (that is, two parents, both white of the same ethnicity, but not Polish, Italian, Irish, or German), had rates of drug use which far exceeded other white and nonwhite ethnic groups.

Reported Use by Friends

The reported use of drugs by friends has been used as a proxy variable to determine drug-use patterns within different populations. Table 20-5 presents data collected from the NCUEA sample on the use of drugs by friends. As might be expected, the subjects reported that most of their friends used marihuana and alcohol, followed by amphetamines and barbiturates, and then opiates, inhalants, and hallucinogens. The pattern within each of the ethnic groups differs considerably in regard to the specific drugs used and rates of use. The white-same and Native American populations reported higher rates of use than the total sample in all drug categories, while the Polish and black populations were always below the total sample. The white-same subsample had the highest reported rate of alcohol, marihuana, and inhalant use, while the Native American subsample was highest in barbiturates, amphetamines, opiates, and hallucinogens.

Patterns of Drug Use by Drug and Age

Table 20-6 shows the regular/heavy current use of substances for each of the ethnic groups and for both younger and older cohorts within each group. The data clearly demonstrate that urban inner-city youths are engaged in a variety of drug-using behaviors. Because the patterns of use vary from group to group, the

Table 20-5
Reported Substance Use by Friends by Ethnic Group from the NCUEA Community Sample

Substance	*Total Population (n = 1,151)*	*Other White Same (n = 251)*	*White Different (n = 96)*	*Polish (n = 203)*	*Italian (n = 98)*	*Irish (n = 46)*	*German (n = 43)*	*Black (n = 177)*	*Hispanic (n = 70)*	*Native American (n = 83)*	*Mixed Racially (n = 84)*
Alcohol	64.5%	79.5%	68.0%	61.0%	67.3%	65.3%	71.0%	53.6%	63.7%	71.3%	61.7%
Marihuana	64.6	81.1	68.8	53.7	63.1	62.1	65.2	54.3	69.4	76.4	73.1
Barbiturates	30.6	41.7	36.0	18.6	31.9	33.1	30.4	17.6	35.2	49.9	39.7
Amphetamines	25.2	42.5	24.2	13.1	31.9	30.3	24.3	17.1	28.1	45.1	28.1
Opiates	14.0	20.3	14.2	5.5	18.3	17.2	13.0	9.9	13.5	25.4	22.5
Inhalants	19.1	35.8	22.5	6.4	16.1	16.6	23.5	11.3	19.0	34.0	30.6
Hallucinogens	17.4	28.5	17.5	8.8	19.7	26.9	7.4	11.6	13.9	34.0	20.6

Table 20-6
Regular/Heavy Current Use of Drugs by Ethnic Groups by Age from the NCUEA Community Sample

Substances	*Total (n = 1,151)*	*Other White Same (n = 251)*	*White Different (n = 96)*	*Polish (n = 203)*	*Italian (n = 98)*	*Irish (n = 46)*	*German (n = 43)*	*Total White (n = 737)*	*Black (n = 177)*	*Hispanic (n = 70)*	*Native American (n = 83)*	*Total Nonwhite (n = 414)*	*Mixed Racially (n = 84)*
Alcohol													
18 or under	20.8	33.8	22.2	17.5	18.6	35.7	8.7	21.9	13.3	24.2	28.1	19.0	25.8
Over 18	37.0	37.5	34.5	30.3	28.6	56.3	52.4	35.6	33.3	10.0	40.0	31.4	54.5
Marihuana													
18 or under	28.7	56.3	30.6	22.2	30.0	39.3	13.0	30.9	19.5	29.5	41.3	26.4	38.7
Over 18	35.9	33.3	42.4	21.9	39.3	37.5	52.4	37.8	28.6	10.0	25.0	27.5	52.2
Barbiturates													
18 or under	5.9	5.7	4.1	2.9	4.3	7.4	0.0	3.9	5.1	4.8	11.1	6.3	9.7
Over 18	12.3	8.0	10.5	12.5	14.3	12.5	14.3	11.7	19.0	0.0	15.8	13.7	26.1
Amphetamines													
18 or under	3.6	5.6	0.5	2.3	1.4	11.1	0.0	2.3	3.8	1.6	11.1	4.9	6.5
Over 18	10.1	12.0	10.5	0.0	17.9	12.5	4.8	9.4	14.3	0.0	5.6	7.8	21.7
Heroin													
18 or under	2.5	2.8	1.0	0.6	0.0	7.4	0.0	1.3	2.5	0.0	5.6	3.5	6.9
Over 18	9.1	4.0	3.5	6.1	7.1	18.8	14.3	7.2	19.0	11.1	10.5	13.7	26.1
Illegal Meth.													
18 or under	2.5	2.8	0.5	0.6	2.9	7.1	0.0	1.4	2.5	0.0	12.7	4.2	6.3
Over 18	6.8	8.0	3.5	3.0	0.0	11.8	4.8	4.4	19.0	0.0	15.0	13.7	17.4
Inhalants													
18 or under	4.7	7.0	3.6	2.3	2.9	3.6	0.0	3.4	3.2	4.8	10.9	5.3	11.3
Over 18	5.0	4.0	5.4	0.0	0.0	11.8	4.8	3.9	14.3	0.0	15.0	5.9	13.6
Tranquilizers													
18 or under	4.0	4.2	3.6	2.3	2.9	3.6	0.0	3.1	1.3	1.6	15.6	4.6	4.8
Over 18	7.8	8.0	9.1	3.1	3.6	11.8	4.8	6.7	23.8	0.0	20.0	17.7	13.0
Hallucinogens													
18 or under	2.9	1.4	1.0	1.2	1.4	7.1	0.0	1.3	2.6	3.2	12.5	4.9	4.8
Over 18	4.4	8.0	5.4	6.0	3.6	11.8	4.8	5.0	14.3	0.0	0.0	5.9	4.5

data suggest that sociocultural factors do influence both the types of drugs used and the frequency of use.

One of the most interesting figures in the table is the extremely high rate of reported illicit drug use within the Native American urban youth population. The younger cohort of this group had higher percentages of use in most drug categories. There were some exceptions in that the Irish and white-same groups were higher for alcohol, the Irish and racially mixed groups were higher for heroin, the racially mixed group was higher for inhalants, and the white-same group was higher for marihuana. In the hierarchy of use, the Germans had the lowest usage rates while the Native Americans were the highest and the Irish were the highest of the white ethnic groups represented.

Regular/Heavy Use by Sex

Table 20-7 presents data on the reported rates of drug use for each ethnic group by sex. It can be seen that the reported rate of drug abuse among males is substantially higher than among females; however, there are some instances in which females of one ethnic group have higher rates than males of another ethnic group or, as in the case with the Native Americans, the use rates of females are even higher than males in their own group for specific drugs.

Overall, the use of alcohol among males is 2.2 times greater than among females, while the use of marihuana is 1.7 times greater. The greatest difference in alcohol use between sexes is found in the male and female Irish group, while the most similarity occurs in the white-same group (with both rates being well above average). Marihuana use follows a different pattern—significant differences exist between the sexes among the Irish but similar male-female patterns exist among the other populations, for example, the Native American group, where the female rate of use for marihuana, amphetamines, tranquilizers, and inhalants exceeds the male. Italian males were the youngest users of barbiturates and amphetamines, although they exhibited rates which approximated sample averages. The data indicate that marihuana is the drug of choice for both males and females and is now used more regularly than alcohol by both male and female inner-city youths residing in ethnic communities.

It is important to note that the Native American subsample comprised tribes from the Southwest part of the United States who had settled, with their families, in the cities of Baltimore and Cincinnati. To our knowledge, this is the first time that drug use by Native Americans residing in an inner-city environment has been reported. Because of the limitations of this study, it is not possible to speculate on the significance of this finding, but the need for further study of this population is clear.

In summary, the data in the NCUEA Ethnic Drug Study suggests that there is considerable variability in adolescent drug use based on ethnicity, age, and sex. While differences in prevalence rates were found between the sexes in the relatively small samples in this study, it should be pointed out that the review of

Table 20-7
Regular/Heavy Recent Drug Use by Ethnic Group by Sex

Substance	*Sex*	*Total (n = 1,151)*	*White Same (n = 251)*	*White Different (n = 96)*	*Polish (n = 203)*	*Italian (n = 98)*	*Irish (n = 46)*	*German (n = 43)*	*Black (n = 177)*	*Hispanic (n = 70)*	*Native American (n = 83)*	*Mixed Racially (n = 84)*
Alcohol	M	21.3%	36.6%	28.8%	24.1%	26.3%	52.9%	12.5%	16.5%	37.5%	30.3%	34.2%
	F	12.4	31.0	13.8	10.0	10.3	9.1	7.1	10.3	13.5	21.4	9.5
Marihuana	M	35.0	63.9	35.9	28.7	36.8	58.8	12.5	20.2	47.8	33.3	39.5
	F	20.6	41.4	25.0	13.8	20.7	9.1	7.1	20.0	16.2	50.0	28.6
Barbiturates	M	8.1	10.0	5.8	3.4	7.9	6.3	0.0	7.1	4.2	12.1	7.9
	F	2.6	0.0	2.5	1.3	0.0	9.1	0.0	2.9	5.4	7.4	0.0
Amphetamines	M	3.5	7.3	1.0	1.1	2.6	12.5	0.0	4.8	0.0	6.1	2.6
	F	2.4	3.4	0.0	2.5	0.0	9.1	0.0	2.9	0.0	14.8	0.0
Heroin	M	3.0	4.9	1.9	1.1	0.0	6.3	0.0	3.6	4.2	6.3	5.3
	F	1.2	0.0	0.0	0.0	0.0	9.1	0.0	1.4	0.0	7.4	0.0
Illegal Meth.	M	3.2	4.9	1.0	1.1	2.6	5.6	0.0	4.7	0.0	6.1	5.1
	F	1.0	0.0	0.0	0.0	0.0	9.1	0.0	0.0	0.0	14.8	0.0
Inhalants	M	6.0	12.2	5.8	4.6	2.6	5.9	0.0	4.7	0.0	9.1	7.9
	F	2.2	0.0	1.3	0.0	3.4	0.0	0.0	1.5	5.4	10.7	5.0
Tranquilizers	M	4.2	7.3	6.7	2.3	2.6	5.9	0.0	0.0	4.2	12.1	5.1
	F	2.3	0.0	0.0	1.3	0.0	0.0	0.0	3.0	0.0	14.3	0.0
Hallucinogens	M	3.3	2.4	1.9	2.3	5.3	5.9	0.0	3.6	4.2	9.1	2.6
	F	1.2	0.0	0.0	0.0	3.4	9.1	0.0	1.5	0.0	10.7	0.0

the literature on sex differences in chap. 7 indicates that sex differences are not substantial for the general youth population.

Correlation of Perceptions of Parents to Drug-Use Patterns

Another analysis of the NCUEA sample focused on a comparison between users' and nonusers' perceptions of their parents. Each respondent was asked to rate each parent on ten traits. Recent drug users were then compared with nonusers in their perception of parents to determine if there were any differences. Alcohol, marihuana, and other illicit drugs were used as the substance categories for comparisons.

Polish and Hispanic users (regardless of the drug used) and nonusers did not exhibit a sense of alienation from either parent except in some minor instances. However, these were the only two groups in which users and nonusers reported no sense of alienation (negative perceptions).

German, male marihuana users felt less positive toward their fathers than did nonusers and indicated some alienation toward their mothers. When German males did feel alienated from their mothers, they were likely to be using a substance which fell in the other illicit drug category.

The Irish respondents, who exhibited higher drug usage rates than other white ethnic adolescents, did not tend to exhibit negative perceptions of their parents, except for male alcohol users who had negative attitudes toward their fathers.

Italian users, on the other hand, had stronger reactions to each parent. Both male and female Italian alcohol users had less positive perceptions of their mothers than did nonusers. In addition, Italian male illicit drug users had less positive perceptions than nonusers of their mothers and fathers. Italian female marihuana users had less positive perceptions of their fathers than did nonusers.

The black alcohol and illicit drug users, both male and female, felt less positively about each parent than did the nonusers. Both male and female marihuana users felt a distance from their mothers compared with the nonusers, but did not feel alienated from their fathers.

The Native American female illicit drug user reported feeling alienated from both her mother and her father compared with her nonusing counterpart.

Thus we see from these data that there are differences in the way different ethnic populations perceive their parents. While black or Native American drug users may have negative perceptions of one or the other parent, Polish and Hispanic users either do not have negative perceptions or, if they do, are less willing to report these attitudes. At a minimum, one could infer different treatment needs among these populations and a need for differing approaches to prevention strategies from this data.

The NCUEA White/Nonwhite Comparison

Youthful drug use is clearly not simply a phenomenon among nonwhites. One apparent difference is the tendency among whites to use predominantly "soft" drugs (alcohol and marihuana) and to be less involved in the use of "hard" drugs (heroin and barbiturates). Although the percentages of hard drug use among youth may appear to be small, the actual number of youths involved in using hard drugs at an early age is large. It should also be pointed out that this is self-report data, and young people may be reluctant to report involvement with illegal drugs.

NCUEA Compared with NYPS

In the examination of regular/heavy drug use patterns for three white ethnic groups–Italians, Irish, and Germans–striking parallels are found between the NCUEA and NYPS samples.

Because the NYPS sample is composed of adolescents who have been admitted to treatment programs and the NCUEA sample represents a general inner-city (nontreatment) population, it was assumed that the NCUEA population would have lower prevalence rates. However, some interesting similarities in the drug use patterns were found. For example, marihuana was the most frequently used drug (NCUEA, 30.9 percent; NYPS, 46.6 percent) while alcohol was second (21.9 percent; and 18.6 percent, respectively). Barbiturates and amphetamines were the third and fourth ranked drugs in both studies. Illegal methadone and hallucinogens were the least used drugs.

In comparing the two samples, two major differences were found. Heroin use in the NYPS sample was relatively large (4.2 percent) compared with the NCUEA group (1.3 percent). Conversely, inhalant use in the NCUEA sample (3.4 percent) was over twice that found in the NYPS sample (1.5 percent). The heroin use discrepancy can probably be attributed to the fact that heroin abusers are more likely to be drawn into drug treatment programs. It has been reported that drug programs find attracting and retaining inhalant abusers extremely difficult (Mason 1978). Table 20-8 shows how each substance ranks in each of the studies.

Further comparison between the two studies are made in tables 20-9, 20-10, and 20-11. Within the three ethnic groups (Italian, Irish, and German), distinct patterns of use emerge. Irish adolescents are clearly the heaviest drug users in both samples. Italians and Germans exhibit use patterns which are markedly lower than for the total sample in both studies.

Table 20-8
Rank of Substance Use, NCUEA Compared to NYPS Sample

Substance	*NCUEA*	*NYPS*
Marihuana	1	1
Alcohol	2	2
Barbiturates	3	3
Inhalants	4	7
Tranquilizers/sedatives	5	5
Amphetamines	6	4
Illegal methadone	7	8
Heroin/opiates	8	6
Hallucinogens	8	7

Observations, Conclusions, and Recommendations

As emphasized earlier in this chapter, the NCUEA study was intended to be exploratory, directed at investigating the nature and scope of drug use in inner-city ethnic communities, and to determine any relationship to family and cultural factors. Not only did the study confirm the fact that drug use is widespread among groups of inner-city, white, ethnic youths, it also showed specific variations in the patterns of use between specific ethnic groups.

The exploratory nature of the study did impose certain methodological limitations. Sample populations, rather than being chosen randomly, were selected on the basis of their availability and willingness to participate, introducing a selective volunteer bias. The study raises an interesting question that could be addressed, perhaps, in a future, more broadly based study: What patterns of substance abuse can be detected among individuals from highly structured ethnic families who live in nonethnic communities?

Another point which evolves from the data relates to the composition of

Table 20-9
Regular/Heavy Use of Substances for Italians, Comparison of NCUEA and NYPS Samples

Substance	*NCUEA %*	*NYPS %*
Alcohol	18.6	23.7
Marihuana/hashish	30.0	38.2
Barbiturates	4.3	7.9
Amphetamines	1.4	3.9
Heroin/opiates	0	11.8
Illegal methadone	2.9	2.6
Inhalants	2.9	1.3
Tranquilizers/sedatives	2.9	7.9
Hallucinogens	1.3	1.4

Table 20-10
Regular/Heavy Use of Substances for Germans, Comparison of NCUEA and NYPS Samples

Substance	*NCUEA %*	*NYPS %*
Alcohol	8.7	17.5
Marihuana/hashish	13.0	48.2
Barbiturates	0	4.4
Amphetamines	0	2.6
Heroin/opiates	0	0.9
Illegal methadone	0	1.8
Inhalants	0	0
Tranquilizers/sedatives	0	2.6
Hallucinogens	0	0.9

inner-city neighborhoods. While the 1970 census showed strong ethnic homogeneity, our survey showed that ethnic neighborhoods were made up of many different groups. In addition, we can only speculate on the role that generational and intercultural differences and conflicts play. It is obvious that further research is needed in this area.

Although some preliminary investigation of attitudes associated with patterns of drug use in various ethnic groups was undertaken, a far more comprehensive study is needed if we are to attempt to understand the underlying factors that contribute to these differences. Understanding the role played by ethnicity in personal development is an important consideration in the design and implementation of prevention, intervention, and treatment programs. The results of this study, because of its limited focus and small sample size, cannot be generalized to the entire population. Rather, it is the responsibility of local programs and coordinating agencies to gather information about the specific populations they serve which will enable them to develop appropriate

Table 20-11
Regular/Heavy Use of Substances for Irish, Comparison of NCUEA and NYPS Samples

Substance	*NCUEA %*	*NYPS %*
Alcohol	35.7	12.4
Marihuana/hashish	39.3	44.3
Barbiturates	7.4	7.2
Amphetamines	11.1	5.2
Heroin/opiates	7.4	5.2
Illegal methadone	7.1	0
Inhalants	3.6	3.1
Tranquilizers/sedatives	3.6	6.2
Hallucinogens	7.1	3.1

intervention strategies. This will require a new sensitivity to the existence of sociocultural differences and ethnicity.

Important information could be gathered and analyzed in the future utilizing existing drug-related data bases. To accomplish this, the following should be encouraged:

Where possible, future research instruments should request information on ethnic identification.

The data collected on both federal and state treatment forms should include ethnic group and geographic (ZIP code or census tract) designations.

References

Barrabe, P., and Von Mering, O. October 1953. Ethnic variation in mental stress in families with psychotic children. *Social Problems* I.

Breton, R. 1964. Institutional completeness of ethnic communities and the personal relations of immigrants. *American Journal of Sociology* 70:193-205.

Cantril, A.H., and Roll, C.W., Jr. 1971. *Hopes and Fears of the American People.* New York: Universe.

Dodson, W.W., Alexander, D.F., Wright, P.S. and Wunderlich, R.A. 1971. Patterns of multiple drug abuse among adolescents referred by a juvenile court. *Pediatrics* 47:1033-1036.

Fromm, E. 1955. *The Sane Society.* New York. Holt, Rinehart and Winston, Inc.

Giordano, J. 1973. *Ethnicity and Mental Health.* New York: American Jewish Committee.

Giordano, J. November 1974. *Testimony Submitted to the Select Committee on the Mental and Physically Handicapped.* Washington, D.C.: 94th Congress.

Glazer, N., and Moynihan, D.P. 1974. *Ethnicity: Theory and Experience.* Cambridge, Mass.: Harvard Univ. Press.

Glazer, N. September 1971. The limits of social policy. *Commentary* 52:3.

Glenn, S., and Warner, J. 1977. *The Development Approach to Preventing Problem Dependencies.* Washington, D.C.: Social Systems, Incorporated.

Greeley, A. February 1978. Alcohol Dependency Patterns Among Euro-Ethnics. Unpublished paper presented at the Conference on the American Family and Cultural Pluralism, Washington, D.C.

Green, G., and Baroni, G. 1976. *Who's Left in the Neighborhood?* Washington, D.C.: National Center for Urban Ethnic Affairs for the Office of Minority Business Enterprises.

The Group School. 1977. *Neighborhood, Youth and Class: An Introductory High School Course on Ethnic and Class Identity.* The Group School and the National Center for Urban Ethnic Affairs.

Gurin, G., Veroff, J., and Field, S. 1958. *Americans View their Health.* New York: Wiley, p. 95.

Hollingshead, A., and Redlich, F. 1958. *Social Class and Mental Health.* New York: Wiley, p. 95.

Kandel, D., Single, E., and Kessler, R.C. 1976. The epidemiology of drug use among New York State high school students: Distribution trends, and change in rates of use. *American Journal of Public Health* 66:43-53.

Kolm, R. 1973. *Bibliography on Ethnicity and Ethnic Groups.* Rockville, Md.: National Institute of Mental Health.

Koloday, R. January 1969. Ethnic cleavages in the United States. *Social Work,* XIV.

Kornhauser, A. 1962. The mental health of factory workers: A Detroit study. *Human Organization* 21.

Krug, S.E., and Henry, T.J. 1974. Personality, motivation and adolescent drug use patterns. *Journal of Consulting Psychology* 21:440-445.

Levine, I.M. 1973. *Ethnicity and Mental Health.* New York: Institute for Human Relations.

Levy, N. 1972. The use of drugs among teenagers. *Canadian Psychiatric Association Journal* 17:31-36.

Litwok, E. April 1961. Voluntary associations and neighborhood cohesion. *Sociological Review* 26:2.

MacAndrew, C., and Edgerton, R.B. 1969. *Drunken Comportment: A Social Explanation.* Chicago, Ill.: Adline.

McCarthy, A. April 1961. Our search for our roots. *Commonwealth* II (3).

Mills, J. 1951. *White Collar, The American Middle Class.* New York: Oxford Univ. Press.

Myers, J., and Bean, L. 1965. *A Decade Later: A Follow-up of Social Class and Mental Health.* New York: Wiley.

National Institute on Drug Abuse. 1977. *Manpower and Training Strategy.* Rockville, Md.: NIDA, p. 32.

National Youth Polydrug Study. 1977. Philadelphia Psychiatric Center. Special data analysis performed for this chapter.

O'Donnell, J.A., Voss, H.L., Clayton, R.R., Slatin, G.T., and Room, R. 1976. *Young Men and Drugs–A Nationwide Survey.* NIDA Monograph No. 5. Rockville, Md.: National Institute on Drug Abuse.

Opler, M. 1967. *Culture and Social Psychiatry.* New York: Atherton.

Parsons, T. 1967. Some Theoretical Considerations on the Nature and Trends of Change of Ethnicity. In N. Glazer and D. Moynihan (eds.), *Ethnicity, Theory and Experience.* Cambridge, Mass.: Harvard Univ. Press, pp. 53-83.

Pittman, D.J., and Synder, C.R. 1962. *Society, Culture and Drinking Patterns.* New York: Wiley-Interscience.

Rosencrans, C.J., and Birgnet, H.P. 1972. Comparative personality profiles of young drug abusers and non-users. *Alabama Journal of Medical Sciences* 9:397-402.

Seltzer, C., Friedman, G.D., and Suegelaub, A.B. 1974. Smoking and drug consumption in white, black and Oriental men and women. *American Journal of Public Health* 64:466-473.

Slater, P. 1970. *The Pursuit of Loneliness: American Culture at the Breaking Point.* Boston: Beacon Press.

Spiegal, J. 1965. Some cultural aspects of transference and counter-transference. In M.W. Zold (ed.), *Social Welfare Institutions,* New York: Wiley.

Srole, L., Langner, T., Michael, S., Opler, M., and Rennie, T. 1962. *Mental Health in the Metropolis: The Midtown Manhattan Study.* New York: McGraw-Hill.

Vaillant, G. 1966. Parent-child cultural disparity and drug addiction. *Journal of Nervous Mental Disorders* 142:534-539.

Warren, D. 1971. Neighborhoods in urban areas. In *The Encyclopedia of Social Work.* New York: NASW.

Yankelovich, Skelly and White, Inc. 1975. *Students and Drugs.* Drug Abuse Council, Inc., Washington, D.C.

Zborowski, M. 1964. *People in Pain.* San Francisco, Calif.: Jossey-Bass.

Part VI
Youths in Drug Abuse Treatment

21 Treatment Services for Youthful Drug Users

David Smith,
Stephen J. Levy, and
Diane E. Striar

Drug treatment services—from chemotherapy to acupuncture—and drug treatment environments such as methadone clinics and therapeutic communities provide a variety of helping approaches for drug abusers. However, most of these services/environments are not suited for the treatment of adolescent drug users. Many drug treatment programs, for example, have been designed for the older, hard-core heroin addict. Furthermore, many "drug programs" structured to serve youths are small components of a total service system offered in a general youth service or mental health agency, resulting in a low visibility and a low priority. As an added limitation, even the apparently successful drug programs have not been able to offer proof of their effectiveness, since few youth-serving agencies have the research capacity or resources to conduct adequate program evaluations. As a result, there are limited treatment options for youthful drug abusers, their families, and for the community or court referral systems who must arrange for drug treatment without adequate assurance of its suitability.

Compulsory Treatment

The existence of court referral systems has further complicated the situation. Many drug-abusing youths do not choose to enter treatment—nor are they given freedom to select a specific modality. According to the National Youth Polydrug Study, the criminal justice system—parole or probation officer, judge, or police—refers 22.5 percent of all youth clients into drug treatment. Furthermore, 22.4 percent of all criminal justice system referrals are admitted into residential therapeutic communities, compared with 13 percent of other referrals. Moreover, the whole concept of identifying drug abusers and users as criminals has been questioned. The issue of compulsory treatment has been a controversial one since the Federal Narcotic Treatment and Rehabilitation Act (NARA) of 1966, which provided for a long-term inpatient drug program in federal treatment centers. Certain apprehended addicts were able to choose treatment in lieu of criminal prosecution. The federal centers were known for their high recidivism rates and never accomplished the goal of constituting a viable rehabilitation system.

Today, more than thirty-four states provide for involuntary commitment of drug-dependent people under various circumstances. One program, Treatment Alternatives to Street Crime (TASC), allows successful "graduates" of drug treatment the chance to have charges dropped against them. If they abscond or fail to cooperate with the treatment program, a bench warrant may be issued, and the normal criminal justice proceedings will begin.

Questions arise as to the effectiveness of compulsory treatment. While clinical experience has shown that no one can be effectively treated against his will, some individuals do become interested in treatment after they have been required to enter into a program. A distinct advantage to diverting youths into treatment rather than prison is that the latter tends to reinforce criminal lifestyles.

Getting into Treatment

Only a small percentage of youths get into federally supported treatment programs compared with the percentage of adults in these programs. The Client Oriented Data Acquisition Process (CODAP), the federal reporting system for drug programs, recorded 224,959 clients in its admissions files during 1975. Clients under 18 years of age accounted for only 12.3 percent of all admissions. The CODAP system also found marked differences in the types of treatment environments that actually served youths and adults. A significantly higher proportion of youths were admitted to outpatient settings–73.6 percent of all youths compared with 63.1 percent of all adults; and a significantly higher proportion of adults were treated in hospitals–14.7 percent compared with 2.3 percent of all youths.[1]

In an analysis of the three types of outpatient treatment modalities–detoxification, methadone maintenance, and drug free–it was found that an almost negligible number of youths under 18 years of age are served in outpatient detoxification and outpatient methadone maintenance treatment. A higher proportion of youths received the drug-free modality of treatment within every type of treatment environment. The small numbers of young people in chemotherapy programs can be explained by the FDA and state regulations which discourage these treatments for patients under 18 years of age. This fact also accounts for the significantly smaller proportion of adults found in drug-free outpatient treatment relative to youths under 18 years of age. More young adults addicted to heroin would probably apply for drug-free outpatient treatment if methadone maintenance treatment and outpatient detoxification using methadone were not available to them.

The remainder of this chapter will describe different treatment services and programs generally thought to be successful with youths. It is apparent to us that youthful drug users need access to a variety of helping services because they have a wide range of values, class backgrounds, types of drug involvement, and social, psychological, and medical needs. Some young people, for example, feel more comfortable in the traditional social service clinic, while others prefer to try alternative agencies with a counterculture atmosphere and approach.

Youth Services

Emergency services provided in hospital inpatient units, emergency rooms, and crisis centers give immediate medical or psychological intervention for drug abusers. Specific problems dealt with on an emergency basis are adverse drug reactions, related psychological crises, and other medical problems which are directly related to drug abuse: precipitous withdrawal, ill health, sores, hepatitis, poor dental hygiene, gynecological problems, nutritional problems, stabbings, and shootings.

According to the Drug Abuse Warning Network (DAWN), a national data system that monitors drugs, the total number of youth (6 to 19 years of age) drug "mentions" between April 1976 and April 1977 was 25,302 for hospital emergency rooms, 9,952 for crisis centers, and 243 (deaths) for county medical and coroner offices.[2] *Mentions* are instances in which an individual interviewed at a reporting facility refers to a substance. Because people are not the unit of reporting and the system is anonymous, it is difficult to describe the demographic characteristics of the sample, and there is no way to estimate the number of people who are associated with more than one episode. However, the DAWN data support a trend toward a heterogeneity of substances abused by youths. There were 743 different substances mentioned by the subjects. Of the leading drugs mentioned, for emergency room cases, marihuana headed the list with 12 percent of the total; alcohol in combination with any other substances ranked second with 5 percent; and PCP (phencyclidine) ranked third with 3.3 percent. (PCP mentions increased radically from the tenth rank in frequency for the previous year.) For the youth subsample, the leading cause of death was heroin-morphine, and alcohol in combination with other substances was second.

The most common motivation for drug use reported by all race/sex youth groups interviewed at crisis centers and emergency rooms was "psychic effects." Proportionally more females than males in both white and black races reported "suicide attempt or gesture" as their motivation. Regardless of the motivation presented by individuals in emergency rooms, hospital facilities have demonstrated negative attitudes toward drug abusers. Long waits have been standard procedure for both alcoholics and drug abusers. Furthermore, young people brought to the hospital may not be treated unless they are accompanied by an adult, usually a parent or legal guardian. As a further problem, in many states, hospitals and private practitioners are required to report drug episodes to the police. Finally, many hospital emergency rooms until recently did not have adequate knowledge of how to treat overdose and acute withdrawal problems.

However, the development of such narcotic antagonist drugs as naloxone (Narcan) have made the task somewhat easier.

Originally, emergency detoxification services such as those provided in traditional hospital settings were targeted for alcoholics and opiate addicts whose toxic condition and other medical conditions were serious or acute enough to require detoxification or whose habits had become too expensive or otherwise unmanageable. Later on, similar programs were made available for barbiturate and amphetamine addicts, and more recently for those in a toxic state due to PCP (phencyclidine). The maximum goal of the detoxification program for an opiate addict is to eliminate the habit under medical supervision. The procedure generally involves administering decreasing dosages of methadone to ease withdrawal.

Detoxification clients in the past would often leave the program against medical advice, whether or not counseling and other services were provided, once they had reached a detoxification level that eliminated all withdrawal symptoms. The addict could then return to the street with a greatly reduced and less expensive habit. Some clients today still try to use the detoxification service the same way, but the programs are less likely to admit them if they have a history of such use of detoxification service—without negotiating a contract in advance for continuing drug-free outpatient treatment after the detoxification is completed. There are hopeful signs, in some detoxification programs, that the staff has learned from experience to understand the addicts better and provide more meaningful counseling and treatment programs, and that some addicts have developed a positive therapeutic relationship during the detoxification phase, so that they are more likely to continue in therapy during an outpatient "after-care" phase—and less likely to get into another toxic and acute crisis situation.

Additional challenges in detoxification programs have included preventing inpatients from sneaking drugs while on the ward, and developing a therapeutic relationship with "detox" outpatients so that they will be less likely to use drugs during or after clinic hours in an illegal and harmful way. A problem that has limited detoxification services, as well as other drug treatment services, for adolescent abusers has been the required consent for treatment from parents or legal guardians, who are sometimes reluctant to admit the need for such services. The adolescent frequently tries to hide his drug use and addiction from his parents for as long a period as he can.

Despite some problems, detoxification programs provide an essential service for the client and serve as a referral service for those rehabilitation and after-care programs that utilize their services. Unfortunately for many clients—and to the frustration of workers in drug treatment programs—these clients pass through a detoxification program many times while never wanting or seeking rehabilitation.

Crisis Intervention Centers and Hotlines

Drug emergencies are also handled by community "hotline" services and by crisis centers that may have a "hotline" telephone component. The most common types of services provided by telephone hotlines are a sympathetic listener, drug information, and information on available community resources:

> Drug crisis intervention generally operates along ground rules of establishing strong rapport with the client through maintaining a reassuring, nonjudgmental attitude and providing immediate tangible help. Occasionally, included in the crisis intervention is an offer for ongoing treatment if indicated. For example, after a drug crisis a chronic abuser may be unusually motivated to seek help and this motivation sometimes can be translated into an effective after-care program.[3]

In an analysis of over 1,500 calls to a drug-crisis intervention service in St. Louis, Missouri, Levy and Brown found that most calls concerned a request for drug information.[4] These were made by individuals (median age 16) either contemplating use or already using a particular drug. Drug-crisis calls (median age 17) most commonly involved LSD, other hallucinogens, and amphetamines. The symptoms presented included flashback, persecutory delusions with insight maintained, unrealistic fears, severe free-floating anxiety, and situational problems.

Professional Counseling (Individual)

There is a voluminous literature on the many philosophies of individual counseling and individual psychotherapy and on a broad spectrum of approaches and techniques, all of which probably have been tried with the adolescent drug user. These approaches include the traditional psychoanalytically oriented "intensive" or "deep" interpretive psychotherapy, as well as the nondirective and reflective; the informational, instructional and problem solving; the behavior modifying; the active-supportive; the reality oriented; the environmental manipulative; authoritative-persuasive; confrontative; relationship therapeutic; affect expressive; encounter; gestalt; psychodrama; role playing; and so on. Given this bewildering array of types and forms of individual counseling and psychotherapy, little has been done to establish the relative effectiveness of these various methodologies with young drug-abusing clients. Even for clients in therapy or counseling who are not involved in drug abuse, the only characteristics that have been firmly established as effective by objective research study are the warmth and the empathic understanding of the therapist and the unconditional regard for the client by the therapist.

In recent years, the role of the individual therapist in work with the young drug abuser has probably tended to become more active, supportive, expressive, and open, in a "gestalt" sense, than in the past, and has focused more on the "here and now" (the client's current feelings, relationships, and behavior), than on the uncovering and restructuring the client's past experience. The less professionally trained, paraprofessional, and ex-addict individual counselors tend to be relatively active, supportive, persuasive, and confrontative, and tend to assume the roles of friend, equal, and model for the young clients.

The sine qua non for counseling—whether by a professional, paraprofessional, or peer—is that a condition of basic trust and rapport must be developed, with mutuality and respect for each other as people and for each other's language, particular cultural framework, values and beliefs. It is also crucial that the young client move toward making a voluntary commitment to the therapy process and feel that he wants help for himself. A very frequent problematic situation for therapy is one in which the young client does not perceive his use of marihuana or other drugs as a "problem" at all, but his parents consider it very serious and have sent him for individual therapy. The young client may only be participating in the individual counseling sessions to keep his parents "off his back." In many of these cases, it may be that the attitudes and behavior of the parents are in some way related to the underlying problems that led to the youngster's drug use. In any event, it is obvious that a family therapy approach stands a better chance of making progress in such a situation than does individual counseling or psychotherapy.

Group Therapy (Group Counseling)

Although individual counseling or psychotherapy is offered in most youth drug programs, many programs believe that, overall, group therapy is more effective for adolescents, and that many young drug clients are more likely to be influenced by group pressure and peer influence than through a one-to-one relationship with an adult. The group structure has elements that may be essential for getting many of the young drug users to respond and to commit themselves to the therapy and to the change process. The initial reaction of some young drug users to the older professional individual therapist is one of distrust and antagonism, and the assumption that the therapist is antiyouth, and antidrugs, and disapproves of them—a reaction similar to the one they have toward their parents. In group therapy, the peer group provides more of a counter and a balance to the older professional leader and may render entering the new therapy situation more comfortable for the adolescent.

Peer group therapy is a widely used and popular modality for young drug-abuse clients in drug-free clinics. In groups that stress openness and honesty, peers can share common interests, begin to feel at home, establish relationships, make friends, learn communication skills, and learn how to deal more constructively with parents, with adult authority, and with society.

In group therapy, the patient not only receives support and guidance from others with similar problems, but he or she is also able to help others as well, thereby improving his or her self-image. Group therapy for drug users emphasizes building confidence and understanding through strong group identification. The harsher forms of the group approach (the authoritative confrontation group, for example) tend to enforce rigid standards of conformity that may be useful in treating some addicts who require more structure and control to deal with their drug problem and change their life behavior patterns. As employed most often in the past in therapeutic communities, group therapy is a confrontation between an individual and his or her peers in which he or she is sometimes challenged or taunted by the others to admit weaknesses, face reality, and promise change. The standard therapeutic community group confrontation technique is now recognized as being inappropriate in certain situations. For example, sex or alcoholism counseling for juveniles may be managed better for some people in an individual approach. It has been learned that some drug clients do not respond well in a group situation to either the requirements of confrontation and aggressiveness or even to a supportive group atmosphere that requires open expression of feelings.[5]

The variety and diverse array of types of approaches, modalities, and techniques used in group therapy with young people, some of which have also been advanced as unique theories or structures for group therapy, is indicated by the following names and descriptions found in the group therapy literature: informational (rap groups, drug education, sex education, etc.); instructional; authoritative-persuasive; values clarification; cognitive; problem-solving; task-oriented; activity group therapy; reality group therapy; behavior modification group therapy; sensitivity "T" groups; "human laboratory" training groups; assertiveness training groups; transactional analysis (TA) groups; guided interaction groups; structured interaction; psychoanalytic; existential groups (Zen); confrontation (Synanon) groups; encounter groups; gestalt groups; sensory awareness; mind-body connection; relaxation groups; Yoga; human enrichment; affective-expressive groups; cathartic groups; primal scream groups; psychodrama; role-playing; self-directed "leaderless" groups; and so on. The development of such an array of group therapy types and techniques indicates that there exists a healthy capacity to meet the different treatment needs of various young client populations. Of course, not all the approaches are of equal appropriateness for working with youths. However, there has not been sufficient experience in utilizing these approaches with youth groups to be able to evaluate their relative effectiveness. There are no systematic studies of the outcome of group therapy with young drug-abuse clients conducted with adequate research controls that we have been able to find reported in the literature. There are some reports of beneficial effects of group therapy with drug abusers, based on clinical impressions and uncontrolled program evaluations.[6] In a large-scale treatment demonstration with Philadelphia inner-city delinquent male youths, the majority of whom were involved in drug abuse, a controlled research evaluation of the effects of group therapy was summarized by one of the editors of this book, as follows: "We found that all the groups experienced a change process in the direction of less chaos and tension, better organization, greater self-control and a more relaxed group atmosphere. In the end, the groups' interactions clearly looked much more like the traditional picture of a therapeutic discussion than they did in the beginning, and there was a greater sense of group identity and cohesion."[7]

While individual counseling provides the client a confidential, ongoing relationship, peer group therapy provides the client a setting in which his or her concerns and problems can be expressed and validated among peers. Experience has shown that adolescent drug users will accept the structure of peer group therapy with an appropriate leader—if the group purpose and process are relevant to the topics and issues that are important to them. Some may first want to use the group to exchange drug information and share their experiences in using drugs. A beneficial aspect of this can be their alerting each other to dangerous and harmful experiences they have had with certain drugs. Gradually, as the group members get to know and to be more comfortable with each other, the ground rules and the contract for the working relationship of the group with the leader begins to develop, both implicitly and explicitly.

When a constructive working relationship or set is established, the group members are in a position to discuss, negotiate, and decide upon specific targets for change and specific treatment goals for each group member. The declared public commitment by the individual in an ongoing group setting—to improve or better control his or her behavior (a method popularized by Alcoholic Anonymous)—has been shown to be effective for some individuals in implementing appropriate behavior change. In a behaviorally oriented group, there can be weekly scheduling of practice (behavioral rehearsal) of the specific behaviors that are individually prescribed for group members. There can be group-established contracts for performance by members of some adaptive behavior in relation to a specific situation that occurs or exists outside the therapy situation during the week.

A theoretical rationale for a behaviorally oriented group therapy, derived from basic behavioral principles and from experimental small group social interaction research, is that the specific behaviors of the other group members operate as discriminating and reinforcing stimuli. The process is conceptualized primarily as a reciprocal or feedback mechanism. The practical advantage of conducting behavior therapy in small groups rather than with an individual is economy of therapist's time; in addition, this method utilizes group influence on each member (prompting and reinforcing individual behavior) and provides the attractive features of group belongingness, loyalty, and cohesiveness. The group has also been found to be an effective setting for observing interpersonal behavior problems and for influencing, shaping, and modifying behavior.

Among the important life skills that can be taught, practiced, role-played, and worked on in various other ways in the behaviorally oriented group process are (1) anxiety management, (2) assertiveness behavior, (3) maintaining self-esteem, (4) clarifying personal values, (5) decisionmaking, (6) communication skills, (7) interpersonal skills, (8) life-career planning, and (9) overcoming loneliness, personal loss, self-defeat, etc. Modern group therapy tends to focus on the "here and now" in interpersonal interactions and communication, while they are occurring within the group therapy sessions, and on the relationships, feelings, and problems between group members. It is also a guided group interaction procedure for eliciting the expression of thoughts, attitudes, and feelings; for learning the optimum degree of control of such feelings; and for working on the relationships that each group member has with other group members and his or her peers outside the group and with family, authority figures, and institutional staff. Thus it is reality and problem oriented and focuses less on the intrapsychic, on the past, and on developing psychological or intellectual insight.

Family Therapy (Family Counseling)

The fact that most adolescents still live emotionally, socially, and economically as part of their families has led to the development and use of various types of family intervention in treating youthful drug users. Drug using/abusing youths not only follow the examples of their peers but of family members as well. In an evaluation of forty-seven families of drug addicts participating in a program, Hirsch and Imhof found that "with dramatic regularity the families studied had an historical multigenerational excessive use of alcohol as a coping device. . . . The future addict has long been exposed to the use of chemicals in his family. . . . Often the family constellation may have greatly contributed to initially setting the patient on the road to excessive drinking or drug taking. Whatever the cause, the drug addict's behavior can exert considerable influence and have wide repercussions on the attitudes, feelings and behavior of the whole family. Thus, the family often needs help as much as the patient himself."[8]

Recently, there has been increased interest in the possibility of integrating family therapy into youth drug treatment programs. In a NIDA-funded national study of drug-abuse treatment agencies, out of 1,986 agencies surveyed, 93 percent reported that they provided some services to families of clients, but only 8 percent made this a mandatory service.[9]

In "conjoint" family therapy, all family members meet on a regular basis. The family unit is seen either as the "patient" or as a small social system that can be modified by a variety of approaches, including therapeutic support, guidance and leadership, clarification of communication, expression and working through of unexpressed feelings existing between family members, task negotiation, behavior modification, and so on. With a new emphasis on more open and honest communication, the family is able to start to make more constructive use of its potentially powerful interactional processes.

A common approach for drug programs is to combine family therapy with individual and/or peer group therapy. Several authors, Laqueur among them,[10] have reported on the use of "multiple family therapy" in which a number of families are treated conjointly. Working with a group of several partial families together, such as several father-son dyads or mother-daughter dyads, can also be effective in cases in which whole intact families are not available for treatment.

There are practical problems associated with the attempt to implement this type of treatment in drug programs. Some drug treatment programs have experienced difficulty in getting family members into treatment and have had to make extensive outreach efforts. Often the parents want to turn the problem of the drug-using adolescent over to the treatment agency, and they do not want to come in to expose their own individual or family problems in a family therapy process. When the family lacks transportation or the resources and initiative required to come to the treatment facility, family sessions are sometimes conducted in the home. Funds have not been readily available to support this therapy, since most funding agencies have not compensated drug treatment programs for the time required to work with non-drug-using family members.

This treatment modality may be particularly indicated for those families in which the degree of conflict and lack of healthy family milieu are conducive of delinquent and drug-use behavior by an adolescent member. In a vicious cycle, the drug-use behavior that results leads to an intensification of the discord and conflict in the family. Fixed, repetitive, and interactional family patterns develop and become pathological family "systems" that are difficult for the family to alter on their own initiative. Each family member adjusts to this situation and has some investment in maintaining the status quo.

Drug abuse as a behavior pattern of an adolescent family member may not only serve that adolescent's personal needs, but may also be maintained by that adolescent, wittingly or unwittingly, in order to serve a family function or to solve a family problem. For example, just at the time that a young addict senses that his or her parents may split up, or that one parent may leave and break up the family, he or she may demonstrate loyalty to parents and rescue the family, by creating, either intentionally or not, his or her own crisis, such as by an OD, in order to bring the parents together to focus on or to rescue the addict. Thus the addict saves the parents' marriage by allowing them to unite in their concern over his or her drug-abuse problem. Continued drug use may also ensure for the adolescent that he or she will continue to receive the attention and concern of parents in those families in which the parents have a tendency to be more interested in problems and in "bad" behavior rather than in rewarding and encouraging constructive behavior with attention and praise.

Some parents of young drug abusers have been known to encourage continuing drug-abuse behavior by giving money to their offspring abuser or addict to purchase drugs. They may do this to protect the adolescent from stealing to buy drugs, but often there are additional parental needs to maintain control over the addicted child by this means and to keep him or her dependent on a parent for support.

Davis and Klagsbrun postulated from their review of the literature on factors associated with drug abuse that increased disorganization of the family system would be found prior to drug taking and that this increased disorganization would be manifested in the following ways: increased affect and anxiety without resolution, dyadic conflict, blurring of the role relationships within the family, and changes in self-perceptions.[11] Following the drug taking they expect to find a decrease in disorganization in the family with resolution of conflict and with the drug taker's behavior becoming the "focus for previously unresolved feelings of frustration, anger, blame and contempt."

Stanton associated the high mortality and suicide rate of young drug addicts to a death wish in which other members of the family participate with the addict by placing him or her in the family role of the martyr and savior who has become the receptacle of the family's pain, suffering and sins; thus it is fitting that he or she sacrifice life: "If he dies, it is as if his mother can have him forever without the fear of losing him to others."[12] While such a family dynamic constellation might in fact contribute to the deaths of a small percentage of drug addicts, it is not necessarily to be considered typical of families of drug abusers and addicts. Nevertheless, some of the parents of drug addicts are seriously disturbed individuals, emotionally and mentally, and the extent of their disturbance may only become apparent after they are observed interacting with other family members during family therapy sessions.

Some of the principles of the family therapy technique discussed in the literature include the following: the therapist should (1) be aware of the essentially reciprocal nature of human relationships; (2) be keenly aware of and alert to the current "here and now" interactions, transactions, and covert feelings between the family members occurring during the session and help clarify them and intervene to make constructive use of them; (3) work to clarify communication and understanding between family members (for which some of the systematic, structured behavioral procedures are effective and can be taught directly to the family members); (4) work for spontaneous, open, pleasant, and affectionate communication and expression of emotions and reduce tendencies for rigid suppressions, denials, and facades; (5) by his or her own empathy increase gradually the empathy, caring, and concern of family members for each other; and (6) be a "real person" to the family and make constructive use in the therapy of himself or herself, his or her personal feelings toward and about family members, his or her knowledge, experience, and technical knowhow.

One of the most frequently used approaches in family therapy involves a combination of enhancing and clarifying communication and individual psychodynamics wherein the restructuring of communication processes naturally leads to exploration of individual psychodynamics within the family system. This approach makes possible the working through of individual conflicts and concerns within the ready-made communication structure of the family system.

Peer Counseling

Peer counseling, a major component in such alternative agencies as hotlines, runaway houses, and free clinics, relies on young people who identify and want to help or who have recently been through personal difficulties themselves. Untrained ex-addicts and paraprofessionals are frequently used, and these individuals are accepted by certain drug abusing youths who are difficult to reach by the trained professionals. These addict and ex-addict counselors are more often from the same ethnic, racial, cultural, and social class background as the clients ("indigenous to the community being served") and therefore have a ready and natural understanding of the clients' life experience. On the negative side, ex-addict counselors are frequently minimally trained in the counseling area and bring with them a knowledge of drugs and drug-taking behavior based on their personal experiences that is sometimes less than accurate and comprehensive. They tend to have a strong bias against the use of chemotherapy (such as methadone) to the extent that they would withhold drugs from clients who could benefit from their use. These problems have been overcome by some programs by providing supervision for the ex-addict and the peer counselor by a trained professional such as a senior-level psychologist or social worker.

In another type of peer counseling, particularly in rural and suburban areas where qualified peer ex-addicts may not be readily available for staff positions, youth drug programs may be partially staffed by young people who have never used or abused drugs. These individuals can serve as role models for their drug-using peers.

Meditation

Transcendental Meditation (TM) has been used as a drug treatment technique in a variety of treatment environments. Although the effectiveness of this mind-control technique has not been evaluated in a major controlled drug abuse study, several smaller studies suggest its usefulness. Proponents of TM cite the physiological changes occurring during the practice as proof of its relaxation benefits. Studies have found TM to lower the metabolic rate, reduce the lactate concentration in the blood (the reverse is associated with anxiety and high blood pressure), produce a synchronous brain wave pattern distinguishable from other states of consciousness and exert a balance in the autonomic nervous system.[13] "The evidence on TM suggests that the meditative state is a fourth major state of consciousness; wakefulness, dreaming and deep sleep are the other three distinct states. The TM state is characterized by very deep physiological rest and a state of mental alertness."[14]

The technique can be taught in four 2-hour sessions held on consecutive days. In some programs, clients spend 15 to 20 minutes meditating twice a day. A "mantra" with a resonating quality is repeated to allow the mind to reach "pure consciousness," a state in which the mind is awake and alert but not conscious of any particular object or thought. As one practices TM, the conscious capacity of the mind is increased, carrying over into daily activity.

A relatively inexpensive and simple technique, TM provides an alternative to drug abuse for some youngsters since it "meets the drug abuser in the very forum he or she has selected for dealing with problems. The drug abuser's mental experience is mere alteration of consciousness, often with negative effects."[15]

Yoga therapy components, combining meditation, body exercises, and special diets, have been implemented by many drug treatment agencies. Structured as an alternative to drug use, Yoga provides an opportunity for clients to invest in a different lifestyle that includes exercise to strengthen the body, meditation to stimulate the mind and relieve stress, and emphasis on nutritional diet to improve one's health.

Supervised Work Experience (TC)

Most residential facilities teach skills used in the everyday functioning of the home and the commune. These include simple chores such as maintaining the grounds, preparing and cleaning up after meals, and shopping for food. In therapeutic communities, clients may ultimately have responsibility for helping to manage facilities and program operations. Although these are not the skills generally needed to earn a living, they are structured to help the client gain confidence and self-respect during the rehabilitation process, as well as learn good and responsible work habits, so that he or she will be able to perform better in the outside world.

Vocational Training

The failure of many treatment facilities to deal with rehabilitation and reentry into society of the drug abuser has been a major factor in the high recidivism rate. Impaired ability to obtain and hold a job is obviously serious for an adult who has the responsibility to support a family, but the problem may also be serious and acute for the young abuser. Very often, drug involvement began early in adolescence and contributed to a youngster's failure in school and failure to learn the skills required to compete in the job market. It is quite unlikely that such adolescents will have developed work or educational skills to which they can return after drug treatment "rehabilitation." Thus for the young drug abuser these skills may have to be learned for the first time during the treatment process. As a result, many programs are placing greater emphasis on youth "habilitation" in the vocational area.

In addition to vocational counseling and vocational testing, some of the more typical approaches used by drug programs include role rehearsal for job interviews, resumé preparation, attitudinal training around issues such as employer authority, "job readiness" training, practice in "tinker trades" or alternative industries, genuine skills training and vocational workshops, and placement in "supported work" arrangements and apprenticeship arrangements in private industry and in public and private agencies and institutions. In some areas, specific organizations and businesses have been formed to provide job opportunities for drug clients. One such organization is Provide Addict Care Today (PACT) in New York City. With a small staff of professionals, PACT works closely with business and industry leaders to create job openings and training opportunities. Wildcat Industries, which grew out of the high unemployment rate of methadone maintenance patients in New York, provides a variety of building and maintenance services and a messenger service.

Educational Services

These are often provided by treatment programs and may include counseling about educational opportunities and alternatives or instruction for dropouts who want to take the high school equivalency exam (GED courses) to learn the basic practical skills in reading, writing, and arithmetic for better adjustment to work and life. Some drug treatment agencies have schools on the premises for those who have dropped out, have been expelled from school, or have learning problems. Some drug treatment programs for young Spanish-American school dropouts have developed bilingual school programs within the drug program facilities.

Referral Services

Hotlines, schools, free clinics, other medical clinics, youth centers, social agencies, and community mental health centers may provide referral services to drug treatment for their clients. Hospital emergency rooms may refer patients to drug programs following emergency treatment. In addition, school guidance counselors and probation officers can provide an important referral service for youngsters who are identified as drug users in the school systems and in the criminal justice system.

To be successful, those who provide referral services must establish relationships with established drug treatment agencies and make some attempt to understand the strengths and weaknesses of different service providers so that they are in a position to make appropriate referrals. Referral services appear to be different for the various treatment environments according to the findings of the National Youth Polydrug Study concerning 2,750 clients admitted to treatment in 1976-1977 (see table 21-1); in fact, self-referral is the most frequent type of referral for outpatients. The family, or a member of the client's family, is the most frequent referral source for inpatient detoxification and daycare treatment; and among residential clients the criminal justice system is the most frequent source of referral.

Youth Programs

Runaway Houses and Group Homes

For the adolescent drug user who has left home, a "runaway" house may be the first source of help. These houses report many of their clients are heavy users of a wide variety of drugs. According to a recent survey conducted by the National Youth Alternatives Project,[16] 54 percent of youth aged 10 to 17 years questioned at seventeen runaway centers were alcohol abusers or heavy drinkers. Turned off by traditional treatment, this population has a tendency to shy away from any agency that may report their status as runaways to their parents or to the authorities. Many of these programs, however, notify the "authorities" (mainly police), and they either require or encourage the runaway to notify his parents of his whereabouts. Most runaway houses provide individual counseling.

Table 21-1
Type of Referral Source by Type of Treatment Environment in the National Youth Polydrug Survey (n = 2,750)

Referral Source	*Outpatient (Drug Free) Col. %*	*Residential (TC etc.) (Drug Free) Col. %*	*Day Care (Drug Free) Col. %*	*Hospital Detox Col. %*
Self	24.2	21.8	16.4	17.2
Family	22.6	22.4	22.8	26.5
Criminal justice system	17.2	33.4	21.0	21.5
Peers	16.7	7.5	15.1	3.4
School	10.8	1.6	12.8	4.5
Social service agencies	6.2	10.3	9.1	11.9
Medical-mental health	2.4	2.7	2.7	15.3

Some attempt to provide family counseling, as well as help runaways obtain social and medical services. These temporary shelters (few days to several months) strive to help adolescents understand their feelings, make them aware of their options, promote understanding and communication between them and their parents, and work toward a reconciliation between parents and children if possible and desirable.[17]

When the adolescent and parents cannot or will not get together—either due to the youth's attitude or the unsuitability of the parents' home—a runaway house may arrange for the individual to stay in a group home or a small residential program for teens staffed by professionals. Unfortunately, few localities have these kinds of residential arrangements available. If the parents will not cooperate in finding an alternate living arrangement for their child, the runaway house may have to initiate court proceedings to remove the child from their custody—often a sticky legal situation—or to place the child in an institution.

Alternative Agencies

Free Clinics. The free clinic movement, which began in 1967, has evolved as a symbol for alternative, nonjudgmental, humanistic health care delivery for "alienated" individuals and those who experience difficulty obtaining needed services from traditional health delivery systems. The problems experienced by hospital emergency rooms in treating drug problems discussed earlier in this chapter, along with other deficits in the traditional health care delivery system, led to the development of free clinics. These agencies, designed to treat clients with dignity and respect, are generally staffed by physicians knowledgable of the community and the local drug scene.

The free clinic philosophy implies a minimum of red tape and other barriers between doctors and patients—and freedom from applying conventional labels and values to individuals regarded as "deviant" by the dominant culture. Socially stigmatized individuals, such as drug addicts, unmarried pregnant teenagers, and homosexuals, generally feel more comfortable in a free clinic than in traditional medical clinics. While the traditional medical clinics may focus only on the physical illness, free clinics attempt to relate to the entire individual and his or her needs. This difference becomes immediately apparent to the patient and is conveyed by the attitude of the clinic staff. Although there have been a number of definitions of free clinics and their services, most provide medical, dental, psychological, and social services; individual and group therapy and counseling services; and such nonmedical treatment alternatives as talking patients down from bad trips.[18]

Most free clinics make service available to everyone without a "means test," and there are generally no direct fee charges, although some free clinics may request small charges for specific services such as pregnancy tests. In addition to providing direct medical and drug rehabilitation services, free clinics also serve as an important source of credible drug information for the young user who feels that "Establishment drug education" is dishonest. Some free clinics have played an important prevention role, discouraging individuals from dangerous drugs. The Haight-Ashbury Free Clinic in San Francisco, for example, disseminated accurate information about the dangers of methamphetamine. Such slogans as "Speed kills" helped turn youths away from using amphetamines by injection. Free clinics also serve as social institutions where alienated youths can find a place to participate in a meaningful work experience. Many young people have acquired skills as medical paraprofessionals, drug counselors, and administrators of medical programs. Furthermore, free clinic staffs, by going out into the community and discussing a variety of health and neighborhood issues, have served as a valuable source of public health education and preventive street medicine.

The free clinic movement is not without its problems, however. Some members of the American Medical Association have been critical of the quality of the care delivered by free clinics, citing lack of peer review, poor continuity of care resulting from the volunteer physician situation, and long waiting room periods. Other physicians point out some of these same problems exist within the emergency room and outpatient medical departments of county hospitals and other hospitals. Still other groups have criticized free clinics, saying they propagate a discriminatory two-layered system of health care: an adequate high quality one for the middle class and rich and another less adequate one for the poor or disaffiliated. They also claim that the clinics are "counterrevolutionary" because they decrease whatever pressure to change that might otherwise impact on the existing Establishment system.

In the seventies, however, free clinics have evolved toward community-oriented neighborhood clinics that are probably more acceptable to the mainstream of medicine as well as to various health care critics. Large numbers of youthful drug abusers still seek primary care at free clinics for a variety of services.

In addition to free clinics, there are other programs, whether self-supporting or not, which characterize themselves as "alternative" programs. In this context, the term *alternative* refers to the providing of a viable option to the benefits and satisfactions of drug use and the street peer drug culture. It may also, secondarily, refer to an "alternative" to traditional forms of treatment (medical or psychological), since these programs consist primarily of various kinds of organized group activities for youths, of "milieu" and action therapy modalities, and are not heavily weighted with "talking" forms of treatment, such as individual, group, or family counseling. The various organized activities are planned to have some intrinsic appeal for young people, to teach interesting and useful life skills, and to become "laboratories" or workshops for guided learning about how to deal effectively with life's problems. The type of setting or "environment" in which these alternative programs are structured is most often a daycare center, which schedules 6 or more hours of program activities on each of 6 or 7 days per week and may also offer evening programs. Obviously, such alternative activity programs can also be offered in residential communities and, to a lesser extent, in drug-free outpatient clinics. There is an endless variety to the combinations of ways that treatment environments, facilities, and programs can be organized.

The rationale for the use of "alternative high" activities in the treatment of youth drug abuse was formally presented at least as early as 1971 in a paper by A.Y. Cohen.[19] In this rationale, the thesis is that people take drugs because drugs make them feel better by changing their moods, shifting their emotions and their levels of consciousness (including providing escape by inducing oblivion and sleep), modifying their energy state, facilitating visions, transcendental states, spiritual and mystical experiences, removing inhibitions, and enhancing sponteneity and creativity. However, these effects of drugs tend to be temporary and "siphon off energy from long-term constructive growth." The rationale for the "alternative high" treatment experience, then, is that "basically, individuals do not stop using drugs until they discover 'something better.' . . . The key to meeting problems of drug abuse is to focus on the something better, and maximize opportunities for experiencing satisfying nonchemical alternatives." This model emphasizes the development of new attitudes, life styles, and improved skills in the art of living in order to diminish the desire and the need for drugs to attain legitimate personal effects, states, experiences, and goals.

Some of the types of alternative activities and new learning experiences which have been found to appear to be appealing, useful, and effective with young drug abusers are such cultural experiences as workshops in music, art, theater, crafts training (hobbies), carpentry, photography, creative writing, physical education, body awareness training, relaxation techniques, Yoga, sex-education, homemaking, family life education, health education and nutrition, music with movement, dance, training in community involvement, educational assistance, and vocational training courses. Some of the more usual pleasurable, healthful, and recreational activities for adolescent boys and girls are also relevant for this type of program, such as athletics, exercise, hiking, outdoor projects, gardening, special trips, games, and hobbies. Such recreational programs may include such standard facilities as reading rooms, game rooms, movies, music rooms, and service club projects. When these programs are conducted in a positive and understanding atmosphere, therapeutic and rehabilitative support is provided to adolescents with drug-abuse and other problems.

The Door, An Innovative Center for Alternatives. A truly innovative model of an alternative agency, The Door, has been developed in New York City. The

Door has gone beyond the scope of most free clinics, gaining nationwide recognition for its multimodality program, and as a model for reaching and providing quality services to youths, since 1972. The Door can best be classified as a daycare center with regard to type of treatment environment, but it has combined the best features of a therapeutic community, a drop-in center, a drug treatment center, a free medical clinic, and a community youth center.

Young drug abusers and potential drug abusers between the ages of 10 and 21 receive a variety of free services at the program now housed in a mammoth old department store in Manhattan, New York. These services, provided by a large professional, paraprofessional, and volunteer staff, include medical/gynecological services, drug and psychiatric counseling, sex counseling, nutrition counseling, an information and contact center, educational/vocational counseling, legal counseling, a rap line/hotline, creative workshops, an in-service training program, and a drug education and community outreach program. Many of these services are alternatives to drug use. The Door program, according to its founders, means "getting into something other than drugs, turning on to people or to learning, taking up an art or craft, getting into music or photography, getting a job, going to school, working in the community, dealing with environmental or poverty problems. It means doing things, building things, creating things. . . . It means finding channels for the energy and the creativity that otherwise is wasted, dissipated or misused."

The Door's program places equal emphasis on prevention, treatment, and rehabilitation, based on the assumption that only a "total approach" will ultimately provide an effective response to the contemporary drug problem. An individual's drug abuse is viewed as a symptom of a larger problem that may involve physical, economic, social, legal, vocational, emotional, and interpersonal difficulties. Using an individualized treatment plan, The Door deals with the causes and problems of drug abuse in the individual's total life situation. There are various treatment plans operating within The Door. One is the intensive long-term drug treatment and rehabilitation program (12 months) for young people in need of a highly structured and intense therapeutic and rehabilitative program. Another is the short-term crisis intervention program for the young client who wants immediate help only to solve a specific, current life problem (approximately 3 months). Third is the preventive intervention and treatment program (length of time varies) for young people only tangentially or occasionally involved in drugs and for those who are not ready to commit themselves to a more structured drug treatment program. All these programs use the entire range of services, activities, and personnel available at the center. By following one adolescent through a typical involvement in The Door's intensive drug treatment and rehabilitation program, we can fully appreciate the total approach offered.

In Phase I of the intensive program, the youth (let's call him John) will be totally immersed in the therapeutic process of The Door for about 6 months. He will spend five evenings a week there for 5 hours each evening. The evening program will allow John to resume or continue his education. John will participate in community group meetings, group therapy, individual counseling, education counseling, study groups, tutoring, creative workshops, Hatha Yoga, Tai Chi Chuan or karate, and other services. Every activity will be structured in a way that will best support John in breaking out of his destructive pattern of living and the drug scene.

At the community group meeting, which is composed of staff and other participants in the intensive program, daily problems of interaction among the participants will be explored and resolved. Peer pressure will be used in dealing with acting out and inappropriate behavior both at The Door and in the outside community. Therapy and encounter will concentrate on the relief of anxiety and depression and will facilitate the ongoing exploration of viable positive alternatives to drugs. After 3 months, and at regular intervals throughout the entire 12-month program, members of a treatment planning conference will meet to evaluate the relevance and effectiveness of John's current programming plans and make any necessary changes. After 6 months, when he has begun to develop a healthier self-image, greater self-understanding and awareness, as well as improved general health, he will enter Phase II of the program. During the "reintegration" phase, which lasts about 3 months, John will attend The Door a minimum of four nights a week for 5 hours each evening.

Activities will be similar to those in the first phase but will also include an "identity group" to explore central life questions, relevant education counseling, job placements, and referrals to training programs. John will spend one evening each week in the outside community, where he will be involved as an individual or as a member of a group in a community project or activity. When The Door staff witnesses an improved social-interpersonal functioning in John and an ability to make healthier choices in his daily life, he will enter Phase III of the program. In "aftercare," which lasts about 3 months, John will attend The Door at least three full evenings each week. Individual and group therapy will work to resolve fears and anxieties induced by the prospect of separation from the supportive environment of the program. In the final year-long follow-up phase of the program, John will attend the center once a week for the first 6 months, and then gradually decrease this level.

The Door, then, provides a form of substitute family at the community level in which the goals are a discontinuation of the destructive use of the drugs, giving up a drug-oriented lifestyle, and becoming involved in a more creative and constructive way of living. Improvement in the client's psychological well-being, development of a positive self-image, and a sense of self-worth and self-confidence, with freedom from disturbing symptoms such as anxiety, depression, confusion, or fear (which frequently interfere with or inhibit a process of growth), are all considered part of these long-term goals.

The Door is not a residential program and therefore is able to treat a much larger number of clients than the innovative therapeutic community programs that provide a total residential involvement. The Door also implemented an "experimental learning laboratory" demonstration project. In cooperation with the International Center for Integrative Studies, the laboratory was designed as a model to demonstrate the drug treatment and rehabilitative effects of an alternative educational program. Young drug abusers who have failed in school and/or who have learning difficulties attend a structured, individualized learning/treatment program. Each client is assigned to a primary teacher responsible for the coordination and frequent evaluation of his or her program and progress. Preliminary results from an evaluation of the program have shown that involvement in such an educational process appears to help reduce or eliminate drug abuse.

Therapeutic Communities

Since Synanon was established in Southern California in 1959, the therapeutic community (TC) has developed into a standard treatment modality for drug users. Today more than 100,000 clients participate in this form of treatment. When the TC was developed, the average drug client was a male heroin addict in his thirties who had spent time in prison and was from a ghetto environment. To treat such an individual, traditional TCs developed "the game"–encounter and attack group therapy aimed at encouraging honesty in interpersonal relationships and to provide a system through which the addicts would be forced to deal with their problem. According to Yablonsky, the TCs believed that eliciting anger and hostility and attacking interpersonal defenses are necessary in breaking through the barriers and defense mechanisms of drug addicts–and their false sense of pride and ego.[20]

Other characteristics of the early traditional TC include:

Reinforcement of a substitute family organization in which senior staff occupied the transferred roles of father and mother, and other clients were siblings; at the same time, the client was encouraged to separate from his or her natural family.

An elaborate system of social sanctions to shape and control behavior.

Total absence of individual privacy.

Privileges involving some basic rights, given out and taken away often in an arbitrary manner as lessons in "personal growth."

Punishments often taking the form of humiliating and degrading rites such as shaved heads, the wearing of signs and costumes, and verbal reprimands.

No medication unless it was to be used in treatment of a serious physical illness.

It was learned that the harsh therapeutic techniques worked only with a small percentage of the addicts, and the early TCs had high dropout rates. In an attempt to increase the retention rates and serve younger people, most TCs began modifying their methods and techniques in the early 1970s. Some attempted to segregate their younger clients from the older hard-core heroin patients. Others opened up new facilities designed specifically for youthful drug users. Recently, "modified" therapeutic communities have reported a much greater success in attracting and holding younger clients. Bourne and Ramsay, who conducted a nationwide study of TCs, concluded that the modified TCs has more potential for reaching and treating youths.[21] Some of the more rigid, arbitrary, and authoritarian aspects of the traditional TC have been dropped in these programs. Unlike their traditional counterparts, these TCs do not require total separation of the youth from the family. Many have incorporated family therapy into their programs. Additionally, they believe that youthful drug abusers, many of whom self-medicate to alleviate anxiety, depression, and mood disorders, respond better in a nurturant setting in which psychoactive drugs are available on a controlled and prescribed basis to help them cope with their symptoms.

Furthermore, in contrast to traditional TCs, which have created their own subculture and fostered the clients' long-term continuing involvement with the TC, many of the modified TCs are placing a greater emphasis on reentry into the community and vocational rehabilitation. In addition to educational/vocational concerns, some TCs have been placing more of an emphasis on nutrition, physical well-being, and individual counseling. Although many of the therapeutic communities have in the past vigorously resisted scientific evaluation, there is a growing trend to support evaluation efforts, particularly for those programs that are federally funded.

Halfway Houses

These are usually designed for those clients who are to be discharged from residential and inpatient facilities who need help to adjust in the community. Although they may be used as an alternative to hospitalization, they are usually intended to be "after-care" programs to allow the patient to ease back into the life of the community. There are very few programs for youths that are designated as halfway houses, and those which exist are very similar in their programs to daycare centers, emphasizing "alternative" types of activities and vocational services.

Outpatient Clinics

Drug-free outpatient programs (DFOP) range from completely unstructured drop-in or teen rap centers in storefronts to highly structured diversified socialization activities and programs, in addition to a regular schedule of ongoing individual, group, and family therapy and counseling sessions. These sessions are usually scheduled for once or twice per week, and a fairly typical plan is to have one individual and one group session per week. Outpatient programs may provide "rehabilitative" services or they may serve as referral centers to other agencies who provide these services. Referrals may be made to agencies providing welfare, housing, food, child care, medical and dental services, legal services, and vocational/educational services.

Many drug rehabilitation programs operate one or more outreach components, such as storefront facilities, in various communities as a way to induct prospective clients into more formal treatment environments. Street workers—affiliated with a drug program are young people living in a community who may seek out drug abusers at such places as coffee houses, encouraging them to participate in the drug program.

Some outpatient programs attempt to educate clients on the dangers of drugs. They may provide confidential analyses of street drugs, warning clients away from dangerous drugs. The Haight-Ashbury Free Clinic in San Francisco, for example, was instrumental in deterring the use of phencyclidine and other drugs considered harmful. Some programs do not require any commitment by the drug abuser, while others insist on regular participation.

The major problem facing drug-free outpatient programs is that the temptations of the street and peer influence await the client after he or she leaves the clinic each day. Some workers see this problem as insurmountable and set patient goals appropriate for low-motivation individuals. Other workers perceive the need for a long-range induction process that helps the client "buy" time to consider a more serious commitment to treatment and abstinence. During this long period, there is a consistent effort to develop a relationship of trust and acceptance, in which the worker may become friend, supporter, counselor, advisor, and problem solver. Many of these clients leave treatment and then return from time to time when his or her life problems become more acute or when his or her drug abuse gets more out of control. Eventually, and gradually, some of these clients begin to face their life behavior patterns and their drug abuse problem more responsibly, and they begin to work seriously in therapy in trying to change it.

Thus a major objective of treatment staff in drug-free outpatient programs is to engage the client at a strategic point in his or her drug-taking career or during a personal crisis, when involvement in treatment and positive life change become more likely. The percentage of youth clients that has successfully been engaged at these periods of susceptibility and crisis, and that has received beneficial effects from these programs, is difficult to determine, since systematic evaluation of drug-free outpatient treatment has rarely been conducted. Nevertheless, several large-scale treatment evaluation studies have credited outpatient treatment with improving employment and effecting reductions in levels of drug use and illegal behaviors for young-adult client populations.[22,23,24] Chaps. 22 and 23 of this book report on the effectiveness of outpatient treatment with adolescents.

Special Services

Among the more innovative types of outpatient programs are mobile clinics. Usually housed in large street vans, these clinics attempt to bring drug and treatment information to the clients in their natural environment in the hope of engaging them in discussion, assessing problems experienced, and arranging for ongoing treatment and services at a permanent location. Mobile vans have also been used for prevention projects, primarily reaching into areas where addicts are known to congregate.

The popularity of large counterculture rock concerts–Woodstock and Watkins Glen, for example–led to the development of a new style of health care delivery service at the gatherings. Often, with thousands of young people in attendance, the traditional first aid station does not provide an adequate response to the health needs. The problems of youngsters who participate in the rock concerts range from emergency medical problems to alcoholic stupor, drug reactions and overdoses. Because there is a very high degree of deception in the street drug scene, drug analysis programs can provide an important source of information to medical staff caring for the concert attendees. Youth-oriented rock concert medical teams also have utilized innovative methods of talking down bad LSD trips. Talk-down methods not only serve a young person with adverse psychedelic drug reaction in a more humane fashion, but they also greatly reduce the need for hospitalization, making such situations more cost-efficient.

School Programs

School systems are often reluctant to attempt to engage the drug problem directly, because of a concern that acknowledging a drug problem will give the school a bad name. However, there are occasional school-based programs that use group work, affective education, values clarification, peer counseling, and professional counseling modalities to treat drug users. Often, they try to avoid giving the program a "drug" identity, since it is likely to be a social stigma for those students who participate. However, there are some school-based programs where the school officials have publicly acknowledged the drug problem and where the program is popular with some of the students and thus has very little social stigma attached to it. It has been learned that strong support by the school administration, principal, and faculty are also essential to effective programming in a school-based program.

Youth Centers

Youth or "teen" centers such as the YMCA and YMHA usually work with young people who are "joiners." However, adolescents who are heavy drug users tend to stay away from such programs. Traditional recreation and social centers have had to either avoid the more serious drug abusers or develop new methods of serving them. Although few such agencies have adopted full-scale drug-abuse programs, many have developed drug education programs or alternative programs that counteract drug abuse as a peripheral activity. Carp has described one such program at the Bernard Horwich Jewish Community Center in Chicago.[25] The center's approach includes the use of a "T-group experience as well as providing opportunity for linking groups into a larger caring network in which participants are able to develop considerable interpersonal and group skills."

Distribution of Youth Drug Clients in Treatment Settings

The Client Oriented Data Acquisition Process (CODAP) provides the most extensive data base on the characteristics of clients in federally supported drug treatment facilities. During 1975, there were 27,118 youths (12 to 18 years of age) admitted into CODAP. Of them, 73.6 percent were admitted into an outpatient treatment setting, 14.1 percent into residential facilities, 8.7 percent in daycare, 2.3 percent in hospitals, and 1.2 percent in treatment while imprisoned (see table 21-2).

The more recent and smaller national sample of the National Youth Polydrug Study (NYPS) was found to have a not too different distribution of clients across the various treatment settings. NYPS, however, did not include any clients in prison. Second, NYPS contained more clients in the residential setting (18 versus 14 percent) and more clients in hospitals (5.3 percent in the NYPS versus 2.3 percent in the CODAP) (see table 21-3).

The distribution of the CODAP youth group across treatment environments and by sex and race is shown in table 21-2. There are proportionately more white than nonwhite youths admitted to hospital (phi = .069) and proportionately more black youth than nonblack youths treated in daycare centers (phi = .114). There were proportionately more females in outpatient treatment as compared with other modalities.

Table 21-3 presents the demographic characteristics of the NYPS sample of young drug-abuse clients in treatment in five different types of treatment environments. Those in the outpatient environment were shown to be younger at admission and to have a similar proportion of blacks and Hispanics. In contrast, youth clients in the residential therapeutic communities tended to be older; and a relatively greater proportion of the black clients were in therapeutic communities as compared with Hispanics. The inpatient environment was the only environment in which females outnumbered males. The overwhelming proportion of the inpatient youths (86 percent) were white.

Youths' Reasons for Applying for Treatment

The NYPS clients were asked at intake to respond to a list of thirty-three possible reasons for entering a drug treatment program. The thirty-three items

Table 21-2
Distribution of CODAP Youth Admissions in 1975 by Treatment Environment, Race, and Sex
(Column Percentages)

	White Under 18		*Black Under 18*		*Hispanic Under 18*		*Other Under 18*		*Total Under 18*
	Male	*Female*	*Male*	*Female*	*Male*	*Female*	*Male*	*Female*	
Prison	1.6	0.9	1.9	1.1	0.3	0.6	0.4	0.3	1.2
Hospital	3.0	2.6	1.2	1.1	1.2	1.9	–	1.5	2.3
Residential	16.6	13.2	11.9	11.0	14.1	14.8	8.3	7.1	14.1
Daycare	8.0	6.4	14.4	14.2	9.1	9.9	7.6	4.7	8.7
Outpatient	70.8	76.9	70.5	72.5	75.3	72.8	83.7	86.4	73.6

Table 21-3
Demographic Characteristics of Clients across Five Treatment Environments in the National Polydrug Youth Study

	Sex				*Age of Admission*		*Race*					
	Male Row %	*Female Row %*	*Total n*	*Column %*	$\overline{X}$	*S.D.*	*White Row %*	*Black Row %*	*Hisp. Row %*	*Am. In. Row %*	*Others Row %*	*Total n*
Outpatient	62.2	37.8	1,834	(70.3)	16.2	1.4	65	13	15	4	3	1,828
Residential-counseling psychotherapy	64.9	35.1	151	(5.8)	16.2	1.5	80	12	6	21	1	157
Residential-therapeutic communities	65	35.1	317	(12.2)	16.7	1.2	78	18	2	1	1	322
Daycare	57.1	42.9	168	(6.5)	16.5	1.3	59	34	5	0	2	167
Inpatient	49.3	50.7	138	(5.3)	16.5	1.3	86	8	1	4	1	138
Totals	1,609 (617%)	999 (38.3%)										

$\chi^2 = 12.7$, d.f. = 4, $p < .02$; $F = 16.3$, $p < .001$.

were classified, or clustered, into nine types of problems. The percentages of the total sample of clients that gave each of the nine types of problems as one of the reasons for applying for admission to the program or for treatment, in rank order, was as follows: (1) substance abuse problems, 53 percent; (2) family-related problems, 49 percent; (3) school-related problems, 39 percent; (4) legal problems, 35 percent; (5) psychiatric problems, 27 percent; (6) social-peer relationship problems, 22 percent; (7) economic problems, 18 percent; (8) medical and health problems, 5 percent; (9) basic human needs (housing, etc.), 5 percent. The variety and frequency of problems, other than their serious degree of substance abuse, for which these young people reported they were applying for help, is impressive. Nearly all of them admitted that they were seeking help for at least one type of problem other than substance abuse; and almost half of them stated at intake that their substance abuse was not one of the reasons that they were applying for admission to the program. Probably multiple types of problems and forces impact on the client, and then when a minor or major crisis occurs in the client's life, he decides or is prevailed upon to apply for treatment.

A comparison was conducted of the two major treatment environments (outpatient versus residential) in the NYPS sample with regard to a number of client background factors and reasons for applying for treatment. It was found that residential clients, to a statistically significant degree, used more drugs, had been more involved with the criminal justice system (number of arrests and legal offenses), and were generally under a greater pressure to enter treatment in the sense that they reported more reasons for applying for treatment. Significantly more residential clients reported family problems, legal problems, social/peer relationship problems, and basic human need problems (lack of food, clothing and shelter). Residential clients had significantly more drug overdoses (ODs), but it was found, conversely, that outpatient clients had a significantly higher rate of "intentional suicidal attempts." (Incidentally, this suicide attempt rate for young outpatient clients was also higher than for inpatient detox clients, which is an unexpected finding.)

Typical Problems Experienced by Youth Drug Programs

The problems existing in youth drug programs are as numerous as the different types of services and modalities previously described. Difficulties in treatment goals, staffing, evaluation, and funding sources have been identified. It has been learned that many treatment approaches, particularly the harsher forms of group therapy and behavior modification, are generally inappropriate for treating youthful drug users. These therapeutic approaches enforce a rigid standard of conformity that can stifle the personal growth and development so important in adolescence. Therefore, great care should be taken in selecting a drug treatment to which to refer a youth drug abuser.

Adolescents directed by the criminal justice system into treatment may demonstrate a lack of motivation or interest in participating in a serious and authentic way in the therapeutic process. Thus the treatment experience may be a failure for a young drug abuser who views it only as "something better than jail." On the other hand, some individuals who have entered into treatment involuntarily have developed motivation during the treatment process and have been known to find the treatment useful to themselves. There is a need for additional research in this area to determine the effectiveness of compulsory treatment.

Unfortunately, individualized treatment planning is still foreign to some drug programs serving youths, with many providing custodial rather than good clinical care. The large number of paraprofessionals working in drug programs often are not providing skilled individual counseling or being sufficiently sensitive and responsive to the depression, anxiety, and disturbed emotional and mental states of their young clients. Nonindividualized treatment usually fails to look at a particular adolescent's learning problems. Many of these youths report feeling "stupid" and unable to learn. Furthermore, clients who have not finished school are often not guided to seek proper help to continue their schooling. Many of them end up with inappropriate jobs because vocational testing and evaluation are not done by professionals who can assess skill and interest areas that might lead to more creative work. It is recognized that there is not a large job market for young people, particularly those who have had problems with drugs. However, that does not mean that a youngster should be pushed into a job with the possibility of experiencing one more defeat or letdown.

If drug abuse is considered symptomatic of underlying problems (many of which began before drug usage), then treatment programs must be prepared to address these problems or have the capability of making appropriate referrals. In efforts to treat young drug users, there should be more emphasis on such treatment methods as family therapy. We speculate that the majority of adolescent clients entering drug treatment programs have experienced or are currently experiencing serious family disruption both as a cause and a result of drug-taking behavior. Forty-nine percent (49 percent) of the young clients in the NYPS sample reported that "family related problems" were among their reasons for applying for treatment. This was the most frequently cited type of reason, after "substance abuse problems."

An innovative "total approach" such as The Door's, which relies on a variety of therapies (including family therapy), counseling, and other activities, increases the adolescent's chances for resolving the problems that led to drug abuse. Few communities have been able or willing to make the investment in this type of approach. The lack of professionally trained staff members in many drug programs poses a serious problem, too. As mentioned previously, ex-addict counselors often have minimal training in counseling as well as inadequate knowledge of all the types of drugs abused. Counselor intuition, while important, is not a substitute for proper training. Furthermore, when budgets are cut, in-service staff training (where it exists) is often the first item to be excised.

Despite efforts to educate the public, a stigma still surrounds an individual with an emotional, social, or substance-abuse problem. Parents are reluctant to refer youngsters to drug programs for the stigma it may create for them. Not only are they sometimes hesitant to admit the nature of their child's problem, but they may be unaware of the resources that are available and confused as to which treatment setting or modality is most appropriate or best qualified. It is not easy to select a program since there is generally little information available about the treatment alternatives available to youthful drug users. Instead, the publicity has been focused on the more controversial programs designed to treat hard-core heroin addicts.

Drug programs designed for youths are less likely to generate third-party payments for their clients. A study conducted by the NIDA Services Research Branch found this problem to be beyond the control of the programs, since most youths are not eligible for third-party coverage under Medicaid or private health insurance.[26] In some cases where third-party payments might be available, the adolescent clients do not make those available to the program because they do not want to inform their parents of their drug problems or that they are in treatment. Although Title XX funds would cover some clients in substance-abuse treatment programs, these funds are allocated by state governments, and drug treatment is one of many programs competing for funds.

The limitations on research and evaluation in the drug treatment area derive not only from a lack of funds but from a concern to protect the confidentiality of clients. Most youth treatment programs do not have the staff qualified to conduct adequately controlled research and careful scientific analysis. Perhaps university departments can be encouraged to get more involved in this important area of research.

Conclusions

A drug rehabilitation program designed to serve youths must provide comprehensive and integrated services. Since resources are generally limited, programs must develop and maintain adequate working relationships with other agencies and institutions in the community. A program that is self-contained is less likely to be in a position to provide the social, medical, and psychological services required by young drug abusers.

There has been a great diversity of services and modalities established to treat adolescent drug abuse, but thus far there has been a failure to design and test distinct treatment models that can be replicated in the field. Most youth programs in existence have not evaluated their services because of a lack of resources and research capability. The literature on the evaluation of treatment and rehabilitative methods and approaches for youthful drug abusers is limited.

The result has been a reliance on hearsay and "plain common sense" in attempting to determine the most appropriate services for youngsters with drug problems. Often there is a failure to diagnose the individual's needs before he or she is referred to a treatment program, adequate for the determination of the most appropriate referral. The youngster is often forced to conform to the program rather than having the services structured or adapted to address his or her unique problems and needs.

Frequently, youngsters with drug problems are referred to unsuitable programs designed for older, hard-core heroin addicts. Furthermore, the presence of the older drug abusers may provide an undesirable influence on these youngsters who are at a vulnerable age. It has been found that in many programs, a high percentage of youthful polydrug abusers who use marihuana, alcohol, amphetamines, and hashish are likely to drop out of drug treatment programs within a 3- to 6-month period.

Many of the agencies successful in serving youthful drug users look upon drug abuse as a symptom of other life problems, do not limit their services to drug abusers, and do not refer to themselves as drug agencies. Funding is a major problem for these agencies, since it is often difficult to demonstrate that they serve only individuals with serious drug problems and funding is generally limited.

Federal and state agencies discourage program support for problems out of their jurisdiction; NIDA discourages drug treatment programs from serving those whose primary substance of abuse is alcohol, although many youths who use other drugs use alcohol most frequently because of its easier availability. Surveys also show that youngsters are likely to use different types of drugs in different periods of their life. Successful treatment with youthful drug users is hampered by policies that discriminate on the basis of the type of drug used and tend to split the treatment effort.

Add these difficulties onto the problems of limited funding, untrained staff, and lack of evaluation of the treatment outcome, and drug treatment for adolescents emerges as an imperfect system. Certainly there is a need for a more coordinated approach to the problems of youthful drug use. To be successful in this endeavor, communities must promote more interagency and intraagency coordination between service systems capable of addressing the underlying social, psychological, and medical problems experienced by youngsters who misuse or abuse drugs. There must also be more support and resources devoted to the evaluation of treatment efforts to determine what works best for youngsters with differing needs.

Notes

1. Polydrug Research Center. *A Statistical Report on Youth Admitted to Treatment in Calendar Year 1975 from the Client Oriented Data Acquisition Process (CODAP) National Data File*, p. 15, April 1977.

2. Polydrug Research Center, *DAWN IV Statistical Report on Youth Sample,* Submitted to NIDA, January 1977.

3. Donald R. Wesson, David E. Smith, and Lauren Kabat Linda, Drug crisis intervention: Conceptual and pragmatic considerations, *Journal of Psychedelic Drugs* 6 (2):135-142, April-June 1974.

4. R. Levy and A. Brown, An analysis of calls to a drug-crisis intervention service, *Journal of Psychedelic Drugs* 6 (2):143-152, April-June 1974.

5. George DeLeon and George Beschner, The Therapeutic Community, *Proceedings of Therapeutic Communities of America Planning Conference, January 29-30, 1976,* DHEW Publication No. (ADM) 77-464.

6. Frances E. Cheek, *Behavior Modification Program,* New Jersey Department of Health, Division of Narcotic and Drug Abuse Control, Trenton, N.J., 1973.

7. A.S. Friedman, *Three Treatment Models for Delinquency,* Report to U.S. Children's Bureau, 1969.

8. R. Hirsch and J. Imhof, A family therapy approach to the treatment of drug abuse and addiction, *Journal of Psychedelic Drugs* 7 (2):181-185, April-June 1975.

9. NIDA, *The Use of Family Therapy in Drug Abuse Treatment: A National Survey,* ADM 78-622, December 1977.

10. P.H. Laqueur, "General Systems Theory and Multiple Family Therapy." In J.H. Masserman (ed.), *Current Psychiatric Therapies,* vol. VIII, New York, Grune & Stratton, 1968.

11. Donald I. Davis and Micheline Klagsbrun, The family and drug use symposium, *Family Process,* 16 (1977):141-173.

12. M. Duncan Stanton, The addict as savior: Heroin, death and the family, *Family Process* 16 (1977):191-197.

13. R.K. Wallace and H. Benson, The physiology of meditation, *Scientific American* 226:84-89, February 1972.

14. J. Marcus, Transcendental Meditation: Consciousness expansion as a rehabilitation technique, *Journal of Psychedelic Drugs* 7 (2):169-179, April-June 1975.

15. Sat Nam Singh Khalsa, Mukta Kawr Khalsa, and Hukam Singh Khalsa, The Application of Yoga Nutrition and Meditation in Overcoming Addictive Behavior, paper presented at National Drug Abuse Conference 1978, Seattle, Washington.

16. National Youth Alternatives Project, National Directory of Runaway Centers, January 1974.

17. Ibid.

18. C. Bloomfield, M. Levy, R. Kotealchuck, and M. Handelman, Free Clinics, Health Policy Advisory Bulletin No. 34, pp. 1-16, October 1971; and D. Smith, D. Bentel, and J. Schwartz, (eds.), *The Free Clinics: A Community Approach to Health Care and Drug Abuse,* Beloit, Wisc.: STASH Press, 1971.

19. A.Y. Cohen, The journey beyond trips: Alternatives to drugs, *Journal of Psychedelic Drugs* 3 (2):16-21.

20. L. Yablonsky, *Synanon–The Tunnel Back,* New York: MacMillan, 1964.

21. P. Bourne and A. Ramsay, The therapeutic community phenomenon, *Journal of Psychedelic Drugs* 7 (2):203-208, April-June 1975.

22. M.R. Burt, Drug Treatment in New York City and Washington, D.C.: Followup Studies. DHEW Publication No. ADM (77-506). Services Research Monograph Series, Rockville, Md.: National Clearinghouse on Drug Abuse Information, 1977.

23. MACRO Systems, Inc., Three Year Follow-up Study of Clients Enrolled in Treatment Programs in New York City, NIDA report, Silver Springs, Md.: MACRO Systems, Inc., 1975.

24. D.D. Simpson, L.J. Savage, M.R. Lloyd, and S.B. Sells, Evaluation of Drug Abuse Treatments Based on the First Year after DARP, IBR report 77-14, Forth Worth, Texas Christian University, Institute of Behavioral Research, 1977.

25. J.M. Carp, Youth's need for social competence and power: The community building model, in E. Senay, V. Shorty, and H. Alksne (eds.), *Developments in the Field of Drug Abuse. Proceedings of the National Drug Abuse Conference,* Cambridge, Mass.: Schenkman, 1974.

26. NIDA Services Research Branch, *Utilization of Third-Party Payment for the Financing of Drug Abuse Treatment,* DHEW Publication No. ADM 77-440, 1977.

22 Evaluation of Treatment Outcome for Youths in the Drug Abuse Reporting Program (DARP): A Follow-up Study

Saul B. Sells and
D. Dwayne Simpson

Introduction

This chapter presents some results of a special study of outcome effectiveness of drug-abuse treatment for the youth subsample of the NIDA-TCU Drug Abuse Reporting Program (DARP) file. Although it is limited by the data available and the resources provided for conducting the study, it has been possible, by review of previous DARP research, further examination of a subset of during-treatment data for black and white youths in the DARP, and a summary of as yet unpublished data on youths in the DARP cohort 1 and cohort 2 follow-up study samples, to provide a substantial set of results. The treatments included were not designed specifically for youths, but more generally for the spectrum of drug users in the various communities. As such, they have important implications for the understanding of drug abuse treatment for youths and the results can be compared with evaluation data on youth-specific treatments as they become available.

The DARP was established to create a data base for research on the evaluation of drug-abuse treatment. Between June 1969 and April 1973, this program recorded approximately 44,000 admissions to treatment at fifty-two agencies located throughout the United States and in Puerto Rico. These data have been analyzed in relation to outcomes during treatment (see Sells 1974*a*, and *b*; Sells and Simpson 1976*a*, *b*, and *c*), and more recently, in conjunction with follow-up studies of samples of 1969-1971 and 1971-1972 admissions in relation to posttreatment outcomes (Sells et al. 1976).

Two data sets were analyzed in the present study. The first consists of 5,405 black and white youths aged 19 and under drawn from the DARP final research tape (see Simpson et al. 1976). The second includes 587 black and white youths who were interviewed in the DARP cohort 1 and cohort 2 follow-up studies; Puerto Rican and Mexican-American youths were excluded because of insufficient numbers.

The organization of the chapter is as follows. The section following this introduction describes the data source and includes a discussion of the DARP data system, the treatments provided, the treatment population, and the characteristics of the youths sample. This is followed by a review of the previously published DARP results concerning youths, based on studies reported in the five-volume series edited by Sells (1974*a* and *b*) and by Sells and Simpson (1976*a,b,* and *c*). The fourth section summarizes retention and termination data for a youth sample of black and white DARP admissions aged 19 and under (n = 5,405). Section five presents some impressive new posttreatment follow-up results based on 587 black and white youths who were interviewed 1 to 6 years after termination from DARP. A discussion of the results and the conclusions that appear to be justified are presented in the final section.

Data Source and Samples

The DARP Data System

Between 1969 and 1974, the Institute of Behavioral Research at Texas Christian University collected patient reports on 43,943 clients who were admitted to treatment for drug abuse at fifty-two agencies located throughout the United States and in Puerto Rico. This massive data collection was implemented under the Drug Abuse Reporting Program (DARP), supported by NIDA and previously by NIMH, for the purpose of creating a data base for research on the evaluation of treatment. The DARP admission record was completed on all patients at intake and provided demographic, classification, and individual developmental and background data, as well as baseline information on variables used as outcome criterion measures (drug and alcohol use, productive role activities and employment, and criminality). The status evaluation record was completed bimonthly up to termination and included data on family and living arrangements, each of the criterion measures, and a summary of treatment experience and components attended during each 2-month period. The status evaluation record also served as a termination report, indicating date and reason for termination, and as a readmission report, when patients returned to treatment at the same agency following a period out of treatment. DARP admissions were reported from June 1, 1969 through March 31, 1973, when the DARP system was supplanted by the federal CODAP reporting program. However, status evaluation records continued for a final period of 12 months to enable the collection of during-treatment criteria for a full year on all patients then in treatment. Copies of the DARP forms are included in Sells (1974*a*).

To protect the confidentiality of the records, all forms were identified by agency code numbers; names, addresses, and other personal identifiers were excluded from the DARP forms. This system worked well throughout the 5 years of data collection, but necessitated difficult special negotiations with the

DARP agencies to enable the posttreatment follow-up studies, which were initiated in 1975. Nevertheless, throughout DARP, major emphasis was given to respect for the individual, protection of privacy, and protection of the confidentiality of the data. It is believed that the strict enforcement of this policy contributed greatly to the reliability and validity of the data.

For convenience in analysis of the data, DARP admissions were grouped into three admission cohorts, as follows:

Cohort 1: 11,383 patients from twenty-three agencies, admitted between June 1, 1969 and May 31, 1971.

Cohort 2: 15,831 patients from thirty-six agencies, admitted between June 1, 1971 and May 31, 1972.

Cohort 3: 16,729 patients from fifty agencies, admitted between June 1, 1972 and March 31, 1973.

The Research Population and Study Samples

The total DARP population of 43,943 admissions is described in detail in the five volumes cited earlier and in Simpson et al. (1976). The total population included 9,877 individuals whose records were inappropriate for inclusion in the during-treatment evaluation studies for a variety of substantive reasons. Some of these people were hospitalized, in jail, or otherwise not at risk during the preadmission baseline period; others entered DARP treatment, either by transfer or after moving from another city, while on a regimen of methadone maintenance; a substantial number were in experimental or mixed treatments that could not be classified for inclusion in the DARP research design; and others were found to be nondrug users, in prevention programs, or otherwise disqualified, as discussed in detail by Simpson et al. (1976, p. 41).

An additional subset of exclusions consisted of 6,074 people who went through all intake procedures and were formally admitted to treatment but never reported to any treatment appointments. This group, identified subsequently as "intake only," had no treatment data and was necessarily excluded from the during-treatment research but was retained for inclusion in the posttreatment follow-up studies as a comparison group.

Since the DARP files represent the only available large-scale research source that provides detailed prospective data on patients through at least one drug-abuse treatment episode, it has been consulted extensively for normative and comparative information. To meet the needs of groups seeking such information, as in the case of the present study, a master research file was created (see Simpson et al. 1976) that included all cases not excluded for substantive reasons, as previously explained, or because of absence of treatment data (the "intake only" group). The resulting master research file includes 27,460 patients who were drug users and received treatment at one of the forty-six DARP agencies retained for research analysis.

For the present study there were 6,259 patients in the master research file who were 19 years of age or younger at admission. The distribution of these patients by sex, age, and race is shown in table 22-1. This sample is divided approximately one-third female to two-thirds male, about equally between patients under 18 and those aged 18 or 19, and is mainly composed of blacks (26 percent) and whites (60 percent); Puerto Ricans (8.8 percent), Mexican-Americans (3.4 percent), and others (1.4 percent) represent small minorities in the youth sample as well as in the total DARP file. In order to present reliable results for males and females by racial as well as age breakdowns in the follow-up and the during-treatment phase of this study, it was necessary to restrict the analyses performed to black and white youths. The subsample of black and white youths in the during treatment phase included 5,405 patients (see table 22-1); the corresponding follow-up subsample from the cohort 1 and 2 follow-up studies included 587 patients.

DARP Treatments

Four treatment modalities, each with at least two characteristic variants, were provided by the agencies that participated in the DARP. The modalities were outpatient methadone maintenance (MM), therapeutic community (TC), out-

Table 22-1
Distribution of the Youth Component of the DARP Research Sample, by Sex, Race/Ethnic Group, and Age

	Number of Males	*Number of Females*	*Total*
Race/ethnic group			
Black	1,211	432	1,643
Puerto Rican	414	139	553
Mexican-American	138	76	214
White	2,307	1,455	3,762
Other	60	27	87
Age at admission			
<15	284	297	581
15	359	295	654
16	583	334	917
17	725	337	1,062
18	958	410	1,368
19	1,221	456	1,677
Total sample	4,130	2,129	6,259

patient drug free (DF), and detoxification (DT). Because of the emphasis on specification of the treatment provided in the DARP research design, much attention was devoted to the goals, policies, processes, staffing, procedures, components, and facilities of the participating programs, and a treatment typology was developed (see Cole and Watterson 1976; James et al. 1976) that identified discrete treatment approaches within the major modalities.

Both MM and DF programs were divided between change-oriented treatments (MM-CO and DF-CO) and adaptive treatments (MM-A and DF-A). Change-oriented programs generally sought to socialize their patients to values, beliefs, and lifestyles consistent with those of the majority in society through the use of group therapy, encounter groups, and other means. They made heavy demands in terms of time participation, used strict discipline and sanctions (including expulsion for noncompliance), and expected abstinence from drugs as a major outcome. Adaptive programs generally featured low dosages and trial detoxification during treatment. Methadone maintenance in the MM-CO types of program was regarded as a therapeutic strategy toward achieving an eventual drug-free status; methadone maintenance treatment in the MM-A type of program has the practical goal of maintaining the addict patients on a licit drug while endeavoring to teach practical adaptive, vocational, and social skills.

Three types of TC were identified: TC-T, the traditional, long-term (at least 1 year) regimen in the tradition of Maxwell Jones (1953), Synanon, and Day Top; TC-M, a modified type of program of somewhat shorter duration than TC-T, with more professional and institutional oversight; and TC-ST, emphasizing in particular a short-term (frequently 2 months) intensive socialization program. The residential aspect of all TCs implied isolation from the community, and as a result TC patients were minimally at risk with respect to behavioral outcomes during treatment.

Two types of DT programs were also described. DT-IP is the standard inpatient program, usually of 21 days duration, involving hospitalization and use of methadone or other drugs during the withdrawal period. DT-OP, outpatient or ambulatory detoxification, was apparently initiated during the early 1970s, when maintenance "slots" were taken and waiting lists were common. Outpatient detoxification usually involves decreasing doses of methadone, but in practice it is longer in duration than inpatient, although usually not over 3 months in duration.

Characteristics of the Black-White Youth Sample

Table 22-2 presents distributions of the 5,405 black and white youths by age at admission, sex, and race/ethnic group. Although not a representative sample of drug-using youths or of drug-using youths in treatment in the United States, they include all black and white youths in the age range designated in the DARP research sample.

Table 22-2
Distributions of Black and White Youths by Age at Admission, Sex, and Race/Ethnic Group (Panel 1: Numbers in Groups; Panel 2: Age-Level Percentages by Race/Ethnic Group; Panel 3: Sex Percentages within Race-by-Age Groups; Panel 4: Age Percentages within Race/Ethnic Groups by Sex)

		Age at Admission					
Race	*Sex*	*Under 16*	*16 to 17*	*18*	*19*	*Total*	*% of Total*
1. Numbers in Groups							
Black	Male	98	358	325	430	1,211	22
	Female	50	105	109	168	432	8
	Total	148	463	434	598	1,643	30
White	Male	471	808	462	566	2,307	43
	Female	486	493	240	236	1,455	27
	Total	957	1,301	702	802	3,762	70
Both	Male	569	1,166	787	996	3,518	65
	Female	536	598	349	404	1,887	35
	Total	1,105	1,764	1,136	1,400	5,405	100
	% of Total	20	33	21	26	100	
2. Age Level Percentages by Race/Ethnic Group							
Black		13	26	38	43	1,643	30
White		87	74	62	57	3,762	70
3. Sex Percentages within Race by Age Groups							
Black	Male	66	77	75	72	74	
	Female	34	23	25	28	26	
	Total	100	100	100	100	100	
White	Male	49	62	66	71	61	
	Female	51	38	34	29	39	
	Total	100	100	100	100	100	
Both	Male	51	66	69	71	65	
	Female	49	34	31	29	35	
	Total	100	100	100	100	100	
4. Age Group Percentages within Race by Sex Groups							
Black	Male	8	30	27	35	100	
	Female	12	24	25	39	100	
	Total	9	28	26	36	100	
White	Male	20	35	20	25	100	
	Female	33	34	17	16	100	
	Total	28	32	19	21	100	
Both	Male	16	33	22	28	100	
	Female	28	32	19	21	100	
	Total	20	33	21	26	100	

Panel 1 of table 22-2 shows the numbers of patients in each age x race x sex category and marginal percentages for race x sex totals and age group totals. This sample is divided 70 to 30 percent between white and black and 65 to 35 percent between male and female. In these respects it differs from the total DARP sample (all ages), in which blacks (46 percent) outnumbered whites (35 percent) and the male/female ratio was 75 to 25 percent. As shown in panel 2, whites particularly dominated the younger age groups (87 to 13 percent at under 16 and 74 to 25 percent at 16 to 17), and they represented a clear majority at every age level. This relationship of age and race/ethnic group has implications for the interpretation of the distributions of pretreatment drug-use pattern and treatment assignment, as discussed later.

Panel 3 shows further comparisons of percentages of males and females within age by race/ethnic groups; overall, females were relatively more numerous among whites (39 percent) than blacks (26 percent). This is apparent at every age level, but particularly at the two younger age levels. In addition, the percentage of white females even exceeded that of white males in the youngest age group. Panel 4 shows the percentage of each race/ethnic group by sex at each age level. The only age group in which the percentage of females exceeded that of males is under 16; this occurred in both race/ethnic groups, but was more pronounced among whites than blacks.

In summary, the whites outnumbered the blacks (70 to 30 percent), tended to be younger, and included proportionately more females. There was a fairly consistent trend, over the range of the age of admission (from 15 to 20 years of age), for the proportion of males to increase gradually, relative to females, and for the proportion of blacks to increase gradually, relative to whites. These trends were observed to continue in the adult treatment sample over 20 years of age (as shown in table 22-5).

Percentage distributions of the total youth sample are shown in table 22-3 for four categories of pretreatment drug use (during the 2 months preceding admission) by age, race/ethnic group, and sex. The four drug-use categories presented are (1) use of daily opioids only (16 percent), as shown in panel 4; (2) daily opioids plus any use of other illicit drugs (24 percent); (3) less-than-daily opioids, with or without other illicit drugs (17 percent); and (4) nonopioids only (43 percent). As might be expected in this youth sample, the highest frequency is for nonopioids only; nevertheless it is noteworthy that 40 percent of this sample were daily users of opioids prior to admission and an additional 17 percent used opioids at frequencies less than daily.

As shown in table 22-3, no remarkable sex differences were seen in drug-use patterns, but the variations associated with age and race/ethnic group were substantial. Both categories of daily opioid use increased with age, with a major jump from under 16 to 16 to 17 and then another major jump from 16 to 17 to 18. Although daily opioid use increased from age 18 to 19, it appears meaningful to distinguish this variable in terms of two age ranges, under 18 and 18 to 19. Fifty-five percent of 18-year-olds and 66 percent of 19-year-olds, compared with 30 percent of 16- to 17-year-olds, were using opioids daily. The sharp increase in percentage that occurred between 16 to 17 and 18 is probably partly a function of the fact that methadone maintenance treatment, by FDA regulation, usually becomes available at 18 years. Daily opioid users are more likely than less than daily users to apply for and be accepted into methadone maintenance treatment.

Table 22-3
Pretreatment Drug Use of Black and White Youth Sample by Age at Admission, Race/Ethnic Group, and Sex

	Percent by Pretreatment Drug Use				
	Da Op Only	*Da Op Plus*	*<Da Op Plus*	*NonOp Only*	*Number in Group*
1. Age at Admission					
Under 16	3	4	14	79	1,105
16 to 17	12	18	19	51	1,764
18	22	33	18	27	1,136
19	28	38	15	19	1,400
2. Race/Ethnic Group					
Black	35	39	14	12	1,643
White	8	16	19	57	3,762
3. Sex					
Male	18	25	16	41	3,518
Female	14	21	18	47	1,887
4. Total Number					
Total Number	897	1,276	903	2,329	5,405
Percent	16	24	17	43	10

Note: The explanations given below can be utilized as a key to the abbreviated column headings in the table.

Da Op only = Use of daily opioids only.
Da Op plus = Daily opioids plus any use of other illicit drugs.
<Da Op plus = Less than daily opioids plus any use of other illicit drugs.
NonOp only= Nonopioids only.

No discernible age trend was apparent for the "swing" category, involving less than daily opioids; this category is viewed as an important transition stage between experimentation and light drug use (nonopioids only) and harder drug use. The greatest variation appeared for the fourth category, nonopioids only, in which the percentage was 79 percent for the under 16 group, followed by a steady decline to 19 percent at age 19. Thus daily opioid use was found to be a phenomenon mainly involving the older youths, with nonopioid use (usually less than daily) mainly involving the younger youths.

The association noted in table 22-2 between race/ethnic group and age should be recalled since the data are examined for drug-use pattern by race/ethnic group (table 22-3, panel 2). Here it appears that daily opioid use was the major pattern among the blacks, while nonopioids only was the major pattern among whites. Elsewhere, Sells (1976) presented evidence that age at onset of first drug use occurred earliest among nonopioid users (77 percent under age 18), and on the average it occurred over a year later among daily opioid users (59 percent under age 18). Median transition time from first drug to first opioid, and from first opioid to first daily opioid (for those who had used opioids), was also longer among nonopioid than daily opioid users. In relation to the present sample, these data are in agreement with the results that indicate later onset for the black subsample, who were older at admission and predominantly daily opioid users, and earlier onset for the younger, white, nonopioid user subsample. With regard to indications for prevention and treatment, these data suggest the desirability of early intervention.

The data on treatment assignment, shown in table 22-4 by age at admission, race/ethnic group, sex, and pretreatment drug-use category, are consistent with the foregoing information concerning these characteristics of the sample. As expected, the majority were assigned to DF treatments and had a characteristic representation with respect to age (under 18), race (white), and drug-use pattern

Table 22-4
DARP Treatment Modalities for Black and White Youth Sample by Age at Admission, Race/Ethnic Group, Sex, and Pretreatment Drug-Use Classification

	Percent by Type of Treatment				*Number in Group*
	MM	*TC*	*DF*	*DT*	
1. Age at Admission					
Under 16	1	14	82	3	1,105
16 to 17	5	23	60	12	1,764
18	19	26	33	22	1,136
19	22	26	29	23	1,400
2. Ethnic Group					
Black	24	22	25	29	1,643
White	6	23	62	9	3,762
3. Sex					
Male	13	22	49	16	3,518
Female	9	23	54	14	1,887
4. Pretreatment Drug Use					
Da Op only	28	23	17	32	896
Da Op plus	25	29	18	28	1,254
<Da Op plus	4	36	51	9	917
NonOp only	1	14	81	4	2,338
5. Total Number					
Total number	616	1,222	2,,745	822	5,405
Percent	11	23	51	15	100

Note: Key to row labels abbreviated in the table.

Da Op only = Use daily opioids only.

Da Op plus = Daily opioids plus any use of other illicit drugs.

<Da Op plus = Less than daily opioids plus any use of other illicit drugs.

NonOp only= Nonopioids only.

(nonopioids only and less than daily opioids). Similarly, the assignments to MM and DT reflect the selection of older, black, daily opioid users for those treatments. As in the total DARP sample, the residential TC programs included both opioid and nonopioid users. However, the comparatively low frequency in TCs of patients under age 16 and of nonopioid only users probably reflects the fact that the younger patients were often considered too young for those programs; apparently many of them were also encouraged to attend school.

Evaluation of Treatment in the DARP

The DARP evaluation studies based on during-treatment data for the three admission cohorts included three retention studies (Joe 1974; Joe and Simpson 1976*a* and *b*), three major analytic studies focused on behavioral criteria (Spiegel and Sells 1974; Gorsuch et al. 1975; and Gorsuch et al. 1976), and several multiple discriminant analysis studies focused on patient and treatment factors that discriminated among groups defined by specific outcome patterns (Demaree et al. 1976; Demaree and Neman 1976).

Comparisons across modalities and treatment types within modalities were extremely difficult, in part because of the different time frames involved and in part because of the differences in characteristics of patients assigned. MM programs provided extended treatment, and substantial percentages of MM patients were still in treatment after 12 months in all three cohorts. TCs varied from the traditional programs, designed for a year or longer, to the short-term programs, some only 2 months in planned duration of treatment. DF programs varied in planned duration, but generally involved considerably less than a year. Finally, DT programs were of 3 weeks (inpatient) to 3 months (outpatient) planned duration. In view of these variations, average tenure was not comparable across treatment.

Table 22-5 shows variations in treatment assignment related to age, race/ethnic status, and sex. With regard to black and white youths under 18, 38 percent of the blacks and 76 percent of the whites were in DF, the most common modality for this age group. The predominance of whites in DF was matched by greater numbers of blacks in MM, TC, and DT. Another feature of table 22-5 is the steady increase with age of the proportions of both blacks and whites who were in MM treatment.

Retention and Termination in DARP

Table 22-6 summarizes treatment dispositions in terms of percentages terminated for various reasons, referred, completed treatment, and still in treatment at 1 year after admission, as well as days in treatment for patients who terminated within the first year for the total DARP research sample of 27,460. Patients are grouped by treatment type. The upper panel of this table refers to disposition. Except for MM treatments, where the highest percentages were still in treatment, the highest percentages for all other treatment types were patients who terminated by quitting; these ranged between 50 percent in TC-M and DF-CO to 71 percent in DT-OP. Referrals were comparatively high in only one treatment type, DF-CO (14 percent), and completions were substantial in TC-M and TC-ST (both 15 percent), DF-CO (18 percent), DF-A (19 percent), DT-IP (34 percent), and DT-OP (16 percent).

The lower panel of table 22-6 shows distributions of days in treatment by treatment type for patients who terminated within the first year after admission. It is apparent that only the MM programs retained any substantial percentages of these patients over 6 months. In the TC and DF programs, which were among the highest in percentages of quits, over half their patients terminated within the first 3 months.

Table 22-7 breaks down the termination percentages for treatment types by sex, age, race/ethnic group, and pretreatment drug-use category. Here it can be seen that there were few significant differences attributable to sex or drug-use pattern. With respect to age, the under 18 group had a substantially higher termination rate than all other groups in both MM types but were notably lower in both DF types and also in both DT types (although it approximately tied with the over 40 group in DF-A and DT-IP). Whites and users of nonopioids only also had low termination rates in DF-CO.

In general, the retention studies on DARP cohorts indicated superior retention in MM programs compared with other modalities. The relatively low tenure and high termination rates in TC and DF programs raised questions concerning the general effectiveness of these treatment, but it was recognized (1) that the tenure of youths in DF and of whites, females, and nonopioid (polydrug) users at least in DF-CO was encouraging, and (2) that the significance of these data depended ultimately on the results of posttreatment follow-up studies. Blacks who remained longer in DF-CO were found to be those who did not use heroin daily and whose age of onset of drug use was relatively older. Whites who remained longer in DF-CO tended also not to be daily heroin users and could be described as having fewer previous treatment episodes, later age of onset, little criminal history, a better employment history, and above-average education. Whites who remained longer in DF-A were younger, not daily heroin users, and late in onset of drug use (as in the case of DF-CO) but also were involved with law enforcement agencies at admission and had less education.

During-Treatment Criterion Performance

The gross outcome results in all three DARP cohorts showed substantial reductions of drug use and criminality during all treatment and smaller but

Table 22-5
Distribution of DARP Research Sample by Treatment Type for Patients Grouped by Sex, Age, and Ethnicity

	Percent of Patients by Age at Admission and Ethnic Group																			
	Black				*Puerto Rican*				*Mexican-American*				*White*				*All Ethnic Groups Combined*[a]			
Type of Treatment	*Under 18*	*18 to 22*	*23 to 30*	*Over 30*	*Under 18*	*18 to 22*	*23 to 30*	*Over 30*	*Under 18*	*18 to 22*	*23 to 30*	*Over 30*	*Under 18*	*18 to 22*	*23 to 30*	*Over 30*	*Under 18*	*18 to 22*	*23 to 30*	*Over 30*
Male																				
MM-CO	1	10	19	24	2	57	66	67	0	5	6	7	0	4	10	13	0	13	21	23
MM-A	12	30	34	43	2	2	3	4	29	50	47	36	2	14	19	25	5	20	27	36
TC-T	18	10	7	3	29	10	6	6	0	2	1	1	6	14	12	5	10	11	8	3
TC-M	3	3	2	4	10	11	5	2	8	2	2	2	6	10	8	4	6	7	4	4
TC-ST	4	3	2	2	0	0	0	0	8	7	2	1	5	6	4	4	4	4	2	2
DF-CO	21	7	4	2	43	8	4	4	16	2	0	0	58	19	7	4	47	12	4	2
DF-A	14	8	7	5	3	1	2	1	23	12	11	10	19	13	12	12	17	10	8	7
DT-IP	6	7	6	5	4	4	4	6	6	12	25	36	2	7	10	21	4	7	9	12
DT-OP	21	22	19	12	7	7	10	10	10	8	6	7	2	13	18	12	7	16	17	11
No. of Patients	456	2,716	3,471	2,800	136	877	883	372	51	332	765	805	1,279	2,850	1,942	600	1,951	6,855	7,139	4,618
Female																				
MM-CO	3	16	21	23	0	48	55	52	0	8	7	7	0	5	13	10	1	13	20	20
MM-A	6	29	36	41	0	4	3	6	25	36	40	31	1	14	17	20	2	20	28	34
TC-T	24	9	4	1	48	30	12	12	2	2	1	0	8	11	9	5	12	11	6	2
TC-M	5	2	3	4	1	1	1	0	0	3	1	1	7	9	8	8	6	5	4	5
TC-ST	2	3	2	3	0	0	1	4	10	9	2	1	4	8	5	3	4	5	3	3
DF-CO	29	5	3	2	47	4	3	4	5	2	0	0	61	15	7	6	55	9	4	2
DF-A	15	8	6	5	1	2	4	2	44	13	12	17	15	14	16	18	15	11	9	9
DT-IP	4	9	8	7	1	4	8	4	7	19	29	33	2	9	12	21	2	10	11	12
DT-OP	12	19	17	14	2	7	13	16	7	8	8	10	2	15	13	9	3	16	15	13
No. of Patients	155	983	1,189	715	71	165	151	50	41	103	157	72	979	1,116	617	238	1,263	2,399	2,150	1,085

Males and Females Combined

MM-CO	1	12	20	24	2	56	65	65	0	5	6	7	0	4	11	12	0	13	21	23
MM-A	10	29	34	42	2	2	3	4	27	47	46	36	1	14	18	24	4	20	28	36
TC-T	19	9	6	3	35	13	7	7	1	2	1	1	7	13	12	5	11	11	7	3
TC-M	4	3	2	5	7	9	4	2	4	2	2	2	7	9	8	5	6	7	4	4
TC-ST	4	3	2	2	0	0	0	1	9	8	2	2	5	6	4	4	4	4	3	2
DF-CO	23	6	4	2	44	7	4	3	11	2	0	0	59	18	7	4	50	11	4	2
DF-A	15	8	6	5	2	2	2	1	33	12	11	10	17	14	13	14	16	10	8	7
DT-IP	5	8	7	5	3	4	4	6	6	14	25	35	2	8	10	21	3	8	9	12
DT-OP	19	22	19	12	5	7	11	11	9	8	7	7	2	14	17	11	6	16	16	11
No. of Patients	611	3,699	4,660	3,515	207	1,042	1,034	422	92	435	922	877	2,258	3,966	2,559	838	3,214	9,254	9,289	5,703

Source: Simpson et al. 1976, Table 6.A2.

[a]Also includes "other" ethnic groups.

Table 22-6
Treatment Disposition of DARP Research Sample 1 Year after Admission and Days in Treatment for Terminees (Patients Grouped by Treatment Classification)

	Percent of Patients by Treatment Type									
	MM-CO	*MM-A*	*TC-T*	*TC-M*	*TC-ST*	*DF-CO*	*DF-A*	*DT-IP*	*DT-OP*	*Total*
Treatment Disposition 1 Year after Admission										
Terminated										
Deceased	1	1	0	0	0	0	0	0	1	1
Jailed	4	4	2	1	2	1	3	2	4	3
Hospitalized	0	0	0	1	1	0	0	1	1	0
Expelled	10	5	4	9	6	5	7	4	5	6
Quit	22	32	68	50	64	50	59	57	71	47
Other	2	0	0	0	0	1	1	0	0	1
Referred	3	5	3	5	3	14	3	2	1	4
Completed	1	5	2	15	15	18	19	34	16	12
Still in treatment	57	48	21	19	9	11	8	0	1	26
No. of Patients	4,451	6,572	2,221	1,393	891	3,185	2,600	2,354	3,793	27,460
Days in Treatment for Patients Terminating within 1 Year after Admission										
1 to 15 days	2	7	25	16	23	16	5	58	20	18
16 to 30 days	2	8	11	11	8	15	7	6	15	10
31 to 60 days	7	12	15	20	14	18	19	18	22	16
61 to 90 days	9	12	11	14	12	14	17	11	22	14
91 to 120 days	12	10	8	8	9	10	15	4	9	10
121 to 180 days	20	18	14	13	16	11	20	2	8	13
181 to 240 days	18	13	7	9	9	8	9	1	3	9
241 to 300 days	16	12	5	5	6	5	5	0	1	6
301 to 365 days	14	8	4	4	3	3	3	0	0	4
No. of Patients	1,698	2,769	1,656	854	655	1,828	1,827	1,507	3,095	15,892

Source: Simpson et al. 1976, Table 7.D1.

Table 22-7
Numbers of Admissions and Percentages of Patients in DARP Research Sample Terminated within 1 Year after Admission (Patients Grouped by Treatment Classification, Sex, Age, Ethnicity, and Pretreatment Drug Use)

	Type of Treatment Classification																	
	MM-CO		*MM-A*		*TC-T*		*TC-M*		*TC-ST*		*DF-CO*		*DF-A*		*DT-IP*		*DT-OP*	
	No. Adm.	*% Term.*	*No. Adm.*	*% Term.*	*No. Adm.*	*% Term.*	*No. Adm.*	*% Term.*	*No. Adm.*	*% Term.*	*No. Adm.*	*% Term.*	*No. Adm.*	*% Term.*	*No. Adm.*	*% Term.*	*No. Adm.*	*% Term.*
Sex																		
Male	3,486	41	5,086	43	1,659	74	1,049	60	618	73	2,155	60	1,844	72	1,748	64	2,918	82
Female	965	42	1,486	43	562	78	344	66	273	74	1,030	51	756	67	606	63	875	82
Age																		
Under 18	12	75	115	62	352	70	188	69	140	76	1,607	47	521	57	96	51	183	76
18 to 20	465	40	869	48	620	75	360	64	237	76	706	65	541	72	348	57	741	81
21 to 22	758	41	1,010	45	417	75	236	65	153	76	339	68	378	80	351	65	725	82
23 to 25	934	45	1,176	45	420	77	226	55	121	80	259	73	420	75	412	67	866	84
26 to 30	1,002	41	1,368	43	247	78	154	62	110	72	145	76	347	80	448	69	634	81
31 to 40	912	38	1,472	41	115	74	174	54	93	62	94	77	275	68	523	66	508	82
Over 40	368	41	562	33	50	80	55	55	37	49	35	54	118	55	176	56	136	74
Ethnic Group																		
Black	2,180	41	4,225	44	834	72	401	58	298	72	627	77	877	77	815	64	2,228	81
Puerto Rican	1,531	37	72	35	310	75	164	62	9	78	223	87	44	73	110	63	242	89
Mex.-American	140	67	965	45	23	96	46	41	74	77	22	64	274	63	614	70	168	64
White	548	44	1,245	42	1,020	76	772	65	494	75	2,268	49	1,363	68	789	60	1,122	83
Other	52	42	65	46	34	74	10	50	16	69	45	51	42	62	26	54	33	85
Pretreatment Drug Use																		
Da Op only	1,945	41	3,035	43	526	75	313	61	185	76	365	87	647	78	1,337	67	1,631	82
Da Op+NonOp	2,242	41	3,140	44	953	74	572	61	277	75	366	77	647	79	649	62	1,800	82
<Da Op+NonOp	214	44	297	42	473	74	258	62	179	74	548	59	429	70	118	61	198	84
NonOp only	50	36	100	39	269	77	250	65	250	70	1,906	48	877	58	250	56	164	72

Source: Simpson et al. 1976, table 7.D2.

statistically significant improvements on other criteria as well (productive activities, employment, beer and wine consumption). Overall, the MM treatments showed more effects than other types, particularly no opioid use and criminality. Sex differences were noted on pretreatment mean scores on some variables, but these were slight, and for the most part the changes observed during treatment were comparable for male and female patients.

In all treatments it was noteworthy that most changes observed occurred early, within the first 2 months of admission; only productive activities and employment, which changed minimally and typically only in MM treatments, registered change later. In addition to the initial change from pretreatment levels, further changes throughout the first year of treatment were found on productive activities, employment, opioid use, and criminality. Patient groups that remained in treatment longer improved more than short-term patients on these outcomes.

Ethnic group differences were also striking. Overall, whites had the most favorable mean pretreatment, during treatment, and change scores; blacks had the most unfavorable mean scores; and Puerto Ricans and Mexican-Americans were in between.

The age differences found were complex in that they varied among performance measures. Within age groups there were no remarkable sex differences, but there were differences between age groups on productive activities, opioid use, nonopioid use, beer consumption, and criminality. The cohort 3 research sample included a substantially increased proportion of youths compared with the previous cohorts. Among the under 18 group in this cohort, there was a substantial number of beer drinkers; this group had the highest scores (both at admission and during treatment) on nonopioid use, included a relatively large number still attending school, and had the lowest scores on the criminality indicators. The older groups (26 to 30 and over 30) were most deviant at admission on opioid use and criminality but showed the largest decreases during treatment; the over 30 group was the highest on wine drinking both before and during treatment.

In relation to pretreatment drug-use pattern, when the daily heroin and other opioid users were compared with the primarily nonopioid users, the latter were found to be disproportionately young and white, and the differences found at admission and during treatment reflected the fact that daily opioid users tended to be older and black and were typically in MM treatment, while the nonopioid users tended to be younger and white and typically in DF treatments.

The gross changes just discussed served the purpose of illuminating the mean levels of deviance at which the research sample entered treatment and the average amounts of change that occurred during treatment within the first year following admission. However, every group and subgroup was differentially composed of varying numbers of patients with respect to sex, age, race/ethnic group, and drug-use pattern at admission, and neither these factors nor individual background profiles were controlled in these initial comparisons. Since the various groups were not comparable and the effects of their varying compositions could not be discerned, these analyses were mainly of descriptive interest.

A series of differential analyses was carried out, addressed to questions not answered in the gross analyses. These involved analyses of variance and covariance using linear model multiple regression procedures. Specifically, they focused on the effects of pretreatment baseline levels, sex, race/ethnic group, age, drug-use pattern, treatment type, and time in treatment, as well as the effects of certain interactions among these factors, on during-treatment outcomes for each criterion separately. These analyses were computed for outpatient treatments only since it was considered inappropriate to apply them to residential (TC) or inpatient (DT-IP) treatments in which treatment effects were confounded with the effects of isolation from community exposure. Five sets of analyses were completed; for females in MM, males in MM, females in DF, males in DF, and males in DT-OP. The objective of the analyses performed was to isolate the effects of treatment per se from those accounted for by the other factors which were known to be associated with differences in life situations, lifestyles, motivations for treatment, and potential for change during treatment. The emphasis was on identification of significant differences among subgroups defined by the factors mentioned. Where significant differences were found in the amount of change occurring among subgroups defined by a factor (for example, between older and younger patients), this was interpreted as evidence of differential influence of that factor on treatment outcomes. Findings of no significant differences were interpreted as indicating that the respective factors did not contribute differentially to treatment outcome at whatever level of change was observed.

The differential analyses revealed that the large general reduction of opioid use appears to be generalizable in drug-abuse treatment regardless of patient type, modality, or treatment type. This was most apparent in MM, where only time in treatment accounted for any substantial portion of the criterion variance of opioid use, but also in DF, where the baseline level accounted for 26 percent of the criterion variance for females and 21 percent for males. A similar conclusion appears warranted for nonopioid use, although it is noteworthy that opioid use was more salient to MM and DT treatments, where patients were predominantly opioid addicts, whereas nonopioid use was more central to the DF treatments, where patients included significant proportions of nonopioid users as well as opioid addicts.

Time in treatment was a differential factor of major importance in every treatment, particularly with respect to productive activities, employment, and opioid use. Patients who remained in treatment longer generally showed greater improvement on these criteria than shorter-term patients and showed similar results occasionally on other criteria as well. The differences associated with time in treatment were unrelated to pretreatment levels and therefore suggest significant treatment effects. It was also suggested that taking into consideration the differential retention rates of MM, DF, and DT treatments previously discussed, patients in DF and DT who remained in treatment over 6 months showed as much improvement as patients in MM who remained that length of time, even though the average improvement in DF for all patients was lower than that of patients in MM, whose overall tenure was considerably longer.

The gross results indicated quite clearly that, with the exception of productive activities and employment, on which improvement occurred somewhat later, the major improvements obtained during treatment occurred during the first bimonthly report period and were reflected on the first status evaluation record. The analysis of time in treatment revealed further that improvements on opioid use increased throughout the period of treatment. Improvement on productive activities and employment, which generally appeared not before 3 to 4 months after admission, also tended to continue over the entire period that patients remained in treatment. This finding is of major importance since it points to what appears to be a valid therapeutic effect. The widespread early reduction on opiate use, on the other hand, could be interpreted as compliance with agency surveillance.

Retention of Youths in DARP Treatments

This section presents data on time in treatment and type of treatment termination for the DARP black and white youth sample (n = 5,045) in relation to MM, TC, DF, and DT treatments. Particular attention has been given to the comparisons judged to be of most importance as a result of research discussed earlier. These include (1) comparisons of the youth sample with the total DARP research sample (in which the youths are included);[1] (2) comparisons of blacks under 18 with whites under 18, blacks 18 to 19 with whites 18 to 19, and blacks in both age groups with whites in both age groups; (3) comparisons of younger with older patients within ethnic groups and combining ethnic groups; and (4) comparisons across modalities by age and ethnic group breakdowns.

Time in Treatment

The length of time in DARP treatment (by days) is presented for each modality in table 22-8 for the youth sample (including age by ethnic group breakdowns) and the total DARP research sample. Days in treatment are shown without reference to reason for termination.

Comparison of Youth Sample with Total DARP Research Sample. To aid in the comparisons of the youth sample with the total research sample, rough estimates of *median days in treatment* were calculated for each treatment modality and are shown below:

	MM	*TC*	*DF*	*DT*
Youth sample	267	96	117	39
Total research sample	380	90	108	34

These data illustrate the tendency for the youth sample to have a much shorter tenure in MM than that observed for the total research sample (due particularly to the longer tenure for older patients) and a somewhat longer tenure in the TC, DF, and DT treatments. In DT, the longer tenure of the youth sample primarily reflects the fact that a higher proportion of youths were in outpatient DT (generally having longer tenure) than in inpatient DT.

The same trends are observed in comparisons of the percentages of each sample that remained in treatment *over 60 days.* These data are shown below:

	MM	*TC*	*DF*	*DT*
Youth sample	87%	61%	75%	36%
Total research sample	91%	61%	70%	31%

Although the median days in MM treatment figure was much lower for the youth sample than for the total research sample, this difference is much less marked when one considers only retention rates for over 60 days (87 versus 91 percent). Thus the youths had lower overall tenure in MM than the total sample. As can be seen in table 22-8, this reflected higher rates of termination among youths throughout the first year after DARP admission. The over-60-day retention rate in TC was the same for the youth sample and total sample (61 percent) but was slightly higher for youths in DF (75 versus 70 percent) and DT (36 versus 31 percent).

Comparisons of Age by Ethnic Group Breakdowns within Modalities. A summary of retention data for the black and white under 18 and 18 to 19 age groups in MM is as follows:

Days in DARP MM	*Black, under 18*	*Black, 18 to 19*	*White, under 18*	*White, 18 to 19*
Over 60 days	84%	87%	93%	86%
Over 240 days	42%	57%	45%	52%
Over 360 days	32%	41%	15%	41%

The principal group variation within MM reflects age differences, with the 18-19-year-olds generally showing greater retention rates than those under 18 (the

Table 22-8
Percentage Distributions of Days in Treatment for Black and White Youths under 18 and 18 to 19, Total Youth Sample and Total DARP Research Sample, by DARP Treatment Modality

	Percent by Days in DARP Treatment						
Sample	*1 to 30*	*31 to 60*	*61 to 120*	*121 to 240*	*241 to 360*	*Over 360*	*Number in Group*
Methadone Maintenance							
Black:							
<18	10	6	9	33	10	32	69
18-19	6	6	10	21	16	41	329
White:							
<18	7	0	30	19	30	15	27
18-19	7	7	16	18	11	41	191
Youth total	7	6	13	21	14	39	616
DARP total	4	5	10	17	12	52	11,023
Therapeutic Community							
Black:							
<18	27	11	17	15	11	19	162
18-19	24	13	17	15	7	24	194
White:							
<18	21	13	22	22	7	16	403
18-19	30	14	18	16	9	14	463
Youth total	26	13	19	18	8	17	1,222
DARP total	25	14	17	18	8	18	4,505
Outpatient Drug Free							
Black:							
<18	21	18	22	20	11	9	233
18-19	29	16	21	19	9	6	181
White:							
<18	9	12	27	34	9	10	1,731
18-19	11	15	26	28	11	10	600
Youth total	12	13	26	30	10	9	2,745
DARP total	15	15	25	27	9	9	5,785
Detoxification							
Black:							
<18	37	19	37	4	3	0	147
18-19	47	20	24	7	2	0	328
White:							
<18	52	15	23	9	1	0	97
18-19	41	24	27	7	1	0	250
Youth total	44	21	27	7	1	0	822
DARP total	48	21	23	8	1	0	6,147

white, under 18 group was too small to reflect reliable trends since it included only twenty-seven patients).

A summary of retention data for TC, including the percentages of each group in treatment over 60, over 120, and over 240 days, is presented below:

Days in DARP TC	*Black, under 18*	*Black, 18 to 19*	*White, under 18*	*White, 18 to 19*
Over 60 days	62%	63%	66%	56%
Over 120 days	45%	46%	45%	39%
Over 240 days	30%	31%	22%	23%

Age differences associated with retention rates in TC were typically small, but there was a tendency within both age groups for blacks to have higher rates (particularly for over 240 days in treatment) than whites.

Retention in rates in DF are summarized next, including the same categories used earlier to report MM and TC:

Days in DARP DF	*Black, under 18*	*Black, 18 to 19*	*White, under 18*	*White, 18 to 19*
Over 60 days	62%	55%	79%	73%
Over 120 days	40%	34%	53%	49%
Over 240 days	20%	15%	18%	20%

The data for retention in DF indicate that among blacks and whites, the under 18 age group tended to remain in treatment somewhat longer than the 18 to 19 age group. Even more striking, however, was the trend for whites to show better retention than blacks; this trend was the opposite of that observed for TC treatments. These trends observed in DF were most notable in the retention rates of the over 60 and over 120 days in treatment.

The following summary presents selected retention rates for DT. Because of the short-term nature of this treatment, rates are shown only for over 30 and over 60 days in treatment:

Days in DARP DT	*Black, under 18*	*Black, 18 to 19*	*White, under 18*	*White, 18 to 19*
Over 30 days	63%	53%	48%	59%
Over 60 days	44%	33%	33%	35%

For DT, the data show no consistent age or ethnic group trends. The highest retention rate was for blacks under 18, and the next highest was for whites 18 to 19.

Comparisons of Age by Ethnic Group Breakdowns across Modalities. The overall retention rates for the DARP treatment modalities were highest for MM and lowest for DT; DF and TC were intermediate, with DF slightly higher than TC. The relative differences in these retention rates, however, reflect variations in the intended durations of the treatment modalities. Age and ethnic group comparisons across modalities, therefore, should be considered in light of these variations.

Several suggestive trends among age and ethnic group combinations were previously noted concerning retention rates in the four separate treatment modalities, even though the percentage differences were not always striking. To examine the statistical significance of these differences, days in treatment in MM, TC, DF, and DT were analyzed by analysis of variance. For each modality, the measure of days in treatment (scaled to a 5-point ordinal scale) was analyzed with respect to age (under 18 versus 18 to 19), ethnic group (black versus white), and sex (male versus female). Using the .01 confidence level, the only statistically significant difference in retention rates was observed in DF. This involved the ethnic group differences emphasized previously, showing whites to have higher retention than blacks in DF [$F\ (1{,}2737) = 28.33, p < .001$]. The other trends already pointed out for each treatment modality were significant at or near the .05 level of confidence. Retention in treatment was not previously presented with regard to sex, but it may be noted that in these analyses, males in MM and TC had slightly higher retention rates than females ($p < .05$). No interactions were statistically significant.

The conclusions based on comparisons across modalities which appear to be warranted are (1) the under 18 group had better retention than the 18 to 19 group in DF but poorer retention in MM, and (2) whites had better retention than blacks in DF but poorer retention than blacks in TC.

Termination from Treatment

Table 22-9 shows the final DARP treatment disposition or type of termination for younger and older black and white youth groups in each treatment modality. The categories of final treatment disposition include Terminated-Expelled, Terminated-Quit, Terminated-Other (deceased, extended hospitalization, extended jail sentence, etc.), Referred (to other programs), Completed Treatment, and Still in Treatment at the time the DARP was discontinued (each of these patients had at least 1 full year in DARP treatment). Comparative percentages for blacks and whites and for all patients in each modality, including those over 19 years of age, are given for the total DARP research sample.

Comparison of Youth Sample with Total DARP Research Sample. The major categories of interest in table 22-9 involve Completed Treatment (as defined by individual treatment programs) and Terminated-Quit, since these were generally the most prevalent reasons reported for leaving treatment and have special interpretative significance. Summary data representing percentages reported as having completed DARP treatment are as follows:

Completed Treatment	*MM*	*TC*	*DF*	*DT*
Youth sample	14%	15%	27%	25%
Total research sample	7%	16%	22%	23%

These data suggest that the youth sample generally realized more successful treatment outcomes (defined by completions) in MM and DF compared with the total research sample; differences were minimal for TC and DT.

Summary data showing the percentages that quit treatment are presented below:

Terminated-Quit	*MM*	*TC*	*DF*	*DT*
Youth sample	49%	67%	48%	63%
Total research sample	41%	65%	56%	66%

These data are generally consistent with the previous tabulations for treatment completions; the differences were very small in TC and DT, but the youth sample in DF included a substantially lower percentage of people who quit (along with more who completed, as noted before) than found in the total research sample. In MM, however, an interesting and seemingly contradictory finding is observed, in which the youth sample showed a higher percentage of "quitters" than in the total sample and also a higher percentage of completions. It is important to note that this is related in part to the size of another category, Still in Treatment (that is, in 1974 when the DARP was discontinued); 21 percent of the total research sample was in this category, compared with only 12 percent of the youth sample. Taking into account the shorter retention rates among the youth sample in MM (discussed previously) and their higher completion rates, it appears that those younger DARP patients who were discharged as having completed MM treatment tended to do so in shorter time than older patients. The data available at the time of this analysis did not provide information on what the eventual treatment disposition was for people still in DARP during the last report period, but the completion rates in both samples would probably have increased since those individuals all already had at least 1 full year in treatment.

Comparisons of Age by Ethnic Group Breakdown within Modalities. Table 22-9 shows that age-related differences in treatment disposition in MM were small and inconsistent; but as noted previously, there were relatively few under-18-year-olds included in this treatment. As a group, blacks in MM tended to have a higher proportion of treatment terminations by quitting, and whites had a higher rate of treatment expulsions. Quitting was also slightly more frequent among blacks in TC than among whites, and whites showed higher completion rates.

Table 22-9
Percentage Distributions of Final DARP Treatment Disposition for Black and White Youths under 18 and 18 to 19, Total Youth Sample and Total DARP Research Sample, by DARP Treatment Modality

	Percent by Final DARP Treatment Disposition						
Sample	*Term.: Expel.*	*Term.: Quit*	*Term.: Other*	*Referred*	*Complete*	*Still in Treatment*	*Number in Group*
Methadone Maintenance							
Black:							
<18	6	59	7	6	16	6	69
<18-19	8	48	9	8	14	13	329
White:							
<18	15	44	7	4	19	11	27
18-19	12	44	10	8	13	13	191
Youth total	9	49	9	7	14	12	616
DARP total	10	41	11	10	7	21	11,023
Therapeutic Community							
Black:							
<18	4	74	2	8	8	4	162
18-19	6	71	1	4	13	5	194
White:							
<18	6	65	2	7	17	3	403
18-19	8	66	1	4	19	2	463
Youth total	6	67	2	6	15	4	1,222
DARP total	7	65	3	5	16	4	4,505
Outpatient Drug Free							
Black:							
<18	7	58	4	8	19	4	233
18-19	10	65	7	3	13	2	181
White:							
<18	3	43	1	18	30	5	1,731
18-19	6	53	4	9	24	4	600
Youth total	5	48	2	14	27	4	2,745
DARP total	6	56	3	9	22	4	5,785
Detoxification							
Black:							
<18	6	65	4	2	23	0	147
18-19	3	65	5	3	24	0	328
White:							
<18	5	51	4	1	39	0	97
18-19	5	65	3	3	24	0	250
Youth total	5	63	4	3	25	0	822
DARP total	5	66	4	2	23	0	6,147

Age-related and ethnic group differences both stand out in the treatment disposition tabulations for DF. Blacks had higher rates of unfavorable termination (that is, quitting, expulsion, and other) and lower rates of treatment completion or referral than did whites. Within each ethnic group, the under-18-year-olds had more favorable outcomes, compared with the 18- to 19-year-olds, the under 18 group had lower rates for unfavorable terminations (particularly quitting) and higher rates of referral and treatment completion. For DT, few differences were observed among the groups, although the white, under 18 group had a higher rate of completion and a lower rate of quitting than other groups.

Comparisons of Age by Ethnic Group Breakdowns across Modalities. Final DARP treatment dispositions were substantially different across treatment modalities, especially with regard to the cteagories of completing and quitting treatment. Rates of completion were highest in DF and DT treatments and lowest in the longer-term MM. Rates of quitting were highest in TC and DT, and lower in DF and MM.

Comparisons across these modalities for age and ethnic groups indicate that e principal treatment in which clear age or ethnic group advantages recurred was DF. Whites had more favorable treatment disposition outcomes than blacks (fewer terminations and more completions), and the younger age groups within both blacks and white groups also had more favorable outcomes. Group differences within other modalities were much smaller than in DF.

Posttreatment Follow-up of DARP Youths

In 1975, field work was initiated to obtain posttreatment follow-up data on a sample of cohort 1 (1969-1971) admissions and later that year on a cohort 2 sample (1971-1972 admissions). These samples were designed carefully to represent the ethnic group times age times sex times treatment times time-in-treatment times agency subgroups that comprised substantial components of the respective cohort populations; youths were included as part of the implementation of the design. Although a sample designed to be representative of all youths in the DARP was not investigated, there were completed interviews on 587 black and white youths aged 19 and under, and these were used as a basis for the present study. The following tabulations show their distribution by age and race/ethnic group:

Age	*Black*	*White*	*Total*
Under 18	78	164	242
18 to 19	143	202	345
Total	221	366	587

This youth follow-up sample represents 21 percent of the interviewed sample for cohorts 1 and 2. (The composition of the total follow-up sample is presented in table 22-10, showing the black and white components and the numbers on which interviews were completed.) It will be noted that blacks and whites represented approximately 90 percent of the total sample in each cohort and that the percentages of blacks and whites for whom interviews were

Table 22-10
Blacks and Whites in DARP Cohort 1 and Cohort 2 Follow-up Samples

	Cohort 1	*Cohort 2*	*Total*
Number in total sample	1,853	2,254	4,107
Number interviewed	1,409	1,722	3,131
Percent interviewed	76%	76%	76%
Number of blacks in sample	881	948	1,829
Number of whites in sample	777	1,089	1,866
Subtotal	1,658	2,037	3,695
Percentage of total sample	89%	90%	90%
Number of blacks interviewed	668	723	1,391
Number of whites interviewed	586	824	1,410
Subtotal	1,254	1,547	2,801
Percentage of Total	76%	76%	76%

completed (76 percent) were identical in both cohorts. The total location rate for the follow-up samples was 87 percent, including 11 percent who were located but not interviewed, classified as deceased, out of the country, or who refused to participate. Thirteen percent of the total sample could not be located within the time available.

The results presented in this section involve comparisons of baseline measures representing, except where noted otherwise, the 2-month period immediately preceding admission. The data reported here afford only a partial, descriptive picture of the outcomes at two points in time, pre-DARP baseline and post-DARP at interview (representing the 2-month period before the follow-up interview). The follow-up interview occurred between 4 and 6 years after DARP admission, depending on actual dates of admission and interview. For the present study it was not possible to utilize additional post-DARP information covering month-by-month data on the separate criterion items or to utilize a composite criterion profile developed for the DARP follow-up studies. These were not available at the time that the present tabulations were prepared. In addition, variations in criterion scores attributable to baseline, background, and demographic variables are presented only by comparison of subgroups formed by partition of the sample on several critical variables. The full DARP follow-up study, currently in progress, will analyze quantitatively the contributions of these and other variables to various outcome indexes in order to isolate effects attributable to treatment from those accounted for by other factors. Nevertheless, the descriptive results on the youth sample presented later are of much interest and afford insights into the effects of DARP treatments for youths that have not been available previously.

The data presented in this section consist of two tables of gross results, showing breakdowns of age by race/ethnic groups and treatment groups, and of five additional tables of results for each treatment group separately by race/

ethnic group (black versus white) and age (under 18 versus 18 to 19) divisions. In these treatment group tables, the numbers available were too few to permit cross-tabulation of race/ethnic group and age. The tables included in the text present mean scores converted to a uniform scale of 0 to 100 for each criterion variable. These were first computed from index numbers representing the various criteria on ordinal scales, as explained in the definitions that follow, and then converted to a common scale.

Comparison tables, showing percentage distributions for each level of the criteria for each subgroup, are included in appendix 22A. It will be seen that the tables of means reflect the information in the tables of distributions in appendix 22A quite accurately and facilitate rapid inspection of the data. All scores are based on scales on which the *high extreme is deviant* and the *low extreme is favorable.* Hence negative differences imply improvement, and positive differences indicate outcome changes in an unfavorable direction.

The specific criterion measures selected, with the exception of the last two discussed below, are comparable in respect to the time periods covered. Definitions of these measures, the scales used, and the periods of reference are as follows:

Opioid Use. Frequency of use of heroin or other illicit opioid drugs during the 2-month period (preceding admission to DARP treatment or preceding the follow-up interview), scaled 1, none; 2, less than weekly; 3, weekly; and 4, daily.

Nonopioid Use. Frequency of use of cocaine, sedatives, stimulants, psychedelics, and other illicit drugs except marihuana, with same scale and same reference periods.

Marihuana Use. Frequency of use of marihuana, with same scale and same reference periods.

Alcohol Problems. Dichotomous variable indicating presence or absence of a major problem involving excessive use of alcohol that interfered with work, family, health, or other life situation; scaled 1, no; 2, yes, with same reference periods.

Alcohol Use. Frequency of use of alcohol; scaled in terms of ounces of 80-proof equivalent: 1, none to 4.0; 2, 4.1 to 8.0; and 3, over 8.0; with same reference periods.

Employment. Number of days worked full- or part-time on legitimate jobs; scaled 1, 40 to 60; 2, 30 to 39; 3, 20 to 29; 4, 10 to 19; 5, 1 to 9; and 6, none, with same reference periods.

Productive Activities. Dichotomous variable indicating active participation or nonparticipation in productive role activities, such as legitimate jobs, homemaking, or school attendance, during the reference period. This variable was constructed to compensate for the unfairness of employment in relation to females and youths for whom the base rates are significantly lower than for adult males; scaled 1, yes; 2, no, with same reference periods.

Illegal Support. Dichotomous variable included in criminality criterion cluster, indicating whether the individual received major or secondary support from illegal activities; scaled 1, no; 2, yes, with same reference periods.

Arrests. Dichotomous variable included in criminality criterion cluster, indicating whether the individual was arrested by law enforcement personnel one or more times during the reference period. *Arrests* were defined to include times picked up as well as times booked on a charge; scaled l, no; 2, yes; pre-DARP figures represent lifetime data (that is, all arrests at any time prior to admission), while at-interview arrests refer to the 2-month period preceding the interview.

Treatments. Dichotomous variable indicating whether the individual had or had not been in treatment for drug abuse prior to DARP (at any time) or during the 2-month period preceding the follow-up interview; scaled l, no; 2, yes. Difference scores are not warranted and were not included in the tables; however, in the present setting, post-DARP treatment is considered to be a negative outcome.

It should be noted that the means for *dichotomous variables* can be read as percentages. For example, if a group mean for Alcohol Problems is 11, this implies that 11 percent of the group had alcohol problems during the reference period.

Gross Results for the Youth Follow-up Subsample

Tables 22-11 and 22-12 (and Appendix 22A tables 22A-1 and 22A-2) show pre-DARP and at-interview data on the ten criterion variables, just defined for the total youth subsample included in the DARP cohort 1 and cohort 2 follow-up studies. In table 22-11 (and table 22A-1), the sample is divided into four race/ethnic groups by age, regardless of DARP treatment, and in table 22-12 (and table 22A-2), the sample is divided into five treatment groups (four DARP treatments and the comparison group), regardless of race/ethnic group or age. The group sizes in table 22-11 are all relatively large (n = 78 to 202); those in table 22-12 are substantial for MM, TC, and DF but small for DT (n = 34) and IO (n = 38). Interpretations based on the small DT and IO groups must be considered cautiously.

Table 22-12
Adjusted Means (to Scale of 0 to 100) of Five Treatment Groups on Ten Criteria within the Youth Sample at Pre-DARP and At Interview and Mean Differences

	MM (*n = 119*)			*TC* (*n = 238*)			*DF* (*n = 158*)			*DT* (*n = 34*)			*IO* (*n = 38*)		
Criterion Measure	*Pre-DARP*	*At Int.*	*Mean Diff.*	*Pre-DARP*	*At Int.*	*Mean Diff.*	*Pre-DARP*	*At Int.*	*Mean Diff.*	*Pre-DARP*	*At Int.*	*Mean Diff.*	*Pre-DARP*	*At Int.*	*Mean Diff.*
Opioid use	90	20	−70	63	03	−60	40	10	−30	70	17	−53	73	17	−56
Nonopioid use	33	20	−13	40	10	−30	40	13	−27	40	27	−13	27	27	0
Marihuana use	30	47	+17	37	47	+10	47	43	−04	37	47	+10	53	57	+04
Alcohol problems	02	02	0	10	06	−04	06	06	0	12	06	−06	08	11	+3
Alcohol use oz. 80 proof equiv.	15	25	+10	20	20	0	20	15	−05	15	35	+20	15	25	+10
Employment	68	60	−08	80	38	−42	78	44	−34	80	54	−26	70	60	−10
Productive activities	55	34	−21	64	21	−43	44	17	−27	53	28	−25	61	29	−32
Illegal support	55	21	−34	44	17	−27	22	19	−03	33	22	−11	51	46	−05
Arrests	77	25	−52	82	27	−55	61	20	−41	69	26	−43	81	37	−44
No. of treatments[a]	35	33	–	48	16	–	29	10	–	22	26	–	42	38	–

[a]Mean differences were not computed for number of treatments.

Table 22-11
Adjusted Means (to Scale of 0 to 100) of Four Race/Ethnic Groups by Age on Ten Criteria at Pre-DARP and At Interview and Mean Differences

	Black, under 18 (n = 78)			*White, under 18 (n = 164)*			*Black, 18 to 19 (n = 143)*			*White, 18 to 19 (n = 202)*		
Criterion Measure	*Pre-DARP*	*At Int.*	*Mean Diff.*	*Pre-DARP*	*At Int.*	*Mean Diff.*	*Pre-DARP*	*At Int.*	*Mean Diff.*	*Pre-DARP*	*At Int.*	*Mean Diff.*
Opioid use	70	13	–57	40	10	–30	80	13	–67	70	07	–63
Nonopioid use	27	13	–14	50	17	–33	27	17	–10	43	13	–30
Marihuana use	30	57	+27	53	50	–03	33	47	+14	47	40	–07
Alcohol problems	0	10	+10	10	0	–10	10	10	0	10	0	–10
Alcohol use oz. 80 proof equiv.	20	15	–05	20	20	0	05	20	+15	20	15	–05
Employment	80	54	–26	80	46	–24	76	56	–20	72	38	–34
Productive activities	53	33	–20	48	16	–32	68	35	–33	55	20	–35
Illegal support	36	25	–11	29	23	–06	40	22	–18	50	17	–33
Arrests	75	37	–38	62	23	–39	82	31	–51	79	18	–61
Other treatment episodes[a]	26	22	–	38	11	–	29	24	–	50	20	–

[a]Mean differences were not computed for number of treatments.

Comparison of Race/Ethnic Groups by Age. Prior to admission, all four groups compared in table 22-11 showed substantial drug use, unemployment, and criminality. Alcohol use and problems were generally low, and over a fourth of each group reported one or more previous treatments for drug abuse. The young whites (under 18) were lowest on opioid use and highest on nonopioids and marihuana. Both black groups showed an opposite pattern (high on opioids and relatively low on nonopioids and marihuana), while the older whites (18 to 19) tended to be high on all three. The younger whites had the most favorable scores on productive activities (involving school attendance, work, or homemaking), illegal support, arrests, and previous treatments. Overall, the pretreatment criminality indicators were lower for the younger than the older groups and for whites compared with blacks. Some of the differences between age groups can be understood as effects of age; that is, the younger group had less time to develop records of arrests, prior treatment episodes, illegal income sources, and to obtain employment.

The posttreatment results for opioid and nonopioid use were favorable in all four groups, but marihuana use showed no change among whites and an increase among blacks to the same level maintained by the whites. Alcohol use increased slightly among the older blacks only. Employment improved in all four groups, but most among the older whites. Still the level of unemployment was relatively high at the follow-up interview. Criminality declined in all four groups, more among the older groups, but most among the older whites. Finally, the younger whites had fewer post-DARP treatments than the other three groups. Since the proportions of the four race/ethnic groups by age were unequal in the five treatment groups followed, no definitive conclusions can be drawn. However, the impressions obtained from table 22-11 are, first, that favorable changes were obtained in all four groups with regard to reduction of opioid and nonopioid drug use, and second, that favorable but less impressive changes occurred also in employment and reduction of criminality. The increase in marihuana use among blacks brought them up to the level of use by whites. Overall, the greatest change toward favorable outcome occurred among the older whites and the least among the younger blacks.

Comparison of Treatment Groups. A glance at table 22-12 will show that in terms of pretreatment profile on the criteria, the DF group stands apart as dissimilar to the other four groups. It differs from them mainly on opioid use, productive activities, illegal support, and arrests, on which it was lowest. At the same time, this group ranks among the highest on nonopioid and marihuana use. Variations in pretreatment profiles among the other treatment groups were considerably smaller and generally reflect specific variables, such as the high score of the IO group on marihuana use and the extremely high score of the MM group on opioid use.

Although all five groups showed much favorable change from pretreatment to the follow-up interview, particularly on opioid use, variations in the gross results were noteworthy. Overall, the most favorable scores at interview were found for the DF group, with TC second, and the poorest results in the IO group. The results for MM and DT were generally similar and in between those for TC and IO. In the area of drug use, (1) the group with the highest pretreatment opioid use, MM, decreased most on opioid use (although all groups did well on this variable, including the IO group); (2) only IO showed no change on nonopioid use, while TC and DF performed better than MM and DT on this variable; and (3) only DF showed a slight decrease in marihuana use, while the IO group had the highest level of both pretreatment and posttreatment marihuana use. As noted earlier, alcohol use was comparatively low in this sample, but posttreatment increases were found in three groups, MM, DT (the largest), and IO. TC showed no change, while DF was the only group with a small decrease. By contrast, 12 percent of DT, 10 percent of TC, and 8 percent of IO patients had alcohol problems at admission, slightly higher than the 7 percent recorded for the total DARP population. Only the IO group reported an increase in alcohol problems at interview (from 8 to 11 percent). MM and DF, both comparatively low at admission, showed no change, and TC and DT showed noticeable reductions. Overall, the results for employment were poor, but substantial improvements were reported in TC and DF (and to a lesser extent in DT). All groups, including IO, showed meaningful improvements on productive activities and frequency of arrests; and, also all, except IO, improved on illegal support. It is noteworthy that the DF group had fewest members who entered post-DARP treatment, while the IO group had most. In this respect, TC was close to DF, while MM and DT were closer to IO.

The results shown in table 22-12 imply that among the DARP treatments, DF was most effective overall in this youth sample. The small IO group, which was admitted to DARP program but had no DARP treatment, was by comparison the poorest in overall outcomes. However, these data did not take account of differences among the treatment groups with respect to patient characteristics, and they must be regarded as giving only gross indications. More detailed examinations taking into account these characteristics are provided later.

Posttreatment Results for Treatment Subsamples

Separate comparisons for black versus white and for the under 18 versus 18 to 19 subsamples are shown for each of the five treatment groups in tables 22-13 through 22-17 (and Appendix tables 22A-3 through 22A-7). The subgroup sizes exceeded fifty for all subgroups in MM, TC, and DF, except for the under 18 group in MM (n = 27); regrettably the numbers were very small (all less than 25) in DT and IO, but they have been included nevertheless and appear to present a consistent picture.

MM. The MM results are shown in tables 22-13 and 22A-3. Although the results for both the black and white and the younger and older groups were uniformly substantial and favorable on opioid use, even in the small under 18 group (presumably including juvenile heroin addicts), and to a lesser extent on the criminality indicators. They were unfavorable and unimpressive on the other criteria. All groups increased their marihuana use; the younger age group showed an increase in alcohol problems as well as in level of alcohol use, and increase in unemployment and in the percentage not involved in productive activities, and were high in the percentage entering post-DARP treatment. In general, the younger group did most poorly in MM, and whites did more poorly than blacks.

TC. Within the TC modality there were very few black-white or younger-older differences, as indicated in tables 22-14 and 22A-4. Blacks and the younger age group had higher posttreatment marihuana use and increased over pretreatment levels. Blacks also increased from 6 to 9 percent with alcohol problems, and blacks and the older age group increased somewhat their alcohol use. On the other hand, whites and the younger age group had fewer in post-DARP treatment. Overall, however, the results for TC were superior to those for MM, as noted earlier.

DF. It has already been mentioned that DARP youths appeared to have the best outcomes in DF treatments. Within DF, the data in tables 22-15 and 22A-5 indicate that white youths had more favorable outcome profiles at interview (posttreatment) compared with blacks, although both ethnic groups tended to show favorable improvements. No clear differences occurred with respect to age, with outcome profiles at interview fairly similar for both groups.

DT. The small numbers in this modality preclude any definite conclusions (see tables 22-16 and 22A-6). However, it is noteworthy that substantial reductions were reported in all groups on opioid use but not on nonopioid use or marihuana use. Indeed, three of the four DT subgroups increased on marihuana use, and the posttreatment levels on this variable were quite high and second only to those of the IO patients. All DT groups increased their alcohol use somewhat, and the younger age group also reported an increase in alcohol problems (of 17 percent, or 2 people out of twelve). Unemployment and post-DARP treatment were generally high in DT.

IO. The IO sample is also small (see tables 22-17 and 22A-7). As a comparison group that went through intake procedures at admission but did not return for treatment, it nevertheless shows quite substantial improvements on several variables, although not of the order of the major treatment groups previously reviewed. Substantial reductions can be seen on opioid use in all groups and to a

Table 22-13
Adjusted Means (to Scale of 0 to 100) for Black and White Youths under 18 and 18 to 19 in DARP Methadone Maintenance Treatment on Ten Criteria at Pre-DARP and At Interview and Mean Differences

	Ethnic Group						*Age*					
	Black (n = 67)			*White (n = 52)*			*Under 18 (n = 27)*			*18 to 19 (n = 92)*		
Criterion Measure	*Pre-DARP*	*At Int.*	*Mean Diff.*	*Pre-DARP*	*At Int.*	*Mean Diff.*	*Pre-DARP*	*At Int.*	*Mean Diff.*	*Pre-DARP*	*At Int.*	*Mean Diff.*
Opioid use	93	20	–73	87	17	–70	80	20	–60	93	17	–76
Nonopioid use	23	17	–06	43	20	–23	33	17	–16	33	20	–13
Marihuana use	23	47	+24	40	50	+10	33	57	+24	30	47	+17
Alcohol problems	10	0	–10	0	0	0	0	10	+10	0	0	0
Alcohol use oz. 80 proof equiv.	15	15	0	10	25	+15	0	30	+30	20	15	–05
Employment	72	72	0	62	46	–16	60	70	+10	70	54	–14
Productive activities	60	40	–20	50	20	–30	40	50	+10	60	30	–30
Illegal support	40	20	–20	70	30	–40	40	30	–10	60	20	–40
Arrests	70	30	–40	80	20	–60	80	40	–40	80	20	–60
No. of treatments[a]	30	30	–	50	40	–	30	40	–	30	30	–

[a]Mean differences were not computed for number of treatments.

Table 22-14
Adjusted Means (to Scale of 0 to 100) for Black and White Youths under 18 and 18 to 19 in DARP Therapeutic Community Treatment on Ten Criteria at Pre-DARP and at Interview and Mean Differences

	Ethnic Group						*Age*					
	Black (n = 69)			*White (n = 169)*			*Under 18 (n = 102)*			*18 to 19 (n = 136)*		
Criterion Measure	*Pre-DARP*	*At Int.*	*Mean Diff.*	*Pre-DARP*	*At Int.*	*Mean Diff.*	*Pre-DARP*	*At Int.*	*Mean Diff.*	*Pre-DARP*	*At Int.*	*Mean Diff.*
Opioid use	73	0	−73	60	07	−53	57	07	−50	70	03	−67
Nonopioid use	30	07	−23	47	10	−37	47	13	−34	37	10	−27
Marihuana use	37	53	+16	50	43	−07	47	53	+06	47	37	−10
Alcohol problems	06	09	+03	11	05	−06	11	05	−06	09	06	−03
Alcohol use oz. 80 proof equiv.	20	25	+05	20	20	0	25	25	0	15	25	+10
Employment	82	40	−42	52	38	−14	88	42	−46	74	36	−38
Productive activities	72	28	−44	61	19	−42	69	21	−48	61	22	−39
Illegal support	43	19	−24	44	17	−27	39	18	−21	48	16	−32
Arrests	87	39	−48	79	22	−57	76	28	−48	85	26	−59
No. of treatments[a]	41	25	–	52	12	–	46	12	–	50	18	–

[a]Mean differences were not computed for number of treatments.

Table 22-15
Adjusted Means (to Scale of 0 to 100) for Black and White Youths under 18 and 18 to 19 in DARP Outpatient Drug-Free Treatment on Ten Criteria at Pre-DARP and at Interview and Mean Differences

	Ethnic Group						*Age*					
	Black (n = 54)			*White (n = 104)*			*Under 18 (n = 88)*			*18 to 19 (n = 70)*		
Criterion Measure	*Pre-DARP*	*At Int.*	*Mean Diff.*	*Pre-DARP*	*At Int.*	*Mean Diff.*	*Pre-DARP*	*At Int.*	*Mean Diff.*	*Pre-DARP*	*At Int.*	*Mean Diff.*
Opioid use	57	13	−44	30	07	−23	30	10	−20	53	07	−46
Nonopioid use	23	17	−06	47	13	−34	43	17	−26	37	10	−27
Marihuana use	37	53	+16	53	40	−13	47	47	0	47	47	0
Alcohol problems	04	07	+03	08	06	−02	05	06	+01	09	07	−02
Alcohol use oz. 80 proof equiv.	25	10	−15	20	15	−05	20	10	−10	25	15	−10
Employment	84	48	−36	76	42	−34	80	46	−34	78	38	−40
Productive activities	56	30	−26	38	11	−27	32	13	−19	59	23	−36
Illegal support	24	26	+02	20	16	−04	18	20	+02	26	18	−08
Arrests	76	31	−45	53	13	−40	48	22	−26	76	17	−59
No. of treatments[a]	14	19	–	36	06	–	29	08	–	28	13	–

[a]Mean differences were not computed for number of treatments.

Table 22-16
Adjusted Means (to Scale of 0 to 100) for Black and White Youths under 18 and 18 to 19 in DARP Detoxification Treatment on Ten Criteria at Pre-DARP and at Interview and Mean Differences

	Ethnic Group						*Age*					
	Black (n = 12)			*White (n = 22)*			*Under 18 (n = 12)*			*18 to 19 (n = 22)*		
Criterion Measure	*Pre-DARP*	*At Int.*	*Mean Diff.*	*Pre-DARP*	*At Int.*	*Mean Diff.*	*Pre-DARP*	*At Int.*	*Mean Diff.*	*Pre-DARP*	*At Int.*	*Mean Diff.*
Opioid use	80	17	–63	63	13	–50	67	27	–40	70	10	–60
Nonopioid use	27	23	–04	43	27	–16	33	33	0	40	23	–17
Marihuana use	43	63	+20	37	37	0	33	50	+17	40	57	+17
Alcohol problems	17	10	–07	09	05	–04	0	17	+17	14	0	–14
Alcohol use oz. 80 proof equiv.	06	16	+10	04	12	+08	0	16	+16	08	14	+06
Employment	68	50	–18	86	54	–32	70	56	–14	86	52	–34
Productive activities	33	20	–13	64	32	–32	25	25	0	68	30	–38
Illegal support	45	20	–25	27	23	–04	17	42	+25	43	10	–23
Arrests	73	33	–40	67	23	–44	64	25	–39	71	27	–44
No. of treatments[a]	17	25	–	25	27	–	08	42	–	30	18	–

[a]Mean differences were not computed for number of treatments.

Table 22-17
Adjusted Means (to Scale of 0 to 100) for Black and White Youths under 18 and 18 to 19 Who Were Admitted to Treatment in DARP but Never Reported to Any Treatment Session on Ten Criteria at Pre-DARP and at Interview and Mean Differences

	Ethnic Group						*Age*					
	Black (n = 17)			*White (n = 19)*			*Under 18 (n = 13)*			*18 to 19 (n = 23)*		
Criterion Measure	*Pre-DARP*	*At Int.*	*Mean Diff.*	*Pre-DARP*	*At Int.*	*Mean Diff.*	*Pre-DARP*	*At Int.*	*Mean Diff.*	*Pre-DARP*	*At Int.*	*Mean Diff.*
Opioid use	87	27	–60	60	10	–50	73	13	–60	77	17	–60
Nonopioid use	17	37	+20	40	20	–10	23	27	+04	30	27	–03
Marihuana use	30	43	+13	73	67	–06	60	73	+13	47	50	+03
Alcohol problems	0	0	0	16	19	+03	0	11	+11	12	11	–01
Alcohol use oz. 80 proof equiv.	10	25	+15	20	40	+20	20	20	0	15	30	+15
Employment	74	44	–30	68	40	–28	70	46	–24	72	50	–22
Productive activities	68	42	–26	53	19	–34	46	22	–24	68	32	–36
Illegal support	50	58	+08	53	37	–16	54	67	+13	50	37	–13
Arrests	83	42	–41	79	32	–47	77	38	–39	83	36	–47
No. of treatments[a]	29	21	–	53	26	–	15	23	–	56	24	–

[a]Mean differences were not computed for number of treatments.

lesser extent on unemployment, productive activities, and arrests. However, on nonopioid and marihuana use, alcohol use and problems, illegal support, and post-DARP treatment, the results were poor.

Discussion and Conclusions

The DARP treatments were not particularly oriented to youth as a target population, but treated them along with older drug users in the various programs. Youth were disproportionately distributed among the treatments available, as shown in the following comparison.

	MM	*TC*	*DF*	*DT*
Youth sample (*N* = 5,405)	12%	22%	51%	15%
Total Darp research sample (*N* = 27,460)	40%	17%	21%	22%

The lower percentage of youth in MM reflects (1) the fact that daily opioid use was relatively low among youth compared to the total DARP population, and (2) the effect of federal guidelines with respect to minimum age for admission to MM. Since DT in the DARP was concerned primarily with opioid addiction, the lower percentage of youth in DT is also related to the age distribution of drug use patterns. The drug-free environments of TC and DF have, as expected, a higher percentage of youth than the total DARP, but the TC environment was unsuited to many, particularly the younger youth, and DF was clearly the treatment of choice for the age groups nineteen and under.

In general, the retention data presented for the DARP youth sample indicated that youth remained in all treatments except MM for longer periods than the total DARP sample. Retention rates and percentage of treatment completions were best for the youth sample in DF, particularly for whites and the under eighteen group.

The follow-up results for all DARP treatments generally showed favorable outcomes four to six years after admission, particularly in respect to drug use. Although average tenure in MM was appreciably longer than in the drug-free treatments, the posttreatment results for DF were best overall and those for TC there were not enough DF patients in cohort 1 (1969-1971 admissions) to justify this inclusion in the sample. As a result, the DF sample includes only cohort 2 patients. Table 22-18 shows overlap as well as differences among the groups and reminds the reader that the numbers of patients, particularly in DT and IO, were very small. Considering this information, together with the criterion baseline scores in tables 22-13 through 22-17, it is not surprising that the DF youths appeared most favorable overall at follow-up evaluation. However, substantial gains were realized in MM and TC as well on opioid and nonopioid use, productive activities, and the criminality indicators. The youths in MM had very poor outcomes on employment compared with TC and DF.

In general, the retention data presented for the DARP youth sample indicated that youths remained in all treatments except MM for longer periods than the total DARP samples. Retention rates and percentage of treatment completions were best for the youth sample in DF, particularly for whites and the under 18 group.

The follow-up results for all DARP treatments generally showed favorable outcomes 4 to 6 years after admission, particularly with respect to drug use other than marihuana and alcohol. Although average tenure in MM was appreciably longer than in the drug-free treatments, the posttreatment results for DF were best overall, and those for TC were in many ways superior to those for MM in this youth sample.

The DARP treatments apparently failed to influence youths with respect to marihuana and alcohol and were at best only moderately successful in improving employment, although here both DF and TC were superior to MM. Comparisons on criminality were difficult because of variations in pretreatment levels between treatments, but overall the results were favorable, if not impressive.

Post-DARP treatment appears to be an indication of negative outcome in the DARP follow-up research, although it is related in part to the type of DARP treatment involved. The data presented on this variable indicated that fewer members of the drug-free DF and TC groups entered post-DARP treatment; by comparison the MM, DT, and IO groups had considerably more patients who entered treatment after DARP.

In sum, and with the qualifications mentioned earlier in this section, the posttreatment data supported the conclusion that the drug-free treatments in DARP were most effective for the youths assigned to them. By comparison, the

Table 22-18
Description of the Follow-up Study Treatment Subsamples in Terms of Background and Baseline Characteristics (n = 587)

Background and Baseline Characteristics	*Treatment Subsamples*				
	MM	*TC*	*DF*	*DT*	*IO*
Percent black	56	29	34	35	50
Percent under age 18	23	43	66	35	35
Percent with high background criminality	25	30	14	7	31
Percent with high background socioeconomic status	30	44	42	34	29
Percent with low background family responsibility	58	73	73	76	69
Percent with high baseline nonopioid use	26	51	56	41	49
Percent with high baseline opioid use and criminality	43	35	11	31	40
Number in subsample	119	238	158	34	38

small IO group had the poorest record. However, since the reduction of use of hard drugs is only part of the problem, the results with respect to marihuana, alcohol, and employment must be considered. The poor record in these areas probably reflects the fact that these aspects of patient adjustment received less emphasis in DARP treatment than may be required for patients in the youth age range.

Note

1. It should be noted that comparisons between the youth sample and total DARP research sample are partially confounded by the fact they represent part-whole comparisons. The youths, however, comprise only about 20 percent of the total sample.

References

Cole, S.G., and Watterson, O. 1976. A treatment typology for drug abuse in the DARP: 1971-1972 admissions. In S.B. Sells and D.D. Simpson (eds.), *Effectiveness of Drug Abuse Treatment*, Vol. 3. Further Studies of Drug Users Treatment Typologies and Assessment of Outcomes during Treatment in the DARP. Cambridge, Mass.: Ballinger.

Demaree, R.G., and Neman, J.R. 1976. Differential use of illicit drugs by outpatients admitted to methadone maintenance treatment programs in the DARP during 1972-1973. In S.B. Sells and D.D. Simpson (eds.), *Effectiveness of Drug Abuse Treatment,* Vol. 5. Evaluation of Treatment Outcomes for the 1972-1973 Admission Cohort. Cambridge, Mass.: Ballinger.

Demaree, R.G., Neman, J.F., Long, G.L., and Gant, B.L. 1976. Patterns of behavioral outcomes over time in methadone maintenance treatment. In S.B. Sells and D.D. Simpson (eds.), *Effectiveness of Drug Abuse Treatment,* Vol. 4. Evaluation of Treatment Outcomes for the 1971-1972 Admission Cohort. Cambridge, Mass.: Ballinger.

Gorsuch, R.L., Abbamonte, M., and Sells, S.B. 1976. Evaluation of treatment for drug users in the DARP: 1971-1972 admissions. In S.B. Sells and D.D. Simpson (eds.), *Effectiveness of Drug Abuse Treatment*, Vol. 4. Evaluation of Treatment Outcomes for the 1971-1972 Admission Cohort. Cambridge, Mass.: Ballinger.

Gorsuch, R.L., Butler, M.C., and Sells, S.B. 1976. Evaluation of treatment for drug users in the DARP: 1972-1973 admissions. In S.B. Sells and D.D. Simpson (eds.), *Effectiveness of Drug Abuse Treatment,* Vol. 5. Evaluation of Treatment Outcomes for the 1972-1973 Admission Cohort. Cambridge, Mass.: Ballinger.

James, L.R., Watterson, O., Bruni, J., and Cole, S.G. 1976. Studies on the development and validation of checklists for classification of drug abuse treatment programs. In S.B. Sells and D.D. Simpson (eds.), *Effectiveness of Drug Abuse Treatment,* Vol. 5. Evaluation of Treatment Outcomes for the 1972-1973 Admission Cohort. Cambridge, Mass.: Ballinger.

Joe, G.W. 1974. Retention in treatment of drug users in the DARP: 1969-1971 admissions. In S.B. Sells (ed.), *Effectiveness of Treatments for Drug Abuse*, Vol. 1. Evaluation of Treatments. Cambridge, Mass.: Ballinger.

Joe, G.W., and Simpson, D.D. 1976. Retention in treatment of drug users admitted to treatment during 1971-1972. In S.B. Sells and D.D. Simpson (eds.), *Effectiveness of Drug Abuse Treatment,* Vol. 4. Evaluation of Outcomes for the 1971-1972 Admission Cohort. Cambridge, Mass.: Ballinger.

Joe, G.W., and Simpson, D.D. 1976. Treatment retention for drug users: 1972-1973 DARP admissions. In S.B. Sells and D.D. Simpson (eds.), *Effectiveness of Drug Abuse Treatment,* Vol. 5. Evaluation of Treatment Outcomes for the 1972-1973 Admission Cohort. Cambridge, Mass.: Ballinger.

Sells, S.B. (ed.). 1974*a*. *Studies of the Effectiveness of Treatment for Drug Abuse,* Vol. 1. Evaluation of Treatments. Cambridge, Mass.: Ballinger.

Sells, S.B. (ed.). 1974*b*. *Studies of the Effectiveness of Treatment for Drug Abuse,* Vol. 2. Research on Patients, Treatments, and Outcomes. Cambridge, Mass.: Ballinger.

Sells, S.B. 1976. Reflections on epidemiology of heroin and narcotic addiction from the perspective of treatment data. *Proceedings of the Conference on the Epidemiology of Heroin and Other Narcotic Drugs.* Stanford Research Institute, San Francisco, February 1976.

Sells, S.B., and Simpson, D.D. (eds.). 1976*a*. *Effectiveness of Drug Abuse Treatment*, Vol. 3. Further Studies of Drug Users Treatment Typologies and Assessment of Outcome during Treatment in the DARP. Cambridge, Mass.: Ballinger.

Sells, S.B., and Simpson, D.D. (eds.). 1976*b*. *Effectiveness of Drug Abuse Treatment,* Vol. 4. Evaluation of Treatment Outcomes for the 1971-1972 Admission Cohort. Cambridge, Mass.: Ballinger.

Sells, S.B., and Simpson, D.D. (eds.). 1976. *Effectiveness of Drug Abuse Treatment,* Vol. 5. Evaluation of Treatment Outcomes for the 1972-1973 Admission Cohort. Cambridge, Mass.: Ballinger.

Sells, S.B., Simpson, D.D., Joe, G.W., Demaree, R.G., Savage, L.J., and Lloyd, M.R. 1976. A National followup study to evaluate the effectiveness of drug abuse treatment: A report on cohort 1 of the DARP five years later. *American Journal of Drug and Alcohol Abuse* 3(4):545-556.

Simpson, D.D., Savage, L.J., Joe, G.W., Demaree, R.G., and Sells, S.B. 1976. *DARP Data Book–Statistics on Characteristics of Drug Users in Treatment*

During 1969-1974. IBR Report 76-4. Fort Worth: Texas Christian University, Institute of Behavioral Research, 1976.

Spiegel, D.K., and Sells, S.B. 1974. Evaluation of treatments for drug users in the DARP: 1969-1971 admissions. In S.B. Sells (ed.), *Effectiveness of Treatments for Drug Abuse,* Vol 1. Evaluation of Treatments. Cambridge, Mass.: Ballinger.

Appendix 22A: Percentage Distribution Tables Comparing Four Youth Groups in Five Different Treatment Modalities at Pre-Treatment and Follow-up on Criteria Measures

Table 22A-1
Comparison of Black and White Youths, under 18 and 18 to 19 for 2-Month Period Pre-DARP and at Follow-up Interview on Ten Criterion Measures

	Pre-DARP				*At Interview*[a]			
	Under 18		*18 to 19*		*Under 18*		*18 to 19*	
Criterion Measure	*Black*	*White*	*Black*	*White*	*Black*	*White*	*Black*	*White*
Opioid use								
None	21	48	13	23	77	82	79	85
<Weekly	1	12	3	5	11	9	10	9
Weekly	24	14	17	15	5	6	5	4
Daily	54	26	67	57	7	3	6	2
Nonopioid use								
None	56	25	56	30	72	67	67	72
<Weekly	18	19	18	29	18	20	21	22
Weekly	19	39	19	25	5	8	8	5
Daily	7	17	7	16	5	5	4	1
Marihuana use								
None	47	26	50	31	21	31	29	37
<Weekly	22	16	14	17	19	16	19	24
Weekly	22	35	24	30	26	26	34	23
Daily	9	23	12	22	34	27	18	16
Alcohol problems[b]								
No	96	92	94	91	95	93	95	96
Yes	4	8	6	9	5	7	5	4
Alcohol use (in oz. 80-proof equiv.)								
None	67	72	73	74	25	9	15	12
0.1-4.0	8	8	6	5	53	64	57	61
4.1-8.0	11	5	4	6	12	12	18	14
>8.0	14	15	17	15	10	15	10	13
Employment								
None	72	71	72	59	47	29	45	27
1-9 days	6	2	3	6	0	8	4	4
10-19 days	1	7	3	5	5	7	2	5
20-29 days	4	5	3	8	2	9	10	6
30-39 days	8	5	6	7	14	11	9	10
40-60 days	9	10	13	15	32	36	30	48
Productive activities								
No	53	48	68	55	33	16	35	20
Yes	47	52	32	45	67	84	65	80
Illegal support								
No	64	71	60	50	75	77	78	83
Yes	36	29	40	50	25	23	22	17
Arrested[b]								
No	25	38	18	21	63	77	69	82
Yes	75	62	82	79	37	23	31	18
Drug treatment[b]								
No	74	62	71	50	78	89	76	80
Yes	26	38	29	50	22	11	24	20
No. in group	78	164	143	202	57	154	110	180

[a]Persons confined in jail, hospital, or therapeutic community at interview were excluded from these calculations.

[b]Pre-DARP measure refers to lifetime and not just the last 2 months.

Table 22A-2
Comparison of Treatment Groups for 2-Month Period Pre-DARP and at Follow-up Interview on Ten Criterion Measures

	Pre-DARP					*At Interview*[a]				
Criterion Measure	*MM*	*TC*	*DF*	*DT*	*IO*	*MM*	*TC*	*DF*	*DT*	*IO*
Opioid use										
None	7	24	51	24	16	66	91	85	72	75
<Weekly	4	8	7	6	0	20	5	7	13	11
Weekly	3	24	14	9	29	7	3	4	13	4
Daily	86	44	28	61	55	7	1	4	2	10
Nonopioid use										
None	43	37	36	32	55	63	76	71	56	54
<Weekly	29	18	23	32	8	23	20	19	19	24
Weekly	16	31	27	24	35	10	4	6	16	11
Daily	12	14	14	12	2	4	0	4	9	11
Marihuana use										
None	52	34	30	38	29	29	33	34	31	18
<Weekly	14	15	20	24	13	20	22	17	22	21
Weekly	24	29	32	24	32	20	21	31	25	32
Daily	10	22	18	14	26	21	24	18	22	29
Alcohol problems[b]										
No	98	90	94	88	92	98	94	94	94	89
Yes	2	10	6	12	8	2	6	6	6	11
Alcohol use (in oz. 80-proof equiv.)										
None	74	76	66	76	67	15	10	14	25	4
0.1-4.0	9	3	8	9	14	58	61	68	31	57
4.1-8.0	6	5	8	3	8	15	14	11	19	25
>8.0	11	16	18	12	11	12	15	7	25	14
Employment										
None	61	70	69	71	68	51	28	31	38	28
1-9 days	2	4	6	3	0	3	3	5	9	15
10-19 days	3	6	3	6	3	3	4	6	6	7
20-29 days	5	6	6	3	0	5	8	8	6	11
30-39 days	9	6	4	12	5	10	13	9	9	3
40-60 days	20	8	12	5	24	28	44	41	32	36

Table 22A-2 continued

Productive activities										
No	55	64	44	53	61	34	21	17	28	29
Yes	45	36	56	47	39	66	79	83	72	71
Illegal support										
No	45	56	78	67	49	79	83	81	78	54
Yes	55	44	22	33	51	21	17	19	22	46
Arrested[b]										
No	23	18	39	31	19	75	73	80	74	63
Yes	77	82	61	69	81	25	27	20	26	37
Drug treatment[b]										
No	65	52	71	78	58	67	84	90	74	76
Yes	35	48	29	22	42	33	16	10	26	24
No. in group	119	238	158	34	38	103	197	141	32	28

[a]Persons confined in jail, hospital, or therapeutic community at interview were excluded from these calculations.

[b]Pre-DARP measure refers to lifetime and not just the last 2 months.

Table 22A-3
Comparisons in DARP Methadone Maintenance of Black and White Youths and under 18 and 18 to 19 for 2-Month Period Pre-DARP and at Follow-up Interview on Ten Criterion Measures

	Ethnic Group				*Age*			
	Pre-DARP		*At Interview*[a]		*Pre-DARP*		*At Interview*[a]	
Criterion Measure	*Black*	*White*	*Black*	*White*	*<18*	*18 to 19*	*<18*	*18 to 19*
Opioid use								
None	6	8	67	65	18	3	57	69
<Weekly	3	6	18	23	4	4	30	18
Weekly	1	4	6	8	0	3	9	6
Daily	90	82	9	4	78	90	4	7
Nonopioid use								
None	60	21	65	60	52	40	70	61
<Weekly	19	42	24	23	22	32	17	25
Weekly	12	21	7	13	4	19	4	11
Daily	9	16	4	4	22	9	9	3
Marihuana use								
None	63	38	31	27	48	53	22	31
<Weekly	9	21	22	17	19	13	26	17
Weekly	21	29	27	33	22	25	17	34
Daily	7	12	20	23	11	9	35	18
Alcohol problems[b]								
No	95	100	98	98	100	97	91	100
Yes	73	0	2	2	0	3	0	0
Alcohol use (in oz. 80-proof equiv.)								
None	73	77	22	8	85	71	4	19
0.1-4.0	7	9	58	58	11	8	57	59
4.1-8.0	6	6	15	15	4	7	17	14
>8.0	14	8	5	19	0	14	22	8

Table 22A-3 continued

Employment								
None	69	50	64	38	52	63	65	47
1-9 days	0	4	3	2	0	2	0	4
10-19 days	1	6	2	4	4	3	4	3
20-29 days	4	6	4	6	7	4	0	6
30-39 days	8	11	9	10	15	8	9	10
40-60 days	18	23	18	40	22	20	22	30
Productive activities								
No	61	46	44	23	44	58	48	30
Yes	39	54	56	77	56	42	52	70
Illegal support								
No	58	29	84	73	59	41	74	80
Yes	42	71	16	27	41	59	26	20
Arrested[b]								
No	26	19	73	77	22	23	63	78
Yes	74	81	27	23	78	77	37	22
Drug treatment[b]								
No	74	54	75	58	74	63	70	66
Yes	26	46	25	42	26	37	30	34
No. in group	67	52	55	48	27	92	23	80

[a]Persons confined in jail, hospital, or therapeutic community at interview were excluded from these calculations.

[b]Pre-DARP measure refers to lifetime and not just the last 2 months.

Table 22A-4

Comparisons in DARP Therapeutic Communities of Black and White Youths and under 18 and 18 to 19 for 2-Month Period Pre-DARP and At Follow-up Interview on Ten Criterion Measures

	Ethnic Group				*Age*			
	Pre-DARP		*At Interview*[a]		*Pre-DARP*		*At Interview*[a]	
Criterion Measure	*Black*	*White*	*Black*	*White*	*<18*	*18 to 19*	*<18*	*18 to 19*
Opioid use								
None	17	27	96	89	29	21	90	92
<Weekly	2	10	4	5	11	5	3	5
Weekly	29	21	0	4	26	22	5	2
Daily	52	42	0	2	34	52	2	1
Nonopioid use								
None	51	31	81	74	31	40	72	78
<Weekly	14	19	17	21	14	21	22	18
Weekly	28	33	2	4	38	26	5	4
Daily	7	17	0	1	17	13	1	0
Marihuana use								
None	45	29	24	36	30	36	27	38
<Weekly	19	14	21	22	18	14	16	27
Weekly	22	32	23	21	33	26	25	18
Daily	14	25	32	21	19	24	32	17
Alcohol problems[b]								
No	94	89	91	95	89	91	95	94
Yes	6	11	9	5	11	9	5	6
Alcohol use (in oz. 80-proof equiv.)								
None	74	76	21	7	69	81	10	10
0.1-4.0	3	3	45	65	5	1	62	59
4.1-8.0	7	4	17	13	6	4	11	17
>8.0	16	17	17	15	20	14	17	14

Table 22A-4 continued

Employment								
None	78	66	32	27	80	62	29	27
1-9 days	6	4	2	4	3	5	3	4
10-19 days	3	7	2	4	7	5	6	3
20-29 days	0	8	10	7	2	9	7	8
30-39 days	4	6	9	15	2	8	21	7
40-60 days	9	9	45	43	6	11	34	51
Productive activities								
No	72	61	28	19	69	61	21	22
Yes	28	39	72	81	31	39	79	78
Illegal support								
No	57	56	81	83	61	52	82	84
Yes	43	44	19	17	39	48	18	16
Arrested[b]								
No	13	21	61	78	24	15	72	74
Yes	87	79	39	22	76	85	28	26
Drug treatment[b]								
No	59	48	75	88	54	50	88	82
Yes	41	52	25	12	46	50	12	18
No. in group	69	169	47	150	102	136	87	110

[a]Persons confined in jail, hospital, or therapeutic community at interview were excluded from these calculations.

[b]Pre-DARP measure refers to lifetime and not just the last 2 months.

Table 22A-5
Comparisons in DARP Outpatient Drug Free of Black and White Youths Under 18 and 18 to 19 for 2-Month Periods of Pre-DARP and at Follow-up Interview on Ten Criterion Measures

	Ethnic Group				Age			
	Pre-DARP		At Interview[a]		Pre-DARP		At Interview[a]	
Criterion Measure	Black	White	Black	White	<18	18 to 19	<18	18 to 19
Opioid use								
None	31	61	77	89	61	39	83	88
<Weekly	4	9	9	6	9	4	7	7
Weekly	26	8	7	3	14	14	5	3
Daily	39	22	7	2	16	43	5	2
Nonopioid use								
None	54	26	70	72	31	41	69	74
<Weekly	24	23	16	20	23	24	16	23
Weekly	17	33	9	5	36	16	9	3
Daily	5	18	5	3	10	19	6	0
Marihuana use								
None	41	25	25	38	31	30	35	33
<Weekly	22	18	14	18	19	20	15	20
Weekly	28	34	42	26	33	30	28	34
Daily	9	23	19	18	17	20	22	13
Alcohol problems[b]								
No	96	92	93	94	95	91	94	93
Yes	4	8	7	6	5	9	6	7
Alcohol use (in oz. 80-proof equiv.)								
None	61	67	16	13	66	65	16	11
0.1-4.0	9	8	67	69	9	8	68	69
4.1-8.0	9	8	12	11	10	6	10	13
>8.0	21	17	5	7	15	21	6	7

Table 22A-5 continued

Employment								
None	72	66	42	26	70	66	33	28
1-9 days	9	5	0	7	5	8	6	3
10-19 days	2	4	2	8	3	3	7	5
20-29 days	7	6	7	8	7	6	9	6
30-39 days	6	3	14	7	5	3	5	15
40-60 days	4	16	35	44	10	14	40	43
Productive activities								
No	56	38	30	11	32	59	13	23
Yes	44	62	70	89	68	41	87	77
Illegal support								
No	76	80	74	84	82	74	80	82
Yes	24	20	26	16	18	26	20	18
Arrested[b]								
No	24	47	69	87	52	24	78	83
Yes	76	53	31	13	48	76	22	17
Drug treatment[b]								
No	86	64	81	94	71	72	92	87
Yes	14	36	19	6	29	28	8	13
No. in group	54	104	43	98	88	70	80	61

[a]Persons confined in jail, hospital, or therapeutic community at interview were excluded from these calculations.

[b]Pre-DARP measure refers to lifetime and not just the last 2 months.

Table 22A-6
Comparisons in DARP Outpatient Detoxification of Black and White Youths Under 18 and 18 to 19 for 2-Month Period of Pre-DARP and at Follow-up Interview on Ten Criterion Measures

	Ethnic Group				*Age*			
	Pre-DARP		*At Interview*[a]		*Pre-DARP*		*At Interview*[a]	
Criterion Measure	*Black*	*White*	*Black*	*White*	*<18*	*18 to 19*	*<18*	*18 to 19*
Opioid use								
None	17	27	70	73	25	23	58	80
<Weekly	0	9	10	14	8	4	17	10
Weekly	8	9	20	9	8	9	17	10
Daily	75	55	0	4	59	64	8	0
Nonopioid use								
None	50	23	60	55	33	32	42	65
<Weekly	25	36	20	18	33	32	25	15
Weekly	17	27	10	18	25	23	25	10
Daily	8	14	10	9	9	13	8	10
Marihuana use								
None	33	41	10	41	50	32	25	35
<Weekly	25	23	20	23	17	27	17	25
Weekly	25	23	40	18	17	27	42	15
Daily	17	13	30	18	16	14	16	25
Alcohol problems[b]								
No	83	91	90	95	92	86	83	100
Yes	17	9	10	5	8	14	17	0
Alcohol use (in oz. 80-proof equiv.)								
None	75	77	20	27	83	73	25	25
0.1-4.0	8	9	30	32	17	5	25	35
4.1-8.0	0	5	20	18	0	4	25	15
>8.0	17	9	30	23	0	18	25	25

Table 22A-6 continued

Employment								
None	58	77	40	36	50	82	33	40
1-9 days	0	5	0	14	9	0	17	5
10-19 days	8	5	10	5	8	5	8	5
20-29 days	0	5	0	9	8	0	9	5
30-39 days	25	4	20	4	25	4	0	15
40-60 days	9	4	30	32	0	9	3	30
Productive activities								
No	33	64	20	32	25	68	25	30
Yes	67	36	80	68	75	32	75	70
Illegal support								
No	55	73	80	77	83	57	58	90
Yes	45	27	20	23	17	43	42	10
Arrested[b]								
No	27	33	67	77	36	29	75	73
Yes	73	67	33	23	64	71	25	27
Drug treatment[b]								
No	83	75	75	73	92	70	58	82
Yes	17	25	25	27	8	30	42	18
No. in group	12	22	10	22	12	22	12	20

[a]Persons confined in jail, hospital, or therapeutic community at interview were excluded from these calculations.

[b]Pre-DARP measure refers to lifetime and not just the last 2 months.

Table 22A-7
Comparisons in DARP Intake-Only Group of Black and White Youths under 18 and 18 to 19 for 2-Month Period of Pre-DARP and at Follow-up Interview on Ten Criterion Measures

	Ethnic Group				*Age*			
	Pre-DARP		*At Interview*[a]		*Pre-DARP*		*At Interview*[a]	
Criterion Measure	*Black*	*White*	*Black*	*White*	*<18*	*18 to 19*	*<18*	*18 to 19*
Opioid use								
None	0	32	75	75	23	12	78	74
<Weekly	0	0	0	19	0	0	11	11
Weekly	37	21	0	6	15	36	0	5
Daily	63	47	25	0	62	52	11	10
Nonopioid use								
None	74	37	42	63	61	52	56	53
<Weekly	5	11	25	25	8	8	22	26
Weekly	21	47	17	6	31	36	11	11
Daily	0	5	16	6	0	4	11	10
Marihuana use								
None	53	5	33	6	23	32	11	21
<Weekly	16	11	17	25	15	12	11	26
Weekly	21	42	33	31	23	36	22	37
Daily	10	42	17	38	39	20	56	16
Alcohol problems[b]								
No	100	84	100	81	100	88	89	89
Yes	0	16	0	19	0	12	11	11
Alcohol use (in oz. 80-proof equiv.)								
None	76	58	0	6	61	69	11	0
0.1-4.0	12	16	58	56	15	13	56	58
4.1-8.0	6	10	33	19	8	9	22	26
>8.0	6	16	9	19	16	0	11	16

Table 22A-7 continued

Employment								
None	74	63	42	19	69	68	22	32
1-9 days	0	0	8	19	0	0	22	11
10-19 days	0	6	8	6	0	4	0	10
20-29 days	0	0	17	6	0	0	11	10
30-39 days	0	10	8	0	8	4	11	9
40-60 days	26	21	17	50	23	24	34	37
Productive activities								
No	68	53	42	19	46	68	22	32
Yes	32	47	58	81	54	32	78	68
Illegal support								
No	50	47	42	63	46	50	33	63
Yes	50	53	58	37	54	50	67	37
Arrested[b]								
No	17	21	58	68	23	17	62	64
Yes	83	79	42	32	77	83	38	36
Drug treatment[b]								
No	71	47	79	74	85	44	77	76
Yes	29	53	21	26	15	56	23	24
No. in group	19	19	12	16	13	25	9	19

[a]Persons confined in jail, hospital, or therapeutic community at interview were excluded from these calculations.

[b]Pre-DARP measure refers to lifetime and not just the last 2 months.

23 Predicting Treatment Outcomes for Juvenile and Young-Adult Clients in the Pennsylvania Substance-Abuse System

Thomas Vale Rush

The purposes of this chapter are to identify those characteristics of clients which are significantly related to the desired treatment outcomes and to evaluate the impact of the treatment experience upon substance-abuse clients. It is both important and useful to identify those characteristics of drug-abuse clients which are related to outcomes of their treatment. This information is particularly helpful in the development of appropriate treatment plans tailored to the needs of individual clients. The information would enable a more appropriate assignment of clients to the type of treatment in which the clients are more likely to do well.

Literature Review

Assessing the impact of a treatment on the client receiving that treatment is a very difficult task. Ideally any attempt to do so should contain a control and an experimental group, a random assignment procedure, and at least three different points of data evaluation (preadmission, discharge, and postdischarge). It can also be appropriate and useful to compare the effects of two different treatment programs or two different treatment methods instead of comparing a treatment group with a "no treatment" control group, such as a randomly assigned wait-list group, which has been found to be virtually impossible to achieve.

The data gathered should be complete so as to enable the researcher to assess the degree of the substance-abuse problem, the personal characteristics of the subjects, and the context in which the substance use and abuse occurred (Eichberg and Bentler 1975). This ideal is rarely found in the literature (Sirotnik and Roffe 1977), and there is good reason for this inadequacy. First and

I would like to thank the Governor's Council on Drug and Alcohol Abuse which provided the data, computer programming staff, and time, as well as secretarial services, for the project. Dr. Alfred S. Friedman and members of his staff, Mr. Edward C. Farley, and Mr. Yoav Santo provided the necessary guidance and assistance in the development and direction of this chapter.

foremost, a legitimate control group is virtually impossible to garner, although there have been attempts to establish a quasi-control group (Sells and Simpson 1974; Burt and Pines 1976, Macro Systems, Inc. 1975). It is also very difficult to obtain information on the quality and quantity of the drugs used. Little attention has been paid to the context in which drug use occurs (Eichberg and Bentler 1975). While there has been a long history of follow-up research studies on drug-abuse clients (see Vaillant 1966*a* and *b*; and 1970), they have in the past tended to focus only on those people with the most severe problems (narcotic addicts in treatment at federal hospital programs such as Lexington), who are not representative of the majority of young drug-abuse clients. (An exception is the study reported by Sells and Simpson in chap. 22 of this book.)

This study attempts to overcome the problem of finding a sample of adequate size by reviewing, on a statewide base, clients who received treatment at publicly supported facilities in Pennsylvania. The method of analysis utilized is to determine the degree of association between a client's characteristics at admission and at discharge on selected outcome criteria. Those criteria are productivity at discharge (with additional analysis of the two main components of this index), criminal justice involvement, and successful completion of the treatment program.

The criteria of success selected for this chapter have general acceptance in the field (Norris 1975; Mandell et al. 1975; Collins and Kelly 1975; and Keil et al. 1975). DeLeon (1975) considered retention or time in treatment, opiate use, and employment and legal status at follow-up as outcome criteria. Sirotnik and Roffe (1977) considered just one criterion, length of treatment, which is perhaps better suited as a predictor than a criterion.

Several demographic variables have been found to be related to or to "predict" success in treatment (Eichberg and Bentler 1975; Sirotnik and Roffe 1977; Keil et al. 1975; Cutter et al. 1975), but as Fisher (1975) has indicated, the prediction coefficients should not be expected to be of a high magnitude. The role of the time a client spends in treatment is unclear. It has been argued that a minimum amount of time is necessary for a program to achieve its goals (DeLeon 1975; Zuckerman et al. 1976), yet a program can exert an important positive influence even on those who leave treatment against clinical advice (DeLeon 1975, pp. 148-149). On the other hand, one study found duration of treatment to have only marginal impact on treatment outcome (Macro Systems, Inc. 1975). Most patients leave treatment within the first year. Bardine et al. (1976) reviewed CODAP (Client Oriented Data Acquisition Process) data and found that on a nationwide basis, 44 percent leave after being in treatment 1 month or less, with only 12 percent remaining more than 10 months. The time spent in treatment was also found to be affected by type of substance abused, number of prior treatment experiences, frequency of use of abused drug, and length of habit, as well as, obviously, by the nature of the treatment environment and the type of treatment approach. The most complete recent study on treatment effectiveness has been the major analysis of clients in the DARP (Drug Abuse Reporting Program) system as reported by Sells and Simpson (1974). Of a more limited scope has been the work of Keil et al. (1975 a and b), which used a client data base similar to the one being used here and controlled for primary substance of abuse, comparing opiate abusers with nonopiate abusers who were in treatment. It was found in that study that the variables associated with and predicting to intreatment changes varied according to the success criterion utilized and, to a lesser degree, according to the class of the primary substance of abuse.

Pennsylvania Uniform Data Collection System

The Pennsylvania Data Collection System (UDCS) provided the data used in this analysis. The system was established in June 1973, having as one of its purposes the evaluation of all treatment facilities within the Commonwealth of Pennsylvania.[1] Several concrete goals were promulgated, and they were (1) productive employment, (2) law-abiding behavior, and (3) drug-free existence and appropriate use of alcohol. These three goals of treatment were readily adaptable to a data-collection scheme, in that they are all readily quantifiable.

For the purpose of this chapter, the period between July 1, 1975 and December 31, 1976 was selected for analysis. All youths and young adults in treatment during that time period and discharged from the environment/approaches under study were included in the analysis, provided the following conditions were met. All drug treatment facilities in Pennsylvania were required to submit UDCS client records to the Governor's Council on Drug and Alcohol Abuse. It was necessary to complete both admission and discharge forms for the clients, link[2] them, and send them to the Governor's Council on Drug and Alcohol Abuse. It should be remembered that this study is concerned solely with the youth (under 18 years of age) and young-adult (18 to 19 years of age) segments of the treatment population, two groups which constitute a minority of the clients who received treatment during the study time period.

There is an unknown relationship between the number of clients and the number of admissions in the UDCS. Data collection focuses on treatment admissions, with the consequence that there may be multiple admission and discharge forms for particular individuals. Since a case management system has yet to be instituted, accurate estimates of the true number of clients are unavailable.

The issue regarding the quality of the data must be discussed. The UDCS represents one of the few statewide data systems gathering information on all clients in treatment. A system this large with more than 350 facilities and over 50,000 admissions per year, will have inadequacies. Internal consistency checks have been conducted that indicate that in the aggregate the data is relatively accurate.

All the clients in the treatment system are receiving public-supported treatment. The implications of this are obvious: those who can afford to pay for their treatment are not included in this data base unless they wish to go to a government-supported or government-assisted program. Thus UDCS clients tend to be less likely to have jobs to which they can return, and they are less likely to have family and community support mechanisms to assist them after they leave treatment. It would appear that the UDCS clients should have a more difficult time doing well in treatment.

Defining Successful Treatment Outcome

Success in treatment is a very difficult concept to operationalize in a system like the UDCS. First, there may not be consensus regarding treatment goals and objectives among the system components. Some of the goals established by the Governors Council on Drug and Alcohol Abuse were mandated by the legislature, and some personnel from the rehabilitation field have asserted that the treatment goals of the Governor's Council were not their goals. With this being the case, assessment of client performance according to these goals may be unfair to the projects and their clients. The outcome criteria or indicators are based on self-reported information and are limited in scope. Also, some of the treatment success criteria employed have conceptual difficulties. "Completion of treatment," for example, does not necessarily have a concrete referent or an operational definition; rather, in many projects there is a subjective appraisal as to the client's progress and treatment status. Completion of treatment in one program therefore does not mean the same thing as completion of treatment in another program. Another criterion, the arrests for felonies while in treatment, is not an entirely precise measure of treatment success. The time of arrest generally lags behind the time at which an offense was committed; and on occasion, people are arrested for acts they committed several months earlier. This can occur when people are arrested for drug sales in an areawide narcotics raid or when an accomplice is arrested and later implicates the other individual. Thus, if a client is charged or arrested, after he has started treatment, for an offense committed earlier, he might get labeled, inaccurately, as a treatment failure.

The use in this study of employment status at discharge and educational status at discharge as treatment outcome criteria are not as appropriate for young therapeutic community clients as they are for outpatient clients. Since most of these therapeutic community clients drop out before completion, they will probably be unemployed and out of school at the time, although they may not be so at 6 months *after* discharge. Outpatients have more time and opportunity to look for work and attend school away from the treatment facility. Employment, in any event, is not the most desirable referent criterion for a sample of clients who are under 18 years of age.

Description of the Sample

Of the 4,738 drug treatment clients included in the study, 62 percent are juveniles under 18 years old and 38 percent are young adults 18 or 19 years of age. These two age groups received treatment in two different treatment environments. The age groups are further defined by the type of drug treatment they received. Most of these clients were enrolled in outpatient drug-free programs. Only 17 percent of the juveniles and 25 percent of the young adults came from (residential and drug-free) therapeutic communities. (A detailed description of Therapeutic Communities and their approaches is presented by DeLeon and Beschner, 1976). Table 23-1 reports on a number of characteristics for each of the age and treatment program groups. Males outnumber females in all four age/program groups. The male proportion increases substantially with

Table 23-1
Characteristics of Youth Clients in Pennsylvania's Drug Treatment Program

	Age/Treatment Groups			
	Juveniles under 18		*Young Adults 18 to 19*	
Characteristics	*Outpatients*	*T.C.*	*Outpatients*	*T.C.*
Demographics				
Percentage of males	55.4%	69.8%	70.0%	79.3%
Percentage of whites	86.8%	87.7%	80.6%	79.7%
Percentage of students in an education program	70.6%	37.8%	12.4%	17.2%
Percentage of students in a training program	5.3%	3.3%	4.1%	2.3%
Percentage of clients, no employment in last 2 years	60.8%	40.8%	24.6%	23.8%
Drug history				
Median age of first use	14.3	13.1	14.9	14.3
Percentage of opiate abusers	2.6%	8.0%	14.3%	17.0%
Percentage of nonopiate drug abusers	64.2%	74.6%	50.3%	45.2%
Percentage of multiple-drug abusers	47.2%	76.3%	50.9%	59.2%
Treatment involvement				
Median time in treatment	123 days	36 days	100 days	34 days
Percentage with no previous treatment experience	85.1%	63.6%	72.8%	55.2%
Legal involvement				
Percentage in treatment, legal pressure	17.1%	44.3%	29.3%	44.3%
Percentage with no prior confictions	85.5%	61.4%	70.1%	50.4%
Number of clients	2417 (83%)	503 (17%)	1360 (75%)	458 (25%)
Age group totals	2929 (62%)		1818 (38%)	

Note: Only youth clients from outpatient counseling and/or psychotherapy programs and inpatient therapeutic communities are reported on. These youths compose only 14 percent of the clients in the UDCS system.

either the shift to the older age groups or enrollment in a therapeutic community. Nationally, the Client Oriented Data Acquisition Process (CODAP) also reports a preponderance of male over female clients in the therapeutic communities and an increase in the proportion of males as the client's age increases.

Regarding the racial composition of the groups, we find that the two selected treatment environments have minimal differences. However, the proportion for the minorities is substantially greater in the age group of young adults. CODAP has also found that the proportion of minorities increases with the age of clients in treatment.

As would be expected, the younger group reported a higher proportion of school enrollment and a smaller percent of employment experiences and prior convictions. Further, the younger group generally lasted longer in outpatient treatment, which was for most of them their first drug therapy experience.

In addition to these differences, the two age groups appear to have markedly dissimilar drug use patterns. Only 3.5 percent of the young group indicated opiates as their primary abuse problem, compared with 15 percent reported by the older group. The younger groups reported earlier drug onset ages as well as proportionally more problem use of two or more drugs.

Thus the data indicate that there are salient demographic and drug use history differences between these age groups. While the younger group is at an earlier stage in their drug-abuse and criminal careers, they are already involved in the problem use of a larger number of different types of nonopiate drugs. (Chapter 7 examines in detail the phenomenon of multiple-drug use among youths in treatment.)

Turning to an examination of the differences between the treatment groups, we find that therapeutic community clients, regardless of their age, are more prone to be involved in deviant lifestyles; substantially higher proportions of these clients were found to have dropped out of educational programs and have past legal problems. In fact, almost half the clients in the therapeutic communities were referred by the criminal justice system. Further, more than half of them reported a prior conviction. A lesser proportion of older outpatients reported prior convictions than the proportion of younger therapeutic community residents.

Research Design

Variables Used. This study explores the degree to which five measures (criteria) of treatment success can be predicted by certain client characteristics at admission. The five dependent criterion variables to be predicted are:

1. Being productive at discharge (being either in school, in a training program, or employed).

2. Being employed at discharge.
3. Being enrolled in an education program.
4. Number of felonies committed while in treatment.
5. Completion of treatment.

The variables employed to predict treatment success, or the independent predictor variables, are demographic variables (race and sex), drug-use variables, and the client status at admission regarding education, employment, criminal justice involvement, and previous treatment history. The prediction of treatment success is studied for four groups: juveniles in outpatient counseling/psychotherapy facilities; juveniles in (residential) therapeutic communities; young adults in outpatient units; and young adults in therapeutic communities. Stated differently, the age and treatment environment/approach variables were controlled in this prediction analysis (see figure 23-1).

Therapeutic communities (residential) and outpatient "drug-free" modalities were chosen because they represented contrasting styles of treatment and

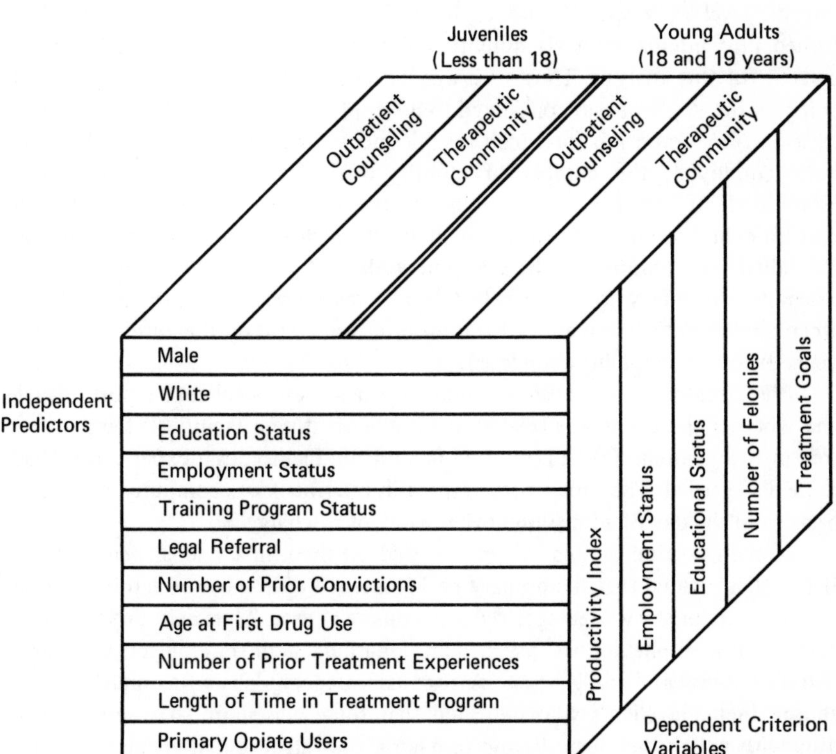

Figure 23-1. Multivariate Design Used for the Pennsylvania Treatment Outcome Analysis.

involved relatively long-term treatment approaches. (Clients under 18 years of age are usually not eligible for admission to outpatient methadone maintenance treatment.) A therapeutic community is defined as a residential environment (a work-in/live-in milieu) which provides services 24 hours a day and which seeks to modify the client's attitude and behavior toward substance abuse, lifestyle, social responsibility, and interpersonal relationships. Medication is not a primary part of treatment, but rather social agents, such as discipline and behavior modification with positive and negative reinforcements, are used to encourage psychological growth and maturity. This contrasts sharply with outpatient treatment programs which have much more limited periods of client contact, ranging from 1 hour per month to 5 hours per day, and usually limited to the basic provision of counseling, psychotherapy, advice, or guidance as a means of dealing with the client's problems.

All independent (predictor) variables, with the exception of time in treatment, were based on the client's status at entry to treatment. The dependent variables were all based on the status of the client at the time of discharge.

The dependent criterion and independent predictor variables were either interval level or a special case of interval level (dichotomized nominal data turned into interval data via dummy variables). Several dummy variables were created for this analysis. Thus, race was defined in terms of being white or not being white. A client was considered to be employed if he or she was working at least part-time on a job for which taxable income was derived. If the client had been employed, the number of months worked in the past 2 years was established. If the person at admission to treatment was enrolled at least part-time in a course of study which led to a degree or diploma, then that individual was considered to be a current student. A current student in a training program was one who was enrolled in a nonacademic or vocational program when admitted to treatment. Education level was based on the number of grade years of formal schooling completed.

Prior treatment for substance abuse was based on the client's report of such and whether the client was treated at a public treatment facility. If the previous treatment experience(s) had occurred in a private facility, that experience(s) had to be disregarded. The time a person spent in treatment was computed on a daily basis from the day of admission until the day of discharge.

A main portion of this analysis focused on the primary substance of abuse. If the client stated that the primary problem was with the use of heroin or other narcotics, he or she was categorized as an opiate abuser. A primary problem with barbiturates, amphetamines, psychedelics, marihuana, or tranquilizers was classified as "nonopiate" drug abuse. A residual category, labeled as multiple drug abuser, included clients who indicated that there was more than one type of drug with which they were having problems, plus alcohol abusers and those for whom the substance-abuse information was inadequate. Regarding the major type of drug of abuse, information was analyzed for both age of first use and the number of years of continued use.

The variables pertaining to the individual's involvement with the criminal justice system (which were used both as predictors and outcome criteria) included total arrests for felonies, total convictions, and commitment to treatment under legal pressure. For a period of 2 years preceding admission to treatment, the client was to indicate the number of times he or she had been arrested for felonies, including drug possession and/or sales. If the individual was arrested for drug possession and that offense was treated as a misdemeanor, it was not to be considered. The number of total convictions was for the 2 years preceding entry into treatment, regardless of the type of arrest. If the client had entered treatment under court order or by some other direct official order, then it was deemed that he or she had entered treatment under legal pressure.

The dependent variables were various indicators of the success of the treatment experience. With two exceptions, these variables were similar to the corresponding independent variable, save for the fact that they referred to the client's status during treatment and at end of treatment. Employment was a yes/no situation, either the individual was employed part-time or full-time at discharge or he or she was not employed. The productivity variable was created from the employment and student status information. An individual was considered to be productive if he or she was either employed or enrolled in an education or training program. The completion of treatment variable referred to whether the client was discharged with his or her goals successfully completed or was considered to have been discharged for some other reason.

Statistical Technique. A multivariate analysis was conducted, with the specific technique being the stepwise regression procedure as found in the Statistical Package for the Social Sciences (SPSS, Nie et al., 1975). In this regression procedure, the customary best-fit linear equation is developed between the criterion (dependent variable) and the predictors (independent variables), with one modification. Each of the predictors is entered into the equation individually, with the entry of the first variable being based on its ability to explain the remaining residual variation unaccounted for by the previous variables in the equation.

It is possible to specify the order in which variables are entered into the equation by forcing some in and holding others back. This was not done for this analysis. The standard regression method of decomposition was used, as opposed to the hierarchical method. The standardized regression coefficient (beta weight) reflects the true contribution of each individual variable, with no provision for the variance (R^2) which might be accounted for by that variable in conjunction with another variable. The alpha acceptance level was established at 0.05. In some instances multicollinearity was present and had to be removed. It was handled by dropping one of the two variables from the analysis. Not all of the variables selected by the final step in stepwise regression were statistically significant; only those which were significant were listed in the accompanying tables.

The procedure was used to describe the relationship between the various predictor variables and each selected outcome criterion. The findings should not be considered to suggest causal connections.

Predicting Five Criterion Variables of Treatment Success for Youths in Outpatient Counseling and/or Psychotherapy (see table 23-2)

Productivity. A client was considered productive at discharge if he/or she was either employed to some degree or was a student in an education or training program at that point. Since the two most important components of productivity among the groups studied were employment and enrollment in an education program, they too will be analyzed and discussed separately. The strongest predictor of productivity for youths under 18 years of age was whether the individual was a student in an education program when he or she was admitted to treatment. (See table 23-2) This was followed by employment status. The less the involvement with drugs and with delinquency at admission, the more likely the client would be productive at discharge. This is reflected in the following predictor variables: the more felony arrests, the longer habit (in years of continuous use), the earlier the initial use of drugs, the abuse of nonopiate drugs, and having abused only one drug. People with no previous treatment experience and people who had formerly been students in training programs also showed greater productivity at discharge. Those factors accounted for a fairly substantial proportion (28 percent) of the variance in the productivity variable. Time in treatment accounted for very little of the variance, and it had a negative effect: the less time the person was in treatment, the better the chance that he or she would be productive at discharge.

Education Status. The configuration of results for this regression was very interesting. As anticipated, the most important variable in predicting whether a juvenile would be enrolled in an education program at the time of discharge was his or her education program status prior to treatment. The next variables entered into the equation dealt with the involvement of the person in drug use. The longer the client had been using the primary drug and the earlier he or she had started using the drug, the less likely was the person to be in an education program at discharge. Even time in treatment was related to this dependent variable, indicating that the longer the client was in treatment, the less likely that he or she would be enrolled in an education program at discharge.

Juvenile male clients were significantly less likely than female clients to be enrolled in an education program, as were people who had previously been arrested for felonious offenses, people with more years of schooling, people who had previously been in treatment, and white clients. Those in treatment for the

Table 23-2
Predicting Treatment Outcomes for Youths (Juveniles) in Outpatient Counseling and/or Psychotherapy

	Dependent Criteria									
	Productivity Index		*Educational Status*		*Employment Status*		*Felony Arrests*		*Treatment Goals Completed*	
Independent Predictors ($\alpha = .05$)	*Beta Weight*	*Changes in* R^2	*Beta Weight*	*Changes in* R^2	*Beta Weight*	*Changes in* R^2	*Beta Weight*	*Changes in* R^2	*Beta Weight*	*Changes in* R^2
Demographics										
Males			–.06	.005	.03	.001				
Whites			–.02	.001	.04	.002	–.04	.002	.04	.002
School status	.43	.233	.55	.379	–.07	.005			.13	.025
Employment status	.14	.017			.40	.177				
Training status	.06	.003	.03	.001	.06	.003				
Grade years completed			–.04	.002						
Treatment history										
Length time in treatment	–.05	.002	–.12	.012	.04	.002			.24	.065
Prior treatment experiences	–.05	.002	–.04	.001						
Drug-use history										
Opiate abuser					–.04	.001			–.06	.007
Nonopiate abuser	.04	.002	.04	.002					.05	.002
Multiple-drug abuser	–.05	.003							–.08	.006
Age at first use primary drug	–.11	.009	–.11	.012					.04	.001
Years continued use	–.12	.004	–.14	.011						
Criminal justice use										
Legal referral							.05	.003		
Prior convictions							.05	.002		
Felony arrests	–.07	.008	–.05	.002			.30	.132	–.04	.002
Total *N*	1778		1774		1794		1810		1810	
Total *R*	.53		.65		.44		.38		.33	
Total R^2	.28		.43		.19		.14		.11	
Net ΔR^2	.05		.04		.01		.01			

abuse of nonopiate drugs and those who had been in training programs when they entered treatment were significantly more likely to be enrolled in an education program at discharge.

This regression equation explained 43 percent of the variance of the education status criterion variable, but 38 percent was accounted for by whether the client was in school at the time of admission to treatment.

Employment Status. Intuitively, it would seem that those people who were employed before entering substance-abuse treatment would have the best chance of being employed when they were discharged from treatment. This was found to be true. The longer the person had been employed preceding entry into treatment, the higher the probability that he or she would be employed when leaving treatment. While other predictors were also significantly associated with the criterion, their explanatory ability was limited in comparison with this predictor. With this younger group, those enrolled in a training program at admission were more likely to be employed when they left treatment. On the other hand, those in school (educational) programs, as distinct from "training programs," at admission were less likely to be employed at discharge. It appears that more of them continued in their school educational programs and did not obtain employment during treatment.

Table 23-2 shows that several other variables were also significantly related to being employed at discharge. Whites, as contrasted with nonwhites, and males, as contrasted with females, were more likely to be employed at the time of their discharge from treatment. It was also found that the longer the juvenile remained in treatment, the better was the chance that he or she would be employed. However, those people who were in treatment for abusing opiates were much less likely to be employed.

Arrests. Among people under 18 years of age, the best predictor of arrests for felonies while in treatment was the number of felony arrests prior to treatment. After the arrest variable had been entered, two more law-related variables were placed in the equation: total convictions and treatment entry under legal pressure. The only other variable found to be significant was race, with whites being less likely to be arrested while in treatment.

Treatment Completion. The final criterion to be considered was completion of treatment according to the goals of the program. The time spent in treatment was the best predictor of completion of treatment for juveniles. What that exactly means is uncertain: does it mean that the longer a person is in treatment the more he or she is effected by the treatment, or does it mean that the longer the person stays in the treatment program, the more likely that the program will say the client has completed the goals just because they have worked with him a long time (a situation analogous to one of the promotion policies of our public school system)? Other significant factors at admission positively related to the completion of treatment were: being enrolled in an educational program, being a nonopiate abuser, being white, and being older when the drug of abuse was first tried. Those juveniles who were opiate abusers and multiple-drug abusers were less likely to complete treatment. The more felony arrests an individual had, the less likely he or she was to complete treatment.

A separate regression was run using the combination criterion of completing treatment or leaving under favorable circumstances (transferred to another facility) as success. The effect was to cut the explained variation in half, drop the number of significant variables, and reorder the rank importance of the variables after the first two.

Predicting Treatment Success for Youths in Residential Therapeutic Communities

Productivity. There was quite a disparity between the regression equations for the productivity criterion for those youths receiving treatment in outpatient counseling and/or psychotherapy compared with the same age group in residential therapeutic communities. Whereas the former had ten significant variables and accounted for 28 percent of the variance in the criterion, the latter had only three significant variables and explained only 12 percent of the variance. This means that the equation for clients in inpatient therapeutic communities was less useful in explaining the variance in the criterion than was the one for the outpatient counseling and/or psychotherapy clients. (See table 23-3)

For these youth clients in the therapeutic communities the best predictor of productivity at discharge was having been a student in an educational program (school status) at admission. Time spent in treatment was the second best predictor even though it has a slightly larger beta weight. This situation can occur when there is a negative bivariate relationship between the two predictor variables. Enrollment in a training program at admission was the only other significant predictor of productivity.

Two items are notable in this regression equation, and they are the significance of the time in treatment variable and the lack of statistical significance of employment status. This is the only regression equation with productivity as the dependent outcome measure in which pretreatment employment status was not significant. The longer the youths remained in treatment, the more likely that they would be productive at discharge. This variable was the best predictor for both youths and young adults in residential therapeutic communities, yet it was negatively related to the productivity criterion among juveniles in outpatient counseling and/or psychotherapy and positively (but not particularly strongly) related to the criterion among the corresponding young adults. Thus it is apparent that for clients in residential therapeutic communities,

Table 23-3
Predicting Treatment Outcomes for Youths in Residential Therapeutic Communities

	Dependent Criteria									
	Productivity Index		*Educational Status*		*Employment Status*		*Felony Arrests*		*Treatment Goals Completed*	
Independent Predictors (α = .05)	*Beta Weight*	*Changes in* R^2	*Beta Weight*	*Changes in* R^2	*Beta Weight*	*Changes in* R^2	*Beta Weight*	*Changes in* R^2	*Beta Weight*	*Changes in* R^2
Demographics										
Males			–.07	.005						
Whites			–.11	.011	.13	.011			.09	.008
School status	.22	.054	.23	.057	–.09	.007			–.09	.009
Employment status										
Training status	.10	.012								
Grade years completed										
Treatment history										
Length time in treatment	.23	.049			.33	.102			.22	.047
Prior treatment experiences							.10	.009	–.06	.004
Drug use history										
Opiate abuser									–.16	.019
Nonopiate abuser			.08	.008			–.09	.009	–.26	.032
Multiple-drug abuser					–.13	.013				
Age at first use primary drug							.07	.004		
Years continued use										
Criminal justice use										
Legal referral										
Prior convictions										
Felony arrests							.12	.019		
Total N	468		477		407		487		487	
Total R	.35		.29		.37		.21		.35	
Total R^2	.12		.08		.13		.04		.12	
Net ΔR^2	.06		.02		.03		.02			

time in treatment is the most important predictor of productivity, be the clients juvenile or young adults.

Education Status. When enrollment in an education program at discharge is the criterion, youths who would do well in residential therapeutic communities are those who had been enrolled in an education program when they entered treatment. Once the effect of that variable was removed, not being white had the next strongest positive association with education status at discharge. Only two other variables were statistically significant: being an abuser of a nonopiate drug and being female.

This was one of the least predictive equations of the set, accounting for only 8 percent of the total variance of the criterion variable, educational status. Why? Maybe the best answer is in comparison of the demographics of the two groups. Nearly three of every four youths in outpatient counseling and/or psychotherapy were in an education program when they entered treatment, compared with only three of every eight youths in the residential therapeutic communities in this analysis. It would appear that the youths in residential therapeutic communities had previously withdrawn from educational pursuits and perhaps did not view reentry into the educational system as a relevant goal for themselves. This is supported by the fact that 44 percent of the youths in residential therapeutic communities were referred by the criminal justice system. Also, considering that the median time in treatment was only 36 days, it may be that most clients were dropping out before a plan for enrollment in an educational program could be completed.

Employment Status. It follows from the productivity criterion that time in treatment should be the best predictor of this criterion, and it is borne out by the data. Interestingly, being white was positively related to this criterion, exactly opposite to the relationship apparent on the education program goal. This largely explains why race was not significant on the productivity criterion measure. Whites were more likely to be employed at discharge and significantly less likely to be in an education program at discharge. Also significantly related to this criterion of being employed at discharge was *not* being a student at admission and not being a multiple-drug abuser.

Arrests. The equation for arrests for felonies during treatment was not particularly effective for juveniles, explaining only 4 percent of the variance. Four variables were significant, and they were relatively equal in their explanatory ability. Total arrests for felonies at the time of admission was the best predictor, with a positive relationship to number of felony arrests during treatment. People who had been in treatment previously were significantly more likely to be arrested for felonies while in treatment, as were people who had started using the abused drug later in life. Individuals in treatment for abusing nonopiate drugs were less likely to be arrested for felonies once in treatment.

Treatment Completion. Nonopiate and opiate juvenile abusers were found to be less likely to complete treatment than those with only alcohol and multiple-abuse problems. The longer time a juvenile spent in treatment the more likely he or she was to successfully complete treatment. Juveniles who were students in an education program were significantly less likely to successfully complete treatment, and similarly for juvenile clients who had been in treatment on previous occasions. Whites were significantly more likely than nonwhites to complete treatment.

As in the case for clients in outpatient counseling and/or psychotherapy, a separate analysis was performed using both completed treatment and left under favorable circumstances as the criterion. This had a particularly strong impact on the juvenile subsample. The regression equation explained more variance (R^2 = .18 versus R^2 = .12), and there was a reordering of the predictors for juveniles. When only completed treatment was considered, the time spent in treatment had the second highest standardized regression coefficient, but as the criterion was expanded, the time spent in treatment dropped to a relatively minor role (it still was statistically significant). The most important predictors remained being in treatment for opiate vs nonopiate abuse (they were negatively related), and there were a number of new significant predictors. The strongest of these new predictors were pretreatment employment status, arrests for felony offenses, and sex status.

Two general observations regarding the findings on predicting treatment outcome for juveniles in outpatient and therapeutic community environments are: first, the predictive power of the regression equation was substantially higher for juveniles in outpatient as compared with those in therapeutic communities; second, in both modalities the overall pattern of the equation showed that the client's status at admission was the key predictor to the client's status at discharge. Other variables generally contributed small amounts of explained variance, once controlling for status at admission on the criterion variable was accomplished

Predicting Treatment Success for Young Adults in Outpatient Counseling and/or Psychotherapy
(See table 23-4)

Productivity. The variable which best predicts a productive status of these young adult clients at discharge from treatment is their employment status at admission. While 39 percent of the total variance of productive status at discharge was accounted for by this regression equation, 29 percent of the total variance was accounted for solely by being employed at admission. An additional 6 percent of the variance in productivity was explained by the client student status. This is to be expected, since the productivity criterion measure is composed of both the employment status and educational status measures.

Other variables which were of importance in explaining productivity

Table 23-4
Predicting Treatment Outcomes for Young Adults in Outpatient Counseling and/or Psychotherapy

	Dependent Criteria									
	Productivity Index		*Educational Status*		*Employment Status*		*Felony Arrests*		*Treatment Goals Completed*	
Independent Predictors (α = .05)	*Beta Weight*	*Changes in R^2*	*Beta Weight*	*Changes in R^2*	*Beta Weight*	*Changes in R^2*	*Beta Weight*	*Changes in R^2*	*Beta Weight*	*Changes in R^2*
Demographics										
Males										
Whites	.11	.018			.16	.026			.07	.004
School status	.23	.061	.58	.346			–.04	.001	.12	.017
Employment status	.51	.293			.31	.122			.12	.109
Training status					.06	.003				
Grade years completed			.05	.003						
Treatment history										
Length time in treatment	.10	.012			.09	.010			.29	.097
Prior treatment experiences	–.04	.001			–.07	.004				
Drug use history										
Opiate abuser	–.06	.005								
Nonopiate abuser	.04	.001	.07	.006	.04	.001				
Multiple-drug abuser									–.05	.002
Age at first use primary drug										
Years continued use										
Criminal justice use										
Legal referral										
Prior convictions							–.09	.005		
Felony arrests							.34	.092	–.06	.005
Total N	1167		1167		1172		1186		1186	
Total R	.63		.60		.41		.32		.38	
Total R^2	.39		.36		.17		.10		.14	
Net ΔR^2	.10		.01		.04		.01			

included being white and time in treatment (both positive) and the abuse of opiate drugs (negative). It is interesting to note that only one of these three variables (time in treatment) had been found to be significant among the juvenile group, and in that instance the direction of the relationship was reversed. Perhaps the juveniles in outpatient treatment who tended to get jobs or to get into school programs did not want to, or need to, stay in treatment very long.

Education Status. As expected, the best predictor of enrollment in education program at discharge was an enrollment in that type of program when the individual was admitted to treatment. Only two other variables were statistically significant predictors of educational status for the young adults, and their contribution to the explanatory ability of the regression equation was slight.

Employment Status. The best predictor, as expected, was preadmission employment status, but the predictor variables entered in the equation after this first variable did add some predictive strength to the equation. Being white was associated with being employed at discharge, as was true of more time spent in treatment, the lack of previous treatment experience, and enrollment in a training program at admission.

Arrests. As was anticipated, the best predictor of arrests at the time of discharge was the client's pretreatment arrest history. Those who had been arrested before treatment were more likely to be arrested during treatment. Interestingly, however, more convictions before admission appeared to predict to less arrests during treatment. But it is possible that this inverse relationship was a statistical artifact of the statistical technique adopted, since the bivariate correlation between prior convictions for young adults and felony arrests at discharge was positive ($r = +.12$).

Treatment Completion. More time in treatment was the most powerful variable in predicting whether the young adult outpatient client would be reported as having completed treatment. The next two variables suggest that constructive societal involvement on the part of the client was a good prognostic sign; more of those who were employed and who were in education programs at admission were reported to complete their treatment goals. Whites were discharged significantly more often than nonwhites with their treatment goals reported as completed. Also, clients with prior arrest records were significantly less likely to complete treatment. All these variables, with the exception of employment status at admission, had also been found to be significant for the juveniles in outpatient settings which suggests that on this criterion the two groups were relatively similar.

Predicting Treatment Success for Young Adults in Residential Therapeutic Communities
(See table 23-5)

Productivity. Similarly to the pattern found in the juvenile sample, the regression equation for the young adults in residential therapeutic communities was far less predictive or useful than the one for clients in outpatient counseling and/or psychotherapy, explaining substantially less of the variance in the productivity criterion (13 versus 39 percent). The ordering of the significant variables did show a change (see table 23-3 and table 23-5). Among clients in outpatient counseling and/or psychotherapy treatment employment status was by far the best predictor, followed by educational program status and race. Only after these variables were controlled for did time in treatment impact on the criterion. On the other hand, for young adults in residential therapeutic communities, time in treatment was the most important predictor, followed in order by employment status, education program status, and surprisingly, arrests for felonies prior to treatment. Clients who had been arrested for a felony before admission were more productive at discharge. Approximately one-half the explained variance in productivity at discharge is accounted for by employment, school status, and felony arrests at admission, once time in treatment is controlled.

Education Status. Those young adults who had been arrested for felonies prior to treatment were more likely to be enrolled in an education program at discharge. Nonwhites did significantly better than whites on this criterion. Only after those two variables had been controlled did the pretreatment education program status enter into the equation. A comparison of these young adults with the other (outpatient) sample of young adults (see tables 23-4 and 23-5) reveals that the two differed in the ordering of the variables and in the power of the regression equation to predict.

Employment. Young adults who remained in treatment longer were also more likely to be employed at discharge, as were clients who had been enrolled in a training program at admission. Only after these variables had accounted for most of the explained variance did pretreatment employment status account for an additional 0.7 percent of the variance. Since employment status at admission predicted better to employment status at discharge for the young adult outpatient clients it can be assumed that these TC clients showed more change on this criterion after admission. Most of this change may have been in a negative direction, from employment to nonemployment status, since there is relatively little opportunity to be employed while in a residential program. For

Table 23-5
Predicting Treatment Outcomes for Young Adults in Inpatient Therapeutic Communities

	Dependent Criteria									
	Productivity Index		*Educational Status*		*Employment Status*		*Felony Arrests*		*Treatment Goals Completed*	
Independent Predictors ($\alpha = .05$)	*Beta Weight*	*Changes in* R^2	*Beta Weight*	*Changes in* R^2	*Beta Weight*	*Changes in* R^2	*Beta Weight*	*Changes in* R^2	*Beta Weight*	*Changes in* R^2
Demographics										
Males			–.08	.004						
Whites	–.10	.007	–.16	.025	.13	.014	.09	.011	.10	.009
School status	.12	.014	.15	.023						
Employment status	.18	.030			.08	.007				
Training status			–.06	.006	.15	.022				
Grade years completed			–.08	.006						
Treatment history										
Length time in treatment	.19	.055			.24	.049			.12	.012
Prior treatment experiences			.08	.005					–.13	.016
Drug use history										
Opiate abuser							–.20	.023	–.23	.040
Nonopiate abuser							–.21	.011	–.26	.025
Multiple-drug abuser					–.08	.006				
Age at first use primary drug							.21	.012		
Years continued use	.08	.007	.09	.016			.11	.007		
Criminal justice use										
Legal referral			.07	.003						
Prior convictions							–.14	.009		
Felony arrests	.12	.013	.18	.035			.25	.019		
Total N	415		431		417		442		442	
Total R	.36		.36		.31		.31		.32	
Total R^2	.13		.13		.10		.10		.10	
Net ΔR^2	.07		.09		.05		.07		.06	

this reason, as was stated earlier in this chapter, employment status at discharge (rather than at a later follow-up period) is an inappropriate and unfair criterion for evaluating the effects of treatment in residential therapeutic communities.

Arrests. Having been an opiate abuser before admission and having had felony arrests during the 2 years prior to admission were the two best predictors to being arrested for a felony during treatment. Nonopiate drug abusers were significantly less likely to be arrested while in treatment.

Treatment Completion. The findings for these young adults in residential therapeutic communities resemble more the findings for the juveniles in therapeutic communities than those for the other group of young adults in outpatient facilities when we examine their respective regression prediction profiles. For both TC age groups, the best predictor to completing treatment was the fact that the client was not involved in opiate abuse at admission. This variable was not even statistically significant for young adult outpatients. The young adult TC clients who had had prior treatment experiences were less often reported to have "completed" the current treatment experience. An unexpected finding was that time in treatment played only a secondary role for this group in predicting to this particular outcome criterion (treatment completion).

Treatment Approach as a Predictor

The preceding analyses consider the treatment environment/approach to be a control variable, thus removing it as a source of variation. This is useful for analysis of the variables predicting to outcome within each environment/approach group, but it precludes any determination of the relative effectiveness of the treatments in different environment/approaches. One way to accomplish this latter objective is to treat the environment/approach as a predictor to treatment outcome and then to assess its significance and importance in the stepwise regression procedure. As reported in the following section, this is precisely the procedure we followed.

There were three different environment/approaches considered: counseling and/or psychotherapy, therapeutic community, and halfway house. The effects of treatment on the group of clients in each of the three treatment environments were compared, in turn, with the effects on the combined group of clients who were in the other two treatment environments. A control was placed on the type of substance abused. Since relatively few juveniles in the sample were heavy opiate users, it was decided that only those clients in treatment for abusing nonopiates would be included in this analysis. Only two outcome measures were analyzed: enrollment in an education program and felony arrests at discharge. It was not considered appropriate to use employment and productivity at discharge as outcome criteria for the purpose of this comparison, since clients in residence have much less opportunity to secure employment during treatment than do outpatient clients. Completion of treatment goals was also not considered appropriate as a criterion since the goals of outpatient treatment might be different from those of residential treatment. All the variables used in this section were defined and scored in the same manner as those reported in the preceding analyses.

The most significant predictor to enrollment in an education program at discharge for juveniles was found to be enrollment in an education program at admission (see table 23-6). Since many treatment programs encourage their juvenile clients to continue the formal education process, it is only logical that those clients who were in those programs when they were admitted to treatment would be in such programs at discharge.

Neither of the two treatment approaches was found to have a differential significant effect on the juvenile clients with regard to this criterion. For the total juvenile sample, the longer the history of continued nonopiate drug use before admission, the more *likely* the client was found to be enrolled in an education program at discharge.

The best predictor to the number of felony arrests while in treatment was being a client in an outpatient counseling and/or psychotherapy program. The fact that these clients were more likely than the other clients to be arrested for felonies can be explained by the greater opportunity that outpatients have for criminal behavior, compared to residential clients, who are usually not permitted to leave the physical location.

For the young-adult, nonopiate users, the treatment setting predicted outcome, to a significant degree, for each of the two outcome criteria. For the criterion of enrollment in an education program at discharge, it was found that young adults who were in therapeutic communities were significantly less likely to succeed than those treated in the other two settings. Indeed, this was the strongest predictor, once the effect of pretreatment education status was controlled. Clients in TCs may have less opportunity to enroll in educational programs, as well as less opportunity to be employed. On the other hand, clients in TCs also have less opportunity to commit crimes and get arrested and they were, in fact, found to get arrested significantly less often while in treatment than the other young adult clients.

Summary

Two features were apparent in the data. People receiving treatment in outpatient counseling and/or psychotherapy seemed to have different sets of significant predictor variables than did the clients in therapeutic communities. It would seem that this is because the former had not been as heavily involved before treatment either in the drug scene or in criminal behavior and were more identified with mainstream society. This was especially true for the juveniles;

Table 23-6
Predicting Treatment Outcomes by Age for Clients Abusing Nonopiate Drugs

	Juveniles				*Young Adults*			
	Education Status		*Felony Arrests*		*Education Status*		*Felony Arrests*	
Predictors ($\alpha = .05$)	*Beta Weight*	*Change in* R^2	*Beta Weight*	*Change in* R^2	*Beta Weight*	*Change in* R^2	*Beta Weight*	*Change in* R^2
Demographics								
Whites								
School status	.50	.304	.05	.002	.46	.200		
Training status							–.05	.004
Grade years completed	.06	.003						
Treatment history								
Length of time in treatment	.06	.003	–.08	.007	–.05	.002	–.10	.007
Drug-use history								
Multiple-drug abuser	.04	.002						
Years of continued use	.12	.018	–.04	.002				
Criminal justice history								
Legal referral								
Prior convictions	.04	.003	.14	.009				
Felony arrests			.24	.066			.31	.049
Treatment approach								
Therapeutic community					–.12	.014	–.08	.003
Counseling and/or psychotherapy			.29	.039			.11	.024
Total N	1,466		1,144		809		643	
Total R	.58		.36		.47		.30	
Total R^2	.33		.13		.22		.09	
Net ΔR^2	.03		.06		.02		.04	

and while also true for the young adults, the differences were not as pronounced.

The different set of predictor variables is related to the type of clients treated and the manner in which they were treated. Those individuals who are able to function in society while still receiving treatment will have a better chance of doing well in treatment than those who need a more insulated environment in which to work on their problems. The therapeutic community has the added burden of integrating an individual back into society. Consequently, it should be expected that predictor variables for clients who remain identified with and attached to society and who receive outpatient counseling and/or psychotherapy treatment should reflect the more usual and accepted societal criteria of success and status; and the predictor variables for clients in therapeutic communities should reflect somewhat different factors. This in fact was what seemed to occur. For clients in outpatient counseling and/or psychotherapy, the best predictors of success for productivity, education status, and employment status were pretreatment employment or education status. In contrast, for clients in residential therapeutic communities, the best predictors were time in treatment, pre-treatment number of felony arrests, and education status at admission.

The productivity criterion was probably the single most important index used in this chapter, since it combined education, training, and employment in a meaningful way. For both age groups in therapeutic communities, the time spent in treatment was the best predictor of productivity at discharge. Time in treatment was also a significant predictor for clients in outpatient counseling and/or psychotherapy, but its effect differed radically when compared with therapeutic communities. First, it was not as important a variable in the equation, since several other variables had more predictive power. Second, its direction was not uniform. Among the outpatient juveniles, time in treatment was negatively related to the productivity outcome criterion, meaning that the less time the youths remained in treatment, the more likely that they would be doing well at discharge. Probably some of the juveniles who have the best potential to become more productive in education and employment do not need to stay in treatment very long to achieve these particular goals. Juvenile outpatient clients who stay in treatment longer may have more severe problems and be less capable of making constructive changes in productivity. In contrast, juveniles in therapeutic communities had more serious problems on the average, and those who remained longer in the protective environment were apparently better able to restructure their lives and then become productive at discharge.

A profile emerges of a special subgroup of juveniles in the outpatient counseling and/or psychotherapy setting who were productive at admission, had started using a nonopiate drug later in life with consequently fewer years of continued use, were not multiple-drug users, and had less felony arrests in the 2 years preceding the treatment experience.

Juvenile abusers of nonopiates treated in TCs were significantly less likely than opiate abusers to be arrested for felonies while in treatment, while clients who first used the drug of abuse later in life were more likely to be arrested while in treatment. The explanation for this latter finding could possibly be that those clients who used opiates tended to start drug use somewhat later in their young lives.

The finding that young adults in TCs who had been arrested for a felony before treatment turned out to be more productive at discharge appears on the surface to be quite unexpected. At least part of the answer must be situational and may be considered as an artifact rather than a very meaningful finding. Since some of those arrested for a felony were probably in jail and may even have been admitted to the TC directly from jail, they could not have been employed or in training at the time. They thus had more opportunity to improve or increase their productivity score during treatment.

On the final outcome criterion, completion of treatment, time in treatment was the best predictor for clients of both age groups in outpatient counseling and/or psychotherapy, but not for the clients who were in therapeutic communities. This appears to be somewhat ironic, since time in treatment tended to be the best predictor to the more specific productivity outcome criteria of enrollment in education and employment status for clients in TCs. Also, those clients who had previous treatment were less likely to complete treatment. Finally, for both youths and young adults who were being treated in therapeutic communities, those who were white and those who stayed in treatment longer were more likely to complete the goals of the program. These and the other findings reported earlier on factors that predict to completion of treatment are considered to be less reliable, valid, and useful than the findings reported on the productivity outcome criterion, since completion of treatment is a poorly defined, subjective criterion that is used in a variety of ways in different treatment programs around the Commonwealth. It is not too surprising, then, that a variable which is found to predict to success in completion of treatment predicts in the opposite direction to a failure in productivity. It is possible, of course, that a client who has not become gainfully employed or entered training could be considered by his therapist or counselor to have grown or matured emotionally or to have better control of his drug-abuse behavior and thus to have completed treatment.

Finally, the impact of the type of treatment setting and approach was assessed with some interesting results. Both juveniles and young adults in counseling and/or psychotherapy treatment were found to be significantly more likely to be arrested while in treatment. Young adults in therapeutic communities were significantly less likely to do well on the education criterion, but they did significantly better on the felony arrest criterion, in that they were less likely to be arrested.

An attempt was made to offer some plausible explanations for some of the findings reported in the chapter, while at the same time being careful to stay reasonably close to the data and to limit the amount of speculation.

Notes

1. It should be noted that the UDCS was not limited to client-level data. It was to be the umbrella term for any routinized data-gathering effort undertaken by the Pennsylvania Governor's Council on Drug and Alcohol Abuse. However, for the purposes of this chapter, UDCS will be considered only with regard to the client data-gathering effort.

2. For the data system which served as a base, there were 58,782 linked records (this file was created in April 1977). When the initial file was created in September 1976, the following breakdown existed. There were 81,551 total records, of which 50,119 were linked (of those 50,119 linked records, 5,033 had to be adjusted). A total of 8,489 were old admissions (prior to July 1975) and they were deleted.

References

Bardine, A., Ferris, W.H., and Greene, B.T. 1976. Explaining Length of Time in Treatment for Drug Abuse Clients. Paper presented at National Drug Abuse Conference, New York.

Burt, M.R., and Pines, S. 1976. Evaluation of the District of Columbia's Narcotics Treatment Administration Programs 1970-1973. Draft manuscript, Burt Associates, Inc.

Collins, W.P., and Kelly, W.P., Jr. 1975. Methadone treatment and crime reduction-Differential impact: An analysis and a case study. In E. Senay et al. (eds.), *Developments in the Field of Drug Abuse.* Cambridge, Mass.: Schenkman.

Cutter, H.S.G., Samaraweera, A., Price, B., Haskell, D., and Schaeffer, C. 1977. Prediction of treatment effectiveness in drug-free therapeutic community. *International Journal of the Addictions* 12(2-3):301-321.

DeLeon, G. and Beschner, G. (eds.). 1977. The therapeutic community. *Proceedings of Therapeutic Communities of American Planning Conference January 29-30, 1976*. NIDA Services Research Branch Report, Publication No. 77-464.

DeLeon, G. 1975. Phoenix House: Influence of time in program. In E. Senay et al. (eds.), *Developments in the Field of Drug Abuse.* Cambridge, Mass.: Schenkman.

Eichberg, R.H., and Bentler, P.M. 1975. Current issues in the epidemiology of drug abuse as related to psychosocial studies of adolescent drug use. In D.J.

Lettieri (ed.), *Predicting Adolescent Drug Abuse: A Review of Issues, Methods and Correlates.* Washington: U.S. Government Printing Office.

Fisher, S. 1975. The quest for interpersonal predictors of marijuana abuse in adolescents. In D.J. Lettieri (ed.), *Predicting Adolescent Drug Abuse: A Review of Issues, Methods and Correlates.* Washington: U.S. Government Printing Office.

Governor's Council on Drug and Alcohol Abuse, Commonwealth of Pennsylvania. 1975. *The Uniform Data Collection System.* Harrisburg, Pennsylvania.

Kandel, D. 1975. Some comments on the relationship of selected criteria variables to adolescent illicit drug use. In D.J. Lettieri (ed.), *Predicting Adolescent Drug Abuse: A Review of Issues, Methods and Correlates.* Washington: U.S. Government Printing Office.

Keil, T.J., Rush, R.V., and Dickman, F.B. 1975*a*. Client Demographics and Therapeutic Approaches as Predictive Factors in the In-Treatment Outcome of Opiate Users. Paper presented at Alcohol and Drug Problems Association of North America Conference, Chicago.

Keil, T.J., Rush, T.V., and Dickman, F.B. 1975*b*. Pre-Treatment Client Roles and Therapeutic Environment as Correlates of In-Treatment Client Success: The Case of the Non-Opiate Users. Paper presented at American Society of Criminology Conference, Toronto.

Lettieri, D.J. (ed.). 1975. *Predicting Adolescent Drug Abuse: A Review of Issues, Methods and Correlates.* Washington: U.S. Government Printing Office.

Lofchie, S., Davenport, D., Turner, J.J., and Rafalsky, T. 1975. Early performance as a predictor of treatment outcome in a methadone maintenance program. In E. Senay et al. (eds.), *Developments in the Field of Drug Abuse.* Cambridge, Mass.: Schenkman.

Macro Systems, Inc. 1975. *Three-year Follow-Up Study of Clients Enrolled in Treatment Programs in New York City.* Phase II. Final Report. Report submitted to National Institute of Drug Abuse, Macro Systems, Inc.

Mandell, W., Goldschmidt, P., and Jillson, I. 1975. Evaluation of treatment programs for drug abusers. In E. Senay et al. (eds.), *Developments in the Field of Drug Abuse.* Cambridge, Mass.: Schenkman.

Nie, N.H., Hull, C.H., Jenkins, J.G., Steinbrenner, K., and Bent, D.H. 1975. *SPSS: Statistical Package for the Social Sciences,* 2d ed. New York: McGraw-Hill.

Norris, T.L. 1975. The role of program evaluation in therapeutic communities. In E. Senay et al. (eds.), *Developments in the Field of Drug Abuse.* Cambridge, Mass.: Schenkman.

Rabin, J. and Stimmel, 1975. A follow-up of patients discharged from methadone maintenance In E. Senay et al. (eds.), *Developments in the Field of Drug Abuse.* Cambridge, Mass.: Schenkman.

Sadava, S.W., and Forsyth, R. 1977. Turning on, turning off, and relapse: Social psychological determinants of status change in cannabis use. *International Journal of the Addictions* 12(4):509-528.

Sells, S.B., and Simpson, D.D. 1974. *The Effectiveness of Drug Abuse Treatment,* Vol. I through V. Cambridge, Mass.: Ballinger.

Sirotnik, K.A., and Roffe, M.W. 1977. An investigation of the feasibility of predicting outcome indices in the treatment of heroin addiction. *International Journal of the Addictions* 12(6):755-775.

Vaillant, G.E. 1966*a*. A twelve-year follow-up of New York narcotic addicts. I. The relation of treatment to outcome. *American Journal of Psychiatry* 122:727-737.

Vaillant, G.E. 1966*b*. A twelve-year follow-up of New York narcotic addicts. IV. Some characteristics and determinants of abstinence. *American Journal of Psychiatry* 123:573-584.

Vaillant, G.E. 1970. The natural history of narcotic drug addiction. *Seminars in Psychiatry* (2):486-498.

Zuckerman, M., Sola, S., Masterson, J., and Angelone, J. 1976. MMPI Patterns in Drug Abusers Before and After Treatment in Therapeutic Communities. Prepublication copy (mimeographed).

Index

About the Contributors

Carl Akins, *Ph.D.* is currently the executive director of the National Association of State Alcohol and Drug Abuse Directors, Inc. He has been a consultant for the Office of Management and Budget, Executive Office of the President; a research associate at the Brookings Institution; an instructor at the AFL-CIO, Labor Studies Center, Washington, D.C.; an associate professor at American University; and a teaching fellow in social science at Harvard University.

Ann F. Brunswick, *Ph.D.* is a senior research associate at Columbia University (Public Health-Sociomedical Sciences and Center for Sociocultural Research on Drug Use); director, Adolescent and Young Adult Health Project; program chairperson, Conference on Social Sciences in Health, American Public Health Association; and a past officer for the American Association for Public Opinion Research.

R. Stanley Burns, *M.D.* is a research associate at the National Institute of General Medical Sciences, Bethesda, Maryland. His clinical research interests are in neurology, pharmacology, and drug abuse.

John A. Carlisi, *M.B.A.* is director, Planning and Systems, The National Center for Urban Ethnic Affairs. He has served on a panel of the President's Commission on Mental Health and has had consultantships with federal agencies and drug abuse programs.

Richard R. Clayton, *Ph.D.* is associate professor of sociology, University of Kentucky. He was Visiting Scientist at the National Institute on Drug Abuse from 1977 to 1978; associate editor for the *Journal of Marriage and the Family*; and associate editor of *Pacific Sociological Review*. He is author of *The Family, Marriage and Social Change*; and co-author of *Young Men and Drugs: A Nationwide Survey*. He has published numerous journal articles on drug use, religion, and other topics.

Allan Y. Cohen, *Ph.D.* is currently executive director of Pacific Institute for Research and Evaluation, Walnut Creek, California. He is professor of psychology and philosophy and assistant to the president for Research Planning of John F. Kennedy University in Orinda, California. He co-authored *Understanding Drug Use: An Adult's Guide to Drugs in the Young* with Peter Marin, and recently completed *The Mastery of Consciousness.*

Sidney Cohen, *M.D.* has degrees in pharmacy and medicine and was awarded a Doctor of Sciences degree from Columbia University in 1976. He is editor of the

Drug Abuse and Alcoholism Review Journal and the *Drug Abuse and Alcoholism Newsletter* and is on the editorial board of *Psychosomatics,* the *International Journal of Addictions, Drug Dependence,* and the *American Journal of Drug and Alcohol Abuse.* Dr. Cohen served as director of the Division of Narcotic Addiction and Drug Abuse, NIMH from 1968 to 1970. He is now a clinical professor of psychiatry at the Neuropsychiatric Institute, UCLA. He has researched LSD for the past twenty years and marihuana for the past five. He has published over 200 articles and four books in the areas of psychopharmacology and drug abuse. He has spoken on all aspects of the drug problem in the United States and abroad.

Robert L. DuPont, *M.D.* is a practicing psychiatrist, president of the nonprofit Institute for Behavior and Health, Inc., and appears on ABC-TV's "Good Morning America" show. He holds the positions of associate clinical professor of psychiatry and behavioral sciences at the George Washington University School of Medicine and visiting associate clinical professor of psychiatry at Harvard Medical School. Dr. DuPont was the director of the National Institute on Drug Abuse from September 1973 until July 1978. In June 1973 he was appointed by the President to direct the White House Special Action Office for Drug Abuse Prevention (SAODAP), where he designed and coordinated the $1 billion a year federal drug abuse prevention and treatment program.

Edward C. Farley, *M.S.W.* is a senior research associate for the Polydrug Research Center of the Philadelphia Psychiatric Center. Prior to his work there, he contributed to the National Polydrug Collaborative Study; and before that, he evaluated drug rehabilitation programs at Temple University.

George S. Goldstein, *Ph.D.* is secretary for health and environment, state of New Mexico. He has been a professor at Dennison University, and director of Program Development and Evaluation with the Indian Mental Health Service.

Judith Green, *Ph.D.* is currently associate professor, Departments of Biology and Psychology, The William Paterson College of New Jersey. She is director of the Biopsychology Honors Program at the college, where she teaches courses in psychopharmacology, neuroscience, and biological rhythms in physiology and behavior. Dr. Green is conducting research into the relationship between biological rhythms and consummatory disorders.

Leon Gibson Hunt, formerly senior research professor, Dixon Institute for Public Health Research, Antioch College, is a consultant in applied mathematics. His principal area of research is mathematical epidemiology. He acts as advisor to the White House, the United Nations, the World Health Organization, and the National Institute on Drug Abuse. Some of his books and monographs include

Recent Spread of Heroin Use in the United States: Unanswered Questions (1974), *Incidence Analysis* (1975), *The Heroin Epidemics* (with Carl Chambers) (1976), and *Assessment of Local Drug Abuse* (1977).

Raymond S. Kirk, *Ph.D.* is currently vice president of Research and Evaluation Specialists of Vermont, Inc., and assistant professor of psychology at the University of Vermont. He formerly was director of research at the Washington County Youth Service Bureau (Montpelier, Vermont).

Robert A. Ladner, *Ph.D.* is executive director, Behavioral Science Research Institute, Coral Gables, Florida.

Marvin A. Lavenhar, *Ph.D.* is professor of preventive medicine and community health and Director, Division of Biostatistics, College of Medicine and Dentistry of New Jersey, New Jersey Medical School. He has published fifteen scientific papers on problems of drug abuse.

Steven E. Lerner, *M.S.* is currently training coordinator, California PCP Training Project, University of California, Los Angeles.

Carl G. Leukefeld, *D.S.W.* is currently the deputy director, Division of Resource Development, National Institute on Drug Abuse. His drug abuse career started in 1967 with the National Institute of Mental Health, and he has held positions with responsibilities for treatment, prevention, and training.

Stephen J. Levy, *Ph.D.* is currently director, Alcoholism Treatment Program, Beth Israel Center; and assistant professor of psychiatry, Mount Sinai School of Medicine of the City University of New York. As director of Planning and Development of the Training for Living Institute he developed training programs for the personnel of the Addiction Services Agency of New York City. Many of his papers on topics related to drug abuse and addiction have been published in professional journals and books.

Duane C. McBride, *Ph.D.* is co-director of the Center for Social Research on Drug Abuse, Division of Addiction Sciences, Department of Psychiatry, School of Medicine, University of Miami. He is the co-author of a recent book on emergency room drug overdoses.

Clyde B. McCoy, *Ph.D.* is co-director of the Center for Social Research on Drug Abuse, Division of Addiction Sciences, Department of Psychiatry, School of Medicine, University of Miami. After an initial adventure with the Christian ministry he taught at the University of Kentucky for three and a half years. His latest research efforts are forthcoming in the book *Appalachians in Urban Areas* (University of Kentucky Press).

John A. O'Donnell, *Ph.D.* is professor, Department of Sociology, University of Kentucky. He is author of *Narcotic Addicts in Kentucky* (1969); co-author of *Young Men and Drugs: A Nationwide Survey* (1976); co-editor of *Narcotic Addiction* (1966); and the forthcoming *Handbook on Drug Abuse*.

E.R. Oetting, *Ph.D.* is professor and chairperson, counseling section, Department of Psychology, Colorado State University. He has conducted research on the assessment of the impact of social action programs on disadvantaged populations.

Thomas Vale Rush, *Ph.D.* was a Bureau of Research Associate in the Pennsylvania Governor's Council for Drug and Alcohol Abuse when he conducted the work for his chapter. He is currently research associate in the Office of Research and Statistics analyzing drug and alcohol abuses in the Supplemental Security Income Program. He was author of the Incidence and Prevalence Survey for Pennsylvania, and he presented numerous papers on drug and alcohol abuse.

Yoav Santo, *M.A.* is the research supervisor of the Polydrug Research Center of the Philadelphia Psychiatric Center. Previously he conducted research in the areas of multiple substance abuse, at Eagleville Hospital; in fertility behavior at Chilton Research Services; and in industrial sociology at the Center for Research on the Acts of Man. He is completing his Ph.D. work at the University of Pennsylvania.

Sidney H. Schnoll, *M.D., Ph.D.* is medical director, Eagleville Hospital and Rehabilitation Center, and assistant professor of pharmacology and psychiatry and human behavior at Thomas Jefferson University. He is author of a number of journal articles and books on pharmacology and drug addiction.

Saul B. Sells, *Ph.D.* is research professor and director of the Institute of Behavioral Research at Texas Christian University, with biographic listings in *American Men and Women of Science, Who's Who in America,* and *Who's Who in the World.* He is managing editor of *Multivariate Behavioral Research* and editor of *Behavioral Science Monograph.* His research interests and publications focus on evaluation of treatment, epidemiology of drug use and abuse, and organizational and industrial psychology. Dr. Sells received the National Institute on Drug Abuse 1978 Pacesetter Award for his contributions in the field of evaluation on drug treatment effectiveness.

D. Dwayne Simpson, *Ph.D.* is associate professor in the Institute of Behavioral Research at Texas Christian University, with biographical listings in *Men of Achievement, American Men and Women of Science,* and *Who's Who in the*

South and Southwest. His research interests and publications have dealt with social and health-related problems, focusing particularly on drug use and evaluation of treatment.

David E. Smith, *M.D.* is founder and medical director, Haight-Ashbury Free Medical Clinic, and associate clinical professor of toxicology, University of California at San Francisco. He has been health advisor to President Jimmy Carter; founder and former president of the National Free Clinic Council; consultant on drug abuse, SAODAP; advisory council, U.S. Department of Health, Education and Welfare; and chairperson, National Drug Abuse Conference 1977, San Francisco. He is founder and editor of the *Journal of Psychedelic Drugs*; a member of the editorial board, *The Journal,* the official publication of the Toronto Addiction Research Institute; and a Member of the editorial board of *Clinical Toxicology.*

Jose Szapocznik, *Ph.D.* is director of research at the Spanish Family Guidance Clinic and research assistant professor of psychiatry (Psychology) at the Department of Psychiatry, University of Miami. He is a consulting editor for the *Journal of Hispanic Behavioral Sciences,* is a member of the American Psychological Association's Ad Hoc Committee on Ethnic and Cultural Affairs and is chairman of COSSMHO's National Hispanic Committee for the Implementation of the President's Commission on Mental Health Reports and Recommendations.

Kerry G. Treasure is the vice-president of Birch & Davis Associates, Inc., a management consulting firm that specializes in health care delivery systems. She is the author of publications concerning the treatment of rape victims and management information systems in the drug abuse treatment setting.

About the Editors

George M. Beschner is deputy chief of the Services Research Branch, National Institute on Drug Abuse (NIDA). An official of NIDA since 1971, he has planned, implemented, and coordinated research and demonstration projects designed to improve drug-abuse rehabilitation services. Previously he was on the faculty of the University of Maryland School of Social Work and Community Planning. He has directed community action programs in Washington, D.C., and southern Maryland and has served as a training director with the Office of Economic Opportunity. He began his career in the delinquency field with the New York City Youth Board in 1958. He has published numerous journal articles and monographs and is co-editor of the recent volume entitled *Polydrug Abuse*.

Alfred S. Friedman is director of Drug Treatment Programs and of the Research Department of the Philadelphia Psychiatric Center. He has served as president of the Family Institute of Philadelphia, chairman of the American Psychological Association's Committee on Relations with the Social Work Profession, and director of the Clinical School of Family Therapy, Family Institute of Philadelphia. Dr. Friedman has developed and directed large-scale federally funded research projects on schizophrenia, depression, drug therapy, marital therapy, juvenile delinquency, and youth drug abuse. He has published numerous clinical-research papers and books.